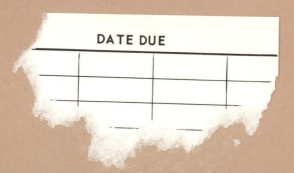

THE PAPERS OF

WOODROW WILSON

VOLUME 28
1913

SPONSORED BY THE WOODROW WILSON
FOUNDATION
AND PRINCETON UNIVERSITY

THE PAPERS OF

WOODROW WILSON

ARTHUR S. LINK, *EDITOR*

DAVID W. HIRST AND JOHN E. LITTLE

ASSOCIATE EDITORS

EDITH JAMES, *ASSISTANT EDITOR*

SYLVIA ELVIN, *CONTRIBUTING EDITOR*

PHYLLIS MARCHAND, *EDITORIAL ASSISTANT*

Volume 28 · 1913

PRINCETON, NEW JERSEY
PRINCETON UNIVERSITY PRESS
1978

Note to scholars: Princeton University Press
subscribes to the Resolution on Permissions of
the Association of American University Presses,
defining what we regard as "fair use" of copyrighted works. This Resolution, intended to encourage scholarly use of university press publications and to avoid unnecessary applications
for permission, is obtainable from the Press or
from the A.A.U.P. central office. Note, however,
that the scholarly apparatus, transcripts of
shorthand, and the texts of Wilson documents
as they appear in this volume are copyrighted,
and the usual rules about the use of copyrighted materials apply.

Publication of this book has been aided by a
grant from the National Historical Publications
and Records Commission.

Printed in the United States of America
by Princeton University Press
Princeton, New Jersey

INTRODUCTION

THE opening of this volume (June 23, 1913) finds Wilson still embroiled in the struggle for tariff reform. The House of Representatives has passed the Underwood bill on May 8 by a strict party vote, but Wilson's insistence on free wool and free sugar has made the outcome in the Senate unpredictable because of the slim Democratic majority in that body. However, Wilson prevails through steady pressure and moral suasion: the Senate approves the Underwood bill on October 2.

"We shall go the rest of the journey," Wilson said upon signing the tariff bill on October 3. He referred to the battle now reaching its height in the Senate over the Federal Reserve bill. That controversy begins in earnest with Wilson's address to Congress on currency and banking reform. Bankers denounce the measure as socialistic and confiscatory; agrarian spokesmen say that it ignores the needs of farmers. Patiently and deftly, Wilson steers the bill through the House of Representatives, compromising on details and holding firm to the basic principles of the bill. New troubles break out in the Senate when insurgent Democrats combine with Republicans on the Banking Committee to block the bill. The close of this volume finds the struggle in the final stages, with Wilson again prevailing by patient but unrelenting pressure upon the Senate.

Meanwhile, Wilson has been facing one of the most difficult challenges of his entire career—working out a policy toward Mexico after the overthrow of its constitutional government and the murder of its president by the usurper, General Victoriano Huerta. At first he tries the course of friendly persuasion, by sending former Governor John Lind of Minnesota to Mexico City with proposals for new elections and the re-establishment of constitutional government. Huerta seems willing to cooperate; however, on October 10, after a military disaster at the hands of his opponents, the Constitutionalists, Huerta dissolves Congress, arrests most of the deputies, and establishes a military dictatorship. Wilson, reacting furiously, announces to the powers that the United States would depose the tyrant by peaceful means if possible and by force if necessary.

A dire diplomatic crisis erupts at the same time. Great Britain, along with the European powers, had earlier accorded Huerta *de facto* recognition. The ostentatious reception in Mexico City of a new British minister, Sir Lionel Carden, on the day after the arrest of the deputies, convinces Wilson that the British government is determined to thwart his policy. He prepares a message to Congress hurling defiance at Europe and announcing a new corollary to the Monroe Doctrine. Only the quick retreat of the British government, threatened in Europe by Germany and not daring to lose the friendship of the United States, prevents a direct confrontation.

At the end of this volume (December 1, 1913), Wilson has not found a solution to the Mexican dilemma. Huerta is not only hanging on but gaining strength at home. Wilson has sought to come to an understanding with the Constitutionalist leader, Venustiano Carranza, only to meet rebuff because Carranza will permit no outside intervention.

Most of the documents in this volume are published for the first time. Noteworthy are the many letters between the President and Ellen Axson Wilson—the last such extended series. Different but equally important are the press conferences, private and political letters, and diplomatic reports and correspondence. They reveal Wilson in intimate detail as parliamentary leader, diplomatist, leader of public opinion, husband, and friend.

All correspondence is reproduced *verbatim et literatim*, with typographical and spelling errors corrected in square brackets *only* when necessary for clarity and ease of reading.

Readers are reminded that *The Papers of Woodrow Wilson* is a continuing series and that persons, events, and institutions that figure prominently in earlier volumes are not ordinarily re-identified in subsequent ones; and that cumulative indexes and tables of contents are published from time to time (thus far, Volumes 13 and 26). The table of contents for this volume reflects the increase in and diversity of correspondence (letters, telegrams, reports, memoranda) in this period of Wilson's life. We have divided the correspondence into three categories: diplomatic, personal, political. The subdivisions of these categories are the same as in previous volumes, namely, collateral, from Wilson, to Wilson. Correspondence is listed alphabetically by name, and chronologically within each name by page.

We take this opportunity to thank James S. K. Tung, Curator Emeritus of the Gest Oriental Library and East Asian Collection of Princeton University, for translating Japanese documents. Dr. Michael A. Lutzker of Richmond College, CUNY, spent the academic year with us as a National Historical Publications Commission Fellow in Advanced Historical Editing. We express our appreciation for the work that he did on this and the following volume. We continue to be grateful to Judith May, our editor at Princeton University Press. Finally, we extend a warm welcome to Professor John Milton Cooper, Jr., of the University of Wisconsin to the Editorial Advisory Committee.

N.B. Since the essay, "Editing the Presidential Volumes," in Volume 27, was set in pages, we discovered that the letters between Wilson and Edith Bolling Galt Wilson had been transferred from her papers into his, and that the location ascribed to her papers in the essay is incorrect.

THE EDITORS

Princeton, New Jersey
May 10, 1978

CONTENTS

ILLUSTRATIONS

Following page 330

ABBREVIATIONS

AL	autograph letter
ALS	autograph letter signed
CC	carbon copy
CC MS	carbon copy of manuscript
CCL	carbon copy of letter
CCLI	carbon copy of letter initialed
CLSsh	Charles Lee Swem shorthand
CLST	Charles Lee Swem typed
EAW	Ellen Axson Wilson
EMH	Edward Mandell House
hw	handwriting, handwritten
HwI	handwritten initialed
JRT	Jack Romagna typed
MS	manuscript
RFhw	Rudolph Forster handwriting
T	typed
T MS	typed manuscript
TS MS	typed manuscript signed
TLI	typed letter initialed
TLS	typed letter signed
TS	typed signed
WHP	Walter Hines Page
WJB	William Jennings Bryan
WJBhw	William Jennings Bryan handwriting, handwritten
WW	Woodrow Wilson
WWT	Woodrow Wilson typed
WWT MS	Woodrow Wilson typed manuscript
WWhw	Woodrow Wilson handwriting, handwritten
WWsh	Woodrow Wilson shorthand
WWTL	Woodrow Wilson typed letter
WWTLS	Woodrow Wilson typed letter signed

ABBREVIATIONS FOR COLLECTIONS AND REPOSITORIES

Following the National Union Catalog
of the Library of Congress

BIA	Bureau of Insular Affairs
CtY	Yale University
DLC	Library of Congress
DNA	National Archives
EBR	Executive Branch Records
FO	British Foreign Office
FR	*Papers Relating to the Foreign Relations of the United States*
JFO-Ar	Japanese Foreign Office Archives
MH	Harvard University
MH-Ar	Harvard University Archives

NNC	Columbia University
NjP	Princeton University
PRO	Public Record Office
RG	Record Group
SDR	State Department Records
TDR	Treasury Department Records
WDR	War Department Records
WHi	State Historical Society of Wisconsin
WC, NjP	Woodrow Wilson Collection, Princeton University
WP, DLC	Woodrow Wilson Papers, Library of Congress

SYMBOLS

[July 4, 1913]	publication date of a published writing; also date of document when date is not part of text
[*July 28, 1913*]	composition date when publication date differs
[[Sept. 9, 1913]]	delivery date of speech if publication date differs
* * * *	elision by author of document

THE PAPERS OF
WOODROW WILSON
VOLUME 28
1913

THE PAPERS OF
WOODROW WILSON

To David M. Flynn

My dear Colonel Flynn: [The White House] June 24, 1913

It is with deep and genuine regret that I find myself unable to be present at, and participate in, the celebration of the One-hundredth Anniversary of the Incorporation of the Borough of Princeton. My affection for Princeton draws me very hard. If I send only this message of warm greeting and congratulation, you may be sure that it is because I am prevented by public duty from showing in any other way my deep interest. The stout little borough is to be congratulated upon its history of slow and peaceful development and of growing distinction. Will you not convey to my friends and neighbors there greetings that come direct from my heart?

Cordially and sincerely yours,   Woodrow Wilson

TLS (Letterpress Books, WP, DLC).

To Alonzo Barton Hepburn

My dear Mr. Hepburn: [The White House] June 24, 1913

Allow me to thank you for your courtesy in sending me a copy of the answers prepared by the Currency Commission of the American Bankers' Association to the questions formulated by a subcommittee of the Banking and Currency Committee of the United States Senate.[1] I shall examine them with great interest.

Sincerely yours,   Woodrow Wilson

TLS (Letterpress Books, WP, DLC).

[1] This document is missing. The Senate subcommittee had prepared thirty-three questions soliciting information and sounding opinion to be sent to the bankers and businessmen of the country. The Currency Commission of the American Bankers' Association met at Atlantic City June 18-19, 1913, to prepare its answers to the questions. Copies of the resulting document were sent to Wilson, McAdoo, Owen, and Glass. See *Journal of the American Bankers Association*, VI (July 1913), 2-5.

To William Jennings Bryan

My dear Mr. Secretary: [The White House] June 25, 1913

The chief vacancies on our foreign list still waiting to be filled are Germany, Russia, Austria (to which I assume we shall send Penfield), Turkey, Belgium, China, Spain (if we transfer Girard to Germany), Ecuador, Greece, Haiti, Honduras, Paraguay, Uruguay, Persia (unless Birch[1] changes his mind), Portugal, Sweden (which Mr. Lind does decline), the Balkan States (to one of which I think we should send Charles J. Vopicka,[2] of Chicago), and Liberia.

The following assignments have occurred to me as the best in the circumstances: Perhaps Mr. Bernstein, of New York, to Turkey; Professor Reinsch, of the University of Wisconsin, a great student of world politics and particularly Oriental relationships, to China (Ross's politics having turned out to be unsatisfactory); McGoodwin,[3] of Oklahoma, to Ecuador; Smith, as you suggested, pro tempore, to Haiti; DeSaulles to Paraguay; and Senator Bacon's friend, Hitch,[4] to Uruguay.

Cordially and faithfully yours,   Woodrow Wilson

TLS (Letterpress Books, WP, DLC).

[1] Thomas Howard Birch was appointed Minister to Portugal on September 4, 1913.

[2] Charles Joseph Vopica, Bohemian-born brewer of Chicago, active in civic affairs and Democratic politics. Appointed Minister to Roumania, Serbia, and Bulgaria, September 4, 1913.

[3] Preston Buford McGoodwin, managing editor of the Oklahoma City *Oklahoman*, 1910-1913. He was appointed minister to Venezuela on August 6, 1913.

[4] Calvin Milton Hitch of Atlanta, who served as executive secretary to three governors of Georgia between 1898 and 1907, and as private secretary to Senator Augustus O. Bacon, 1907-10. General agent of an insurance company in Georgia, 1910-1913. Appointed assistant chief of the Division of Latin-American Affairs, Department of State, July 2, 1913.

From William Jennings Bryan

My Dear Mr President,   Washington [c. June 25, 1913]

I am very much interested in the list of diplomatic positions yet to be filled & shall be pleased to confer with you at any time. How would it do to send Hurst of Ill[1] to Russia with the understanding that he will resign when Crane is ready? We need some one in Russia now.

As to Ecuador, that is one of the most delicate situations to deal with & I am anxious to have a good man—that is one whom whom [sic] we *know* to be good. McGoodwin ought to have a place but I would rather have him go to Venezuela (Gray[2] says he can not take the place) or to Honduras than to Ecuador. If you have have [*sic*] no one for Ecuador whom you know *personally* I beg to bring again to your attention Hon Chas Hartman (former congressman) from Montana[3] for the place. I have known him for some 20 years. He is so good a man that I had thought of him for a place on the Philippine Commission. If you do not think he will be needed there I would like to see him selected for Ecuador.

Ohio has been left out & I venture to suggest that we leave Portugal for Ohio—the man to be agreed upon. And can we not give Arkansas either Venezuela or Honduras, whichever Oklahoma does not receive?

We have not done much for New England[.] Why not go to N. E. for the minister to Greece? Am willing to consider Vopica settled on for the Balkan States if you wish—but it might be well to *see* him first. Have you asked any of the prominent Jews about Bernstein, or do you know him personally. We ought to be sure that he is satisfactory to his own people—a thing that can not always be taken for granted. Shall I enquire of Simon Wolfe[4]— one of the leading Jews of the country who lives in Washington? Am on track of an Indiana colored man for Liberia[.] Have heard Reinsch highly spoken of but do not know him personally & do not know how much interested he may be in missionary work. Would like to talk with you about China. Hitch is to come into the Dept as asst to Long[5] in Latin Am Bureau. That leaves us Urugua[y] open & I am anxious [to] include Ky & Kansas in the states favored. We have no diplomatic places for them so far.

Will talk with you about DeSaulles when I see you. Pardon pen but Rose[6] is just now in another building. With assurances of respect etc I am   Yours truly   W. J. Bryan

ALS (WP, DLC).
[1] Elmore W. Hurst, wealthy lawyer, businessman, and Bryan Democrat of Rock Island, Ill. According to his obituary in the *New York Times*, July 22, 1915, he was offered the post and declined on account of ill health.
[2] Probably James Richard Gray, editor of the *Atlanta Journal*.
[3] Charles Sampson Hartman, lawyer of Bozeman, Mont., Republican congressman, 1893-97; "Silver Republican" congressman, 1897-99; joined Democratic party in 1900. Appointed Minister to Ecuador, July 18, 1913.
[4] Simon Wolf, German-born lawyer of Washington, active in defense of the civil rights of Jews of all countries.
[5] Boaz Walton Long, proprietor of a commission company with offices in San Francisco, Chicago, and Mexico City, 1900-1913. Appointed chief of the Division of Latin-American Affairs, Department of State, May 14, 1913.
[6] Robert Forrest Rose, former newspaperman and shorthand expert, private secretary to Bryan in the campaigns of 1900 and 1908. Appointed clerk to the Secretary of State, May 8, 1913, and Foreign Trade Adviser, June 5, 1913.

To William Howard Thompson

My dear Senator: [The White House] June 25, 1913

Allow me to acknowledge the receipt of your letter of June eighteenth about the post office at Coffeyville.[1]

You will understand, I am sure, from our conversations that I have the most sincere and earnest desire to meet your wishes in every possible way, but I think you will also appreciate the fact that there are instances in which it seems to me only just that I should appoint men of whose record I am personally cognizant and whom I personally desire to draw into the public service. The choice which the President exercises in all these matters is a very responsible one, and I feel that I am exercising it not only as President but as leader of our party; that it is incumbent upon me, therefore, to exercise a personal judgment in the matter wherever I have the material to do so.

Of course, in all such instances I make my choice with entire respect for my colleagues who have taken the burden of recommending persons to me for appointment and who are generously ready to share the responsibility, but I do not feel that I can divest myself of a constitutional function which in the last analysis resolves itself into a personal judgment.

I have had only a word with the Postmaster General with regard to the postmastership at Coffeyville, but my judgment after that interview was that Mr. Jones[2] should be appointed at Coffeyville.

I am, my dear Senator, with great respect,

                Sincerely yours,   Woodrow Wilson

TLS (Letterpress Books, WP, DLC).
    [1] W. H. Thompson to WW, June 18, 1913, TLS (WP, DLC), urging the appointment of Elliott Irvin, secretary of the Chamber of Commerce of Coffeyville, Kan., as postmaster of that city.
    [2] Paul A. Jones, editor of the Coffeyville *Sun.* Jones's nomination was rejected by the Senate on July 29, 1913.

From William Jennings Bryan

My dear Mr. President: Washington June 25, 1913.

I enclose a despatch just received from del Valle.[1] He does not seem to be favorably impressed with Carranza. Possibly Carranza is irritated because of our refusal to allow them to take arms across the border, or possibly he is irritated because of our warning in regard to the Americans who were arrested.

You will note that del Valle is now on his way to the City of Mexico. I think it might be well to ask him to go down into

Zapata's country,[2] which is just below the City of Mexico, and get an idea of what is going on there. It might also be worth while to have him go to the capitals of some of the states around the City of Mexico so that we can have a more complete knowledge of the sentiment of the country.

With assurances of respect, etc., I am, my dear Mr. President,
Very sincerely yours,   W. J. Bryan

TLS (WP, DLC).

[1] Reginaldo Francisco Del Valle, lawyer and Democratic politician of Los Angeles; member of an old southern California family of Spanish-Mexican descent; at this time a member of the Los Angeles Public Service Commission. Bryan sent him to Mexico early in June 1913 to gather information on the situation there from both revolutionary and anti-revolutionary sources. He began his investigations in the Constitutionalist state of Sonora and proceeded eastward from there. The most recent and thorough study of Del Valle and his mission is Larry D. Hill, *Emissaries to a Revolution: Woodrow Wilson's Executive Agents in Mexico* (Baton Rouge, La., 1973), pp. 40-60.

[2] Del Valle never got as far as Zapata's territory in Morelos. He was so indiscreet in Mexico City (see WJB to WW, July 8, 1913) that Wilson and Bryan, on July 15, 1913, ordered him to end his mission.

Two Telegrams from William Bayard Hale

[Mexico City, c. June 25, 1913]

Resignation, Brown, president National railways, brings to a head long fight against political interference in the conduct of the road. To-night Brown consented to remain tentatively but the probability is that he will soon go. Issuing a statement which will put absolute end to all financial hope (?) of Huerta government, a panic narrowly averted to-day. Financial strain together with fall Durango[1] collapse campaign in Sonora and increasing seriousness the situation Guatemalan frontier have caused general change sentiment. Last night a conference of influential men debated propriety of proposing resignation of Huerta. It would be the pschyological moment for any positive policy you may contemplate to end intolerable conditions. Fact that Huerta dines by invitation American Embassy next Thursday, irritating, causing comment.   Hale.

I think Wilson should be recalled.   W.W.

What do you think of Huerta dining with Wilson?   WJB

Think it most seriously unwise[.] Probably make it worse to interfere.   W.W.

[1] Durango fell to Constitutionalist forces under General Tomás Urbina on June 18, 1913.

[Mexico City, c. June 25, 1913]

Huerta supporters continue to use every means to impress argument that the U. S. Government, by refusing recognition is giving Mexico over to anarchy for native comsumption. The argument runs that this is being done deliberately in order to make intervention and annexation justifiable and anti-American feeling is really becoming ground for serious apprehension. Sentiment of foreigners here, especially French is strong against us. In my judgement it is true that Huerta end cannot be far off and that to follow there is nothing in sight but anarchy. Rebels have developed no leaders and there is not in evidence man capable of ruling Mexico without the moral support of the United States. Is there not abundant justification for United States to take hand, not by according recognition asked but by declaring the conditions upon which it would later on accord recognition, such as a free election and Huerta self-elimination. I believe proposals somewhat of this nature have been (?) hinted by Ambassador Wilson. It would be difficult to make firm representations on the definite understanding that (?) was completely determined and fully prepared to compel if necessary their being carried out. After many talks with Mexicans and after a conversation with (?) man on whom Huerta now appears much to depend for political advice, I incline to the opinion that only moral determined compulsion would be necessary to carry these points. To put it safely, there would be strong hope of the Secretary to settled Government in Mexico without resort to force while if matters be allowed to drift, there is very little hope of escaping the eventual necessity of a military occupation. I have noted your instructions. Very important publicity should be avoided. You may depend on me absolutely.

Hale.

T telegrams (WP, DLC).

Remarks at a Press Conference

June 26, 1913

Mr. President, you saw yesterday, I believe, some bankers on the currency bill?[1]

Yes, sir.

I have been told that they proposed to you, or rather suggested, I mean, the bill was to include bankers on the central board.

A minority representation of bankers.

Would you say whether your opinion has been changed at all by the representations they made?

Well, frankly, it would not be fair to express too hasty an opinion. They presented their case in a very fair way, and so fair that I felt that I ought to say I will take it under consideration. . . .

Returning to currency once more, Mr. President. The conference here last night with the members of the Senate Committee on Banking and Currency, did you get any helpful suggestions from them?

Well, I found that the time had been so short since they had received copies of the proposed bill, they hadn't acquainted themselves with the text of it, and therefore all they were interested in was to exchange views as to the general idea of the bill, so that we didn't get anywhere.

At the conference with these bankers yesterday, was their protest as emphatic as you expected to receive from bankers?

I would regard part of it as emphatic. They expressed a very confident opinion about the effect of the omission of what they suggested—I mean, the effect on their interests. But they conveyed it in such a way that it didn't have any particular emphasis of any kind.

Mr. President, do you expect other bankers to visit you?

No, sir. You see, these gentlemen had semi-official status. Whether they were deputized by their colleagues to come or not, I don't know. But they are members of the commission.

Do you expect, Mr. President, to have a similar conference with the House committee?

I have had one with the subcommittee last week—last Friday night. I dare say we may have future conferences, but none is arranged for yet. . . .

Mr. President, some of the critics of the currency bill are making a great point—seem to try to make a great point of calling it the "Bryanesque" bill, saying that Mr. Bryan is dominant in all this proposition that has entered into the political side of the discussion. Is there anything you could tell us about that?

Those things don't count. It will be called all kinds of a thing before they get through with it. Of course they expected his approval these first two or three weeks while they are examining it. You can hear anything you choose to listen to, but when they get down to the solemn consideration of it, I haven't any doubt as to the result; because, you see, it's a question of suggesting something better.

Nothing has transpired to shake your confidence in getting it through this summer?

Nothing.

You really expect to get it considered this summer?

I feel confident.

JRT transcript (WC, NjP) of CLSsh (C. L. Swem Coll., NjP).
¹ About this meeting with representatives of the Currency Commission of the American Bankers' Association, see Arthur S. Link, *Wilson: The New Freedom* (Princeton, N.J., 1956), p. 217.

To Charles Ernest Scott

My dear Mr. Scott: [The White House] June 26, 1913

Accept my cordial thanks for your very interesting letter of May 31st and its enclosures. And let me send a word of thanks to Mrs. Scott for the photograph; it is a most charming picture.

With appreciation of your courtesy in writing me at such length and with every good wish for you and yours, pray believe me   Sincerely yours,   Woodrow Wilson

TLS (Letterpress Books, WP, DLC).

To William Jennings Bryan

My dear Mr. Secretary: The White House June 27, 1913

I entirely approve of the suggestion that Mr. del Valle be requested to continue his journey southward from Mexico City into Zapata's country.

Cordially and sincerely yours,   Woodrow Wilson

TLS (SDR, RG 59, 812.00/23649, DNA).

To William Gibbs McAdoo

My dear McAdoo: The White House June 27, 1913

I had a long talk with Senator Gore the other day, who was very anxious to obtain some recognition for Oklahoma in the general appointments which we are making. He urged upon me a colored man named Patterson¹ for Register of the Treasury. I wonder if you would not be kind enough to see the Senator about it and consider the matter for me.

Always   Faithfully yours,   Woodrow Wilson

TLS (WP, DLC).
¹ Adam Edward Patterson, a lawyer of Muskogee, Okla., who had campaigned actively for Wilson in 1912.

A Telegram and a Letter
to Ellen Axson Wilson

[The White House June 28, 1913]

Find so long as I am President, I can be nothing else. Have felt constrained to consent to be present at the fiftieth anniversary of the Battle of Gettysburg on the 4th of July. Could not leave here until Monday afternoon at the earliest because of business here. It would be foolish to spend forty-eight hours on the train between now and Wednesday when I would have to return. Will write fully tomorrow.

T transcript of WWsh telegram (WC, NjP).

My darling Sweetheart,   The White House 29 June, 1913.

I can hardly keep back the tears as I write this morning. It is a bitter, bitter thing that I cannot come to my dear ones; but the duty is clear, and that ought to suffice. I cannot choose as an individual what I shall do; I must choose always as President, ready to guard at every turn and in every possible way the success of what I have to do for the people. Apparently the little things count quite as much as the big in this strange business of leading opinion and securing action; and I must not kick against the pricks. I am feeling physically quite fit again; the weather has freshened and grown comfortable once more; there are many ways in which I can make things easier; and so duty wears a by no means intolerable aspect. The President is a superior kind of slave, and must content himself with the reflection that the *kind* is superior!

It came about in this way. I had declined the invitation to Gettysburg along with all others and very much as a matter of course, and it had practically gone out of my mind, as I think you know. But yesterday Mitchell Palmer called me up and sought an interview with me about it, saying that at first he had looked upon the matter with a good deal of indifference, as something I could afford to put opon [upon] the same footing with other invitations, but that, as the event drew near and he listened to the talk about it, among our friends in the two houses and out of them, he came to see that it was something we had to take very seriously indeed. It is no ordinary celebration. It is the half-century anniversary of the turning battle of the war. Both blue and gray are to be there. It is to celebrate the end of all feeling as well as the end of all strife between the sections. Fifty years ago, almost, also on the fourth of July, Mr. Lincoln was there (in the midst of business of the most serious and pressing kind, and at great personal cost and sacrifice to himself). If the President should refuse to go this time and should, instead, merely take a vacation for his own refreshment and pleasure, it would be hotly resented by a very large part of the public. It would be suggested that he is a Southerner and out of sympathy with the occasion. In short, it would be more than a passing mistake; it would amount to a serious blunder. And so I surrendered—the more readily because all this would have been so serious a misapprehension of my own real attitude. Nothing, while I am President must be suffered to make an impression which will subtract by an iota from the force I need to do the work assigned me. I can do this without any real risk to my health, and shall lose, not what I need but only what I want (ah, how much!).

My glimpse of Harlakenden is only postponed, my sweet one; and I shall study to get a little pleasure and frequent refreshment here. I shall probably go off a couple of days this week, before the fourth, on one of the boats, for a sniff of the sea. I shall play golf more often. I shall curtail as much as I dare the weary interviewing at the office. In brief, I shall thrive, *if only I surrender my will to the inevitable.*

How shall I tell you what my heart is full of? It is literally full to overflowing with yearning love for you, my incomparable darling, and for the sweet daughters whom I love with so deep a passion, and admire as much as I love! I dare not pour it out today. I am too lonely. I must think quietly and not with rebellion. The big house is very still: I must copy its stately peace, and try to be worthy of the trust of those whom I try to serve and those who make me happy by their wonderful love!

Your own   Woodrow

WWTLS (WC, NjP).

To Mary Allen Hulbert

Dearest Friend,   The White House 29 June, 1913.

Here I am marooned in the White House, alone in my majesty and discontent. The family left for Cornish on Friday. Of course I intended to go with them, and fancied in my simplicity that since this week was to contain the fourth, and the Houses were sure to adjourn over the holiday and all that, I might stay with them for a week or ten days before settling down here to my lonely vigil over legislation and the affairs of State. No such

luck! Within a few hours of the starting hour questions of the
first importance turned up (as only questions of the first importance are smart and mean enough to know how to do) which
no man in his senses would think of trying to settle off hand or of
turning over to some one else to settle; and so I gave up going then
and flattered myself I would follow next Monday. Again stern
visaged Duty lifted its hand and said "Not on your life, my dear,
sanguine boy! You seem to forget that you are my lad, that you
are President of the United States and not your own master,—
no not for a minute." "What is it now?" I said, savage like, and
with scant manners. "You forget, lad, that this fourth of July is
the fiftieth anniversary of the battle of Gettysburg, the battle that
turned the tide of the civil war. A big celebration is on. Old men
both in blue and in gray are to be there. It would be nothing less
than a scandal were the President to prefer a personal holiday
instead of being present. Besides they would say, This is what
comes of making a southerner President: he is not in sympathy,
deep down in his heart, with this celebration at all." Again I
clapped my heels together, saluted, and prepared to obey orders,
not give them. I may take a turn down the river on one of the Government's boats to get a whiff of the sea before Friday; but to
Cornish I cannot go. I shall have to content myself with a week
end later on.

I suppose,—I fervently hope,—that you do not know how hot this
huge continent has been during the past week. A little life and
freshness has come into the air again now, within the last
twenty-four hours and we breathe freely again, but it was a fierce
trial while we were in it. It was hard to keep one's head cool, and
one's temper! You would have smiled to see me at church this
morning. All alone I sat there, a secret service man directly
behind me; and when the service was over the whole congregation waited till I walked out, trying to look unself-conscious and
at ease, but feeling very miserable indeed. All day long I have
been fighting against the weakness and silliness of feeling sorry
for myself. I feel more than ever like a prisoner, like a sort of
special slave, beguiled by the respect and deference of those about
me, but in fact in durance vile and splendid. Congress is quite
certain to sit all summer,—probably until the first of October, and
here I will sit also. The most I can hope is, that by the end of the
session I shall have learned not to tug at my chain and lacerate
my,—feelings! It's a fine discipline, but it comes so late in life! I
learn hard. I am not so pliable as I once was.

Washington is quite empty of everybody who can get away.
Most of the houses on the best residence streets are closed. One

has to go where the other working people live to see any life stirring and get over the sensation that he is forgotten and left behind, as if the population had forgotten to take him away with them. Ah, but it's grand being President and running the Government. Advise all your friends to try it.

I am well, perversely enough. I try to make myself and my doctor believe now and again that I am overworked and likely to go bad if I do not get away; but my symptoms will not conform. I look as ruddy and husky as I feel. It is chiefly sun-burn, acquired during an occasional game of golf in the broiling sun, but I cannot explain that to everybody, and, besides, it's none of their business anyway.

I suppose you read of me in the papers; but remember that you are to believe none of it. And permit me to remind you that I do not read of you in the papers, but am dependent upon letters, which I wish for more and more, simply because I am

Your devoted friend,   Woodrow Wilson

WWTLS (WP, DLC).

From John Bassett Moore

Personal   Washington
My dear Mr. President: 7 p.m., Sunday, June 29, 1913

In performance of my promise of the 27th inst., I beg leave to enclose the draft of a reply[1] to the last Japanese note.

In reading in its final form this Government's reply of May 19 to Japan's original protest, I observe that an amendment made, as I infer, in Cabinet discussion, to a particular passage, misquotes the Constitution of the U. S. and misrepresents its meaning. "Your Government," says the reply, "is no doubt advised that by the Constitution of the U. S. the stipulations of treaties *made in pursuance thereof* are the supreme law of the land," etc. The Constitution does not so read. It (Art. VI) says:

"This Constitution, and the *Laws* of the United States which shall be *made in pursuance thereof*; and all *treaties* made, or which shall be made, *under the Authority of the U. S.*, shall be the Supreme Law of the Land."

By design and in fact the treaty-making power is not subject to the constitutional limitations imposed on the law-making power. The maintenance of this distinction is vital to the preservation of the constitutional supremacy of the Gov't of the U. S. in foreign affairs.

Very respectfully & truly yrs   J. B. Moore.

ALS (WP, DLC).

1 This note cut the ground from under the Japanese government's legal case and blunted its argument that the California legislation was motivated by racial prejudice. While admitting that racial and cultural differences might provoke antagonisms, Moore argued that "the racial difference is a mere mark or incident of the economic struggle." All nations recognized this fact, and it was for this reason that each nation was permitted to maintain exclusive control of immigration into its territory. The Japanese government restricted most foreigners to designated areas. In 1907 it singled out Chinese laborers for exclusion on the ground that they would undercut Japanese workers. The American government was confident that this had been done for economic, not racial, reasons.

Reviewing the negotiation of the Japanese-American Commercial Treaty of 1911, Moore pointed out that the Japanese government, in its own draft, had deliberately omitted any reference to ownership of land. It was the American government's understanding that the Japanese preferred to regulate this matter "wholly by domestic legislation." (This was correct. See n. 3 to the remarks at a press conference printed at April 11, 1913, Vol. 27.) The treaty itself provided only for the mutual right to own or lease houses, manufactories, warehouses, and shops and to lease land for residential and commercial purposes.

The question of the ownership of land was dealt with in an exchange of notes in 1911, Moore continued, when the Japanese government agreed to grant American citizens the right to own land when they came from states that granted the same right to Japanese subjects. In fact, Moore went on, California, by permitting aliens ineligible to citizenship to lease agricultural land for three years, went beyond the measure of privilege established in the treaty. The Japanese government could exercise the principle of exact reciprocity if it so desired.

Continuing, Moore said that, for historical reasons, denial of citizenship to Japanese subjects by the United States did not constitute racial discrimination, adding that he would not go further into the matter because the Imperial government had admitted that the question of naturalization was "a political problem of national and not international concern."

In the final two paragraphs, Moore assured the Japanese government that the United States Government stood ready to guarantee that no Japanese subject would suffer economic loss on account of the California statute. In addition, the Washington government stood ready to use its good offices to assure that all Japanese subjects received fair treatment in cases arising from the California legislation. The Secretary of State to the Japanese Ambassador, July 16, 1913, *FR 1913*, pp. 641-45. Wilson went through Moore's draft and made a few changes, clarifying and tightening its language.

To Paul Samuel Reinsch

White House June 30 1913

Would it be possible and convenient for you to come to Washington the middle of next week   I should like to have a brief co[n]versation with you on a matter of important public business.[1]

Woodrow Wilson.

T telegram (P. S. Reinsch Papers, WHi).

1 Wilson offered Reinsch the ministership to China on July 16, and he accepted.

To Andrew Furuseth[1]

My dear Mr. Furuseth: [The White House] June 30, 1913

I thank you sincerely for the paper you send me under date of June twenty-sixth.[2] I think I appreciate fully the deep significance

of the seamen's cause, and you may be sure that I will espouse it
in every way that is possible.

                    Cordinally yours,   Woodrow Wilson

TLS (Letterpress Books, WP, DLC).
    1 President of the International Seamen's Union. He had been fighting for over
twenty years for legislation to improve the lot of seamen.
    2 A. Furuseth to WW, June 26, 1913, TLS (WP, DLC), an eloquent plea for
Wilson's support of the seamen's bill.

From William Jennings Bryan

My dear Mr. President: Washington June 30, 1913.

    I have read the draft of the answer to the Japanese Ambassador
as prepared by Mr. Moore and have discussed the various points
with him. I think that the answer is a strong one and that the
principal points are presented with great force and conclusive-
ness. There are only two points on which my judgment would
differ from his, and in discussing the matter with him I find that
he is not disposed to be insistent on those points. I have asked him
to prepare two amendments which he thinks could be accepted.
These points are respectfully called to your attention for such
action as you may deem wise.

    The first has reference to the suggestion made by Mr. Guthrie.
I believe it would be advisable to insert the amendment which
Mr. Moore has prepared (at my request) covering this point. It
is not likely that many Japanese would avail themselves of this
offer, and we could well afford to purchase whatever land they
are willing to sell. It seems to me that to make this offer so completely answers their claim that injustice may be done them as to
make it worth while to consider the advisability of including it in
the reply.

    The other point has reference to the naturalization question. I
think that the position taken by Mr. Moore is a sound one and
well fortified with argument and precedent, but am disposed to
believe that it would be better not to discuss the question at this
time. It is quite evident that the question of naturalization is
really the thing that they feel most interested in and if, after the
argument presented on the other questions, we were to present
the argument which Mr. Moore has embodied in your reply it
would seem to close the question. Time is valuable in the matter, it seems to me, and by assuming that the Japanese Government did not intend to press this question, we could prolong the
discussion and give further time for excitement to subside. If they
leave the question without a positive answer, so much better for

us. If they come back with a request for a discussion of this point, we can then offer the argument prepared by Mr. Moore. These points I submit for your consideration.

Just as I am ready to prepare this note, the Japanese Ambassador has called to say that he had received notice of supplemental matter, now on its way, which his government desired to have included in its answer and I told him that the delivery of your answer to his last communication would be delayed until we have received the supplemental matter and had time to consider it.

With assurances of respect, etc., I am, my dear Mr. President,
Very sincerely yours,   W. J. Bryan

Amendments not ready this evening, will send them tomorrow.

TLS (WP, DLC).

From James Watson Gerard

S.S. Imperator, June 30, 1913.

If wireless report correct[1] you have done me great honor of appointing me to Germany. If so permit me to express my gratitude for designation to this most important point. I arrive in Paris July second and shall await your commands.

James W. Gerard.

T telegram (WP, DLC).
[1] It was. Wilson sent his name to the Senate on July 11, 1913.

To William Jennings Bryan

My dear Mr. Secretary: The White House July 1, 1913

The document from Hale[1] is indeed extraordinary. I should like, upon my return from my little outing, to discuss with you very seriously the necessity of recalling Henry Lane Wilson in one way or another, perhaps merely "for consultation" until we can have a talk with the man himself.

With warmest regard,
Faithfully yours,   Woodrow Wilson

TLS (SDR, RG 59, 812.00/7864½, DNA).
[1] Printed at June 18, 1913, Vol. 27.

From William Jennings Bryan

My dear Mr. President: [Washington] July 1, 1913.

When I sent you my letter yesterday afternoon in regard to the Japanese matter, I had not received the amendments from Mr. Moore. I beg to enclose them at this time.[1]

The first amendment is a substitute for that part of the answer which relates to the question of naturalization. The part to be stricken out is the last three lines on page ten, all of pages eleven and twelve, and the first five lines on page thirteen. This postpones for future consideration the question of naturalization.

The second amendment is a very short one, and is added at the end of the fourth line on page fourteen. This, as you will see, incorporates the idea suggested by Ambassador Guthrie. If you approve of it, the answer to the point in regard to damages will be that "this Government stands ready to compensate him (the Japanese subject) for any loss which he might be shown to have sustained or even, in order to avoid any possible allegation of injury, to purchase from him his lands at their full market value prior to the enactment of the statute."

With assurances of respect, etc., I am, my dear Mr. President,
Very sincerely yours,   W. J. Bryan

TLS (WP, DLC).
[1] A two-page CC MS. Bryan describes the amendments in his letter.

From Henry Lane Wilson

Personal to the President

Dear Mr. President: Mexico, July 1, 1913.

I send you, herewith, for your private and confidential information a copy of an interview had with Dr. William Bayard Hale by the Political Secretary to General Diaz, who is also an American and correspondent of the NEW YORK SUN.[1] This report was furnished to me by General Diaz, who informed me at the same time that he had received other reports of a similar character and that both he and the Government had taken note of Dr. Hale's antagonistic attitude toward me and toward the present Government from the very moment of his arrival and before he had any opportunity to make proper investigation.

I have assumed that Dr. Hale has no official mission in Mexico and that he is not charged with the making of any report to you concerning conditions in Mexico, but in the event that information should be offered you from this source I deem it my duty, as your personal representative here, to say to you that this person is by temperament and habit entirely unfit to form a just and clear idea of the situation here. His mind appears to me, from the conversations which I have had with him, to be unevenly balanced, and the questions which he asks relative to events which have occurred here indicate a complete failure to grasp the underlying causes of the unrest in Mexico and absolute ignorance, or, rather, misinformation as to the true history and chronology lying behind the scenes of the Mexican drama.

I know there is a disposition at this time in the United States to make of Madero a martyr to democratic ideals. Whatever may have been the history of his taking off, and I am not prepared to accept without reserves the opinion that the Government was privy thereto, the fact remains that the Madero family despoiled and corrupted every avenue of Government and business in Mexico; that they talked glibly of liberty and human rights but gave none to the people; that they robbed the Government; seized without process of law the property of foreigners and Mexicans; debauched, silenced and censored the press; established secret political societies which maintained a reign of terror; and made illegal arrests without warrant of law. All of the true and secret history of their brief rule in Mexico and prior thereto is known to no one but to me. Others may have it in part but I have it all and eventually I shall place it before the world together with clear demonstrations not only of the anti-American policy of these people but of their deliberate and organized efforts to attack almost every American interest in the country by legal conspiracies in collusion with the courts, and of the absolute inability of this Embassy to secure the punishment of the murderers of Americans or of those who had deprived them of their property by violence or by stealth.

I feel, my dear Mr. President, that whatever may be your final attitude towards this Administration, and it has its bad points as well as its good points, that it is my duty to you to see that you are in no wise misled, either by the reports of sentimental idealists or by those who are endeavoring to bring about conditions which will force intervention, as to the real character of the Madero Administration.

I do not expect to be in charge of this post very long. I have served my Government in the diplomatic service honorably and usefully for seventeen years. I had the absolute confidence of Presidents McKinley, Roosevelt and Taft and the last named has placed in my hands a letter relative to my work at this post up to and including the last day of his Administration which would appear to justify my hope of receiving your confidence during such period as I may have the honor to serve under you. Beyond having the truth made known I care nothing.

I beg to remain, my dear Mr. President,

Very sincerely yours,   Henry Lane Wilson.

TLS (WP, DLC).
    1 It is missing.

From William Gibbs McAdoo

Dear Mr. President: Washington July 1, 1913.

I have yours of the 27th of June in reference to a colored man named Patterson, whom Senator Gore has recommended for the office of Register of the Treasury. I have seen the Senator, as you requested, and have asked him to tell Patterson to come to Washington so that I may look him over and discuss the matter with him.   Very sincerely yours,   W G McAdoo

TLS (WP, DLC).

From Ellen Axson Wilson[1]

                                      Williamstown, Massachusetts
My own darling,   Saturday July 2 1913

I am very sad that no letter went to you yesterday. We had luncheon at 12.30 starting immediately after; I meant of course to write before, but "owing to a combination of circumstances which it would be more interesting not to mention," it was unexpectedly crowded out.

Yesterday was an absolutely perfect day, so that we really enjoyed the *whole* drive,—and the first fifty miles or so were pure bliss. After 36 hours of rain there was no dust, the air was fresh and soft, and the colour glorious. We reached here at 7.45[,] had a delicious little dinner,—no guests,—and went to bed at nine. We have spent this whole morning looking at houses; it is very difficult to find anything that will do.

We are just about to leave again to see another, then to drive and take tea in the open. I must also stop to see Mrs. Nott[2] and later some other old friends come here. The Lewis Perrys[3] come to dinner, but there is no party proposed. This is a most interesting family.[4] I wonder if you remember that Jessie told us that Mrs. Carter was that charming Miss Henry who used to visit Mrs. Fine at Princeton when we first went there. She is just as vivacious and almost as pretty as she was then, though she has

seven children, six boys and one girl. She is a wonderful mother,—
and just as bright and amusing as possible,—makes good-natured
fun of everybody. She says Mrs. Hopkins[5] told her I had "done
more good in Washington in four months than any other President's wife had *ever* done in four years—had completely changed
the conditions of life for 12,000 people,—or was it 12,000 alleys?"[6]
Mrs. H. certainly takes the will for the deed. "It *is* to laugh!"

Am *so* sorry to stop,—they are all waiting. I love you, *love* you,
love you!—you adorable one!

Your devoted little wife   Nell.

ALS (WC, NjP).

1 Mrs. Wilson and Jessie Wilson had just motored over to Williamstown, Mass.,
with Francis Bowes Sayre, a young lawyer of New York. Jessie and Sayre had
become engaged on October 29, 1912. He had agreed to become assistant to
President Harry A. Garfield of Williams College and to do some teaching in the
Political Science Department during the coming academic year, and he and
Jessie were looking for a house. See Francis B. Sayre, *Glad Adventure* (New
York, 1957), pp. 39-45.

2 Alice Effingham Hopkins (Mrs. Charles Cooper) Nott. Mrs. Nott was originally from Williamstown. Her husband was the former chief justice of the
United States Court of Claims. The Notts had retired to Princeton in 1905.

3 B.A., Williams 1898. A.M., Princeton 1899. Professor of English Language
and Literature, Williams College. He was the brother of Bliss Perry.

4 The family of the Rev. John Franklin Carter and Alice Henry Carter. Carter
was the rector of St. John's Episcopal Church of Williamstown. Their seven children were Henry, Sallie, John, Percival, Paul, Lewis, and Lawrence. They were
close friends of Francis Sayre.

5 Charlotte Everett Wise (Mrs. Archibald) Hopkins of Washington. Archibald
Hopkins, A.B., Williams 1862, was the clerk of the United States Court of Claims,
1873-1914. Mrs. Hopkins was chairwoman of the Washington section, woman's
department, of the National Civic Federation and president of the city Home for
Incurables.

6 About Mrs. Wilson's work in the slums, see Grace Vawter (Mrs. Ernest Percy)
Bicknell, "The Home-Maker of the White House, Mrs. Woodrow Wilson's Social
Work in Washington," *Survey,* XXXIII (Oct. 3, 1914), 19-22.

Two Letters to William Jennings Bryan

Dear Mr. Bryan: [The White House] July 3, 1913.

I am sending you with this the note which Mr. Moore prepared
in reply to the last Japanese note. I think it is admirable. I do not
see how it can be answered.

At the same time, I am perfectly willing that the amendments
you suggested to Mr. Moore should be embodied, particularly the
one regarding the purchase by the Government of the lands now
owned by Japanese which they are willing, or desire, to sell.

I have some doubt as to the omission of the passage concerning naturalization. I would not like to seem to avoid or dodge any
of the points made in the last Japanese note, and Mr. Moore's
reply to the portion concerning naturalization seems to me quite
as excellent and quite as conclusive as the rest of the paper. It

throws a new light upon the whole subject, and should certainly make it very difficult for them to press the point any further.

Always cordially and faithfully yours,

[Woodrow Wilson]

CCL (WP, DLC).

My dear Mr. Secretary: The White House July 3, 1913

After reading Hale's report and the latest tel[e]grams from Henry Lane Wilson, I hope more than ever you will seriously consider the possibility of recalling Wilson, as I suggested in a recent note, and leaving matters in the hands of O'Shaughnessy,[1] who, you will notice, is commended as a perfectly honest man by Hale.

Cordially and faithfully yours,   Woodrow Wilson

TLS (W. J. Bryan Papers, DNA).
[1] Nelson O'Shaughnessy, career diplomat, Secretary of the American embassy, Mexico City. He was appointed Chargé d'Affaires on July 17, 1913.

From John R. Mott

Mr. President: Williamstown, Mass., July 3rd, 1913.

When I was with you I volunteered to make some special inquiries regarding Professor Ross of the University of Wisconsin, especially with reference to his attitude toward Christianity and the Church. It has taken me longer to do this than I had expected, as I thought it best to make face to face inquiries rather than by correspondence. I have had opportunity in my recent trip to the West as well as elsewhere to confer with a few persons who are in a position to know. I find that his attitude to Christianity is one of friendliness. I am told that he is not a Church member, but that he attends Church occasionally. I have received the impression from three or four sources that during his visit to China his attitude to Christian missions changed from one of comparative indifference to one of growing sympathy. He seemed to be more impressed, however, by such practical work on the field as that of the Young Men's Christian Association, than the work of the different denominations. Since his return he has been more active in advancing the interest of the Christian Association in his own university. I have heard nothing but favorable comment regarding his own character and that of his wife.

I have wondered whether you have ever considered Professor Ernest D. Burton of the University of Chicago in this connection. He spent the larger part of one year recently making an exhaustive investigation of all phases of the life of the Chinese people from the point of view of Christian missions. He visited nearly all parts of China. I have had occasion to read his confidential reports as well as to confer with him repeatedly at great length, on educational and other problems in China. To my mind he has acquired a really wonderful grasp of the situation. Mr. Brockman[1] shares with me this estimate. If you have not yet arrived at a decision we would take the liberty of suggesting the desirability of considering him. He is a member of the Baptist Church. During his tour he formed a personal acquaintance with practically all of the leading missionaries of all the Churches working in China as well as with Government officials, Chinese educators and other prominent men.

With highest regard,   Faithfully yours,   J. R. Mott

TLS (WP, DLC).
    [1] Fletcher Sims Brockman, general secretary of the National Committee of the Young Men's Christian Associations of China, 1901-15.

An Address at the Gettysburg Battlefield

[July 4, 1913]

Friends and Fellow Citizens: I need not tell you what the battle of Gettysburg meant. These gallant men in blue and gray sit all about us here. Many of them met here upon this ground in grim and deadly struggle. Upon these famous fields and hillsides their comrades died about them. In their presence it were an impertinence to discourse upon how the battle went, how it ended, what it signified! But fifty years have gone by since then, and I crave the privilege of speaking to you for a few minutes of what those fifty years have meant.

What *have* they meant? They have meant peace and union and vigour, and the maturity and might of a great nation. How wholesome and healing the peace has been! We have found one another again as brothers and comrades in arms, enemies no longer, generous friends rather, our battles long past, the quarrel forgotten—except that we shall not forget the splendid valour, the manly devotion of the men then arrayed against one another, now grasping hands and smiling into each other's eyes. How complete the union has become and how dear to all of us, how unquestioned, how benign and majestic, as state after state has been added to this our great family of free men! How handsome the vigour, the maturity, the might of the great nation we love with undivided hearts; how full of large and confident promise that a life will be wrought out that will crown its strength with gracious justice and with a happy welfare that will touch all alike with deep contentment! We are debtors to those fifty crowded years; they have made us heirs to a mighty heritage.

But do we deem the nation complete and finished? These venerable men crowding here to this famous field have set us a great example of devotion and utter sacrifice. They were willing to die that the people might live. But their task is done. Their day is turned into evening. They look to us to perfect what they established. Their work is handed on to us, to be done in another way but not in another spirit. Our day is not over; it is upon us in full tide.

Have affairs paused? Does the nation stand still? Is what the fifty years have wrought since those days of battle finished, rounded out, and completed? Here is a great people, great with every force that has ever beaten in the lifeblood of mankind. And it is secure. There is no one within its borders, there is no power among the nations of the earth, to make it afraid. But has it yet squared itself with its own great standards set up at its birth, when it made that first noble, naive appeal to the moral judgment of mankind to take notice that a government had now at last been established which was to serve men, not masters? It is secure in everything except the satisfaction that its life is right, adjusted to the uttermost to the standards of righteousness and humanity. The days of sacrifice and cleansing are not closed. We have harder things to do than were done in the heroic days of war, because harder to see clearly, requiring more vision, more calm balance of judgment, a more candid searching of the very springs of right.

Look around you upon the field of Gettysburg! Picture the array, the fierce heats and agony of battle, column hurled against column, battery bellowing to battery! Valour? Yes! Greater no man shall see in war; and self-sacrifice, and loss to the uttermost; the high recklessness of exalted devotion which does not count the cost. We are made by these tragic, epic things to know what it costs to make a nation—the blood and sacrifice of multitudes of unknown men lifted to a great stature in the view of all generations by knowing no limit to their manly willingness to serve. In armies thus marshaled from the ranks of free men you will see, as it were, a nation embattled, the leaders and the led, and may know, if you will, how little except in form its action differs in days of peace from its action in days of war.

May we break camp now and be at ease? Are the forces that

fight for the nation dispersed, disbanded, gone to their homes forgetful of the common cause? Are our forces disorganized, without constituted leaders and the might of men consciously united because we contend, not with armies, but with principalities and powers and wickedness in high places? Are we content to lie still? Does our union mean sympathy, our peace contentment, our vigour right action, our maturity self-comprehension and a clear confidence in choosing what we shall do? War fitted us for action, and action never ceases.

I have been chosen the leader of the nation. I cannot justify the choice by any qualities of my own, but so it has come about, and here I stand. Whom do I command? The ghostly hosts who fought upon these battle fields long ago and are gone? These gallant gentlemen stricken in years whose fighting days are over, their glory won? What are the orders for them, and who rallies them? I have in my mind another host, whom these set free of civil strife in order that they might work out in days of peace and settled order the life of a great nation. That host is the people themselves, the great and the small, without class or difference of kind or race or origin; and undivided in interest, if we have but the vision to guide and direct them and order their lives aright in what we do. Our constitutions are their articles of enlistment. The orders of the day are the laws upon our statute books. What we strive for is their freedom, their right to lift themselves from day to day and behold the things they have hoped for, and so make way for still better days for those whom they love who are to come after them. The recruits are the little children crowding in. The quartermaster's stores are in the mines and forests and fields, in the shops and factories. Every day something must be done to push the campaign forward; and it must be done by plan and with an eye to some great destiny.

How shall we hold such thoughts in our hearts and not be moved? I would not have you live even today wholly in the past, but would wish to stand with you in the light that streams upon us now out of that great day gone by. Here is the nation God has builded by our hands. What shall we do with it? Who stands ready to act again and always in the spirit of this day of reunion and hope and patriotic fervor? The day of our country's life has but broadened into morning. Do not put uniforms by. Put the harness of the present on. Lift your eyes to the great tracts of life yet to be conquered in the interest of righteous peace, of that prosperity which lies in a people's hearts and outlasts all wars and errors of men. Come, let us be comrades and soldiers yet to serve our fellow men in quiet counsel, where the blare of trumpets is neither heard nor heeded and where the things are done which make blessed the nations of the world in peace and righteousness and love.

Printed reading copy (WP, DLC).

To Violet Sopwith Grubb

[Cornish, N. H., c. July 8, 1913]

My deepest sympathy.[1] I grieve most sincerely that we should have lost so true and noble a gentleman and soldier. I wish I could have done something to cheer and brighten his last days.

Woodrow Wilson.

T telegram (Letterpress Books, WP, DLC).
[1] Her husband, Edward Burd Grubb, had died on July 7.

From William Jennings Bryan

Washington
My dear Mr. President: July Eight, Nineteen thirteen.

The following telegram came from Hale this morning:

"Mr. Del Valle is here giving elaborate newspaper interviews announcing himself as a special envoy commissioned by his friend President Wilson to take important steps. Comports himself as a plenipotentiary. Allows himself to be described as the next Ambassador. I have no doubt that it is all right but the atmosphere here is electric and possibility of a grave indiscretion is distressing."

I will wire Del Valle to keep away from newspapers and that the success of his mission depends upon his exercising care not to allow himself to be considered as an official.

I am, my dear Mr. President,

Very truly yours,   W. J. Bryan

P.S. The situation in Mexico is giving me a good deal of concern. Do you think it is time to offer our good offices to secure a conference of the representatives of the various factions with the government with a view to securing a basis for peace? I am inclined to think it worth while to try. If not why not invite Ambassador Wilson here *for conference*? You suggested this and it appeals to me. I am perfectly willing to share with you responsibility for accepting his resignation, but am inclined to think that it would be better to bring him here for conference and decide on resignation after conference, but it might be well to have him sound Huerta about a conference before starting. What do you think?

W.J.B.

Am also enclosing copy of additional telegram received from Mr. Hale today.[1]

TLS (WP, DLC).
[1] W. B. Hale to B. G. Davis, July 8, 1913, T telegram (WP, DLC), saying that there were rumors that Huerta might take to the field in person, turn the government over to a lieutenant, and run for the presidency himself.

A Report by William Bayard Hale

July 9, 1913.

MEMORANDA ON AFFAIRS IN MEXICO.

Summary of Conditions.

At this writing, the Government of Victoriano Huerta has been in power for nineteen weeks.

For three months the city lay in part terrorized by the methods through which Huerta had siezed power and partly persuaded that the only hope for peace and order lay in the rule of such a man.

At the end of three months, it was apparent that Huerta was not pacifying the country. The revolt of the Madero sympathizers in the North spread, until it reached from the Atlantic to the Pacific and extended far down into the interior of the Republic. In the South, three States have passed entirely out of Federal control, and as many more are overrun with bandits. The most daring of these, the Zapatistas, bring their operations within sight of the Capital, frequently descending into the Federal District (closely corresponding to the District of Colombia). It is to-day unsafe to motor fifteen miles out on any road leading from Mexico City. The suburbs of Tlalpam, Coyoacan, San Angel, six or eight miles from the National Palace, are subject to frequent alarms and constant apprehension.

Less than forty percent of the railroad mileage of the country is in operation.

Maps marked to show the division of the country between Federals and Insurrectos, are misleading and of little avail. Because the ordinary conditions of rebellion and the customary methods of warfare are not to be found. The "Rebel" forces are mainly wandering bands. It is not their aim to occupy or hold territory—they revage and demoralize it; they capture a town or city, raise forced loans, do a certain amount of looting, and then generally evacuate, passing on to another town.

The most considerable city most recently looted was Zacatecas, which yielded large spoil. Matamoras, important as the key to the Northeast, and Durango, one of Mexico's richest cities, the rebels continue to hold at this writing. Bands now appear to be gathering about Guadalajara, a city of immense wealth, but the movement made be a feint, with another point as its real object. Another concentration appears to be taking place around Ciudad Juarez.

The chief seat of rebel operations, however, is in the country. Two thirds of the land is overrun with bands, which appear, levy tribute, and disappear, to the utter demoralization of the Government's authority. In the North, they frequently act in considerable force, but in the South they have the character of mobile guerillas.

All are mounted—or practically all. They live in the saddle, off the best they can find in the land, and the life is so attractive that recruits are constantly joining. It is perhaps idle to attempt to form any estimate of the number of bandits in the saddle throughout the Republic, but it can hardly be guessed as less than Forty Thousand.

The Government troops cannot, and do not pretend, to follow these bands into the country. The Federal forces, which General Huerta last Sunday said numbered Seventy One Thousand, and which may possibly amount to Forty Thousand, stick closely to the cities and follow the lines of the railroads. They are far superior in the possession of artillery, but they have few horses, and are without pack or wagon transportation facilities.

The Government forces are made up entirely of conscripts— captured rebels, released jail-birds and impressed peons. They can be handled only when kept together. To despatch a column of even four or five hundred into the country after the enemy, is equivalent to making them a present of so many recruits.

The bandits will sweep over a State, take half a dozen towns and occupy them until a Federal force appears; then, breaking up into squads and making their way across country, they suddenly turn up reunited in another district, where the program is repeated.

There is very much less fighting than the official reports indicate. Many of the published battles are known never to have been fought. The corruption of the Government officers is past belief: Many "engagements" consist of conferences between officers and rebel chiefs, as a result of which arms, and more particularly cartridges, are sold to the insurgents, who thereupon decamp with a pretence of flight. The very highest military officers are undoubtedly participants in acts like these. The whole scene of "war" as conducted in Mexico is, as much as anything else, a gigantic opportunity for graft. The Government pays (or is supposed to pay) its soldiers $1.50 (silver) per day, out of which they provide for themselves. Muster rolls are kept padded until they do not represent the true strength of the Army in the most remote degree. Commissions are exacted on every purchase; provisions withheld; horses, arms and ammunition sold, and fictitious battles with an imaginary enemy fought by non-existent troops.

It is one of the hopeless features of the situation that the officers of the Army and the War Department have every incentive to prolong the war and not to end it.

The brigand leader, Zapata, seldom more than forty miles from the City of Mexico, is never so much as seen by the Federal troops. "Battles" with his men are reported daily, and daily a few hundred Zapatistas prisoners are marched into the Capital. They are in reality harmless peons, for the most part. The reconcentrado policy, made familiar by General Weyler in Cuba, has been put into effect in the State of Morelos, and that rich district is being swiftly depopulated, and is returning to jungle, haunted by outlaws who have reverted to the type of savages. Thousands have been torn from their homes and sent to penal colonies in Yucatan, and hundreds more have been pressed into the army. The day before this page was written, the Government "captured" and brought to town the mother-in-law and the four sisters-in-law of Zapata, who were taken along with a gang of other victims, to a military prison, and who will be held as hostages.

The operations in Morelos make one of the three campaigns in which the Government forces are chiefly engaged. The other two are: one in the Northwest against General Alvaro Obregon, and the Sonora Rebel Army; the other in the Northeast against General Venustiano Caranza. General after general, in the Government Service, has returned disgraced from these campaigns; in the latest chapter of the Sonora fighting, General Pedro Ojeda seems to have been frightfully punished, though he has managed to retain the Port and City of Guaymas. As this is written, the Government is building high hopes of the success of the most elaborate campaign it has yet organized against Carranza, under Generals Joaquin Tellez and Rubio Navarette. Carranza is declared to be surrounded at Monclova by overwhelmingly superior forces. Already, however, particulars have leaked through which arouse the suspicion that something has gone wrong again. . . .

Again, let it be repeated that there is no definite demaracation between the sections of territory in control of the Huerta Government and those out of its control. The "rebels" as a rule do not regularly occupy and organize a Government for the territory they ravage. They have done this, as has been said, in Sonora, and probably to some extent in Chihuahua, Sinaloa, Coahuila and Durango, though little accurate information is obtainable in Mexico City as to the character of the authority, or the degree of organization, if any exists, in those regions.

The general picture is that of a country "on the loose"; "out of hand"; with a Government which may be said actually to be in control of perhaps one third of its territory, conditions in that third being disorderly; and utterly unable to maintain anything approaching order, except along a few railroad lines—unable, indeed, to send its troops, except in large bodies, prepared to fight their way through constant harrassing guerillas.

It is hardly necessary to dwell on the hard lot of the unfortunates who inhabit the ravaged regions. There is no security for any sort of property or life. Lands are going out of cultivation; mines are closed down; only the most necessary labor and trade is carried on. Bandits and Government troops vie in cruelty to each other and towards the population. The Mexican is a savage and finds sport and pleasure in horrible excesses of cruelty. Except in its chief cities, life in Mexico counts for nothing to-day; non-combatants are shot to death merely by way of amusement, and at the least excuse death is administered with refined cruelty. There can be no doubt that sportive barbarities are common. I have the testimony of eye-witnesses of such acts. The abuse of women is extremely common. Prisoners are shot by both sides. After every battle skirmish, captured officers are "executed" by both sides.

The mass of the population take no sides. That is the peculiarity of the case. They submit, apparently without thought of the possibility of resistance. A band of a dozen free-booters ride into a town of several thousand, shooting at everything in sight, and the place is captured. A city like Durango, with a population of forty-five thousand, made no resistance to the attack of eight hundred or a thousand rebels. The National Palace is visited by streams of petitioners from towns and the cities, begging Federal troops for their protection. "There was one delegation to-day," said General Huerta, "from a town of five thousand, begging to be protected from a band of seven that had threatened them." Nothing ever suggests to the average Mexican that he could get a gun and defend his own home, or that it is any business of his

to put down rebellion, except by criticizing the army that is paid
to do it. Alike in war and politics, the mass of the Mexican people
never dream of mixing.

Such is the condition of Mexico to-day. Sentiment toward the
Huerta Government has completely changed within the weeks I
have been here. A month ago, no one breathed a doubt of its
triumph. Newspapers printed nothing but victories and eulogies.
It was hard not to accept the universal opinion, but even then
the facts were too clear.

The change of sentiment came with the fall of Zacatecas
and Matamoras and the revelation of the truth about the big
loan, in celebration of which the business men of the city gave
the Secretary of Hacienda a $10,000 dinner. The Government
was to get 200 millions; it actually gets less than ten. Then came
the fall of Durango, the revolt of Campeche, and the collapse of
the Sonora campaign.

From the depression following these events, the Huerta Government has now indeed partly recovered. It is actively sending
out more troops. The new Minister of War is inspiring new confidence. Frantic efforts to open the railroad to Laredo give some
real promise of success. If Carranza should be caught at Monclova, it will give the Huerta Government new life for a little
while. If he gets away as usual, the fact will not appear in the
papers here.

A new policy was adopted towards the Press last week: The
editors of the city were summoned to the Minister of Governa-
cion and given their choice between full support of the Government in news and editorial columns—or immediate suppression.
It was not necessary to suppress a single newspaper.

Financially, the prospects of the Government could scarcely
be worse. Expenses are greater than ever; for not only is the cost
of the war inevitably heavy, but war-time conditions multiply all
forms of graft. Receipts, meantime, have fallen off fully one-
half. The Veracruz and the Tampico Custom-houses alone yield
any revenue to the Government. The taxes on the State have
generally had to be remitted. The mining taxes have fallen off
one-third; the hacienda taxes two-thirds or more. The stamp taxes
are greatly decreased. . . .

Who's Who in Mexico.

General Huerta is an ape-like old man, of almost pure Indian
blood. He may almost be said to subsist on alcohol. Drunk or only
half-drunk (he is never sober), he never loses a certain shrewd-
ness. He has been life-long a soldier, and one of the best in

Mexico, and he knows no methods but those of force. It is now believed by some who come into contact with him that Huerta is finding the presidency a hard and an uncongenial task. He is too old to learn to devote himself to work at the desk and in the Cabinet; and his drunken habits are against him. But he is a hard fighter, glories in the exercise of power, and I see no signs that he will abandon his office, except, as is possible, to take the field for a few months, so as to render himself legally eligible to take the presidency again under the pretence of election. . . .

Shall We Abandon Mexico?

on July 2, I sent a despatch commenting upon the feeling aroused here by the circulation of a telegram, representing Secretary Bryan as saying, with supposed significance, that the Taft instructions to Americans to get out of Mexico had never been revoked. The purpose of my despatch was to suggest that the conception, very widely entertained, that American interests here were mainly of the Standard Oil or Guggenheim type, with employees who could readily leave the country, did not correctly represent the case.

I do not know what proportion of the American capital invested in Mexico is controlled by absentee corporations, but it is the fact that vastly the more substantial element of our interest here consist in men and women from the United States who live and work here.

Of these there are thousands—in the Capital City alone, now perhaps three thousand, in normal times perhaps eight thousand. Some of them are in business in a small way; some are clerks; some are in the professions—men of whom the United States should be proud, leaders in the law, in medicine, in surgery. There are teachers and stenographers, and trained nurses and missionaries; there are engineers, assayers, chemists, mechanics, blacksmiths, shoemakers and shoedealers, bakers, barbers, printers, engravers, newspaper men, garage-keepers, druggists, haberdashers, plumbers, dressmakers, small contractors and builders, tailors, typewriting agents, automobile agents, hotel and boarding house keepers, carpenters, news dealers. There are grocery keepers, milk-men, real estate dealers, proprietors of book-stores, electrical repair shops, confectionery shops. A surprising number have prospered until they are among the chief figures in the financial, commercial and industrial life of the city and the country. Leading banks are owned and managed by citizens of the United States. Citizens of the United States are employed on railroads, in every position from Switchman to General Manager and President. All kinds of business enterprises and industrial enterprises—foundries, steel works, fruit canneries, telephone systems, planing mills, amusement enterprises—have been conceived and built up and are operated by citizens of the United States in the City of Mexico. I do not speak of enterprises by big American combinations of capital; I speak of individuals, who have come here from the United States, and, by their industry, have established themselves in business and brought it up to importance.

These people are Americans of our own type and with our own sentiments and ideals. They live in American houses; they practice and hold up American standards of morality and rectitude.

No one could become acquainted with our people here, as I have become acquainted with them, sober, high-minded men and women, and observe how they are regarded in the community, without understanding their tremendous influence for good. To ask these people to withdraw from Mexico would be to push civilization backward; to desert the standards they have planted here; to abandon outposts and pioneers, not of any political ambitions of the United States, but of our higher civilization, our better ways of living. Surely, Mr. Bryan, with his warm sympathy for all that uplifts, cannot be willing to see this done. Surely, the United States will not thus betray the cause of civilization and humanity.

We are, in spite of ourselves, the guardians of order and justice and decency on this Continent; we are, providentially, naturally and unescapably, charged with the maintenance of humanity's interest here. Civilization and humanity look to us, and have a right to look to us, for protection on this Continent. Civilization is more important than the conventional claims of nationality. It is more necessary to maintain civilization than to pay fantastic deference to the formal prerogatives of a Government that has lost the ability to maintain civilization.

This is no argument of intervention in Mexico. Intervention is not necessary. Firm representations, politely made, as by a perfectly friendly, yet a fully determined and powerful neighbor, would, I believe, save Mexico. To frame the exact plan, to hit upon just the fashion and manner in which the necessary influence can be brought to bear, without involving us too deeply, may take long and hard thought. Then, let the Government of the United States give it that thought. But let it not abandon

Mexico and the ideals our people have set up here, extinquish the torch, lay down the staff of leadership committed to our hands. Wm. B. Hale

T memoranda (SDR, RG 59, 812.00/8203, DNA).

Sir Edward Grey to Sir Cecil Arthur Spring Rice

Sir, F.O., 11 July, 1913.

I told the American Ambassador to-day that I wished to ask him unofficially about Mexico. The European Representatives there had expressed a great desire that the United States should recognise General Huerta provisionally in the interests of stability. We ourselves could not do more than we had done, which was to give a provisional recognition till the next election should take place. This recognition would expire after the election, and we should then be free to consider the question of giving permanent recognition to whatever was the outcome of the election. I did not wish to instruct Your Excellency to make any representation in Washington that would be embarrassing to the Government of the United States; but it did seem to me that it was in every one's interest to have as much stability as possible up to the next election, and I should be very glad if the Ambassador would ascertain whether his Government saw any insuperable objection to their giving provisional recognition.

The Ambassador said that his Government were most reluctant to intervene in Mexico. He could tell me privately that the President had been taking exceptional steps to ascertain what really was the state of things in Mexico. But, as the United States were a neighbour of Mexico, they were affected by considerations that did not arise in the case of European Powers.

I admitted this readily, but said that these considerations might cut both ways: the United States might be compelled by disorder on their frontier to intervene; but on the other hand, if they desired not to intervene, they might have still more reason than European Powers to do what they could to promote stability without intervention.

The Ambassador said that he did not know the view of his Government, but he would ascertain privately. E.G.

TLI (FO 371/1674, No. 32722, PRO).

To John Randolph Thornton[1]

My dear Senator: [The White House] July 15, 1913

Thank you sincerely for having let me see the enclosed.

Let me say that I fully recognize the difficulty of your position in the matter of the sugar schedule and do not wish to minimize it in any degree. You will, I am sure, understand me, however, if I say that the conclusion I, myself, draw from the circumstances is different from that which you evidently draw. Undoubtedly, you should have felt yourself perfectly free in the caucus[2] to make every effort to carry out the promises you had made to your own people, but when it comes to the final action, my own judgment is perfectly clear. No party can ever for any length of time control the Government or serve the people which can not command the allegiance of its own minority. I feel that there are times, after every argument has been given full consideration and men of equal public conscience have conferred together, when those who are overruled should accept the principle of party government and act with the colleagues through whom they expect to see the country best and most permanently well served.

I felt that I owed it to you that I should express my own judgment as frankly as you have done me the honor of expressing yours. Cordially and sincerely yours, Woodrow Wilson

TLS (Letterpress Books, WP, DLC).
    [1] Democratic senator from Louisiana.
    [2] The Senate Democratic caucus debated the Underwood bill from June 20 through July 7, 1913. The members voted on the latter date to make the bill a party measure.

From William Sulzer

Personal

My dear Mr. President: Albany July 15, 1913

I respectfully ask you to see and to hear Commissioner Van-Kennan,[1] and Mr. Lucey,[2] of our State. They come to see you about a matter of much moment to your administration, and to mine. You can rely implicitly on just what they tell you. I am very anxious to have Mr. Lucey appointed United States District Attorney for the Northern District of New York. It will be in the interest of good government, and honest and decent administration. He is peculiarly qualified for the duties of the office by ability, by honesty, and by long experience. A more capable man could not be selected, and his appointment will be exceedingly gratifying to our friends. I commend Mr. Lucey to your favorable consideration, and hope you can spare the time to go over matters with these gentlemen regarding this whole situation.

With best wishes, believe me,

Very sincerely your friend,   Wm. Sulzer

TLS (WP, DLC).

[1] George E. Van Kennen, a lawyer of Ogdensburg and mayor of that city since 1910.

[2] Dennis Benedict Lucey, a lawyer of Ogdensburg, mayor of the city, 1885-87, and for many years chairman of the St. Lawrence County Democratic Committee. Wilson appointed him United States district attorney in 1916.

From Ellen Axson Wilson

My own darling,   Cornish, New Hampshire July 15, 1913.

Many, many thanks for the dear telegram![1] God bless the man who invented the "night letter" and the "day letter,"—telegrams that really *say* something. I have been living on that one, —was tempted to kiss it, in spite of the fact that it was really Coates[2] who wrote it down! We have had two very interesting afternoons, yesterday at Miss Slade's[3] and today at Mr. Platts[4] the architects. They are both *enchanting* places. The Slade house and garden is one of Platts best and it is to me simply perfection! The house is set very high and the view is magnificent. I had no idea that the river made such a grand sweeping curve. The house is Italian and practically all the furniture is old Italian, really museum pieces; and yet it looks as if one could live in it. The garden is a *dream*, and is surrounded by old spreading beech trees.

The Platt house & garden are charming too—though of course much simpler than the Slade, but the *view* there absolutely takes your breath away! It is a matter of composition,—of glorious long sweeping lines and one splendid simple valley leading on and on into it as if from earth to Heaven! *I* consider it one of the most beautiful views in the world! And as if that were not enough for one family to own they have a pine grove that makes all the others here look like toy trees. It is perfectly clean of underbrush, just the deep, deep carpet of pine needles, and it stretches along a high ridge with absolutely nothing beyond it but the blue mountains. These great trees from the roots up were in si[l]-houette against an intense violet blue. It was unearthly in its beauty. I am wild for you to see it.

But it is after seven & I must close in haste. We are all perfectly well & as happy as we can be without you. I love you beyond all words   Yours always & altogether,   Nell.

ALS (WC, NjP).
1 It is missing.
2 A White House butler.
3 The summer home of Emily and Augusta Slade of New York.
4 Charles Adams Platt, an architect and landscape artist of New York.

To William Sulzer

My dear Governor: [The White House] July 17, 1913

There is such an excessive pressure upon me at the present time, with regard to important matters from which I cannot conscientiously turn away even for a moment, that I do not see how it would be possible for me to see Mr. VanKennan and Mr. Lucey at present, but I should be very glad to have them make an appointment with Mr. Tumulty or send me memoranda of any sort that they choose.

I suggest this course with the greatest reluctance, but I do not see anything else to do in the extraordinary circumstances of my present days.

Cordially and sincerely yours,   Woodrow Wilson

TLS (Letterpress Books, WP, DLC).

Remarks at a Press Conference

July 17, 1913

Gentlemen, I wanted to say a few words to you about the Mexican situation, so that nothing might be done or said which will make it more difficult to handle than it is now, and I want to say this in our capacity as confidential friends, so that you will know exactly what is in my mind and for your guidance. The trouble is that we don't know what is going on in Mexico. I have reason to believe—I always have to say that with regard to Mexico, because nothing appears to be certain—but I have every reason to believe that the reported demonstrations in Mexico City against Americans are fomented and manufactured by a small group of persons who are trying to force this government to recognize the government of Mr. Huerta; and there is an equal artificiality attaching to a good many other things that are said to be happening in Mexico. Upon examination, they don't turn out, so far as can be ascertained at this distance, to be genuine. I will give you an instance: The other day it was reported, upon the capture of some town, that a number of women were assaulted and afterwards committed suicide. We immediately tried, through the State

Department, to get a confirmation of that or some means of judging whether it was true or not, through our consuls on the spot and in the neighborhood. We could not get any verification of it at all, and in my opinion it never happened. But the very phraseology I am using shows you our embarrassment—I say, in my opinion it never happened. I don't know. And I wish you gentlemen might cooperate with me, not only in trying to get the most exact information obtainable, but also in trying to keep the public from being misled by the rumors. It has been said, among other things, that foreign governments are making representations which constitute a pressure on this government. Now, that isn't true. In the most informal way possible, they have conveyed to us the impressions as to the situation on the part of their representatives in the City of Mexico, which, you see, is a very different matter. And, if I may say so, in entire confidence, I think that one or two of their representatives in Mexico City are very excitable and unwise gentlemen. But that is just part of the whole confusion and uncertainty of the situation. So that I can say to you that I am in search of the real facts, as is shown by the fact that we have asked Mr. Henry Lane Wilson to return to Washington at once so that we can by intimate conversation with him, instead of through telegrams, which he may feel may leak at any time, get his direct and genuine impressions in the situation. I think that that is all that I can say, because I am searching for the facts and don't believe I have got them. Now, when we get the facts, it will be possible, I hope, to formulate some definite course of action, provided things don't change overnight and throw everything into confusion after we have got the information that Mr. Wilson may be able to bring us. . . .

Mr. President, do you have any other sources of information than the diplomatic and consular service in Mexico?

>Well, you know I told you that Mr. Hale, being a long time friend of mine, and having gone down there in the interest of two or three papers, promised to supply me with any information he could get; and I received one or two telegrams from him, but, of course, they are entirely of an unofficial character—just conveying his impressions.

Mr. President, is it your intention of sending Mr. Ambassador Wilson back to Mexico?

>That will depend on his own advice and account of the situation. . . .

Mr. President, do you care to indicate what was the nature of Mr. Hale's impressions?

Well, mixed, like the others. Because, there again, the impressions differ from time to time. . . .

Mr. President, would you care to say, in the same confidential way, what you believe to be the extent of the duty of the United States towards the situation in Mexico?

No, my opinion would be conjectural until I am sure of the situation. . . .

Pending further more dependable information, there will be no change in the administration policy of "hands off," pending a constitutional election?

No.

So there is a determination that the government shall not be recognized there until after the election?

No, there isn't. I can't say that there is a determination about anything. I mean, we hold our minds perfectly open to do the right and necessary thing, until we find out what it is.

Mr. President, do you feel that Ambassador Wilson has been too friendly to the Huerta government?

Oh, I don't permit myself to feel anything about it.

Is this summoning of the Ambassador here in the nature of a recall?

No; I have stated just exactly the nature. . . .

Mr. President, of course, we all know you are not inclined to give any formal recognition to the Huerta government; but the Huerta government is having all the rights that we would accord to any de facto government outside of formal recognition. For example, they have the right to bring in arms and ammunition from the United States, and the Constitutionalists, who control, or apparently control, all of northern Mexico, don't seem to have that right. Now, I have understood that there had been no recognition of the Huerta government even as a belligerent. They have simply permitted the recognition of the Madero government to continue. Now, the Constitutionalists are anxious to have this government grant them that right to bring in arms and ammunition or else to rescind it with reference to the Huerta government. Has that matter been considered?

No, it hasn't. . . .

Mr. President, will this government tolerate the landing of foreign troops in Mexico?

I am not going to answer that; that is too big an "if."

We have to take that into consideration in writing?

I don't see why you have to take that into consideration,

because there is no most distant intimation of that possibility yet.
I understand that there have been a good many outrages on
foreign subjects down there.

> I have seen that stated; there again, I don't know whether
> it is so or not. I doubt it myself. Of course, in a state of civil
> war, property may undoubtedly suffer, and the nation under
> which it suffered will have to render indemnity finally for
> it; but international law does not recognize any right other
> than the right of final indemnifications in circumstances of
> that sort.

Did I understand you to say in the early part of the interview
that, after conferring with Ambassador Wilson, there will be an
announcement of some definite plan?

> I don't know whether our minds will be crystallized by what
> we hear from him. . . .

Mr. President, is a man named Del Valle of California furnishing
you with any information?

> He did indirectly through a gentleman with whom he was
> corresponding, but not directly.

Can you state where he is now, Mr. President?

> I don't know.

Mr. President, have you any intention of sending anyone down to
Mexico?

> No present intention. I hold myself ready to do anything at
> any time, though.

T MS (C. L. Swem Coll., NjP).

To Edward Mandell House

The White House July 17-18-13

Wellcome back with every affectionate welcome   It is delightful to have you in reach again   We have missed you every day
and valued every message and letter   Most cordial greeting to
Mrs House.   Woodrow Wilson.

T telegram (E. M. House Papers, CtY).

From William Gibbs McAdoo

Dear Mr. President: Washington July 18, 1913.

As a result of our conversation day before yesterday about the
position of Register of the Treasury, I respectfully recommend

the appointment of Adam E. Patterson, of Muskogee, Oklahoma. He is endorsed by Hon. R. S. Hudspeth, Member of the Democratic National Committee from New Jersey, Charles L. Barnes, Secretary of the National Colored Democratic League, and by Senators Owen and Gore. I have spoken to each of the Senators about him and they approve of his appointment, so it will not be necessary for you to see them about the matter unless you care to.   Very sincerely yours,   W G McAdoo

TLS (WP, DLC).

From Cleveland Hoadley Dodge

My dear Mr. President: New York July 18th, 1913.

During the past two weeks (part of which time you were on your vacation) I have sent to Mr. Tumulty a number of letters and telegrams from Judge Haff from the City of Mexico, asking Mr. Tumulty to use his discretion in showing them either to you or the State Department.

I do not know how valuable Judge Haff's information has been, but it has thrown some light upon the situation in Mexico which may have been of service. Meanwhile in the last few days the papers which are opposed to your policy have been so energetic in trying to force you to recognize the Huerta Government that I want to express to you how thoroughly I approve of your course and how unwise I think it would be for you to recognize the nominal president of the Mexican Republic.

Many of the large American interests in Mexico would like to see our government recognize the Huer[t]a regime, and they, as a rule, make a great hue and cry. On the other hand I have met many men who have interests in Mexico who thoroughly approve of your policy. I had a call yesterday from Mr. E. D. Morgan,[1] the grandson of the late Governor Morgan,[2] who is interested in a large ranch in Chihuahua and large silver properties further south, both of which have suffered considerably from the present unrest. He called to impress upon me the fact that Ambassador Wilson was strongly in favor of recognition, and to express his very decided hopes that our government would not be influenced by the views of the Ambassador when he reaches Washington.

After he had left the office he wrote me the enclosed letter, which expresses his sentiments very clearly, and, as he is an influential, well-informed man, I have obtained his consent to forward his letter to you, which I think will interest you.[3]

In talking the matter over with Mr. Vanderlip two days ago

he expressed the same sentiments, stated that he did not see how the Huerta Government could continue much longer as only fifteen per cent of the loan to his government has been subscribed, and apparently the bankers do not intend to give him much if any of the money unless the United States recognizes him.

I am very glad that you were able to get a good week's vacation, and sincerely trust that you will not be worn out by the severe strain that you are having in Washington during this summer weather.

With warm regards,
                    Very sincerely yours,   Cleveland H. Dodge

P.S. I am going off next Tuesday for a ten days cruise (how I wish we could fly the President's flag at our forepeak) & if anything of interest should come from Mexico when I am away, I will have it forwarded to Mr. Tumulty by my secretary   CHD

TLS (WP, DLC).
  [1] Edward Denison Morgan, president of the Corralitos Co., which owned 900,-000 acres of land in Mexico, and of the Candelaria Mining Co. He was also a director of banking, coal, and power companies in New York and New Jersey. He was named Alfred Waterman Morgan, but he took the name of his father, Edward Denison Morgan, Jr., a physician, after his father's early death.
  [2] Edward Denison Morgan, Sr., Governor of New York, 1859-62, and United States senator, 1863-69.
  [3] E. D. Morgan to C. H. Dodge, July 17, 1913, TLS (WP, DLC). Morgan stated that the *Huertistas* had gained power by "unspeakable treachery," had no money, and could get none without the recognition of the United States. It was evident to any intelligent man, he added, "what use they would make of the money obtained by loans through the endorsement of the United States."

From Ellen Axson Wilson

                              Cornish, New Hampshire
My own darling,   Friday morning [July 18, 1913]

Your second "day letter"[1] has just arrived and has made us all happy. You speak of my letter. I am wondering if you would like me to write every day. I would of course be glad to do it. Somehow I had a feeling that perhaps you were too busy to be bothered with the daily letter now!

I am *so* pleased about the result of the White House Conference on the labour trouble.[2] It really is a great success, is it not, dear? A Mr. Saunders of New Jersey,[3] who is in Windsor, was actually saying yesterday that he thought it the greatest thing you had accomplished since you went to Washington. Is it true that Mrs. Borden Harriman had something to do with suggesting it? Don't forget to answer this question for I am very interested to know.

The girls have just started to meet Frank who comes on the

10.30, and will stay over Sunday of course. The weather remains just as it was when you were here and has been ever since,— absolutely perfect—like Sept. How I hope that means fairly cool weather even in Washington!

Our days keep rather full in one way or another for of course I paint every morning. Yesterday I had my first little tea and it was very pleasant,—such nice people! I had half the Cornish crowd yesterday and shall have the other half today—about 25 each day. On Monday I shall have all the Windsor people who have called,—about 35. I am sorry to say that several of the interesting men of the Colony are not here now,—among them Platt the architect & Kenyon Cox.[4] Mrs. Platt[5] is charming;—also a Mrs. Hand,[6] wife of a distinguished New York lawyer, Judge Hand. He too is away. She presided at the little Club[7] this week with a charming mixture of real ability, modesty and a quiet, soft, feminine charm. It seems she was a class-mate and friend at Bryn Mawr of Florence Hoyt.

Mr. Vonnoh[8] has begun his group of the four of us. We are "composed" in his studio window with the grape vines and columns outside. I am pouring tea at a tiny table. It bids fair to be a nice thing of the sunny impressionist sort. It is going to take a lot of our time I fear, but fortunately we do not all have to pose at once.

Well I must get this off so that it will reach you tomorrow morning. Oh how I wish I could tell you how *intensely* I love you & how constantly I think of you!—but it is impossible.

Yours devotedly,   Nell.

ALS (WC, NjP).

[1] It is missing.

[2] On July 14, the President, the Secretary of Labor, and congressional leaders met at the White House with representatives of railroad companies and unions and averted a strike of nearly 100,000 trainmen and conductors on fifty-four eastern roads. Union and management leaders agreed to arbitration under terms of the pending Newlands bill.

[3] William Laurence Saunders of Plainfield, engineer and inventor of devices for drilling rock under water and for pumping with compressed air; president of the Ingersoll-Sergeant Drill Co. and of the Ingersoll-Rand Co. He was active in the state Democratic party, was twice mayor of North Plainfield, and was appointed by Wilson to the New Jersey Harbor Commission.

[4] Kenyon Cox, an artist of New York City. He executed portraits, sculptures, building decorations, mosaics, and murals.

[5] Eleanor Hardy Platt.

[6] Frances Amelia Fincke (Mrs. Learned) Hand, Bryn Mawr 1898.

[7] Mrs. Wilson attended two clubs in Cornish. One consisted of local artists; the other was what she called a "discussion group."

[8] Robert William Vonnoh, portrait and figure painter of New York City, winner of the Thomas R. Proctor Portrait Prize of the National Academy of Design and of several exhibition medals. Vonnoh's portrait now hangs in the Wilson House in Washington. It is also reproduced in this volume.

To Ellen Axson Wilson

My precious Sweetheart,   The White House 20 July, 1913.

What shall I say to a little girl whom I love with all my heart and yearn for almost more than I can stand who *asks me if I would like a daily letter*; saying that she had hesitated to write every day because she was afriad I was too busy to be "bothered" with a daily letter now! I do not know how to explain things to such a dull person! You dear, dear goose! Why I have not begged for a letter every day, and do not beg for it now, only because I cannot return the infinite favour in kind. I do not wish to be selfish, and it would be selfish to ask for more than I can give: for I am vain enough to believe that you would like a letter every day from me! What a treat it would be: for the loneliness of being without you is sometimes more than I can bear, it seems to me,—but your days are full, very full, and I want them to be, of painting and driving and seeing interesting people and making friends, and of anything and everything that may make the summer rich with refreshment and of the things that you do not and cannot get here. I am so happy, for your sake, that you are there and not here. I am well, perfectly well. I do not wither under the heat, even when it is hot; and I do not need to be taken care of,—indeed I fancy that I need as little as any man in Washington, outside the things that affect my heart; and my heart is quietist when things are as I would have them for you. So there is the whole matter, madam,: write me whenever you *feel* like it and as often as you can without interfering with the things I most want you to have and do!

Yes, it was largely through Mrs. Borden Harriman's initiative, Tumulty tells me, that the conference was brought about which will lead, I still hope, to a settlement of the difficulty between the railroads and their trainmen and conductors, and I am so glad that she got the credit that was due her! I say "I still hope" because the railroad authorities have, since the conference, introduced matters of controversy which may again throw matters out of joint, in what seems to me entire disregard of the strict good faith of our understanding of last Monday.

Monday morning! less than a week ago! It seems a month since I left Cornish! The days are so full of matters of consequence and even anxiety that they count for quite four times the hours they contain. And yet they have a certain relish in them too. I would not have you think that it is all burden or that the burden distresses. It is heavy, very heavy, but the strength to carry it seems to go along with it, and there is the satisfaction of the task set forward. Things continue to go on the whole very well indeed. We have a difficult Banking and Currency Committee to deal with in the House;[1] but by constant watchfulness and tact and suggestion we manage to keep things going as they should go; and the tariff matter is at last in a way to approach its conclusion.

Yesterday Dr. Grayson[2] and I took a long ride, after a morning of golf. This morning I went to our church as usual. The Dr. Asks me to say that your white slippers will go to you early this week.

Thank dear Helen for her note, enclosing the limericks from Mrs. Adams.[3] I was glad to get the limericks, but so much more glad to receive Helen's own sweet note. I hope she will be obliged to write to me frequently! Give her a heart-full of love.

Ah! my sweet, sweet Nelly! how shall I tell you what those eight days at Cornish meant to me! They were like a new honeymoon! All the days were days of contentment, renewal, and delight. I begin to think that I am just learning what a holiday means. Perhaps when we were college people we were a bit spoiled. We had so much liberty that we did not realize how precious it was. Now I know. And it pleases me to learn of the friendships you are making, and the new experiences you are having. Bully for Mr. Vonnoh! I hope the picture will be a success, even if it must be "impressionistic." Is he up to a really good thing?

Give to my dear ones as much love as they can wish for or imagine from their father, and keep for yourself, my adorable darling, whatever is your heart's desire from

Your devoted   Woodrow

Tell Nennie I have sent the left-hand golf clubs I promised.

WWTLS (WC, NjP).

[1] Wilson was having great difficulty at this time with southern agrarian members, who were demanding broader benefits for agriculture in the Federal Reserve bill. About this controversy, see Link, *The New Freedom*, pp. 218-22.

[2] Cary Travers Grayson, M.D., surgeon of the President's yacht and attending and consulting physician of the Naval Dispensary, Washington, during the Roosevelt and Taft administrations. Wilson appointed him White House physician and aide to the President in 1913.

[3] Adeline Valentine Pond (Mrs. Herbert) Adams of New York. She was an artist, and her husband was a noted sculptor.

To Mary Allen Hulbert

Dearest Friend,   The White House 20 July, 1913.

The eight days I spent in New Hampshire with that happy, adorable family up there did me a lot of good. I had grown stale down here. Washington is, I should judge, the worst place in America to keep normal. One's perspective goes wrong along with one's nerves, and there are a lot of people here who get on your nerves! Since I got back I have worked off the physical strength I got up there on the golf links and on the open country roads and in the still pine woods with their perfume of peace, but I have not worked off the refreshment of mind. The visit brought the United States back into my consciousness, with its plain folks and all its normal, everyday life, and I am a better President for it! Every day has its anxiety and its trying piece of an unending task, which it takes it out of a man to carry forward steadily and without too serious error of judgment; but it's good to think of the people I am working for. And they are generously grateful for a very little. If only a man keep honest and steer by a principle of action which they know to be genuine, they will stand by him and confuse his enemies.

Meanwhile, how is my dear friend faring? I need not tell you how often I think of her, and wonder what message I could send her to quicken the process by which she is now surely finding herself, up there amidst the things she is near kin to, by the sea and in the garden and out in the open sky and the endless waters. You are a child of nature, if ever there was one, and nothing pleases me more in your letters than those passages in which you turn to her. You never fail to be eloquent when you do, with a sort of inevitable, unconscious eloquence that is the more delightful because not deliberate, but just the instinctive response of your nature to the great out-of-doors where you are most at home. Here *I* sit about as far from nature as it [is] possible for a man to get, and think of the long curve of the shore and the free sky and the stretch of quiet beech upon which you look out, and try to reconstruct, by instinctive sympathy, for myself, the thoughts you must be thinking and share the inspiration you must be drinking in, even when you are least conscious of it. Not that there are not beautiful stretches of cultivated natural beauty just outside my own windows here: I have only to turn my head as I sit here now to see them. But the city and the men it contains and the questions that come to me out of it almost every hour constitute a glass through which I see these simpler, more natural things darkly only. I get away from them only when, in imagination, I join those far away friends through whom I can renew my contact with what I love best. What You have about you is, I cannot help thinking, just what you need now; and yet it is whimsical, too, that you should be marooned away from the throng. It is a singular contradiction, but it is a fact that, child of nature though you are, you were intended also for the delectation of your fellow beings. Nobody was ever better fitted for society! You have a positive genius, not only for being delightful yourself, but also for drawing others out and making them appear at their best. The very sympathy, the very lovely and touching sympathy, which enables you to understand simple, poor people, which enables you to help them so and to win their friendship so instantly, makes you the best possible companion and mediator in the more sophisticated circles where *natural*, spontaneous force, such as you always contribute, is generally so sadly lacking. You refresh and stimulate such people as Democracy itself invigorates society, by a constant return to the big, generous sources of mutual sympathy and mutual helpfulness. When you come out of your retreat you will be more vital than ever with those forces which are your glory. How do you like the idea of being *Democracy personified*, the living, vital embodiment of the natural forces of society? I never thought of you in that way before! but it's the fact, if I know you at all; and it delights my imagination. I shall hereafter resort to you as to the priestess of Democracy! How different this from the idea of you that those have who do not know you, and how absolutely square with the real facts! I am glad that my slow head has worked it out at last!

I am well and fit. The work is not hurting me. If my friends will only stand by me in utter loyalty, I shall be happy and all things will go well with me. My love to Allen.

Your devoted friend, the loyal servant of Democracy,
Woodrow Wilson

WWTLS (WP, DLC).

From William Jennings Bryan, with Enclosure

My Dear Mr President   [Washington c. July 20, 1913]

I beg to submit for your consideration a memorandum on the plan suggested for aiding the neighboring Republics. No hurry but am anxious to have your opinion after consideration[.] With assurances of respect etc. I am my dear Mr President
Yours truly   W. J. Bryan

ALS (WP, DLC).

E N C L O S U R E

MEMORANDUM.

The advantages of the plan proposed are:

1. That we confer a material and substantial benefit upon the small republics to whom the offer is made. They are now compelled to pay a high rate of interest and to sell their bonds at a discount. The interest runs from five to six per cent. or more, according to money conditions, and the bonds sell at a discount of eight or ten or more per cent. If the United States offers to loan them its credit to the extent that such a loan is safe, the bonds could be made to draw four and a half per cent, which would be an immediate saving to them in the way of interest, and the difference of a cent and a half between their bonds and ours could go into a sinking fund which would, in a reasonable time, at compound interest, pay off the debt and leave them free. We could, in this way, relieve them of the debts which embarass them, and enable them to construct such railroads as are imperatively necessary for the development of their countries.

2. The second advantage would be that the plan would give our country such an increased influence—and an influence welcomed because obviously beneficial—that we could prevent revolutions, promote education, and advance stable and just government.

These two advantages would be derived from the plan without the incurring of any real risk, and we would in the end profit, negatively by not having to incur expense in guarding our own and other foreign interests there, and, positively, by the increase of trade that would come from development and from the friendship which would follow the conferring of the benefits named.

The plan could be offered to Nicaragua first, in view of the fact that she has offered to embody the Platt amendment in the treaty. But I am sure that the plan would be so attractive that other countries of Central America, and with them Santo Domingo and Haiti, would soon be asking for us to extend the same neighborly assistance to them.

I have set forth the plan more fully than I had time to when I talked over the subject with you, so that you may the better form an opinion as to its merits.

T MS (WP, DLC).

From William Jennings Bryan, with Enclosure

My Dear Mr President,   [Washington c. July 20, 1913]

I take the liberty of submitting a memorandum on Mexico. It is a matter of such grave importance that I am sure you will pardon me for offering an outline of a plan which I believe we could defend before the public. I can not say how the plan would be received but no one else can tell. It is easier to decide that a thing is right than to decide upon its reception. We can not tell until we try & I am willing to *try* anything that I believe to be right. Will see you next Friday or Saturday according to your convenience. With assurances etc I am my dear Mr President

Yours truly   W. J. Bryan

ALS (WP, DLC).

ENCLOSURE

MEMORANDUM.

The tender of our good offices with a view to restoring order and establishing permanent peace in Mexico, can be justified:

First: On the ground of our proximity.

Second: On the ground of our deep interest in the conditions in North America; and

Third: Because of the large number of Americans residing in Mexico, persons who have been invited to invest their money there in the development of the resources of the country. Such an invitation implies a promise of protection to the lives and property of those who accept the invitation, and we must assume that any one aspiring to the government of the country desires that such protection shall be given in the fullest sense—a protection which is impossible under existing conditions and so long as conditions remain as they are.

We have no reason to believe that our good offices would be refused or that the tender of them would, under the circumstances, be resented, especially if such tender was accompanied by the assurance that we desired to recognize the Government as soon as we have proof of its acceptability by the people—the only basis upon which stable government is possible.

The wishes of the people can be tested by an election fairly held and we may be able to exert an influence with the Constitutionalists to bring about a suspension of hostilities until such election can be held, provided such reforms are pledged as will satisfy those who are resisting the Central Government.

If Huerta does resent the suggestion of mediation, we have then to consider the reiteration of the call made by President Taft upon all Americans residing in Mexico to leave their property in the hands of agents and retire from the country. The exact number of Americans in Mexico is not known, but it has been stated by Henry Lane Wilson as thirty thousand. This is probably a maximum estimate, but the number does not alter the principle involved. Americans who go from our country into another country for the purpose of making money, must leave their country to decide the conditions under which they remain if they would claim their country's protection. We have a law, passed not many years ago, limiting the time during which the naturalized citizen can claim the protection of this country if he returns to the country of his birth; and so we have a right to prescribe the conditions upon which an American citizen, going abroad, may claim his country's protection. If, after being notified by our Government, he decides to stay in the country and risk the dangers, he cannot justly charge to his country injuries that may be due to his lack of judgment. If an American citizen, having property in Mexico, refuses to leave Mexico because he is afraid that his property will suffer, he puts his property interests above his own welfare, but he cannot rightfully ask this Government to put his property in another country above the lives of American citizens who may be sacrificed in the attempt to protect that property.

Any property rights that may be violated by the Mexican government can be dealt with when order is restored. But a distinction ought to be made between the propection [protection] of citizens passing through a country on legitimate business, and those who, for business reasons, remain in a country in times of war when extraordinary risks have to be taken and after warning has been given them.

If any American citizen, desiring to leave the country, is unable to do so without danger to himself, we can demand safe conduct at the hands of the Government, and in view of our paramount position, we would also be justified in asking safe conduct for foreigners of other nations desiring to leave Mexico. This safe conduct would not likely be refused.

If safe conduct was refused, it would be a confession, either of the Government's inability to protect foreigners residing there, or of its unwillingness to do so. In either case, we would be justified in sending such a force as might be necessary to rescue American citizens and citizens of other countries and bring them out of the country, notice being given at the time that this was the only reason for sending forces into the country. If war follow as the result of our effort to bring out of Mexico those who desire to come, and whose safety the Government could not or would not guarantee, we would be acquitted before the world if the war was continued only for that purpose and only until the purpose was accomplished.

When we have first exhausted our efforts to assist in the restoring of peace by friendly counsel; second, recalling American citizens and others looking to us to [for] protection from the war zone; third, demanding safe conduct for our citizens and others looking to us for protection; and, fourth, furnishing safe conduct for our own citizens and those looking to us for ptotection, we have done all that duty requires of us. In the doing of these things, we will be justified in using whatever force is necessary. To go farther, and send a force into the country to protect property which Americans are not willing to leave, is, first, to allow such Americans to declare war, whereas the constitution has vested in Congress, and in Congress only, the right to declare war; second, to send a force into a country to protect property merely because American citizens are not willing to leave it, is to put property rights above human rights—to put the dollar above the man—and war entered into for this purpose would put this country upon a level with those nations which have extended their territory by conquest, first allowing their citizens to go abroad in quest of gain and then sending an army to guarantee the profits sought. To do this in the case of Mexico would be to become responsible for the blood shed in the undertaking and to fasten upon our country the burden of administering for generations to come a foreign government over a hostile people to their own injury and to our own demoralization.

Our nation claims to stand in the forefront of the world's civilization and aspires to be the greatest moral influence in the world. We cannot hope to realize our ambition or to support our claim if we are willing to engage in war with a neighboring people merely to protect property which has been acquired with a full knowledge of the risks attendant upon it.

Property can be compensated for in money—it cannot be measured in the lives of human beings, even if the number of lives necessary could be estimated—a thing impossible, for when a war is commenced no one can foresee the end. Neither can any one foresee the foreign complications that may follow a war or the far-reaching influence of national and race antagonism. The Mexicans are a Spanish speaking people, and what we do in Mexico will go far toward fixing in the minds of the people in Central and South America their estimate of us. In proportion as Mexico is made to suffer for having permitted Americans to assist in the development of the country, in that proportion will the other undeveloped countries to the south of us be suspicious of American citizens coming among them to do business.

In addition to these tangible and material dangers involved in a war, there is the immeasurable loss of prestige which must come if we can no longer be looked to as the leader in the peace movement and as the exponent of human rights, not to speak of our moral responsibility for the lives lost in such a war.

T MS (WP, DLC).

From Walter Hines Page

My dear Wilson: London. July, 20. 1913

I am writing you this personal note, man to man, about a subject that is none of your business nor mine, and is, therefore, the more fascinating. If you have any influence in that quarter, I pray that you will persuade your daughter and her fiance when they are married to accept the invitation that Mrs. Page[1] took great pleasure in sending a little while ago to make us a visit. We have a house large enough to entertain the King (in fact, I have had to take one for that very purpose, because His present Majesty expects the American Ambassador to ask him to dinner), and it is, therefore, quite big enough for them to make themselves at home in. We now know some of the most interesting people here, and we can, I hope, really contribute to their pleasure and give them an interesting experience.

If they are married in the Autumn and come immediately, they will be here out of the London season, which does not begin till Spring. There will be no court functions, but there'll be plenty of other things; and we can make as much or as little fuss about them as they wish. You and I will not publicly confess it, but a little well-ordered fuss gives much fun to the young—of all ages.

We American folk come here by the thousand and see the outside of London and of English life. A few see a little of the inside. Very few ever see much of the inside. But this inside is very well worth seeing. They are a noble race yet—these dukes and earls and knights as well as the commoners. You forget their amuzing ceremonies and decorations on close view. For instance, one day not long ago I met Lady Philip Sidney and her son (another Sir Philip to-be); the next day a Lady Somebody-else, who is sprung in direct line from John Hampden, and her son; the next week, Lady Darwin and Charles Darwin III, as fine a young fellow as any Kingdom can show. These folk and their like we seldom see in the United States or on mere summer visits to England. They are very simple and genuine; and I can think of nothing more interesting than to come to know them. Such an experience I should like to give your fine and genuine young couple as they start forth. And at the same time we should give these folk here an experience with young Americans that would be worth their while.

Or, if they prefer to come later and be presented at Court and see the finest show of that sort now left in the world—very good: let them come then. There may never be such a sight again after this reign and after Lloyd-George gets his work done. (I was at the Palace looking on at the gaudy ball when the King and Queen were dancing, and the highly bedecked nobleman of "the silver stick" who walks backwards before the king, having a moment of rest while the dance went on, came up to me and whispered: "Your Excellency, I should like to know your real opinion of all this damned tinsel." I told him and we became firm friends.) It's a great show, worth seeing. One of my boys,[2] who was here on a visit and was in the dance, hoped to have the pleasure to tell your daughter about it.

This plan, for the young couple to come, good and sufficient for its own sake, is also a prelude to a more swelling plan. Later, when the first big tasks are done, you and Mrs. Wilson must come here—I mean during your Presidency. Then you'll smash a precedent to some purpose!

The whole subject of American-British relations is the most fascinating and important thing imaginable. The peace of the world hangs on it. They have their Germany and we have our Mexico and we both have our Japan. Of course we want no alliance: we need not engage ourselves to their troubles. Perhaps we can do even without treaties: no great matter. But there is a deeper kinship than we realize so long as we are absorbed in our domestic problems. These people of the real ruling class are conscious of it and proud of it and they wish to learn from us and to keep close to us. I went the other day with a fine specimen of Englishman to look at the grass-grown, outdoor theatre where the Saxons held their first moot—the real mother of parliaments. It is kept as it was when they sat there and made laws. "Your newest State legislature at Tucson," said he, "runs back to this: do you realize it as we do?"

There is a way, if we can be so fortunate as to find it, to do a great piece of constructive work in the right adjustment of world-forces by using just right this English admiration of our greatness and strength—using it positively, without boast or formal alliance, with no artificial force at work, with perfect naturalness. I believe it would help greatly if you should find a perfectly natural occasion to come here—I will say, to accept the gift of the old Washington homestead which will be made next year as a part of the celebration of our hundred years of peace, or your presence here in April 1916 (tho' that's too far off) when the tercentenary of Shakespeare will be celebrated all over the world. Either of these or some other occasion could be used which would make your coming here natural and would relieve you of any reason to visit any other European country. I have a feeling that such a visit, made as quietly as it could be made, might possibly prevent an Anglo-German war, which seems almost certain at some time, and an American-Japanese war which is at least conceivable a decade or so hence. I think the world would take notice to whom it belongs and—be quiet.

I mentioned this to House when he was here, and his imagination took fire. Talk with him about it.

To return to the young couple—further our plans.

With all good wishes for your health and continued mastery

Yours affectionately,   Walter H. Page

ALS (WP, DLC).
  [1] Alice Wilson Page.
  [2] The Pages had three sons: Ralph Walter, Arthur Wilson, and Frank Copeland Page.

From Ellen Axson Wilson

Cornish, New Hampshire

My own darling,   Sunday [July 20, 1913]

It is six o'clock and the two lovers have just started for the station, Jessie of course to see Frank off. So now I have time to write to *my* lover before dinner.

We have had a Sunday in some respects a repetition of the last "but oh!—the difference is to me"! We went to the little Cornish church again and had another nobly simple sermon from Dr. Fitch.[1] Of course we were in time today and so found as we expected that he is (to use the old phrase) "as much gifted in prayer" as in preaching. He and Mrs. Fitch[2] were at our second little tea on Friday and he is delightfully human and simple. We are planning to see something of them alone.

Our tea was really very interesting. There were a large number of men, some of whom possibly take themselves too seriously. These were mainly the "literary fellows." The artists were, as

usual, of an engaging simplicity. Mr. Stephen Parrish[3] is an old
dear. Maxfield Parish[4] is such a shy bird that he never goes into
a crowd[.] His wife[5] begged that he and she might come alone
someday. Our nearest neighbour, Miss King,[6] (at "The Inn"[7] you
know) said something that not only pleased me in itself but made
me like *her* because it showed sympathetic observation. She said
it was a pleasure to watch you pass every day because you had
such an unusually *happy* expression—"like a boy out of school"
and something more. You darling! I can't express to you what a
delight it was to me to see you so happy, or what a wonderful
warm feeling about the heart that blessed week has left me. We
were so close to each other that I hardly feel even yet as if we
are really separated. I am with you in spirit constantly. I hope
you too have some little consciousness of that left in spite of all
the burdens. As ever   Your little wife   Eileen.

ALS (WC, NjP).
  [1] The Rev. Dr. Albert Parker Fitch, Bartlet Professor of Practical Theology
and president of the faculty at Andover Theological Seminary, Cambridge, Mass.,
who was supplying the Cornish Congregational Church during the summer.
  [2] Flora May Draper Fitch.
  [3] Philadelphia-born artist who specialized in etchings of New England scenes.
  [4] [Frederick] Maxfield Parrish, also Philadelphia-born, a painter but best
known for his illustrations in books, popular magazines, and posters.
  [5] Lydia Austin Parrish.
  [6] Unidentified.
  [7] Churchill Inn, a farmhouse across the road from Harlakenden House, also
owned by the Winston Churchills.

Remarks at a Press Conference

July 21, 1913

Mexico and Nicaragua? . . .
I mean, as to what the policy with regard to Nicaragua is?
>   This is a proposal, you know, with regard to obtaining from
>   them a concession on the canal route so that we may have
>   the option of opening it if it seems wise to do so. That is the
>   subject matter of the negotiations.

I have been away two days, and according to the papers on which
I have been compelled to rely, a much broader policy is involved.
That is what I mean to ask you about.
>   Of course, there always is the problem with regard to those
>   Central American states of making such arrangements as
>   will enable them to float their loans and soften ours. I am
>   now speaking to you gentlemen just for your information,
>   not for the newspapers. We are sincerely desirous of finding
>   some way by which we can render them some assistance
>   without submitting ourselves to the suspicion of our taking
>   possession of them or preventing them from acting. Of

course, at the outset, we would be open to that suspicion. It
is up to us in the long run to show that there is nothing in it.
Mr. President, do you think that in announcing that policy or in
looking after our Latin American sisters the European powers
would think we are working for, perhaps, the military—

Very possibly they would, but what we have to look at are our
own purposes and our own consciences in the matter. The
question would be if any European power would have any
right to object with the Monroe Doctrine in view, and also
that we have the canal to look after—well, speaking freely to
you in confidence, they would have a right to object but—
(laughter)

Mr. President, did the suggestion for this treaty or understanding
with Nicaragua originate with you or with Nicaragua?

I am sorry to say I can't answer that. I am under the impression that it grew out of the conversations of the Secretary of State with the representatives of Nicaragua.

One of the papers this morning states that the same proposition
was submitted to Honduras and El Salvador and that it aroused
considerable excitement on the part of the gentlemen who represent those countries here, and that Mr. Bryan made that offer to
them also.

If so, I didn't know anything about it.

Of course, I don't suppose you would be willing to answer questions whether this policy would extend over the entire of Central
America?

I don't want you to exaggerate anything in your minds in
thinking of it. We are not adopting a general policy with
regard to Central America. We are trying to deal in as helpful and friendly a way as we can in each particular case as it
arises. Of course, if the state we are dealing with doesn't like
the idea, we wouldn't impress it for a moment.

It would seem almost necessary for it, then, that the idea must
originate with the other countries.

At any rate, it must be thoroughly acceptable to the other
countries.

Mr. President, in regard to the purpose. I don't know whether you
want to say anything about those countries or anything of that
kind—the purpose is really to foreclose that canal proposition with
reference to any other country?

With regard to the main method of the negotiations, yes. . . .

Would it be fair to assume, Mr. President, that the administration
is going as far as it can to influence and exercise relations with
those countries to protect American interests?

That is to protect American interests in the large sense—to advance American interests, to show our friendliness, to help in every legitimate way. I think that is the way to help American interests—to be real friends, and not try to exploit them or use them to our own selfish advantage. . . .

Mr. President, referring to Mexico, there is a general feeling and I think—at any rate, I am willing to speak it for myself—that Ambassador Wilson is at any rate inclined to be favorable to the recognition of Huerta. I think that can be stated as a known condition. Are you receiving from any source the other side of the question, the so-called Constitutionalist side?

I can't say that we are. Indeed, so far as I know, we are not. By the other side, at first I thought you meant the side against the recognition of Huerta.

Well, I meant more specifically that—I mean the *Carrancistas*.

No, we are practically getting nothing with regard to that.

They are a pretty responsible element of the people there.

They are indeed. I would be very glad indeed to know exactly what is in their minds, but—

Haven't they a representative in the city here, like the Huerta representative?

If so, he hasn't been to see me.

Would you be willing to see him?

That is a question for the Department of State.

Is there anything authentic or authoritative that would lead you to believe that the dispatches are correct which state that the Huerta government is toppling?

Well, there again, I don't know. I shouldn't be surprised if that is true. I am not sufficiently informed.

The question was raised in an editorial in the New York *World* last week that seemed to me very much to the point. The administration states—in fact, I think you have said this to us—that they have not been able to get entirely trustworthy information. We have a sufficient amount of diplomatic representatives down there, and the *World* asks what the truth is.

I remember that question. It was a very pertinent one. When I covered that one, I was saying to you gentlemen the other day that local circumstances color a man's judgment in what is going on in the rest of the country, and you get one impression in one part, I mean, and in another part another impression.

That would be the case with Mr. Wilson, I presume?

Yes. He has got this, that, and the other set of rumors in the different parts of the country. For example, as I understand it, there is constantly fighting going on. At first, the Huerta government represents every fight as resulting in a victory of its troops. Sometimes that is true and sometimes it is not. But it changes the point of view, and so it goes from day to day. I don't think the most active inquiry on the spot would determine very much more than we get. I am beginning to get now from people who have long been resident in Mexico the judgment of persons who have been used to traveling that road and who seem to know a little bit about it.

Well, can you give us any intimation as to the general color of that information?

Well, just among ourselves, it is to the effect that the Huerta government certainly can't last.

Have there been a great many reports coming here about the activities of Ambassador Wilson toward the support of the Huerta government? Have any of those been well founded?

What?

Or have you found them to be true in any sense?

I don't feel at liberty to discuss that. I don't think it would be fair to Mr. Wilson.

JRT transcript (WC, NjP) of CLSsh (C. L. Swem Coll., NjP).

To Cleveland Hoadley Dodge

My dear Cleve: [The White House] July 21, 1913

Thank you warmly for sending me Mr. Morgan's letter, and also the reports from Judge Haff. They jump entirely with the best information I get and with my own judgment about the perplexing Mexican business, and you need not fear that we shall be misled or influenced by any advice we may get from Henry Lane Wilson when he returns to Washington. His position in the matter is already only too well marked.

How my heart echoes the wish that I might be with you on your cruise! I hope it will do you no end of good and bring you back as refreshed as I was when I got back from New Hampshire. I have worked it off again, but retain the delightful recollection.

I am sure that if the rest of the family were here, they would join me in the most affectionate messages.

Affectionately yours,   Woodrow Wilson

TLS (Letterpress Books, WP, DLC).

Thomas Snell Hopkins[1] to Rudolph Forster

Dear Mr. Forster: Washington, July 21, 1913.

My son and partner, Captain S. G. Hopkins,[2] has a very extended acquaintance in Mexico, having been the late President Madero's legal adviser during the revolution that drove Diaz from power. He now has correspondence with Carranza, who seeks to overthrow Huerta.

Today Mr. Francisco Escudero, professor of political economy and history in the old University of Guadalajara, a member of the Mexican Congress, and Chief of the Department of Finance in the Constitutionalist government, headed by Carranza, called to see him and enquired if there was any way by which he might secure opportunity to lay before President Wilson or Mr. Bryan an intelligent view of the situation in Mexico, from a Constitutionalist standpoint. My son told him he doubted it; but knowing that the President really desired reliable information relative to Mexican affairs, which I think Professor Escudero can supply, I conceived that it might not be improper to tell you of his presence in Washington, and of his wishes, so that should the President care to unofficially receive a visit from him, or should the President wish to have him call on any one else, I might let Professor Escudero know.

With best wishes, believe me, dear Mr. Foster,
                    Sincerely yours,   Thos. S. Hopkins

TLS (EBR, RG 130, DNA).
 [1] Senior member of the firm of Hopkins & Hopkins of Washington, specializing in international law.
 [2] Sherburne Gillette Hopkins. A member of the District of Columbia naval militia, he commanded *U.S.S. Fern* in 1899.

To Rudolph Forster

Mr. Forster: The White House [c. July 21, 1913].

I do not think that it would be wise or proper for me to see Mr. Francisco Escudero, but I appreciate Mr. Hopkins' kind suggestion very much and feel that it would be very valuable to me if I might get a statement of just what Mr. Escudero believes to be the present situation in Mexico, the present and most settled purposes of the Constitutionalists and the prospects and grounds for a settlement. I wonder if Mr. Hopkins would not be kind enough to get a memorandum about these matters from Mr. Escudero which I might have the privilege of seeing without committing the impropriety of having any direct communication with Mr.

Escudero. In brief, I am very anxious to know the facts and yet to ascertain them in the right way.   The President.

Phoned Col Hopkins[1]

TL (EBR, RG 130, DNA).
  [1] RFhw.

From Oswald Garrison Villard

PERSONAL

Dear President Wilson: New York July 21, 1913.

A number of protests, of which the enclosed are samples,[1] are pouring upon me in my capacity of Chairman of the Executive Committee of the National Association for the Advancement of Colored People. The colored people everywhere are greatly stirred up over what they consider the hostile attitude of the Administration in regard to colored employees in the government departments. In the Bureau of Engraving and Printing colored people have been segregated at their work where colored and white were together before. General Burt[2] touches upon the segregation in the Treasury Department. In the Bureau of the Census and the Post Office Department segregation is going on steadily. Some of this segregation works great hardship upon the colored clerks. The ruling of the Treasury Department upon which General Burt touches[3] is particularly humiliating to them because it seems to imply that there is something degrading and demoralizing in associating with these American citizens, as if they were lepers to be set apart.

Before taking action, or permitting the Association to take action officially, in regard to these matters I think it but fair and just to you to ask for some authoritative expression from you as to whether this policy is a deliberate one on the part of the Administration, or whether it is due, as I believe, to the individual initiative of department heads without your knowledge and consent.

I cannot exaggerate the effect this has had upon the colored people at large. The colored press, which is mostly Republican harps upon it in every issue; I enclose a sample from the most influential New York newspaper.[4] The *Crisis*, the organ of our Association, has the largest circulation ever attained among colored people. I enclose herewith its editorial in support of you last fall; its readers are now asking whether it means to keep silent in the face of these discriminations at Washington at the hands of men it helped to put in office. The colored men who voted and worked for you in the belief that their status as American citizens was safe in your hands are deeply cast down, and know not how to answer the criticisms they receive on every hand. Should this policy be continued we should lose all that we gained in the last campaign in splitting the negro vote, and in teaching a part of the race to vote nationally and not with regard to their own immediate interest, or appeals to the issues of the war.

You have, as first Southern-born President of the United States since the war, a wonderful opportunity to win the confidence and interest of these people who ask nothing by [but] fair play,— nothing but what they are entitled to under the Constitution. They followed your speeches in the campaign with thrilled interest; they got from your "New Freedom" the belief that your democracy was not limited by race or color; that the fundamental scientific political truths which you have therein expressed, being truths, applied to every human being whatever his situation, whatever his color. If they are wrong in this theirs will be the severest disappointment which has come to them during the fifty years of freedom in which they have been loyal patriotic citizens; during which they have added enormously to the wealth of the country, although starting with nothing but the clothes they wore when the shackles fell from their scarred limbs.

As one who has supported you in season and out, at Princeton, at Trenton and in Washington, you will appreciate my own great embarrasement in this situation; it is, I feel sure, not too much to ask that you will let me know just how the Administration stands in relation to the colored man that I may be instrumental in putting the facts in the case before the colored people.

Sincerely yours,   Oswald Garrison Villard.

TLS (WP, DLC).
    [1] A. S. Burt to O. G. Villard, July 16, 1913, TLS (WP, DLC), and A. W. Clifford to O. G. Villard, July 16, 1913, ALS (WP, DLC).
    [2] Andrew Sheridan Burt, brigadier general, U.S.A., Ret.
    [3] An order of the Treasury Department, issued on July 15, 1913, which limited black employees of that department in the City of Washington to the use of specified toilets.
    [4] It is missing, as is the clipping from *The Crisis* mentioned in the next two sentences.

Two Letters from Ellen Axson Wilson

Cornish, New Hampshire
My own darling,   Monday [July 21, 1913].

We have just finished dinner which we took rather hurriedly because Jessie and Helen were going to meet Adeline and Mary Scott[1] on the 8 o'clock train. They are to stop until Friday; and Ruth Hall[2] comes over from Hanover to spend tomorrow night.

We had the last of our three teas this afternoon, the Windsor people,—chiefly an assorted lot of Evarts of all ages and conditions.[3] With them were three Conovers from Princeton, including Mrs. Bradford.[4]

The house is full of the most beautiful flowers sent by various people. One of todays guests brought a magnificent basket with her. She was Mr. Kennedy's daughter, Mrs Babcock,[5] a stunning six-footer of a woman.

I don't like to allude to politics in my letters when you are so surfeited by it all the time; but I *must* speak of the increased duty on books and pictures! I saw in a paper that you yourself had not known that it was being done and were shocked at it. Is that so? It seems to me quite dreadful that they should during *your* Administration raise the duties on those things on the ground of their being luxuries! It is so incongruous. I hope and pray it is not too late to change it. It is so different from anything else because the supposed beneficiaries, the native authors and artists are of all men most opposed to it. John Alexander[6] had a long letter about it in today's paper. He is President of the Academy.

We are all perfectly well and are still having perfect weather. I paint every morning, though thanks to the mail and Mrs. Jaffrey's flow of language, I do not get at it until late,—ten or after. I have engagements for every afternoon this week—to see gardens, to go to the club to pose for Mr. Vonnoh, &c.

I am hungrying dearest for another little "day-letter" from you. Of course I don't expect real letters,—wouldn't *wish* you to take that much extra burden. I *love* you with all my heart,—tenderly, passionately, devotedly, I am always and altogether,

Your own   Nell.

ALS (WC, NjP).

1 Adeline Mitchell Scott and Mary Blanchard Scott, daughters of Wilson's former colleague, William Berryman Scott.

2 Ruth Preble Hall, who lived at 11 Cleveland Lane, Princeton, with her widowed mother, Mary Hepburn Hough (Mrs. William Richardson) Hall. Ruth was a close friend of the Wilson girls.

3 The children and grandchildren of William Maxwell Evarts (1818-1901), United States senator and Secretary of State. Their large estate, Runnemede, was at Windsor, Vt.

4 Mary Field Conover Bradford, wife of Willard Hall Bradford, Princeton 1891, proprietor of a coal brokerage firm of Philadelphia. The other two "Conovers from Princeton" were Mrs. Bradford's sister, Juliana Conover, and their mother, Helen Field (Mrs. Francis Stevens) Conover. The Conover ladies were old friends of the Wilsons.

5 The Editors have been unable to identify her.

6 John White Alexander, one of the best known and most successful American painters of his era; an officer in many artistic associations including, at this time, the National Academy of Design and the National Institute of Arts and Letters.

Cornish, New Hampshire

My own darling,   Monday *No–Tuesday*! [July 22, 1913]

Your *adorable* letter came this morning and you may well believe that my heart has been full to overflowing with the joy of it ever since. How wonderful you are to take time to write such a letter when things are pressing so upon you! I shall keep this special letter among my chief treasures always. Of course I knew you would like a little love message daily. What I was really thinking, I suppose, was that a longish letter giving the little details of our days here might take too much of your time and attention. And I am sure you do not crave a daily comment from me on the political situation!

I have just come back from the club. It was much more interesting because the subject was one about which we would all naturally know something, viz. the education of girls. There really are a number of very attractive and interesting women among them. It was at Mrs. Hands,—Florence Hoyt's old classmate; and that clever interesting Miss Goldmark[1] was there on a visit. She was on her way to the old cottage on the side of "Noonmark."

I was interrupted by the arrival of the five girls from Hanover. I am finishing this while they dress for dinner.

I suppose since things press so in Washington now that there is no hope of your coming this week. If by any wonderful good fortune there is, telegraph me when you receive this, for otherwise I shall go to Williamstown on Friday afternoon with Jessie & Frank, returning on Sunday. We will get there at night so that I can go almost at once to bed and so rest from my trip. That is already arranged for with Mrs. Carter. Then we will have Saturday for our sight-seeing & house-hunting, and start back in the fresh early morning, Sunday. We will reach here at lunch time and I can if I wish go to bed just after. So it will be an easy and a beautiful trip, and I am looking forward to it with pleasure.

I "laid in" today my first large Cornish canvass. It is rather promising,—if I can keep the present freshness and vigour. It is rather stunning colour,—deep blues and strong sunlight and shadow. I rather like it now, but I may be utterly disgusted tomorrow night. But I must stop at *once*! With devoted love,

Your little Wife,   Nell.

ALS (WC, NjP).

[1] Josephine Clara Goldmark, Bryn Mawr 1898, publication secretary of the National Consumers' League.

From William Sulzer

Confidential

My dear Mr. President: Albany July 22, 1913

Your letter received. Of course I appreciate all you say. However, I am very sorry you could not see Commissioner VanKennan and Mr. Lucey when they called at the White House. The latter gentleman is a candidate for United States District Attorney for the Northern District of New York. He is your friend, and well qualified for the position he seeks. A better appointment, all things considered, could not be made. I commend his application to your favorable consideration.

Mr. Antisdale of Rochester, Mr. Burgard of Buffalo, Mr. Perkins of Poughkeepsie,[1] Mr. VanKennan of Ogdensburg, and Collector Mitchel of New York City, desire an interview with you at your earliest convenience, to go over matters of moment in the Empire State.

We are, in this State, in a struggle for good government; for decent Democracy; and for direct primaries to carry out our pledges to the people in the last campaign. Our friends can rely on me to go forward in the cause—come what may.

In the last analysis, the fight here is very similar to your fight in New Jersey—only the bosses here are more powerful, and more strongly entrenched. To nullify much of the work we are doing, they are relying upon patronage from the Federal administration. Of course if they get appointments to important offices, it will practically negative our efforts, and defeat the purposes that all our friends have in view.

The real, true Democrats of western New York have agreed upon appointments to the offices in that section of the State. They want to talk it all over with you, and I earnestly beseech you to grant them an audience and hear what they say.

We need your help and your moral support in our fight for the right. Do not fail us. Will you be good enough to let me, or Assistant Secretary of the Navy Roosevelt, know when you will see the gentlemen I have mentioned, as a Committee of prominent Democrats from the State of New York?

With best wishes, My dear Mr. President, believe me as ever,
Very sincerely your friend,   Wm. Sulzer

TLS (WP, DLC).
[1] Louis Marlin Antisdale, editor of the *Rochester Herald*; Henry P. Burgard, chairman of the Erie County Democratic Committee and Democratic state committeeman; and Edward E. Perkins, lawyer, financier, newspaper publisher, chairman of the Dutchess County Democratic Committee, and treasurer of the New York State Democratic Committee.

To Oswald Garrison Villard

My dear Mr. Villard: The White House July 23, 1913

Your letter of July first, I must say, distresses me. It is true that the segregation of the colored employees in the several departments was begun upon the initiative and at the suggestion of several of the heads of departments, but as much in the interest of the negroes as for any other reason, with the approval of some of the most influential negroes I know, and with the idea that the friction, or rather the discontent and uneasiness, which had prevailed in many of the departments would thereby be removed. It is as far as possible from being a movement *against* the negroes. I sincerely believe it to be in their interest. And what distresses me about your letter is to find that you look at it in so different a light.

I am sorry that those who interest themselves most in the welfare of the negroes should misjudge this action on the part of the departments, for they are seriously misjudging it. My own feeling is, by putting certain bureaus and sections of the service in the charge of negroes we are rendering them more safe in their possession of office and less likely to be discriminated against.

Cordially and sincerely yours,   Woodrow Wilson

TLS (O. G. Villard Papers, MH).

To Henry Otto Wittpenn

My dear Mr. Mayor: [The White House] July 23, 1913

It has given me a great deal of concern that, in view of your having been generous enough to consult me with regard to the advisability of your becoming a candidate for the nomination for Governor at the primaries, it was clearly incumbent upon me to form and express an opinion. I felt, as I explained to you at the time you requested my opinion, that your desire to know my judgment forced me to make a practical political choice as between friends, friends who had been of great service to me personally as well as to the public in the political contests of the past two years. But there was nothing else for it, and I yesterday told Mr. Grosscup, as had been agreed, what my judgment was. It is that we ought to support Mr. Fielder's candidacy.

Fielder backed me so consistently, so intelligently, so frankly and honestly throughout my administration and has followed, on the whole, so consistent a course that I feel I would have no ground whatever upon which to oppose his candidacy. My analysis of the political situation in New Jersey makes me feel that a three-cornered fight would be most unwise and that, probably, in such a fight your own strength would not be great enough to count decisively.

I cannot state this conclusion without also saying to you how greatly I have admired the course you have pursued from time to time and the stand you have taken for the rights of the people. Moreover, your generous friendship for myself and your aid, again and again rendered in effective fashion, have won not only my admiration but my deep appreciation. I am sure that you will not think the conclusion I have come to as the leader of the party is in any way a subtraction from my cordial personal regard or from my acknowledgment of the distinguished services which you have rendered the party.

Cordially and sincerely yours,   Woodrow Wilson[1]

TLS (Letterpress Books, WP, DLC).
[1] Wittpenn replied that he felt it his duty to withdraw from the contest in view of Wilson's belief that a continuation of his candidacy would cause factional strife and jeopardize the progressive Democratic movement. H. O. Wittpenn to WW, July 25, 1913, TLS (WP, DLC).

From Ellen Axson Wilson

Cornish, New Hampshire

My own darling,   Wednesday [July 23, 1913]

I am just back from a visit to the Maxfield Parrishes and from posing afterwards for Mr. Vonnoh. The posing was interrupted by a storm, leaving, while it lasted, no light to paint by.

The Maxfield Parrish ménage is *charming* in every respect. In the first place they are all so good-looking! He is really a beautiful young man and charming too, and she is *lovely*, with deep dark eyes, and a sweet, rather worn look like a young madonna. She has four beautiful young children,[1] and is evidently a devoted mother. She was an artist herself[.] The house is set high on a hill and is altogether fascinating,—very artistic and at the same time unpretentious. The garden is a delightful tangle like the Boxwood garden. The[y] have a few magnificent trees,—and a really stupendous view,—too panoramic to paint of course, but a glorious scene. Altogether it is an ideal artist home. And they live there all the year round. It must be very wonderful in winter.

The girls go to a little dance there next week.

They go tonight—all five of them—to one of the Evarts houses for impromptu charades. The charades ought to be good with Nell, Ruth and Mary Scott, besides the lively Evarts girls.

How I wish I knew how the railroad affair is actually getting on, and if there is very serious danger of the arbitration plan falling through! I can't help being a little anxious.

I see from other letters that Mr. Alexander rather exaggerated as regards the duty on pictures,—that they are not actually *raising* the duty but only restoring it in part,—when the house had made them free. Still the papers are full of protests about it,—and I do hope they can be made really free. Everyone who knows anything about the subject wants them free.

I have just escaped,—I hope,—a visitation from the suffragists —those who are on their way to Washington. I heard rumours that they were coming to Windsor and would ask me to receive them; but they did not write me. They simply *came*, and called up on the telephone to know if I would see them. Helen told them I was just leaving the house to meet an important engagement, which was literally true,—it was this afternoon. They were extremely disappointed of course, saying that they did not expect me to put myself on record as for them, but it would "help them greatly for me just to receive them." Doubtless it *would*, for it would be considered putting myself on record!

I also had a letter on the subject from an anti-suffragist.

I fear my darling is suffering from the heat now for it is rather stifling here. We are all well, and I love you with all my heart and soul. I think of you all day and sometimes have the good luck to dream of you by night. Devotedly   Your own   Nell.

ALS (WC, NjP).
  1 Jean, John Dillwyn, Maxfield, and Stephen.

To Ellen Axson Wilson

[The White House] July 24, 1913

The weather here continues fine and it is no hardship at all to work. I am perfectly well and fit. Your letters are a great delight to me and are all that I need to keep me going. Doctor Grayson and Tumulty are both living with me and we are a congenial and jolly company. It was delightful to read the accounts of your teas which appeared in the newspapers. They seemed this time to be correct for they sounded like what must have happened, though I dare say they were based upon conjecture. With dearest love for all   Woodrow.

T telegram (Letterpress Books, WP, DLC).

To Augustus Octavius Bacon

My dear Senator: [The White House] July 24, 1913

I have conscientiously tried to reconstruct the enclosed resolution[1] in such a way as to relieve it of the implication which it obviously carries. That implication is that the rights of American citizens on the border and in foreign countries are not being diligently or properly safeguarded by the Government of the United States, and that is, of course, not the case.

The resolution involves an entirely untenable position. American citizens can not have "constitutional" rights outside their own country. They can have only international rights, the rights guaranteed them by international law. These rights do not include, as we were agreeing the other day, the right of the American Government to enter a foreign territory in order to protect property, or even, except in certain unusual circumstances, to protect life. To do so would be a declaration of war or, at the least, an intervention with armed force. The Government of the United States has the right, on the other hand, to hold every foreign government strictly responsible for its violation of international law in every respect with regard to American citizens, and the present government will certainly be diligent to do that. I think that the Democratic members of the Senate can safely vote against this resolution or any resolution equivalent to it as involving a virtual impeachment of the faithfulness of the present administration.

If I could have reconstructed it to mean anything else, I would gladly have done so.

Cordially and sincerely yours,   Woodrow Wilson

TLS (Letterpress Books, WP, DLC).

[1] On July 19, Republican Senator Albert Bacon Fall of New Mexico, heavily interested in Mexican mining enterprises and a persistent critic of the Mexican policy of both the Taft and Wilson administrations, introduced in the Senate the following resolution: "*Resolved*, That the constitutional rights of American citizens should protect them on our borders, and go with them throughout the world, and every American citizen residing or having property in any foreign country is entitled to and must be given the full protection of the United States Government, both for himself and his property." This was a clever political move, for, as Fall himself pointed out in debate, except for the necessary addition of the words "Resolved, that," the resolution was a verbatim transcription of a plank in the Democratic platform of 1912. In an acrimonious debate on the resolution on July 22, Fall admitted that the measure was directed specifically to the Mexican situation and made it clear that he regarded armed intervention by the United States as inevitable. See *Cong. Record*, 63d Cong., 1st sess., pp. 2548-49, 2591-2600.

To Newton Diehl Baker

My dear Mr. Mayor: [The White House] July 24, 1913

. . . I often think of you and often wish that I might have you at hand to ask your advice. There is one service which you could do us immediately and which I am going to take the liberty of suggesting to you. Mr. Bulkley[1] of the House Committee on Banking and Currency, I know, has the greatest confidence in your judgment, and if you could stimulate him a little bit to support the administration heartily in its present bill, it would be immensely serviceable, because the difficulties (so far as they exist) seem to be in the Committee and not in the House itself.

Cordially and faithfully yours,   Woodrow Wilson

TLS (Letterpress Books, WP, DLC).
[1] Robert Johns Bulkley, Democratic congressman from Cleveland, who had been attacking the Federal Reserve bill on the ground that it vested too much power in the Federal Reserve Board. See the *New York Times*, July 24, 1913.

From William Bayard Hale

[Mexico City] July 24, 1913.

I have received visit from de la Barra,[1] sometime President, lately Minister for Foreign Affairs, et cetera. He desires me ascertain whether it would be convenient for the President to see and talk with him in purely private capacity. His idea is that if he visited New York with his wife on the way to Europe the President might invite him to Washington simply as a distinguished personage. The request really comes from Huerta. De la Barra declares that Huerta is anxious to come to an understanding with the U. S. Government and is prepared to discuss measures to satisfy revolutionists. I beg to suggest there could be no better opportunity and means for the President to communicate his attitude to this Government. De la Barra would leave on next ship.

Hale.

T telegram (WP, DLC).
[1] Francisco León de la Barra, who had served as ad interim President of Mexico from the resignation of Porfirio Díaz on May 25, 1911, until the swearing in of Francisco I. Madero on November 6, 1911. De la Barra was Huerta's Minister of Foreign Relations from February to June 1913.

A Memorandum by Francisco Escudero[1]

M E M O R A N D U M

RELATIVE TO CONDITIONS IN MEXICO.

Washington, 24th of July, 1913.

Mexico is a country of intermingled colonization, composed of people of quite different races, traditions and civilizations. As a people they may be regarded as a genuine national unity, yet such has only come into existence during recent years. Mexico was the principal colony founded by Spain in America, and so it was here that the conservative classes, the aristocracy, the clergy and the military, gained their highest development and stood in opposition to the humble conditions of life in which the great mass of the inhabitants lived. These facts have been the cause of the several convulsions that have afflicted the Mexican nation in its struggle for life, during the last hundred years.

The war of independence was rather a social than a political strife, its main object having been to emancipate, from a social point of view, the Indians, the mixed bloods and the peasants, whom the wealthier classes, too jealous of their own privileges, had denied the right to mingle in public affairs. This war for independence lasted for over eleven years, and it did not come to an end until the aristocracy gave it their own support in hopes of becoming more powerful under the new regime, than they had been under the crown of Spain.

Once the political, but not the social, independence was accomplished, the struggle was renewed between the conservative and the liberal classes. This struggle covered a long period of time and was full of dramatic events, such as the French intervention, and the subsequent establishment of the so-called Empire, an enterprise which ended in the death of an Austrian prince, and which brought about the final establishment of a democratic government and the separation of the Church from the State. The clergy were granted full liberty in respect to their own welfare and ecclesiastical duties, but were thereafter not allowed to meddle in government affairs.

The country, now almost exhausted by long internal strife, was willing to tolerate the dictatorship of Porfirio Diaz who maintained a state of peace for thirty years, during which public wealth increased considerably; a middle class, never known before, was created, and public instruction began to be imparted, though in a scant manner. Diaz, however, utterly neglected to give the people a political education and to protect the latter

classes from the oppression of the aristocracy and the ambitions
of the Church, which had already been abundantly reimbursed
for its former losses. He also failed to bring about a distribution
without discrimination of the public wealth, and to satisfy the
appeals for justice which were made throughout the country.
Diaz failed to understand that after the thirty years of his dictatorship, the social conditions of the country had undergone important changes; the cost of living had increased, while wages
had not been raised proportionally. Thus the people lived under
unbearable conditions, their earnings, in later years, being hardly
sufficient to afford them existence.

Francisco I. Madero embodied the aspirations of the newer
generation of the Mexican people, who, having no legal means
of redressing their wrongs, were compelled to resort to arms.

The revolution headed by Madero was, like the wars of Independence and of the Reform, a social, rather than a political,
struggle. Public opinion, constantly supporting the revolutionary
movement, brought Madero quickly to the Presidency. Unfortunately, Madero's pure ideals and magnanimity brought about a
compromise with the tottering administration of Diaz, by means
of which a provisional president was named, Mr. De la Barra.
During De la Barra's administration all the reactionary elements
of the country, quite sure that they would be harassed no more,
prepared to regain power and, in advance, to undermine both the
administration of Madero and the principles of the revolutionary
party.

In fact, Madero never ruled at all; he was constantly prevented
from doing so by the reactionary party which, through the press,
entirely under its control, and a majority in the hold-over Congress, proceeded to foment revolt and excite the public. His administration was finally overthrown by virtue of joint action on
the part of all the reactionary elements, and by means of one of
the most cowardly betrayals ever recorded in history.

The government, having been forcibly seized by the military
chief charged with the defense of its institutions and the protection of the persons representing the Executive Power, and having
sealed that usurpation with the assassination of President Madero
and vice-President Pino Suarez, the nation, in a solid mass, experienced a strong sentiment of exasperation, outrage and despair,
because it understood the character of the betrayal, realizing,
as a people aspiring to be considered as enlightened, what had
befallen them; that their structure was once more in the hands
of the reactionaries, and that it was now a human impossibility
to satisfy the aspirations that formed the ideals of the revolution

of 1910. The interests that strengthened the arm of Huerta were the same that at first opposed the independence of Mexico; that, still later, in their selfish anxiety to hinder the social reforms of progress, called foreign forces to their aid; that industriously perverted the dictatorial will of Porfirio Diaz (who divided among a very limited number of persons the riches of the country) and that next treacherously conspired to betray Madero, and consequently the people, to the extent of sacrificing them, and usurping the powers of government.

During the moments of surprise and horror that followed the overthrow of the constituted government, the Governor of the State of Coahuila, Señor Venustiano Carranza, and after him the Governor of the State of Sonora, Señor José Maria Maytorena, and a group of members of Congress, had the courage to boldly protest against the crime, and in favor of the constitution. In order to render these protests more effective, they rose in arms.

At this point it is desirable to note that the pretended government set up by those who overthrew Madero, has never been legal. In the first place, the resignation obtained from him was secured, if it existed, through misrepresentation as well as by moral and material pressure; by duress. In the second place, the Chamber of Deputies, before which he ought to have appeared, and by which he should have been received, during the night of the extraordinary session, when it was given notice of the existence of that document, lacked in a legal quorum, having no more than ninety of the one hundred and twenty members, which, according to the law, constitutes its relative majority. In the third place, when the acceptance of the resignation of Madero was obtained from the Chamber, prior to the taking of the oath of office as Provisional President by Huerta, moral and material violence were employed against its members, to whom were communicated cynical threats that if they did not forthwith accept the resignation of Madero, he would at once be sacrificed without mercy. Simultaneously a battalion of troops was stationed under the arches of the Legislative Palace, and the galleries of the Chamber were filled with soldiers, a demonstration of armed force intended to intimidate, as it did, the members in the free exercise of their duty. The writer himself was a member from the State of Guadalajara, and protested against all and each of these unlawful acts; and there were five others who, in spite of the menace, voted against the acceptance of the resignation of Madero. But, I repeat, that the Chamber was not legally constituted at the time, and was under moral and material pressures, so that, consequently, by deed and by right, its action was void, rendering the government of Huerta illegal.

On the other hand the authority of Carranza and Maytorena, representing the executive power of the sovereign States of Coahuila and Sonora, respectively, as well as that of Castillo Brito, Governor of the State of Campeche, is sustained by the Constitution and the law. Therefore, they are not rebels; on the contrary, they are, as in duty bound, promoters of an effort to vindicate the Constitution. They are the remnant of the Constituted Government of Madero. Those who are really rebels are Huerta and his co-usurpers who have tramped the Constitution under foot and defied society.

The prompt determination of Governor Carranza to take up arms rather than submit to Huerta, impelled the proclamation of what is known as the "Plan of Guadalupe," which was, at the same time, approved by a large number of military chiefs who rallied about him with their respective commands.

This plan reads more or less as follows:

1. We repudiate Gen. Victoriano Huerta as President of the Republic.

2. We repudiate also the legislative and judicial powers of the Federation.

3. We repudiate the governments of the States which, thirty days hence, shall recognize the Federal authorities which form the present administration.

4. For the organization of the military forces necessary to make compliance with our purposes, we name as First Chief of the Forces which shall be called "Constitutionalists" Don Venustiano Carranza, Governor of the State of Coahuila.

5. On the occupation by the Constitutionalist forces of the City of Mexico, the Executive Power shall be taken charge of by Don Venustiano Carranza, First Chief of the forces, or who ever may be substituted in command.

6. The President *ad interim* of the Republic shall convoke general elections as soon as peace shall have been established, delivering the power to the person who shall be elected.

7. The person acting as First Chief of the Constitutionalist forces will assume charge as Provisional Governor of such States as have recognized Huerta, and shall convoke local elections, after which the persons elected shall assume their duties. * * *

Signed at the Estate of Guadalupe, Coahuila, on the 26th day of March, 1913.

This rather simple but direct declaration, devoid of high sounding phrases and complex considerations, met with a high approval at once by a vast majority of the people of the northern States, and later by those of other parts of Mexico when its terms became known.

From a political standpoint the leaders of the Constitutionalist party have no personal ambition. This is not a quarrel of personalities; it is not a struggle to place a given individual in power. Both leaders and followers aspire to be austere and devoted democrats who are fighting for respect for the law and for the honor of the country.

While the political aspect of the present revolution is important, it is less important, however, than its social aspect.

At the bottom, the social ideas of the present movement are the same as those of the Revolution of 1910, and it can be stated that every event which has taken place since, is nothing more than an episode of that same great drama.

In the first place, the whole nation, tired of a regime of special privilege and of a policy that had degraded the judiciary, transforming it into a simple instrument in the hands of a Dictator, to serve only the interests of the rich, demands the establishment of a new regime founded on real justice, without discrimination against the poor; also, that the Department of Justice be purified and a revision of the laws made for the better protection of all from the influence of politics.

The Constitutionalists wish to improve the conditions of the farmer, doing away, once for all, with certain abuses which, in some sections, transform the peasant into a slave; in others, they are deprived of all hope of ever acquiring a piece of land for themselves, the land-holder absorbing all the product of their work. There are, indeed, parts of the country where the laboring classes are held in such miserable and pitiful conditions, that it can be said they live in far inferior conditions to beasts of burden, which are sometimes better cared for and better fed.

The Constitutionalists want a more equitable distribution of all public taxation, because through old corrupt methods, the whole burden rests almost exclusively on the poor, the wealthy bearing but a very small proportion of it.

The Constitutionalists want that certain class of individuals who, by unclean means, during the Diaz regime, deprived even towns, to say nothing of many poor individuals, of their lands, compelled, by due process of law, to return them.

The Constitutionalists demand that certain estates of immense area, which are in the hands of individuals who cannot cultivate them, and who have not even seen them, shall be divided up, enacting the necessary laws for equitable compensation, and which will harmonize private interests with those of the community. They want new legislation which may favor, either by private enterprise supported by the State, or undertaken by the State itself, a system of irrigation and water supply to help the farmer cultivate his land. They declare the necessity for a new financial system, which, in a similar way, may provide funds, at low interest, so that the farmer may, by giving suitable security, borrow modest amounts to enable him to cultivate his lands. They also wish to impart education on a large scale; to build roads and turnpikes, and to establish schools of agriculture and industry in sufficient number.

The Constitutionalists want the land holdings fixed and respected, and, at the same time, that legislation may be enacted to facilitate the transfer of property. The condition of working-men must also be improved by means of a better relationship between capital and the working classes. And it is specially desirable to protect, educate and redeem the neglected Indians.

Finally, the social ideas of the Constitutionalist movement may be condensed by saying that Mexico wishes to take another step forward in the road of moral, political and social improvement. This movement is one of progress, and in view of the knowledge that the writer has of the present conditions of the country, he considers that if the present crisis can be solved in a way favorable to the popular will, in a day not very far distant, Mexico will call the attention of the world by the harmonious development of her resources and by the democratic exercise of her rights. The people are already practically prepared for democracy, though they lack experience, and, above all, confidence in their ruler to execute their express will.

I may say, in a rough way, that all honest men in Mexico are on the side of the Constitutionalist faction; but as I may be considered partial in such a general statement, I consider myself obliged to rectify it only in the sense that few are the honest men who are against us, and these are only those individuals who sincerely believe in a dictatorial and oppressive regime. Thus, with the exception of these few, who may be convinced, the remainder of those who are on the side of Huerta are only those who may have, with him, common interests; these are old followers of Diaz, known by the name of "cientificos," among whom are those who became rich with the money of the nation, others are large land-holders who consider their estates in danger, or that they may be obliged to emancipate the workmen whom they exploit in tilling their fields, in case the Constitutionalists are successful. There are a few still belonging to the military class, and others who are religious fanatics. We may have to add to these, the professional politicians, who fear to lose their places, and who would be quickly displaced were the popular vote consulted, due to the fact that they are invariably unpopular. But the good element of Mexico, the country people, the middle class, the working men, the intellectual man who has not gone into politics as a means to get a living, and the great Liberal Party as a whole, are united with the Constitutionalist movement, which is favored, it may be said, by no less than 90 per cent of the population.

Among the leaders of this great party are counted in the first rank Mr. Venustiano Carranza, who belongs to one of the leading and oldest families of the State of Coahuila. He was educated at the City of Mexico, and began a course of study at the National School of Law, but was caused to abandon it because of trouble with his eyes. But his splendid preparation put him in a position to become a highly cultured man. In his personality he is a thinker; he speaks but little; he is famously honest and is well to do. He is about fifty-five years old, greatly admired and beloved by his fellow citizens. He was engaged in the management of his estate when he was elected mayor of his own town, after which he was made a judge, a Senator in the National Congress, and finally was unanimously elected as Governor of his State, which position he still holds. He believes that the cause for which he is fighting is the cause of righteousness; he knows that the burden he assumed is a very heavy one, but he has a clear consciousness of the great need of the present movement, on which depends the establishment of lasting peace in Mexico. He is not impulsive, nor is he unfair in his decisions; but, on the contrary, is humanitarian and a man of repose; but, at the same time, he is endowed with a firmness of character which has made him noted among the leaders of the country.

Mr. Jose Maria Maytorena, Governor of the State of Sonora, is also a man of very good social position, and he is well to do. He has spent his life developing his estate. He is also admired and beloved by his people. Around these two great leaders, and Governor Castillo Brito, of Campeche, there are all the really influential men of their respective States.

Out of the 235 Congressmen who were elected to form the present Mexican National Congress, more than one-half sympathize with the Constitutionalist movement. During the last day's of Mr. Madero's administration, many of them were in great danger of death, and were compelled to leave the Capital for safety. About forty of them are already in the army of the Constitutionalists. Nearly one-half of the Senators are, at heart, also sympathizers with the movement, and if their number is not greater it is due to the fact that many of them belong to the old ranks of Porfirio Diaz.

Many of the leaders of the movement are still in the capital, unable to leave.

The state of war in which the country finds itself at present has developed the military qualities of many citizens who were un-known before. Thus we have among the prominent leaders and officers of the Constitutionalist army, many merchants, farmers, manufacturers and men of various professions. Obregon, Cabral, Calles Bracamontes in Sonora; Toribio Ortega, Francisco Villa and many others in Chihuahua; Pablo Gonzalez, Jesus Carranza, Francisco Cos, Atilano Barrera and others in Coahuila; Roque Gonzalez Garza, Lucio Blanco, Mujica and many others in Nuevo Leon and Tamaulipas; Orestes Pereira, Calixto Contreras, Pablo Nateras, Santos Coy, Novoa, Iturbe, Martin Espinoza, in Durango, Zacatecas, Tepic, Sinaloa, and Jalisco; Gertrudis Sanchez, Rentería Lubiano, Castrejon and many others in Michoacan and Guanajuato. Besides, there are many new leaders in all the states enumerated, and others who have just received their commissions in San Luis Potosi, Vera Cruz, Guerrero, Hidalgo, State of Mexico, Puebla, Tabasco, Campeche and Tlaxcala. Zapata with his many followers, in the State of Morelos, would gladly submit to Carranza.

In brief, it may be said that the revolutionary movement has on its side intellectual and enterprising men in sufficient number to absolutely secure the general peace of the Republic, to organize the administration, to arrange a proper plan of reform in order to systematically establish the same throughout the Republic. The principal characteristics of these men is, in general, that all of them are morally sane, and are moved by a common desire to work for the benefit of their country.

In the first place, we count on the good will and the active co-operation, according to circumstances, of the great majority of the inhabitants of Mexico. The Constitutionalists control nearly the whole of the States of Sonora, Coahuila, Durango and Campeche, in which States the troops of Huerta control only a very few towns. Chihuahua, Tamaulipas, Nuevo Leon, Zacatecas, and the greatest part of San Luis Potosi; Michoacan, Guerrero and Sinaloa are also controlled, in a general sense, by the Con-stitutionalists. In the States of Tabasco, Jalisco, Tepic, Tlaxcala,

Puebla Veracruz, Hidalgo and Mexico, several organized movements have been started, spreading with such a facility that within 30 days these States will be entirely under control.

It is easy to foresee that the few States in which the movement has not yet started will very soon follow the others. In the city of Mexico our followers are actively at work, counting on the public opinion, especially among the middle classes and among the working men.

The soldiers of Huerta only amount to anything where they stand. As soon as they leave a town or city, the latter turns to the Constitutionalist side; any railroad line that they leave unprotected comes immediately to their power. A new opportunity will come to show the weakness of the so-called government of Huerta, and that opportunity will come when he begins to concentrate his troops, leaving great sections of the country entirely in the hands of the Constitutionalists, choosing to fight his last battle in the valley of Mexico.

It is a fact that war supplies have not been very abundant in the Constitutionalist camps, the greater part of the arms and ammunition in their possession being taken from the troops of Huerta. If the Constitutionalists could purchase the necessary elements to arm the volunteers who offer their services, they would readily make up an army of more than 100,000 men, within 30 days, doing away with Huerta's administration in short order.

This time the leaders of the movement intend to bring it to a final success, in order that when the needs that produced it shall be satisfied, a definite and organic peace may be established. Thus they are perfectly decided to enter into no negotiations of any kind with either Huerta or with the followers of Felix Diaz, or with the Cientificos, or with the Catholic party, nor with any other reactionary faction, whose tendencies are more or less concealed. A compromise, which was really a sign of weakness, determined the partial failure of the revolution of 1910, the disaster to the Madero policy, the murder of Mr. Madero, and caused the present situation. Thus it is for humanity's sake and for the sake of the most elementary patriotism that the Constitutionalists feel in duty bound not to enter into any compromise with the enemy. No compromise would insure peace.

Therefore, the Constitutionalists will not look with favor on any endeavors that may tend to promote such a compromise, as, for instance, the suggestion in behalf of General Treviño, a very old man, closely tied with the Cientificos, and therefore persona non grata.

When the movement shall have achieved its triumph, it is intended to keep sound and whole the strength that gave it victory. Therefore, we will not muster out our men, but will retain them in service, in order to maintain peace throughout the Republic and to do away with any bands of brigands who, under pretext of political ideas, may operate in the country.

Therefore, the Constitutionalist forces will be retained under arms to maintain order throughout the Republic, while the army which now supports Huerta will be disbanded under suitable precautionary conditions.

The intervention of any foreign power in our internal affairs would only favor the interests of Huerta and the reactionary party. The interests of the people would be greatly prejudiced, inasmuch as it would compel them to enter into some unjust compromise with their oppressors. Furthermore, the idea of intervention is highly unpopular among the people, and it would surely originate evils far greater than those it intended to remedy.

Among the people at large there is no anti-American feeling; on the contrary there is a feeling of true friendship. The great majority, as heretofore stated, have their sympathies with the Constitutionalists, and, therefore, the failure to recognize the so-called government of Huerta has been considered by them as a justification of their attitude, and has been regarded as an indirect help to them, which has been greatly appreciated. The anti-American demonstrations which have taken place in the city of Mexico are known to be mere artificial manipulations intended to force recognition, for the purpose of floating a loan in Europe, which, we believe, could only serve to protract unnecessarily a struggle, whose final outcome is easy to predict. Millions of dollars would in this way be squandered by some well known men, never regarded as honorable, and the interests of the nation would be to this extent further impaired.

In this connection it must be said, however, that the Constitutionalists will never be disposed to recognize such a loan.

The Constitutionalists have never asked, and never will ask, any help from foreign powers. All they desire is that these powers consider their cause with justice and calmness. The lives and property of foreign subjects and citizens have been protected by every possible means within their jurisdiction, and it is fair to say that no honest man need have fear. The only men who now run any risk in Mexico are those who have been charged with committing crime, or those who have plundered the national treasury.

In spite of the great difficulties encountered in maintaining communication between the different States now in arms, as well as between the different military chiefs, the whole constitution-alist movement follows strictly the same ideals and is under the general control of Mr. Carranza. Persons who have a keen interest in misrepresenting the cause have reported that this movement is chaotic and lacks systematic co-ordination, but these reports are absolutely false. Representatives from all over the country are constantly arriving in Piedras Negras—Carranza's headquarters—to receive orders and instructions.

Carranza has already begun to form an embryo government and to appoint a cabinet. At the beginning, military organization was most important, and he, therefore, devoted all his attention to the needs of his army; but now he has created two new depart-ments, one of War and one of Finance, the latter under the direc-tion of the writer, and in a very few days other departments will be created to meet the necessities incident to the occupation of new territory and fresh responsibilities.

On the 15th day of May, last, Carranza, without pressure of any sort, issued a decree binding the Constitutional government to the principle of international arbitration for the immediate set-tlement of claims of American citizens and other foreigners against Mexico, upon the triumph of his cause. This affords an excellent example of the practical side of his character.

To sum up: The Constitutionalists conceive that the seizure of the Government of Mexico by Huerta, and his assumption of power, did violence to the constitution and justifies the people in a resort to arms in an effort to vindicate not only the fundamental law, but the national honor.

The masses support this movement for the restoration of con-stitutional order; the aristocracy and the reactionary elements oppose it, favoring Huerta.

The movement is rapidly gaining ground, with at present about ninety percent of the people in its favor.

In event of triumph, a military government will be maintained in Mexico City until peace is an accomplished fact and brigand-age completely suppressed, when a general election will be called, in accordance with the terms of the constitution, for the election of a President.

All disloyal elements of the army will be disbanded under suit-able precautions, and a new army, effective and well paid, will be formed in order to guarantee public order.

The personnel of the government, including the judiciary, will be materially changed, in all grades.

Reforms will be pressed on Congress, free elections guaran-teed, and present financial methods suppressed.

An administration of the strictest economy and diligent application to internal necessities will follow.

Francisco Escudero.

TS MS (WP, DLC).
    [1] A representative of Venustiano Carranza in Washington and, as he indicates in this memorandum, head of Carranza's department of finance. Thomas Snell Hopkins sent this memorandum to Rudolph Forster in T. S. Hopkins to R. Forster, July 25, 1913, TLS (WP, DLC).

From Ellen Axson Wilson

Cornish, New Hampshire

My own darling,   Thursday [July 24, 1913].

We are having a regular rainy day, to everyone's satisfaction for rain is still needed and it was very dusty again. So all engagements were off, and we have been quietly at home. At least Jessie and I are. The others have gone to take Ruth Hall back to Hanover. I painted all morning and got on very well. I hope this will mean a fresh pleasant day and fine "effects" tomorrow on our long drive.

But I must confess that my mood is not quite idyllic, because I am so concerned about my darling, and the way in which anxieties and "crises" of all sorts seem to be heaping up about you. I am so anxious about the Mexican situation,—merely as it affects *you* I am afraid! Which is of course a shockingly selfish narrow way to regard it. I know just how steady you are in the midst of it all, but still I would give anything to *see* you and hear you say that it is all right. It is almost better never to look at papers at all when away from you, than to read them and never know what to think. But enough of this.

The girls are having a very happy time together and they all enjoyed their party last night. There seems to be a very nice crowd of young people here; much superior to the "Lyme set." Adeline and Mary are to go with us in the car tomorrow as far as Bellow's Falls. They are certainly three delightfully interesting girls.

I wonder how many times I have read that last letter, sweetheart, I wish I could tell you how I love you; but I was never good at that, you know. I shall never find that "great hearts word." The love is so great that it overpowers even the concern about *you* and fills me always with a deep joy. Always and altogether

Your own   Nell.

ALS (WC, NjP).

To James Levi Barton

My dear Dr. Barton: [The White House] July 25, 1913.

I have learned with deep interest that beginning on November 7th next there will be celebrated at Bombay the centenary of the establishment of the first American mission in India.

I feel that I should not let the occasion pass without a word of recognition of the great educational, christianizing and civilizing benefits which have accrued to that part of the world through the devotion of those self-sacrificing and self-forgetting men and women who, for the sake of a righteous cause and the good of humanity, exiled themselves from home and friends and country.

I should be very glad if the gentlemen who will represent your Board at the coming celebration could find occasion to make known my entire sympathy with the great work which the Christian missionaries have done and are still doing for the advancement of the welfare of the people of India.

Sincerely yours,   Woodrow Wilson

TLS (Letterpress Books, WP, DLC).

To Robert Marion La Follette

My dear Senator,   [Washington, c. July 25, 1913]

I forgot to ask if you thought John R. Commons[1] all right for the Industrial Commission. Don't take the trouble to come out:— just indicate your opinion below.[2]   Woodrow Wilson

ALS (La Follette Family Papers, DLC).
[1] John Rogers Commons, Professor of Political Economy at the University of Wisconsin.
[2] La Follette must have come out from the Senate chamber to give his response. He did not write it on this note.

From Augustus Octavius Bacon

Dear Mr. President: Washington, D. C. July 25th, 1913.

I am this morning in receipt of your note of yesterday relative to the Fall resolution making declaration as to the "constitutional" rights of American citizens in Mexico. I fully agree with the view presented by you, and will actively exert myself in the effort to see that the resolution in this or in any other form does not pass the Senate.[1]

I beg, Mr. President, to remain,

Very truly yours,   A. O. Bacon

TLS (WP, DLC).
  1 There was no further discussion of, or action upon, the Fall resolution.

From George Mason La Monte

                                            Bound Brook New Jersey
My dear Mr. Wilson: July 25th, 1913.

Upon my return from Saranac Lake, I sent you a telegram yesterday morning.[1] Since then I have met with Mr. Wittpenn, Mr. Grosscup, Mr. Hudspeth and other friends of Mr. Wittpenn; and your letter to Mr. Wittpenn was read to us. Needless to say I am extremely disappointed.

Last Spring, you thought that if I resigned my position as Commissioner of Banking & Insurance in New Jersey that Mr. Fielder would name an improper successor. He is precisely the same man now that he was then.

You and I have frankly talked over Mr. Fielder's limitations in the past, and we then agreed in regard to him.

I see no chance of his being an aggressive Governor, and I think many hundred aggressive Democrats will seek an opportunity to support some one else.

I thought a way out of the difficulty would be the selection of a third man, with your approval, which would have taken the bitterness out of the present situation.

Mr. Fielder will enter the campaign with your endorsement and with that of James Smith, Jr. I cannot see that his election, under the circumstances, will be any credit to the National Administration, not [nor] can it be construed as a Wilson victory. It looks to me like a surrender.

I more than ever regret that I have not had an opportunity to talk over the New Jersey situation with you, for I cannot believe that if you knew all the facts you would ask your friends to get back of Mr. Fielder at this time. Certainly, I am not prepared to do so at present, but am going to wait further developments.

I know we have let a great opportunity go by and the democracy is weaker because of it.

                          Yours very truly,   Geo. M. La Monte

TLS (WP, DLC).
  1 G. M. La Monte to WW, July 24, 1913, T telegram (WP, DLC).

From William Jennings Bryan

My Dear Mr President   [Washington July 26, 1913]

I enclose statement by Ambassador Wilson.[1] Thought you might like to read it Sunday. Have not read it myself—will read it tomorrow. Had a long talk with him. Will you please let me know what hour you would like to see Wilson[2] also whether you desire me to come with him.

With respect etc my dear Mr President I am

Very truly   W. J. Bryan

I enclose also his *advice*[3]

ALS (WP, DLC).

[1] A nineteen-page typed memorandum (WP, DLC) reviewing events in Mexico since 1910, particularly the coup which resulted in Madero's overthrow and murder.

[2] The President received Ambassador Wilson, accompanied by Secretary Bryan, at the White House on July 28. During a conference lasting fifty minutes, the Ambassador reported on affairs in Mexico. *New York Times*, July 29, 1913.

[3] Two two-page typed memoranda entitled "Recognition" and "Intervention" (WP, DLC), listing the concessions which should be exacted from the Huerta regime before recognition was accorded, and advising that military intervention should be undertaken if recognition was not granted.

To Ellen Axson Wilson

My darling,   The White House 27 July, 1913.

How incomparably sweet and dear you are! Your letters warm my heart so and give me so constant and vivid a realization of you that even this barren house seems full of you, my heart is serene and strong for every turn of the day, and even the loneliness is tempered with a delightful sense of moving in an atmosphere of assured love and comradeship. Bless you for it all! Something of the way I feel must have stolen into my letter of last week to make you speak of it as you do. It seems to me that I never loved you as I do now! It would be strange if none of the feeling which moves me so deeply and governs me so constantly got into my letters, written with my whole mind and heart intent upon you. Please do not be anxious about me. There is absolutely nothing to cause anxiety. The weather is excellent. Even when it is hottest there is some life in it and I am never overcome by it, but always rest and am revived very easily. The strain is great, very great: eternal watchfulness, incessant shifts of personal sensitiveness and jealousy, incalculable currents to be watched for and offset and controlled [and] an infinite drift of talk and comment and conjecture about affairs in Mexico and elsewhere, where we cannot control and cannot foresee; but it is not a breaking strain. Discount what you see in the papers. The difficulties in handling the currency question are not as great as the papers would have the country believe. It happens, by very hard luck, that practically *all* the men likely to oppose and give trouble, whether in the House or in the Senate, are on the committees now

handling the matter. When once it is out of their hands, I believe
that we shall have comparatively plain sailing. At any rate, everything is well in hand up to date. I will tell you if anything really
goes wrong. The Senate is infinitely slow, but even it is feeling
the impatience of the country and is likely to act sooner than
was expected. To-morrow I am to see that unspeakable person
Henry Lane Wilson; but even he is not impossible to handle. We
are merely giving him decent dismissal. We already knew what
he thought and what he had to advise. It is trying to have to
deal with such a fellow at all, but it is not in the least difficult to
decide what to do with him or with his advice. The sum of the
whole matter is, therefore that so long as you and the dear ones
with you keep well and are happy, and so long as you continue
to feed me with the sweet affection upon which I live, I shall
fare excellently,—just as well as a man could who was never
intended to be a bachellor for so much as seven days together.
Both Tumulty and Dr. Grayson are living with me, and they wear
extremely well. Tumulty is an exceedingly poor bachellor. He *cannot* stand it for seven days together. By Saturday his staying
powers are exhausted and he makes straight for Avon where his
little flock are. I'm not saying I would not do the same, if mine
were so accessible! The Doctor and I played golf three times this
week, and are great chums. He went to church with me this morning. Last week I went alone.

But I do not sit down here on Sunday afternoon to think and
speak of this dull place or this dull life here, but to think and
speak of you: the dearest indulgence I can allow myself. It was so
sweet, the other night, to pick up a New York afternoon paper
and see the picture of you I enclose.[1] And the story with it is most
attractive, whether true or not. Bless you, how everybody up there
will love and admire you before the summer is over. The glimpses
you give me of what you are doing enable me to see just how
charming and natural and genuine a friend and neighbour you
are making of yourself. I like to sit and imagine how pretty and
charming you are in it all! I adore you! No President but myself
ever had *exactly* the right sort of wife! I am certainly the most
fortunate man alive! I go to the theatre twice a week (this week
the plays were delightful and delightfully played), I take long
rides, I play golf as often as possible, I do everything I can to keep
elastic and young, but the real source of youth and renewal for
me is my love for you, the sweetheart I picked out the moment
I laid eyes on her and who has been my fountain of joy and comfort ever since. The reason it is like a new honeymoon whenever
we are together again after a separation and are free to enjoy

one another is that it is on such occasions that the deep, abiding spirit of our life and intercourse is brought fresh to our consciousness. We are wedded sweethearts. If there be any sweeter thing in life, I have not found it. De[e]pest love to all.

Your own   Woodrow

WWTLS (WC, NjP).
¹ The enclosure is missing.

To Mary Allen Hulbert

Dearest Friend,   The White House 27 July, 1913.

I wish you could see this house, and the lone bachellor in it! Not that he is literally alone. Tumulty and Dr. Grayson are living with him, and capital companions they are, wearing as well as any mere men can wear. But a chap not intended by nature to be a bachellor at all is a "lone" bachellor no matter how many men are with him, moving in and out in the same desolate house. Two of the rooms upstairs (The one you occupied and the one across the hallway, next my bedroom) are in the hands of the paperers and decorators; the East Room is similarly dismantled, bescaffolded, and possessed; the third story is presently to be occupied by the workmen who are to reconstruct it and add numerous guest chambers; and the rest of the house is stripped of rugs and carpets and hangings. The furniture everywhere in it is in ghostly summer attire. Altogether it is as much like a home as the show parts of the Trianon. I feel like a ghost myself as I move about its echoing rooms and corridors. I can imagine myself an historical character come back to revisit the glimpses of the moon and haunt the places where I played my part! The two other men seem quite real; but nothing else does, myself included. In the office it is natural enough,—desperately natural, speaking from the point of view of one who has come to find politics familiar in most of its aspects! Most of what you read in the newspapers is not true; but other things are which are almost as perplexing: so that I do not have much time to think of the desolate house in which I sleep. I only eat and sleep in it. Dr. Grayson and I try to get over into Virginia, to a little country club nearby, to play golf two or three times a week; I go twice a week to the theatre; and I take long rides in the country: I spend precious little time sitting about the house and bemoaning my desperate bachelorhood. The theatres here, by the way, maintain excellent stock companies during the summer. I have a hard time trying not to fall in love with one or two of the players! How very care-

ful and circumspect a President must be! He must indulge in
nothing natural and inevitable, in nothing that is not official and
dull and regular. The only fun he can get he must steal by doing
the regular things in an unexpected and irregular way. Tumulty
is, I must say, a less submissive and well behaved bachelor than
I. His family is at Avon, near Sea Girt on the Jersey coast. When
Friday afternoon comes, He can't stand it any longer. He runs
for an early afternoon train and is off to be with them till Sunday
night. On Sunday night it often proves possible for him to miss
the train that would bring him back! I'm not saying what I would
do if Cornish, New Hampshire, were within six hours ride of
Washington, instead of eighteen or twenty! Imagine your friend,
then, moving about his business with a straight face and a perfectly orthodox addiction to his office duties, going to his meals,
and to his bed, at the right and appointed time, taking a house full
of ghosts and ghosts' furniture quite as a matter of course and as
good enough appointments for any man's home in this world of
sin and sorrow, but with a private eye out for all the fun available
and for every escape not regarded as scandalous,—especially seeking to see all that is amusing in the frailties of his fellow
politicians. You need not be told that one of his chiefest solaces
is to think of the friend who has stimulated and delighted him so
much, the friend who knows so perfectly how to lighten such
things as he is now trying with due philosophy to endure and
survive, and to interpret them, too,—the priestess of Democracy
who yet seems, to those who see only the surface, to have been
meant for gayety and light intercourse and the circles where interesting talk is the law of life and of pleasure. How delightful her
talk is, in fact; how perfectly she reigns in whatever she attempts
amongst whatever people she mingles with; and how perfectly
the secret is her own: namely, sympathy and insight and a passionate love of the deep, simple, fundamental things that make
all men and all women kin and in need of one another. She is at
home and at ease everywhere because she everywhere understands those about her and experiences to the full the things that
move and govern them. Universal sympathy, universal insight,
and an instinctive knowledge of the moving powers of life,—what
better analysis could there be of the spirit of Democracy? The
present leader of the Democratic party would be deeply indebted
to the priestess of Democracy for frequent messages of sympathy
and inspiration   Your devoted friend   Woodrow Wilson

WWTLS (WC, NjP).

From Ellen Axson Wilson

Williamstown, Massachusetts

My own darling,   Sunday Morning [July 27, 1913].

I am writing a hurried note before starting for church—for we have changed our plans and leave here at 1.30. It was impossible to finish the house business on any other schedule. The only two unfurnished houses that offered proved so out of repair and without modern conveniences that we had to take a furnished one, just from Feb. (when they are due in Williamstown—beginning of the second term) to Sept. It of course belongs to a professor who is leaving for his Sabbatical year. They pay $500.00 for that time, and it is a *charming* house,—has every convenience and is in perfect taste. I think they are lucky to get it; and I really think it better for them not to furnish beforehand. It would be such a difficult, complicated thing to achieve. Now they will have no trouble at all,—will simply walk into a clean, sweet little home.

Louis Perry has a lovely young wife and a pretty six months old boy.[1] They are a dear little family. Mrs. Perry senior and Miss Perry[2]—the mother and sister of Bliss[—] will be Jessie's next door neighbours.

This town is really enchantingly pretty. They are fortunate to begin their life amid such surroundings and such devoted *friends*. It is evident that Frank and Mr. Garfield himself expect that his work will be to a large extent what you got Luke Miller[3] for—"to get at the boys." Partly too to make up for Mr. Garfields own misfortune in alienating their affections by trying to reform things. He is splendid and they have really been more unreasonable than Princeton, for *they* resented his introducing the group system and raising the standard. The church bell rings and I must stop. I love you passionately.   Your devoted little wife,   Nell.

ALS (WC, NjP).
  [1] Margaret Lawrie Hubbell Perry and a second Lewis Perry.
  [2] Mary Brown Smedley (Mrs. Arthur Latham) Perry and Grace Perry.
  [3] Lucius Hopkins Miller.

From Thomas Dixon, Jr.

Dear Mr President: New York July 27 [1913].

I am heartsick over the announcement that you have appointed a Negro to boss white girls as Register of the Treasury. Please let me as one of your best friends utter my passionate protest. Unless you can withdraw his name the South can never forgive this.

We have travelled many leagues from the Negro Equality ideas in vogue when Cleveland, a Democratic President did this thing.

The establishment of Negro men over white women employees of the Treasury Dept. has in the minds of many thoughtful men & women long been a serious offense against the cleanness of our social life. I have confidently hoped that you would purge Washington of this iniquity.

I sincerely hope you can withdraw the appointment.

Sincerely,   Thomas Dixon

I have no axe to grind. I am only a citizen & your friend.

ALS (WP, DLC).

Remarks at a Press Conference

July 28, 1913

Mr. President, can you not, in view of the rather psychic condition of newspaper headlines and the public mind, permit yourself to make some sort of statement in our papers today in reference to Mexico?

> Well, to tell you the truth, I don't think that the public mind is in the least agitated. I think the newspaper headlines are headlines, but the agitations are confined for the most part to that part of the United States. And I don't think that there is any uneasiness to be allayed except in certain quarters where uneasiness is justified, where people have employees, or friends, or relatives in Mexico. About their condition, you may assume us to be in sympathy with their uneasiness. I don't see· anything. Nothing, certainly, has developed in the last week or ten days that increases my anxiety.

May we indirectly use that in our newspapers, and what can we say in the newspapers?

> Why, I think you can justly say this, that nothing has developed there which seems to make the situation either better or worse than it was ten days or two weeks ago.

And that so far as the administration of this country is concerned, what course is it pursuing?

> It is pursuing a course of diligent inquiry, to see just what is the right thing to do.

When that information is gathered, Mr. President, will there be some definite and direct action on the part of this country?

> That I can't say, how definite and direct, because that is just the point under debate. . . .

[Break in Swem's notes]

> No sir—checking in that. I mean, returning to that banking

and currency question for a moment, I would like you gentlemen to give out the impression in some way that will occur to you as well as myself that there has not been the slightest wavering or supplicating on the part of the administration in its support for the bill as proposed, and that there is no likelihood of changes of any essential kind being made in the committee.

JRT transcript (WC, NjP) of CLSsh (C. L. Swem Coll., NjP).

From Joseph Patrick Tumulty

The White House.
Memorandum for the President: July 28, 1913

Representative Glass advises that the following nine members[1] of the Committee are certainly all right:

Glass   Patten   Seldomridge
Korbly   Stone   Wilson
Brown   Phelan   Weaver

Mr. Glass thinks that Representative Wingo[2] may come into line. He has been very unwilling but is apparently disposed to join the majority.

Representative Bulkley may also come into line, although he has made a great deal of trouble heretofore.

Mr. Glass thinks it would be a very good idea if the President would, over the 'phone or in some other way, communicate to the above nine members his appreciation of their attitude.[3]

T MS (WP, DLC).
[1] Carter Glass of Virginia; Charles Alexander Korbly of Indiana; William Gay Brown, Jr., of West Virginia; Thomas Gedney Patten of New York; Claudius Ulysses Stone of Illinois; Michael Francis Phelan of Massachusetts; Harry Hunter Seldomridge of Colorado; Emmett Wilson of Florida; and Claude Weaver of Oklahoma, all Democrats.
[2] Otis Theodore Wingo, agrarian Democrat of Arkansas.
[3] Wilson made check marks by each name listed above.

A News Report

[*July 28, 1913*]

WILSON PLAN IS ADOPTED.

Currency Bill to be Reported to House Caucus Aug. 11.

Washington, July 28.—President Wilson's quiet intervention in the currency legislation produced results in to-day's conference with the Democratic members of the Banking and Currency Committee of the House of Representatives. Here are the developments:

First—An agreement was reached to report a currency bill to a caucus of the Democrats of the House to be held on Monday, Aug. 11, two weeks hence.

Second—A resolution was adopted by a narrow marginal vote imposing absolute secrecy on future conferences of the Democratic members of the Glass committee.

Third—Chairman Carter Glass, acting, it is understood, with the approval of President Wilson, cast the vote which broke the tie in favor of secret sessions for future conferences, while the Democrats of the committee are considering the measure.

Fourth—The decision to submit the measure to a caucus of the House Democracy means that the bill will be presented as a partisan and not as a non-partisan one.

The agreement to report "a bill" to the Democratic caucus on Aug. 11 is regarded by friends of President Wilson as a long step in the direction of obtaining favorable action on banking and currency legislation by the House Representatives, and that the leaders of the House will put through the caucus, by a large majority, and by steamroller methods, if necessary, the kind of bill that President Wilson wants.

It is understood that President Wilson has disliked very much the publicity given to the haggling and bickering that took place behind the closed doors of the Glass committee conferences. Friends of the Administration believe that such dissension about the measure has had a bad effect upon business men and financiers and caused them to become uneasy over the prospects of favorable action on the President's proposals for currency legislation.

The fact that Chairman Glass cast the vote which broke the tie on the motion to impose secrecy upon members regarding the work of the Glass committee conferences is accepted as indicating that the President approved that action.

Printed in the *New York Times*, July 29, 1913.

From Ellen Axson Wilson

Cornish, New Hampshire

My own darling,   Monday, July 28 [1913].

Your wonderful, your adorable Sunday letter has just come and has made me fairly drunk with happiness. I would give anything to be able to *express* my love as perfectly as you do, dear heart, for then indeed I might hope to make you as happy as you make me. But then no one else in the world can express *any*thing so perfectly as you,—so there is no help for it, unless when you write those "great heart words" you will say to yourself "her *heart* is as great as mine, and it echoes all I say, though she has not the genius for expression." Oh how I *adore* you! I am perfectly sure that you are the greatest, most wonderful, most lovable man who *ever* lived. I am not expressing an opinion, I am simply stating a self-evident fact. Certainly such love is the real source of youth and renewal for women,—for me,—and it is a joy too deep for words to hear you say and feel that it is the same for you. God bless you, my darling, my darling!

Nell and I enjoyed especially what you say about Henry Lane Wilson for we loathe him so that we want everyone else to, and are very glad to know positively that his days are numbered. How exactly his appearance seems to fit,—so contemptable, and mean looking,—such a shifty, furtive eye! I would not trust him with a brass farthing. The "World's" editorial today[1] suited us exactly, and how we raged over the one in the "Times."[2]

There was not a word of truth in the story about the old ladies tea. I am dismayed to think what my real guests "the best families of Windsor" (chiefly Evarts) will make of it,—for I am afraid the average New England woman does not laugh as easily as we do.

Really, I believe the reporters up here are the worst we have yet encountered, the most shameless liers.

We had another pleasant ride yesterday back from Williamstown and saw some even finer scenery than on our way. To do it, we made a detour, and ascended various high places, making the journey 125 miles in all, instead of the 111 the other way.

We reached home at 8.30, very tired, of course, but not exhausted. It was a *beautiful* day, though not quite so wonderful as Saturday. As per schedule we picked up Adeline and Mary at Walpole, where we left them on Saturday. Their grandmother[3] is spending the summer there, and Mrs. Scott[4] is also there at present. We saw her and stopped for tea with them. It is 35 miles away, so it gave the Scotts quite a nice motor trip, and they enjoyed it intensely.

I stayed in bed all the morning, painted in the early afternoon and then posed for Mr. Vonnoh an hour. The light for his picture is best from 4.30 to six. It rained most of the day clearing suddenly and completely about five. The picture is developing charmingly. He did a lot of work on Nell while we were away, and is beginning to get something of a likeness. It is really a very interesting composition and a lovely piece of colour. And today he made great progress on my head. It is in profile, with the eyes down, the face in shadow with a warm light along the edge of the face and hair; so of course it is not a "portrait" but will probably have more charm because of that fact; we all like it, even at this stage. Jessie's ought to be a portrait for it is full face and in the light; but he has not gone very far with it.

I found in my room at Williamstown a book called "The Story of Two Noble Lives," by Augustus J. C. Hare,[5] one of those leisurely English biographies that are so delightfully readable. It is out of print but not very hard to get, they say. I am sure you would *love* it,—and I want it. Will you ask some one to try and get it for you. It can be had in either two or three vols. All send love. *I love you* intensely. As ever   Your own little wife   Nell.

ALS (WC, NjP).
[1] "Underwriting a Tyranny?," New York *World*, July 28, 1913. It castigated Henry Lane Wilson for his opposition to and contempt for the Wilson administration, his low opinion of the character of the Mexican people, support of the tyrant Huerta, and complicity in the overthrow and murder of Madero.
[2] "Recognition of Gen. Huerta the Practical Course," *New York Times*, July 28, 1913. As its title suggests, this editorial accepted completely the view of the Mexican situation set forth by Henry Lane Wilson, who had done "heroic work for his Government in Mexico in the last three years." Armed intervention was unthinkable; mediation would be between the "established government" and "armed bandits"; hence the only practical course was recognition of the "reasonably efficient" Huerta government. In any event, the editorial concluded, "The character of Gen. Huerta is none of our business."
[3] Their maternal grandmother, Adeline Furman Mitchell (Mrs. Edwin Fredine) Post.
[4] Alice Adeline Post (Mrs. William Berryman) Scott.
[5] Augustus John Cuthbert Hare, *The Story of Two Noble Lives, Being Memorials of Charlotte, Countess Canning, and Louisa, Marchionesse of Waterford* (3 vols., London and New York, 1893). This book is in the Wilson Library, DLC.

To George Mason La Monte

My dear La Monte: [The White House] July 29, 1913

I am sincerely sorry you feel as you do about the opinion I felt obliged to give as to the gubernatorial situation in New Jersey. You are mistaken in supposing that I acted without sufficient information. I made very diligent inquiry in many quarters from many sorts of people, and it was perfectly clear that it was my duty as the leader of the party to analyze and act upon the facts as I found them. It was a case when I had to choose between friends, very good friends and very true friends. I had to choose with the coolness of one who does not allow his heart to play any part in the matter, and I am confident, in view of what I know of the situation, that I judged rightly. I can only hope that you will agree with me as the situation develops.

It was very pleasant to hear from you, and I am sure Mrs. Wilson and my daughters would join in cordial messages to the family if they were with me.

Faithfully yours,   Woodrow Wilson

TLS (Letterpress Books, WP, DLC).

To Thomas Dixon, Jr.

My dear Dixon: [The White House] July 29, 1913

I do not think you know what is going on down here. We are handling the force of colored people who are now in the departments in just the way in which they ought to be handled. We are trying—and by degrees succeeding—a plan of concentration which will put them all together and will not in any one bureau mix the two races. This change has already practically been effected in the bureau in which I proposed the appointment of Patterson.

It would not be right for me to look at this matter in any other way than as the leader of a great national party. I am trying to handle these matters with the best judgment but in the spirit of the whole country, though with entire comprehension of the considerations which certainly do not need to be pointed out to me.   Cordially and sincerely yours,   Woodrow Wilson

TLS (Letterpress Books, WP, DLC).

To William Sulzer

My dear Governor Sulzer: [The White House] July 29, 1913

Your letter of July twenty-second has brought very vividly to my mind again the difficulties we labor under here in making federal appointments. Of course, the systematic effort in the matter of recommendations is always made by the local organization. We have not the opportunity or the means to go out and look for candidates or for information about those who are candidates, and very often information by which we would wish to have been guided comes to us after a nomination is sent to the Senate.

I can assure you that we are doing our best to show our appreciation of the best elements in the party and that we will welcome the fullest information for our guidance.

Whether, in the present circumstances when I am staggering under a burden of work which there are not hours enough for me to dispose of, I can see the gentlemen you speak of who wish to come down for an interview, I can not now say, but certainly I shall manage in some way to learn what their advice is.

Cordially and sincerely yours,   Woodrow Wilson

TLS (Letterpress Books, WP, DLC).

To Henry De La Warr Flood

My dear Mr. Flood: [The White House] July 29, 1913

I greatly appreciate the message you were kind enough to leave at the office the other morning. It gives me a sense of confidence to feel that the members of the Foreign Affairs Committee are behind me, and I shall be very glad to avail myself of your kind offer to confer with me at any turning point of the matter.

Cordially and sincerely yours,   Woodrow Wilson

TLS (Letterpress Books, WP, DLC).

To John Barrett[1]

My dear Mr. Barrett: [The White House] July 29, 1913

Thank you sincerely for your paper of July twenty-sixth,[2] which I have read with a great deal of attention and with genuine interest and appreciation.

Cordially yours,   Woodrow Wilson

TLS (Letterpress Books, WP, DLC).
[1] Director General of the Pan American Union, Washington; former Minister to Siam, Argentina, Panama, and Colombia.
[2] J. Barrett to WW, July 26, 1913, TLS (WP, DLC), urging Pan-American mediation in Mexico.

From Ellen Axson Wilson

Cornish, New Hampshire
My own darling,   Tuesday [July 29, 1913]

Im wae[1] to think how hot it must be in Washington today for it has been intensely close here as well as hot. However it is late afternoon now, there has been a light shower and things are better.

I am just back from the club where they discussed—what do you suppose?—"the Monroe doctrine"! It was too political for me of course! I was in fact afraid of being indiscreet so I said nothing until they began to be irrelevant, as they always do. It was quite harmless to talk about trade with South America, &c. &c.

But I saw another pretty place, that of our nearest neighbour Mrs. Nichols,[2] niece of St. Gaudens, the rambling white house with the many fine hedges that really joins ours.

Nothing else has happened since I wrote. Nell & Mary Scott ride every day and find the horse good. Two of them nearly died from the journey—the doctor was up with them all night,—bu[t] they made a most rapid recovery and are in fine shape now.

They are perfectly delighted to have horses. The Scotts leave to-morrow, much to our regret. They are splendid girls.

We are all more or less absorbed in the Mexican situation,—Nell and I especially. I am so proud of you. How splendidly "the World" put it this morning! ["]In the poise, patience and patriotism of the Chief Magistrate, who can be rushed no more than Lincoln or Cleveland could be rushed, the hope of a peac[e]able solution of the problem now rests." I should judge that "The Times" too feels rather differently about Wilson today, though it has no editorial[.]

All the family join me in love beyond measure. How devotedly you[r] children love you, my darling!—as for me words fail as usual. I *idolize* you,—I love you till it *hurts*. As ever

Your little wife   Nell.

ALS (WC, NjP).
    ¹ A Scottish word meaning woe.
    ² The property mentioned here belonged to Arthur Howard Nichols, a physician of Boston. His wife was Elizabeth Fisher Homer Nichols, a sister-in-law of Augustus Saint-Gaudens. Mrs. Wilson must have been referring either to Mrs. Nichols or to one of her two unmarried daughters, Rose Standish Nichols and Marian Clarke Nichols.

From George Mason La Monte

My dear Mr. Wilson: Bound Brook New Jersey July 30, 1913.

I was very glad to receive your letter of the 29th inst this morning. It is a source of satisfaction to me to know that I can write to you frankly and that you like to have me do so.

The fact is, every anti-Wilson man that I have met in the State of New Jersey is in a jubilant frame of mind. For instance, I know that Mr. Smith has expressed great satisfaction because the only thing that he wished to accomplish was the elimination of Mr. Wittpenn.

Yesterday morning Teddy Edwards¹ entered my office wreathed in smiles and invited me to take a front seat on the band wagon, saying that "this shows what will happen to any man who bucks up against the influence of the First National Bank and its ramifications." So there seems to be a general impression that your friends have suffered and have to eat "crow" for their health's sake.

Of course, I know that you meant to get all the information that you could before acting, but here at least is one man who thinks he could have contributed to the fund of information if he had been given an opportunity to do so. I know perfectly well that your time is occupied, and therefore, I do not intend at any time to push my views forward unless they are asked for; but I am always ready to be at your service, and if it were not for my intense interest in the administration I probably would not feel as badly as I do at the present time.

Mrs. La Monte and I were talking the other day about how different this Summer was from last Summer and were wishing that you were nearer by and that we might have the pleasure of dropping in on you occasionally as we did then.

Yours very sincerely,   Geo. M. La Monte

P.S. In looking over the above I find that I have not said all I wanted to. I think that Mr. Fielder will undoubtedly be nominated and elected, but that will be largely because of the weakness of the opposition and not because of the Democratic strength. I wish we could win because we deserve to.

The Independent Progressive Democratic vote is now headed toward Colby. I do not see how Mr. Fielder's campaign is going to be made to appeal to the independent voter. He will undoubtedly get some of the stand-pat Republican vote and some of the vote of the Smith Republicans, but he will not get the entire Democratic vote.

I also feel that I ought to say that I think there is not any human relationship in which the heart should not play a part, and perhaps it is because of the coldness of your letter to Mr. Wittpenn that it hurts so much.

TLS (WC, DLC).

1 Edward Irving Edwards, cashier of the First National Bank of Jersey City and State Comptroller of New Jersey since 1911. For the somewhat complex story of his opposition to Wittpenn's gubernatorial candidacy, see James Kerney, *The Political Education of Woodrow Wilson* (New York and London, 1926), pp. 253-58.

From Adam Edward Patterson

My Dear Sir: Washington, D. C. July 30th, 1913.

In view of recent developments caused by my name having been submitted to the United States Senate for confirmation as Register of the Treasury,[1] I beg to request that you withdraw my nomination for that position. I consider that you have paid me a high tribute and an honor well worth cherishing in appointing me Register of the United States Treasury, for which I heartily thank you. I had hoped that the nomination and confirmation would be made without protest. This hope, it seems, was unfounded.

I feel like our Savior must have felt when he was handed the bitter cut [cup], it meant life and death. Yet I take it and cheerfully stiffle my personal ambitions and surrender back to you, Mr. President the appointment of Register of the United States Treasury, the prize for which I have striven all my life.

I begun my political career when a very young man in Colorado by speaking throughout that state in the interest of the present Secretary of State, in 1896, and since that time have continued steadfastly in the Democratic faith for which I am justly proud. I will be found working for the supremacy of the Democratic party in the future as I have in the past, and, in the future as in the past, without expectation of remuneration or reward.

I refuse to embarrass your administration, Mr. President, by insisting upon my confirmation, and I also believe it is best for my race that I withdraw my name from further consideration for this position. I am anxious that the spirit of harmony and good-will exist between the two races, and by taking this step I believe it will go far towards bringing about a more friendly racial feeling.

Again thanking you for the honor of the appointment, and assuring you of my future loyalty to the Democratic Party,
I remain very truly yours,   A. E. Patterson
Address—R.F.D. No. 2, Spokane, Wash.

ALS (WC, DLC).
    [1] Patterson's nomination had set off loud denunciations from southern Senators, including Hoke Smith of Georgia, Benjamin R. Tillman of South Carolina, and James K. Vardaman of Mississippi. They declared flatly that Patterson would not be confirmed and that they would not permit any black to be confirmed for an office which would give him authority over white women. See George C. Osborn, "The Problem of the Negro in Government, 1913," *The Historian*, XXIII (May 1961), 331.

From Ellen Axson Wilson

Cornish, New Hampshire
My own darling,   Wednesday July 30 [1913]

I sincerely hope that you in Washington are like ourselves having some relief from yesterday's intense heat. It is still hot but not murky, and we had a fine night. The girls all went to a dance at Maxfield Parrish's—"a small and early." This morning they took the Scotts as far as White Plains [River] Junction and put them on the train.

It is now the middle of the afternoon. I have been resting after my morning in the studio and reading the papers. When I finish this I shall dress and go to visit *Mr* (!) Stephen Parish and Mrs. Louis St. Gaudens.[1] Mr. Stephen is "the original democrat," the father of Maxfield, and he has a lovely garden and view. Mrs. St. Gaudens is a sculptor and wants me to see her latest picture,—

just finished. She is the widow of Augustus St Gaudens brother, but looks young enough to have been his daughter, such a quaint little thing, at once fearless and very shy—like a bird.

I am sorry to see that the Mexican[s] reject mediation.[2] Perhaps it would save us trouble in the long run to give them arms and let them exterminate each other if they so prefer. I am also sorry that Kahns of Calif,[3] who was our very good friend in the alley matter is behaving so detestably now as regards McReynolds.[4] Will it injure the latter much that he has been shown to have telegraphed delaying the case long *before* Sec. Wilson spoke to him about it? I have been rather uneasy since seeing that.

I was interrupted here and am finishing after my return from my visits. Both were unusually interesting. Mrs. St. Gaudens was the assistant of Augustus for some years before she married his brother Louis (who died last winter). He of course was a distinguished sculptor too,—only overshadowed by his greater brother. He did all the great figures for the station in Washington and she worked with him. It gives one quite an insight into the ways of sculptors to see their studio and its contents. She does charming bas-reliefs, all her own, and very much in St. Gaudens style.

But the Stephen Parrish house and garden is a perfect idyl, and he is the *dearest* old man,—so mellow and wholesome & interested in what is worth while, *you* for instance! He & his daughter live there most of the year. We took tea with them & had a beautiful time.

Good-bye, dear, *dear* heart. I love, I adore you, in fact I am mad about you. When oh, *when* am I to see you again.

As ever   Your own   Nell

ALS (WC, NjP).

[1] Annetta Johnson (Mrs. Louis) Saint-Gaudens.

[2] A curious statement. There were no reports in the newspapers on or about this date about any Mexican rejecting mediation.

[3] Representative Julius Kahn, Republican from California.

[4] A reference to the Diggs-Caminetti cases. Farley Drew Caminetti and Maury I. Diggs, both of California, were indicted in March 1913 for violating the Mann Act prohibiting the transportation of women across state lines for immoral purposes. Caminetti's father was Anthony Caminetti, the head-designate of the Immigration Service in the new Department of Labor. On May 16, Attorney General McReynolds sent a telegram to John L. McNab, federal district attorney in San Francisco, directing him to send a full report on the cases and to take no further action until advised. After reading McNab's report, McReynolds wired him again on May 27, ordering him to proceed with the cases.

In June, Anthony Caminetti asked Secretary of Labor Wilson for a leave of absence to attend his son's trial, then set for July. The Secretary, feeling that the elder Caminetti's absence would seriously impede the work of his department, requested the Attorney General to order a postponement of the trials until autumn. Secretary Wilson later insisted that he had done so entirely on his own initiative and not at the request of the elder Caminetti or anyone else.

McReynolds wired McNab on June 18, ordering him to postpone the trials until autumn. McNab, a Republican, responded on June 20 by telegraphing his resignation to President Wilson, charging that attempts had been made to corrupt government witnesses, that friends of the defendants openly boasted that the prosecutions would be stopped by appeals to Washington, and that the Department of Justice was yielding to improper influences. McNab's telegram appeared in the press on June 22 and caused a furor both in Congress and the country. After requesting and obtaining a report on the circumstances of the postponement from McReynolds, President Wilson, on June 24, ordered the Attorney General to proceed with the trials with "the utmost diligence and energy." Diggs and young Caminetti were eventually convicted and sent to prison.

Julius Kahn led the Republican denunciation of the administration's handling of the Diggs-Caminetti affair on the floor of the House of Representatives. He introduced a resolution on July 25 directing the Attorney General to transmit to the House a copy of his telegram of May 16, which had not been included in the documents on the cases previously transmitted. Kahn made a lengthy speech in the House on the affair on July 29, denouncing the administration in bitter and sarcastic terms and also presenting many of the relevant documents. See J. C. McReynolds to WW, June 24, 1913, and W. B. Wilson to J. C. McReynolds, June 24, 1913, both TLS (WP, DLC); and WW to J. C. McReynolds, June 24, 1913, TLS (Letterpress Books, WP, DLC); *Cong. Record*, 63d Cong., 1st sess., pp. 2776, 2876-86; and Link, *The New Freedom*, pp. 117-18.

From William Jennings Bryan

My dear Mr. President: Washington July 31, 1913.

We have struck a snag in the matter of the Nicaraguan treaty. I have been before the Committee twice, and they have had a separate meeting for considering the matter, but there is quite a determined opposition on the part of the minority of the Committee against the Platt amendment idea—in fact, against any extension of our authority over these countries. I believe that a majority of the Committee will endorse the treaty, but Senator Bacon says that, under existing conditions, it would be impossible to secure a ratification of the treaty at the special session in the face of any considerable opposition. According to the rules of the Senate, a minority can delay action, at a time like this, when most of the Senators want to go home and are only prevented from going by the pressure that is back of bills that must necessarily be considered. Senator Bacon thinks that we would have no trouble with a bill providing for the purchase of the canal option and the naval base on Fonseca Bay.

I write, therefore, to ask you whether it might not be wise to separate the two and put the treaty through now providing for the purchase of the canal site and the naval base and then, at the regular session, try to secure a treaty extending our authority along the lines of the Platt amendment? The matter could then be decided upon its merits and time taken to overcome any opposition the minority might be disposed to offer. You could decide whether, in submitting the second proposition relating to the Platt amendment, you would also recommend the plan I laid before you of lending our financial credit. It might be that the lending of our credit, with an agreement as to the appointment of an inspector of customs, and permission to protect our interests there in case of disorder, would be sufficient, and the offer of a real material advantage might—I think it would—overcome the objections that have been made against the proposal; at least, it would give us an opportunity to present a matured policy and invite the judgment of the country on it without delaying the acquisition of the canal option and naval base. I have asked the Nicaraguan Minister[1] to tell his Government of the situation and see whether they are willing to separate the two propositions and act now upon the canal option and naval base. He promises to let me know in the morning, and I write you now so that you may have time to think it over and let me know, if possible, tomorrow morning.

I expect John Lind to arrive tomorrow.[2]

The despatches today from the City of Mexico are more encouraging. O'Shaughnessy reports that the spirit of the present administration toward the United States has changed in a marked degree in the last three days. He also says that there is a report that Huerta will resign the Presidency in favor of the Minister of Gobernacion and that Felix Diaz will not proceed further than San Francisco. The Minister of Finance resigned because he refused to consider the suggestion of certain bankers that there should be a foreign inspector at the Treasury Department in case the said bankers advance the present administration funds. The President is hastening his message giving relief to the prisoners at Chihuahua. . . .

With assurances of my respect, I am,

My dear Mr. President,

Very truly yours,   W. J. Bryan

Mr Quodra,[3] of Nicaragua thinks that the signing of the treaty as it is would greatly help them even though its ratification was delayed until fall.

TLS (WP, DLC).
   [1] Emiliano Chamorro.
   [2] Wilson and Bryan had decided to ask Lind to go on a special mission to Mexico City. Following documents will make their purposes clear.
   [3] Pedro Rafael Cuadra, Nicaraguan Minister of Finance.

Three Letters From Ellen Axson Wilson

Cornish, New Hampshire

My own darling,   Thursday, July 31 [1913].

I have just returned from posing for Mr. Vonnoh, rather stiff and tired. I fear we are in for a rather exacting and serious undertaking. But it will at least be a real work of art. The girls have also just returned from playing tennis with some of their new friends. We spent the morning as usual and nothing else has happened.

We are all much concerned about the terrible storm in Washington and the wrecked trees in the White House grounds. Do make someone write us just what the damage really is—how *many* trees suffered.

I am also concerned at the report in the "Times" that Congress is disposed to take a different view from your own as regards Wilson and the Mexican situation. He is said to have made "a very favourable impression" on it. I don't want *you* to be troubled to write me on these points—make Mr. Tumulty do it!

Your family is beginning to have the wanderlust again, alas! Nell goes tomorrow to stay two days at Hanover with Ruth Hall. And next week we may *all* four go to the White Mts.! It is only 65 miles to Franconia Notch,—(which is the heart of them), and the girls are wild to see them. If we go at all it must be before the middle of the month for then the Smiths[1] come and the car would not hold us all. We would probably leave on Thursday, spending one night at the Flume House and one at "Crawfords." Murphy[2] insists upon going with us. He has been looking it all up. We can't go before Thursday because I have promised to go to some gathering of farmers wives on Wednesday.

It is fairly cool here again. I hope and pray that you are not suffering. I am fair wearing for the sight of you, my darling, my darling! I always did despise those Mexicans. Now I fear I shall hate them too because they prevent your coming even for a week-end. I suppose they have knocked Mr. Bryan's lecture schedule into a cocked hat! With love inexpressible

Your devoted   Nell.

[1] Lucy Marshall Smith and Mary Randolph Smith of New Orleans.
[2] Joseph E. Murphy, chief of the White House detail of the Secret Service.

Cornish, New Hampshire
My own darling,   Friday, Aug. 1 [1913]

I have been out to luncheon with Miss Evarts,[1] (daughter of Wm. M.) at the old home. It was all very interesting and patriarchal, for W. M. had a *very* beautiful estate in Windsor of many hundred acres and all his sons still live on it, in separate houses, of course. There is a large pond,—(really a beautiful lake) with splendid *clean* woodland on one side and the houses and gardens on the other—also a large farm. After luncheon we took a ride in their automobile, saw their estate first and then a new and very pretty road called "the brook road." Then they brought us home—Jessie and I,—and took tea with us. So it practically took the day. When they left I had to rest off a headache which I had picked up on the way and then dress for dinner; for Helen and I dine at the Platts tonight.

We are just back from the Platts where we had a delightful time. I had not met Mr. Platt before and I like him exceedingly. Of course you remember that he is the artist-architect,—of this house among others. I saw there a large and *very* beautiful picture by him of the mountain—(Ascutney) in winter,—a most noble composition and so poetical! I knew nothing of his work as a painter. The other guests were the H. O. Walkers[2] and Mr. Stephen Parrish and his niece, a delightfully congenial little party for me and for Helen too.

I am appalled at the tales of destruction in Washington; some one sent us today some pictures of the White House grounds. It is heart-breaking. I can only hope that the papers are, as usual, exaggerating.

Good-night dear, *dearest* love. I hate to stop but it is quite late. I am hoping for a "day letter" tomorrow, but if it does not come I can still live on that last wonderful precious letter. I love you with all my heart and I am in every breath,

Your own   Eileen.

Don't forget to deposit your salary for I am going to invest some of it at once. So it should be in bank.

[1] Mary Evarts, the only surviving unmarried daughter of William Maxwell Evarts.

[2] Henry Oliver Walker and Laura Margaret Marquand Walker of Lakewood, N. J. He was a painter specializing in portraits and murals.

Cornish, New Hampshire

My own darling,   Saturday [Aug. 2, 1913]

I am just back from a tea at Miss Steeles[1] in Windsor. She has a pretty place on the Evarts estate,—I don't know whether she is related or not; but she belongs to their set and is very nice,—kindly and rather humorous. She is a pillar of the "old church." The Evarts are all Episcopalians. I met piles of New England spinsters,—and I must say I like them, Mrs Peck notwithstanding! They are all friendly and kindly, if one is cordial with them,—just as the Middletown people used to be. And so unaffected. It was a hot day so we rode afterwards, with the result that I shall have to finish this after dinner. We are missing Nell horribly;—we will go and get her just after lunch tomorrow, probably taking *Dudley Malone* with us! He telegraphed that he wanted to call tomorrow. We asked him to luncheon but do not know if he will get here that soon or not. Of course we will keep him over night if we can. I am very glad to have someone from Washington to question about many things!

By the way, I suppose Dr Grayson knows that the missing box of medecines *never* came! Please ask him if he does? A box of medecines meant for the Tumultys came here by mistake & was returned to them[.] But Helen wrote about that.

It is settled about our little White Mt. trip. We leave here Thursday morning & go that day about 50 miles to Holderness where we spend the night at the Asquam House. The next morning we go 35 miles to the Flume House in Franconia Notch where we will find Frank waiting for us[.] His train comes in from N. Y. at 8 A.M. We hope to get there by 10 and have the day to see the beauties of the Notch. I was there as a girl and it is very wild and lovely. We spend the night at the *Flume House* and the next day go 35 miles to the *Crawford* House via Bethleham and Bretton Woods. That of course takes us through the heart of the White Mts. and we will have an afternoon for the drive through the famous Crawford Notch. We spend the night there and return home the next day, about 100 miles. Frank has to take the train back from here about six in the afternoon. Oh, how I wish you were to be with us! But of course I know that if you were here you would much rather *stay* here. Goodnight, dear heart. I love you *I love you*, deeply tenderly passionately,—in every way that you would like to be loved   Your own   Eileen.

ALS (WC, NjP).
¹ Unidentified.

To Ellen Axson Wilson

My precious darling,   The White House 3 August, 1913.

How I look forward to Sunday and to my little chat with my darling! The weeks between are very long. I feel so ungrateful reading your daily letters, which are the tonic that keeps me going, and yet sending nothing in return but this, a weekly letter. How sweet you are in what you say of these letters! I can only explain their satisfying you by the fact that they are indeed the outpouring of my heart to you. All the longing of the week is concentrated in them: all the sweet thoughts I have of you; all the consciousness of what you mean, and have always meant, in my life; all the thoughts both of the past and of the future that are the food of my heart's life. I can think of nothing, I can feel nothing, while I write, but only *you*. My days are not half so full of anxiety and of the sense of deep responsibility as they are of you, my absent darling who yet plays the leading part in my life every minute of the day. Bless you for the letters! They are meat and drink to me. Each day, as one of them is laid before me on my table in the office, as the tide of business swirls about me, a certain brightness comes into everything and the immediate task is made easy.

Do not worry about the storm. It was bad enough. It was terrible, indeed. The whole air grew black as night and the whole air was filled with terror. The destruction among the noble trees of the city was camparable to nothing I have myself ever seen except that ice storm in Princeton.[1] The grove around the White House and the streets of the city presented just such a scene of ruin as that was. It looked complete and irreparable. Some of the finest trees on these grounds were uprooted entirely and others were twisted to pieces: for it was not a hurricane but a cyclone, which picked and chose which it would torture amongst the trees. But the debris is being slowly cleared away, and it is already evident that things will look almost as they did. I am hoping that you had not got sufficiently familiar with the several trees to miss those that are gone, when you see the place again. And the streets will not look bare: there were so many trees that most of those destroyed will not be missed very much. There has not been such a storm here since 1897.

And do not worry about the Mexican situation, either. It is bad enough, in all conscience, as the storm was, but the newspapers do not know what they are talking about. The Senate is inclined to form an opinion of its own, but it is not inclined to interfere with me, so far as the Democratic members are concerned; and my policy will soon be too clearly disclosed to be interfered with. Tomorrow or next day ex-gov. Lind, of Minnesota, will start for Mexico City, commissioned to advise the embassy there as my personal representative, and with definite instructions of mediation in his pocket; Henry Lane Wilson's resignation will be asked for and accepted; and foreign governments will presently be informed what we are about in a way which will make it very rude for them to interfere or advise. They have left us a perfectly free hand so far, the papers (that is, the Hearst papers) to the contrary notwithstanding. It looks a little as if the situation were clearing up a bit of itself. It is an anxious business, but not impossible, and my head has never been as muddled about it as the heads of some editors seem to be. There is never an hour that I do not have to be watchful; but so far all is as well as could have been expected. And the situation with regard to the currency seems satisfactory, too. There is no reason in the world why on Sundays I should not take time to make love to my sweetheart. What an adorable family I have, and how incomparable is the dear little lady who is its crown and glory! I shall never understand how such fortune feel [fell] to me: such a wife, such lovely daughters, such sweet cousins as Helen, such friends as Lucy and Mary: such faith and confidence and unselfish love to sustain me: such a glow of love keeping my own heart fresh and fit for every turn! I am more happy and more fortunate than any man whose life I have known. It seems to me that I have been lifted to such things as I have accomplished merely by the inspiration of love and faith and sweet example. I am not half as good as those who have loved and sustained me. I am not good at all. I am only the fruit and reflection of noble loving women and faithful friends. And *you*, my darling, what can I ever say that will put into words what you have been in my life? I have loved you, ah how deeply and with what joy and satisfaction; but my love is only an imperfect expression of what you *are*, my dear, adorable, intimate and darling, from whom I take all that is sweet and pure in my life. God bless and guard you. I need and love you more and more. Immeasurable love to all.

Your own   Woodrow.

I am perfectly well.

WWTLS (WC, NjP).
 ¹ Described in WW to Edith G. Reid, Feb. 25, 1902, Vol. 12.

To Mary Allen Hulbert

Dearest Friend,   The White House 3 August, 1913.

I hope that your silence does not mean that you have not been well or that you have not been in good spirits and did not wish to distress your friend by disclosing your depression to him. Please never hesitate on that ground. What is a friend for if not to receive confidences of that kind and help raise the siege? You know what happens when you write to me in the midst of depression. If you do not, I do. After a page or two the very consciousness that I understand and sympathize begins to soften the pain and release the spirits, and out there gleams, in the most delightful way, if only for a sentence or two at a time, the gayety and playfulness so characteristic of you when you speak with freedom and intimacy and know that you can let yourself go. And, look, if you please, madam, at the other side of the picture also. How is a man to get through with days of unbroken anxiety and continuous responsibility of the heaviest kind if he does not have constant evidence that his loyal and loving friends are thinking about him, —thinking such thoughts as ought to make any man strong and confident and happy? What is to keep *his* spirits from sinking and the blue devils from getting him? Is he to be left helpless and defenceless from them? The President of the United States is not, at any rate in this year of grace, made of steel or whip cord or leather. He is more utterly dependent on his friends, on their sympathy and belief in him, than any man he has ever known or read about. Do you not see that there are great and infinitely difficult questions to be unravelled and settled! Does he not have to determine what is to [be] done in Mexico, how that murderous Castro is to [be] choked off and kept in cold storage, how California is to be restrained from embarrassing us with most of the nations of the world, how the currency is to be reformed and the nations of the world kept at peace with the United States? And how, do you suppose, he is going to do all these things, or any important part of them, if his friends do not stand close about him, do not keep in touch with him, do not constantly whisper in his ear the things that will cheer him and keep him in confidence and steadiness of heart? Will you not kindly join in the enterprise of governing the country we love? He cannot do it alone. Both his head and his heart need strengthening,—his heart even more than his head. He has many counsellors, but few loving friends. The fire of life burns in him only as his heart is kept warm. This is not a lecture: it is just an appeal!

Do not believe what you read in the newspapers[.] According to them everything is in a pretty coil and tangle here; but, as a matter of fact, there is no tangle that cannot easily be unravelled, if I am not mistaken. One has constantly to be on the job, it would appear. It is not safe to withdraw one's attention even for an hour. No one but the President seems to be expected, or to expect himself, to look out for the general interests of the country. Everybody else is special counsel for some locality or some special group of persons or industries. Everybody, but he, is to look out for something in particular. He alone has the acknowledged duty of studying the pattern of affairs as a whole and of living all the while in his thoughts with the people of the whole country. It is a lonely business. He needs company. Where is he to find it in Washington? His friends are his constitutents in that difficult and responsible matter. I am very well. I was born in the tropics,— begging dear Virginia's pardon, and have been bred in them,— begging the pardon of her sister States to the south of her; so that the heat (which I must admit to be intense) does not get under my skin. I was never in a tropical cyclone (it was hardly less!) until the other day; but I even sat through that and talked currency with a doubting member of the committee of the House[1] that has charge of the bill without turning a hair. So that you see I am tough and physically fit for the job. I play ten or eleven holes of golf almost every day, heat or no heat, and on as hilly and sporty a course as one could wish, for beauty or fun, and twice every week I go to the theatre, clad in white and looking, I would fain believe, as cool and care free as I often am on those occasions. Fortunately I have a special gift for relaxation and for being amused. But even then it is lonely, very lonely. And it is then that I have *time* to miss my friends and consciously wish for them. What fun it would be if I could summon them about me on some Aladin's carpet, when public business relaxes its hold upon me for a brief space now and again. I would indeed be happy and ready and fit for anything! My love to Allen. How does he fare, these days?

Your devoted friend   Woodrow Wilson

WWTLS (WP, DLC).
[1] Charles A. Korbly. The electrical storm, which "took the form of a small tornado" (as the weather bureau officially described it), began about 3 P.M. on July 30, 1913. *New York Times*, July 31, 1913.

From Ellen Axson Wilson

Cornish, New Hampshire

My own darling,   Sunday Aug. 3 [1913]

If is half past four. Dudley Malone and Mr. Childs[1] who brought him over from Dublin and lunched with us have just returned; and I am waiting now to welcome Nell who ought to be here at any moment. Helen and Mrs. Jaffrey went over to Hanover just after luncheon, partly for the ride and partly to get her.

It was good to see Dudley because he had so recently seen you, but I could have no satisfactory talk with him because of the stranger. But he said that he thought decidedly the worst was over as regards Mexico. That Huerta would be finally discouraged by the collapse of his friend Wilson and your policy of master[l]y inaction,—that in short *he* and not *you* were doing the worrying now! He also confirmed my own impression that things were looking better as regards the currency bill. But we had alas! no confidential talk.

We went again to hear Dr. Fitch and had another delightful sermon. He read the story of the three children in the fiery furnace in a way that made us feel as if we had never heard it before. Of course the world and its troubles is the fiery furnace into which we are all flung, but if the Son of God walks there with us we will pass through unhurt. His picture of 'our human predicament' was very touching—of how we were thrown in *bound*. I only thought he failed to bring out the finest touch in the story if he used it as a human allegory, viz., that it was the fire test that loosed their bonds and set them *free*! "Did we not cast three men bound into the midst of the fire[?]" They answered and said unto the king, "True oh King." He answered and said, "Lo, I see *four* men *loose* walking in the midst of the fire, and they have no hurt; and the form of the fourth is like the Son of God."

Little Nell has just arrived, looking very sweet and dear. I must go and have tea with them, and then undress and cool off before dinner. It is a very hot day.

I hope you had a good rest yesterday and today,—a good rest and a good game. Dudley was very amusing about that manikin Wilson. The sum of it all was merely, "God made him and therefore let him pass for a man."

Dear love, it is very hard to be content without you, especially on a quiet Sunday like this. It won't bear talking about too much, I find. If you can't come again fairly soon please, oh *please* let me go to Washington for a few days. Indeed, dear, I must go! I want you! I love you unspeakably I am always and altogether

Your little wife,   Nell.

ALS (WC, NjP).
¹Ralph David Childs of Dublin, N. H.

To Whom It May Concern

To Whom It May Concern: The White House August 4, 1913

This will introduce the Honorable John Lind, who goes to Mexico at my request and as my personal representative, to act as advisor to the American Embassy in the City of Mexico. I bespeak for him the same consideration that would, in other circumstances, be accorded a regularly accredited representative of the Government of the United States.¹

Woodrow Wilson
President of the United States.

TLS (J. Lind Papers, MnHi).
¹ There is a WWT draft of this letter in WP, DLC.

Instructions to John Lind

Instructions (Mexico)   [Aug. 4, 1913]

Press very earnestly upon the attention of those who are now exercising authority or wielding influence in Mexico the *following considerations and advice*:

The Government of the United States does not feel at liberty any longer to stand inactively by while it becomes daily more and more evident that no real progress is being made towards the establishment of a government at the City of Mexico which the country will obey and respect.

The Government of the United States does not stand in the same case with the other great governments of the world in respect of what is happening or what is likely to happen in Mexico. We offer our good offices, not only because of our genuine desire to play the part of a friend, but also because we are expected by the powers of the world to act as Mexico's nearest friend.

We wish to act, in these circumstances, in the spirit of the most earnest and disinterested friendship. It is our purpose, in whatever we do or propose in this perplexing and distressing situation, not only to pay the most scrupulous regard to the sovereignty and independence of Mexico,—that we take as a matter of course, to which we are bound by every obligation of right and honour,—but also to give every possible evidence that we act in the interest of Mexico alone, and not in the interest of any person or body of persons who may have personal or property claims in Mexico which they may feel that they have the right to press. We are seeking to counsel Mexico for her own good and in the interest of her own peace, and not for any other purpose whatever. The Government of the United States would deem itself discredited if it had any selfish or ulterior purpose in transactions where the peace, happiness, and prosperity of a whole people are involved. It is acting as its friendship for Mexico, not as any selfish interest, dictates.

The present situation in Mexico is incompatible with the fulfilment of international obligations on the part of Mexico, with the civilized development of Mexico herself, and with the maintenance of tolerable political and economic conditions in Central America. It is upon no common occasion, therefore, that the United States offers her counsel and assistance. All America cries out for a settlement.

A satisfactory settlement seems to us to be conditioned on

(a) An immediate cessation of fighting throughout Mexico,—

a definite armistice solemnly entered into and scrupulously observed;

(b) Security given for an early and free election in which all will agree to take part;

(c) The consent of General Huerta to bind himself not to be a candidate for election as President of the Republic at this election; and

(d) The agreement of all parties to abide by the results of the election and cooperate in the most loyal way in organizing and supporting the new administration.

The Government of the United States will be glad to play any part in this settlement or in its carrying out which it can play honourably and consistently with international right. It pledges itself to recognize and in every way possible and proper to assist the Administration chosen and set up in Mexico in the way and on the conditions suggested.

Taking all the existing conditions into consideration, the Government of the United States can conceive of no reasons sufficient to justify those who are now attempting to shape the policy or exercise the authority of Mexico in declining the offices of friendship thus offered. Can Mexico give the civilized world a satisfactory reason for rejecting our good offices? If Mexico can suggest any better way in which to show our friendship, serve the people of Mexico, and meet our international obligations, we are more than willing to consider the suggestion.[1]

T MS (WP, DLC).
[1] There is a WWT outline and a WWsh draft of this document in the C. L. Swem Coll., NjP, and a WWT draft, dated July 30, 1913, in WP, DLC.

From William Jennings Bryan

My Dear Mr President   [Washington] Aug 4 [1913]

It occurs to me that Henry Wade Rogers of Yale might be a good man for France & that Pindell of Ill might like a year in Russia while you are waiting for Crain.[1]

If you decide against Bernstein why not speak to Lewis[2] about Sigmond Zeisler[3] of Chicago. He would be an excellent man. I *think* Simon Wolf of the District is a Dem but am not sure.

Am glad we are nearly through with our diplomatic list. Since Lind thinks it best not to send a Swede to Sweden I wish you would offer Sweden to Arkansas & ask the Senators to agree upon a man. We have not done any thing for Arkansas & Clark[4] is chairman of the caucus & Robinson[5] is one of our best friends in the Senate. If we can take a man from Arkansas that will about finish our list of Democratic States. Am not sure but it might be better to change Leavell of Miss [to] Sweden & give Arkansas Gautaumala. With assurances etc I am My dear Mr President

Yours truly   W. J. Bryan

ALS (WP, DLC).
  1 Charles R. Crane.
  2 Senator James Hamilton Lewis of Illinois.
  3 Sigmund Zeisler, Austrian-born lawyer and civic leader of Chicago.
  4 Senator James Paul Clarke of Arkansas.
  5 Senator Joseph Taylor Robinson of Arkansas.

From Ellen Axson Wilson

Cornish, New Hampshire

My own darling   Monday Aug 4 [1913]

The three girls are all out to dinner. I had mine quite alone,—it consisted of a glass of milk, some biscuit and a peach,—and now I am very comfortably disposed in a wrapper sitting by a fire in my room. Too comfortably indeed, for I went to sleep over the paper before I had even begun the various letters I was planning to write. I have had an active day and this is the result. I painted all morning, standing of course,—posed early in the afternoon,— came home and had some out of town people who wanted to call to tea—then went myself to tea at the Goodyears.[1] They are the rubber tire people[2] who have bought the beautiful Norman Hapgood place. It is an *enchantment*. It is a Platt house in Italian villa style, with an adorable garden of course and perhaps the greatest view of all. It has the great swinging lines of the Platt view with the curving river in the centre. The house you may remember as it is set high on a hill. It adjoins the Platt place,—and personally I still like the latter best. But it is great fun to go around and compare the various places.

Dear, will you let someone write me, just to end my troubles how the matter stands as regards changes in the tariff now. I have the impression that since the caucus the bill is finished, and they can't risk trouble by reopening questions of detail. My neighbours here are most considerate and have not said a word to me about that duty on art,—but I am getting letters; and now I [am] being annoyed by the "bird-lovers."[3] I have *had* to consent to bring the latter matter to your attention,—chiefly because Jessie herself is rather excited about it. So I just want some secretary to write me a plain statement of how matters stand on those two points so that I can know what to say to people. If, as might well be, *you* did not know anything about those two details I should be glad to know that. Of course you could not be expected to weaken your influence by meddling with everything.

And by the way, I said that box of bottles from Dr. Grayson had not come. I now find they *did*—but no one had told me!

Goodnight, dear sweetheart,—I wonder what you are doing! Oh how I long for you! I am fair wearying for the sight of you and the sound of your dear voice. I love you to distraction. Always & altogether.   Your own   Eileen.

ALS (WC, NjP).
  [1] Anson Conger Goodyear and Mary Martha Forman Goodyear.
  [2] Mrs. Wilson was mistaken. Anson C. Goodyear was not closely related to Charles Goodyear of the rubber company which bears his name but was president of two lumber companies in Buffalo.
  [3] A demand to put a prohibitive duty on bird plumes, used in the manufacture of hats.

To Ellen Axson Wilson

My precious darling,   The White House 5 August, 1913.

This being "Cabinet day" and there being no Cabinet here, I am surprised to find myself with a few minutes during which I have no engagement, tho' one is liable to pounce upon me unbeknownst at any moment; and my heart is so full of you that I must send just a few lines to unburden it. I am all right; the heat has lightened considerably; I play golf now almost every day and keep in fine shape; but oh! the difference to me that my darling is not here. Do'nt beg to come down here to see me, *please*, my darling! How am I to say No? And yet if I were to say Yes and you were to come, I should in fact be unhappy. When I look into the very centre of my thoughts I know that my real peace of mind depends upon your being where you are, engaged as you are. That my heart is set upon. My steadiness here depends in reality upon the programme being seen through to the end. There is even (our feelings apart) a dramatic effect upon the imaginations of the members of the Houses that comes from my sticking it out alone, with a sort of Stoical sternness: and I must lose no atom of advantage. If I succeed this session, the rest is easy. We must act together and without a touch of weakness. I shall feel happiest if we yield nothing, in action to our hearts. But that does not prevent the tears coming to my eyes with every word of love and of self-revelation in your dear letters. How dear they are, because so like yourself in every sentence; and I love you with all my heart. I have just received and read the letter about Dr. Fitch's sermon on the three children in the fiery furnace, and your own comment on the sermon, or, rather, on the passage, touched me as deeply as the sermon could, if I had heard it. What a beautiful thought it is as you complete it. The sweetest, noblest thing about you, my darling, is the way in which you are touched and moved by noble, illuminating thought. You are such a quick register of all that moves the spirit and makes life vital and significant! I am deeply in love with you. I live on your love for me. Be a Spartan wife (whom I can see only by stealth!) and it will make it easy for me to be a Spartan statesman. And yet how am I to get two incompatible things? I give you this advice (or, rather, beg this kind of love of you) and yet want *also* just the opposite. I *want* you to beg for me (without getting me!). I *want* you to long for me and to be an insurgent against the circumstances that separate us! In short I am a doting lover, and yet at the same time a man trying to live out his ideals, the ideals he has dreamed of ever since he was a boy, in regard to public life and political duty. May I not be the better lover on that account? "I could not love thee, dear, so much loved I not honour more." The little cry for me you utter in this letter that came this morning, and so nearly broke me down, is sweet to my ear: I should be unhappy if I did not hear it once and again; but you are for the nonce a soldier's wife. How deeply I love both the soft and the stern aspects of life, the romantic and the harshly real! This letter is written to pour out my heart to you: the tenderest and deepest things it contains, my loyalty and admiration and love and longing,—to relieve my heart of a strain which words will a little ease. And yet I speak the mere truth when I say that all is well with me. I am strong, confident in my work, effecting a routine of labour and amusement of which the doctor thoroughly approves; and willing to stick at it for the whole summer without a moment of repining or looking back. I prefer it so to any moment of weakness or repining!

I am so much interested in your journey to Franconia Notch. I am so glad that you are going. Fill yourself with the beauty of the mountains, my dear little sensitive plate! Feast your dear eyes on what will not be half so beautiful as they are as you gaze upon it. I have seen the White Mountains and they are fit for you: they afford just such settings as you ought to have. My thoughts will travel with you. My deep love will be with you every moment, and with the dear ones who are to go with you. God bless you and keep you. My heart lives with you, droops with you, will die with you.   Your own   Woodrow

A heartful of love to all. How I love *them*.

WWTLS (WC, NjP).

To Adam Edward Patterson

My dear Sir: [The White House] August 5, 1913

Allow me to acknowledge the receipt of your letter of July thirtieth and to say that it does you great credit. I want you to know how sincerely I appreciate the spirit and motives which led you to write it.

Cordially and sincerely yours,   Woodrow Wilson

TLS (Letterpress Books, WP, DLC).

From Robert N. Wood [1]

Mr. President, Sir: New York August 5, 1913

On behalf of the United Colored Democracy as a political organization and in order to voice the feeling and thought of the ten million persons of Negro blood who justly aspire to the maintenance of their privileges as citizens in this great democracy, I am reluctantly compelled to express to you a respectful, but none the less earnest, protest at the course your administration is pursuing with regard to the status of the colored people of this country.

In taking this step I have in mind the fact that never, perhaps, since the first term of Abraham Lincoln has a President of the United States found himself obliged to face, immediately after his inauguration, questions of such momentous importance as have successively occupied your attention since the Fourth of March, last. But while the Tariff, the California Alien Lan[d] Laws, the Mexican Government, the compensation of the family of an Italian who was lynched in Florida[2] are certainly matters deserving of the consideration of the Chief Executive of the Nation, I feel that no question can be of more urgent concern to you than the future of ten million citizens within the borders of the United States. The apparent complacency which has marked the attitude of the colored people towards the campaign for their reduction to serfdom which certain reactionary elements in the Democratic Party have inaugurated coincidentally with your assumption of the Presidency[3] cannot by any means be regarded as an indication of our satisfaction with the movement to place us in the condition which was ours before the Civil War. Your scholarly training and your breadth of observation have made you cognizant of the wonderful change that has taken place in the condition of the colored people in this country during the past fifty years. Your clear perception of the importance of this progressive element in the American population has led you to express your determination not to allow any act of wanton injustice or retrograde legislation to be aimed at us during your tenure of office. Knowing and believing, as I do, that you are a man of courage, and mindful of your own personal assurance to me that you are a Christian and a gentleman, I feel that I can no longer disregard the insistent demands of those of my race who expressed their confidence in you by casting their vote to help secure your elevation to the Chief Magistracy, as well as of those whose fears for the safety of our citizenship under a Democratic Administration now seem only too well to have been justified, that I appeal to you for some expression by word or deed that will discourage and discountenance the enemies of the colored man at Washington.

You are not, perhaps, aware that the colored men whose intelligent grasp of the facts of history led them to abandon the superstitious reverence for the Republican Party which has characterized our race are among the leaders of thought in their communities. To me, who can claim the record of having voted none but the Democratic ticket for the last sixteen years, the satisfaction of our triumph in last year's election is all the keener with the appreciation of the difficulties which we have had to face in removing from the mind of the colored voters the insidious prejudice and dread of the Southern Democrat. But at last we induced them to meet the Southerner half-way, assuring them that between honorable and deserving participation in the rights and duties of American citizenship on the one hand and subjection to the yoke of the untraveled, provincial, self-seeking politician from the South on the other hand, there stood in the person of Woodrow Wilson a man of Southern birth whose purpose was to unite the country in the bonds of good-will and mutual respect and whose comprehensive insight had taught him that the country could never be united except the colored people were considered part thereof.

As a man of Southern birth you are well aware, Mr. President, that the attitude of the best teacher in the South toward the colored population is not the attitude represented by those persons in and out of Congress whose sole aim in life seems to be the suppression of the just aspirations of colored poeple, after centuries of residence in this country, to the maintenance of "the right to life, liberty and the pursuit of happiness" in this land, so rich in opportunity to the most degraded refuse of Europe. But even if the sentiment of the Southern people were really represented by men like Vardaman, the Senator from Mississippi who proudly boasts of having murdered a white man in· cold blood,

and Heflin the Representative from Alabama who declared that
another Czolgosz[4] should have attached a time fuse to a bomb and
placed it under the table from which the then President of the
United States partook of a sandwich with the most useful resident
of Alabama,[5] you would not therefor be justified in disregarding
the feeling of the colored people under the treatment which has
been accorded to them. As Chief Magistrate you cannot refuse
to hear our side of the case, even if your own personal sympathies
should lean rather toward the other.

The colored people deeply resent the segregation of clerks in
the Civil Service at Washington, in the Post Office and in other
departments of the Federal Government. We resent it, not at all
because we are particularly anxious to eat in the same room or
use the same soap and towels that white people use, but because
we see in the separation in of the races in the matter of soup and
soap the beginning of a movement to deprive the colored man entirely of soup and soap, to eliminate him wholly from the Civil
Service of the United States. For just as soon as there is a lunch-
room or a work-room which the colored man may not enter in a
government building, there will be separate tasks assigned the
colored men and these will be, as the promoters of segregation
have declared, the tasks which white men do not want. Intelligence and efficiency cannot now be measured according to the
color of the skin. In past administrations individual colored clerks
of superior training and ability have been held back to permit of
the promotion of white men of inferior attainments. In such cases
there was always recourse to the proper authorities and the vic-
tim of such discrimination could thus abtain redress. But the
present system of segregation is surely tending toward the total
elimination of colored people from honest employment in the
Civil Service of the United States. We see no reason why the
status quo of the past fifty years cannot be maintained without
depriving white Civil Service employees of the fullest opportunity
for advancement according to their merits.

We protest against segregation because our interests are at
stake. We protest against it none the less because of the absurd
inadequacy of the reasons given for the change in the depart-
mental service. As a Southern man you well know, Mr. President,
that it is no more a crime for a colored adult to eat a meal in the
same room with a white adult than it is a heinous offense for a
white person to eat a meal prepared by a colored person or drawn
from the bosom and blood of a colored woman. No white man was
ever degraded by the fact that a colored woman performed for
him a duty and a service hardly less sacred than that of mother-

hood itself. No white man will ever be degraded by the fact that a person perhaps just as white as himself, but called black, eats in the same room with him. Finally, Mr. President, as American citizens sincerely interested in the welfare of the country as a whole, we resent the segregation and the discrimination in the Federal Civil Service because, however necessary and important the enforced separation of the races may be to the voters in rural communities in Alabama or Mississippi and to their candidates for office, it is not a business in which this great nation can engage with any profit to the people as a whole, and it can be productive only of evil and ill will among a large and important minority.

In asking you in some way to express your disapproval of the repressive and reactionary measures taken against the colored people, we do not expect you, Mr. President, to do anything beyond your authority or out of keeping with your sense of justice. If some innocent colored man should be pulled off a train and lynched—a fate which a traveling secretary of the Y.M.C.A., barely escaped two years ago in a village in Georgia—we should not consider it your duty to ask Congress to provide an appropriation for the relief of his family. For maintaining a dignified silence you would have ample precedent in the case of the six farmers in Florida who were murdered by a mob because one of them had been accused of killing a white man in self-defense. The *Spectator*, of London, and other influential foreign papers think that you could render no greater service and to civilization than in taking action looking toward the suppression of lynching. As an American citizen and a Democrat, I do not expect you to achieve so signal a triumph against the forces that make for the degradation of white people far more than of colored people, for I know the limitations placed upon you by the Constitution of the United States, by the Democratic Doctrine of States' Rights, and by the complacency of your Republic and [Republican] predecessors. But I do know that it is within your power to impress upon the reactionary elements within the Democratic Party, and especially at the seat of the Federal Government, that you will not be a party to any action leading to the re-enslavement of the colored citizens of this country.

I am, Mr. President,

Very respectfully yours,   Robert N. Wood

For the United Colored Democracy and the Colored People of the United States.[6]

TLS (WP, DLC).

[1] President of the United Colored Democracy of the State of New York; mem-

ber of the New York Democratic State Committee; active in Tammany Hall; employed as an inspector in the Bureau of Highways of the Borough of Manhattan.

2 Angelo Albano, an Italian citizen, was lynched by a mob in Tampa, Florida, on September 20, 1910. After the usual investigations, the Governor and other state and local officials in Florida professed themselves unable to identify the perpetrators of the crime. The Italian government requested the Taft administration to pay an indemnity to the family of the deceased, but Secretary of State Philander C. Knox declined to do so. When the Italian embassy called the matter to the attention of the Wilson administration, Wilson on June 26, 1913, sent a message to Congress recommending an indemnity of $6,000. Congress approved the indemnity on November 14, 1913. See *FR 1913*, pp. 613-24.

3 Numerous bills had been introduced in the House of Representatives in the early part of the special session of the Sixty-third Congress calling for segregation of black and white employees in the civil service, prohibiting racial intermarriage in the District of Columbia, and requiring separate accommodations for whites and blacks on public conveyances in the District. See the entries under "District of Columbia" and "Negroes" in the Index to the *Cong. Record*, 63d Cong., 1st sess., and Morton Sosna, "The South in the Saddle: Racial Politics During the Wilson Years," *Wisconsin Magazine of History*, LIV (Autumn 1970), 35-38.

4 Leon Franz Czolgosz, the assassin of President McKinley.

5 A reference to President Theodore Roosevelt's entertainment of Booker T. Washington at dinner in the White House on October 16, 1901.

6 Tumulty attached the following note to this letter: "The Secretary suggests that the President read the whole of the attached letter." Wilson did not answer it.

From Ellen Axson Wilson

Cornish, New Hampshire

My own darling,   Tuesday Aug 5 [1913]

Many, many thanks from us *all* for your *dear* letter! It has made us all happy. You assuredly are the most *lovable* person in the world,—not to mention any of your other traits. So naturally you live in an atmosphere of "love and faith and confidence." I am glad, darling, that you feel and enjoy the glow of it. You make me happy all the time just by being what you are,—but superlatively so when you show that *you* are happy and that you think I have some part in making you so. I love you until my heart fairly aches with it!

How very interesting Mr. Ormond's letter is![1] Oh! I am so glad, *so glad* that an opportunity has come to him and one that fills him so with hope and enthusiasm. I feared it was too late for him to get a worthy opportunity. How I hope you will be able to speak at it, his inauguration! It will be giving him indirectly the help you gave Daniels directly, and tried to give Fine.

They are to have here a little "masque" written by the playwright Percy MacKye[2] in the interests of some society for bird conservation. It is to be given in the forest, no one present but invited guests, and to be a very "high-class" thing altogether. There are to be only some six actors besides a band of children and they came today to ask Nell to be the "bird spirit." I do not see the least objection but to make sure I told them I would ask you before committing myself. So please drop me a line about it as soon as you read this. It is really to be very idyllic and classic. You know of course that this colony is rather famous for its ["]high class" pageants and such things. But this is quite a simple little affair,—not like its elaborate pageants.

I went to the Club today & they discussed the duty on pictures, and decided to follow the example of many other artist organizations and send a petition to the Senate. It seems to me that this duty is really ridiculous in view of the fact that the very persons to be supposedly benefitted by in [it] are to a man opposed to it, and that the revenue derived from it is *admitted* to be so small as to be almost negligible. Can't something be done about it? It is actually *worse* than the one it replaces, for that admitted pictures free if they were 20 years old and this requires that they shall be 50 *years old*. It is well known that the persons back of this change in the bill since it went to the Senate are certain rich art dealers in N. Y. who do a thriving trade in "antiques" largely faked. Really, dear, it is the sort of job that ought to be looked into. You know the regular House bill admitted all art *free*. This trouble only began in the Senate. I think the artists in working so hard for free art are really giving the country a wonderful & beautiful example of real patriotism and of unselfish devotion to the ideal. For it would of course be to their *personal* advantage to have the foreign stuff kept out. So they are setting a great example.

But I have had a full day and must stop now and go to bed. We were so absorbed in Mexican affairs and other news, that we read the papers until ten o'clock! We do not get the papers until lunch time; and today Helen & I lunched at the Croly's[3] and went straight from there to the club. I really had a delightful time, —such a charming little group of women. The club met at Miss Elizabeth Slade's,[4]—still another beautiful place with a charming garden and a glorious view. It is the most extensive view of all; —is on such a mountain that I was nervous going up to it in the car, for the car distinctly *balked* at it. It was a gorgeous violet and green and gold day, with splendid clouds. It fairly took ones breath away. Ah but the world is a beautiful place in spite of all drawbacks. I love you, *darling*!   Your own   Eileen.

Your Mexican plan is *so* interesting. Thank you for writing me about it. If you had not, I should not have known whether to believe a word the papers said on the subject. It all sounds very hopeful.

ALS (WC, NjP).

¹ Alexander Thomas Ormond's letter to Wilson is missing, but it informed the Wilsons of his election to and acceptance of the presidency of Grove City College, in Pennsylvania, and requested them to attend his inauguration in October. See WW to A. T. Ormond, Aug. 1, 1913, TLS (Letterpress Books, WP, DLC).

² Percy Wallace MacKaye, prolific poet and playwright who resided in Cornish.

³ Herbert [David] Croly and Louise Emory Croly, who maintained a summer home in Cornish.

⁴ Elizabeth Slade, formerly of New York, owned a home in Cornish with her sister, Fannie J. Slade.

From William Jennings Bryan, with Enclosure

My dear Mr. President: Washington August 6, 1913.

I enclose an amendment which Mr. Ragsdale[1] offered in the committee and which he desires to offer in the caucus which is to be held on the 11th. He seems to be very deeply interested in this amendment and thinks if it is adopted he will be able to defend the bill before his constituents. I have stated to him what I have to all of the Democrats who have asked my opinion, namely, that there is so much good in the bill that it ought to be supported regardless of the action of the committee on particular items, but that I would bring the matter to your attention. What he asks is a statement from you that, *without expressing an opinion for or against the amendment*, you have no objection to having it acted upon by the caucus and that if the caucus acts upon it you desire to have it acted upon upon its merits, with the understanding that you will be satisfied with whatever action the caucus takes on the subject, whether it accepts it or rejects it, provided, that *if it is accepted* you would be free to advise its being taken out in case it should be found at any time to jeopardize the passage of the bill.

Mr. Ragsdale does not ask you to endorse the amendment, but desires to have it voted on upon its merits, without being put in the attitude of urging it against your wishes. He is willing to have it taken out of the bill at any time that its presence in the bill would in your judgment jeopardize the passage of the bill. I have examined the proposed amendment and I do not see that it would do any harm to have it adopted upon these conditions. I think instead of mentioning *cotton* specifically, which might seem to discriminate against other farm products, it might be well to substitute for "cotton and other staple commodities" the words "the more important staple farm products."

You will notice that the amendment does not say that warehouse receipts *must* be accepted as security, but that they *may* be accepted, leaving the matter to the discretion of the reserve boards. The amendment also provides that the central board shall determine the conditions, fix standards, etc. It seems to me that this gives the board so much latitude in determining whether the certificates shall actually be used as security and, if used, gives the board such unlimited discretion in fixing terms upon which they shall be used that no harm can come from the amendment if it is adopted. And then, too, it is not certain that the caucus will adopt it, even though you express a willingness to have it acted on upon its merits. I think you will have enough support in the caucus to carry the bill through as you want it, but I am enough of a harmonizer to desire to avoid any opposition that can be avoided by a concession that can be made without harm. I believe that the concession asked for by Mr. Ragsdale might bring in one or two other objectors so as to make the committee practically unanimous.[2]

Wingo and Neeley[3] would, I think, support this amendment, and it might conciliate them. If we can judge Eagle by the statement which he made in last Sunday morning's paper,[4] his opposition to the bill could hardly be overcome by any concessions which it would be wise to make.

Ragsdale feels hurt because he has not received more consideration in the matter of patronage, and his latest grievance is that he was invited to the White House and because of the invitation refused to present his objections to the bill until after he had seen you, and was then notified on Monday that the engagement had been cancelled and that you could not see him.

I have presented the amendment to McAdoo and he is considering it. I have not yet had his opinion upon it, but in order to get the matter before you as soon as possible I write this letter now and will send you his opinion when it is received.

I have advised Neeley not to press the resolution which he introduced calling for an investigation of the charges made by Secretary McAdoo against the bankers. I have told him that a Democratic Congress should not investigate a Democratic Cabinet Officer *without first consulting the officer* so long as the relations between the two are *friendly*. Neeley is a good man and means well and I think he realizes that he made a mistake in introducing the resolution without first consulting Mr. McAdoo. I shall see Mr. Henry as soon as I can get into communication with him —he has been out of town—and urge upon him the objections to having the resolution considered.

If at any time you see anything I can do to assist you in this or other matters, you have only to call upon me.

With assurances of respect, etc., I am, my dear Mr. President,
            Very sincerely yours,   W. J. Bryan

TLS (WP, DLC).

[1] James Willard Ragsdale, Democratic congressman from South Carolina, a member of the House Banking and Currency Committee.

[2] Wilson did not reply in writing; nor do the White House appointment diaries reveal any conference with Ragsdale or Bryan at this time. However, Wilson must have accepted the amendment in principle, as one similar was approved by Glass and Underwood on August 14 and adopted by the House Democratic caucus on August 25. See Link, *The New Freedom*, p. 222.

[3] That is, Representatives Otis T. Wingo of Arkansas and George Arthur Neeley of Kansas, Democratic agrarian members of the Banking and Currency Committee.

[4] Representative Joe Henry Eagle of Texas released to the press a blast against the Federal Reserve bill on July 31, charging that there was practically no difference between it and the Aldrich Plan. "Congressman Eagle Analyzes and Opposes the Glass Banking and Currency Bill," dated July 31, 1913, mimeographed statement in WP, DLC. See also the *New York Times*, Aug. 1, 1913.

E N C L O S U R E

Notes and bills satisfactorily endorsed having a maturity of not exceeding four months and secured by warehouse certificates, issued by individuals or corporations establishing the ownership of cotton or other staple commodities suitably standardized and stored, may be admitted to discount by the Directors of any federal reserve bank. It shall be the duty of the Federal Reserve Board to fix the conditions under which such certificates shall be accepted as collateral, to prescribe a standard from [form] for their issue, and to issue regularly an official list of the individuals or corporations eligible for the purposes of this section.

T MS (WP, DLC).

From William Jennings Bryan

My dear Mr. President: Washington August 6, 1913.

I had an interesting experience yesterday. Mr. John R. MacArthur of the firm of MacArthur Brothers, who are now building the New York aquaduct and are among the largest contractors in the world, was here in regard to the sanitation of Guayaquil. In the course of our conversation I said to him that the greatest obstacle in the way of the development of the small Latin-American countries is their inability to get money at a low rate of interest; that the rate of interest being determined partly by the value of the money and partly by the risk that the lender takes, the Latin-American countries instead of being able to get their money at three per cent, as we can, were paying six per cent or more. He at once approved of the statement of the difficulty and suggested that, in the case of Ecuador, if this Government could guarantee four per cent those dealing with Ecuador might be willing to carry the additional risk. To this I replied that there would be no additional risk and that the benefit ought to be given to Ecuador and not to the financiers. This was an addition to his proposition, which struck him favorably. Without intimating to him that the same idea had been under consideration by us, I asked him to develop his thought in a letter in order that I might show it to you. In pursuance of this suggestion, he dictated a letter which I herewith enclose.[1] You will notice that he lays the foundation for our action in this case by calling attention to our interest in the sanitation of Guayaquil because of its proximity to the Canal. He then, on page four, says

"In these circumstances, and having concern chiefly for our own interests, would it not be a friendly and helpful act for this Government to offer its assistance in the carrying out of this great and humane work by standing sponsor for the bonds to be emitted to meet the cost thereof?"

On page five he says, in reference to the sinking fund

"If it were possible to carry out your magnanimous suggestion that Ecuador be permitted to itself profit by the much lower rate of interest and charges involved in this plan, we feel sure that much of the unfair criticism now directed by South and Central American countries against our Government and people would cease, and in its stead a feeling of loyalty and appreciation arise."

Later in the afternoon I had occasion to talk with a New York banker, Mr Jarvis,[2] who is interested in Cuba and the Dominican Republic and who is considering taking an interest in the Nicaragua National Bank. In discussing the question of interest, I asked him whether it was not possible to separate the value of the money from the cost of the risk in the matter of interest and give the people of Nicaragua the benefit in case the risk could be eliminated. He at once took hold of the proposition as a new one and one of great importance. I did not suggest to him that our Government could aid in any way in eliminating the risk but merely suggested that that portion of the interest which was intended to cover risk might be set apart as a sum to be applied upon the principal in case the interest and principal were paid promptly.

I mention these two instances to show how these two men, one a business man of great experience and the other a banker of large experience, accepted the idea of rendering some service to these countries by reducing the interest charge.

It occurs to me that this Ecuador matter might furnish us an opportunity to test the plan, because we have a deep interest in the sanitation of Guayaquil (I do not know whether you have the place in mind, but if you will look at your map you will find that it is the first place that ships stop going south on the Pacific coast and the last place that they stop coming north, and that sanitary conditions are of the gravest importance to us because of our control of the Isthmus. Pres Taft sent Colonel Gorgas[3] down there to examine into the situation not long ago, but unfortunately he went at a time when the country was irritated over this railroad difficulty which we are trying to settle, and the spirit of co-operation was not then what it ought to be).

I believe that a proposition to Ecuador to the effect that we would accept her four-and-a-half per cent bonds at par and hold them as security for three per cent bonds issued by us, the difference of one and one-half per cent to be turned into a sinking fund to retire the bonds, would be accepted gratefully; at least, it would be a way to show our good will that would at once strike the people down there as well as the people of our country as a practical means of rendering a neighborly favor. If the plan was accepted by Ecuador, I have no doubt that we would be solicited by the Central American countries to do the same thing and that we would soon have these countries bound to us by the strongest of obligations and that, too, without the incurring of any substantial risk, for a favor so obviously beneficial to them and so disinterested on our part could not help but create a profound impression. Considering the manner in which these poor countries have been plundered by financiers who first demand a high rate of interest and a big discount *to cover risk taken* and then appeal to their governments to *eliminate the risk* and leave them in possession of the tax levied because of the risk—in view of these experiences we would furnish a modern example of the Good Samaritan.

With assurances of respect, etc., I am, my dear Mr. President,
Very sincerely yours,   W. J. Bryan

TLS (WP, DLC).

[1] J. R. MacArthur to WJB, Aug. 5, 1913, TLS (WP, DLC).

[2] Samuel Miller Jarvis, vice-president of the National Bank of Cuba with offices at 60 Broadway, New York; also heavily interested in banking operations in the Dominican Republic. For his proposal concerning Nicaragua, see Dana G. Munro, *Intervention and Dollar Diplomacy in the Caribbean, 1900-1921* (Princeton, N. J., 1964), p. 393.

[3] William Crawford Gorgas, colonel, U.S.A., at this time chief sanitary officer of the Panama Canal Zone.

From Ellen Axson Wilson

Cornish, New Hampshire
My own darling,   Aug. 6, 1913.

Your dear, *dear, dearest* letter written yesterday has already reached me, and you may imagine what a delightful surprise it was, for I was not expecting another for a week. Oh, how ineffably lovable and splendid you are. Words fail me entirely; only the greatest of the great poets could do justice to you. You may yet get letters from me composed entirely of extracts from Milton, Browning, Wordsworth or Shakespere!

I am just starting to receive at the reception given to the Farmer's wives by the women of the Colony. The latter started a Club and arranged a simple Club-house for these meetings years ago. But this is a special annual affair given at one of the charming places, Mrs. Louis Shipman's.[1] I shall have to finish this on my return. Am waiting now for the girls.

Just back from the tea which was a great success. Mrs. Shipman's garden is one of the most beautiful in its solid masses of bloom,—like the "Prospect" garden. The house was equally full of flowers, and the affair was quite a love feast. Mrs. Walker was much amused over one difficult old person who had quarreled with most of the others, would not speak to her or them on the street. But she made it all up in order to be at this tea, and meet me and the girls!

I was at the Walkers this morning to see the place, Mr. Walker's work in the studio, and Miss Schauffler, our doctors sister,[2] who is visiting them. The Walkers live at Lakewood in the winter. I had a delightful time of course especially seeing Mr. Walker's work, which is beautiful,—ideal figures such as his fine series at the Washington library. Mrs. Walker is a very brave splendid woman. She has two children, sons, one extraordinarily tall and beautiful. He is really Jessies type. The younger, Oliver, is no taller than a child of three & terribly twisted besides. He has a fine head & is very intelligent,—is now 20 years old. He can walk a little on the level floor, but must be carried chiefly. Until a year ago she herself carried him about in her arms and did everything for him. Then it was discovered that she had wrecked her health doing it and she had to undergo all sorts of complicated operations. Her love and devotion to him is heroic.

But I *must* write some *necessary* letters to other people before we leave Cornish. Lucy & Mary come a week from Friday—the 15th. By the way will you look in that old Russia leather address book of yours and send me the name and address of the firm of stock brokers who used to buy for us,—Mrs. Ricketts[3] firm. I don't know who else to consult,—even Ned Howe seems to have vanished into space; so I think those brokers will do quite well for the present.

I can't tell you how glad I am that you are playing so much golf and feeling so well in spite of everything. But now that John Lind has gone to Mexico *could* you not come up for a few days next week? I know I must be a soldier's wife—but I was just wondering!

Goodbye, my darling. I love [you] with my every heart-throb. Always and altogether,   Your own   Eileen

ALS (WC, NjP).
  [1] Ellen McGowan Biddle Shipman, wife of Louis Evan Shipman, author and playwright, at this time residing in Plainfield, N. H.
  [2] A sister of William Gray Schauffler, physician of Lakewood, N. J. Schauffler had several sisters.
  [3] That is, Eliza Getty (Mrs. Palmer Chamberlaine, Sr.) Ricketts.

Remarks to a Delegation of Southern Bankers

Gentlemen: August 7, 1913.

I have been told by Mr. McAdoo that you expect me to say a few words, and, having had the practice of a great many campaigns, perhaps it will be possible for me to do so on such short notice, particularly since my mind is very full of the matter upon which you have come to Washington. I believe I can say that, almost for the first time, if not literally for the first time, the Government of the United States has thought that perhaps the rank and file of the bankers of the United States were entitled to the use of the people's money, rather than a special group who had subsequently doled it out to them on their own terms. You see, I am speaking with perfect freedom, because I am speaking only within the walls of this room.

I feel that a new era is going to come to American business because the vitality of the business of the country is now going to come from all quarters, instead of from one quarter. What we are trying to do in the currency bill, we are trying to do in every way. In the currency bill we want to mobilize the financial resources of the country. I want to mobilize the energies of the country. I want to see those energies originate, as they can so abundantly originate, from every quarter of this country, so that every fiber of the body politic and of the body mercantile and the body industrial shall be quick with life. It is for that reason that I welcome this opportunity of saying a word or two to you. I have never been sure in past years when I heard and when I did not hear the business of the country speak. Because we have not heard the business of the country; the business of the country has not been vocal. It has not spoken out. There have been times when some of the big businessmen of this country have spoken to me about the real conditions behind their hands and have been obviously nervous lest I should quote them somewhere. They did not say where. An absolutely abnormal condition of affairs! The business of this country thrives by the energy and initiative of men throughout the whole nation who undertake its enterprises. And so the financial situation of this country is so full of vitality in proportion as it proceeds from the brains and initiative of the bankers, rank and file, from one end of the country to the other.

I bespeak your support in this sense. I believe that action such as we are now taking will enable you to understand the temper of the present administration, and, having once caught our object, we will have the sympathy of your minds and the sympathy of your energies. What we are seeking to do in this currency bill is to disperse the energy of the United States. It should be dispersed; it is not energy until it is dispersed—until it thrills at the very tips of the country. So that we are seeking your counsel; we are seeking your support—your intellectual support; and we are seeking to draw you into connection and partnership with those of us who have no other function, as I understand it, than to serve the people of the United States. That is the simple message I have for you this afternoon, and I beg that you will regard it as my confidential utterances in your own ears, to sink, I hope, so deep that you will henceforth have no reason to question what the object of the Government of the United States is, whether we have the wisdom to accomplish that object or not.

T MS (WP, DLC).

To Joe Henry Eagle

My dear Mr. Eagle: [The White House] August 7, 1913

Thank you sincerely for taking the trouble to write out for me your views on the currency question.[1] I had been promising myself, as you know, a long talk with you, but have simply been euchred out of it by constant demands upon my time from which I could not escape. I hope we shall yet become even better acquainted.

Cordially and sincerely yours,   Woodrow Wilson

TLS (Letterpress Books, WP, DLC).
[1] J. H. Eagle to WW, Aug. 1, 1913, ALS (WP, DLC), enclosing his statement denouncing the Federal Reserve bill.

To Ellen Axson Wilson

Darling,   The White House 7 August, 1913.

I have no objection in the world to Nell's taking the part they want her to take in the little forest play. I only wish I were going to see her in it. I know that she will be fascinating.

I shall of course do what I can to get the duty on art and the objectionable provisions about the birds taken out of the bill when it gets into conference. I have not yet had a chance to take the matter up; and this is not yet the moment.

God bless you all, as your love blesses me!

In desperate haste,   Your own,   Woodrow

WWTLS (WC, NjP).

From Ellen Axson Wilson

                                    Cornish, New Hampshire
My own darling,   Aug. 7, 1913 7.45 A.M.

We are leaving this morning at 9.30. It is a brilliantly beautiful day and cool besides. So we are all in high spirits and sure to have a delightful time. We have so broken the journey that the return trip will be the only fatiguing one,—and then we can go to bed and stay as long as we please. We choose our stopping place today partly to break the journey and partly because it leads through Bridgewater and "Hebron" where the Hoyts[1] came from. They (the towns!) are on the shores of Newfound Lake, a beautiful sheet of water, and also on the shores of the lake is a little grave-yard in which my great-grandfather and mother[2] and their forebears are buried. I had an interesting letter from a first cousin of my mothers in Boston telling me all about it. So it is "a pious pilgrimage" as well [as] pleasure trip! How perfectly enchanting it would all be and how entirely happy we would be if our darling were here starting off with us! My eyes fill with tears, in spite of myself as I think of it. Is that very bad for a soldier's wife? But I must stop and finish dressing.

                    Your devoted little wife.   Nell.

God bless you, *my darling*. I love, *love*, _love_ you.

ALS (WC, NjP).
[1] The family of her maternal grandfather, Nathan Hoyt.
[2] Nathan Hoyt and Meribah Perkins Hoyt.

A Circular Note to the Powers

The White House August 8, 1913.

This Government will soon communicate with the Mexican authorities with a view to aiding in a friendly and disinterested way in the restoration of peace. The contents of this communication will be made known to you when it is ready. In the meantime it is respectfully suggested that your Government consider the propriety of asking its representative in Mexico to confer with Huerta and advise him of its view with regard to the propriety and necessity of giving very serious consideration to any suggestions this Government may make and of the situation which might arise should these good offices be rejected.

With assurances of respect, etc.,[1]

T MS (SDR, RG 59, 812.00/8284A, DNA).
[1] There is a CLST draft of this note, with WWhw emendations, in WP, DLC.

From Josephus Daniels, with Enclosure

Dear Mr. President: [Washington, c. Aug. 8, 1913]

Enclosed you will find a brief letter from Admiral [Frank Friday] Fletcher,[1] in command of our ships on the East Coast of Mexico. He is one of the ablest and wisest of our Admirals. The article he refers to is long and not illuminating. Therefore I do not trouble you with it.

I also send at his request a note from Assistant Secretary of War Breckinridge which he wished you to see.

The Mexican situation will improve and I feel sure your course will be both justified and approved.

Faithfully yours,   Josephus Daniels

ALS (WP, DLC).
[1] Not found.

E N C L O S U R E

A Memorandum by Henry Skillman Breckinridge

[c. Aug. 8, 1913]

In case intervention is determined upon the Chairman of the Committee on Military Affairs of the House should be apprised as soon as possible so that he can arrange for the immediate passage of a Volunteer Bill which has the approval of the war department and which is absolutely essential to the efficient execution of such an enterprise. This bill applies the lessons of former wars and should be on the statute books now even though no special exigency existed. But of course any military legislation will cause comment at such a time.

We have sufficient munitions and equipment for at least 200,000 men except ammunition for certain heavy field guns.

There are about 40,000 regular troops including 4500 Coast Artillery which could be used.

There are 112,000 militia, paper strength, only 88,000 present at last federal inspection. A very liberal estimate of the number of militia who would volunteer for service out of this country 60,000.

Time required to get regular troops to Vera Cruz
    3,000 in 7 days
    20,000 in 14 days
    40,000 in 25 days.
40,000 is minimum force for expedition against Mexico City.

The above will depend upon having the power to hire transports immediately—no funds available for such hire—no funds available for purchase of animals or to increase ammunition supply for mobile artillery. An appropriation will be necessary for expenses in addition to present funds.

Detailed plans are in existence for the assembly of the regular troops and for operations in Mexico—also for the mobilization of the militia.   H.B.

HwI memorandum (WP, DLC).

From Ellen Axson Wilson

Flume House, Franconia Notch, N. H.

My own darling,   Friday night [Aug. 8, 1913]

We are, as you see, carrying out our schedule and we have had two great days. The weather has been superb especially yesterday. Today there has been more mist in the air, and so less of the splendid blues in the mountains. I am afraid it is going to rain tomorrow. But perhaps it will be so good as to do it tonight instead.

We went to Bridgewater & saw the old Hoyt graves & then to Hebron where they were born. Both villages are on "Newfound Lake," one of the most beautiful sheets of water I ever saw ringed around with glorious mountains; and the little grave yard is also on the shore of the lake. It has a beautiful sandy beach backed by fine woods and is a paradise for "camps" but has not yet been much exploited by the regular summer crowd. There is one little Inn called "Elm Lawn," and it is known as "the old Hoyt Stand"— that is "tavern." In the old coaching days it was kept by my grandfather's brother, Abraham.

The Asquam House where we spent last night is on the shores of another superb lake called "Squ[a]m." The house is on a high hill and from its roof commands one of the noblest views I have ever seen. We took our own lunch with us yesterday, and ate it in a real wilderness, quite out of the beaten track, on a hill that commanded an indescribably lovely view. The sense of being quite solitary—"the world forgetting, by the world forgot"[–]was delicious. I should like a house there, where there was not even a nice simple Cornish Colony to invite one to teas.

Today of course we have done the regular thing, and have greatly enjoyed it all. We left Asquam at 8 and reached here at ten, finding Frank awaiting us. We scrambled to the "flume," came back & had lunch, then drove to Profile Lake & Bethlehem, 32 miles there and back. We are among the Giants of the range here and they are truly majestic.

But I am very tired now & must not exceed my sheet. We are all well & love you inexpressibly. With all my heart
Your devoted little wife,   Nell.

ALS (WC, NjP).

To Ellen Axson Wilson

My own darling,   The White House 10 August, 1913.

How sweet is this Sunday afternoon hour! All the turmoil of the week still for a little space; a quieting sleep in the morning, a church service that takes me back to the days when I was a boy in the South, and then an hour all my own when I can sit down and think of nothing *but* the little lady who carries my happiness in her heart, talk only to her, live in the full consciousness of all that she is and of all that she has been to me! She is away, but she lives and, in her sweet generosity, lives for me, and is as real to me as if she were this moment in my arms and I were breathing all that I feel into her ear. Ah! my sweetheart, my sweetheart! I can never tell you how much, how deeply, how passionately I love you, but it is balm to my spirit, a keen refreshment to my spirits, to try. I must (whatever Nature may have indicated to the contrary in my ornery appearance) have been meant for a lover. I am not happy unless I am opening my heart to those I love and look to for my life. I cannot tell you how constantly my thoughts follow you every day! In the midst of the most engrossing business, I am conscious of what you are doing,—at any rate, conscious of *you*, and your image lurks all the while just about me in the dim spaces of my imagination. How I enjoy your life at Cornish! I could not be happy if I were there, because I would know all the while that it was my duty to be here, where affairs wait upon me, for some decision or other, every hour of the day. That knowledge would spoil even the sweet content of being with you. But I share your life up there, none the less. My mind is full all day long of happy images of what you are doing, how you are dressed, how you look, how you move among the people who are learning to know and love you, how the dear ones move round about you, how your sweet eyes look when you feel that you must go up-stairs and write to your waiting lover. *I* am not bound so long as you are free! The airs that give you strength sustain and refresh me, too. I live in my heart, not in my body. This labour and this heat does not depress or injure me, chiefly because you are not in it. And so, all day long, everything is translated into terms of love, and all the pulses in me go strong and free. In order to serve me you have only to go through each day with zest, grow more brown in the good air, with that delicious mellow blend of red and brown that is so characteristic of your dear cheeks when you are a great deal in the open in the summer time,—the blend that somehow makes me think of mediaeval songs with a strong tang of the wholesome peasant loves and forest adventures which are so far away from the modern sophisticated world that there are few left to understand them or to take their full relish. I am perfectly well; full of the consciousness that the last two or three days have given you a feast of beauty among the mountains and many a draught of tonic air; struggling with difficulties (chiefly the difficulty of dealing with a man,— Huerta,—whose mind and passions I cannot understand and am therefore at a loss to meet) but with no moment of dismay and with a calm and resolute purpose as I feel my way from step to step; and ready to enjoy the game out at the country club or the play at the theatre whenever the hour of momentary release turns up. In short, thanks to the freedom of those I love and my reassuring thoughts about them, I am in fine fettle. And my game of golf at last shows slight signs of improving. I am learning a *little* from day to day, with numerous disheartening back-slidings, but a movement for the better which can be seen even with the naked eye if the measurement be from week to week and not from day to day. On Sundays Tumulty is not here. He makes a bee line every Friday afternoon, lucky dog, for his little family at Avon, and it's hard to get him back for Monday. The doctor goes to church with me and is a very sedate and excellent imitation of a Presbyterian.[1] He is a sterling enough character to make a good Christian of whatever name or sort the label may be! His golf is improving as fast as mine, if it is not improving faster, so that I have stimulation enough; and we try it now about six times a week. There is no personal news. I do not know which paper you read, and therefore cannot tell you which parts of the general news you think you know is false. Believe very little that you read in the Times! How I drink in your sweet letters! And they are *so* sweet and dear. I can hear your voice as I read each sentence,– the sweetest voice in the world, assuring me of the sweetest things. My dearest love to Cousin Lucy and Cousin Mary. *How* I wish I could see them! As for the others I love them "more than tongue can tell." I am the most fortunate father and cousin (tell Helen) in the world!

With love unspeakable   Your own,   Woodrow

WWTLS (WC, NjP).
[1] Dr. Grayson was an Episcopalian.

To Mary Allen Hulbert

Dearest Friend,   The White House 10 August, 1913.

Your letter,[1] scribbled with pencil from your bed, reassured me and made me feel so much more at ease in my mind about you. I need not tell you how deeply distressed I was about the accident. I hope that you have a really competent doctor and can be sure that the fall resulted in nothing worse than painful strains and bruises. If that is really all that came of it, you may get as much rest as suffering out of it, and your friends can only implore you to be more careful. You certainly make a most entertaining and attractive patient. Your account contains delightful evidence of that, all "unbeknownst" to yourself. You scribbled more of a picture, more of a self-portraiture, than you knew. What made me say that the letter reassured me was that it showed the strain on your spirits which had made me so anxious since your experience in Bermuda to be at last relaxing. You wrote so much more like your old self. You spoke with so much more confidence of Allen. You showed that all your old, naive interest in the people about you was reviving,—your natural affection and sense of comradeship for them. There was something in the sentences that made me feel the old delightful, happy, irresponsible swing from one interesting thing to another in your thought, many of the things wholly irrelevant, apparently, if one had not seen intimately into

your mind and did not know its delectable way of going a journey
of fancy. It was more like the letters you used to write and more
like the free mind I used to enjoy so much in Bermuda: a mind
ready for many things and with a zest in many adventures. By the
way, speaking of Bermuda, I have been deeply interested in what
the papers have had to say in recent weeks about the plans of the
British government to make Bermuda an important naval station
again, in view of its being on the road to the canal. Maybe Ad-
miralty House will open its doors again and something of the old
glory return to the little islands. That would be fine. I should like
to see it come about. It would be a very natural change of policy
in view of the way in which the trade and passenger routes of the
world are sure to shift. There must be a general looking up of the
"first families" down there, if the streams from the imperial treasury are likely to be turned that way again. The chief beneficiaries,
however, will be the American visitors who will soon convince
the British officials down there that all this is being done for their
entertainment, to supply their daughters with dancing partners
and make a "season" when things have fallen dull in The States,—
particularly, to make a season for those for whom there *is* no
season, or for whom seasons have been used up, in America. Must
they do it all for us? But I ought not to indulge in such unchar-
itable reflections on Sunday, after I have been to church in a dear
old-fashioned church such as I used to go to when I was a boy,
amidst a congregation of simple and genuine people to whom it
is a matter of utter indifference whether there is a season or not,
either in New York (or Washington) or Bermuda, or anywhere
else between the ends of the earth. On Sundays only my faithful
aide and companion, Dr. Grayson, is with me. Tumulty has sent
his little family to the seashore, at Avon, near Sea Girt, on the
Jersey coast, and skips off every Friday, lucky dog! to spend the
week end with them. I do not get out of bed on Sundays until
about ten o'clock, just in time to get a little breakfast and get to
church; and after my letters are written in the afternoon the
doctor and I go off for a little drive in the motor,—unless, as this
afternoon, a thunder storm comes up out of mere exasperation
that there should have been so sultry a day. It seems to come up
after such a day exactly as if in a bad humour, to drive the mad-
dening airs away, chasing them with its great angry breath and
growling the while like a wild beast in the chase. The Sunday
afternoon letter writing gives me a delightful renewal of the
normal thoughts and feelings that belong to me, not as President
trying to handle an impossible president of Mexico, but as a
friend and home-loving companion, who is never so deeply con-

tent as when talking to those whom I love and respect, whom I understand and who understand me,—without explanations of any kind! I am perfectly well, calm in my mind and purposes, and thankful to the bottom of my heart that there are those to whom I can subscribe myself

Your devoted friend,   Woodrow Wilson

Love to Allen.

WWTLS (WP, DLC).
¹ All of Mrs. Hulbert's letters during this period are missing.

From William Jennings Bryan

[Washington]

My Dear Mr President: Sunday night Aug 10 [1913]

The Mexican question has been on my mind today to the exclusion of all else and as a result I venture to make a suggestion for your consideration. The time has now come for action.

A.

We have been delayed 1st by lack of information—we now have that. 2nd by having no one in the City of Mexico through whom you could act with the necessary freedom—now we have Lind there to advise with the Chargé. 3d by the desire to allow a reasonable time for those supporting Huerta to prove their ability —or inability—to restore order and establish peace—they have now had nearly 6 months.

B.

If the time has come for action, what action should be taken? There are four courses which have been discussed. 1st Recognition of Huerta—this is indefensible on both material and moral grounds. 2nd Assistance to the Constitutionalists by permitting them to import arms—this would add to the confusion and increase the destruction of life and property. 3d Intervention—the cost of which in life and money no one could calculate, not to speak of consequences even more far reaching and more difficult to estimate. 4th Mediation—the tender of our good offices, as a neighbor and disinterested friend, with a view to assisting in the establishing of peace on a permanent basis.

If we are not willing to adopt the first course—the recognition of Huerta—we must try the 4th—mediation—even though we contemplated the 2nd or 3d as a possibility later

C.

If mediation is is [sic] decided on, what steps are necessary?

We do not know how the offer of mediation will be received—

Huerta has announced in advance that he will not consider it[1]—but there are two things which will have weight—1st Proof that the American people are back of you—the unfriendly papers are attempting to make it appear that you do not reflect public sentiment on this subject. While definite action is likely to bring most of the papers to your support, still those opposing you will magnify whatever opposition there is unless you have a congressional endorsement back of you. Huerta will, secondly, be influenced by the views of the diplomatic representatives of other nations—and other nations will in turn be influenced by evidence of unity on the part of our nation.

D.

Hence it would seem to be very desirable that there should be an endorsement of your policy by the Senate and House, and, if there is to be an endorsement, it will be better to have it in advance of your action so that Huerta can not use the time to aggravate the situation before Congress can act.

The suggestion which I would respectfully submit is that, when you are ready to act, you go before Congress—as you did in presenting tariff and currency problems and stating your plan and the reasons for it, ask a resolution endorsing it. It compels each Senator and member to join you in taking responsibility for the course adopted or register his protest.

I have no doubt that such a request would bring a nearly unanimous endorsement—and this would have its influence upon both Huerta and the foreign governments—possibly a deciding influence because exerted before adverse action is taken. It would also prevent criticism if mediation fails.

Pardon me for using my pen but I was alone at the Department when I began to write

With assurances of respect etc. I am my dear Mr President,
Very truly yours   W. J. Bryan

P.S. Here is an answer to Huerta. He says he will not consider mediation because it is a reflection on the dignity and sovereignty of the nation. Question: If he was willing to go to the Am Embassy and make an agreement with an insurrectionist General in order to become provisional President, why not accept our good offices to restore peace?

ALS (WP, DLC).
   [1] Huerta stated in strong and unequivocal language to a correspondent of the *New York Times* on August 5, and again to a correspondent of the *Washington Times* on August 8, that he would accept neither mediation nor intervention of any kind by the United States. *New York Times*, Aug. 6 and 9, 1913.

From Ellen Axson Wilson

Cornish, New Hampshire
My own darling,   Sunday [Aug. 10, 1913]

We are back from our trip all well and in good shape. We reached here at five, leaving Crawford at ten. We stopped for half an hour at the Mt. Washington House to see the Whitmans, Frank's "boss"[1]; and another hour for our luncheon, which we had put up for us at the Crawford House. We ate it in a most charming and romantic spot on the pine needles under some great pines on a ledge commanding a charming bit of the mountains and over-looking a ravine from which came to us "the little noiseless noise" of a hidden brook. We had gorgeous blues again during the morning, and indeed until we left the White Mts. far behind us. In the afternoon we had some splendid rainclouds and one shower; but it was a beautiful day from first to last.

I have had my bath am about to go to bed instead of to dinner but am not in the least over tired. It has been a really enchanting trip from first to last, and I am glad to find not very expensive either. Frank is a *perfect dear*,–he wears splendidly. He seems entirely one of us now, and he is completely our kind in every respect. It is beautiful to see how perfectly happy they are together,–what good comrades. He really adores her! I am quite satisfied now that he loves her as much as he should.

But it is so dark I cannot see to write. I am supposed to be in bed! I did not sleep very well last night because I was silly enough to worry over Mexico and the tariff bill! But it seems to me there *must* be enough to pass it without Johnson,[2] with Marshall's vote. Only "The Sun" said that, for some reason which I could not understand, Marshall could not cast the deciding vote. Ah well! I *won't* worry any more until I know more about it all!

I love you, sweet-heart, with all my heart and all my might. We kept wishing a hundred times a day for you on this beautiful tour. Do you think you would like to take it? One could really do it comfortably in three days & two nights. Believe me, *darling*, always and altogether.   Your own   Eileen.

ALS (WC, NjP).
  [1] Charles Seymour Whitman and Olive Hitchcock Whitman. Whitman, a Republican, was district attorney of New York County. Francis B. Sayre at this time was a deputy assistant district attorney in Whitman's office.
  [2] Joseph Forney Johnston, Senator from Alabama, who died in Washington on August 8.

From the Diary of Colonel House

[Beverly, Mass.] August 10, 1913.

Dudley Malone brought McAdoo from Boston, and we went over the Massachusetts situation regarding Federal appointments. . . .

McAdoo had all the happenings to tell me since he was last here. He said the President is deeply concerned over the Mexican situation. The last words he said to him as he was leaving were: "God grant that no war shall come to this country during my administration." McAdoo said he spoke with deep feeling. This is another evidence as to what responsibility of office does for a man. The last time the President and I talked of Mexico, soon after he was inaugurated, he was not in this frame of mind.

McAdoo complained that the President took no one into his confidence, that there were now no Cabinet meetings because so few of the Cabinet were in Washington and that he, McAdoo, did not know what instructions were given Governor John Lind before he left for Mexico.

He told the President that it was unfair to himself not to allow the Cabinet to bear a part of the responsibility, because if the people knew he was not discussing these questions with them and things turned out badly, he would be severely censured.

McAdoo thought the President did not realize the importance of having Massachusetts go democratic this Autumn. He, McAdoo, told him if Massachusetts elected a Progressive, Governor, it would indicate to the country that Wilson had not come up the the progressive standard. We shall leave no stone unturned to carry this election.

McAdoo considered that Tumulty was advising the President badly regarding New York. We both think the President should allow his friends to come out boldly for Mitchel for Mayor so as to indicate his preference. His action in this does not accord with his attitude before he became President. Malone tells me that if the President does not consent for him to take an active stand for Mitchel he, Malone, will resign.

T MS (E. M. House Papers, CtY).

Remarks at a Press Conference

August 11, 1913

We are just as anxious to hear about Mexico as you are. We are here in large numbers.

Some mornings there's nothing new. This morning, I see a

good many dispatches from Mexico City in the papers, but I don't know which of them are well founded and which are not.

When do you expect to hear from Mr. Lind, Mr. President?

I can't say that there is any time we expect to hear from him. Of course, he will speak when he has something to say.

Mr. President, the proposal that he carries with him, the suggestion or whatever it is, will it be made public here or in Mexico?

I don't know, sir. Of course, you understand that our instructions to Mr. Lind are chiefly to let us know how this thing stands there, and just what the opportunities for offering our good offices in the interests of peace there are. Then anything that we instruct him to do that is susceptible of being made public will be made public, when we instruct him. So there is no fixed time.

He goes with a sort of blanket instruction to look over the ground and keep you closely advised? It may be that he will not present any—

Well, sooner or later the embassy there will make some suggestions to Huerta's government. Just when and in what circumstances, we can't yet foresee.

Has Mr. Hale reported any more that we might know?

No, he hasn't reported anything in the last forty-eight hours.

On the whole, the situation is materially improved in the last forty-eight hours?

I think it has. In other words, I think all the rather excited expectations are dissipated as to something unfortunate happening.

Mr. Huerta's attitude towards the presence of your representative there. Your conference with the Foreign Relations Committee had quite a good effect on both sides.[1]

I think so, yes. In my conference with the senators, I found they were quite ready to fall in with the program, once it was explained to them.

Mr. President, there has been a great deal of discussion lately, and it was voiced in the Senate by Senator Williams on Saturday, that most of this war scare talk was an organized attempt on the part of certain American interests who had interests in Mexico to stir up a war between this country and Mexico. Are you inclined to that view at all?

Oh, I have no views as to where it's coming from. There is evidently an organized desire somewhere to have a war with Mexico, but where it comes from, I can't even [conjecture]. There could not be such colossal lying going on if there

wasn't something the matter—the most colossal and impudent lying.

Was that so extensive, Mr. President, as to justify you in saying
that it is an organized desire?

> Organized is just a carelessly used word. It is not so exten-
> sive as to justify that as a serious statement, I should think,
> and of course I wouldn't say that as contravening anything
> Senator Williams has said, because he very likely has infor-
> mation that I haven't got.

He used that word in the Senate Saturday.

> So I understand.

Mr. President, I think he expressed the belief that an organized
moneyed effort was—

Mr. President, has the Huerta government made any overtures to
this government at all, suggesting any alternatives?

> No. None whatever of any kind.

Mr. President, have you heard in any way, directly or indirectly,
from Carranza since Mr. Lind [left]?

> Neither before or since.

Never. Have you had a note, as I understand it?

> No, sir.

I would rather like to know what the *Carrancistas* have in mind.

> I would like to know, indeed, what they have in mind.

The dispatches published in the papers [say] that they would advise you.

> They haven't as yet.

Have there been any suggestions from any foreign governments?

> Not the slightest.

Has there been any consideration of a congressional committee's suggestion that we invite Argentina, Chile, and Brazil to
cooperate with us?

> I didn't know that Mr. Kahn had made it.[2]

It was printed in all the newspapers yesterday.

> There hasn't been anything of that sort.

There has been no change, has there, Mr. President, with reference to the embargo on arms?

> No, none at all.

Mr. President, has your attention been directed to a statement
put in the *Congressional Record* by Senator Sheppard of Texas,
giving the history and purposes of Carranza?[3]

> Yes. Senator Sheppard himself called my attention to it,
> and I read it with a great deal of interest.

It says that three fourths of Mexico is under the control of the
Constitutionalists.

Yes, of course, it is very difficult to make those estimates. I dare say that is as telling an estimate as could be made in the circumstances. I have been getting reports at various times as to the extent of the territory controlled by those forces, and I dare say that is quite correct. At any rate, with regard to the northern half of Mexico, of course. They have no hold on the south of Mexico where the *Zapatistas* are.

A determination was made that 90 per cent of the people of Mexico are in sympathy with the Constitutionalists themselves.

You know, the peculiarity of Mexico is that 90 per cent have nothing to say about the government. It is only about 10 per cent that has been running it, time out of mind. . . .

Is there a diplomatic possibility of the recognition of the revolutionists or the Constitutionalists of Mexico?

Nothing of that sort has been considered yet.

Their movement is not strong enough to suggest even a recognition of their belligerency?

Well, I dare say that in proportion to the power of the government in Mexico City, it is strong enough, but just as a matter of fact, we haven't taken the question up. . . .

How soon do you expect the tariff bill to be through?

The Lord only knows, I don't.

JRT transcript (WC, NjP) of CLSsh (C. L. Swem Coll., NjP).

[1] Wilson and Bryan conferred for two hours on the evening of August 9 with the twelve members of the Senate Foreign Relations Committee who were in Washington at that time. The President himself told reporters afterwards that there had been a full exchange of opinions and information on the Mexican situation. Lind's mission was a principal topic of discussion. It was also made clear that the administration had no intention of recognizing the Huerta regime. For a lengthy report of the conference, see the *New York Times*, Aug. 10, 1913.

[2] Representative Julius Kahn of California on August 9 issued a statement deploring the present situation in Mexico and urging that Chile, Brazil, and Argentina be invited by the United States to participate in any effort to restore peace to that troubled nation. *New York Times*, Aug. 10, 1913.

[3] "Memorandum Relative to the Mexican Situation," put in the *Record* on August 6, 1913, by Senator Sheppard. It was the memorandum by Francisco Escudero printed at July 24, 1913, with detailed new information about the Constitutionalist army. *Cong. Record*, 63d Cong., 1st sess., pp. 3129-3133.

To Josephus Daniels

My dear Daniels: The White House August 11, 1913

Thank you warmly for your letter enclosing Admiral Fletcher's letter. I hope that you feel sure that Admiral Fletcher will do nothing on his own initiative and without orders. He is so decidedly of an opinion which does not correspond with ours that I have been wondering about that point a little since seeing in the papers yesterday that Lind spent a couple of hours with him.

It is a great comfort and support to have you agree with me in what I am doing.

Cordially and faithfully yours,   Woodrow Wilson

TLS (J. Daniels Papers, DLC).

From Ellen Axson Wilson

My own darling,   Cornish, New Hampshire Aug. 11, 1913.

I hope you are getting the same "cool spell" that has come to us. It is rather like October today, and very clear and beautiful,—makes even Helen and me feel something like walking. Yet I wasted much of the beautiful morning in bed getting rested completely after the trip. I feel *splendidly*, of course.

I must go and pose later in the afternoon, and then go out to dine with the Kenyon Coxes. I am getting too many invitations for the evenings,—three already for this week. They are all too nice and informal for me to assume the high presidential attitude and decline. Also I must give two more teas, one on Saturday and one next week;—and the "discussion club" next Tuesday! The subject is "Does Human Nature Change?" What do you think about that?

Mrs. Jaffrey has gone,—not to return until shortly before we leave. But she has everything in such good running order that she does not think I need have any trouble, Martha the cook and Coates being so well trained and reliable.

Did I mention that the Smiths were coming on Friday? Miss Hagner[1] comes on Sunday, & Helen leaves for two weeks. Margaret comes on Tuesday.

The papers this morning seem less panicky about Mexico, and more as if they and the Senate were beginning to have some faint understanding and appreciation of your plan and policy; which I take it, is to try to give the Mexicans, (if they can be induced to take it) a great lesson in self-government; to show them that they could an[d] "they would settle their affairs without shooting each other up." Oh how I hope and pray, pray, pray that you may succeed! If only John Lind had your eloquent tongue, and great personality *and* a command of Spanish. But I must dress *at once* —am already late I fear.

With love inexpressible, believe me my own darling, as ever
Your devoted little wife   Nell

ALS (WC, NjP).
[1] Isabella L. Hagner, social secretary to Mrs. Wilson.

To William Cox Redfield

My dear Mr. Secretary: The White House August 12, 1913

I hate to burden you with extra tasks, but we have a most important and interesting Congressional election pending in Maine and nobody could be more serviceable in the speaking campaign which is about to begin up there than you, yourself. The issue is to be the tariff. We are to be challenged to justify the pending action of Congress about the import duties. Nobody can expound that matter better than you can, and it is the unanimous opinion of the executive committee of the national committee (who have just appealed to me in this matter through their chairman, Mr. Mitchell Palmer) that it is indispensable that you should devote several days to speaking in the district. I wonder if you would be willing to do this for the cause. I am sure that they do not exaggerate the importance of it or the service that you could do.

        Cordially and faithfully yours,   Woodrow Wilson

TLS (W. C. Redfield Papers, DLC).

To Ellen Axson Wilson

My precious darling,   The White House 12 August, 1913.

Your dear letters written from Crawford Notch and from Harlakenden just after your return came this morning, to relieve and delight me: for my thoughts waited anxiously for the trip to be over and my darlings safe again at home. How glad I am that the little tour was such a success. Every word you wrote of it was delightful, and I could see your enjoyment of it all shining all through. What a darling you are, and how the things you most enjoy interpret you. I must steal a few minutes to reassure you about Mexico and about the death of one of the Democratic senators. Huerta was bluffing, of course, and nothing has come of it but to make him a little more ridiculous. Lind is in no sort of danger, and is just the well balanced sort not to be disquieted by what goes on about him. The demonstration for Huerta got up on the night of his arrival fell flat and made no impression on anybody. In brief, the situation is not changed. Huerta may not consent to entertain our proposals, but that is not the end of our peaceful program, so far as action by the United States is concerned. We shall then bring pressure of various kinds from various quarters to bear on him. As for the majority in the Senate that is not imperilled. The Vice President can vote, of course, the *Sun* to the contrary notwithstanding, but we shall not need his vote. We shall have a majority of one without the Louisiana men. No one here has expressed any fears on that score. So you see you might as well have slept Saturday night as not! You darling, how I love you for your deep concern to see my leadership sustained! You are the dearest, truest wife that ever lived, and I adore you!

I am perfectly well. The weather has turned quite cool, and this morning there is a steady gentle, soaking rain falling, which all this countryside needed sorely. We have had nothing for weeks but an occasional thunder-storm. All goes serenely in the household; and the work in the house goes on with dignified deliberation!

Love unbounded to you all. My love for you possesses my life.

Your own　Woodrow

WWTLS (WC, NjP).

To John Lind

Washington, August 12. 1913

Gratified to receive your two messages.[1] Hope your wife's[2] reported illness is not serious. Instructions from the President will follow this very shortly allowing a little time for them reflect on the fact that recognition is not to be expected. If matter comes up again remind them that European recognitions were provisional and extend only to date fixed for elections. Report anything you think should be known here.					Bryan

CLST telegram with WWhw emendations (SDR, 812.00/10638A, DNA).
[1] N. O'Shaughnessy to Secretary of State, Aug. 11, 1913, T telegram (WP, DLC), and J. Lind to Secretary of State, Aug. 12, 1913, T telegram (SDR, RG 59, 812.00/8314). In the first message, Lind reported that he had arrived without incident, that he did not intend to communicate with the Mexican Foreign Ministry for "a couple of days," and that Hale, O'Shaughnessy, and he agreed that his instructions should not be published in the United States until about two days after they were delivered to the Foreign Ministry. In his second message, Lind reported that he had spent an hour with Federico Gamboa, the Mexican Foreign Minister, on August 12, and that Gamboa hoped that Lind's instructions included a recognition of the Huerta government and was eager to have the instructions communicated to him as soon as possible. Lind had replied that President Wilson did not contemplate recognition in the present circumstances. Lind again urged that nothing concerning his instructions be made public in the United States.
[2] Alice Shephard Lind.

From Ellen Axson Wilson

Cornish, New Hampshire

My own darling,					Tuesday, [Aug.] 12 [1913]

This alas! is a crowded day! and it is rather alarming to find my Cornish days beginning to be crowded. A pile of mail in the morning; then painting until lunch. (I *won't* let it be crowded out!) Now after luncheon I am writing to you before dressing for the club. We have supper at 5.45 and then go over to Hanover to see a sylvan pageant. This whole New England seems to have gone mad over pageants. Mrs. Hall[1] says this one is very beautiful and artistic. It is a glorious day and we will have bright moon-light, so it will be a pleasure. Oh this perfect, perfect weather! I almost hate it because *you* can't be here to enjoy it! I don't know whether it is an ideal summer everywhere or whether we have found an ideal spot. I had a *very* pleasant evening at the Kenyon Coxes last night. The Coxes themselves are not attractive at first sight, but improve on acquaintance. But the only other guests, Mr. & Mrs. Herbert Adams, are among the choice spirits of the Colony,—both intelle[c]tually and spiritually. I could really *love* them both. He you know is the sculptor whom I met in Wash-ington. They are Boston people. She also "studies art," but I do not hear of her doing anything now. It is pretty to see how much they are loved and honoured by the younger people here.

I have your beloved letter and I could almost "wear it in my bosom" like a lovesick girl—it makes me so happy. And I can't tell you how my spirits rise to see your healthy interest in *golf* in spite of all complications. Oh but you *are* splendid! Did you see that fine editorial about you in the "Evening Post"?[2] Them's my sentiments! But I must dress now and help the women of Cornish decide "What constitutes a good citizen"(!) The meeting is at Maxfield Parish's. All send oceans of love. *I* adore you!

With all my heart and soul I am,

Your little wife,   Nell

ALS (WC, NjP).
1 Mary Hepburn Hough (Mrs. William Richardson) Hall.
2 "Wilson and Legislation," New York *Evening Post*, Aug. 9, 1913. It discussed at length Wilson's role in the writing and consideration of the two great measures before the special session of Congress—the tariff bill and the Federal Reserve bill. It was still too early to comprehend the exact source of Wilson's personal power, the editorial concluded; however, it was clear that he had thus far "more power-fully shaped more important legislation than any Executive of our time."

A Statement

[Aug. 13, 1913]

Statement with regard to Rural Credits[1]

Again and again during the discussion of the currency bill it has been urged that special provision should be made in it for the facilitation of such credits as the farmers of the country most stand in need of—agricultural credits as distinguished from ordi-nary commercial and industrial credits. Such proposals were not adopted because such credits could be only imperfectly provided for in such a measure. The scope and character of the bill, its immediate and chief purpose, could not be made to reach as far as the special interests of the farmer require.

Special machinery and a distinct system of banking must be provided for if rural credits are to be successfully and adequately supplied. A government commission is now in Europe studying the interesting and highly successful methods which have been employed in several countries of the old world, and its report will be made to Congress at its regular session next winter. It is confidently to be expected that the Congress will at that session act upon the recommendations of that report and establish a complete and adequate system of rural credits. There is no subject more important to the welfare or the industrial development of the United States; there is no reform in which I would myself feel it a greater honor or privilege to take part, because I should feel that it was a service to the whole country of the first magnitude and significance. It should have accompanied and gone hand in hand with the reform of our banking and currency system if we had been ready to act wisely and with full knowledge of what we were about.

There has been too little federal legislation framed to serve the farmer directly and with a deliberate adjustment to his real needs. We long ago fell into the habit of assuming that the farmers of America enjoyed such an immense natural advantage over the farmers of the rest of the world, were so intelligent and enterprising and so at ease upon the incomparable soils of our great continent, that they could feed the world and prosper no matter what handicap they carried, no matter what disadvantage, whether of the law or of natural circumstance, they labored under. We have not exaggerated their capacity or their opportunity, but we have neglected to analyze the burdensome disadvantages from which they were suffering, and have too often failed to remove them when we did see what they were.

One of the chief and most serious of these disadvantages has been that he has not been able to secure the extended bank accommodations he every year stands in need of without paying the most burdensome rates of interest and saddling himself with mortgages and obligations of every kind which he fairly staggered under, if he could carry them at all. In other countries systems of rural credit have been put into operation which have not only relieved the farmer but have put his enterprises upon a footing of easy accomplishment. Countries in which agriculture was fatally languishing because wholly unprofitable have seen their farming lands blossom again and their people turn once more hopefully to the soil for a living. Our farmers must have similar means afforded them of handling their financial needs, easily and inexpensively. They should be furnished these facilities before their enterprises languish, not afterwards.

And they will be. This is our next great task and duty. Not only is a government commission about to report which is charged with apprising the Congress of the best methods yet employed in this matter but the Department of Agriculture also has undertaken a serious and systematic study of the whole problem of rural credits. The Congress and the Executive, working together, will certainly afford the needed machinery of relief and prosperity to the people of the countrysides, and that very soon.[2]

Mimeographed MS (WP, DLC).
   [1] Issued to the press while the House Democratic caucus was considering the Federal Reserve bill, in an obvious effort to answer agrarian protests against that measure. See Link, *The New Freedom*, pp. 221-22.
   [2] There is a WWsh draft of this statement in WP, DLC.

To John Lind

Washington, Aug. 13. 1913

The President directs that unless some change has taken place of which we know nothing you now present his proposals very frankly and fully to the Mexican officials. He suggests that by way of preface you make it clear to them that we have canvassed and are familiar with the whole situation in its international aspects as well as with regard to the circumstances which especially affect Mexico; that we feel that we cannot wait longer to speak very frankly; that we therefore approach this conference in the most solemn and earnest spirit, the spirit of those who desire above all things else to serve Mexico and all those who are to have dealings with her, that we know that we have the sympathy and moral support of the governments of Europe in what we are now doing and that we are offering Mexico the only possible plan by which she may find a way out of her difficulties and avoid worse ones; that this is the turning point in the whole business so far as the United States are concerned and that we are now to know whether or not Mexico will accept the United States as her friend and helper; and that the proposals we are now submitting include in effect nothing more than was originally agreed upon when General Huerta assumed his present office, as shown by the despatches at that time received and now on file from Henry Lane Wilson. We have waited longer than the time set in that agreement for the elections. We have notified foreign governments of the nature of your errand but have not communicated to them the contents of your instructions. Would it in your judgment be wise and helpful to you if we were now to communicate the detail of those instructions to them in confidence, allowing the Mexican authorities full time for consideration as you suggest before making proposals public. That we would do when advised by you. Do you think it would soften and aid the business to have leading South American states join us in our present representations.   Bryan[1]

WWT and WWhw telegram (SDR, RG 59, 812.00/15335a, DNA).
[1] There is a WWsh draft and a WWT draft of the first part of this telegram in WP, DLC.

To William Robinson Pattangall[1]

My dear Mr. Pettengall: [The White House] August 13, 1913

I am taking the liberty of writing you just a line to say how deeply interested I am in your candidacy for Congress. Like all other Democrats, I shall watch the result with the greatest interest as well as with the greatest confidence. My immediate object in writing is to congratulate the party in having a representative in this contest who, they can feel, represents the principles and the policy of the party so truly and with so much ability.

Cordially and sincerely yours,   Woodrow Wilson

TLS (Letterpress Books, WP, DLC).
[1] Lawyer, mayor of Waterville, Maine, and former state attorney general. He was the Democratic candidate to fill a vacancy in Congress created by the death of Forrest Goodwin. He did not win the election in September.

From Ellen Axson Wilson

My own darling,   Cornish, New Hampshire, Aug. 13, 1913.

I have just finished reading the papers and feel distinctly cheered about Mexico, & other things too. The papers come just before luncheon and I can hardly wait to eat before getting at them—everything is so exciting just now. Isn't it terrible about Sulzer.[1] I suppose it is very serious for the party in N. Y. as well as for him. Is it? And now with Mrs. Sulzer's confession[2] injected it seems more like a modern play than real life.

I shall probably finish this tonight as I must dress and go to pose for Mr. Vonnah;—I hope for the last time. I have (I think) finished one of my larger pictures this morning and I think it is pretty good for me!

Who do you think is coming to luncheon tomorrow? Gov.

Bullock of Bermuda![3] He telegraphed today from the Crawford House that he would like to do so. His wife and daughter[4] are in England.

We went over to Hanover last night and saw the pageant which was really beautiful. It was given out of doors in a very romantic glade, and some of the scenes,—especially scarf dances by the spirits of the winds the brooks and the shadows, were exquisite. They have a large summer school there in connection with the college, and the play was given by the young women who attend that,—together with all the pretty little children of the place as fairies. I hope none of them have pneumonia today, for they were all bare-footed and had next to nothing on, and it was a *cold* night, though a very beautiful one with the bright moonlight. I slept under *six* blankets!

I have just returned from a little dinner at Mr. Stephen Parrishs's. Helen and I were invited and we had a delightful time. There were just that perfect old dear, Stephen himself, the sweet young cousin who keeps house for him,—(and does it to perfection) the adorable Maxfield (Mrs Max was not well) and Judge and Mrs. Hand. I think I have already written about her and how fine and unusual she is. He is very interesting too; I had not met him before. He is a bull-mooser, but seems to be infatuated with you in spite of it;—he can talk of nothing else. He says he met you some years ago and you impressed him then as the most powerful personality he had ever seen.

I posed for Mr. Vonnah until it was time to start for the dinner, so the letter was delayed until late. I am eager to get the posing done with, so I stay as long as possible. He *is* almost through with mine, and it is a pretty pose and a charming bit of colour,—face, hair and dress, the latter all soft silver grey and lavender. They say it looks rather like me too. None of them are real *portraits*, you understand. I love you passionately my darling, and oh how I want you!　　　　　　　　　　　　　　Your own　Eileen

ALS (WC, NjP).
　1 Governor William Sulzer of New York had just been impeached (on the morning of August 13, after an all-night session) by the New York Assembly, as the result of the findings of a special legislative investigating committee which held hearings in July and August. The principal charges against Sulzer were that he had failed to report numerous contributions to his gubernatorial campaign as required by state law, had committed perjury in swearing that his statement of campaign contributions was correct, and had used some of the campaign funds for speculation in the stock market. Though Sulzer and his followers charged, and many progressive leaders and newspapers believed, both at the time and later, that the impeachment was engineered by Charles F. Murphy and Tammany Hall, the fact remained that Sulzer was unable to provide any convincing refutation of the charges. Sulzer's trial began on September 18, before a high court of impeachment, consisting of the members of the state Senate and the judges of the Court of Appeals. He was found guilty of three of the eight articles of impeachment and removed from office on October 17, 1913. The standard mono-

graph in this affair is Jacob Alexis Friedman, *The Impeachment of Governor William Sulzer* (New York, 1939).

2 During the debate in the New York Assembly on Sulzer's impeachment in the early morning hours of August 13, it was suddenly alleged that Clara Rodelheim Sulzer, the Governor's wife, had "confessed" that she had, without her husband's knowledge, diverted some of the campaign contributions to stock market speculations. It was also reported that she had had a nervous breakdown over the affair. However, an effort to postpone the impeachment proceeding as a result of this "confession" was voted down, and later testimony indicated that there was no truth in her "confession." *Ibid.*, pp. 161, 173-74.

3 Lieutenant General Sir George Mackworth Bullock.

4 Bullock's wife was Amy Isabel Thomson Bullock. The Editors have been unable to identify their daughter.

Remarks at a Press Conference

August 14, 1913

Mr. President, would you care to say anything about this proposed recess of Congress?

Nothing, except that I mean—I mean it.

Mr. President, have you taken any action this morning, or today, with reference to stopping the effort to have a recess?

No, none at all. Oh, I am confident that will take care of itself, as a matter of fact.

Your idea is, then, that Congress should stay right through until the currency legislation is completed?

Yes, that is my idea, and I think that is what is more than my idea, I think that is the idea of the country.

Have you got any communications to indicate that?

I have had—I can't say how many, but a very considerable number of communications from many parts of the country. All indicate that they think it is just as important that we should stay here and complete the currency bill as that we should stay here and complete the tariff bill, and not take the one without the other; which is, in a sense, complete—that the business of the country needs the assistance of the currency act just as it needs to get the relief of tariff aid.

Have you had correspondence largely from bankers, Mr. President?

Not quite a large number of bankers. If I were to sum it up in one word, I would say that it was the general business feeling of the country—merchants and importers, and men of representative businesses of various kinds. . . .

Mr. President, the idea of this recess is to simply take a little rest and then take up the currency bill before the regular session begins.

Yes, after the forces of opposition have gotten a little breather—got their second wind.

Mr. President, has your attention been directed to the statements frequently made on the floor of the Senate by some Republicans, to the effect that the tariff bill will take up so much time it is very doubtful if they can get to currency legislation?

Yes, my attention has been called to that.

Do you think such a program could be carried out?

I think we could well take care of that, sir.

Mr. President, have you any hope that the tariff will be accelerated, the way it is going now?

Of course, you are privileged to see things about it that I am not.

I mean, what are the prospects of its being hastened?

I really don't know that. I can't say I have any definite expectations of it today. But it is incredible to me that the committee should continue to go as splenetically as it is now.

Mr. President, is this government communicating with foreign governments in regard to the Mexican situation?

Only sufficiently to let them know what the character of our efforts is.

They say there are no exchanges, they are really communications from this government.

For information. There are no exchanges.

Mr. President, along that line, have we had any communications from foreign governments as to their attitude toward it?

No.

Can you tell us, Mr. President, anything about Mr. Lind's reports, what he has found in Mexico City?

Well, he hasn't made any reports on anything new that he has found. He has simply reported the very agreeable relations which he has already set up.

Mr. President, does that indicate that we are getting closer to a recognition of Huerta, or are we getting further away from that?

I am not prophesying today. Well, that is in the nature of a prediction, and I don't think you can find any indication that things are going in that direction.

You are still in the same position with reference to that question?

Yes, sir. I have been anchored there for some time.

Mr. President, would you say, is there any prospect that this government will make a declaration that the Huerta government will not be recognized?

Oh, I can't say that. That will depend entirely on the developments, on the sort of declaration we should make.

I think—

By the way, you gentlemen, I am sure undesignedly, did me

a considerable injustice the other day by reporting that I
said that there was a war lobby.

Now I want to call your attention to what I did say, because
I am generally very careful to speak by the cards. I did not
say that. You called my attention to the charge made by one
of the senators that there was an organized syndicate—I
think that was the expression—intended to bring war on,
and asked me if I was of that opinion. I said I had no evidence to that effect—I think you will remember that—and
that all I could say was that it did look like a concerted effort
in some quarters to produce a state of opportunity which
would have that result.

Now any man can see, on the face of the thing itself, that
I did not say there was a war lobby, and I don't want the
country to get the impression that I make statements of that
sort unless I have a large number of documents in my
pocket.

Mr. President, that brings up a point that I would like to make
and inquire about. I was not here the other morning when that
occurred and my—they hadn't said anything to me about a lobby,
but that you certainly shared the idea of Senator Williams.

The impressions I have are those I simply share with the
public. I have no impressions, no private information.

As I understand these inferences here, we are not to represent
you as saying anything that is not quite right? You desire to
correct the impressions that you did, either that there was a lobby.
Now are we to use that?

No, I really was not suggesting that you correct the impression. I simply said this by way of a confidence, so that—just
as a more indirect way of asking you to be more careful
about that sort of thing in the future. Such damage as was
done has been done. I can't say it would wreck [things],
though it would chagrin me to read a number of editorials on
my statement that there was a war lobby.

Mr. President, of course, in regard to an editorial, there is a
chance of us misunderstanding, and always a chance—a lot more
than a certainty, with editorials of misunderstanding.

I know how some editors have to be watched.

I think there were a good many newspapers who did not credit
you with saying that there was a war lobby.

But some papers have a very bewildering effect on things,
and they are just as likely to have editorials on them.

Mr. President, will Mr. Lind see General Huerta?

I don't know.

Mr. President, outside of the official statement that was made at the State Department, which was very brief, describing Mr. Lind's functions, would you be good enough or can you tell us more definitely what is his mission to Mexico?

> Why, I don't see that I can add to what the State Department said.

That was my difficulty. I wanted to add something to it.

> There isn't anything to be added. That is the literal statement of the facts. He has gone there in the only way he could go there in the existing circumstances.

Mr. President, as the imagination focuses on the questions, and one of your answers, one of the possibilities now is the recognition of Mr. Huerta.

> Well, you have much more advantage with your imagination, but I can't see anything to hang that imagination on.

Mr. President, I think that the time for the elections—the constitutional elections in Mexico—was October 25.

> Twenty-six.

Now, is there any prospect, do you think, that an arrangement will be reached for elections at a date sooner than that?

> I can't say that there is. I can only say that I hope there might be an earlier election than that. I think it would help to clear the decks immediately.

There was a suggestion in one of the press dispatches from Mexico City that the Constitutionalists had sent some communication to Mr. Lind.

> I had not heard of that. I had not heard of that.

Mr. President, there is a good deal of confusion about your statement as taken from the State Department some time ago with regard to a communication that Mr. Lind took with him. The State Department said—referred to the President's communication being taken by Mr. Lind to Mexican leaders. When you were asked here by someone about Mr. Lind's presenting that communication to President Huerta, I understood you to say that that communication was to the Chargé, or at least to the American embassy.

> Well, the confusion must have arisen because of perhaps too critical attention to the language used. What I was meaning to say was that Mr. Lind, not being accredited to the Mexican government, would naturally communicate with them or at least get into communication with them through the Chargé d'Affaires down there.

The only point I wanted to clear up is what the communication was, whether it was a communication intended for the informa-

tion of President Huerta or to send to his envoy instructions to
Chargé O'Shaughnessy.

> It would naturally be both. It was a communication in-
> tended to fix in writing for Mr. Lind's use the views of this
> government. Of course, he would naturally communicate
> the views of this government, as he got the opportunity.

Mr. President, in other words, you have a plan, but no choices?

> Well, we have various ideas which we would like to sug-
> gest to the Mexican government.

Nothing inflexible about those views? They could be changed,
based on investigation?

> Well, they could well be changed in part.

Mr. President, was the purport of those suggestions communicated to the Foreign Relations Committee the other
evening?

> No sir, except so far as I have indicated what we were after.

Are your views being communicated to Huerta or to his cabinet
since Mr. Lind's arrival?

> I don't know, sir.

Mr. President, what you have said just now I think has cleared
up a great deal of confusion in our minds in regard to the
administration's program, I take it, from what you say.

> The administration has a program. Yes, it has a definite set
> of views with regard to the situation down there.

And Mr. Lind knows those views in writing?

> Yes sir—knows them in writing. What we are really after,
> you see, is to make perfectly clear to General Huerta what
> our views are. They are entirely friendly views, and views
> intended to help the situation in Mexico without any inter-
> vention or meddling on our part.

The success of this program depends upon the voluntary acceptance of the views by him?

> Of course. Yes.

Has Mr. Lind reported anything so far in the way of any
obstacles in the way of these?

> No, he has not.

Mr. President, have you ever seen any formal report from Mr.
Henry Lane Wilson, or anybody else, that justified the statement
that Huerta had promised that he would not be a candidate for
constitutional President?

> No, sir.

But it is generally accepted that he did make such a statement.

> You know, the dispatches I think were published at the time
> I was not in office and therefore I can't speak with con-

fidence; but, as I remember, before I came into office, I had the distinct impression that, by implication, that would be part of the understanding arrived at at the outset by plain implication. But I never understood that that was a definite, binding, and explicit promise.

JRT transcript (WC, NjP) of CLSsh (C. L. Swem Coll., NjP).

Remarks to a Group of Western Bankers

August 14, 1913

Gentlemen: It is a real pleasure to see you here for many reasons, not only that I may have the pleasure of greeting you individually, but because we have felt that the government had too few points of contact with the businessmen and bankers of the country, and that, therefore, it is a real benefit and service to us to have the opportunity to consult a body of men like yourselves with regard to what are the necessities of business. Mr. McAdoo's action in offering to assist in moving the crops of the country is singular in being original.[1] It is such a common-sense thing that one would have supposed it would have occurred to somebody sooner. Its originality consists in its obviousness. Therefore, I think that we may congratulate ourselves that we are to do the obvious, plain, common-sense thing. But one of the incidental advantages is that it brings you to Washington and enables us to realize what are our ideals of a government, namely, that it is an instrumentality, not a master; that we are not determining what the need of the country is, but are trying to serve the need of the country as we understand it. I feel that though I may not perhaps have the privilege of conferring with you directly myself, I can get a very great advantage from it by subsequent conference with the Secretary of the Treasury, who has had that pleasure.

T MS (WP, DLC).

[1] McAdoo announced on July 31 that he would deposit $25,000,000 to $50,-000,000 of government funds in national banks in the agricultural states of the South and West in order to facilitate the movement of crops during the coming harvest season. Furthermore, he would accept prime commercial paper as security for the deposits. McAdoo held conferences in Washington on August 7, 8, and 14 with groups of bankers from these areas in order to ascertain the exact sums of money needed. Wilson's remarks printed above were delivered to the last of these groups. As it turned out, only $37,386,000 was actually needed and distributed. See *New York Times*, August 1, 2, 8, and 15, 1913; William G. McAdoo, *Crowded Years: The Reminiscences of William G. McAdoo* (Boston and New York, 1931), pp. 245-47; and John J. Broesamle, *William Gibbs McAdoo: A Passion for Change, 1863-1917* (Port Washington, N. Y., 1973), pp. 169-71.

John Lind to William Jennings Bryan

Mexico City [Aug. 14, 1913].

I have just completed a very extended interview with Gamboa at which I delivered the President's proposal. He read it carefully and with marked attention. He at once noted and commented on the last paragraph in the proposal and said that that justified him in presenting the side of his Government. He also called my attention to the absence of any language which justified my statement the other day in regard to recognition. I said that the whole document implied the impossibility of recognition; besides there were some things that could better be said than written if further expression on that question was deemed necessary; that the President had no desire to irritate by assigning reasons in writing for his determination in that regard at this time but that I felt justified in saying to him that that question was foreclosed so far as our Government is concerned. He argued that if the good will professed in this document had been exercised in the past Mexico would not have suffered the loss of eighty thousand lives and been burdened with the number of orphans and widows incident thereto; that if the United States had not directly and indirectly aided the rebels, the Diaz rebellion would not have succeeded; that the United States was party to creation of present Government and the present state of affairs could have been avoided if the United States had recognized the Government now existing legal in form at least (he excused himself from discussing the features of its origin to which we take exception) and felt that we unduly magnified a point that in the nature of things can only be academic in the intercourse between nations. He said that while he would not charge our Government with any organized or methodical aid to the rebellion we had in many instances aided the rebels as well as by the acts of our citizens. He instanced the improper use of the searchlights of battleships in Mexican waters at Guaymas to disclose the position of Federal troops at night and that attacks by the rebels immediately followed resulting disastrously to the Federals. He also charged that national vessels had delivered arms and ammunition to the rebels on the west coast of which fact he had absolute proof. I denied absolutely any conscious or intentional act on the part of the Government to aid the rebels and suggested it would be a waste of time to discuss charges new to me and which I could not refute. I briefly called attention to the burden imposed on our Government to guard a boundary line of fifteen hundred miles. That that work had been done more efficiently than required either by international law or the most faithful neutrality; that our laws in regard to supplying munitions of war were much in advance of the requirements of international obligations. He said that Mexico could not regard this as anything but an unwarranted meddling in their domestic affairs and instanced the suggestion of England at the time of our rebellion which was spurned by our Government. I answered that that suggestion involved the territorial as well as political integrity of the United States and was not parallel; that I did not desire to discuss abstract questions or historical precedents; that this was a situation that the President sought to solve in a manner as practical as it was friendly and wholly for the good of Mexico. He again referred to the dissimilarity of the conditions. That Mexican conditions should be viewed from Mexican standpoint and not by our standpoint; that the maintenance of any government necessitate[d] or at least palliated political action here that would not be tolerated in the United States. He also referred to our political situation and said that the Democratic Party which was now in power was on trial; that it could not afford to make a mistake the consequence of which could not be foreseen; that he had the most positive assurances that a large portion of the Republican Party and many Senators would not support the President in this attitude; that the administration had offers from many Republican papers to voice the cause of Mexico but added significantly that the government was too short of funds to expend in that direction. These questions I did not argue in detail except to suggest that I came from a state and section strongly Republican; that I could speak from personal knowledge that ninety per cent of the population would stand by the President enthusiastically in any policy even to intervention; that it was to avoid the possibility of such eventuality and the consequences to Mexico that might follow which prompted this earnest and justifiable proposal.

I will not attempt more than this sketch of our conversation. He will have to advise me through Mr. O'Shaughnessy by eleven a.m. tomorrow whether or not he desires that the press be informed that we having had conferences. He also accepted my statement that I had recommended to you that my instructions be not given to the press before Monday. He did not specifically ask extension of that time but said, "For God's sake keep this out of the press for your sake and ours." This one expression I deemed the most significant of the interview. He asked me how long I was to remain. I said I had no instructions on that point; that I came prepared to remain as long as I could be of service to the cause of peace and international good will. He promised to inform me when further conference was desired.   Lind.

T telegram (SDR, RG 59, 812.00/10639, DNA).

From Ellen Axson Wilson

My own darling,   Cornish, New Hampshire Aug. 14, 1913

It is 11.15 and I am just free to write to you! Alas! for those quiet first days at Cornish! But I have had a most interesting day. After painting one hour, (from ten to eleven,) having seen first to my mail of course, I went to the train to get Sir George & take him for a little drive before luncheon. He came from "Crawfords" expressly to lunch with us and went back on the four o'clock,— three hours to come and three to go. He was really a delightful guest.

After leaving him at the train we all went to tea at Mrs. St Gaudens. She is in deep mourning for her little grandson, who you know poisoned himself accidentally shortly before we came up, so I had not expected to see her; but she, of course, wanted us to see her husband's work and the place; and it ended in her inviting quite a little group of her best friends to meet us. It was a pleasant intimate little party, and there are copies of most of her husband's best works in the two great studios. All *that*, together with the very beautiful garden and house and view, made it an afternoon to be remembered always. But I have raved over so many "gardens and views" in my letters, that I will spare you further details.

After getting back from that I had barely time to rest a bit and read the paper, and then dress for dinner at the Arnolds,[1] our neighbours down the road. There are only women in the family and it was exclusively a woman's dinner. We had a delightful time, for Miss Grace Arnold is one of the finest, sweetest people here,—and she has a perfectly beautiful and highly trained contralto voice, and exquisite taste in music. She sings the same sort of things that Margaret does. So we have had a regular concert, and that is why I am late getting back. She had another musical friend visiting her who both sang and played. *She* had heard Margaret sing in N. Y. and greatly admired her voice.

Thank you so much, dearest, for your reassuring letter about the various crises, political & diplomatic. That incredible Wilson has certainly finished himself now, as completely as poor Sulzer. I suppose even the "Times" will no longer defend him, or even the most stupid Senators regard him. I am glad he *has* so completely exposed his folly. I had a little fresh panic about the Alabama vacancy because it seemed that O'Neal was doing the wrong thing so that the vote of his appointee might be questioned and thrown out. Is that so?[2] And the paper also says that Senator Culberson is at a sanatarium with a serious nervous break down. How about that? But I can scarcely keep my eyes open, so must say good night, dear heart!

Oh how I want you!

With love unspeakable, I am always and altogether

Your own   Eileen

ALS (WC, NjP).

[1] Charlotte Bruce Arnold, Grace Arnold, and Fannie Arnold (Mrs. Clendenen) Graydon of New York, who rented a place in Cornish known as The Butternuts.

[2] Governor Emmet O'Neal of Alabama, wishing to avoid calling a special session of the state legislature, on August 12 appointed Congressman Henry D. Clayton to fill the unexpired term of the late Senator Johnston. Both Republican and Democratic spokesmen in the Senate immediately expressed doubts as to whether Clayton could be seated, arguing that the second clause of the Seventeenth Amendment provided that a governor could make a temporary appointment to the Senate only if specifically empowered to do so by his state legislature. O'Neal countered with the argument that the third clause of the amendment stated that the amendment should not be construed so as to affect the term of any senator chosen before the amendment itself took effect; he thus had the right to appoint Clayton to fill the unexpired term of Johnston, who had been chosen under the old procedure. Clayton's credentials were presented to the Senate on August 20, at which time they were referred to the Committee on Privileges and Elections. The committee seems to have procrastinated about taking any action. For Clayton, at least, the impasse was broken in October, when President Wilson requested him to remain in the House of Representatives and he agreed to do so (see WW to H. D. Clayton, Oct. 10, 1913, and H. D. Clayton to WW, Oct. 11, 1913). That the threat to deny Clayton his seat was not an idle one was proved by subsequent events. On November 17, 1913, O'Neal appointed Wilson's old friend, Franklin Potts Glass, to fill the vacancy. After another protracted interval, a lengthy report from the Committee on Privileges and Elections, and a debate on the Senate floor, the Senate voted on February 4, 1914, to deny Glass his seat. See the *New York Times*, Aug. 9-15, Sept. 6, and Nov. 18, 1913, Jan. 18 and Feb. 5, 1914; and *Cong. Record*, 63d Cong., 1st sess., pp. 3553-54, and *ibid.*, 2nd sess., p. 2886.

To Edith Gittings Reid

My dear, dear Friend,   The White House 15 August, 1913.

I cannot tell you what delight your letter[1] gave me. I wish Ellen had been here to share the joy and relief of seeing your handwriting again and knowing that you were at last confident of entire recovery. We have been seeking news of you throughout your illness with an anxiety that made us sick at heart. I think you do not realize what a part you play in our thoughts and affection. Now that you are well again one of my burdens of anxiety is lifted and I can go through these trying days with a lighter heart and freer spirits. How fine it is! and how sweet it was of you to write yourself and give me proof in your own words of your recovery! I bless you for it.

Please do not fancy that this is a dictated letter. I long ago wore out my pen hand and for years this little machine has been my pen, when there was writing to be done that I wanted to do myself. One of my correspondents swore once that he could recognize my typewriting!

The days go hard with me just now. I am alone. My dear ones went away almost at my command. I could not have been easy about them had they not gone; and we have found a nest for them in New Hampshire (though their address is Windsor, Vermont) which is ideal, where they have just the right airs, a beautiful country around them, and most interesting neighbours. They are in the midst of a colony of artists and literary people,—just where they belong. And so my mind is at ease about them. And yet, oh! the difference to me! It makes the situation complete, however, I must admit. These are stern days, and this all but empty house fits well with them. My Secretary is living with me and the young naval doctor who is of my staff; and they are lovely fellows, both of them, and good company all the while. They are no substitutes, but in themselves most satisfactory. I work hard, of course (the amount of work a president is expected to do is preposterous), but it is not that that tells on a fellow. It's the anxiety attending the handling of such "things" as that scoundrel Huerta and all other affairs in which you seem to be touching quicksilver,—matters for which your own judgments and principles furnish no standards, and with regard to which you can only frame conjectures and entertain hopes. I play golf every afternoon, because while you are playing golf you *cannot* worry and be preoccupied with affairs. Each stroke requires your whole attention and seems the most important thing in life. I can by that means get perfect diversion of my thoughts for an hour or so at the same time that I am breathing the pure out-of-doors. And I take Saturdays off, as nearly as may be when a telegram or a piece of news may waylay you and hold you up at any moment. Even Sundays are not safe. On the whole, however, I have myself well in hand. I find that I am often cooler in my mind than some of those about me. And I of course find a real zest in it all. Hard as it is to nurse Congress along and stand ready to play a part of guidance in anything that turns up, great or small, it is all part of something infinitely great and worth while, and I am content to labour at it to the finish. I keep perfectly well. My young aide looks after me as a mother would look after a child, and is with me practically all the time. So far things go very well, and my leadership is most loyally and graciously accepted, even by men of whom I did not expect it. I hope that this is in part because they perceive that I am pursuing no private and selfish purposes of my own. How could a man do that with such responsibilities resting upon him! It is no credit to be sobered and moralized by a task like this!

But while I speak of myself I am really thinking about you, and speaking of other things only because I know you want to hear. My heart is full to overflowing with gratitude for your recovery. Be good to all of us who love you and take extraordinary care of yourself, so that there may be so [no] setback and no ifs or buts of any kind about your complete restoration to strength. We shall count on you for that. Meanwhile remember how many follow you with their thoughts in deep and abiding affection. I know that I may couple Ellen's messages with my own. How eagerly she will read your letter (which I shall send to her) and with what joy! They are all well at Cornish, and we love our prospective son in law more and more. He is almost good enough for Jessie. Warmest messages to Mr. Reid and Doris and Francis.

Your devoted friend,   [Woodrow Wilson]

WWTL (WC, NjP).
¹ It is missing.

William Jennings Bryan to John Lind

Washington, Aug. 15 1913.

We are willing to wait a reasonable time if Mexican government requests it. We regard Gamboa's expression as very significant of what publicity might accomplish, but will await your advice. President congratulates you upon manner in which you have presented the matter. You can not too strongly emphasize the fact that the entire country is behind President Wilson, as will be shown the moment the matter is made public. Caution Gamboa against being misled by opposition reported by sensational newspapers.   Bryan

T telegram (SDR, RG 59, 812.00/10639, DNA).

From William Jennings Bryan

My dear Mr. President: [Washington] August 15, 1913.

Senator Bacon has telephoned me what I believe to be a good suggestion, namely, that you call some of the Republican Senators and talk with them about the Mexican situation. He mentioned La Follette, Smoot, Borah, Sutherland, Burton, Crawford, and Nelson¹ as men whom he knew to be friendly to your policy.

I think you have already talked with Smoot. Borah, Sutherland, and Burton are members of the Foreign Affairs Committee. Crawford made a speech on your side the other day. Senator Bacon thinks they would feel complimented to have you send for them and it might be well just now to have them feel as friendly as possible, because some attacks are being made in the Senate. For instance, Penrose[2] made a speech to-day attacking Hale and giving notice of a speech next week on some outrages.

I send you the report that we have received from Durango.[3] I am not sure that you have read it. I think it gives the most horrible story that we have received officially. It might be well for you to read this tonight if you can.

I also suggest that you have Mr. Tumulty call up Senator Bacon and give him any information you desire to about Hale. I have told Senator Bacon that I thought the resolution[4] ought to be referred to his committee and that any criticism of Hale should be replied to as merely an indirect attack upon you and an evidence of partisanship rather than of interest in the public good; but I think it would be well for Tumulty to talk to him over the 'phone in regard to Hale so that he will be prepared tomorrow should the matter come up again.

With assurances of respect, etc., I am, my dear Mr. President,
Very sincerely yours,   W. J. Bryan

TLS (WP, DLC); P.S. omitted.
1 Robert Marion La Follette of Wisconsin; Reed Smoot of Utah; William Edgar Borah of Idaho; George Sutherland of Utah; Theodore Elijah Burton of Ohio; Coe Isaac Crawford of South Dakota; and Knute Nelson of Minnesota.
2 Senator Boies Penrose, Republican of Pennsylvania.
3 T. C. Hamm to Secretary of State, June 4[-25], 1913, TLS (WP, DLC). Because of the difficulty of communication with Washington before and after the capture of Durango by Mexican rebel forces on June 18, Hamm, the American consul in the city, presented his report in the form of a diary kept during the period. The entries from June 18 to 20 described in graphic detail the orgy of looting and arson which took place following the capture of the city. Hamm was also particularly concerned about the hostility of the rebel bandits, especially General Tomás Urbina, toward foreigners, and their reluctance to provide any protection for them or their property.
4 During his speech in the Senate, Penrose introduced a resolution requesting the President to inform the Senate whether Hale was or had been employed as an agent of any executive department of the government, and if so, at what rate of compensation and under what instructions. Penrose permitted the resolution to be referred to the Foreign Relations Committee on August 21, with the tacit understanding that nothing would come of it. Cong. Record, 63d Congress, 1st sess., pp. 3385, 3572.

From Moorfield Storey and Others

Dear Mr. President: New York [Aug. 15, 1913]

The National Association for the Advancement of Colored People, through its Board of Directors, respectfully protests against the policy of your Administration in segregating the colored employees in the Departments at Washington. It realizes that this new and radical departure has been recommended, and is now being defended, on the ground that by giving certain bureaus or sections wholly to colored employees they are thereby rendered safer in possession of their offices and are less likely to be ousted or discriminated against. We believe this reasoning to be fallacious. It is based on a failure to appreciate the deeper significance of the new policy; to understand how far reaching the effects of such a drawing of caste lines by the Federal Government may be, and how humiliating it is to the men thus stigmatized.

Never before has the Federal Government discriminated against its civilian employees on the ground of color. Every such act heretofore has been that of an individual State. The very presence of the Capitol and of the Federal flag has drawn colored people to the District of Columbia in the belief that living there under the shadow of the National Government itself they were safe from the persecution and discrimination which follow them elsewhere because of their dark skins. Today they learn that, though their ancestors have fought in every war in behalf of the United States, in the fiftieth year after Gettysburg and Emancipation, this Government, founded on the theory of complete equality and freedom of all citizens, has established two classes among its civilian employees. It has set the colored people apart as if mere contact with them were contamination. The efficiency of their labor, the principles of scientific management are disregarded, the possibilities of promotion if not now will soon be severely limited. To them is held out only the prospect of mere subordinate routine service without the stimulus of advancement to high office by merit, a right deemed inviolable for all white natives as for the children of the foreign born, of Italians, French and Russians, Jews and Christians who are now entering the Government service. For to such limitation this segregation will inevitably lead. Who took the trouble to ascertain what our colored clerks thought about this order, to which their consent was never asked? Behind screens and closed doors they now sit apart as though leprous. Men and women alike have the badge of inferiority pressed upon them by Government decree. How long will it be before the hateful epithets of "nigger" and "Jim-Crow" are openly applied to these sections? Let any one experienced in Washington affairs, or any trained newspaper correspondent answer. The colored people themselves will tell you how soon sensitive and high-minded members of their race will refuse to enter the Government service which thus decrees what is to them the most hateful kind of discrimination. Indeed, there is a wide-spread belief among them that this is the very purpose of these unwarrantable orders. And wherever there are men who rob the Negroes of their votes, who exploit and degrade and insult and lynch those whom they call their inferiors, there this mistaken action of the Federal Government will be cited as the warrant for new racial outrages that cry out to high Heaven for redress. Who shall say where discrimination once begun shall cease? Who can deny that every act of discrimination the world over breeds fresh injustice?

For the lowly of all classes you have lifted up your voice and not in vain. Shall ten millions of our citizens say that their civic liberties and rights are not safe in your hands? To ask the question is to answer it. They desire a "New Freedom," too, Mr. President, yet they include in that term nothing else than the rights guaranteed them by the Constitution under which they believe they should be protected from persecution based upon a physical quality with which Divine Providence has endowed them.

They ask therefore that you, born of a great section which prides itself upon its chivalry towards the humble and the weak, prevent a gross injustice which is an injustice none the less because it was actuated in some quarters by a genuine desire to aid those now discriminated against.

Yours, for justice,   The National Association for the
                      Advancement of Colored People
   By   Moorfield Storey, President
        W. E. B. DuBois, Director of Publicity
        Oswald Garrison Villard, Chairman of the Board[1]

TLS (WP, DLC).
[1] This letter was published widely.

From Ellen Axson Wilson

My own darling,   Cornish, New Hampshire Aug. 15, 1913.

I have had another whirling day, not at all what should be expected of quiet Cornish, and it is now after eleven at night, alas! I lunched with Mrs. Beaman[1] who is the eldest daughter of Maxwell Evarts and one of the great ladies of the region. She is a widow of many years, and owns some 2,000 acres on the Cornish side of the river. Needless to say she has a beautiful house and a great view and a garden! Her house, you know, is the one on the heights on the left above Blow-me-down pond. We saw it whenever we came from town. I had a very pleasant time; but had to leave a little early, to come home for Jessie and then go to meet the Smiths on the 3.45.

They arrived all right and it is delightful to see them again. They are very well and just as dear and funny as ever. They had expected to come one [on] the 7.45; and we had an engagement to see the Adams and Hart gardens[2] and take tea with the former; so we "called Mrs. Adams up" explained and took the Smiths with us; and we all had a charming time. We saw another beautiful view of course, and one of the prettiest because simplest and most restful of the houses and gardens. Mr. Hart is a bachelor who has a tiny but adorable cottage and a very large garden to which he practically devotes *all* his time. He is really Browning's "pictor ignotus," doesn't care for fame, is a serene philosopher who doesn't even take time to paint in the gardening season. A very pleasant shy man, who I should think would be an extremely good friend and neighbour. He lives in the "back-yard" of the Adams, but is well to do and has a motor-car; and Mr & Mrs. Prellwitz, both of whom are well-known painters,[3] board with his chauffer; and they are all very intimate and happy together!

But in the meantime, before we started for this tea, Cousin John [Adams Wilson] had telephoned that they were motoring over from,—somewhere with two friends and they were all invited to dinner. They reached here sooner than was expected, so that we found them all here when we returned from the tea. We left them to amuse themselves while we all made hurried toilettes. They have just left after a very pleasant evening. But of course my back is the worse for wear after all this, so I must say goodnight and turn in.

I really think you ought to return to Cornish to break the drought again! It is *very* bad,—everyone is getting anxious about the water supply.

I love you my darling beyond expression, and I am so inordinately proud of you that I find it very hard to "behave myself before folk,"—but I do!

Devotedly   Your own   Eileen.

ALS (WC, NjP).
  [1] Hettie Sherman Evarts Beaman, widow of Charles Cotesworth Beaman, a distinguished lawyer of New York.
  [2] William Howard Hart, artist of New York.
  [3] Henry Prellwitz and Edith Mitchill Prellwitz of New York.

John Lind to William Jennings Bryan

Mexico City, Aug. 16, 1913.

Yesterday I had many I think inspired callers, Mexicans and Americans, who urged that the Huerta Government is all there is to save the country from anarchy, that to attempt an election in the present state of affairs would be farcical, that the United States could best serve Mexico by recognizing Huerta and thus facilitate and expedite pacification. Today the British Minister[1] called and really urged the same considerations. Of course he did not suggest any course of action. He thought I ought to see Huerta and offered his good offices to secure an interview. This I declined courteously saying that I was in touch with Gamboa, that if it was agreeable to have me call then the suggestion had best come through the proper channel. I gathered from Minister's conversation that he had had no instructions beyond a suggestion received probably Thursday that he ask the Mexican Government to carefully consider the representations made by the United States. My impressions on general situation may be summarized as follows: The views that have come to me group themselves into three classes. First, those indicated above held by the great landowners, the foreigners, and some Americans with large business interests. This class denies that there is any agrarian or other factor to account for present conditions, except the perversity of the lower classes—military dictatorship is their remedy. Second class, which includes Mexicans and many Americans, the most thoughtful and some of large property interests, who believe the agrarian question is at bottom of trouble aggravated by misrule. They believe that an efficient, liberal government, if such could be secured either through our good offices or by intervention, which would inaugurate necessary reforms would solve the problem. The third class composed of both Mexicans and Americans see no hope except in intervention and American control for an indefinite period. All concur that the situation is very precarious and fraught with all sorts of menace. In this I concur. If the President's proposals be finally accepted the real task begins. Cooperation of all the rebels cannot be hoped for with Huerta in the saddle; without some degree of cooperation from him little can be done without invoking other force.

These are my views in brief at the end of the first week. I am not discouraged, not without hope, but the situation is sufficiently grave to justify preparation for every contingency. I discuss no politics, I ask some questions, I listen patiently.

Have just learned that reply to President's proposition will be delivered tomorrow morning.   Lind.

T telegram (WP, DLC).
  1 Francis William Stronge.

Federico Gamboa to John Lind

Sir: Mexico, August sixteenth, nineteen thirteen.

On the sixth instant, pursuant to telegraphic instructions from his Government, the Charge d'Affaires ad interim of the United States of America verbally informed Mr. Manuel Garza Aldape, then in charge of the Department of Foreign Affairs, of your expected arrival in this Republic with a mission of peace. As, fortunately, neither then nor today has there existed a state of war between the United States of America and the United Mexican States, my Government was very much surprised to learn that your mission near us should be referred to as one of peace. This brought forth the essential condition which my Government ventured to demand in its unnumbered note of the sixth instant addressed to the aforesaid Charge d'Affaires, "that if you do not see fit to properly establish your official character," your sojourn could not be pleasing to us according to the meaning which diplomatic usage gives to this word.

Fortunately, from the first interview I had the pleasure to have with you, your character as confidential agent of your Government was fully established, inasmuch as the letter you had the kindness to show me, though impersonally addressed, was signed by the President of the United States, for whom we entertain the highest respect.

It is not essential at this time, Mr. Confidential Agent, that I should recall the whole of our first conversation. I will say, however, that I found you to be a well informed man and animated by the sincerest wishes that the unfortunate tension of the present relations between your Government and mine should reach a prompt and satisfactory solution.

During our second interview, which, like the first one of the fourteenth instant, was held at my private (#),* you saw fit, after all interruption, honest and frank exchange of opinion concerning the attitudes of our respective Governments which did not lead us to any decision, to deliver to me the note containing the instructions, also signed by the President of the United States. Duly authorized by the President of the Republic, pur-

* Omission.

suant to the unanimous approval of the Cabinet, which was, for the purpose, I have the honor to make a detailed reply to such instructions.

The Government of Mexico has paid due attention to the advice and considerations expressed by the Government of the United States, has done this on account of three principle reasons: First, because, as stated before, Mexico entertains the highest respect for the personality of His Excellency Woodrow Wilson; Second, because certain European and American Governments, with which Mexico cultivates the closest relations of international amity, having in a most delicate respectful way, highly gratifying to us, made use of their good offices to the end that Mexico should accord you a hearing, inasmuch as you were the bearer of a private mission from the President of the United States; and, third, because Mexico was anxious, not so much to justify its attitude before the inhabitants of the Republic in the present emergency, the great majority of whom and by means of imposing *and* orderly manifestations, have signified their adhesion and approval, as to demonstrate in every way the justice of its cause.

The imputation contained in the first paragraph of your instructions that no progress has been made towards establishing in the capital of Mexico a Government that may enjoy the respect and obedience of the Mexican people is unfounded. In contradiction with their gross imputation, which is not supported by any proofs, principally because there are none, it affords me pleasure to refer, Mr. Confidential Agent, to the following facts which abound in evidence and which to a certain extent must be known to you by direct observation. The Mexican Republic, Mr. Confidential Agent, is formed by twenty-seven states, three territories and one federal district in which the supreme power of the Republic has its seat. Of these twenty-seven states, eighteen of them, the three territories and the federal district (making a total of twenty-two political entities) are under the absolute control of the present Government, which aside from the above exercises its authority over almost every port in the Republic and consequently, over the customs houses therein established. Its southern frontier is open and at peace. Moreover, my Government has an army of eighty thousand men in the field with no other purpose than to insure complete peace in the Republic, the only national aspiration and solemn promise of the present provisional President. The above is sufficient to exclude any doubt that my Government is worthy of the respect and obedience of the Mexican people, because the latter's consideration has been gained at the cost of the greatest sacrifice and in spite of the most evil influences.

My Government fails to understand what the Government of the United States of America means by saying that it does not find itself in the same case with reference to the other nations of the earth, concerning what is happening and is likely to happen in Mexico. The conditions of Mexico at the present time are unfortunately neither doubtful nor secret; it is afflicted with an internal strife which has been raging almost three years and which I can only classify in these lines as a fundamental mistake. With reference to what might happen in Mexico, neither you, Mr. Confidential Agent, nor I, nor anyone else can prognosticate, because no assertion is possible on incidents which have not occurred. On the other hand, my Government greatly appreciates the good offices tendered to it by the Government of the United States of America in the present circumstances; it recognizes that they are inspired by the noble desire to act as a friend, as well as by the wishes of all the other Governments which expect the United States to act as Mexico's nearest friend. But if such good offices are to be of the character of those now tendered to us, we should have to decline them in the most categorical and definite manner.

Inasmuch as the Government of the United States is willing to act in the most disinterested friendship, it will be difficult for it to find a more propitious opportunity than the following: If it should only watch that no material and monetary assistance is given to rebels who find refuge, conspire and provide themselves with arms and food on the other side of the border; if it should demand from its minor and local authorities the strictest observance of the neutrality laws, I assure you, Mr. Confidential Agent, that the complete pacification of this Republic would be accomplished within a relatively short time.

I intentionally abstain from replying to the allusion that it is the purpose of the United States of America to show the greatest respect for the sovereignty and independence of Mexico, because, Mr. Confidential Agent, there are matters which not even from the standpoint of the idea itself could be given an answer in writing.

His Excellency, Mr. Wilson, is laboring under a serious delusion when he declares that the present situation of Mexico is incompatible with the compliance of her international obligations; with the development of its own civilization; and with the required maintenance of certain political and economical conditions tolerable in Central America. *Strongly backing* that there is a mistake, because to this date no charge has been made by any foreign Government accusing us of the above lack of compliance; we are punctually meeting all of our credits; we are still maintaining diplomatic missions cordially accepted in almost all the countries of the world, and we continue to be invited to all kinds of international congresses and conferences. With regard to our interior development, the following proof is sufficient, to-wit: a contract has just been signed with Belgian capitalists which means to Mexico the construction of something like five thousand kilometers of railway. In conclusion, we fail to see the evil results, which are prejudicial only to ourselves, felt in Central America by our present domestic war. In one thing I do agree with you, Mr. Confidential Agent, and it is that the whole of America is clamoring for a prompt solution of our disturbances, this being a very natural sentiment if it is borne in mind that a country which was prosperous only yesterday has been suddenly caused to suffer a great internal misfortune.

Consequently Mexico cannot for one moment take into consideration the four conditions which His Excellency Mr. Wilson has been pleased to propose through your honorable and worthy channel. I must give you the reasons for it: An immediate suspension of the struggle in Mexico, a definite armistice "solemnly constructed and scrupulously observed" is not possible, as to do this it would be necessary that there should be some one capable of proposing it, without causing a profound offense to civilization, to the many bandits, who, under this or that pretext, are marauding towards the south and committing the most outrageous depredations; and I know of no country in the world, the United States included, which may have ever dared to enter into agreement or to propose an armistice to individuals who, perhaps on account of a physiological accident, can be found all over the world beyond the pale of the divine and human laws. Bandits, Mr. Confidential Agent, are not admitted to armistice; the first action against them is one of correction, and when this unfortunately fails and the lives must be severed for the sake of the biological and fundamental principle that the useful sprouts should grow and fructify.

With reference to the rebels who style themselves "Constitutionalists," one of the representatives of whom has been given an ear by members of the United States Senate, what could there be more gratifying to us than if convinced of the precipice to which we are being dragged by the resentment of their defeat, in a moment of reaction they would depose their rancor and add their strength to ours, so that all together we would undertake the great and urgent task of national reconstruction? Unfortunately they do not avail themselves of the amnesty law enacted by the provisional government immediately after its inauguration, but on the contrary, well known rebels holding elective positions in the capital of the Republic or profitable employments, left the country without molestation, notwithstanding the information which the Government had that they were going to foreign lands to work against its interests, many of whom have taken upon themselves the unfortunate task of exposing the mysteries and infirmities from which we are suffering, the same as any other human congregations.

Were we to agree with them to the armistice suggested, they [this] would, ipso facto, recognize their belligerency, and this is something which cannot be done for many reasons which cannot escape the perspicacity of the Government of the United States of America, which, to this day and publicly at least, has classed them as rebels just the same as we have. And it is an accepted doctrine that no armistice can be concerted with rebels.

The assurance asked of my Government that it should promptly convene to free elections is the most evident proof and the most unequivocal concession that the Government of the United States considers it legally and solidly constituted and that it is exercising, like all those of its class, acts of such importance as to indicate the perfect civil operation of a sovereign nation. Inasmuch as our laws already provide such assurance, there is no fear that the latter may not be observed during the coming elections and while the present Government is of a provisional character, it will cede its place to the definite Government which may be elected by the people.

The request that General Victoriano Huerta should agree not to appear as a candidate for the Presidency of the Republic in the coming elections, cannot be taken into consideration, because, aside from its strange and unwarranted character, there is a risk that the same might be interpreted as a matter of personal dislike. This point can only be decided by Mexican public opinion when it may be expressed at the polls.

The pledge that all parties should agree beforehand to the results of the election and to cooperate in the most loyal manner to support and organize the new administration, is something to be tacitly supposed and desired, and that the experience of what this internal strife means to us in loss of life and the destruction of property will cause all contending political factions to abide by the results; but it would be extemporaneous to make any assertion in this respect even by the most experienced countries in civil matters, inasmuch as no one can forecast or foresee the errors and excesses which men are likely to commit, especially under the influence of political passion. We hasten to signify our appreciation to the United States of America because they agree from today to recognize and aid the future which we, the Mexican people, may elect to rule our destinies. On the other hand, we greatly deplore the present tension in our relations with your country, a tension which has been produced without Mexico having afforded the slightest cause therefor. The legality of the Government of General Huerta cannot be disputed. Article Eighty-five of our political constitution provides:

"If at the beginning of a constitutional term neither the President nor the Vice President elected present themselves, or if the election had not been held and the results thereof declared by the first of December, nevertheless, the President whose term has expired, will cease in his functions and the Secretary for Foreign Affairs shall immediately take charge of the Executive power in the capacity of provisional President, and if there should be no secretary for Foreign Affairs or if he should be incapacitated, the Presidency shall devolve on one of the other secretaries pursuant to the order provided by the law establishing their number. The same procedure shall be followed when, in the case of the absolute or temporary absence of the President the Vice President fails to appear, when on leave of absence from his post if he should be discharging his duties, and when in the course of his term the absolute absence of both functionaries should occur."

Now then, the facts which occurred are the following: the resignation of Francisco I. Madero, Constitutional President, and Jose Maria Pino Saurez [Suarez], Constitutional Vice President of the Republic. These resignations having been accepted, Pedro Lascurain, Minister for Foreign Affairs, took charge by operation of law of the vacant executive power, appointing, as he had the power to do, General Victoriano Huerta to the post of Minister of the Interior. As Mr. Lascurain soon afterwards resigned, and as his resignation was immediately accepted by Congress, General Victoriano Huerta took charge of the executive power, also by operation of law, with the provisional character and under the Constitutional promise already complied with to issue a call for special elections. As will [have] been seen, the point of issue is exclusively one of constitutional law in which no foreign nation, no matter how powerful and respectable it may be, should mediate in the least.

Moreover, my Government considers that at the present time

the recognition of the Government of General Huerta by that of the United States of America is not concerned, inasmuch as facts which exist on their own account are not and cannot be susceptible of recognition. The only thing which is being discussed is a suspension of relations as abnormal as without reason; abnormal, because the Ambassador of the United States of America in his high diplomatic investiture and appearing as Dean of the Foreign Diplomatic Corps accredited to the Government of the Republic, congratulated General Huerta upon his elevation to the Presidency, continue[d] to correspond with this Department by means of diplomatic notes and on his departure left the first Secretary of the Embassy of the United States of America as Charge d'Affaires ad interim, and the latter continues here in the free exercise of his functions. And without reason, because, I repeat, we have not given the slightest pretext.

The Confidential Agent may believe that solely because of the sincere esteem in which the people and the Government of the United States of America are held by the people and Government of Mexico and because of the consideration which it has for all friendly nations (and especially in this case for those which have offered their good offices) my Government consented to take into consideration and to answer as briefly as the matter permits the representations of which you are the bearer. Otherwise, it would have rejected them immediately because of their humiliating and unusual character, hardly admissible even in a treaty of peace after a victory, inasmuch as in a like case any nation which in the least respects itself would do likewise. It is because my Government has confidence in that when the justice of its cause is reconsidered with serenity and from a lofty point of view by the present President of the United States of America, whose sense of morality and uprightness are beyond question, that he will withdraw from his attitude and will contribute to the renewal of still firmer bases for the relations of sincere friendship and good understanding forcibly imposed upon us throughout the centuries by our geographical nearness, something which neither of us can change even though we would so desire, by our mutual interests and by our share of activity in the common sense of prosperity, welfare and culture, in regard to which we are pleased to acknowledge that you are enviably ahead of us.

With reference to the final part of the instructions of President Wilson, which I beg to include herewith and which say "If Mexico can suggest any better way in which to show our friendship, serve the people of Mexico and meet our international obligations, we are more than willing to consider the suggestion," that final part causes me to propose the following equally decorous arrangement: One, that our Ambassador be received in Washington. Two, that the United States of America send us a new Ambassador without previous conditions.

And all this threatening and distressing situation will have reached a happy conclusion; mention will not be made of the causes which might carry us, if the tension persists, to no one knows what incalculable extremities for two peoples who have the unavoidable obligation to continue being friends, provided, of course, that this friendship is based upon mutual respect which is indispensable between two sovereign entities wholly equal before law and justice.

In conclusion, permit me, Mr. Confidential Agent, to reiterate to you the assurances of my perfect consideration.

Signed   F. Gamboa,
Secretary for Foreign Affairs of the Republic.[1]

TCL (WP, DLC).
[1] J. Lind to the Secretary of State, Aug. 17, 1913, 10 P.M., T telegram (WP, DLC), was a long summary of this note.

Two Letters from William Jennings Bryan

My Dear Mr President   [Washington, c. Aug. 16, 1913]

I was talking yesterday with Jones of Va & I find that he has a good opinion of Sheuster[1] for Gov Gen.[2] He also spoke of Harrison of N. Y. (Francis Burton). I drop you a line to say that Harrison strikes me favorably. He has ability, experience & loyalty. He is also prominent, being next to Underwood on the Ways & Means Com. I believe he is worth considering. You have spoken of Hartman. He has been appointed minister to Ecuador and will be here next week & you will have a chance to look him over. If you want him for the Philippines he will, of course, be glad to make the change. He would be a reliable man anywhere. If Lind succeeds he might be might not be [sic] a bad man for the place. With assurances of respect etc I am my dear Mr President
Yours truly   W. J. Bryan

ALS (WP, DLC).
[1] William Morgan Shuster, collector of customs for the Philippines, 1901-1906; member of the Philippine Commission and Secretary of Public Instruction, 1906-1909; at this time a lawyer in Washington.
[2] Of the Philippines.

My dear Mr. President: Washington August 16, 1913.

I have been in conference with the Nicaraguan Minister and Financial Agent and also with some parties who are negotiating with them for a loan. In conferring with them I have learned something more in regard to the hardships under which the small Latin-American countries labor. Ecuador, for instance, made a loan a few years ago at 22½% and it was an attempt to make a still larger one at the same rate that caused a revolution there which resulted in the loss of some eight thousand lives.

I heard of one firm in New York that was considering a proposition that would call for 36% interest. The way they do it is this: They will make a short time loan, say for six months, at 6% and place a discount on the amount,—in one case that I heard of it was 15%. 15% on a six months' loan would be at the rate of 30% a year, and the 6% added would make it 36%.

The Nicaragua people owe Brown Brothers about $711,000 and as security they have given not only customs, returns from their railroad, etc., but they have given an option on 51% of the stock of their government railroad, and this at a figure that would amount to a profit of something like a million and a half. Brown Brothers are willing to increase the loan to about two million on a 6% basis, but they want an option on the entire railroad which would mean a profit of about three millions.

I mention this to illustrate what I said in a letter the other day about our being in the position of a Good Samaritan and helping those who have fallen among thieves. I feel that we have an opportunity to help these nations in a disinterested way that will cement them to us and give us a standing among the Latin-American countries which no outside influence can shake.

Nicaragua needs some $750,000 to get rid of the Brown Brothers loan and free their railroad. They need some more for the purpose of paying off present indebtedness. They would use a part of the money from the Canal option to discharge these liabilities, but now that nothing can be done for a while on that subject they are urged to meet this Brown Brothers debt which comes due in October. Have you sufficiently considered the proposition which I laid before you to be able to decide upon its merits? I have no doubt that we can provide that if we hereafter purchase the Canal and the naval base in Fonseca Bay, the money paid by us can be used first in liquidating any loans for which we are security. My recommendation is that we propose to the Nicaraguan Government that we loan them a million and a half or two million—whatever sum to you may seem proper—on the basis that I outlined a few weeks ago, namely, that we take from them 4½% bonds for the amount and hold them as security for 3% bonds of our own, with the understanding that, if their bonds are paid, principal and interest, as due, 1½% of the interest will be used as a sinking fund to retire the principal. This would give them at this time a saving of 1½% over anything they can possibly do outside, and in addition to that it would use 1½% more of the interest to retire the principal, so that at the end of a time that could be easily calculated, their debt would be extinguished. I believe that we can do this with perfect safety, and that it would not even be necessary to stipulate for the appointment of an American to collect and disburse the taxes for the payment of the interest, although there is no reason why they should not agree to this. I believe, however, that our position is such that this need not be put into the contract. I have no doubt that they would, without any such provision in the contract, invite us to send an official there to act as auditor.

I believe that such a proposition would be acted upon favorably by Congress. If we found that there was enough opposition to prevent the authorization of the loan at this special session, it could go over to the winter session and we would have the immediate benefit of the offer. I think, too, that it would help us in Mexico, for it would be a complete answer to any question that might be raised as to our disinterestedness.

In bringing the subject of Nicaragua before you again, I do not mean to withdraw my suggestions in regard to Ecuador—one does not interfere with the other. Nicaragua, however, is the more pressing, and while in the case of Ecuador we could emphasize our immediate interest in the sanitation of Guayaquil, in the case of Nicaragua we could point to the fact that the Committee on Foreign Relations had formally endorsed the purchase of the Nicaragua site and the Fonseca naval base, so that it will be merely advancing money which will soon be covered by a payment which we expect to make.

I beg pardon for bringing this subject to your attention again, but it is pathetic to see Nicaragua struggling in the grip of an oppressive financial agreement. As I think I have stated in a former letter, we see in these transactions a perfect picture of dollar diplomacy. The financiers charge excessive rates on the ground that they must be paid for the *risk* that they take and as soon as they collect their pay for the risk they then proceed to demand of the respective governments that the *risk* shall be *eliminated* by governmental coercion. No wonder the people of these little republics are aroused to revolution by what they regard as a sacrifice of their interests.

With assurances of respect, etc., I am, my dear Mr. President,
Very sincerely yours,   W. J. Bryan

TLS (WP, DLC).

From the Diary of Colonel House

[Beverly, Mass.] August 16, 1913.

Dudley Malone came today with his message to me from the President concerning the New York Mayoralty campaign. The President said: "Mr. House is my second personality. He is my independent self. His thoughts and mine are one. If I were in his place I would do just as he has suggested that he ought to do. If anyone thinks he is reflecting my opinion by whatever action he takes, they are welcome to that conclusion."

From Ellen Axson Wilson

My own darling,   Cornish, New Hampshire Aug 16 1913

I'm wae for you today for I know even you must be suffering in this intense heat. There is no life in the air at all. I hope you are not having a drought too;—that I fancy is rather local. We are all perfectly well however and not at all wilted by it for this is practically the first day when it has been severe.

We are to have another tea this afternoon—just about 25 guests —and I am dressed waiting for half past four. The house looks lovely, for Mr. Hart and old Mr. Kennedy[1] keep it practically full of flowers all the time. I shall finish this later. I am glad to say there are no other engagements today except that Marie Dressler[2] comes to sing after dinner. We invited her to one of the other teas, but, somewhat to my relief, she had to be out of town at the time. Her vacation ends next week.

We have all had a delightful day together picking up fallen stitches and talking things out. The Smiths of course went to the studio with me in the morning so I did not have to lose my time there. But they *have* interfered with my writing to you and reading the papers after luncheon.

I see Huerta may resign in order to run for constitutional president. Will you please tell me, dear, if your Mexican policy does or does not admit of accepting him on those terms? that is as a candidate for elections. I suppose he would lose all if he stepped aside on any other terms; and yet I do not suppose Carranza would lay down arms *on* those terms. So I am puzzled & very anxious to know *what* message Lind bears as regards that point. How hard it is never to be able to ask any question! Hard for me, —but all the better for you, I dare say!

The tea is over and went off well in spite of the heat. The people quite evidently had a good time. I have just received and read the pathetic letter from our dear Mrs. Reid. I too had one written about the same time. I was shocked to learn that she had so long continued desperately ill. How *very* lovely she is!

I wonder what my darling is doing today, if he has had his golf and other diversions and a real holiday. How long do you suppose I can endure to do without even a glimpse of you?

Every-body sends love without measure. I love you to *distraction*! and am in every heart-throb—   Your own   Eileen.

ALS (WC, NjP).
  ¹ Unidentified.
  ² Well-known actress specializing in musical comedy and vaudeville.

To Ellen Axson Wilson

My precious darling,   The White House 117 [17] August, 1913.

Henry McAlpin,¹ of Savannah, dropped in to see me the other day, and what do you suppose he brought me? Our original marriage license, with your grandfather's signature and all the other correct endorsements on it! It seems that all this while, though I did not know it, I have been entitled to the possession of this original, it having been copied into the records of the clerk's office immediately upon its return. I wonder if you can imagine how it made me feel? I was as much thrilled as if the paper itself had been a tangible embodiment of all that has made my life bright and blessed. I never held in my hand anything more thoroughly and wholly romantic than that piece of paper, and it is locked away now as my most precious possession! I put it with the sweet letters that come every day from Cornish. They too are redolent with romance for me. I seem to love my darling more every day of my life, and to realize more clearly what she means to me, what part her love plays and has always played, even when I was least conscious of it, in all that I have ever done or been. Without it the best things in me would never have come out. It has kept my soul awake. The reason I do not speak of anything but love in these weekly letters to you, my sweet one (leaving everything else in my life out of my reckoning) is, not that I am weary of everything that makes my weeks weary and anxious and labourious, but that I am jealous of this brief hour when I seem to be with you to the exclusion of the whole world and need to let the whole pent up passion of my days out into words, in order that my heart may not break. I cannot bear to bring anything in that does not touch directly our intimate selves. It is the single hour when I can be a lover and nothing else; and I am more of a lover than anything else. Love alone keeps my pulses going and makes the world of anxious business endurable.

I seem in my present isolation to feel more than ever my relations of fellowship and innate sympathy with all the unnamed people about me. The little children in the streets and on the roads, the plain people at the cottage doors and in the fields and coming and going in the hot city bring the tears to my eyes. My responsibility to them somehow makes me comprehend them better. I seem to know what they are thinking and what they are longing for. And the lamp that guides my thought in it all is my love for you and for our darling daughters the sweet, incomparable little ladies who are the fruit and sanction of our love for one another,—or, rather, perhaps, what I know of *your* hearts. Loving you, I have learned how to love, and at last the whole world seems to me a lesson in love. And ah! the intimacy and delight of it all! What has it not meant to me to have you at the heart of everything that concerned me! I wonder if you will ever realize how perfectly lovely you are, in person and in heart. When you were here it did not mean much to me that my dressing room was full of pictures of you, for you yourself were there, in your own dear, incomparable person, always ready to give me a sweet kiss or a tender embrace and let me feel the warm, palpitating love that filled you; but now they are to me almost like living images of yourself. It makes me happy to look into their eyes, which seem almost to kindle in response to mine. I[t] relieves me a little of the pain at my heart to kiss them passionately. And they are a sort of history of you, for the enchanting series runs back to the time you were a mere slip of a girl. I keep away from the sitting room. I live in the dressing room, the bed room and the study. I have got used to their stillness; and the dressing room and bed room are full of you, to my imagination! *Please*, my darling, pull up a bit in your social engagements at Cornish! They make me anxious. I want my darling to have *rest* and refreshment. I cannot have a free heart here, if I am to be anxious about her there, where I cannot watch over her or help her, or do anything at all for her except sit here and helplessly love her. My love! my love! you are all the world to me! I fill my thoughts all day long with your lovely person, the happy little household at Harlakenden, your freedom, your growing realization of what you mean to the people about you, old friends and new. There is no thought about you that is not delightful. I think when I get you in my arms again I cannot let you go till I have kissed you out of breath and consciousness, at any rate out of all co[n]sciousness of anything but that you are in my arms.

Your own,   Woodrow

Love unspeakable to all the dear ones. It is such a pleasure of [to] think of dear Margaret there at last. Does she seem well and strong? And dear Cousin Lucy and Cousin Mary, give them as much love from me as they will take. I am *so* happy that they are with you at last!

Yes, the tragical Sulzer business will have a very profound, I fear a very disastrous effect on the party in New York, At any rate in the immediate future. In the long run it will, I hope and believe, purge and redeem it.

Undoubtedly Senator Culberson's illness is a very anxious business. He will never get well. He has been ill for a long time, however, and will probably outlive the present session. While he lives his vote counts, because he is "paired" with one of the opposition.   W.

WWTLS (WC, NjP).
¹ Henry McAlpin, Princeton 1881, judge of the Court of Ordinary (Probate Court) of Chatham County, Ga.

From Ellen Axson Wilson

My own darling,   Cornish, New Hampshire Aug. 17, 1913.

It has actually clouded up, there are mutterings of thunder and we are all waiting breathlessly to see if it will really rain. I have just seen in the paper that the drought is broken in the West and South, but not before the corn crop was reduced by several million dollars worth. Oh, I am so sorry, for anything that goes wrong with the crops will, I suppose, affect the popular view of the tariff, so reasonable are our dear people! But apparently it is not yet a "calamity"!

Thank you *very* much for sending the Dooley article.¹ Isn't it *splendid*? One of his best.

There is quite a nice article about us at Harlakenden in the "Sunday Magazine" of the "World" today.² And as it is written by a woman reporter who came up to get an interview from me, and whom I positively refused even to admit into the house, I think she has rather heaped coals of fire on my head, for she certainly make[s] me a lovable person. It is absurdly sentimental, but there is no other objection to it. A good article about the Cornish Colony came out in the July number of "The Western New England Magazine"³ pub. at Springfield Mass. They write me that they sent a number of copies to you in Washington. I should very much like to have those copies found, to know how many there are, and to have them sent to certain friends. Perhaps you will mention this to Hoover.[4] I should, by rights, have written direct to him at first. And by the way, I do not think it worth while to send the yellow books[5] here. They are all back numbers by the time they reach us, and we cant tell what to believe anyhow; especially of course as each contradicts the other. So they simply make us unhappy when we read them, here with no one to apply a corrective. We have the "World," the "Times," and the "Evening Post."

In answer to your question about the canvasses. I wanted the rest of the *painted* ones to "restudy" as I did those I brought with me. But I *only* wanted them brought in case you & Brooks came again with the private car. *Do not pack and send them.* I am busy with other things now and perhaps would not touch them if they came.

We are expecting Miss Hagner any moment. Helen has gone to the station for her. Her small nephew comes with her. He is to stay with their maid from home down at the farm-house and Roberts will board them. Of course you know, poor Miss Hagner has been in much trouble about the divorce proceedings of her brother and his wife; and she has the child on her hands. Helen goes tomorrow for two weeks, so there are several changes in our household. Margaret does not come now until *Friday* night, the concert in which she is to sing having been put off for a few days.

We had another fine sermon by Dr. Fitch today. He is giving a series making use of the splendid Old Testament stories. This time it was the translation of Elijah and the succession of Elisha, especially his request for "a double spirit of Elijah." The subject was really "The old order passeth giving place to new, and God fulfills himself in many ways." Elijah represented the old, stern almost fierce spirit of *our* forbears, largely engaged, like Bunyans pilgrim, in escaping from the City of Destruction and denouncing the inhabitants. Elijah really *lived* in the wilderness. Elisha was of the new order in which the brotherhood of man is more emphasized—the more "social" religion. At its best it "does not want anything, not even 'salvation,' if it can't share it with the rest."

And by the way if one thinks of it so it it [*sic*] might justify Elisha's rather exacting demand for a *double* spirit of Elijah! One would need a "double spirit" if it is to go *all* around!

But don't you think that after all this "new order" is simply a return to the *oldest* order under Christ. His own religion was of the most modern, "social" type. "John the Baptist came neither eating nor drinking and ye say 'he hath a devil,' the Son of Man came eating and drinking and ye say 'behold a gluttonous man and a wine-bibber, a *friend of publicans and sinner's'* "!

It is interesting to see how the fire and force and eloquence in Dr. Fitch break out more and more. That first Sunday, you know, he talked so very quietly and simply as if to little children. But he can't quit[e] keep that up.

By the way, when we left we asked Lucy if she did not like it; and she said it was "a very interesting *address*"! It is amusing to see how easily they are offended by any slight criticism of that "old order."

I had yesterday a very entertaining letter from Walter Griffin.[6] He says he was "the laugh of Venice" because a few days before while painting in the open he noticed a very beautiful young American pass by. A few moments later he heard a splash and a scream; and it turned out that the young person had been so absorbed in staring at his picture that she had backed into the Grand Canal—fifteen ft. of water. I tell Nell I am sure it was *Henriette Stadleman,*[7] for we had just had a letter from her dated Venice. She and three friends are on a regular European sketching tour.

Dear and dearest one, it is getting very hard to remember *"constantly"* (!) that I am a soldier's wife. Oh, I do want to see you *desperately*! Is there no hope for a week end visit? I *love* you beyond all words.   Your devoted little wife,   Eileen

Poor Helen is still away, waiting I suppose at that horrid station for Miss Hagner. The train must be at least an hour late.

We had ten drops of rain and the cloud, alas! has passed!

ALS (WC, NjP).

1 This was probably Finley Peter Dunne, "How Mr. Dooley Recuperated at Elysium-by-the-Lake," a satire of summer resort life. One of a syndicated series, it appeared in the *New York Times*, July 27, 1913, Part V, p. 9.

2 "Summering with the President," New York *World*, Aug. 17, 1913, Magazine Section, pp. 12-13, 21. The author's name does not appear.

3 Brewer Corcoran, "Cornish—The Summer Capital," *Western New England Magazine*, III (July 1913), 275-83.

4 Irwin Hood Hoover, usually known as "Ike" Hoover, chief usher at the White House.

5 Scrapbooks of newspaper clippings made by the White House staff.

6 American-born landscape painter at this time resident in Paris.

7 Henryette L. Stadelman, painter of Wilmington, Del. She and Eleanor Wilson had studied together at the Pennsylvania Academy of the Fine Arts.

To William Jennings Bryan

My dear Mr. Secretary: The White House August 18, 1913

Thank you for your suggestion about Francis Burton Harrison in connection with the Philippines. It is thoroughly worth thinking of.

Cordially and faithfully yours,   Woodrow Wilson

TLS (W. J. Bryan Papers, DNA).

From William Jennings Bryan

My dear Mr. President: Washington August 18, 1913.

I enclose a tentative agreement which the Nicaragua people have made with Mr. Jarvis[1] for a loan of two or two and a half millions. This money is intended to cover some pressing obligations—obligations that would have been covered by the money that they expected to get from us on the canal site and the naval station at Fonseca Bay.

There are two things about this agreement to which I beg to call your attention.

In the first place, you will note that they stipulate that certain things are to have the approval of the Secretary of State. Do you think it would be proper for us to allow the contract to be signed without protest? While the State Department is not a party to the agreement, still I am not sure that I ought to consent, even orally, to this agreement. The object, of course, is to give them credit, and the State Department can exercise its option as to whether it will make the approvals or recommendations stipulated for, and if you think best to allow the contract to be made, I could notify them in writing that the contract was not binding on the Department and that the Department must be free to exercise its judgment at the time as to whether it would do the things contemplated in the contract.

The second thing to which I call your attention is the rate of interest. You will notice that the interest is to be 6% and that Mr. Jarvis is to receive 1% commission,—which is equivalent to 7% interest. Brown Brothers have a contract for 6% interest, but they have an option on 51% of the shares of the government railroad to secure the $711,000, and they insist upon an option on the entire railroad if they increase the loan to two or two and a half million. The Nicaragua people are very anxious to get back the option on the railroad shares and think it is much more desirable to pay 7% interest than to allow that option to be held.

Having already presented my views in regard to the desirability of our making the loan ourselves, I will not add anything on that point.

I shall make inquiry in regard to Mr. Jarvis. He seems to show more interest in the welfare of Nicaragua than any one else whom I have met. He is largely interested in the bank in Cuba and also has a bank in Santo Domingo. He is not friendly to the group of bankers who control the New York market.

The Nicaragua people are very anxious to act on this at once and would like, if convenient, an answer tomorrow. I have explained to them that you have a great deal on hand and that they must await your convenience.

With assurances of respect, etc., I am, my dear Mr. President,
Very sincerely yours,   W. J. Bryan

Rumor has it that Penrose is going to break loose tomorrow the main object of his attack Hale.

TLS (WP, DLC).
[1] Wilson returned the enclosure.

From Oswald Garrison Villard, with Enclosure

PRIVATE

Dear Mr. President: New York August 18, 1913.

On May 14th you were good enough to accord me an interview at the White House in which I laid before you the project of a Race Commission. You stated your approval of the project in general, but expressed the wish not to pass upon the matter at that time because of your inexperience with Congress and obvious inability in so short a time to ascertain just what your relations with Congress were going to be. This was wholly satisfactory to us, as we did not look for an answer before the middle of summer. Mr. Tumulty has recently urged that I see you at an early opportunity, but now writes me that on account of pressure of other affairs you are not able to make another appointment, but that you would be willing to consider any written proposition from me.

I therefore earnestly renew my suggestion that you approve the printed plan, of which I enclose another copy,[1] in principle; that is, you give me authority to attempt to raise the money necessary for such an undertaking, say $50,000 or $60,000, I to say to possible donors that you will name and appoint the Commission, and if the report is satisfactory to you transmit it in due course to Congress. Such an approval in principle would not commit you, of course, to the names suggested for membership on the

Commission, or to any programme beyond an impartial, non-partisan investigation of the race situation in this country by a joint commission of colored men and women and white men and women. If, by the first of January I can return to you and say that I have received the necessary subscriptions for the work, it would then be in order to discuss the size of the Commission and select its membership. Should the undertaking prove successful it ought to be a very great advantage to your Administration to have been identified with so noble an undertaking on behalf of social justice.

I am particularly urging this upon you now because of the intense dissatisfaction of the colored people at their treatment by your Administration thus far. I attach to this a letter received from Dr. Booker T. Washington in which you will see he says that never in his life has he seen the colored people so discouraged and embittered as they are at the present moment. It seems to me that nothing short of the appointment of such a Commission as this, and the prompt appointment of capable colored men to certain offices will in any way mitigate this feeling. I earnestly hope, therefore, in your own interest, that I may receive from you the approval of this plan. Nothing will be said about this in the public press until I can report to you that I have the money in hand. If I should not be able to raise it I will report this fact to you at the end of the year, and no harm will have been done.

Your Administration has been such a success in every other way that I cannot bear to have ten millions of our citizens feel that you are inimical to their interests.

Very truly yours,   Oswald Garrison Villard

P.S. I have Dr. Washington's permission to show you his letter.

TLS (WP, DLC).
   [1] This enclosure is missing; however it was *A Proposal for a National Race Commission to be appointed by the President of the United States, Suggested by the National Association for the Advancement of Colored People* (n.p., n.d.). A copy of this brochure is in the O. G. Villard Papers, MH.

E N C L O S U R E

Booker Taliaferro Washington
to Oswald Garrison Villard

Personal   Tuskegee Institute,
Dear Mr. Villard: Alabama August 10, 1913

You do not know how very glad I am to see your recent editorial on the racial disc[r]imination in the departments at Washington.[1] It shows a fine spirit and I am sure will do good. I am glad to note that a number of newspapers, especially those in Western New York, have already based editorials on the Evening Post editorial. They all speak in the same tone that you do.

I cannot believe that either President Wilson or Mr. Tumulty realizes what harm is being done to both races on account of the recent policy of racial discrimination in the departments. I have recently spent several days in Washington, and I have never seen the colored people so discouraged and bitter as they are at the present time. I am sure that President Wilson does not realize to what extent a lot of narrow little people in Washington are taking advantage of these orders and are overriding and persecuting the colored people in ways that the President does not know about.

I have always had great faith in President Wilson. Soon after his inauguration I gave out an interview in which I stated that I believed he would be just to the colored people.

As I have come into contact with President Wilson and read his addressed, his whole heart seems to be centered in trying to give every man a chance, especially the man who [is] down. Surely the Negro in this country is the man who needs encouragement from the hands of President Wilson.

I believe that your editorial and a good frank talk with the President and his secretary will result in changing this hurtful policy before it goes further.

The colored people are especially embittered and discouraged over the fact that an Indian[2] was made Register of the Treasury instead of a colored man. Added to this, it seems that a white man has been nominated for Minister to Haiti[3] instead of a black man.

I think that the President ought to know that one of the most hurtful and harmful organizations in Washington is one called the "Democratif Fair Play Association,"[4] composed of a lot of white clerks in the various departments. This organization is constantly seeking to stir up strife between the races and to embarrass the colored people. If the President or somebody else could suggest that they ought to attend to their own business in the departments and let the President run the government it would help immensely.

I think and hope that before President Wilson is in office much longer that he will demonstrate to the world that he is a firm true friend of both races.

Yours very truly,   Booker T. Washington.

TLS (WP, DLC).
1 "The President and the Negro," New York *Evening Post*, Aug. 4, 1913. It also

appeared with slight alterations in the New York *Nation*, xcvii (Aug. 7, 1913), 114. Inspired by Patterson's withdrawal from nomination as Register of the Treasury, the editorial went on to discuss the broader question of segregation in the federal service, as demanded by "the negrophobe Southern Senators—Vardaman, Tillman, Hoke Smith, and the rest." Villard argued that, for once, Vardaman was serving a useful purpose: "He has flung down a challenge to this Democratic Administration which Mr. Wilson cannot avoid. Shall the President give up the historic right of the Executive to appoint to office, to the extent at least of permitting a fraction of the Senate to bar out ten million of American citizens from serving the Government, save in the lowest positions, and then as lepers set apart?" Villard professed to understand Wilson's need of southern votes to enact his legislative program. But he pointed out that both Cleveland and Roosevelt had made lengthy fights for the confirmation of Negro appointees. Could Wilson do less? "We do not see how it is possible for him to steer a course of compromise and expediency in this matter, and we can not believe that he wishes to do so."

2 Gabe Edward Parker, of Choctaw ancestry, superintendent of Armstrong Academy, near Tulsa, Okla.

3 Madison Roswell Smith, lawyer and former congressman of St. Louis.

4 The National Democratic Fair Play Association of the United States, a Washington-based organization which, according to its own letterhead, stood frankly for "Race Segregation in Government Service." Its propaganda put heavy stress on the alleged plight of "deserving white girls" in Washington forced to work alongside of blacks or even to be supervised by black men. Little is known of the composition of the group, beyond what Washington suggests in the above letter. None of the fifteen persons named on the organization's letterhead was prominent enough to appear in *Who's Who in America*. The organization held mass meetings in Washington on May 1 and August 6, 1913, at the second of which Senator Vardaman delivered one of his violently racist speeches. See National Democratic Fair Play Association to "Dear Madam," May 9, 1913, T form letter (WP, DLC); Link, *The New Freedom*, p. 246; and William F. Holmes, *The White Chief: James Kimble Vardaman* (Baton Rouge, La., 1970), pp. 286-87.

John Lind to William Jennings Bryan

Mexico City, August 18, 1913

After cabling last night I called on Gamboa in company with O'Shaughnessy. I expressed to him in the most earnest and vigorous manner not by way of threat but as my personal conviction that the rejection by his Government of the President's proposition was a grave and perilous step: that any hope for division among the American people along partisan lines as he had intimated was utterly futile: that when the President was compelled to communicate to Congress and to the American people as he would be sooner or later all the incidents accompanying the change of Government, no American in or out of public life would dare to publicly defend the character the present Government (I had in mind the effect on Congress of President Harrison's message on the Chilean trouble): 1 that in my personal judgment speaking wholly without instructions but venturing and acting (?)'s opinion based on most intimate knowledge of American character and public opinion which I had been in peculiar position by reason of my birth to study objectively one of three courses would be forced on the administration in spite of any less drastic policy that the President might wish to pursue. First, the modification of our neutrality laws in those respects in which they are more strict than international law; second, granting the rebels belligerency; third, intervention. Each of these alternatives was well within our right under the law of nations. I explained how public sentiment was almost unanimous for action differing only as to which course should be pursued. Mr. O'Shaughnessy agrees with me that my discussion of the first two alternatives made a profound impression; the third in less degree. He expressed hope that the President would modify his views when he saw the full text of his note. He did not in the least resent my earnestness but thanked me for my candor.

I am of impression that the situation can best be held in hand by avoiding press publicity. At present an official communication to Congress of all the facts if such is deemed proper or necessary would cause less irritation and be more impressive here. Text of note will follow. Lind.

T telegram (WP, DLC).

1 On October 16, 1891, during a period of tension between the United States and a revolutionary government in Chile, sailors from *U.S.S. Baltimore* were involved in a brawl with Chileans in Valparaiso. Two of the sailors were killed and seventeen injured. The incident resulted in long and sometimes acrimonious diplomatic exchange between Washington and Santiago. President Benjamin Harrison reported on the unsatisfactory status of the negotiations with Chile in a belligerent special message to Congress on January 25, 1892, concluding with the suggestion that that body should take "such action as may be deemed appropriate." As it turned out, the Chilean government was already preparing to accede to the demands of the United States. See Frederick B. Pike, *Chile and the United States, 1880-1962. . . .* (Notre Dame, Ind., 1963), pp. 73-81, and Harry J. Sievers, *Benjamin Harrison: Hoosier President* (Indianapolis, 1968), pp. 192-97.

From Ellen Axson Wilson

My own darling   Cornish, New Hampshire Aug. 18, 1913

It is such a stifling afternoon, that I fear a letter will be as dull as I feel!

In fact nothing much occurs to me to say,—even to *you*! I managed to paint though in spite of the heat, with the water literally pouring down my face!

Jessie posed all morning for Mrs. Vonnah,[1] and all the rest, Nell[,] the Smiths and Miss Hagner went with Helen to White River Junction to put her on the train. If she had not started from there she would have had to make *four* changes to get to York Harbour.

Coming back their car behaved badly and they did not reach home until 2 P.M., finally telephoning for the landolet.[2] It seems the gasoline up here is of bad quality—too much kerosene and grease in it, so the machinery is clogged. It is to be sent to a Pierce-Arrow place at Woodstock. White has been tinkering with it for days and thought he had it all right.

We are all *very* well and happy, and are having cool nights, so we are not hurt by the heat. I go out to dinner tonight, but luckily have no afternoon engagement for once. Miss Hagner says you are "well an doing well" but in spite of myself I can't but be a little blue about you when these hot waves come. Oh, you are *so* precious, and I love you to distraction! As always,

Your devoted little wife, Nell.

ALS (WC, NjP).
    1 Bessie Potter (Mrs. Robert William) Vonnoh, artist and sculptor.
    2 The landaulet was one of the six White House cars (four Pierce-Arrow touring cars, an electric runabout, and the landaulet).

To Ellen Axson Wilson

My sweet darling,   The White House 19 August, 1913.

I realize how unfair it is not to keep you posted about the essential things, at least, of politics. I ought not to be so selfish as to *confine* myself to love-making when I write. It is so much more important to me than anything else in the world, when you are concerned.

No. Lind was instructed to ask Huerta for assurances that he would *not* be a candidate at the elections; that the elections should occur at an earlier date than that fixed in October; that there should be an armistice agreed upon meanwhile; and that full guarantees of a free and fair election be given. These proposals have been rejected, and we are told, in effect, that the Huerta people regard us, Democrats, as only a temporary arrangement and without the real support of the country. It was our duty to propose a settlement and to offer our good offices to bring it about; but we have been rebuffed, and must choose another course. The absurd and sensational reports in this morning's papers, that we had been given until midnight of last night to recognize Huerta and that the charge d'affaires had been given his passports, were of course utterly and maliciously false. It looks today as if some sort of conferences were still going on between Lind and Huerta. Probably we shall now simply take hands off, isolate Huerta, so far as we are concerned, and give them a certain time in which to settle their own affairs. Intervention must be avoided until a time comes when it is inevitable, which God forbid! This is all that is in my private mind at present.

Fuller advices from Mexico City may point out another practicable course to pursue.

There *are* several (I believe five) copies of the "Western New England Magazine["] here with the article on the Cornish Colony. I sent you the copy you received. Send us addresses and we will post the copies remaining.

I am well and keeping my head, though I am head over heels in love with you. Unbounded love to all.

In haste,   Your own   Woodrow

WWTLS (WC, NjP).

To John Lind

Washington. Aug 19th 1913

Since receiving your dispatch repeating conversation with Gamboa, in which you set forth three alternatives, we have awaited further report indicating impression made. Hearing nothing today the President desires you to ascertain whether we have received their final answer and whether they are willing to invite the judgment of the American people unpon the issue as presented in the President's offer and their refusal. Has there been no sober second thought?   Bryan.

CLST telegram (SDR, RG 59, 812.00/10641A, DNA).

To Oswald Garrison Villard

My dear Mr. Villard: The White House August 19, 1913

Because you are an understanding friend, I took the liberty of sending you word the other day that it did not seem possible to arrange a satisfactory interview at present. I would not venture to do this with any one who I knew would not instantly comprehend the situation. I was not jesting when I said that I had a one-track mind and just now the complications of the Mexican situation are so many and my absorption in it and the currency matter so constant that I knew it would be a mere form to put my mind through if I were to seek an interview with you just now.

Pray believe me

Most sincerely your friend,   Woodrow Wilson

TLS (O. G. Villard Papers, MH).

To Lindley Miller Garrison

[The White House] August 19, 1913

Am seriously considering Francis Burton Harrison, Member of Congress from New York, for Governor General of the Philippines. Would like to know your judgment in the matter. Have concluded that appointment of Crosby[1] would be unwise.

Woodrow Wilson.

T telegram (Letterpress Books, WP, DLC).
[1] Oscar Terry Crosby, an electrical engineer who had headed street railway and public utility companies in Washington, Trenton, N. J., and elsewhere.

From Lindley Miller Garrison

Sheridan, Wyoming, August 19, 1913.

I have no objections whatever to Mr. Harrison. What I know of him is all favorable. If you conclude that he is [has] the peculiar qualifications required for what I consider a post of paramount importance I have no further suggestion to make.

Garrison.

T telegram (WP, DLC).

From William Jennings Bryan, with Enclosure

My Dear Mr President   [Washington c. Aug. 19, 1913]

Here is a letter which Mr Queson asked me to hand you. He spoke to me about Harrison & I asked him to put it in writing. With assurances etc I am

Very truly yours   W. J. Bryan

ALS (WP, DLC).

ENCLOSURE

Manuel Luis Quezon to William Jennings Bryan

My dear Mr Secretary: Washington Aug. 16, 1913.

Refering to our conversation this afternoon, I beg to reiterate hereby in writing my statements with regard to Hon Francis Burton Harrison of New York, whose name has been very recently mentioned for the governor-generalship of the Philippines.

Of all the persons that have been called to my attention in connection with the governor-generalship of the Philippines, Mr Harrison is, in my opinion, the best man for the position. His appointment would be even wiser than that of Mr W. Morgan Shuster, whom I consider as exceedingly fitted to hold that office, because, while one would be as much satisfactory to the Filipinos as the other, Mr Harrison's standing in Congress and in the Democratic Party makes him more valuable than Mr Shuster to the Philippine government.

I have known Mr Harrison for the last four years that I have been in Congress; and for what I know of him, realizing as I do the great difficulties and grave responsibilities attached to the governor-generalship of the Philippines and being familiar as I am with the wishes of my people regarding the qualifications for that office, I do not hesitate to express the opinion that he is equal to the task and that my people will be very much pleased with him.

I beg to submit that the immediate need of the Philippines is to have a man at the head of that government who will command the confidence and respect of the people. The appointment of such a man will at the same time be in perfect harmony with the avowed Philippine policy of this administration. If I am correct in my interpretation of the democratic position with regard to the Islands, the party is loath to administer the affairs of the archipelago because it beli[e]ves in the inherent right of every people to govern themselves; but it has come to power having the burden of governing the Philippines to carry and it must bear this burden until it has had the time to set up an independent Philippine government. While, therefore, as a matter of fact and for the time being, the party must exercise the power and assume the responsibility of governing the Philippines, it should as much as circumstances permit try to do so in accordance with the wishes of the people by appointing for the Philippines administrators that will be satisfactory to them.

In conclusion, I wish to say that if Mr Harrison is appointed, he will have the cordial support of the Filipino people.[1]

Very respectfully,   Manuel L. Quezon.

TLS (W. J. Bryan Papers, DNA).
[1] Wilson sent his nomination to the Senate on August 20, 1913.

From William Jennings Bryan

My Dear Mr. President: Washington August 19, 1913.

I hope you will pardon me if I suggest a thought for your consideration while we await definite news from Mexico. You have spoken of allowing the constitutionalists to buy arms, and Senator Bacon thinks Congress favors such a policy. Mr. Moore seems disposed to oppose this, and I think there are objections to be considered.

First, We supply both sides with arms to use against us if we are finally compelled to intervene.

Second, We seem to *invite* further bloodshed by furnishing arms to both sides.

Third, We increase the risk of Americans in Mexico, and thus make intervention more likely.

Mr. Moore did not present all of these, but I regard them all as worth considering. The third weighs most with me, for I fear the repeal of the special restrictions would endanger our people. If we can not bring them out we must consider their safety. I do not want injury to them to rush us into intervention. The alternative is to refuse to ship to either side; that puts us in a position of neutrality, although the Huerta people, being able to get arms outside, would suffer least from that policy. But unless we can get Americans out of the country I fear the effect of any policy which will add to the horrors of the struggle in Mexico, especially if some outrage may at any time excite a demand for intervention. If we could get Americans out of Mexico, furnishing arms to both sides would be less dangerous to us however hard it might be on the Mexicans.

With assurances etc., I am, my Dear Mr. President,
Yours truly,   W. J. Bryan

TLS (WP, DLC).

From Ellen Axson Wilson

My own darling,   Cornish, New Hampshire Aug. 19, 1913

It is six o'clock and my home meeting of the Club has just ended. It went off quite brilliantly. It was (of course!) a very full meeting, and the tea afterwards was unusually pleasant because everyone was still full of the subject and discussing it eagerly. The subject, which I choose, was "How can we best promote a fuller and more general appreciation of *American* art?" We had one good laugh over it. Someone had said that we must not neglect to talk about "the next generation"—no discussion was complete without *that*! Later it was said (of course) that we should have, like the French, a government bureau of art to purchase works of art, to give prizes, to encourage it in every possible way. Then I said I thought the Congressmen who would take that view were not yet born; so after all we had to drag in that next generation.

I had a very interesting evening yesterday. I dined at Miss Nichols[1] and Mr. George Deforest Brush[2] was there. I had not seen him since I studied under him those first two months at the League[3] before I went from the antique class to J. Alden Weirs[4] "portrait class." I broke it to him gently that I was an old pupil and he was much interested. Mr. Hart, about whom I was writing, the other day, then mentioned that he also was a pupil, and it turned out that we were there at the same time, both in the Brush and the Weir classes. I found out today that Mrs. Prellwitz was also there then.

Well, all this gossip is very well but it is just whistling to keep my courage up, for I [am] consumed with anxiety about the Mexican Situation. Oh, for ten minutes talk with you or Mr. Tumulty! I don't see how I can bear so much suspense, and such blind ignorance about affairs that affect you so nearly. And Miss Hagner said there had been *some* hope that you could come up this week and now I suppose you can't. A plague on the Monroe doctrine! Lets throw it overboard! All the European nations have interests and citizens there as well as we, and if we could all *unite* in bringing pressure upon Huerta we could bring even that mad brute to hear reason

Oh, my darling you are so brave and wise and well poised. To think that you and Bryan alone stand between us and an awful war. But I am sure you will *never* let it happen, whatever the excitement and clamour.

I love you until it *hurts*. I think of you every moment. A thousand thanks for that *wonderful* letter   Your own   Nell.

It is a *beautiful cool* day!

ALS (WC, NjP).
   1 Either Rose S. or Marian C. Nichols, daughters of Dr. Arthur H. and Elizabeth F. Homer Nichols of Boston, who owned a summer residence in Cornish.
   2 George De Forest Brush, portrait and figure painter of New York, best known for his paintings of American Indians.
   3 At the Art Students' League in New York in 1884.
   4 Julian Alden Weir, painter of portraits, still life, and landscapes, much influenced by the French Impressionists.

John Lind to William Jennings Bryan

Mexico City. Aug. 19, 1913.

The situation is perplexing. No predictions are possible. Urrutia's alleged statement last night[1] was made during the time I was with Huerta. He may have given out inadvertently a step actually or tentatively agreed upon at Cabinet meeting which met to pass on form of note. My midnight session with Gamboa possibly impressed them with gravity of step taken and led to modification of program. The President occupied most of the time explaining the strength and disposition of his army and his plan for its increase and the progress of proposed reforms if he once secured pacification. He reported the northern states as virtually "pacified" and stated that Carranza and his two leading associates are fugitives in the United States. Captain Burnside[2] does not concur in this statement. The English Minister called again yesterday and tendered good offices. He is strongly pro-Huerta. The German Consul General[3] called this morning with Potter[4] of New York both urging recognition of Huerta Government in familiar argument. They really and sincerely fear anarchy if his hand is not upheld. With sufficient force he would establish peace, the peace of the grave. The great difficulty that I have to contend with is the conviction in the official mind that partisan opinion divides the American people at home. I have combated this with every argument and illustration I could muster. Nothing, in my judgment, will convince them short of demonstration in Congress such as would follow a communication to that body in a formal way of all the facts.

The President asked me how long I expected to remain. I explained that I had no instructions. He hoped I would stay long and that I would soon be commissioned so that he could receive me as befitted the greatness of the United States. I only said that I hoped that the day was not distant when the conditions would be such that the President would feel justified in sending his Ambassador to Mexico. He suggested, significantly I thought at the time, that when I left he would give me a private car. I thanked him for this. All concerned seem more anxious to talk with me now than before correspondence. Situation is improving. I have expressed my personal sympathy with the President and people on account of this morning's catastrophe.[5]   Lind

T telegram (SDR, RG 59, 812.00/8458, DNA).

1 Aureliano Urrutia, Minister of the Interior in Huerta's cabinet. On August 18 someone gave to the press corps in Mexico City a statement to the effect that the Huerta government, in its note to Lind, had demanded that the United States recognize it no later than midnight, August 18, else it would suspend all diplomatic relations. It was reported on the following day that Urrutia was "supposed" to have given out the statement but that both he and Huerta had requested O'Shaughnessy to report to Washington that it had "no foundation in fact." *New York Times*, Aug. 19 and 20, 1913.

2 William A. Burnside, captain, U.S.A., military attaché at the United States embassy, Mexico City.

3 The German consul general in Mexico City at this time was a Dr. Rieloff.

4 James Brown Potter, financier of New York, who had large holdings in coffee-growing and mining lands in Mexico.

5 On August 19, in Tacubaya, a suburb of Mexico City, a railroad car loaded with explosives ran wild down a hill, jumped the track, hit a trolley pole, and exploded. It was estimated that about one hundred people were killed by the blast. New York *World*, Aug. 20, 1913.

To William Jennings Bryan

My dear Secretary: The White House August 20, 1913

Thank you for your letter about Mr. Queson's attitude with regard to the Governor Generalship of the Philippines. I am more and more inclined to think that Mr. Harrison is the right man.   Faithfully yours,   Woodrow Wilson

TLS (W. J. Bryan Papers, DNA).

From William Jennings Bryan

My dear Mr. President: Washington August 20, 1913.

Mr. Thomson[1] reaches Bogotá tomorrow or next day and the Colombian people are quite anxious to take up the matter of their dispute with the United States.[2] As you will remember, they asked that it be submitted to arbitration and by your direction I replied that we preferred not to consider the question of arbitration at present and asked whether they were not willing to take up the matter by direct negotiation with a view to adjusting all disputes. We have not received an answer to that note yet but are expecting one daily. The Colombian Minister[3] and Mr. Hannis Taylor, their counsel, think there is no doubt about their willingness to negotiate directly. The Minister to-day expressed the opinion that they would rather have a proposition come from us than for one to come from them. He thought, too, that they would rather give a quit claim deed to the United States than to have anything to do with Panama, not intending, however, to limit our right to deal with Panama according as we please. They have two or three times expressed the wish that we might take the land between them and the Canal Zone so as to relieve them from the necessity of being neighbors to Panama. This, however, would doubtless be objected to by Panama, besides involving us in the care of a strip of land some two or three hundred miles long and averaging fifty to seventy-five miles in width. They would also like to change the boundary line between Panama and Colombia, but I am not able to speak definitely as to the exact change they desire to make.

I write to submit two questions:

First. If they are willing to proceed to direct negotiations, have you any objection to our making a proposition to them? I see no objection to it, and in view of the fact that the last administration made a proposition, we would have a precedent for it, unless you think that the rejection of the former proposition would make it incumbent upon them to make the next proposition themselves. I hardly think it would be worth while to stand out on a matter of form in a case where it is so desirable for us to get together and where they feel that they are the injured party.

2nd. If you think there is no objection to our making them a proposition, have you in mind a sum that you think would be fair? Mr. Taft offered them ten million dollars and then Mr. Du Bois,[4] our representative there, on his own responsibility, asked whether they would be willing to take fifteen, twenty, and at last, twenty-five millions. They refused and preferred to wait for the new administration. I think you have not indicated the limit to which you would go and I have no scientific basis upon which to calculate a sum, but I have had in mind twenty-five millions as a sum that we might be justified in paying. I think the Colombian people have about fifty millions in mind. If you think that we could consider twenty-five millions as the outside figure, I think it would be well for us to commence with an offer of fifteen millions, or twenty at most, leaving a chance for a compromise, as they are quite sure to ask for more than twenty-five millions.

It occurs to me that it might be an advantage if in their counter proposition they set forth a necessity for the money for internal improvements, like the deepening or [of] harbors, the building of railroads, and the development of the country. While theoretically we would not have an interest in the use of the money, still as a practical matter we are interested in the development of Colombia and would profit indirectly by a system of internal improvements which would bring more of their land under cultivation. I think they have in mind a railroad running from Bogotá to the Pacific coast which would very much shorten the distance from the water to the Capital and also the distance to the large territory lying east of the capital,—a territory which they desire to colonize.

As soon as you have had time to revolve this subject in your mind, I would like to have instructions as to the course of procedure.

With assurances of respect, etc., I am, my dear Mr. President,
Very sincerely yours,   W. J. Bryan

TLS (WP, DLC).

¹ Thaddeus Austin Thomson, formerly in the real estate business in Austin, Tex.; named Minister to Colombia, June 2, 1913.

² Colombia's "dispute" with the United States stemmed from the Roosevelt administration's support of the so-called revolution of 1903, which separated the province of Panama from Colombia and established it as an independent nation. The central question was that of a monetary payment to Colombia in compensation for the event. For earlier diplomatic efforts to settle the dispute, see E. Taylor Parks, *Colombia and the United States, 1765-1934* (Durham, N. C., 1935), pp. 427-39.

³ Julio Betancourt.

⁴ James Taylor DuBois, Minister to Colombia, 1911-13.

From Ellen Axson Wilson

My own darling,   Cornish, New Hampshire Aug. 20, 1913.

We have had a very interesting and full day. It was "Old Home Day" at the Cornish Centre church,—a sort of grand picnic, with exercises in the afternoon, and we all went to the 12 o'clock dinner carrying a big lot of food ourselves. It was quite amusing; and fortunately we *had* to come away just after dinner because I had another engagement viz. a luncheon party with Miss Slade at 1.30. Of course that was the extreme other end of the Cornish social scale; the most beautiful and elaborate house and garden here. The luncheon was the very perfection of elegance. Afterwards we went into the garden and there, sitting around the fountain, Miss Arnold sang to us deliciously. The whole thing was ideal. We did not get away until four o'clock. The weather is perfection again—a splendid blue day, such as we have not had since we were on our trip. It is too bad that I am never free to paint when those rare days come. I began a picture, weeks ago, on such a day, and have never touched it since. After the luncheon I went to pose for Mr. Vonnoh, I think for the last time. My picture is really very nice in the general effect of it. The other two are almost finished.

Tomorrow afternoon I have a tea from 4.30 to 5.30;—and at 6.30 I take the train for *Washington*! Haha! what is my lord going to do about it? Nothing!—except perhaps meet me at the train. When he gets this it will be too late to say me nay.

I telegraphed Dr. Grayson this morning to make absolutely sure that you were not coming here this week, but of course I knew you could not! His answer came tonight. He says he thinks "it will be fine for me to come at this time[.]" I told him, of course, not to tell you. We reach there about 2 P.M. Murphy is coming with me. Oh, I am so glad to be going! Something tight about my heart seems to have loosened with the decision. Honestly, dear,

I could not have stood it any longer,—especially with things apparently going so badly. I got your letter tonight telling about Huerta's attitude. Of course it is a relief that he is not behaving quite as badly as was reported. Now tonight is a fresh shock. "The World" reports that Owen has "killed the currency bill"![1] Killed the bill that was named for him. Is it false, or has he gone mad? You may imagine how dazed and heartsick I am about *that*.

But anyhow I am going to see my darling, *my darling*, and if he is troubled share his anxieties. Do you think it will help and comfort you a little to see me? Ah, my dear one,—I wonder if you know how tremendously I love you. I don't know if I can sleep tonight because I am to see you! At any rate it [is] time for me to stop and see if I can. In every heart-throb,

Your own   Eileen.

ALS (WC, NjP).

  [1] This news story in the New York *World*, Aug. 20, 1913, stated that Senator Owen, in a meeting of the Democratic members of the Senate Committee on Banking and Currency, had declared himself opposed to the regional reserve bank system on the grounds that it was both unfair and unworkable. This meant sure defeat for the administration's bill, the report concluded. However, a story in the *World* on the following day reported that Owen, after a long conference with Wilson at the White House, had stated that he would support the Federal Reserve bill, including the regional reserve bank plan, "if nothing better developed."

William Bayard Hale to William Jennings Bryan

Mexico City, Undated, Rec'd August 20, 1913.

Governor Lind has courteously given me his confidence and I am able to testify to the extreme tact with which he has performed his mission. His personality made the happiest impression and no one could have succeeded where he has inevitably failed.

The fact is Huerta does not believe that the United States is in earnest. He has been told that the Mexican question is a mere matter of party politics in the United States. He has no conception whatever of the moral earnestness of our people and little conception of our physical power. Minister Gamboa, with whom Lind dealt is a respectable gentleman just returned from abroad and not at all in Huerta's confidence. Minister Urrutia, Huerta's nearest confidant last night indulged in a tirade against the United States which the press reports will dare only to hint at. Urrutia talked about an ultimatum and war. Huerta himself suave to Lind talks to his friends of marching the army to St. Louis without opposition.

After three months spent in studying this people and canvassing the situation I again submit the opinion that there will be no yielding to your suggestions until it has been borne in on Huerta that the United States is resolutely determined and fully prepared to enforce them but that when that is clearly understood the actual employment of physical force will probably be unnecessary. Mr. Lind exhausted the possibilities of politeness. I suggest an object lesson of a different character   Hale.

T telegram (WP, DLC).

John Lind to William Jennings Bryan

Mexico, August 20, 1913

I took liberty to anticipate expression of sympathy, it was published this morning. Have just returned from extended conference with Gamboa in which he repeated former arguments in behalf of recognition. He cited our action in the case of Panama[1] which he had purposely refrained from referring to in his note so as to give no cause for the slightest irritation. I declined to either defend or discuss our Government's action in that instance but I suggested that it had no bearing on the present situation which is in a case by itself by itself [sic] in this that the Embassy of the United States unfortunately had become a quasi party to an agreement which resulted in the present de facto Government,[2] that while our Government had not recognized or confirmed our Ambassador's participation in the formulation of that agreement nevertheless so far as that agreement from [forms] the basis of the de facto Government of Mexico we had the right to insist that General Huerta who availed himself of some of the terms of that agreement must comply with all its terms.[3] I urged these considerations only in reply the argument of precedent. That the vital principle in the attitude of our Government is that it will not recognize a de facto Government which assumes power by the means and under the circumstances of the present case. I gave him to understand that on this point my instructions were conclusive and final, that as to the other points specified by the President they were in a measure means to an end and if a better way to accomplish the object sought in any particular were suggested the suggestion would be considered in the broad spirit of the President's entire attitude on the whole question. He explained his own difficulties and embarrassments, the attitude of his colleagues and the almost total hopelessness of making them appreciate our view point. At the conclusion I asked him whether he had anything to suggest differing from note now that his formal record was made. He answered that with regrets he had not. I then asked him whether or not he desired me to report that answer. His reply was most positive that he did not. He then took up the question of the shipment of arms which has been under discussion with Mr. O'Shaughnessy and wanted to know my views whether it was right to complain of inability to pacify and also deny the means. I said I had had no correspondence on the subject but that I assumed that if there had been a change of policy in that respect such change was probably dictated by prudential considerations as to the government's own necessities. He could not conceive of such possibility and subject was dropped. My report of yesterday still expresses my views.   Lind.

T telegram (WP, DLC).
  1 The precipitate American recognition of the Republic of Panama in 1903.
  2 The *Pacto de la Ciudadela* of February 17, 1913, between Huerta and Felix Díaz.
  3 That is, that by accepting the provisional presidency under the terms of the *Pacto de la Ciudadela*, Huerta was explicitly barred from running for the presidency by the provisions of the Mexican Constitution.

To Oswald Garrison Villard

My dear Villard: The White House August 21, 1913

It would be hard to make any one understand the delicacy and difficulty of the situation I find existing here with regard to the colored people. You know my own disposition in the matter, I am sure, but I find myself absolutely blocked by the sentiment of Senators; not alone Senators from the South, by any means, but Senators from various parts of the country. I want to handle the matter with the greatest possible patience and tact, and am not without hope that I may succeed in certain directions. But just because the situation is extremely delicate and because I know the feeling of irritation that comes with every effort at systematic inquiry into conditions—because of the feeling that there is some sort of indictment involved in the very inquiry itself—I think that it would be a blunder on my part to consent to name the commission you speak of and which we discussed at our conference in Trenton. I never realized before the complexity and difficulty of this matter in respect of every step taken here. I not only hope but I pray that a better aspect may come upon it before many months.
                Cordially and faithfully yours,   Woodrow Wilson

TLS (O. G. Villard Papers, MH).

From Cleveland Hoadley Dodge

Dear Mr. President   New York. August 21st [1913]

How I wish I could help you carry some of your burdens.

The Mexican business is very trying but the great bulk of the American people are with you.

The enclosed[1] may amuse you. There is much truth in it, though the mine owner is not the only sinner

I see by the paper this morning that the tax assessors at Princeton have decided to tax the new Graduate School buildings, on the ground that they are not devoted to educational uses[2]

Have just come back from a bully little cruise. We raced "Corona" around Cape Cod for a $500.00 cup, for Schooners built prior to 1900, given by Robert Tod, who was not considered by Jimmie McCosh "fit for my College."[3] We raced in a half gale & the old boat won hands down

With heartfelt wishes

    Á Dios   Yours affectionately   C. H. Dodge

ALS (WP, DLC).
    [1] This enclosure is missing.
    [2] The item appeared originally in the *Princeton Press*, Aug. 16, 1913. The New Jersey State Board of Equalization of Taxes had instructed the Princeton Borough assessor to include the Graduate College among the ratables for the reason stated by Dodge.
    [3] About this affair, see W. Merle-Smith to WW, Nov. 30, 1909, n. 3, Vol. 19.

From Moorfield Storey

My dear Sir   Boston. August 21. 1913

I hope you will permit me to express the very great satisfaction with which I heard that you have appointed a Governor General of the Philippine Islands, who believes in Philippine Independence, in the person of Mr. Francis Burton Harrison. It has seemed to me extremely important that the government of the islands should be placed in the hands of men who believe in the policy of the Democratic party as declared in its national platforms, and I am very glad that you have been able to fill the principal office so satisfactorily. I appreciate the difficulty you have had in finding the proper man, and I hope you will be able to provide Mr Harrison with as suitable associates.

With this let me say also how much the manner in which the Mexican question has been dealt with has been admired by the persons in this neighborhood, whose opinions you would value.

With high respect   Sincerely yrs   Moorfield Storey

ALS (WP, DLC).

John Lind to William Jennings Bryan

Mexico City, Aug. 21, 1913.

This morning Mr. Gamboa came to the Embassy and requested me to inquire whether the President would view with favor his coming to Washington to discuss with him and with you the propositions suggested in the President's note. He assured me that he would come with ample power. He is very sanguine that by a personal interview he could convince you and the President that the President's position should be modified. He understands perfectly that he could only be received as a Mexican citizen authorized by the de facto Government to hold unofficial communications. I believe that the proposition is made in good faith. Whether he would continue to hold the power he may start with is beyond prediction. I believe Captain Burnside is an accurate observer. His judgment as to military situation should be regarded in the consideration of that aspect. There is a rumor today that the Huerta Government has succeeded in raising a substantial amount of funds. Personally I doubt this. The whole situation financial, military and political is liable to become very acute early in September.

If invited Gamboa would probably reach Washington August thirty-first. I have at no time suggested the trip but I am sure that it is not intended to slight me personally. That it will gain the Mexican Government time is evident whether or not that is to our prejudice I have no judgment. I adhere to all the suggestions in my last two reports. If important instructions should arrive before this is answered I will exercise my judgment whether to defer action.   Lind.

T telegram (SDR, RG 59, 812.00/10642, DNA).

To William Hughes

My dear Hughes: [The White House] August 22, 1913

I am very much concerned, as I am sure you are, to see the committee that has charge of it, get the bill for the relief of the seamen[1] ready for consideration at an early period in the regular session. I understand that the committee is practically doing nothing about it, and I thought I would ask you if you would not be kind enough to find out from Senator Clark[2] just what the disposition of the committee is.

It is delightful to have you to turn to.

Faithfully yours,   Woodrow Wilson

TLS (Letterpress Books, WP, DLC).

¹ Wilson's letter to Hughes was probably inspired by the latest maritime accident, the sinking of the coastal steamer, *State of California*, in Alaskan waters on August 17, with the loss of forty of the passengers and crew. Furuseth quickly charged that the loss of life was at least partly due to a lack of qualified seamen available to launch life boats. See the *New York Times*, Aug. 19 and 20, 1913.
² James Paul Clarke of Arkansas, chairman of the Senate Committee on Commerce.

From William Jennings Bryan, with Enclosures

My Dear Mr. President: [Washington] August 22, 1913.

I enclose a copy of dispatch for Lind's personal information. Am preparing instructions, and hope to have draft ready for your criticism before noon. The enclosed dispatch from Lind is amusing as to the British Ambassador and encouraging as to the general situation.

With assurances of respect, etc., I am, my dear Mr. President,

W. J. Bryan

TLS (WP, DLC).

ENCLOSURE   I

[Washington] August 22, 1913

I am sending you instructions in another dispatch which will follow immediately. They are sent subject to your approval. The conditional acceptance of Gamboa's proposal is not to be communicated unless you consider it wise to do so. The President appreciates most cordially the ability, tact and firmness with which you have conducted the negotiations, and regards it as a substantial victory if you have brought about a reconsideration.

Bryan[1]

T telegram (WP, DLC).

¹ This telegram (SDR, RG 59, 812.00/10642A, DNA) was sent on Aug. 22, 1913.

ENCLOSURE   II

Mexico City Aug. 20 [1913]

Since my report this morning the British Minister has called. He wished to tell me that Huerta was very agreeably impressed and pleased over my call etc. He called my attention to an item in the Herald[1] this morning saying that it was proposed in Congress to afford the rebels opportunity to obtain munitions of war. He deemed this a horrible proposition and hoped there could be no foundation for it. I said it was hardly worthwhile to discuss the question abstractly, that the U. S. were confronted with a condition that demanded action, that if the question was relegated into the hands of Congress there was no predicting what might occur, and finally that there was a strong sentiment in Congress and out in favor of just that course. He then said that I might suggest not quoting him that a *words* of agreement might be arranged without recognition if the U. S. would say for instance to our own bankers that the govt would regard a loan negotiated by Huerta govt in the same light as loans negotiated by Diaz and Madero. He said it was important that the govt be able to raise money. To this I assented. The old gentleman is tolerable only as a conduit for conveying Huerta's reflections. The money situation is probably nearing a crisis. There is a reported shortage of funds even for the payment of soldiers.

Lind.

Hw telegram (WP, DLC).
    1 The *Mexican Herald* of Mexico City.

From William Jennings Bryan, with Enclosure

My Dear Mr. President: Washington August 22, 1913.

I enclose a draft of a dispatch to Mr. Lind[1] setting forth your views as nearly as I am able to reproduce them. Upon the advice of Mr. Moore I cut out two or three phrases from the pencil draft. He thought it was not wise to specifically declare that recognition of Huerta would not be considered. He thought it more diplomatic to say, in the language of the dispatch submitted for your criticism, "with the understanding that the attitude of this Government on the subject of recognition is unchanged." He also thought it best not to state that Huerta must consent specifically to the condition that he will not be a candidate at this election. He thinks that is sufficiently covered by an announcement that he is willing to take your proposals as a basis for discussion. At these two points the dispatch is a little milder but not weaker than the outline which we discussed together. If you will indicate any changes, additions or subtractions I will have them made at once, and send the dispatch as soon as it can be put into cipher.

The enclosed dispatch just received from Hale throws additional light on the situation.

With assurances of respect, etc., I am, my dear Mr. President,
Yours truly   W. J. Bryan

TLS (WP, DLC).
    1 The draft is missing. Wilson's note, which was sent, is printed following the enclosure.

ENCLOSURE

Mexico City. Undated. Recd Aug. 22, 1913.

Governor Lind asks me to send the following. He was visited today by ten American missionaries, seven of whom expressed themselves against recognition of Huerta. Later four native Protestant ministers called protesting against recognition. Three believed that granting belligerent right to rebels would solve all difficulties. All four disliked the idea of intervention.

Hale

T telegram (WP, DLC).

To John Lind

Washington, August 22, 1913.

The President has received your despatch communicating Senor Gamboa's inquiry, and assumes that General Huerta has reconsidered his rejection of the President's proposals, and is willing to take those proposals as a basis of discussion. If this assumption is correct it is gratifying evidence of his readiness to treat the President's proffer of friendly offices in the spirit in which that proffer was made, and of his desire for the President's cooperation in the restoration of order. You may therefore say to Senor Gamboa that upon receiving notice to the effect that the reply to the President's proposals recently transmitted to us is withdrawn, and with the understanding that this Government's attitude on the subject of recognition is unchanged, the President will be pleased to confer with Senor Gamboa in Washington unofficially and informally, but as the personal representative of General Huerta with a view to the restoration of permanent peace.

The President has prepared a message to Congress embodying his recommendations accompanied by copies of his proposals and the reply already received thereto. He expected to deliver this next Monday, but in view of Senor Gamboa's request for further time for consideration, and because of his deep desire to assist in every friendly way our sister republic, he is willing, if he receives immediate notice of the withdrawal of the former reply, to await before proceeding any further your advice after communicating this despatch to General Huerta and Senor Gamboa.

Bryan

CLST telegram (SDR, RG 59, 812.00/10642, DNA).

John Lind to William Jennings Bryan

Mexico, August 22, 1913.
Your two cables received.[1]   Rec'd Aug. 23, 9 a.m.

Present indications are that Gamboa's trip will be abandoned. I feel it unwise for him to leave and I think he is of the same opinion. This morning's press reports of the action in the Senate[2] and the intended message to be delivered has caused the state of feeling here that I anticipated. Whether it has moved Huerta I cannot say but some of his nearest friends are exceedingly solicitous that I should urge upon the President to refrain from delivering his message and to urge utmost endeavors to delay action by Congress in the hope that a satisfactory adjustment may be arrived at. I insisted as a condition precedent to any action on my part that Huerta forthwith agree to the following: First. That the election called for October twenty-sixth shall be held in accordance with the Constitution and laws of Mexico; second that General Huerta either publicly or in some other manner satisfactory to the President and to myself give the assurances called for in Paragraph "C" of the proposal.

I also said that if Huerta concedes these two propositions which are the official ones that he can act on alone then I will urge upon the President to continue to exercise his good offices to prevent precipitate action in Congress and to delay the delivery of the contemplated message for such time as he may deem consistent with his duty to the American people and that the remaining propositions shall be taken up later and resolved as circumstances permit and in the spirit of their proposal.

The need for funds is pressing and will shortly be imperative. In the absence of recognition it is assumed that no loan can be negotiated. To relieve this embarrassment I suggested that if the above be accepted I would request him to give American bankers and their associates assurances in such form as may to him seem proper that the American Government will look with favor upon a loan sufficient in amount to meet the temporary requirements of the de facto Government.

Mr. Gamboa, for reasons that would appeal to you if you knew the situation as I view it, did not deem it prudent for him to make this final proposal to Huerta. It seemed to us best that it should be made by the British Minister Mr. Strong. I have spent much of the day with Mr. Strong. He is willing to take this proposition to Huerta and promised to do so some hours ago. He just informs me however that on reflection he does not feel justified in doing so without the approval of his Government and he is now cabling for its permission. Personally I felt so clear on this proposition that I should have taken this action [before] submitting it to the President fearing unfavorable consequences from delay but now I submit my views for approval or rejection. I declined to make any statement in writing but Mr. Strong made a memorandum of our conversation which corresponds with this report thereon. Since writing the above mentioned I have communicated with Gamboa. He begged me to express his sincere appreciation of the President's cordial consideration of his request. I think it wholly inexpedient to insist on the withdrawal of note as a condition precedent to the consideration by Huerta of the proposition I have outlined.

I sincerely appreciate your expression of confidence and wish to say that if I succeed in any degree it will largely be due to the cordial and efficient cooperation of Mr. O'Shaughnessy and the whole Embassy staff. Lind.

T telegram (WP, DLC).
1 W. J. Bryan to J. Lind, just printed, and W. J. Bryan to J. Lind, Aug. 21, 1913, T telegram (SDR, RG 59, 812.00/10642), saying: "Your Aug 21 3 P.M. was deciphered about eleven tonight, will confer with President early tomorrow morning and answer as soon as possible thereafter."
2 Senator Penrose, on August 21, introduced a resolution requesting the President "to take such steps as are necessary to place a sufficient number of troops, as a constabulary, in the Republic of Mexico wherever and at such points as in his opinion they may be needed properly to police and to protect American citizens and their property." Penrose also introduced an amendment to a deficiency appropriation bill then pending to provide $25,000,000 to be used for this purpose by the President at his discretion and to be available until July 1, 1914. Penrose's resolution and amendment were ordered to be laid upon the table and were never acted upon. *Cong. Record*, 63d Cong., 1st sess., pp. 3567-71.

Alfred B. Cosey to Joseph Patrick Tumulty

Dear Sir: Newark, N. J. August 22, 1913.

Yours of recent date received. Replying thereto, beg to state, that a large number of colored citizens in various states of the Union, for the past three months, have urged me to call the President's attention, through you, to the condition of the colored democrats, and the urging need of a loyal negro democratic association, to offset the unwarranted damaging attacts, upon the President, and our national administration, by the Regular and Progressive Republicans; and the old line, and disgruntled Democrats, of both races.

I hesitated, until convinced that further delay would endanger our cause in New York and New Jersey, at the election in November. Whatever I may say, can be VERIFIED at any time; as the imformation was received from the most authentic sorce, supported by positive proof.

The attitude of some of the Negro candidates for office under our national administration, and their followers, completely distroyed, the usefulness of the National Colored Democratic League; thus leaving us without a national association, or leadership with sufficient courage and loyalty, to issue a statement setting clearly before the whole people, the President's high regard for the colored race, and his disaproval of opression in any form. I have been requested as above stated, to call a national gathering, and organize a Progressive National Negro Democratic Association, that can be relied upon to support the President. THIS IS IMPERATIVE, as we are lossing the colored vote in every state. You know as well as I, we certainly cannot afford to lose this vote, if we expect to renominate, and re-elect, President Wilson for another term; or to elect a democratic Congress, next fall, or the Governor of our state, or our Mayor of New York this fall.

Careful investigati[o]n disclosed the following as the chief grounds of complaint by the Colored Democrats.

1— The appointing to important offices at Washington, D. C. and other places, formally held by negroes, men of other races.

2— The disparaging statements of Senator Vardman, concerning the negroes, as reported by the papers.

3— The alleged separation of the races, in the Government Department at Washington, D. C.

4— The retention of NEGRO REPUBLICANS in important offices at Washington, D. C. and other places. This they construed as a reflection on the ability of the negro democrats to perform the duties of the office.

5— The omission of the President, to appoint negro democrats to office in Washington D. C. and other places before now, whether the Senate confirmed them or not.

6— The administrations southern policy towards the Negroes.

7— The administrati[o]ns seeming indifference as to the political welfare of the Negro Democrats; and its apparent readiness to disregard his sacrifices, past support, and future value, and its willingness to combine with his enemies, the REPUBLICANS, and some Southern Senators, to embarris, and disappoint him, in his political ambitions, upon untrue statements, and prejudice.

AS TO COMPLAINTS.

No. 1— Refers to the places held by the negro republicans, at Washington, D. C. and the Haytain Mission.

No. 2— Refers to the reported statements of Senator Vardman, at the time of Patterson's appointment.

No. 3— Refers specially to the alleged separation of employes in the Treasury Department.

No. 4— Refers to the retention of H. L. Johnson, as Recorder of Deeds of the District of Columbia and C. W. Anderson in the department of Rev[e]nue at New York.

It is urged against Mr. Johnson among other things, that he stumped the state of New Jersey against President Wilson, and used vile language against him, among which was, that President Wilson's election ment a return of negroes to slavery, and sanction of linching, he referred to a picture used by the republicans in a paper, during the campaign of President Wilson for Governor of New Jersey, with negroes hanging to a tree. He is during [doing] all he can, in an underhand way, with Mr Napier, who resigned as Register of the Treasury, to embarris President Wilson's administration, and get campaign literature, for the coming fall elections in New York and New Jersey, and future elections, including the next national election.

It is said that Mr. Anderson stumped against President Wilson, and since the election, used unbecoming language, about the President. It is further said that, certain independent democrats in New York are in a deal with him to try and get the colored vote for Mayor, for retaining him in office. A large number of colored republicans and progressives bitterly oppose this. They say they are afraid to trust a democrat, such as Mr. Mitchel, and would rather vote for a man, such as Mayor Gaynor, who has shown his respect for them in New York, than to take a chance on a Wilson Mayor.

If the negro democrats desert Mr. Mitchel, his chances are slim for election. I am now speaking from investigation on this subject, in New York, Kings, and Queens County. I am connected with a number of associations in New York, and there every week, and had the pleasure of being chairman of the committee of Equity Congress in New York, at which place Mr. Mitchel sopke [spoke] on Wednesday night last. I send you herewith the circular.

No. 5— EXPLAINS ITSELF.

No. 6— Refers to the appointment of Postmaskers and internal revinue collectors in the south.

No. 7— The negro democrats particularly disappointed office seekers, are telling of their sacrifices, and regreting being disappointed. Many believe republicans filed untrue charged against them, for no other reason than to humiliate them, knowing them to be untrue.

Something must be done to clarify the situation. I am willing to undertake the task with the President or your approval. Our State Association is in good working order, and ready for the battle. We will do our part for our cause.

Kindly let me hear from you on all points at an early date, together with any advice you may have.

Sincerely yours,   Alfred B Cosey

TLS (WP, DLC).

A Memorandum by John Bassett Moore

CONFIDENTIAL.

For the Secretary: [Washington] August 22, 1913.

Referring to the conference between the President and yourself on the 18th instant, at which I had the honor to be present by request, I beg leave with all deference hereby to state in writing my opinion on the present situation, the expression of which I deferred till I had had an opportunity to read Governor Lind's dispatch[1] and thus to gain more definite information as to the nature and objects of his mission.

In a memorandum of the 14th of May last, the correctness of whose reasonings and forecasts has, as I think, been confirmed by events, I advised the recognition of the Government at the City of Mexico in a particular manner and for definite ends, the attainment of which I then believed and still believe to be of high importance to the people of the United States. The step which I then recommended would, in my opinion, be the appropriate step to take today, but for certain intervening incidents which it is beyond my province to discuss.

In considering the present situation, I proceed from certain fundamental principles, which may be shortly summarized.

1. The paramount duty of a Government is to its own citizens, at home and abroad.

2. In the conduct of diplomatic relations, the fact should be accepted, as an elementary guide, that we are dealing with peoples who are not subject to our authority and control.

3. Interposition in the domestic affairs of other nations, even for what may seem to be a laudable purpose, is always a delicate matter, and, as it invites rebuff, arouses resentment and tends to defeat its professed ends, never can be admitted as a sound rule of action. Governments, like individuals, being liable to error in their own affairs, may properly practice a prudent reserve as to their inerrancy regarding the merits of political action in foreign countries.

Bearing in mind these fundamental principles, we may lay down with regard to the special situation in Mexico the following propositions:

1. The history of Mexico and the character of its population clearly indicate that the prime requisite in the management of its affairs is the maintenance of order. This essential condition was first attained under the stern rule of Diaz, under whose administration the country made its first real progress.

2. The forces of the present revolution, which, although it covers extensive portions of territory, represents a decidedly minor part of the population, are not coherent and embrace a large bandit element, under leaders such as Zapata and Urbina, whose conceptions are well illustrated by the savage conduct of the latter in the capture and pillage of Durango.

3. Any proposal that the ban on the shipment of arms and ammunition to the revolutionists be lifted, coupled with the admission that the revolutionists cannot be expected to do more than hold their own territory, necessarily assumes the form of a proposal that we shall do what we can to promote the dismemberment of the country. From a legal point of view such a proposal need not be discussed: into the discussion of its merits from any other point of view I am not called upon to enter.

4. If the Northern States of Mexico now in revolt should be able to maintain themselves against the Federal Government, the question of the maintenance of public order would still exist. There is credible information that in Chihuahua there have been at least six independent bands, operating in the name of the revolution, who recognize no allegiance to any authority. There have been and perhaps still are five similar bands in Coahuila. In Durango the number has been much greater. Between these bands there is no coherence. Their forces are mostly hordes of marauders depredating upon property and extorting money, and their leaders except in the case of persons such as Chao and Carranza, have no conceptions of government or of public order.

5. While the Joint Resolution of March 14, 1912, goes beyond what international law requires, its adoption and enforcement have placed this Government in an attitude which cannot be reversed without creating certain unmistakable implications.

By this Act it is made unlawful to export arms and munitions of war to any American country, (except under such limitations and exceptions as the President may prescribe) where the President has by proclamation declared that there exist in such country "conditions of domestic violence" which "are promoted by the use of arms or munitions of war procured from the United States."

On the day on which this Act was passed, namely, March 14, 1912, the President of the United States issued a proclamation declaring that the conditions indicated existed in Mexico, and since that time, under the regulations then adopted, the export of arms and munitions of war from the United States to Mexico, except to the Government at the City of Mexico, has been unlawful.

The lifting now of the ban on the shipment of arms and munitions of war to the revolutionists would in these circumstances constitute, in effect if not in form, a recognition of their belligerency. Besides, it would be equivalent to a declaration that both sides equally represent the cause of public order and that public order would be promoted by contributing to the means of their carrying on hostilities with each other.

6. It is admitted in the dispatch of Governor Lind that the present Government of Mexico has, even under the disability resulting from nonrecognition by the United States, made progress towards the pacification of the country, and this fact is evident from other sources. The reversal of our attitude as to the export of arms and munitions of war to the revolutionists would therefore, besides requiring us to treat their various leaders as lawful de facto authorities, also be tantamount to an avowal of sympathy with them and would manifest a readiness to sacrifice the peace and order of a neighboring country to that sentiment. If we are to be guided by a consideration for our own past, we should recall the fact that, during the four years of bloody war in which the Government of the Union asserted its authority by force over the seceding States, which it eventually conquered, it repeatedly declared that acts of sympathy towards the Confederate States, even though they were not accompanied with material aid to those States, constituted an unwarranted intervention in our affairs and were accordingly and justly to be resented. The Government of the United States, in promoting in any way the dismemberment of an American country, would assume an attitude which the precedents of our own civil war would render embarrassing. It is further to be recalled that, for more than ten years after our civil war, the States of the South, forcibly coerced into submission to the national authority, endured what were to them great humiliations.

7. Regarding the interests of our own citizens in Mexico, it is to be borne in mind that the effect of measures on our part to defeat the progress of pacification and to add to the means and activities of hostile operations, would be to increase the dangers of their situation and the hazards to life and property growing

out of civil strife. It would place arms in the hands of marauders, whose bands are numerous and whose numbers are large, as well as in those of patriots.

8. It is further to be borne in mind that along our border there are important points which are now in the possession of the Federal forces. Any act on our part which would have the effect of encouraging and aiding the revolutionists would therefore necessarily lead to the spread of hostile operations on the frontier and, by exposing life and property on our own as well as on the Mexican side of the line to injury, would greatly augment the chances of hostilities between the United States and Mexico.

9. The policy of bringing all our citizens out of Mexico and then leaving the country to settle its own differences has never seemed to me to be practicable, but has on the contrary always seemed to carry with it certain necessary consequences. One of these is that the American people would not indefinitely stand by and witness the continuance of disorder in Mexico. Another is that such a policy on our part would lead other governments to feel that they should be permitted to do such things as might seem to them to be necessary for the protection of their own interests. Yet another consequence would be that difficulties would attend the actual removal of Americans from Mexico. It might not be safe for those at a particular place to be removed at a particular time. If we should endeavor to correct this condition by sending in our own forces, this would necessarily involve the invasion of Mexican territory; and such a step would inevitably increase the danger to which our citizens were exposed by inflaming native hostility towards them.

10. In view of these considerations, if a change in our present attitude should be deemed to be necessary, the least injurious course would seem to be to forbid all shipments of arms and munitions of war to Mexico. In refusing to recognize the Federal Government as the representative of public order, it would hardly be congruous to ascribe a representative character of that kind to the revolutionary bands, whose operations must in any event be suppressed by force.

Moreover, in view of the always existing possibility of serious trouble between the United States and Mexico, so long as the domestic troubles in the latter country continue, it would not appear to be good policy to increase the shipment of arms and munitions of war which may eventually be used against ourselves.

T MS (WP, DLC).

1 J. Lind to WJB, Aug. 17, 1913 10 P.M., already cited.

Two Letters from William Jennings Bryan

My dear Mr. President: Washington August 23, 1913.

The Nicaragua people are awaiting a final decision in the matter of the loan. I suggest the form of a letter[1] which should, in my judgment, be sent to both parties and made a matter of record here in case the loan does go through. I send this in advance so that we may be able to act promptly when they are ready for action. Please let me know whether you have any changes to suggest.

With assurances of respect, etc., I am, my dear Mr. President,
Very sincerely yours,   W. J. Bryan

TLS (WP, DLC).
  [1] The Editors have been unable to find this enclosure.

My Dear Mr President,   [Washington Aug. 23, 1913]

Referring to Linds offer to advise you to favor a loan I beg to call your attention to Mr Linds note of 22. In that he says that "the need for funds is pressing and will shortly be imperative." Some government is necessary—without it elections could not be held. If Huerta would agree to the elections & bind himself not to be a candidate I think you would be justified in looking with favor upon a loan sufficient to meet "the temporary requirements" of the de facto gov't. The end to be gained thereby was sufficient to justify this—without this he would not be able to do his part toward securing a constitutional president. The offer must be taken in connection with an acceptance of the proposal—it depended on that. I do not think that any one could justly complain & only radical friends of Carranza would & they ought not to. I am awaiting the morning messages—one partly translated indicates that nothing has been done by Huerta. With assurances etc I am my dear Mr President
Yours truly   W. J. Bryan

ALS (WP, DLC).

To Mary Allen Hulbert

Dearest Friend,   The White House 24 August, 1913.

Your illness has filled me with the deepest anxiety and distress. You know so well how to make light of anything that affects yourself, and how to lead my thoughts away from it by all sorts of reassurances, that I fear I do not yet know just how serious your condition was or how far you have come out of danger. But I shall take heart and believe, from the mere fact that the nurse is about to leave you, if from nothing else, that you are really getting well. Pray, *pray* be careful. Your first note about the illness touched me to the quick, where you speak of the fear you had that you might go away without good-byes said! A pang went to my heart that made me realize just what it would have meant to me. So you must not! You must take care of yourself for Allen's sake, and for ours, if not for your own. Your friend in Washington is carrying a great burden just now, and cannot afford to part with any portion of the strength and happiness he gets from the affection and sympathy and loyal faith of his closest friends, who understand, who know what is true and what is false of what they read about him in the papers, and who send him messages of the sort that keep his courage alive and his heart quick with life. Is that a selfish view to take of it? How better could I speak my own affection? How better could I say what your friendship and the consciousness of your sympathy mean to me, from day to day, in the midst of distracting tasks as well as when I can invite my soul to a little pleasure and vacation from strain? Let me know again, please, by your own or some other hand, how you fare,—whether your improvement continues and your strength is confirmed. I shall be anxious until I hear again in confirmation of what you are thoughtful enough to tell me in the little note received to-day.

How I should like to refresh you, and myself, by talking over with you the news of the day. It is not all serious. It has its amusing and gossipy side, and it would not be altogether dull to rehearse it in detail. In much of it our contemporaries are certainly to be seen in their actual habit as they live, without concealment most when they deem their motives most covered and best Dressed. Our friend Huerta is a diverting brute! He is always so perfectly in character: so false, so sly, so full of bravado (the bravado of ignorance, chiefly), and yet so courageous, too, and determined,—such a mixture of weak and strong, of ridiculous and respectable! One moment you long for his blood, out of mere justice for what he has done, and the next you find yourself entertaining a sneaking admiration for his nerve. He will not let go till he pulls the whole house down with him. He loves only those who advise him to do what he wants to do. He has cold lead for those who tell him the truth. He is seldom sober and always impossible, and yet what an indomitable fighter for his own hand! Every day the news from Mexico City unsettles the news of the day before. The whole thing is quicksilver. I dare not finish my message to Congress intended for Tuesday till Tuesday's news comes, for fear the things I say in it might turn out to be untrue in fact! Any hour of the day or night I may have to revise my judgment as to what it is best to do. Do you wonder that I have lost flesh a bit?

And yet, to speak truth, I am quite well. I rejoice to find myself a very tough customer. I do not see how anybody not tough in every fibre, both physical and mental, could ever survive the presidency of the United States, if he took the duties of the office seriously and really tried to discharge them as they ought to be discharged.

I am having a little (most unexpected) holiday to-day. Mrs. Wilson and Nellie, most unexpectedly and without permission, ran away from Cornish on Thursday and came down to see me. You may imagine how overjoyed I was to see them; and yet it makes me uneasy to have them here in this debilitating atmosphere (I refer to the literal atmosphere). It is beyond measure refreshing to see them and unbosom myself to them, after being pent up for the better part of a month for lack of such confidantes and yet I feel guilty about acquiescing in this sacrifice on their part. Not that they consider it such, bless their hearts.

We all unite in affectionate messages and in the joint adjuration and command to take care of yourself.

Love to Allen. I am so glad that he is with you and taking care of you!   Your devoted friend,   Woodrow Wilson

WWTLS (WP, DLC).

From William Jennings Bryan, with Enclosure

My Dear Mr President   [Washington, Aug. 24, 1913]

I enclose some important messages.[1] Lind is evidently waiting for approval of plan submitted by him yesterday Should not an answer be sent today. I shall remain at the Dept until I hear from you. With assurances etc

Yours truly   W. J. Bryan

ALS (WP, DLC).
[1] The other enclosures were W. B. Hale to the State Department, n.d., received Aug. 24, 1913, 9:30 A.M., and W. B. Hale to the Secretary of State, n.d., received Aug. 24, 1913, 11:55 A.M., T telegrams (WP, DLC).

ENCLOSURE

Mexico City, Aug. 23, 1913,
Rec'd Aug. 24, 9:35 a.m.

CONFIDENTIAL. FOR THE SECRETARY OF STATE.

No developments today. Another congressman reported executed. The financial situation is daily growing worse. Huerta is entertaining the German representative tonight. If the President should approve the course outlined in yesterday's despatch and if the British Minister is authorized to present the views suggested to Huerta and if they are presented, say tomorrow or Monday morning, then I would suggest the following program for consideration:

One. I would request Consul Canada[1] to come to Mexico City on Monday.

Two. On Tuesday if no answer had been received from Huerta, I would call on Gamboa and quietly bid him good bye saying that I wanted to spend a few days at Vera Cruz before sailing.

Three. I would take the train for Vera Cruz either on Tuesday or Wednesday according to circumstances and remain there until the President's message and the accompanying incidents had been afforded time to percolate Huerta.

Four. At Vera Cruz I would be within easy reach and Gamboa might call on me if Huerta had anything further to communicate. I suggest this course because I believe it dignified and also because I have become satisfied that silence and action at the opportune time are the most effective arguments that we can use. Let the ultimatum be action not words. They discount words. Unless Huerta accepts and receives the good offices of the United States speedily there will be a crisis. It may not be avoidable if he accepts and if positive action by the United States should become imperative it must be speedy and efficient. It would not be a big task at least in its early aspect. I have discussed this with Hale and O'Shaughnessy and they concur.

What do you direct?   Lind

T telegram (WP, DLC).
1 William Wesley Canada, American consul at Veracruz.

To John Lind

Washington, Aug 24 3 pm

Your messages of yesterday and Friday received. President approves action proposed through British minister also programme suggested for yourself. He does not feel that he can delay his message to Congress later than Tuesday unless you can report decided change of attitude before Tuesday morning. We shall interpret decision of cabinet to publish proposals and reply as an indication that negotiations are for the present ended.

Bryan

WWT telegram (SDR, RG 59, 812.00/8526, DNA).

John Lind to William Jennings Bryan

Mexico City, Mexico, August 24 1913.

I have assurances from Gamboa that there will be no publication tomorrow. I have advised the British Minister that my conversation with him is confirmed. He has not heard from his Government. I wish to withdraw my inadvertent remark about Mr. Stronge and express as my deliberate judgment that he is not only well disposed personally but that he is a man of rare tact and good judgment and that he has rendered me great service in delicate situations. I will report again in the morning.

Lind

T telegram (WP, DLC).

To William Jennings Bryan

My dear Mr. Secretary: [The White House] August 25, 1913

Thank you for the enclosures which I return. I think the letter in the Nicaraguan matter is just what it should be. I approve of it entirely.

The other enclosure[1] certainly contains most significant information.

In haste, with warmest regard,

Faithfully yours,   Woodrow Wilson

TLS (Letterpress Books, WP, DLC).
[1] Probably J. Lind to WJB, Aug. 23, 1913.

To Cleveland Hoadley Dodge

My dear Cleve: [The White House] August 25, 1913

How delightful it was to get your letter. I thank you for it with all my heart. Your letters always cheer me.

Is it not a joke too good to be invented that the tax assessors at Princeton are to tax the new Graduate School buildings on the ground that they are not to be devoted to educational uses? Mrs. Wilson and I had seen the notice in the Princeton Press, and have chuckled over it, as you may imagine.

We rejoice in the victory of the beautiful Corona. We learned to love the yacht when we were on it, and she certainly is fine enough to win anything.

All unite in warmest regards. Mrs. Wilson and Nellie stole down from Cornish without my permission to spend Sunday with me and have made me very happy by their presence.

Always   Affectionately yours,   Woodrow Wilson

TLS (Letterpress Books, WP, DLC).

From William Frank Powell[1]

Mr. President: Camden, N. J. August 25th 1913.

I greatly regret that the statements made by you at an interview granted me prior to the Baltimore Convention at which time you became the candidate of the Democratic Party as its candidate for President. I request you to recall that interview.

I stated to you at the time that when you were candidate for Governor of this State, a number of colored citizens had cast their votes for you. We desired to know if you became the candidate for President and if elected to that office, what would be your attitude toward the colored citizens of this country. I further stated to you during the course of the interview that very many of this class of voters felt the time was propitious to divide their votes between the two great political parties of the country—the Progressive Party not being in existence at the time—so that we might feel that whatever political party might secure the direction of the National Government the civil and political rights of our people would not be endangered thereby, that as far as the emoluments of office was concerned it was a minor consideration inuring to the benefit only of the few. What we desired to secure, was to insure the civil and political rights of our people in traveling, in being accommodated in public places of entertainment which was inseperably connected with travelling, and to prevent the lynching of our people, all of which was so prevalent up to this time in the southern tier of States. You were also informed at that time that it had been held up to us that the Democratic Party was the natural political foe of our people, for a colored man to advocate the principles of that Party, he was looked upon by the members of his race as an apostate to his race and was ostracized for doing so, very many were willing to accept this stigma if in so doing a better relation would be brought about between the two races especially in the South.

You replied to these statements by stating you were very glad to learn that such was the feeling of the colored voters of this State toward yourself and towards the Democratic Party of which you were a member, that if this step had been taken years ago by my people the condition of the colored race in this country particularly in the South would have been vastly different from what it is now; that if I should become the nominee of the Democratic Party and I am elected to the office of President, while I may be unable to correct many of the conditions of your people in this country especially in the South that you complain of, I will use my best efforts to ameliorate such conditions and endeavor to secure a change that would be for the benefit of your people. You further stated to me that all the rights granted to my race under the Constitution and its Amendments would be rigidly enforced by yourself, that you desired the colored men of this country to know and to feel that you was and would be their friend. As to the public offices to be filled should you be elected it might be impossible you stated, for you to appoint colored men to some now held by them, that when this could not be done that there would be others that you would appoint them to which would be equally as honorable and as lucrative as those now held by them. You further stated you could not place your views or expressions in writing as it might be used by your political opponents to your detriment before the convention then soon to meet, but I could rest assured that if elected such would be your course and that I was at perfect liberty to make known your attitude as to your feelings towards the colored voters of this State and Country. . . .

Acting upon these statements made by you, organizations of colored men were established in every Northern and Western State. This fact may not be known to you, but it is well known to those who had charge of your campaign. Many of those who entered this field advocating your election refused to accept any compensation for their services, paying their traveling expenses and in some cases contributing toward your campaign fund. In that election you secured slightly above 30 per cent of this vote, Mr. Roosevelt the Progressive candidate about 40 per cent, the Republican candidate Mr. Taft the remainder.

You are no doubt aware of this fact that without the electoral vote of Massachusetts, New York, New Jersey, Ohio, Indiana, Illinois, and Michigan each of which are considered debatable states and in each of them the Colored vote is the balance of power, you could not have been elected, you therefore owe very largely to this class of voters you now ignore your present place as President of this Country. . . .

Have you, Sir, attempted in the slightest way to fulfill any of the pledges that you have made? Unfortunately up to this date those who have loyally rallied to your standard and supported you have been cast aside. They have asked of you bread, you have handed them a stone instead. . . .

As the pilot of the new Progressive Democratic ship which was launched on November 5th, 1912 and which started on its voyage on March 4th, 1913 laden with the good wishes of thousands of well-wishers and the hopes of other thousands that the dogma of American prejudice was about to end, they hoped for it a safe and successful voyage of four years, that at the. end of it the people might acclaim, "Ye have been faithful on this voyage, the country had prospered under your guidance, peace and good-will had attended the nation, prejudice of race or color had been finally banished from the country forever, in doing this the precious treasures of the Nation, we again entrust to your care for another four years."

This acclamation, Sir, you will not hear unless a change comes in the management of this vessal on the part of yourself and your advisors which you are now steering upon the rocks of unre-deemed pledges and promises, I can assure you that it will be many years hence before the destiny of this Nation will again be entrusted to the care of the Democratic Party.

I have the honor to be, Sir,

Courteously yours,   W. F. Powell

ALS (WP, DLC).
[1] Minister to Haiti and Chargé d'Affaires in the Dominican Republic, 1897-1905; at this time editorial writer for the *Philadelphia Tribune*, a Negro newspaper. He was himself a convert to the Democratic party.

From William Jennings Bryan

My dear Mr. President: Washington August 26, 1913.

Senator Bacon telephoned to-day to lay before me two things which he thought you ought to consider. He thinks that your message ought to hold out a prospect or a promise of something more than you now propose,—that is, he thinks that there should be something in there like this

While we are awaiting developments before deciding upon the course to be pursued in case order is not restored, we shall, &c., &c.,

stating the things that you mention. He says he has talked

with Senators and that, while he thinks you will have a majority of the Senate with you, he believes there will be some opposition upon the idea that nothing definite and final is suggested or spoken of as being held in reserve. I told him that I supposed these suggestions came from those who wanted intervention and wanted a threat of it put in the message. He insisted that, while they would be the most outspoken against your program, some who did not want intervention except as a last resort were not entirely satisfied.

During the course of his conversation, he referred to the matter of arms and seemed to go back to his former position, which was substantially the same as Borah took last night.[1] He also reported one "conservative" Senator as saying that he did not believe that the sympathy of European Governments would be with us. I think that the Senator is unduly alarmed, but I comply with his request and lay the matter before you for your consideration.

I enclose a note which I have just received from the War Department,[2] communicating a cable which they have received from Burnside, who is the Military Attaché at the Embassy. He doubtless has reference to the note sent to the Mexican Government by Lind yesterday.

We have received nothing to-day, not even a despatch announcing that Lind has left for Vera Cruz, although the press despatches so report. I shall see that you receive promptly anything that comes during the evening.

With assurances of respect, etc., I am, my dear Mr. President,

Very sincerely yours,   W. J. Bryan

TLS (WP, DLC).

[1] Wilson and Bryan had a lengthy conference with members of the Senate Foreign Relations Committee and the House Foreign Affairs Committee in the cabinet room on the evening of August 25. Wilson briefed them on the Mexican situation and his policy and read to them his forthcoming address to Congress (printed at Aug. 27, 1913); his instructions to John Lind (printed at Aug. 4, 1913); and the reply of the Huerta government (Federico Gamboa to J. Lind, Aug. 16, 1913). Wilson requested the opinions of those present and, according to newspaper reports of the conference, found all in substantial agreement with the administration's policy thus far. See the *New York Times* and the New York *World*, Aug. 26, 1913.

[2] It is missing.

From William Jennings Bryan, with Enclosure

My Dear Mr President   [Washington, Aug. 26, 1913]

This message does not look good but I think we should grant request of Lind & Gamboa—it only means a days delay & can not do harm. With assurances etc

Yours truly   W. J. Bryan

ALS (WP, DLC).

E N C L O S U R E

Mexico City. Aug. 25, 1913.

No instructions having reached the British Minister at four o'clock and having learned through Mr. Strong that Gamboa had said that he could not conceive of any cessation of negotiations until his note had been answered, I hastily prepared and submitted through Gamboa the note which follows. Gamboa requested that the President's message be delayed until Wednesday. I so request.

I leave tomorrow morning for Vera Cruz. Gamboa kindly offered a squad of police which I accepted. I venture no prediction as to the Government's answer. No one can forecast by our standards. I feel that our record is made and that it is the true record. I am grateful to the President and to you for the opportunity to help make it. If answer is made by Gamboa tomorrow it will be communicated to O'Shaughnessy and forwarded by him. I will sail from Vera Cruz Thursday afternoon unless advised differently in care of Consul Canada:

"Mr. Minister:

The President has not directed me to answer the observations contained in your note of August 16th, 1913, and inasmuch as they are not by me deemed pertinent to the suggestions contained in my instructions communicated to you, I refrain from discussing them. In the original instructions of the President it will be noted that he expressly states,

'We wish to act in these circumstances, in the spirit of the most earnest and disinterested friendship. It is our purpose, in whatever we do or propose in this perplexing and distressing situation, not only to pay the most scrupulous regard to the sovereignty and the independence of Mexico,—that we take as a matter of course, to which we are bound by every obligation of right and honor—but also to give every possible evidence that we act in the interests of Mexico alone, and not in the interest of any person or body of persons who may have personal or property claims in Mexico which they in such matters feel that they have the right to press. We are seeking to counsel Mexico for her own good and in the interest of her own peace, and not for any other purpose whatever. The Government of the United States would deem itself discredited if it had any selfish or ulterior purpose in transactions where the peace, happiness, and prosperity of a whole people are involved. It is acting as its friendship for Mexico, not as any selfish interest, dictates.'

"As to the course of action suggested by you to be taken by the United States, I may say that the President regards the question of the recognition of the de facto Government and of any future Government in Mexico as one wholly for the United States to determine. In the exercise of its sovereign rights in this behalf the United States will not hesitate to suggest the adoption by the de facto Government, seeking recognition, especially in a time of serious domestic disturbances, of such course of action as in the judgment of the United States can alone lead to recognition in the future. In the Present instance the President of the United States sincerely and ardently believes that the de facto Government of Mexico will see in his suggestions the most feasible plan for serving the highest interests of Mexico and for insuring the speedy reestablishment of domestic tranquillity. In that spirit and in the spirit voiced in his original instructions, the President authorizes me to submit for the consideration of the de facto Government of Mexico the following propositions:

"First. That the election called for October 26, 1913, shall be held in accordance with the Constitution and laws of Mexico.

"Second. That President Huerta, in the manner originally indicated by the President, give the assurances called for in paragraph 'C' of my original instructions.

"Third. That the remaining propositions contained in my original instructions shall be taken up later, but speedily, and resolved as circumstances permit and in the spirit of their proposal.

"The President further authorizes me to say that if the de facto Government at once acts favorably upon the foregoing suggestions then, in that event, the President will express to American bankers and their associates assurances that the Government of the United States will look with favor upon the extension of an immediate loan sufficient in amount to meet the temporary requirements of the de facto Government of Mexico.

"It is sincerely hoped that Your Excellency's Government will deem it consistent with the best and highest interests of Mexico to immediately accept these propositions. They are submitted in the same spirit and to the same end as the original propositions, but in this more restricted form so that the de facto Government may act thereon without requiring the cooperation or concurrence of any other factor in the situation. Permit me, also, Mr. Minister, in submitting this final suggestion from the President of the United States, to assure you of my deep personal obligation and my innermost sense of appreciation of the numerous evidences of personal good will of which I have been the recipient

at the hands of Your Excellency, of individual citizens of the City
of Mexico and of the Provisional President.

"It only remains for me to renew to Your Excellency the assurances of my high consideration.   (Signed)   John Lind
Personal Representative of the President of the United States
of America."   Lind

T telegram (WP, DLC).

From Henry Jones Ford

My dear President Wilson: Princeton, August 26, 1913

I arrived home yesterday afternoon, with a complete draft of
my main report. With the exhibits it is so voluminous that with
such secretarial assistance as I can obtain in Princeton it is a
rather formidable task to make a fair copy of the whole. It occurred to me that even then you might desire to have it put in
print for your convenient examination, and that perhaps time
might be saved and expense avoided if I were to go to Washington and get the use of facilities you might be able to provide
for me. The report as it stands consists of typewritten sheets with
corrections and is good enough copy for the printer. I could revise
the proofs.

As I wrote to you from London I shall have a supplemental
report to submit,[1] but it will be brief and it will not take me long
to prepare it as soon as I get the bulky main report out of the
way.

Awaiting your instructions, I am,
Faithfully yours   Henry J. Ford

ALS (WP, DLC).
[1] See H. J. Ford to WW, Jan. 17, 1914.

An Address on Mexican Affairs to a Joint Session
of Congress

Gentlemen of the Congress: [Aug. 27, 1913]

It is clearly my duty to lay before you, very fully and without
reservation, the facts concerning our present relations with the
Republic of Mexico. The deplorable posture of affairs in Mexico
I need not describe, but I deem it my duty to speak very frankly
of what this Government has done and should seek to do in
fulfillment of its obligation to Mexico herself, as a friend and
neighbor, and to American citizens whose lives and vital interests

are daily affected by the distressing conditions which now obtain beyond our southern border.

Those conditions touch us very nearly. Not merely because they lie at our very doors. That of course makes us more vividly and more constantly conscious of them, and every instinct of neighborly interest and sympathy is aroused and quickened by them; but that is only one element in the determination of our duty. We are glad to call ourselves the friends of Mexico, and we shall, I hope, have many an occasion, in happier times as well as in these days of trouble and confusion, to show that our friendship is genuine and disinterested, capable of sacrifice and every generous manifestation. The peace, prosperity, and contentment of Mexico mean more, much more, to us than merely an enlarged field for our commerce and enterprise. They mean an enlargement of the field of self-government and the realization of the hopes and rights of a nation with whose best aspirations, so long suppressed and disappointed, we deeply sympathize. We shall yet prove to the Mexican people that we know how to serve them without first thinking how we shall serve ourselves.

But we are not the only friends of Mexico. The whole world desires her peace and progress; and the whole world is interested as never before. Mexico lies at last where all the world looks on. Central America is about to be touched by the great routes of the world's trade and intercourse running free from ocean to ocean at the Isthmus. The future has much in store for Mexico, as for all the States of Central America; but the best gifts can come to her only if she be ready and free to receive them and to enjoy them honorably. America in particular—America north and south and upon both continents—waits upon the development of Mexico; and that development can be sound and lasting only if it be the product of a genuine freedom, a just and ordered government founded upon law. Only so can it be peaceful or fruitful of the benefits of peace. Mexico has a great and enviable future before her, if only she choose and attain the paths of honest constitutional government.

The present circumstances of the Republic, I deeply regret to say, do not seem to promise even the foundations of such a peace. We have waited many months, months full of peril and anxiety, for the conditions there to improve, and they have not improved. They have grown worse, rather. The territory in some sort controlled by the provisional authorities at Mexico City has grown smaller, not larger. The prospect of the pacification of the country, even by arms, has seemed to grow more and more remote; and its pacification by the authorities at the capital is evidently impossible by any other means than force. Difficulties more and more entangle those who claim to constitute the legitimate government of the Republic. They have not made good their claim in fact. Their successes in the field have proved only temporary. War and disorder, devastation and confusion, seem to threaten to become the settled fortune of the distracted country. As friends we could wait no longer for a solution which every week seemed further away. It was our duty at least to volunteer our good offices—to offer to assist, if we might, in effecting some arrangement which would bring relief and peace and set up a universally acknowledged political authority there.

Accordingly, I took the liberty of sending the Hon. John Lind, formerly governor of Minnesota, as my personal spokesman and representative, to the City of Mexico, with *the following instructions*: . . .[1]

Mr. Lind executed his delicate and difficult mission with singular tact, firmness, and good judgment, and made clear to the authorities at the City of Mexico not only the purpose of his visit but also the spirit in which it had been undertaken. But the proposals he submitted were rejected, in a note the full text[2] of which I take the liberty of laying before you.

I am led to believe that they were rejected partly because the authorities at Mexico City had been grossly misinformed and misled upon two points. They did not realize the spirit of the American people in this matter, their earnest friendliness and yet sober determination that some just solution be found for the Mexican difficulties; and they did not believe that the present administration spoke, through Mr. Lind, for the people of the United States. The effect of this unfortunate misunderstanding on their part is to leave them singularly isolated and without friends who can effectually aid them. So long as the misunderstanding continues we can only await the time of their awakening to a realization of the actual facts. We can not thrust our good offices upon them. The situation must be given a little more time to work itself out in the new circumstances; and I believe that only a little while will be necessary, for the circumstances are new. The rejection of our friendship makes them new and will inevitably bring its own alterations in the whole aspect of affairs. The actual situation of the authorities at Mexico City will presently be revealed.

Meanwhile, what is it our duty to do? Clearly, everything that we do must be rooted in patience and done with calm and dis-

---

[1] Here Wilson repeated his instructions to Lind printed at Aug. 4, 1913.
[2] F. Gamboa to J. Lind, Aug. 16, 1913.

interested deliberation. Impatience on our part would be childish, and would be fraught with every risk of wrong and folly. We can afford to exercise the self-restraint of a really great nation which realizes its own strength and scorns to misuse it. It was our duty to offer our active assistance. It is now our duty to show what true neutrality will do to enable the people of Mexico to set their affairs in order again and wait for a further opportunity to offer our friendly counsels. The door is not closed against the resumption, either upon the initiative of Mexico or upon our own, of the effort to bring order out of the confusion by friendly cooperative action, should fortunate occasion offer.

While we wait the contest of the rival forces will undoubtedly for a little while be sharper than ever, just because it will be plain that an end must be made of the existing situation, and that very promptly; and with the increased activity of the contending factions will come, it is to be feared, increased danger to the noncombatants in Mexico as well as to those actually in the field of battle. The position of outsiders is always particularly trying and full of hazard where there is civil strife and a whole country is upset. We should earnestly urge all Americans to leave Mexico at once, and should assist them to get away in every way possible —not because we would mean to slacken in the least our efforts to safeguard their lives and their interests, but because it is imperative that they should take no unnecessary risks when it is physically possible for them to leave the country. We should let every one who assumes to exercise authority in any part of Mexico know in the most unequivocal way that we shall vigilantly watch the fortunes of those Americans who can not get away, and shall hold those responsible for their sufferings and losses to a definite reckoning. That can be and will be made plain beyond the possibility of a misunderstanding.

For the rest, I deem it my duty to exercise the authority conferred upon me by the law of March 14, 1912, to see to it that neither side to the struggle now going on in Mexico receive any assistance from this side the border. I shall follow the best practice of nations in the matter of neutrality by forbidding the exportation of arms or munitions of war of any kind from the United States to any part of the Republic of Mexico—a policy suggested by several interesting precedents and certainly dictated by many manifest considerations of practical expediency. We can not in the circumstances be the partisans of either party to the contest that now distracts Mexico, or constitute ourselves the virtual umpire between them.

I am happy to say that several of the great Governments of

the world have given this Government their generous moral support, in urging upon the provisional authorities at the City of Mexico the acceptance of our proffered good offices in the spirit in which they were made. We have not acted in this matter under the ordinary principles of international obligation. All the world expects us in such circumstances to act as Mexico's nearest friend and intimate adviser. This is our immemorial relation towards her. There is nowhere any serious question that we have the moral right in the case or that we are acting in the interest of a fair settlement and of good government, not for the promotion of some selfish interest of our own. If further motive were necessary than our own good will towards a sister Republic and our own deep concern to see peace and order prevail in Central America, this consent of mankind to what we are attempting, this attitude of the great nations of the world towards what we may attempt in dealing with this distressed people at our doors, should make us feel the more solemnly bound to go to the utmost length of patience and forbearance in this painful and anxious business. The steady pressure of moral force will before many days break the barriers of pride and prejudice down, and we shall triumph as Mexico's friends sooner than we could triumph as her enemies—and how much more handsomely, with how much higher and finer satisfactions of conscience and of honor![3]

Printed reading copy (WP, DLC).
[3] There is an undated WWsh draft of this address in the C. L. Swem Coll., NjP; a WWT draft, dated Aug. 26, 1913, in WP, DLC, and a CLST draft in *ibid*.

From William Jennings Bryan

My Dear Mr President   Washington Aug 27, 1913

I can not allow this hour to pass without telling you how gratified I am with your message on Mexico and its reception by Congress. If I am competent to judge of merit in the domain of morals and statesmanship you have set a record in both. You have raised our international relations upon the highest possible plane. Your appeal can not fail to bring a response from the conscience of the world. It is an epoc making deliverance.

I have heard nothing but praise from those with whom I have spoken. Accept my dear Mr President the cordial congratulations of your most obedient servant   W. J. Bryan

ALS (W. J. Bryan Papers, DLC).

To William Jennings Bryan

My dear Mr. Bryan, The White House 27 Aug., 1913.

Your note was most generous. It gave me the deepest and truest pleasure. So counselled and supported, a man who did not seek and choose the right path would be inexcusable.

Gratefully yours, Woodrow Wilson

ALS (W. J. Bryan Papers, DLC).

Two Telegrams from John Lind
to William Jennings Bryan

Vera Cruz. Aug. 27, 1913.

August 27, 4 p.m.

CONFIDENTIAL. By special messenger from President Huerta I have received communication which I tentatively interpret as follows:

First. The note of Mexico in reply to President's proposals is reaffirmed in toto.

Second. To [the] second note from myself is equally inadmissible though it is noted that [as] the terms of de facto Government and President Huerta are employed it is desired that the Government be addressed as the Constitutional Provisional Government.

Third. The President of the United States must be wholly unfamiliar with the Mexican Constitution or it would not be possible for him to assume that Huerta, having succeeded to the Presidency by operation of law, could under any circumstances be a candidate at the ensuing election.

Fourth. That for the present Government cannot reply to the suggestion of good offices to secure financial relief, as such action would subject the Government to embarrassing reflections.

Fifth. That request for exchange of Ambassadors is withdrawn, but it is hoped that the Embassies will be continued with present personnel until after October elections.

I have asked O'Shaughnessy to forward note in full.

CONFIDENTIAL. Lind

Vera Cruz, Mexico, Aug. 27, 1913.

August 27, 11 p.m.

Mr. Dantin,[1] the Embassy counsel, is with me. He has completed translation. Every point contended for in the last note is accepted in fact, though not in form. From a diplomatic standpoint the mission is a success, and the press should be cautioned to discuss the subject with care. The Mexican people are very sensitive. I assume that I may be directed to return to Mexico City. I have already requested Burnside to be prepared to advise me as to the character of the revolutionary forces that should be considered as entitled to our good offices in considering measures for the cessation of hostilities. Some good man or men should (#) that in the north. The lesson of non-recognition is our weapon it can be wielded effectively in the north, I believe. The real work commences now. I cannot prophesy success but the possibility of it is worth our best efforts.   Lind.

(#) Apparent omission.

T telegrams (WP, DLC).
    1 Louis D'Antin, clerk in the American embassy, Mexico City.

Nelson O'Shaughnessy to William Jennings Bryan

Mexico City, Aug. 27, 1913.

Referring to my cable four fifty-five, August 27, 4 p.m., The Mexican Foreign Office is giving out the note addressed to Governor Lind under date of yesterday. I am therefore using my discretion and sending the translation thereof to the Department en claire appended hereto.

A synopsis of the President's message has been received here and a special meeting of the permanent commission of Congress is at this moment being held to consider it. I saw the Minister for Foreign Affairs this afternoon but he said that he could not give me the impression made by the message in Government circles until late tonight. I hope to cable later in the evening.

Sir: Yesterday I had the honor of receiving from your hands a note in which you are pleased to state that, although you have no instructions from the President of the United States of America, from the scope of your instructions you reply to the note of this Government, given to your [you] through me, of the 16th instant. You are pleased to repeat from those same instructions the paragraph which translated says literally. "We wish to act in the present circumstances under the inspiration of the most lively and disinterested friendship. We propose, in all that we do or say by reason of this serious and intricate situation, not only to maintain the most scrupulous respect for the sovereignty and independence of Mexico and we consider ourselves obligated to that respect by all the considerations of honor and right but as well to give all possible proofs that we are working only in the interests of Mexico and not for any person or group of persons who might have claims relating to themselves or to their properties in this country and who might consider themselves with a right to demand their settlement. What we intend to counsel Mexico for her own good and in the interest of her own peace and with no other object of any kind. The Government of the United States would consider itself discredited if it had in mind any selfish or ulterior motive, considering that the negotiations in hand concern the peace, welfare and prosperity of a whole people. We are working, not with selfish interest but in accordance with the dictates of our friendship towards Mexico."

In spite of the fact that at the beginning of the note which I now answer you state that you lack instructions from the President of the United States of America after the statement which I have reproduced about you state in the name of that same President that the method indicated in my note of the sixteenth, instant, in so far as it concerns the recognition of the present Government (which I may say in passing is quite far from being a de facto Government, as you have chosen to qualify it) or of any other future Government of Mexico this you add is something which only the United States of America may decide, which in the exercise of its sovereign rights in this respect will not hesitate especially in times of serious domestic troubles to consummate in the judgment of the United States of America and not in that of Mexico, May be best for this matter. You add that the President of the United States of America sincerely and ardently believes that my Government will see in the suggestions of His Excellency Mr. Woodrow Wilson the most feasible plan for serving our vital interests and for insuring the speedy re-establishment of our domestic tranquility. And always in the name of the President of the United States you submit to the consideration of my Government the three following propositions.

(1) That the election called for the 16th of October of the present year (the note sent to the Foreign Office by Mr. Lind stated October 26th and not 16th) shall be held in accordance with the constitutional laws of Mexico.

(2) That President Huerta, in the manner originally indicated by the President of the United States of America give the assurances called for in paragraph "c" of the original instructions. Paragraph which says literally "the consent of General Huerta to agree not to be a candidate in the coming elections for president of the Republic."

(3) That the remaining propositions contained in your original instructions shall be taken up later but speedily and re-

solved as circumstances permit and in the spirit of their proposal.
You add furthermore, Mr. Confidential Agent, that the President
of the United States of America has authorized you to say that if
my Government "acts immediately and favorably upon the foregoing suggestions" that same President express to American
bankers and their associates assurances that the Government of
the United States of America will then look with favor upon the
extension of an immediate loan sufficient in amount to meet the
temporary requirements of the present Mexican administration.
At the end of your note, Mr. Confidential Agent, you express the
hope of your Government that my Government will judge it consistent with the best and highest interest of Mexico to immediately accept such propositions. That they are submitted in
the same spirit and to the same end that my Government may act
within it[s] faculties without the cooperation or aid of any other
outside factor. It appears at once, Mr. Confidential Agent, that
in this case the proposal of His Excellency Mr. Woodrow Wilson
is not to remove himself an iota from the position originally
assumed by him, for notwithstanding the time consumed since
the 16th, the date of my reply to the 25th, in which you delivered
to me your second note which I am here answering, the essence
and even the form of his original instruction are the same with
the aggravating feature well qualified by you as "more restricted."
For my part it would have been sufficient to answer this note in
its totally [totality] by reproducing the whole of my note of the
16th instant as negative as categorical, as I have the honor to
reproduce it in this present note. But the President ad interim
wishes to carry his forbearance to the last point and to the end
that Mexican public opinion, which is so justly disturbed by the
present tension in the diplomatic relations between the two
countries and also to the end that the various foreign governments which offered their good offices in the most delicate possible manner, I am glad to repeat that this has been their
attitude and not less pleased to express grateful acknowledgment
thereof, may be duly informed, has authorized me to reply to you
in the following terms. I will begin by taking notice of a highly
significant fact. Between the night of the 14th instant when I
received the sheets containing your instructions not directed to
any one and calling the present administration "the persons who
at the present time have authority or exercise influence in
Mexico," and yesterday, some progress has been made in that
now the constitutional President ad interim (see paragraph No.
2 of the new propositions) is called "President Huerta" and in the
whole course of the note the personal [personnel] of his adminis-

tration is referred to as the "de facto Government" but inasmuch as this or that qualification in [is] of no importance, upon the ground that all the representations of your Government have not been initiated except with ourselves which gives us, upon the supposition that we have been dispossessed of it, a perfect political and moral personality [responsibility] to clear up the present divergance, I intentionally limit myself solely to point out the facts. If your original proposals were not to be admitted. They are now, in the more restricted form in which they are reproduced, even more inadmissable, and ones attention is called to the fact that they are insisted upon if it be noticed that the first proposals had already been declined. Precisely because we comprehend the immense value which is possessed by the principle of sovereignty which the Government of the United States so opportunely invokes in the question of our recognition or non-recognition, precisely for this reason we believe that it would never be proposed to us that we should forget our own sovereignty by permitting that a foreign government should modify the line of conduct which we have to follow in our public and independent life. If even once we were to permit the counsels and advice (let us call them thus) of the United States of America not only would we as I say above, forego our sovereignty but we would as well compromise for an indefinite future our destinies as a sovereign entity and all the future elections for president would be submitted to the veto of any President of the United States of America. And such an enormity, Mr. Confidential Agent, no government will ever attempt to perpetrate and this I am sure of unless some monstrous and almost impossible cataclysm should occur in the conscience of the Mexican people. We believed, taking into consideration the disproportionate interest that the President of the United States of America has shown concerning our internal affairs that he as well as his Government would know perfectly well the provisions of our consti[tu]tion in the matter of elections. Unfortunately and in view of the insistence with which His Excellency Mr. Wilson sustains his first ideas. We are compelled acknowledge that we have made a mistake. The reform of constitutional article Nos. 78 and 109, put into effect by the congress of the union on November seven, nineteen eleven, provides among other requirements that which is contained in the final part of article seventy eight. "The Secretary of State in charge of the executive power shall not be eligible to the office of either President or Vice President when the elections shall take place."

This transcription which I take the liberty of making Mr. Confidential Agent, in order that the Government of the United States of America may take due note of it, prevents the constitutional ad interim President, of the Republic from being a candidate at the forthcoming elections; and if His Excellency President Wilson, had taken into consideration that paragraph before venturing to impose upon us the conditions in question and which we may not admit the present state of affairs between you and ourselves would have been avoided leaving out of the discussion our decorum and the personal pride of the President of the United States wrongly interested in this discussion without foundation.

It should be well understood the ad interim constitutional President could not be elected President or Vice-President of the Republic at the forthcoming election already called for the twenty-sixth of October because our own laws prohibit him from being a candidate and these laws are the sole arbiters of our destinies. But never through the imposition although friendly and disinterested of the President of the United States of America or of any other ruler, powerful or weak (this does not matter in the case) who would be equally respected by us.

I beg to inform you, Mr. Confidential Agent, that up to the present time, at least only the President of the United States of America has spoken of the candidacy of the Constitutional ad interim President at the forthcoming elections. Neither the solemn declaration of this high functionary or the most insignificant of his acts—all of which have been done with a view of obtaining a complete pacification of the country which is the supreme national aim and which he has decided to bring about in spite of everything—have authorized anyone even to suspect that such are his ultimate intentions. It is perfectly well known that there does not exist in the whole country a single news paper[,] a single club, a single corporation, or group of individuals who have launched his candidacy or even discussed it.

On what then is the gratuitous suspicion of the President of the United States of America based and his demand which is absolutely inadmissable that in order to comply with the ad interim President of the Republic should enter into agreement and contract obligations which have never heretofore been imposed upon the ruler of any sovereign nation.

The question having been set forth as I have had the honor of doing in this reply His Excellency Mr. Wilson, will have to withdraw definitely *of* his present attitude at the risk that his motives which I take pleasure in acknowledging are as he himself quotes them friendly and disinterested altruistic and without ulterior ends at the risk I repeat that they may be wrongly and differently interpreted by all the other nations which look upon our present international conflict with more or less interest. And although the President of the United States of America should take an altogether different stand from the universal viewpoint which considers differently an administration under the conditions in which our own is at present (the best proof of my assertion is the unconditional recognition of the foremost powers of the world amongst which the United States of America occupies such a prominent and legitimately conquered rank) he will have to cease to call us a de facto Government and will give us the title of ad interim constitutional Government which is the only one to which we are rightly entitled.

Permit me, Mr. Confidential Agent, not to reply for the time being to the significant offer in which the Government of the United States of America insinuates that it will recommend to American bankers the immediate extension of loan which will permit us among other things to cover the enumerable urgent expenses required by the progressive pacification of the country; for in the terms in which it is couched it appears more to be attractive antecedent proposal to the end that moved by petty interests we should renounce a right which incontrovertibly upholds us. When the dignity of the nation is at stake I believe that there are not loans enough to induce those charged by the law to maintain it to *permit be* lessened. On the other hand I have seen with great pleasure that the President of the United States of America proposes for a later date and according to what the circumstances permit the solution which was marked with the letter "a" in the original instruction and in the note to which this is a reply with the number three; for this reveals that we are really in the way of arriving at an arrangement equally dignified for both sides.

In view of all this, Mr. Confidential Agent, today more than ever we profoundly hope for an immediate solution of the conflict which unfortunately has separated us. I could go even further. I would renounce on our part that our respective Ambassadors be received immediately since for the end in view the present personal [personnel] of our reciprocal Embassies is sufficient if it remains as it has been heretofore until the elections of October have taken place but I will always stand on the unavoidable condition which declares that we are in reality the ad interim constitutional Government of the Mexican Republic.

In my turn, Mr. Confidential Agent, I beg again to repeat to you the pleasing impression which you leave with me as a citizen of the United States of America, and as an able, righteous and well intentioned personal representative of His Excellency Mr. Woodrow Wilson; I esteem in great the gratitude which you say you profess for the well-deserved treatment which you have received in Mexico at the hands of the ad interim Constitutional President of the Republic from private individuals and from myself and I reiterate to you as in my previous note my perfect consideration. The Secretary for Foreign Affairs of the Republic.

(Signed).   F. Gamboa.

To Mr. John Lind,
Confidential Agent of the President of the United States of America, et cetera, et cetera, A true copy of the original to which I certify: for the sub-Secretary of Foreign Relations the Chief Clerk.   (signed)   Pena y Reyes."

Nelson O'Shaughnessy.

T telegram (WP, DLC).

To John Lind

Washington, August 27, 1913. 11 p.m.

Accept my hearty congratulations. Huerta's announcement that he will not be a candidate is the one thing necessary to the restoration of peace. The President desires you to remain there until situation is fully developed   Bryan

WJBhw telegram (SDR, RG 59, 812.00/8593, DNA).

From Oswald Garrison Villard

Dear Mr. President: New York August 27, 1913.

I am indebted to you for two letters, one of August 19th which touched me greatly, and one of August 21st, which equally disappoints me since it brings me your decision not to appoint the Race Commission. I understand, of course, that the difficulties of the Mexican situation prevented your seeing me, and believe me I have no personal feelings to hurt when speaking for millions of the downtrodden. I am sorry, however, that you could not have found time to let me talk this over with you before reaching a final decision. Since this disappointment has come to us there is nothing left but to go ahead as best we can in another direction.

Frankly, I feel very sorry that you find yourself "absolutely blocked by the sentiment of Senators." I believe that as with your most immediate predecessors, the time will come when you will find it necessary to go ahead and do what is right without considering their feelings. I find it the more difficult to understand this decision because of your promise to stand "for everything by which I could assist in advancing the interest of their race in the United States," and since, as I explained to you, it involves no appeal to all-powerful senators, no asking for financial aid from them, and leaves you free to lay the report before Congress or not as you see fit. How do Senators enter into this? If it is true that inquiry sometimes means indictment, should we, who search for the truth, only hold off, particularly when, as you yourself told me, you felt it was needed and the right thing to do?

But, if we must for the present bow down to the God Expediency, will you not reconsider the matter of the "Jim-Crowing" of the colored clerks in the Departments at Washington? I sent you Dr. Washington's letter in which he said that never had he seen the colored people so discouraged and embittered as they had become since your Administration began. Is that condition to remain? Are they not to be recognized by you in any way? Are you not going to appoint any one of them to office? Are you going to continue the policy of segregation? With all respect, these are questions, it seems to me, that must be promptly answered, unless the feeling of bitterness among the colored people towards your Administration and the Democratic party shall steadily increase. You will remember that you wrote on October 16, 1912,—"Should I become the President of the United States they may count upon me for absolute fair dealing and for everything by which I could assist in advancing the interest of their race in the United States." You will surely not let the Senators manoeuvre you into such a position that the colored people and their friends can say that you have not lived up to this promise? Your own mail must be showing you, if it is laid before you and you have time to run through it, how intense is the feeling, and how wide the protest against segregation.

You have seen so clearly in the Mexican situation that you will forgive me, I am sure, for wishing that a similar vision might be given you in this matter of our colored fellow citizens. Meanwhile, I shall hope, with you, "that a better aspect may come upon it before many months." I can only believe, however, that that aspect can be put upon it by courageous and vigorous action on your part. If I speak very frankly please lay it only to my eagerness to be of service to you and to your Administration, and to the high personal regard I have for you.

Faithfully yours,   Oswald Garrison Villard

TLS (WP, DLC).

Two Telegrams to John Lind

Washington, August 28, 1913.

The President directs me to extend his congratulations upon the success which has accompanied your visit. As you are on the ground he desires that you exercise your discretion as to the time you shall return to Mexico City. As soon as the Mexican people have had time to consider the notes passed between the two Governments, the Mexican Government may be ready to intimate a desire to see you in regard to further negotiations. You can ascertain their wishes and communicate them with your advice. Now that the crisis is passed there will be time for deliberation and consultation as to the various steps to be pursued.   Bryan

CLST telegram (SDR, RG 59, 812.00/8593, DNA).

Washington, Aug. 28, 1913

Venture to caution you against letting the provisional authorities infer that we concede that General Huerta is president ad interim by operation of law. Our attitude towards him is based upon our denial that his authority rests upon law or the constitution.[1]   W.W.

WWT telegram (SDR, RG 59, 812.00/10643D, DNA).
  [1] Wilson had just read a memorandum by David Lawrence quoting the provisions of the Mexican Constitution relating to presidential succession. More to the point, it repeated the argument of Constitutionalist lawyers that Huerta's succession was invalid because of the absence of a quorum when the Mexican Congress accepted Madero's resignation. WW to WJB, Aug. 26, 1913, TLS (SDR, RG 59, 812.00/10483, DNA), enclosing "Memorandum prepared by Mr. Lawrence," T MS.

To Gilbert Monell Hitchcock

My dear Senator: [The White House] August 28, 1913

Your note of the twenty-sixth[1] was peculiarly welcome. For some weeks past I have been wishing that I might have a talk with you about banking and currency. I hesitated to invite an interview, because I shrink more than I think many persons realize from seeming to try to press my own views upon men who have an equal responsibility with myself. I wonder if it would be possible for you to give me the pleasure of seeing you this evening at the White House—at, say, half-past eight. The messenger who carries this will wait for an answer.[2]
            Cordially and sincerely yours,   Woodrow Wilson

TLS (Letterpress Books, WP, DLC).
  [1] It is missing.
  [2] Hitchcock came to the White House that evening.

To Henry Jones Ford

My dear Ford: [The White House] August 28, 1913

I am heartily glad to hear that you are back and shall look forward with the greatest pleasure to seeing you.[1]

I think that the suggestion that your report be printed is an excellent one. I do not know that I have any right to print it as a public document, but I would have a right in connection with what I delegated you to do to have it paid for out of the contingent funds of the War Department. Pray come down when you can and take the matter up.

Hoping that you are very well, in haste
Cordially and faithfully yours,   Woodrow Wilson

TLS (Letterpress Books, WP, DLC).

[1] Ford conferred with Wilson at the White House on September 5 and left his report. The document, ninety-eight pages in length, is in the form of an undated typed letter to the President of the United States and is filed in WDR, RG 350, BIA, DNA.

Ford spent sixty-six days in the Philippines, traveling extensively through several of the larger islands; he also took extended automobile trips to interior towns in northern and central Luzon. He was accompanied by his son, J. Howard Ford, who had served in the Philippines as a district engineer and was fluent in Spanish. Ford conducted interviews with Filipinos and Americans, both in and out of government.

The Filipinos, Ford reported, "are very different from any people of color with whom the people of the United States are acquainted." Their culture could be likened to the older Oriental cultures with regard to such basic characteristics as close family organization, proficiency in arts and crafts, and the value placed upon manners. At the same time, Filipinos differed from other Orientals in that they possessed a vital connection with western civilization through their long-time practice of the Christian religion.

In administering the islands, the United States had aimed at creating the prerequisites of self-government. Foremost among these was a system of public education, which had been created by using a large number of American teachers and by training thousands of Filipinos. There were some 3,660 schools in operation as of 1911-1912. Ford visited several and found them comparable in most respects to those he had seen in the United States. The American authorities had expected that English would become the common language that would knit together the various regions with their different dialects. Instead, Ford discovered that, although English was the sole language taught in the schools, it was virtually never used by students outside the classroom. Those children taught English by Filipino instructors (often somewhat hastily trained) had difficulty making themselves understood to Americans. Despite the best efforts of American teachers, the imposition of English had tended to reinforce the use of native dialects, and, in the case of the older, educated classes, the use of Spanish. Ford found Spanish to be the speech of business and social intercourse everywhere. Its use seemed to be increasing, even on the part of Americans, who found themselves treated with greater courtesy and respect when they addressed Filipinos in Spanish.

Literacy among Filipinos had been defined as the ability to read and write either Spanish or English. Ignoring ability in native languages, Ford emphasized, disregarded a tradition of literacy in the vernacular that reached back to the years preceding the Spanish conquest. On a basis of conversation with well-informed observers, Ford estimated that the actual literacy rate among Filipinos was between 80 and 90 per cent. He saw a considerable body of native literature displayed in Manila bookstores. While acknowledging the difficulties involved in changing the language habits of seven million people, he concluded that the attempt to compel the use of English in place of the native languages had been a failure. "However benevolent the purpose, it certainly does not look well to proclaim as illiterate people who can read and write their own language."

Ford paid tribute to the resourcefulness and adaptability of American officials. Experts had created an excellent currency system, and there were signs of material progress everywhere, particularly road construction and maintenance and better vehicular transportation. Improved sanitation and the use of artesian wells had done a great deal to prevent the spread of disease. The haste with which some construction projects had been undertaken, however, had at times led to waste and loss due to inadequate information as to terrain. One significant grievance on the part of the Filipinos was the very large expenditure of funds for a mountain road to the summer capital of Baguio, which had cost more than $1,900,000. In Baguio, removed from the summer heat of Manila, American administrators and their Filipino co-workers pursued their work and recreation in great comfort—in contrast to the rest of the population—and this, coupled with the exorbitant cost of the access road, had provoked widely expressed resentment.

Ford observed three types of governmental authority operating in different parts of the islands: quasi-military in the Moro country (where occasional skirmishes were fought); direct rule of the Commission in some of the remote provinces; and government by the Commission in conjunction with the elected Assembly in most parts of the country.

Executive authority was vested in the nine-member Philippine Commission, composed of the Governor-General; the secretaries of the four departments into which the Executive was divided—Interior, Finance and Justice, Public Instruction, and Commerce and Police; and four members without portfolio. Americans headed all offices except for the Department of Finance and Justice. The Commission was also the upper house of the Philippine legislature.

The lower house—the Assembly—was composed of members elected for four-year terms from each of eighty-one districts by voters who were literate in English or Spanish. The mixture of different governmental systems for the various parts of the archipelago, Ford reported, had produced "chronic discord." The Commission and Assembly were rival powers pursuing separate aims, while their actual relations were "diplomatic rather than legislative." During the prior three fiscal years, the two houses had failed to agree on appropriations for current expenses, so that each year they had had to be determined by the Governor-General. Ford found universal agreement that this bicameral system had broken down and that change was necessary.

Ford held extended conversations with Emilio Aguinaldo and Sergio Osmeña, Speaker of the Assembly. Both leaders expressed a strong desire for independence rather than increased autonomy under American rule. Both also preferred a simpler form of government, modeled after the Swiss federal system. Ford said that he agreed substantially. For one reason, the heavy costs of maintaining the present governmental system were a great burden upon Philippine commerce. Customs duties at Manila averaged over 22 per cent, far higher than at Hong Kong. Other essentials such as stevedoring, lightering, and landing and storage costs were all substantially higher than in other far eastern ports.

Americans living in the islands believed that, for the foreseeable future, Filipinos were incapable of self-government. The major arguments cited were the lack of a common language, the rivalry of antagonistic tribes, and the prevalence of caciquism, that is, the system under which provincial magnates used their power to manipulate the poorer classes. Evaluating each of these objections in turn, Ford concluded that the linguistic diversity was no greater than the regional dialects of some European nations. The Swiss system, as well as that of other countries, functioned without linguistic uniformity. Similarly, Ford regarded tribal antagonisms as a lesser problem than some Americans alleged. Among the non-Christian tribes, the Igorotes, or "hill peoples," were highly industrious, lived in settled mountain communities, and constituted no peril to the country. Only the Moros, numbering perhaps 300,000, might be considered a threat. They were a warlike people occupying a large part of Mindanao and the Sulu chain of islands. They practiced a fanatical Mohammedanism much adulterated with local superstitions. In times past, they had been dreaded invaders of the other islands, and memories of their depredations were still vivid. However, Ford dismissed them as a serious threat to Filipinos armed with modern weapons and utilizing steam-powered boats.

The system of caciquism, Ford said, was essentially similar to gentry-tenant relations in other predominantly agricultural societies. These relations were characterized by strong patterns of loyalty and dependence on the part of the tenants. In return for various services, the landlord provided assistance, protection from outsiders, and defense in the courts. Given the dependent relationship and the local power exercised by the cacique, Ford was frequently told that any of them who were dissatisfied with the outcome of an election could instigate an insurrection by ordering out their clients. He did not share these fears. The existence of such a system elsewhere had not been incompatible with constitutional government, nor had it prevented "democratic progress." The public order would best be preserved under a decentralized system that employed a permanent (i.e., nonpolitical) civil service.

In general, Ford thought that the marked commercial spirit of the Filipino gentry was a strong encouragement to public order. He could discover no class of military adventurers and observed that "civilian influence seems to have a secure ascendency in public life." "A very important consideration," he added, "is the fact that national control has been thoroughly organized and solidly established by American administration. A native administration, taking over the government as a going concern, would be abundantly supplied with the means to enforce law and suppress disorder."

Ford summarized as follows:

"The main conclusion I have reached is that American administration has been attended by greater success in organizing the Philippines and fitting the country for self-government than I had supposed before visiting the Islands and that both justice and expediency require that we should adhere to our declared policy of conforming the government not to 'our theoretical views' but to 'their customs, their habits, and even their prejudices, to the fullest extent consistent with the accomplishment of the indispensable requisites of just and effective government.' The present temporary form of government has done its work and has quite filled out its term of usefulness. To convert it now, into what with indefinite postponement of self-government would be practically a permanent system, would be a violation of our national pledges for which I could not find sufficient justification. It is a deplorable fact that the people of the Philippines seem inappreciative of our efforts and resentful of our domination, but it is not surprising that this should be the case. The color line is now drawn with a rigor unknown to Spanish rule and a strong racial antipathy has grown up and appears to be increasing. If on the one side there is an attitude which appears to be ungrateful and exacting, on the other side there is an attitude which is regarded as arrogant and insulting. To understand the situation it should be borne in mind that the Filipinos believe that they would have achieved their independence before now but for American intervention, and this opinion is not confined to Filipinos. . . .

"A strong national consciousness had been developed before we appeared upon the scene and all events since have tended to intensify it. The political capacity of the Filipinos has been much underrated, through too narrow a view of the requir[e]ments of constitutional government and through adherence to American political traditions in a country where they have no historical basis and are incompatible with social conditions. The Filipinos may be incapable of maintaining 'just and effective government' under a constitution of the American pattern but they seem to be capable of carrying on successfully a government of the type they desire. Considerations pertaining to the maintenance of peace and order are overwhelmingly in favor of granting them liberty of choice. It would be extremely imprudent to ignore the strength and earnestness of Philippine demands for self-government.

"The narrow basis upon which the representative element in the Philippine government now rests should be promptly enlarged by extending the suffrage to all who can read and write their own language on the same terms as it is now granted to those who are literate in English or Spanish. The present ban upon native literacy is certainly not calculated to inspire good will. It is difficult to reconcile with President McKinley's instructions the Philippine Commission's treatment of the language question. It may be that justification for it can be found in the rapid production of a class of natives sufficiently acquainted with English to furnish clerical aid to American administration. But no such need exists now. Instead of more recruits what the Philippine public service seems to stand most in need of now is economical reform. In expressing this opinion I do so without disparaging the great value of the work that has been accomplished in framing governmental mechanism. In starting any business overhead expenses are temporarily large and after the work of installation has been concluded economical revision is the next step in order.

"Conditions in the Philippines are so radically diverse from those in the United States that to treat the two widely separated countries as parts of the same economic system will be disadvantageous to both. The Philippes should be entirely free to frame their own revenue and navigation laws. Nothing is more important to the welfare of the country than economic independence.

"As regards political independence, that matter is so involved in external considerations that it would be wise to postpone action until after the Filipinos have set up and organized their government, save that we should disavow any intention to hold them subject against their will or any unwillingness to allow them to assume the burden of their national defense as soon as they feel themselves ready to do so. To fix a date at which complete independence should automatically take effect would be wanting in due regard for their situation.

"In pursuance of these suggestions I beg leave to make the following recommendations:

"That the Philippine Commission be abolished, its work having been accomplished, and that its power shall devolve upon such person and persons and shall be exercised in such manner as the President of the United States shall direct, pending the establishment of self-government in the Philippines.

"That native literacy be accepted as a qualification for the suffrage equally with literacy in English or Spanish.

"That a special election be held for delegates to a convention which shall be authorized to frame a constitution establishing a government autonomous in character and republican in form, which constitution shall go into effect when approved by the President of the United States and at such time as he shall designate."

From William Hughes

My dear Mr. President: [Washington] August 28, 1913.

I have consulted Senator Clark about the Seamen's Bill and he assured me that he will be in a position to put the Bill on the calendar just as soon as it is possible for the Senate to give it consideration.   Very truly yours,   Wm. Hughes

TLS (WP, DLC).

To Oswald Garrison Villard

Personal.

My dear Mr. Villard: The White House August 29, 1913

Thank you for your letter of the twenty-seventh of August. I fear that I did not make clear to you my thought both with regard to the commission and the question of segregation. You remember I wrote you some weeks ago that I honestly thought segregation to be in the interest of the colored people, as exempting them from friction and criticism in the departments, and I want to add that a number of colored men with whom we have consulted have agreed with us in this judgment. I dare say that in several instances the thing has been managed in a way which was not sufficiently thoughtful of their feelings, but wherever this has appeared we have tried to set it right, and in more than one instance I could mention have succeeded very pleasantly. With regard to the commission, I was thinking of the efficiency of the work and of the effects that the report would have. I do not want to set in its way prejudices which might shift the whole discussion from the findings of the commission to the method in which it had been set up.

When I differ with you upon practical questions of this sort, I am inclined to question my own judgment very sharply, but I know that you want me in every case to state what is really in my mind.

With warmest regard,
Cordially and faithfully yours,   Woodrow Wilson

TLS (O. G. Villard Papers, MH).

To William Hughes

My dear Senator: [The White House] August 29, 1913.
    I thank you for your note of August 28th, concerning the Seamen's Bill.   Sincerely yours,   Woodrow Wilson

Would be obliged if you would keep tab on this.   W.W.

TLS (Letterpress Books, WP, DLC).

From William Jennings Bryan

My dear Mr. President: Washington September 1, 1913.
    . . . I thought you might be interested in an answer which we received through one of the consuls from Colonel Calles,[1] Military Commander of the Northern District of Sonora. In acknowledging receipt of the note which the consul at Nogales sent him, communicating notice to the authorities that they would be held responsible for harm done to Americans, he declares that protection has been given to Americans and will be given to them, and then he adds a word in regard to intervention, which I think is significant. I quote from his note as follows:
"And therefore we believe that intervention would be an injustice on the part of the United States as all the world knows that today we are fighting for ideals and for the purpose of wiping out forever the revolutionary era which is sweeping our country owing to the ambitions of a few unpatriotic pretorians; but in the remote case that the United States should disregard

the rights of humanity and the principles of international rights be disregarded, which we hope will never happen, all the Mexicans would have to unite to defend the integrity of our country, as in that case there could be no partition or division as we are all Mexicans. I beg of you to transcribe the foregoing to your Government and for which I hereby respectfully thank you."

This confirms what we have believed all along, namely, that intervention would unite the country against us and that we would have a long and difficult work upon our hands.

With assurances of respect, etc., I am, my dear Mr. President,
Very sincerely yours,   W. J. Bryan

I go to Maine Friday noon

TLS (WP, DLC).
  [1] Plutarco Elías Calles, President of Mexico, 1924-28.

From Furnifold McLendel Simmons

Washington, D. C. Sept. 2-13

We are confronted by a troublesome situation. Newlands who is in Nevada sends a disconcerting wire. Differences in our ranks about rate of income [tax][1] and two other important questions are giving us grave concern[.] Hope you can return to Capital tomorrow for conference.[2]   F. M. Simmons.

T telegram (WP, DLC).
  [1] About the demands of progressive senators for a substantial increase in the income tax rates set by the Underwood bill, see Link, *The New Freedom*, pp. 191-93.
  [2] Wilson had gone to Cornish with Mrs. Wilson on August 29. He had decided to go because his daughter Jessie had suffered a minor injury in a riding accident on August 26. See the *New York Times*, Aug. 28, 29, and 30, 1913, and, for Wilson's own description of the accident, WW to Annie J. W. Howe, Oct. 12, 1913.

From Joseph Patrick Tumulty

Washington, D C Sep 2-13

Senator Simmons has asked Mr. Bryan for letter endorsing finance committees action increasing rates on large incomes to seven per cent as a maximum, this being three per cent above the house maximum. Some of the radical democrats desire to go even higher owing to amendments introduced by progressive republicans. Mr. Bryan is inclined to give letter asked for believing it better to have seven per cent maximum with all democrats sup-

porting it than a higher rate with many democrats objecting. He desires to know your wishes before expressing himself on subject.
Tumulty.

T telegram (WP, DLC).

Two Telegrams to Joseph Patrick Tumulty

Windsor, Vermont, Sept. 2, 1913.

I agree with Mr. Bryan's judgment as to letter he should give Senator Simmons.
Woodrow Wilson.

Windsor, Vt., Sept. 2, 1913.

Please exprect me tomorrow Wednesday morning 9:35. Am calling Senator Simmons on long distance phone now.
Woodrow Wilson.

T telegrams (WP, DLC).

A Telegram and a Letter to Ellen Axson Wilson

[The White House] September 3, 1913

Arrived safe and sound. No real difficulties; only some questions about the tariff measure to be discussed and settled. Developments in Mexico favorable rather than otherwise. Dearest love to all.
Woodrow.

T telegram (Letterpress Books, WP, DLC).

My darling sweetheart,   The White House 3 September, 1913.

We reached home this morning all right. Our train was more than two hours late and I had to rush up to the office and plunge headlong into work without so much as a chance to take breath, but that did me no harm, and this evening I can look back on a full day's work done, and a game of golf over in Virginia sq[u]eezed in, besides, this afternoon. We started a half hour late at Windsor, and the delays accumulated all the way down. We had a leaky engine to begin with and had to limp along until we got to a place where an additional engine could be attached. We passed the scene of the wreck in the dark, and could see only heaps of glowing embers. It was not the train that Frank just missed taking, after all, to which the disaster happened. It did the damage; it did not suffer it. I believe no one was hurt on the White Mountain express, not even the engineer and fireman, though their engine telescoped two cars in the train ahead. How unspeakably dreadful it all was![1]

I am not particularly tired. I had a long sleep on the train—all the longer because the train was delayed in arriving; and a good bed tonight will refresh me entirely.

I have had many, many tender thoughts about you, my darling —ah how deeply tender!—since I lost sight of you as the motor passed around the turn of the road and you were lost for a little while from my side; and such discouraged and discomfiting thoughts about myself! It makes me deeply unhappy to think how often and how utterly I act with absolute disloyalty to all that is best and (I believe) most real and permanent in me; how often I make myself seem exactly what I know I am not, and carry grief and consternation to the heart of the one person in all the world to whom I try to show myself completely and truly! I am saddened to think what a poor creature I am when it comes to the task which I hold dearest in all the world, the task of making those I love happy. I am disgusted and disheartened. When I try hardest I fail most ignominiously. I pray God you will understand, and will see truly through all the strange disguises I weave about myself.

Nothing really disturbing came to light on my taking the threads into my hand again. There are some disturbances among the senators about some of the features of the tariff bill, or, rather, the income tax part of it, but I feel confident that they can be adjusted. And the Mexican situation seems to show some slight signs of brightening according to the last despatch, from O'Shaughnessy.[2] They wish to discuss matters with us further, and I think we shall arrange it successfully. There are many weights for my mind to carry, but none of them seems to be a breaking weight.

My dearest love to all. How lovely our dear ones are; how delightful it was to see the dear Smiths again; and how my darling crowns the group. My dearest love to Helen, too, when she comes. I was *so* sorry that I missed her!

With love without end or measure for yourself,

Your stupid but devoted,   Woodrow

WWTLS (WP, DLC).

1 Twenty-one people were killed and many injured in the collision of two trains of the New York, New Haven and Hartford Railroad on September 2.

2 N. O'Shaughnessy to W. J. Bryan, Sept. 1, 1913, T telegram (SDR, RG 59, 812.00/8648, DNA).

From William Jennings Bryan

My dear Mr. President:　　　　　Washington September 3, 1913.

I have the honor to enclose[1] a copy of the letter which the Minister of Finance of Nicaragua, don Pedro Rafael Cuadra, and the Nicaraguan Minister, resident in Washington, don Emiliano Chamorro, have addressed to the Department under date of September 1st,[2] with a copy of the contract referred to therein. You will notice that the provisions of the letter call for sufficient funds to pay off the present bankers (thus cancelling the option on the railroad) and to relieve Nicaragua's present financial stringency.

Mr. Moore revised the form of agreement and we have put in everything that we can think of that will protect Nicaragua. Please note that the Finance Commissioner has no right to be interested in concessions, except the bank. We thought this provision might remove temptation and enable him to act solely in the interest of Nicaragua. You will notice, too, that the compensation of 1% commission is small compared with what financiers have been in the habit of charging these countries in the form of discounts, and that the loans and expenses incurred in securing the same are subject to approval by the State Department.

The Nicaraguan representatives in Washington would have willingly made a contract less favorable to Nicaragua. In fact, they complained a little at the restrictions that I imposed, but I told them that I would not recommend anything to you that could, in my judgment, be criticised. When the new loan is made Nicaragua will insisit upon a clause permitting payment at any time, so that she can pay off any part or all of her debt with money received from the Canal and Naval Base Convention.

I directed Mr. Long on Saturday afternoon last to request the Nicaraguans to write me a letter expressing definitely their preferences and I enclose a copy of their favor of August 30th.[3] It contains many interesting statements, but as it did not define their desires with sufficient accuracy I asked for this supplemental letter.

Mr. Jarvis has not seen the papers in their present form, but as he is willing to act as Finance Commissioner and investigate the affairs of Nicaragua, as well as secure money for her, I do not anticipate that he will object to the consideration the Nicaraguans desire to show to the present bankers by paying them off before appointing Jarvis definitively. He is principal owner of the National Bank of Cuba and is willing to advance $200,000 to Nicaragua for her immediate use at straight 6% and 1% banker's commission if Nicaragua will agree to pay him back out of the money received for the Canal and Naval Base Convention.

I will serve on all parties the notice which you have already approved, reserving for the Department entire freedom as to any action that may be asked for, the Department's decisions to be rendered when its advice or approval is asked. Copy enclosed.

I will await your advice in this matter and in order that you may note what the present bankers claim to have done for Nicaragua, I attach a copy of their telegram dated August 28, 1913. In my inquiry which brought out this message I referred to the option on the railroad as representing concealed profit, as there was no way to determine accurately the value of option on railway, but whatever it was, it represented an additional profit over and above the 6% interest for which the contract called. Please observe that they soberly refer to 18% as a current rate of interest in Nicaragua and that the Nicaraguan Minister points out that 24% is frequently charged, and states that even at these rates loans are not available. It is little wonder that unrest and revolution occur occasionally under such conditions, and it is the Department's desire as soon as the loan of approximately $2,500,000 now desired is arranged to suggest such distribution of same as will relieve existing unfortunate conditions.

If the present bankers should desire to exercise their option on the railroad under the terms of the *existing* contract, they would be compelled to pay $1,000,000 for 51% of the capital stock (which is $3,200,000) and to lend to the railroad a half million dollars for improvements. Should a new temporary loan by them to Nicaragua for the sum of $2,000,000 be necessary, they now desire a new contract, 51% of the railway for $1,000,000, the remaining 49% for $1,250,000, and release from the obligation of advancing the half million to the railroad for improvements.

The Nicaraguans would prefer to retain the railroad but would not interpose objections should Brown Brothers and Seligman[4] endeavor to exercise their existing option, believing that any effort on their part to break this contract, even though it be a bad one, would have an unfavorable effect upon the credit of their country.

As the transfer of this loan may be the subject of comment, I desire your opinion before taking final action.

I have the honor to be, my dear Mr. President,

Very respectfully   W. J. Bryan

TLS (WP, DLC).
[1] Wilson returned all the enclosures mentioned in the letter. Only the significant ones will be identified.
[2] It is printed in FR *1913*, pp. 1050-1052.
[3] It is printed in *ibid.*, pp. 1047-50.
[4] J. & W. Seligman & Co. of New York, merchant bankers.

From Ellen Axson Wilson

My own darling,   Cornish, New Hampshire Sept. 3, 1913

Your telegram reached me at four this afternoon & is very reassuring. I notice that the papers have very little about Mexico for the last two or three days, and that in itself is surely a good sign.

All is going well here. Mrs. Hall & Ruth spent last night with us and we,—that is the Smiths and I[—] took them back to Hanover this afternoon returning just in time for dinner. We enjoyed them very much & Mrs. Hall certainly enjoyed it too. Margaret sang delightfully for an hour last night. This morning just after breakfast Nell rehearsed her "part" with Mrs. Hall as "coach," and it was a very great help to the child. Then we went out, ostensibly to drive, but we had to take Nell first to Mrs. Adams so it ended in our seeing that charming place,—house, garden, view and studio with casts,—and then stopping at Mr. Vonnoh's to see the picture. Mrs. Hall is immensely charmed and impressed with the Cornish environment.

We had an amusing time at Mr. Vonnoh's. Mrs. V. & Mrs. Potter[1] have gone, you know, and as the maids were no good he has dismissed them & is taking his meals across the way. I posed there yesterday afternoon & as there is now no one to answer the bell, I am instructed to walk right into the studio. I left my party outside today and walked in,—to find Mr V. & a friend swimming in the pool,—fortunately in bathing suits! Mr. V. ran upstairs & came down in a bath robe in which he entertained us most gracefully. It was a handsome robe & he looked much better dressed in it than in his dirty blouse. He has much improved my head,—though it is not yet right.

I had rather a feverish day yesterday too,—with the club and the posing just after you left,—and it is very hot today so I am looking forward to a quiet time tomorrow, & I hope a little painting. We have asked the Fitches to dinner tomorrow night but have not yet heard from them. Poor Nell has to leave at *midnight* tomorrow. This trip of hers is most trying in every way.

Jessie insisted upon riding horseback this morning; said that if she did not do it at once she would lose her nerve, & that Dr Grayson had said she could. I was rather miserable but had to bear it of course. She came back radiant & said she had had a splendid time. Her eye is better. I love, *love, love* you, dear, in every way you would like me to love you & I am altogether

Your own   Eileen

ALS (WC, NjP).
1 Mary Elizabeth McKenney (Mrs. Alexander C.) Potter, mother of Bessie Potter (Mrs. Robert William) Vonnoh.

From Furnifold McLendel Simmons, with Enclosures

To the President: [Washington] September 4, 1913.

I inclose you herein a copy of the amendment to the Income Tax rate as proposed by the Committee—also a copy proposed by Senator Reed.

There is very much division in the Caucus. I would be glad, if you think you can afford to do so, to have a letter from you which I may show to my Democratic colleagues with respect to this very much controverted question.

Very respectfully yours,   F. M. Simmons

The Caucus will meet to-morrow, Friday, at 9:30 a.m.

TLS (WP, DLC).

E N C L O S U R E   I

Senator Reed

Strike out all after the word "exceeds" in line 19, page 165, all of lines 20 and 21, page 165; and down to and including "100,000" in line 3, page 166, and insert in lieu thereof the following:

"$10,000 and does not exceed $20,000; and 1½ per centum per annum upon the amount by which the total net income exceeds $20,000 but does not exceed $30,000; and 2 per centum per annum upon the amount by which the total net income exceeds $30,000 but does not exceed $40,000; and 2½ per centum per annum upon the amount by which the total net income exceeds $40,000 but does not exceed $50,000; and 3 per centum per annum upon the amount by which the total net income exceeds $50,000 but does not exceed $60,000; and 4 per centum per annum upon the amount by which the total net income exceeds $60,000 but does not exceed $70,000; and 5 per centum per annum upon the amount by which the total net income exceeds $70,000 but does not exceed $80,000; and 6 per cent per annum upon the amount by which the total net income exceeds $80,000 but does not exceed $90,000; and 7 per centum per annum upon the amount by which the total net income exceeds $90,000 but does not exceed $100,000; and 8 per centum per annum upon the amount by which the total net income exceeds $100,000."

ENCLOSURE   II

Committee

On line 3, page 166, after "$100,000" insert the following: "and does not exceed $250,000; 4 per centum per annum upon the amount of which the total net income exceeds $250,000 and does not exceed $500,000; and 5 per centum per annum upon the amount by which the total net income exceeds $500,00[0] and does not exceed $1,000,000; and 6 per centum per annum upon the amount by which the total net income exceeds $1,000,-000."

100 ⎫
250 ⎬ 3%
250 ⎫
500 ⎬ 4%
500 ⎫
1000 ⎬ 5%
1000 — 6% [1]

T MS (WP, DLC).
  [1] WWhw figures.

To Furnifold McLendel Simmons

My dear Senator: [The White House] September 4, 1913

I have your favor of today enclosing the proposals of Senator Reed with regard to the modification of the pending bill so far as it concerns taxes on incomes, and also the proposals submitted to the caucus by the Finance Committee. I do not wonder that there are wide divergences of opinion regarding this difficult matter. Individual judgments will naturally differ with regard to the burden it is fair to lay upon incomes which run above the usual levels. My own opinion in the matter is that it is much safer to begin upon somewhat moderate lines, and I think that the proposals of the committee are reasonable and well considered. I should think that they would commend themselves to the caucus, particularly where there is, I understand, so considerable a diversity of opinion, because they run along a reasonable, median line. I have every confidence that an accommodation of individual judgments will lead to a conclusion which everybody will support.

I am very much obliged to you for paying me the compliment of asking my opinion in this important matter.

Cordially and sincerely yours,   [Woodrow Wilson]

CCL (WP, DLC).

From William Jennings Bryan

My dear Mr. President: Washington September 4, 1913.

I have just talked with Mr. Henry, of Texas. There have been two resolutions introduced reflecting upon the Department of Justice.[1] Henry asked me to say that no rule would be given in regard to these resolutions until he had conferred with you and learned your wishes in the matter. He also told me to say that his Committee[2] would report any rule that you wanted in regard to the currency bill. The report that he had voted against the bill in caucus is not true. He is very well satisfied with the bill since the amendment has been added in regard to farm loans and wants you to know that he is ready to give any assistance he can.

In regard to the resolutions affecting the Attorney General's office, I told him that I thought he ought to say to any Democrat who wanted to investigate a department that he must *first* take the matter to the department and to the President and find out the Administration's side of the question, and that any Democrat who introduced a resolution looking to an investigation *without first having conferred with the President and the department*, ought to be treated as a Republican rather than as a Democrat, because a Democrat who takes the public into his confidence before he confers with the Administration cannot have the good of the party at heart. Henry agreed with me that that is the position to take.

I think I may be able to reach Fowler, of Illinois, who introduced one of the resolutions, and I may be able to reach Kindel, although I am not so sure about his attitude. I shall try to show them the difference between the attitude of a friend and the attitude of an opponent. No friend will criticise until he has first exhausted every opportunity to ascertain the facts by private investigation, and the first place to go for investigation in such matters is to the department itself and to you. I shall be glad to have any suggestions that you may have to make on this subject.

With assurances of respect, etc., I am, my dear Mr. President,
Very sincerely yours,   W. J. Bryan

TLS (WP, DLC).

[1] Representative George John Kindel of Colorado on August 19 introduced a resolution calling for an investigation of "the alleged dissolution of the Union Pacific-Southern Pacific Railroad merger." Ten days later, Representative Hiram Robert Fowler of Illinois introduced a resolution for an investigation of the dissolution of the American Tobacco Co. Both resolutions were referred to the House Rules Committee; neither ever emerged from it. *Cong. Record*, 63rd Cong., 1st sess., pp. 3531, 3925. For the activities of Attorney General McReynolds which inspired the resolutions, see Link, *The New Freedom*, pp. 417-19.

[2] The House Rules Committee.

From Howard Allen Bridgman[1]

My dear Mr. President: Boston Sept. 4, 1913.

We are somewhat concerned over the segregation of negroes in the departments at Washington, and before commenting unfavorably on it, we should like much to get your own point of view. We have no right to demand a long letter from you but should appreciate just a word telling us whether you approve of this segregation, to what extent it is being practiced, and why there should be such a departure from precedent.

Thanking you much for a reply, and with sincere esteem,
Respectfully yours,   H. A. Bridgman

TLS (WP, DLC).
[1] Editor-in-chief of *The Congregationalist and Christian World.*

From Ellen Axson Wilson

My own darling,   Cornish, New Hampshire Sept. 4 1913

It is nearing eleven so I fear I must write only a little letter in answer to the *dear dear* one just received. Oh how I love you, my darling. It is *I* who ought to ask *your* pardon,—and I do ask it,—for being so sensitive and, so to say, taking you too literally. Of course I know how well you love me, dearest,—how *much* more than I deserve,—and I should not let a mere word hurt me and so, by reaction, hurt you. I will try hard to be more sensible! Certainly it [is] all right with me now.

We have had a beautiful evening. The Fitches dined with us and they are altogether charming. He is in some ways a dear, delightful boy,—the simplest most natural person! I feel as if I had known him for years. It makes me smile now to think that you feared the "strain" of having him here. In five minutes you would be about as much at your ease with him as with Dudley Malone! We are *all* to go and lunch with them on Monday week,— a sort of picnic.

Our darling Nell goes off on the one o'clock train. I can hardly bear it,—it is so dreary, and that road is so horrible. Besides she has been having tooth-ache for days, (though it is better tonight). Chiefly because of the tooth-ache, I am sending Margaret Norton[1] with her as far as New York, for she had a horrible time with it last night. We have arranged for her to stay in N. Y. until the noon train and see a good dentist. Frank goes to the station with her tonight.

I posed for the picture again today and I really think he has it at last. I sat close to the easel and he worked at the face in detail.

I am eager for the others to say it is good and so end my troubles.

But I can scarcely see my paper I am so sleepy—so I must say good-night.

I love you devotedly my darling. I am altogether.

You[r] own   Nell.

Is there fresh trouble about the currency bill?—as the papers report.[2]

ALS (WC, NjP).

[1] Unidentified.

[2] Strong protests against the Federal Reserve bill from both individual bankers and bankers' associations were playing into the hands of Republican and Democratic senators opposed to the measure. They made it clear during the first days of September that they intended to hold lengthy hearings on the bill in the Banking and Currency Committee. The newspapers announced on September 4 that a resolution would soon be introduced in the Senate to postpone enactment of currency legislation at least until December. See the *New York Times*, Sept. 1-5, 1913, and Link, *The New Freedom*, pp. 225-29.

To William Jennings Bryan

My dear Mr. Secretary: The White House September 5, 1913

I think that you have handled most wisely the matters that Mr. Henry of Texas brought to your attention. I think it would be useful for Mr. Henry and our other friends in the House to know that there is something like a concerted effort to discredit Mr. McReynolds because he is known to be formidable, dangerously formidable, to the men who wish to act without sanction of law. Mr. Kindell, I am sorry to say, seems to have some sort of obscure grievance against the administration, which I have tried to fathom and can find no shadow of justification for.

I am heartily glad to know how Henry feels and I would appreciate it very much indeed if he kept in close touch with Mr. Glass about the rule to be reported concerning the currency measure. I am very glad that he is, himself, satisfied with it in its present form.

My general feeling is that the Democrats ought to keep it in mind that the present administration is Democratic and that they ought not to allow members of our own party to assume an attitude towards it such as they used to assume toward an hostile administration. My own personal conviction is that there is no more honest and conscientious man in the public service than Mr. McReynolds, and it distresses me that there should be these repeated attacks upon him.

With warmest regard,

Cordially and faithfully yours,   Woodrow Wilson

TLS (W. J. Bryan Papers, DNA).

From Furnifold McLendel Simmons, with Enclosure

To the President: [Washington] September 5, 1913.

I inclose you herein the Income Tax amendment upon which the Caucus finally agreed.

I think it a magnificent settlement of our differences. It is reasonably satisfactory to everybody.[1]

Very respectfully yours,   F M Simmons

TLS (WP, DLC).
[1] It became part of the income tax provision of the Underwood-Simmons Tariff Act.

ENCLOSURE

CAUCUS AMENDMENT.

Subdivision 2. In addition to the income tax provided under this section (herein referred to as the normal income tax)[1] there shall be levied, assessed, and collected upon the net income of every individual an additional income tax (herein referred to as the additional tax) of 1 per centum per annum upon the amount by which the total net income exceeds $20,000 and does not exceed $50,000, and 2 per centum per annum upon the amount by which the total net income exceeds $50,000 and does not exceed $75,000, and 3 per cent per annum upon the amount by which the total net income exceeds $75,000 and does not exceed $100,000; and four per centum per annum upon the amount by which the total net income exceeds $100,000 and does not exceed $250,000; and 5 per centum per annum upon the amount by which the total net income exceeds $250,000 and does not exceed $500,000; and 6 per centum per annum upon the amount by which the next [net] income exceeds $500,000.

CC MS (WP, DLC).
[1] It was 1 per cent of taxable personal income.

From Ellen Axson Wilson

My own darling,   Cornish, New Hampshire Sept. 5, 1913.

Helen came back today looking very well and lovely in spite of a cold,—the third since she left. She says the sea-shore does not agree with her. The Smiths, Miss Hagner & little Aleck went over to meet her at White River Junction. Margaret was out lunching, posing, and driving with one of her suitors, so I had the whole place to myself all the afternoon and very much enjoyed the profound quiet. I painted on the breakfast porch most of the time. Jessie & Frank were out on a "picnic" alone,—afterwards she posed too;—and both she and Margaret think my picture lovely now and a *real* likeness. Thank heaven! My troubles are surely over at last! I am to go once more however.

Poor Miss Hagner is in fresh trouble over that unspeakable sister-in-law. She threatens to come *here* at once and seize the child if he is not sent to her in N. Y. So Belle feels she must take him at once to Washington and put him under his father's protection both for the sake of the child and to avoid a scene under your roof,—which naturally she feels she has no right to risk. So she leaves tomorrow for Washington. It is *too* bad! The change was doing both her and the child so much good.

We are all going on a picnic tomorrow to please Jessie,—all except Margaret, who has other engagements. We elders are not very enthusiastic about picnics but are doing it to please Jessie. She leaves on Monday for Boston. Her eye is improving with extraordinary rapidity. There is just one little narrow streak of blue under the eye and the red spot on the ball is *much* smaller.

Margaret has *two* suitors here at once, Dr Devolle & Boyd Fisher.[1] But she is not "encouraging" either of them as she did in Washington. She says with evident truth that she is not in the least in love with either.

By the way, you remember that invitation of Walter Page's to Jessie & Frank which she begged you not to answer until they consulted about it. They think they will *accept*; but cannot of course decide positively just yet. So will you please, dear, have your note of acknowledgment written along those lines. Jessie will write to Mrs. Page. They think it will be "broadening" to do it!

Goodnight, dear heart,—how I hope that all goes well with you. With love inexpressible.   Your own,   Nell.

How I wish I knew if the new currency "hitch" is a very serious one! And what is happening about Mexico—and *every*thing that Mr. Hale reported![2] Ah me!

ALS (WC, NjP).
  [1] Boyd Archer Fisher is identified in L. D. Brandeis to WW, May 26, 1913, n.1, Vol. 27. The Editors have been unable to identify Dr. Devolle.
  [2] Hale had just returned to Washington to report to the President.

From Morris Sheppard

My dear Mr. President: Washington, D. C. Sep. 6, 1913.

I appreciate very deeply your note[1] in reference to my speech.[2]

I stated in my address before the Texas Legislature accepting my election to the Senate that I would be proud to support your ideals and policies.

It is both a pleasure and a duty to stand with you and to direct attention to the devotion and the success with which you are guiding the nation.

With every expression of regard, I am,

Most sincerely,   Morris Sheppard.

ALS (WP, DLC).

¹ A WWhw or WWT note, which is missing.

² Sheppard delivered a lengthy speech in the Senate on September 4 praising and defending the Underwood-Simmons tariff bill. Wilson's note of thanks undoubtedly was inspired by Sheppard's final paragraph: "And as this bill pursues its march of triumph through the American Congress the attention of the American people turns to that unassuming figure at the Nation's head, that exemplar of justice and of love, that marvel of patience and of power, Woodrow Wilson. To his genius and his courage must be attributed the elements in this measure that do most to break the sway of privilege." The balance of the paragraph paid a similar tribute to Bryan for his long fight for tariff reform. *Cong. Record*, 63rd Cong., 1st sess., pp. 4212-19.

From Ellen Axson Wilson

My own darling,   Cornish, New Hampshire Sept. 6, 1913

We have had a 97 miles automobile ride today and I am rather tremulous after it—so you must excuse everything. We started out to go over a "pass" which would take us virtually to the Green Mts.,—or within sight of them all; but we lost our way & never achieved the pass. But we had a very successful day all the same. It is such fun to explore—to get out of the beaten track, and we did that with a vengeance! We went through many wild mountain valleys with the great hills crowding close about us and we saw *dozens*,—literally,—of beautiful little lakes. Then we came to a tiny but unusually beautiful little brook and we followed it for *hours* until it developed before our eyes into a broad quiet lovely river at Woodstock,—the Orquaqueechy(?)¹ In short we had a lovely day! "We" were Jessie & Frank, the Smiths & me. Poor Helen's cold was too severe. We found, to our dismay, that she had been quite sick during the day—a severe billious attack—but she is much better now.

I hope from the papers tonight that things are looking better as regards Mexico; but I am *so* concerned at the reports about the currency bill. They say you are fighting desperately with your back to the wall. And I remember what you have said all along about that committee—so I fear it is true for once. Please tell me. I really cannot see the paper—my eyes are so heavy—so I must say goodnight, my *darling*!   Your own Eileen.

ALS (WC, NjP).

¹ The Ottauquechee River.

To Ellen Axson Wilson

My precious darling,   The White House 7 September, 1913.

I enclose two things: a deposit slip for the salary for August and for royalty from Houghton, Mifflin & Co., and an extract from a speech made in the Senate the other day by Senator Morris Sheppard of Texas. I was so much gratified, and indeed touched, by what he was generous enough to say about me that I wanted you to see it and read it also. I know that it will make you a warm friend of Senator Sheppard. He is a most lovable man, whom I want you to know.

No; there is no new trouble about the currency. I have seen all along that it is going to be a hard matter to get it through the Senate Committee on Banking and Currency without radical changes because of Senator O'Gorman and Senator Hitchcock, who happen to be members of the committee and almost the only two serious critics of the bill on our side of the house in the Senate; but there are no new snags, so far as I can see, and I feel confident that things can be guided to a successful issue. Please do not let yourself be disturbed by what the newspapers say. They are all the while looking for something out of the usual. Trouble makes news; the ordinary course of business and of human conduct does not. Pay no attention to them,—particularly since those which are controlled are determined that there *shall* be trouble, and will make it themselves if no one else will. They do not determine what is going to happen in Washington, and so far as I can ascertain nothing new has turned up here in regard to the situation, either with regard to the currency or with regard to the tariff.

Our pastor[1] has returned (very recently, I should judge from the loose structure of this morning's sermon), and I took the liberty of breaking another precedent this morning by going to service in a white suit. It was simply too hot to wear a cloth suit, and I took the rules of propriety into my own hands. We (Dr. Grayson and I) had the Lord Provost of Glasgow[2] to lunch with us, a very juicy and interesting and most unusual man he proved to be: a slim, scrawny little gentleman whose outside did not in the least give intimation of what was inside him; and slimmer than usual, he gave us to understand, because the heat of this handsome continent had taken some eight pounds of flesh off his bones since he landed. An American summer is a terrible ordeal for a Scotsman!

We have fallen back into our old routine and everything goes as usual with us. I am perfectly well, and do not find that the heat makes any real difference to me, except occasionally in the matter of physical comfort. I understand that Miss Hagner is back in the city. Did you not expect her to remain at Cornish for a good deal longer time? Hoover says she intimated to him over the telephone that her return had something to do with an attempt by "the other party" to get hold of the child. Poor lady, she is having a hard and anxious time, I am so sorry.

Sundays are hard for me, dearest. I have time then to think,— about myself,—and to feel lonely, and it is not profitable. It spoils me to go to Cornish. It softens my power of steadfast addiction to my duty. It fills me with a longing which it is impossible for me to conquer. Indeed, I do not know that I can truthfully say that I try to conquer it. It is sweet, even when it hurts, to dwell upon my love for you,—to sit and dream of you, to realize you, to fill all my thoughts of every kind *of you*. It is like drinking my fill at the fountain from which most of my strength and happiness come. I would grow dry and hard, I fear, if I did not. Life would look grey and dun, and I would have no zest in anything. At any rate I can't help it. I must have you one way or another! How I do daily bless you for your letters! Every day, either Fo[r]ster[3] or Pat McKenna[4] comes in and stands one of your letters up on end in front of me about the middle of the morning as I work, evidently knowing perfectly well what it means to me and feeling that it will lighten the labour of the day, which both of them, bless them! want to do when they can. I *know* that it gives them real pleasure to put the letter there. As for me, it is meat and drink to me!

Dearest love to all. My thought dwells upon the whole dear circle with infinite pleasure. Where else in the world are there so many persons in a single household every one of whom is so lovable? I am the most fortunate man in the world.

Your own   Woodrow

WWTLS (WC, NjP).
    [1] The Rev. James Henry Taylor.
    [2] Daniel Macaulay Stevenson, wealthy coal export merchant and philanthropist.
    [3] Rudolph Forster, executive clerk of the White House.
    [4] Patrick E. McKenna, clerk at the White House.

To Mary Allen Hulbert

My dearest friend,   The White House 7 September, 1913.

I wonder if the long interval since your last letter means that you are worse or that you do not recover your strength as rapidly as you expected? I try to reassure myself. I try to reason that if you were worse Allen would have let me know or that some one would have sent me a message, but I do not wholly succeed. I catch myself worrying about you, and am often full of uneasiness. And yet I know that that is unreasonable. I *will* not assume anything of the kind—I cannot work as I should when I do,—for I know, among other things that reassure me, how thoughtful you are and how sure you would be to let em [me] know of anything that seemed serious. I had set my heart, you see, on having this summer, spent quietly on Nantucket, quite set you up again, and bring back all your old spring and vivacity, if only by virtue of the mere rest and refreshment (physical refreshment) you were getting out of the winds and the influences of the ocean and all the things you love so much in Nature that are about you. It would go hard with me to be disappointed. Please write to me presently and tell me exactly how you fare and what you are projecting for yourself when autumn and winter come on.

I spent last Saturday, Sunday, and Monday (Labour Day) at Cornish, and it did me a lot of good to get a few days of freedom from the atmosphere (the figurative article) of Washington; but not so much as if I had had a clear conscience. The fact must be admitted that I cannot have a clear conscinece [conscience] away from Washington so long as Congress is sitting. It's tough to have your conscience in one place and your heart in another; but when that unhappy situation arises the only safe thing is to stay doggedly where your conscience is: for that, after all, is the master of your happiness. And so I came back, in spite of being urged by indulgent associates here to stay away for a week. Weekends are all I can hope for,—and precious few of them!

Every now and again, just to keep my hand in and feel natural, I break a precedent. I broke one to day, feeling a little stale and dull. I went to church in a white linen suit. It was simply so hot that I could not stand any other kind. I created a mild sensation as I entered the church, as I could see by the way the people looked at me; but that of course is what every public man wishes to do, at church or anywhere else, and it did not in the least interfere with my own state of mind during the service. After the first five minutes I lost the self-consciousness I had felt on entering. Is there anything more hateful or more unhandsome and ridiculous than self-consciousness? I would rather have the small pox. It is as fatal to any genuine action as any kind of disease is to acting at all! We are immensely pleased with our little church here. It is so simple and old-fashioned. And the people in it are so genuine and fundamentally self-respecting. We never have had there the sense of being stared at or made capital of for the benefit of the congregation. If I could only go without having a secret service man sit right behind me, and half a dozen secret service men wait about the church while I am in it! What fun it will be some day to escape from arrest!

I am perfectly well, and public affairs go very well,—as well as could be expected, and much better than those who do not like the party would like to see them go. And there are compensations even to official life here. To-day, for example, we (Dr. Grayson and I; he and I and Tumulty keep bachelors hall together, but on Sundays T. runs away to be with his little family on the Jersey shore) had a most delightful man to lunch with us whom I would not have had the pleasure of knowing had he not wished to meet the President, namely the Lord Provost of Glasgow, a Mr. Stevenson, who proved to be full of the kind of things that make the mind of a cultivated & gifted Scotsman one of the most delightful companions of the modern world (since I never belonged to any other). I had him in as a matter of duty, and duty graciously put on the aspect of pleasure the moment he began to talk. There are these incidental and occasional rewards, to keep a fellow from going stale or turning grim and dull and being deadened by it all. How it would brighten everything if some day the friend who has been so much to me might happen this way! But the fairies are not so kind as *that.*

Your devoted friend   Woodrow Wilson

WWTLS (WP, DLC).

From Ellen Axson Wilson

My own darling,   Cornish, New Hampshire Sept. 7, 1913.

These Sundays when, no matter how busy you are, you could be with us if we were only near enough to you, make me feel very sadly that it was a great mistake to take this place *this* year. Oh for a little simple house in the mountains of Va. or Maryland,— within two or three hours of Washington! Don't you think that would have [been] the right thing? If I had only had more experience I would never have been caught in such a trap! Did *you* know when we took this place that things would be as they are? Honour bright? Well, at any rate it has been lovely for the girls here,—perfectly ideal for Jessie and Frank. It will be an enchanting memory for them all their lives,—and that goes far to console me. Margaret too is passionately in love with it all.

Her two suitors both leave tonight or tomorrow. Mr. Fisher has been here as long as she has. He really is a very attractive fellow.

He has such an interesting mind,—so quick to take, not only an idea but a point of view or an impression. Sympathetic without the least sacrifice of truth or independence. I am afraid I think him more interesting to be with than either Frank or Ben![1] He and Margaret are taking a "last ride together" in the car, and Frank and Jessie are driving in the little "buggy."

The Smiths have gone into retreat as usual on Sundays. Helen was up for luncheon and also went out in the car with me after church. She is *very* much better.

I have been painting a little; went down to the studio to show Boyd Fisher my work and of course was tempted to linger after they went off in the car. What *would* I have done this summer without the painting! I could not have endured it! It is beginning to look like fall already, and I shall paint out of doors more.

By the way, dear, have you deposited the check for last month? If so I will get some more of the same bonds from Webb & Prall.

It is good to think that my darling is perhaps writing to me at this very hour! With what inexpressible eagerness I await those Sunday letters! And oh how I love them and *you*,—my darling, *my darling*. Be sure to tell me exactly how you are;—also the facts of the currency situation. With love unspeakable I am, my dear one, always and altogether   Your own   Eileen.

ALS (WC, NjP).
[1] Benjamin Mandeville King, Eleanor's fiancé. King worked for the Weyerhaeuser Timber Co. as manager of a lumber camp near Madera, Mexico. Eleanor had met him while visiting friends in Madera in early 1913.

To Howard Allen Bridgman

Personal and Confidential   [The White House]

My dear Doctor Bridgeman: September 8, 1913

In reply to your kind letter of September fourth, I would say that I do approve of the segregation that is being attempted in several of the departments. I have not always approved of the way in which the thing was done and have tried to change that in some instances for the better, but I think if you were here on the ground you would see, as I seem to see, that it is distinctly to the advantage of the colored people themselves that they should be organized, so far as possible and convenient, in distinct bureaux where they will center their work. Some of the most thoughtful colored men I have conversed with have themselves approved of this policy. I certainly would not myself have approved of it if I had not thought it to their advantage and likely to remove many of the difficulties which have surrounded the appointment and advancement of colored men and women.

Cordially and sincerely yours,   Woodrow Wilson

TLS (Letterpress Books, WP, DLC).

From Ellen Axson Wilson

My own darling,   Cornish, New Hampshire Sept. 8, 1913.

I begin this letter while waiting for the car to return from Hanover with the Smiths, Helen & Ruth. They went with Frank and Jessie to White River Junction first. Jessie took the train there to Boston for her little shopping excursion at the Tedcastles. She will buy all her lingerie and return on Thursday or Friday morning,—in time to see Nell act.

Nell returned on the ten-thirty which was of course late. We were there to meet her with all the family and *both* cars, for a chum of Frank's was to jump off here & go on with him to the Junction. From there they started on a walking tour—to pass the time until Jessie returns. They had a rather wild time carrying out the schedule because of the delayed train. Nell had never met Frank's chum, but last night *he* was asked quite by accident if he "would not give up his lower berth to the President's daughter." So they came out of the car together, already good friends. Nell's tooth has given her practically no further trouble since the N. Y. dentist saw it. He took out a filling.

But her journey was a most extraordinary tragi-comedy. She had to come back home *before* the wedding[1] after taking that long terrible journey to go to it! The marriage does not take place until *tomorrow* the 9th! They wanted her to *be* there by the sixth for some dinners &c. As far as she can recall they never said that the marriage proper was on the ninth. And since the bird-play is to be on the 12th & they have had but two rehersals, she was *forced* to return at the time fixed. Did you ever hear of such a fiasco? Of course they "cried their eyes out" & spent sleepless nights, &c, &c.; but now Nell has reached the stage of thinking it a great joke. She looks very tired, poor child, and she has to reherse all the afternoon. But then we will tuck her in bed & keep her there for 18 hours or so.

Tell the doctor that Jessie went off looking scarcely disfigured at all. The bruise around the eye is practically gone, and the clot is quite small though still intensely red.

Since I began this I have lunched and been for the last time to Mr. Vonnah's. My head is very dainty now and I think sufficiently like me. He is going to do a head of Jessie from that lovely coloured photo, for a wedding present. Isn't that delightful? It is a great secret, by the way! It ought to be *mine*, & perhaps I can get it, for neither Jessie nor Frank like that photograph very much.

I love you dear, *dearest* Woodrow with all my heart and soul. You are my very life. As always

Your own little wife   Nell.

ALS (WC, NjP).
[1] The wedding of a former schoolmate, Nellie Kitner, in Athens, Pa.

A Statement Upon the Passage of the Tariff Bill[1]

[[Sept. 9, 1913]]

A fight for the people and for free business, which has lasted a long generation through, has at last been won, handsomely and completely. A leadership and a steadfastness in council have been shown in both houses of which the Democratic Party has reason to be very proud. There has been no weakness or confusion or drawing back, but a statesmanlike directness and command of circumstances. I am happy to have been connected with the Government of the nation at a time when such things could happen and to have worked in association with men who could do them.

There is every reason to believe that currency reform will be carried through with equal energy, directness, and loyalty to the general interest. When that is done this first session of the Sixty-third Congress will have passed into history with an unrivaled distinction.

I want to express my special admiration for the devoted, intelligent, and untiring work of Mr. Underwood and Mr. Simmons and the committees associated with them.

Printed in the *New York Times*, Sept. 10, 1913.
[1] By the Senate, at 5:40 P.M. on September 9. The vote was forty-four to thirty-seven.

To Ellen Axson Wilson

My darling,   The White House 9 September, 1913.

Just a line to enclose this additional memorandum of deposit. It represents an unexpected royalty on "The New Freedom," of which, it seems, some ten thousand copies have been sold.

I am perfectly well. I am not disturbed about the currency. To say that I have my back against the wall is ridiculous. The Senate is tired, some of the members of its committee are irritable and will have to be indulged with a few days of rest, but there will be no insuperable difficulty in handling the situation, so far as I can see. *Please* pay no attention to what the papers say.

Mexico is *sui generis*. I do not know what to make of it. The apparent situation changes like quicksilver. But the real situation, I fancy, remains the same, and is likely to yield to absent treatment.

I love you with all my heart. I love you all.

In tearing haste,   Your own,   Woodrow

The bills Cosby sends I have approved.

WWTLS (WC, NjP).

From William Jennings Bryan

My dear Mr. President: Washington September 9, 1913.

The Japanese Ambassador is very anxious to get some intimation as to what answer may be expected to the proposition he submitted some weeks ago.[1] He has been quite patient in waiting for the tariff bill to be out of the way, and I think it might be well for me to take the matter up with you Thursday so that I can report progress on Friday. In the meantime we can both be revolving his proposal in our minds with a view to seeing what, if any, concessions can be made.

There seems to be a little outbreak of jingoism in Tokio, the immediate cause being something that happened in China, but those who criticise the Government connect the California question with the China question, and the Ambassador informs me that they are even criticising the action of the Government in not welcoming Diaz.[2]

With assurances of respect, etc., I am, my dear Mr. President,
                    Very sincerely yours,   W. J. Bryan

TLS (WP, DLC).
    [1] See WJB to WW, Sept. 17, 1913.
    [2] Huerta had appointed Felix Díaz as special envoy to Japan, mainly, it was commonly alleged, to get him out of Mexico. The Japanese government had announced that it would not receive him.

From Robert Latham Owen

[Washington]

My dear Mr. President: Sept. 9th [1913] 4.45 p.m.

I enclose a poll of democratic Senators.[1] Hitchcock strongly opposes being "rushed" otherwise except the natural weariness of the flesh our members are about unanimous in favoring prompt action of the Committee on Banking & Currency and as speedy action as practicable by the U. S. Senate.

Yours truly   Robt. Owen

ALS (WP, DLC).
[1] It is missing.

From Ellen Axson Wilson

My own darling,   Cornish, New Hampshire Sept. 9, 1913.

Your dear, *dear* letter letter [*sic*] reached me last night and made me very happy,—for a dozen different reasons. Every word of it exactly met and filled some deeply felt need either of my mind or heart. Bless you for it, dear heart! All you say about the currency was most reassuring and took a weight off my mind.

I am waiting most eagerly now to hear that the tariff bill has passed. Will it be really *settled* then?—no turning back or weakening of it possible? Or can they still do mischief in the "conference" of which you spoke. I find that my ideas about the next steps in the long process are very hazy.

I am just back from the club. It met at Miss Slade's splendid place, and we discussed "the simple life—what is it and is it worth while?" Mary and I went alone. Lucy has a bad cold now and Helen just "cut it"!

Margaret's lovers have both gone, and she was posing. Nell & Ruth were, of course, rehersing. Everyone is *wild* over Nell's performance,—her grace, her beauty and her real gift as an actress. But oh dear me, I don't know what I will do if this cold, shivery weather lasts until Friday night; it will be so dangerous for them with those thin things on. Her costume is charming, —a white shimmering silk slip and fluttering rainbow tinted gauze scarves arranged to suggest wings.

Mr. Vonnoh came around this morning to look at my work and give me a criticism. He was very encouraging. He said he "was very much surprised,["] though he had expected a good deal from the little things he had seen at the White House. He said I "was a real artist, and that if I will go on my work will be really *very* distinguished." He also thought Nell's little picture quite charming. He thought we both had any amount of individuality, and that I had with it a good deal of variety,—that is that I did several sorts of things equally well,—and with equal feeling. He wants to come again after I have made certain little changes in detail. He made only one general criticism and I see myself that he is right. I have been getting my tree trunks and the darkest accents in my foregrounds a little too hot,—I should use more purple & less brown in them. They are not completely "enveloped"!

I *adore* you, dear *dear* love! You make me more happy than I can express—even when you are absent!

Your own   Eileen.

ALS (WC, NjP).

From Edward Mandell House

My dear Friend,   Beverly [Mass.] September 10th, 1913.

I want to add my congratulations to the many that are coming to you today. The passing of such a tariff is truly a great achievement and no matter how generously you give credit to others, it is known to all men that the work is yours. You are so much more efficient than any public man with whom I have heretofore been in touch, that the others seem mere tyros. Then, too, you have a way of getting what is best out of those who are working for the same cause. Everyone connected with your administration is on his mettle striving to emulate his Chieftan's example in unselfish service to his country. It is a splendid future that I see before you, and God grant you strength to carry all your noble undertakings to completion.

Your letter of a few days ago[1] stimulates me anew, and makes me eager to be again at your side. Your confidence in me and your affection for me is the greatest reward that has ever been given me, and I pray that I may prove worthy of it.

Your devoted,   E. M. House

ALS (WP, DLC).
[1] WW to EMH, Sept. 4, 1913, TLS (E. M. House Papers, CtY).

From John Francis Fitzgerald

Boston, Mass., Sept. 10, 1913.

Rumor here tonight that Edward [Edmund] Billings to be named collector port. Billings a commercial Democrat, *if a Democrat* at all, and his nomination particularly at this time would be most injurious to party. His services for years back have been for hire to those engaged in effort to destroy Boston Democracy. A man of ordinary ability his nomination to this office an insult to rank and file of party.

John F. Fitzgerald,   Mayor of Boston.

T telegram (WP, DLC).

From William Gibbs McAdoo

Dear Mr. President: Washington September 10, 1913.

I respectfully recommend for appointment as Collector of Customs at the Port of Boston, Massachusetts, Mr. Edmund Billings, of Boston. Mr. Billings is President of the Paul Revere Trust Company, and is President of the Good Government League. He is strongly recommended by Messrs. Louis Brandeis, Richard Olney, E. A. Grozier,[1] E. M. House, and Dudley Field Malone.[2]

Very sincerely yours,   W G McAdoo

TLS (WP, DLC).
  [1] Edwin Atkins Grozier, editor and publisher of the *Boston Post*.
  [2] Wilson sent Billings's nomination to the Senate on October 7, 1913.

From James Richard Gray

Atlanta, Ga., Sept. 10, 1913.

I beg to offer my warmest congratulations upon the Senate's passage of the tariff bill. The country now understands substantially the basis upon which it must operate and I predict that business which has been to some extent marking time pending this legislation will take on great activity. I trust the currency bill will also pass without needless delay. I cannot refrain from expressing to you my profound admiration for the superb generalship and infinite tact you have shown throughout this trying summer of tariff and currency agitation. These measures were promised by the party. They were indispensible for the country's welfare and you have redeemed your party pledges honestly, wisely and in a manner that reassures those who feared the result of proposed changes. The country applauds your masterful leadership and will I am convinced approve with great unanimity the business conditions that will result from these measures.

James R. Gray.

T telegram (WP, DLC).

From Charles William Eliot

Dear Mr. President: Asticou, Maine, September 10, 1913.

Because of their great and far-reaching importance, I venture to call your personal attention to certain Democratic acts for which the party is liable to be held responsible at the next elections. These acts seem to me to show instability, or lack of conviction, with regard to the consistent application of the merit system.

The first is the party vote in the Senate rejecting Senator Lodge's amendment about the income-tax-collection force.[1] That action seems to fix on the Democratic party the deliberate purpose of making a large number of spoils appointments.

The second is the issue from the Department of the Interior of the circular letter of which I enclose a copy.[2] The last paragraph of this letter is an order to give public advertising to Democratic newspapers.

The third is the violation in a considerable number of instances of the excellent policy set up by the last two Republican Administrations, namely, that of making the diplomatic and consular service a life-career for well-trained men, who should prove themselves efficient and influential. I learn from the public records of the diplomatic officers who have been removed and of their successors, that several ministers, who have come up through the service from the ranks and are trained diplomats, have been displaced by men who have never been in the diplomatic service, and are obscure men at home.

I feel as if it were not only right but also highly expedient to keep the skirts of the party clean from every use of public offices or appointments as party spoils. The convictions of an immense majority of the American voters are against that practice. You seem to be the main stay of Democratic morality in this respect. Do not these matters require, therefore, your urgent personal intervention?   Sincerely yours,   Charles W. Eliot

TLS (WP, DLC).
  [1] On August 29, Lodge proposed to strike out a proviso of an amendment to the tariff bill which exempted the agents, deputy collectors, and inspectors charged with administering the income tax provisions of the bill from the regulations imposed by the Civil Service Act of 1883. After some debate, Lodge's proposal was rejected by a vote of thirty-seven to thirty-two. *Cong. Record*, 63rd Congress, 1st sess., pp. 3873-84.
  [2] F. K. Lane to Register, U.S. Land Office, May 13, 1913, CCL (WP, DLC). Lane reminded the registers that they were charged with selecting newspapers for printing official notices and concluded with the following: "It is considered that the Registers of the Land Service should recognize the propriety of designating newspapers whose political principles are in harmony with the administration."

From Ellen Axson Wilson

Cornish, New Hampshire

My own darling,   April [Sept.] 10, 1913

I am so glad,—so very very happy over the passing of the tariff bill. It was good in you and the doctor to send us the telegram, for no matter how sure we are that a thing is *going* to happen, we are always a little more sure when it has happened! And the majority was so unexpectedly satisfactory. I had just come up to bed last night, when the telegram came and the girls rushed up wildly with it. You may imagine the rejoicing and excitement in the house. The paper today answers one of my questions. It says the bill will actually become law, they think, about the 25th. It that correct? I do hope the *art* blunder will be set right in the conference. I have been so absorbed in the papers— which came *very* late today,—that I have not begun writing until bed-time. All the details were so interesting—the scenes in the Senate &c. &c. What a wonderful six months it has been, dear. It is so splendid that everyone knows now how great you are. Even when they are opposed to you they feel your power.

I think the houses will enjoy so the good taste in their mouths of getting things done that they will not deny themselves the triumph of breaking all records by passing the currency bill in this same session. But I am glad you feel they must be given a little respite by their hard task-master, and that you may share their holiday. We are eagerly hoping to see you on Friday, but trying not to let ourselves set our hearts too much on it this time.

It will be delightful if you can see dear Nell in the masque. The slight confusion attendent upon it will be over by Friday morning, as they are not going to reherse on Friday at all. They will be at it practically all day tomorrow. Ruth Hall is to be in it too—as a brown thrush.

Your note came tonight—also the amusing article. Thank you for sending it. Nell had told us about it & we were eager to see it. It is delightful to have $2500.00 unexpectedly. If this keeps up we will be as rich as Mr. Bryan! I have $6500 to invest now, and I have already invested $8500 since March! It is well to get ahead a little now because the 3 winter months will be very expensive. We are all well & love you more than tongue can tell. I think of you "constantly."—I adore you!   Your own,   Eileen.

Be sure to bring warm things. We had a hard *frost* here last night.

ALS (WC, NjP).

To William Jennings Bryan

[The White House]

My dear Mr. Secretary: September 11, 1913

Will you not be kind enough to say to the Japanese Ambassador that matters of capital importance in our domestic legislation have diverted my attention for a time, but that I am giving serious consideration to the note from his Government and shall hope to communicate with him at a very early date regarding it?

Cordially and faithfully yours,   Woodrow Wilson

TLS (Letterpress Books, WP, DLC).

To Walter Hines Page

My dear Page: The White House September 11, 1913

I greatly enjoyed your delightful letter of July twentieth and have this to say for our young people: They are not only complimented by your desire to have them visit you at the Embassy but they are very much tempted to accept the invitation. That is one of the reasons why my daughter has been so slow in replying to Mrs. Page's kind letter. I think you will hear from her in a short time.

As for your suggestion that I should, myself, visit England during my term of office, I must say that I agree with all your arguments for it, and yet the case against the President's leaving the country, particularly now that he is expected to exercise a constant leadership in all parts of the business of the government, is very strong and I am afraid overwhelming. It might be the beginning of a practice of visiting foreign countries which would lead Presidents rather far afield.

It is a most attractive idea, I can assure you, and I turn away from it with the greatest reluctance.

We hear golden opinions of the impressions you are making in England, and I have only to say that it is just what I had expected.

Cordially and faithfully yours,   Woodrow Wilson

TLS (W. H. Page Papers, MH).

From Edward Mandell House

Beverly, Massachusetts.

Dear Mr. President: September 11th, 1913.

Perhaps you do not know the reason for the Billings recommendation. Lieutenant Governor [David Ignatius] Walsh advised it.

When Dudley Malone told me of this, I insisted that he see both Mr. Brandeis and Mr. Grozier, and find whether they concurred in the advisability of naming him. They both thought it an excellent selection.

There is no substantial opposition to him outside of Mayor Fitzgerald himself. The Congressmen are being told by him, that if they permit Billings to go through that he, Fitzgerald, will hold them accountable. This is the reason for their unusual activity.

I have had lunching with me today Francis Carroll,[1] a man whom you have met and who is clean and fairly able, and whom Fitzgerald likes better than almost anyone.

I believe if you will make Carroll District Attorney, and Reilley,[2] who is now State Chairman, United States Marshal, that the tempest in the teapot will subside.

I will know definitely about this before McAdoo and Tumulty arrive.

The material that you have to appoint from is not of the best, but I think with Billings for Collector of the Port, Maynard[3] for Surveyor, Malley[4] for Internal Revenue Collector, Francis Carroll for District Attorney and Reilly for United States Marshal, you will have done the very best that could be done.

This will give Fitzgerald, and the Boston democracy which he represents, two of the best places, and if he is not satisfied with this consideration I would let it go at that.

Please do not think of it while you are at Cornish, for as a matter of fact it is not as serious as the Massachusetts Congressmen try to make it.   Your very faithful,   E. M. House

TLS (WP, DLC).

[1] Lawyer of Boston, former acting fire commissioner of Boston under Mayor Fitzgerald. He did not become district attorney.

[2] Thomas P. Riley, lawyer of Boston and chairman of the Massachusetts Democratic State Committee, 1912-13. He was not appointed United States marshal.

[3] Joseph Adolphus Maynard, businessman of Boston and president of the Democratic City Committee. He was appointed Surveyor of the Port of Boston.

[4] John Frank Malley, lawyer of Boston and Springfield. He was appointed United States Collector of Internal Revenue for the District of Massachusetts.

From Walter Hines Page

Skibo Castle, Dornoch,
Dear Mr. President: Sutherland. Scotland, Sept. 12. 1913.

Score one! You have done a great historic deed and demonstrated and abundantly justified your leadership.

I have been telling Bagehot's successor in the editorship of *The Economist*[1] that the passing of commercial supremacy to the United States will be dated in the economic histories from the Tariff Act of 1913 just as so many things in this realm are dated from the Reform bill; and that, although nothing sudden and nothing spectacular is going to happen, the freeing of great forces will work this inevitable change by the time he can adjust the thought of his readers to it. The change will come so quietly that it will be here before they are aware.

A large section of British opinion understands this. For example, there are here in this castle of vanity and keep the heads of the Scotch universities, and even they forget their quest of succour long enough to assent to this view. We can still more easily command British capital now—the best proof that we compel their proper envy.

It is so good to be alive at such a time that I have driven my golf ball clean over the greens and lost the game from excitement.

My congratulations!

Most heartily yours,   Walter H. Page

ALS (WP, DLC).
[1] Francis Wrigley Hirst, editor, 1907-16.

To Kenyon Cox

My dear Mr. Cox: Cornish, N. H., September 13, 1913

Thank you sincerely for your note of today.[1] I am entirely with you in the matter of the duty on art and am glad to say that I had a conversation with Senator Simmons and Mr. Underwood just before leaving Washington, in which I took the liberty of expressing to them my views about the matter. Whether I convinced them or not remains to be seen, but you may rest assured of my deep and sincere and continuing interest in the matter.[2]

It was a pleasure to meet and shake hands with you last night.

Cordially and sincerely yours,   [Woodrow Wilson]

CCL (WP, DLC).
[1] K. Cox to WW, Sept. 13, 1913, ALS (WP, DLC).
[2] As it turned out, the conference committee on the tariff bill decided to accept

the House provision which put all original works of art on the free list. *New York Times*, Sept. 20, 27, and 30, 1913.

From Ellen Axson Wilson

My own darling,   Cornish, New Hampshire Sept 15 [1913]

Didn't we have a good time at the Fitches, and aren't they perfect dears! I hope that next summer we and they may be "intimate friends." After you left we wandered about the place a little longer alternately praising the view and *you*. Then we came home and I got in an hour and a half of painting. I put in the sky and the distance in the little Cornish study somewhat to my satisfaction; so I think I see my way now to "the picture" proper.

Now I am writing this little note before dressing for dinner just "to tell you how I love you, dear." By the way, Margaret sang that song "Laddie" just before we left the Fitches,—that and no other. She sang it beautifully and they were perfectly charmed.

This was such a happy little visit, dearest! I wish I could tell you how intensely I enjoyed every moment of it. I was distressed before you came for fear the confusion incident upon the masque would ruin it for you. In a sense of cours[e] it did mar the first 24 hours. Yet I know you were more than compensated in seeing your adorable little daughter reveal *herself* so charmingly. Please make the office collect Sunday papers telling about it. We know that a number of them were going to feature it with pictures, and we shall be sadly disappointed if we miss them all. Are'nt they all *wonderful* girls—and adorable? And how intensely they all love you! It really is a sort of adoration—and Helen is "just as bad as the rest"! If your happiness depends upon being greatly loved, as you say, you surely have every reason to be happy, dear heart. As for me words fail me as usual,—but *you know*!

As always,   Yours in every heart throb   Eileen

ALS (WC, NjP).

From Howard Allen Bridgman

My dear Mr. President: Boston Sept. 16, 1913.

We appreciate much your courteous and prompt reply to our letter of inquiry with regard to the segregation of the races in the departments. While we can not view the issue as you view it, and are frankly expressing our judgment in the paper this week,[1] we thank you for your own frankness and promptness.

    With sincere regard,

                    Yours very truly,   H. A. Bridgman

TLS (WP, DLC).

    [1] "Turning the Negro Back," *The Congregationalist and Christian World*, xcviii (Sept. 18, 1913), 357, 359. It reviewed the progress of racial segregation in the federal service since the advent of the Wilson administration and warned of worse things yet to come if the desires of the most rabid southern racists should prevail. "We do not challenge motives in the President," Bridgman continued. "He takes the Southern point of view and has his reasons for it. These reasons rest upon a fallacy and prejudice. We cannot square them with principles of sound democracy or the Golden Rule. We hope it is not now too late to undo the mischief that has been begun. . . . The black man is the brother of the white man in the sight of God. What, therefore, is the Christian white man's duty in a time like this? Protest against the wrong; demand justice; keep on demanding it until we win."

From Ellen Axson Wilson

My own darling,   Cornish, New Hampshire Sept. 16, 1913.

    It is after ten o'clock; we had Mr. Vonnah to dinner and he has just left after almost talking us to death. Not even Lucy could get in a word edgewise. Nell thought we ought to have him because he was alone in his house and his other friends were doing it. Then *she*, forsooth, fled in the middle of the evening and left the rest of us to complete the endurance test. The result is that I am so sleepy that I can scarcely see the paper.

    It has been a beautiful day but oh so cold! We had the last meeting of the club this afternoon at Highcourt[1] and the Smiths greatly enjoyed seeing the place. We took a nice ride between luncheon & the club hour when the sun was bright and warm. I was busy with accumulated mail most of the morning, but had one hour for painting.

    Your telegram came and was most welcome, darling. I am so glad all is well. I suppose the report that 100 Americans have been captured in Mexico, &c. &c. is false,—is it not? It is interesting to note that the man who was responsible for the famous "ultimatum" has got out of the Mexican Cabinet,—or been turned out.[2] I think it would be worth your while to get Dave Ricketts[3] opinion about the situation in general down there and especially as regards the degree of danger to Americans.

    Everyone at the club today was singing the praises of the two girls; it was very delightful. Mrs. St. Gaudens (Louis) the sculptor says Nell has the dignity of sculpture in her movements. You know she does beautiful figures in low relief on vases. She is going to do one with all the characters of the masque on it. I think it will be charming. Of course she will have to do it from photographs.

Goodnight, my dear, *dear* love. I try not to *think* how much I miss you, much less *tell* you. It is not safe. With love inexpressible. Your own   Eileen

ALS (WC, NjP).
¹ The estate of Anson Conger Goodyear, described in EAW to WW, Aug. 4, 1913.
² About the "ultimatum," see n. 1 to J. Lind to WJB, Aug. 19, 1913. Huerta accepted Urrutia's resignation as Minister of the Interior on September 14. The report in the *New York Times*, Sept. 16, 1913, commented that he was under fire from the diplomatic corps in Mexico City for his anti-foreign sentiments. Urrutia himself was alleged to have given as the reason for his resignation that the post required qualities which he did not possess.
³ Louis Davidson Ricketts, Princeton 1881, consulting engineer for Phelps, Dodge & Co. properties in the southwestern United States and northern Mexico, 1890-1906; president and general manager of the Cananea Consolidated Copper Co. of Sonora, Mexico, since 1907.

To Ellen Axson Wilson

My precious darling,   The White House 17 September, 1913
Ever since I touched this town again yesterday morning I have been so deep in work of all kinds that I am sure that if you were here you could not see the top of my head. Whenever I go away and get back and see the innumerable things to be done which ought not to wait, I wonder that I ever dared leave and how I can ever leave again. But I must stop for a moment to-night before I go to bed to send something more of a love message to my precious ones than I sent yesterday in my telegram. Your dear, dear letter reached me this morning, and how sweet, how deeply sweet, every sentence was! Bless you for your dear love and all its manifestations. They keep me alive and well and happy. Nothing has developed to increase my burdens or anxieties as yet; I am perfectly well; and a happier man in the thought of the character and adorable charm of those he loves does not live in the world. Your own,   Woodrow

WWTLS (WC, NjP).

To Charles William Eliot

My dear Doctor Eliot: The White House September 17, 1913
Thank you for your letter of September tenth. It is certainly the act of a friend to call my attention to the important matters of which you speak.

With regard to the instructions to the Registers of the land offices relative to advertising, I am glad to say you are mistaken in the impression you have received. It was the habit until recently of the Registers to advertise exclusively in the Republican newspapers, and all that the department is trying to do is to correct that abuse by seeing to it that a fair division is made. I think that this is in the interest of the right.

With regard to the other matters, let me say that we are following the merit system in the consular service more strictly even than either of the preceding administrations and shall continue to do so. In the matter of the diplomatic service, there are difficulties which I cannot within the space of a letter more than indicate to you. We find that those who have been occupying the legations and embassies have been habituated to a point of view which is very different, indeed, from the point of view of the present administration. They have had the material interests of individuals in the United States very much more in mind than the moral and public considerations which it seems to us ought to control. They have been so bred in a different school that we have found, in several instances, that it was difficult for them to comprehend our point of view and purpose. I have been genuinely distressed at the necessity of seeming to act contrary to the spirit of the merit system in any case or particular, but there are circumstances which seem to me to make a certain amount of this necessary at the opening of a new order of things.

Cordially and sincerely yours,   Woodrow Wilson

TLS (C. W. Eliot Papers, MH-Ar).

To Hiram Woods

My dear Hiram: [The White House] September 17, 1913

Your letter of the twelfth[1] gave me a great deal of pleasure. The sketch you send of the Graduate College is truly characteristic of the people who have been promoting this thing in which university ideals have been so perverted and distorted.

I cannot tell you what it means to me that my old chums are so generous in their friendship and support, and you may be sure that I will convey to Jessie your generous congratulations.

In haste   Affectionately yours,   Woodrow Wilson

TLS (Letterpress Books, WP, DLC).
[1] H. Woods to WW, Sept. 12, 1913, TLS (WP, DLC).

From William Jennings Bryan, with Enclosure

My dear Mr. President: Washington September 17, 1913.

If you have read the newspaper report of Huerta's speech you will, I am sure, be gratified at the promise which it gives of an early election. He says

"The Mexican Government regards the pacification of the country as an urgent necessity in order to restore the public services to their normal state, to re-establish the political, social, and economic equilibrium, and to make possible a program of reforms which will satisfy the national aspiration.

"I will spare no effort and no sacrifice to obtain the coveted peace and to guarantee fully in the coming elections the free casting of the ballot.

"You may be sure it will constitute the greatest possible triumph for the interim government to surrender office to its successor, if the latter, as is to be expected, enters upon its functions with public peace and order an accomplished fact."

The fact that no reference is made to his being a candidate, taken together with what he says in regard to the greatest triumph of the interim government being to surrender the office to his successor, and his promise of the free casting of the ballot—these give ground for encouragement. The only offensive thing in his message is the suggestion that the relations between his Government and this Government are strained but that this does not apply to the people of the United States. However, we can stand language that is unfriendly if he will only do the things necessary for the restoration of peace.

The enclosed despatch from Lind shows that he places a favorable construction upon Huerta's message. I would suggest a message to Lind something like the following. Please suggest any changes you think will improve it:

"Governor Lind,
Amconsulate,
Vera Cruz.

Your telegram received. Your construction of the message agrees with ours. We feel encouraged, first by the fact that there is nothing in it to indicate a desire on his part to be a candidate; second, he promises free elections; and third, he will regard it as the greatest triumph of his Government to be able to turn it over to an elected successor. Your mission has been successful in very much relieving the situation and it seems likely that you will be called back to the Capital before the election. While it must be monotonous for you and your wife to remain in Vera

Cruz, the President feels that there is so great a probability of your having further opportunity for service, in addition to your valuable reports, that he desires you to remain for the present and await further developments.   Bryan.''[1]

With assurances of respect, etc., I am, my dear Mr. President,
                    Very sincerely yours,   W. J. Bryan

TLS (WP, DLC).
[1] Wilson approved the dispatch.

E N C L O S U R E

                              Vera Cruz, Mexico, September 16, 1913

The message leaves the way open for further negotiations as I expected and I desire your instructions. Huerta is weakening as is evident by the dismissal of Urrutia. The tide of popular approval which seemed strong in his favor two weeks ago is waning in a marked degree. His Government is drifting. The attitude of the Congress is yet to be ascertained. It is not at all clear that it is controlled by the administration. A week or ten days will tend to make clear the situation. Personally I dislike to waste time as I am doing but I also feel quite convinced that in the end time will be gained by compelling them to take the initiative; that the situation is daily becoming more difficult for the Government and that it is only a matter of weeks when help will be sought. In my correspondence with O'Shaughnessy I have said incidentally that I stand ready to return to Mexico whenever it is thought that I may be of service. As to the future I am still at sea what to do. Instruct.   Lind.

T telegram (WP, DLC).

From William Jennings Bryan, with Enclosure

My dear Mr. President: Washington September 17, 1913.

As the Japanese Ambassador is to call on you at 2:30 tomorrow, I send a memorandum, which he left with me to-day, of the interview between Ambassador Guthrie and the Japanese Foreign Office.

You will notice that Ambassador Guthrie is reported as having expressed his personal concurrence in the draft agreement proposed by the Japanese Government.[1] I have explained to the Ambassador that this was Mr. Guthrie's personal opinion and not a concurrence which he has been authorized to give for this Government. The Ambassador recognized that it was purely personal.

I have explained to the Japanese Ambassador the difference between what you did in California and what he asks you to do here, namely, that in California you tried to *persuade* the legislature not to make a discrimination against the Japanese or any other people but that you did not discuss with them their *right* to make the distinction.

In making the treaty which they now ask, you would put yourself in the position of *denying* to the states *the right* to make distinction. He recognized the difference between the denial of a right and the failure to exercise the right. I have explained to him that you would be willing to give any assurance that you could of your readiness to advise other states against discrimination and your willingness to advise California to amend their anti-alien law to the extent of permitting a Japanese land owner to dispose of his land by will and to permit his heirs to take it by inheritance for one generation, but I have also explained to him that you do not feel justified in presenting to Congress a treaty that will *deny* to the states the right to discriminate. I have tried to show him that to present such a treaty without being assured of the support of the Democrats would subject you to the danger of raising a fundamental issue that might impair your ability to secure other legislation needed by our people. I have expressed to him a willingness to confer with the Democratic Senators *after the passage of the currency bill* with a view to ascertaining their opinion, with the understanding that if you were assured of the support of the Democrats of such a treaty you would be willing to enter into it. I have also explained to him that you would not be willing to have this verbal assurance made public, because to do so might put you in opposition to the Senators as effectually as the presentation of a treaty would.

Ambassador Chinda will tell you of several treaties which we have made embodying the provisions which he asks, and for my part, I am perfectly willing to share responsibility for such a treaty if its ratification can be secured, because I do not think that a state should be permitted to discriminate against any particular class of foreigners. If alien land laws are desired, they should be made to apply to all aliens alike. It is not fair for a state to endanger international peace by acting independently of the rest of the states on a matter that concerns other nations.

I have gone over the ground as I discussed it with the Ambassador in order that, when you confer with him, you may be fully informed as to what has been said.

With assurances of respect, etc., I am, my dear Mr. President,

Very sincerely yours,   W. J. Bryan

TLS (WP, DLC).

¹ The Japanese government, on August 19, submitted to Guthrie two articles, in effect the draft of a treaty, for discussion. The first said that in everything concerning the acquisition, disposition, and inheritance of real property, the subjects or citizens, as well as the companies, corporations and associations, of the two contracting parties should in the territories of the other be placed on the same footing as that of the most favored nation. The second article said that it was "well understood" that nothing in the first article should be construed as affecting or superseding the laws now existing in either country in regulation of alien land tenure, "provided however that in the matter of acquisition, enjoyment, transfer, transmission or inheritance of real property or any interest therein in the territories of each contracting party lawfully vested prior to the coming into force of the present agreement in the subjects or citizens of the other party or in the Companies Associations or Corporations of which the whole or a part of the members or stockholders consists of such subjects or citizens, the most favored nation treatment provided in Article one of this agreement shall in all cases be extended to the actual holders of said property rights or any of those upon whom such rights may subsequently devolve by transfer, transmission or inheritance." G. W. Guthrie to WJB, Aug. 19, 1913, T telegram (SDR, RG 59, 811.52/189, DNA).

ENCLOSURE

Baron Nobuaki Makino to Viscount Sutemi Chinda

[Tokyo, received Aug. 19, 1913]

The Americam Ambassador called on me August 19, to discuss the question of the proposed Japanese-American Agreement respecting alien land tenure, copy of which had been forwarded to him for his confidential information.

I called his attention to the fact that the two nations had always placed special importance, in deeds as well as in words, upon the maintenance of their mutual relations of genuine friendship, and I remarked that no serious differences of political significance had ever marred the record of their long standing intercourse, until the questions of immigration and of land ownership came up for adjustment. Fortunately, the problem of immigration, it would be remembered, had been brought to a final and satisfactory conclusion a few years ago, and the only controversy now awaiting solution related to the subject of land ownership.

I refrained muself from discussion on those features of the California alien land law, to which the Imperial Government felt bound to take exception, but I pointed out that the discrimination against Japanese subjects and the disregard of their vested interests, which the new legislation unmistakably implied, created a deplorable impression upon our people of all classes and political affiliations. Agitations of serious magnitude had broken out among certain quarters in Japan, and, while every endeavor was being made to appease popular resentment, it would apparently be imposseble, so long as the cause of grievances was left unremedied, to remove the sentiments of grave concern and dissatisfaction at the unfair treatment to which Japanese people were subjected in California.

I explained that in Japan, the days when statesmen of an exclusive class governed and controlled the foreign policy of the country independently of the trend of public opinion were fast disappearing, and the mass of the people now claimed to have a voice in the determination of the destiny of the nation. I declared that, being apprehensive of the untoward and unfavorable development of the situation, which might be brought about under the new order of things, the Imperial Government were sincerely bent upon every possible exertion, before it was too late, to find a suitable adjustment of the pending dispute, and to remove all causes of misunderstanding from their relations with the Government of the United States.

I then proceeded to say that the Japanese Ambassador at Washington, with that object in view, and, at the same time, having regard to the position of the American Government, formulated a project for the regulation of the question and informally submitted it to the Secretary of State for his consideration. I continued that upon receipt from you reports on your action thus taken subject to the approval of the Cabinet at Tokio, I had decided to accept your plan of adjustment, and had authorized you to present it to the American Administration as official proposals of the Imperial Government.

I embraced this opportunity to assure to Mr. Guthrie the profound appreciation, felt by the Government and people of Japan, of the friendly attitude shown by the President, in urging upon the Californian authorities, while the land bill was under discussion, the advisability of suppression, from that bill, of certain objectionable clauses, and in sending the Secretary of State to Sacramento to give counsel to the State Legislature. I added that those manifestations of good will on the part of the President created an excellent impression in Japan.

Finally, I expressed my earnest hope that the American Administration might find its way clear to accept the proposed Agreement, and to co-operate with the Imperial Government in the solution of the problem, which the high cause of international friendship seemed to demand.

The American Ambassador, in reply, dwelt at great length upon the momentous value which he attached to the relations of good accord and understanding between the two countries. He said that he had always watched with keen interest the furtherance of such relations, and that it was because of his sincere solicitude to contribute towards that desirable end, that he had gladly accepted the responsible post of representing the United States in Japan. He was fully sensible of the importance of bringing to a satisfactory close the difficulties created by the recent legislation in California, and he expressed his personal concurrence in the draft Agreement proposed by the Japanese Government. He added that he would at once telegraph to his Government recommending favorable consideration of the Japanese proposals.

The interview was entirely cordial, and I was deeply impressed with the sincerity and earnestness which Mr. Guthrie displayed in dealing with the question.

T telegram (WP, DLC).

From Ellen Axson Wilson

My own darling,   Cornish, New Hampshire Sept. 17, 1913

We have had a pleasant evening listening to Mary reading Barrie's "Little White Bird," an adorable book, quite good enough for a second reading—especially out loud. Now I am very cosy in my own room, with a beautiful bright fire, to finish the day with my letter to you.

It has been a perfect day and I am glad to say somewhat warmer at last—most fortunately for me, for the furnace in this wing is out of order and the pipe rusted through,—so it will be some days before we can have heat. The heat is on in the main part of the house.

We had a lovely ride today. Early this morning Mr. Vonnoh came at his own suggestion to give me another criticism on my work. He found them all "much improved"—I having carried out all his suggestions! It is very comfortable to have them passed upon favourably by so good an artist. By the way, he is anxious if possible not to sell his picture to anything but a museum, or preferably, the White House. He has done a number of portraits for Mr. Penfield and has a little idea that he might buy it sometime for the White House. But I suppose Mr. Penfield will not be in the country again for a long time.

I have just had a charming letter from Mrs. Yates. She says Fred is very busy with landscape work now. Also that they are all busy picking out a house for us when you are free to go there and rest[.] "Shall it be 'Miller Bridge' under Loughrigg, near Miss Arnold's,[1] or Rydal Mount?" The very question fascinates, does it not?

We are all well, and I have, as you see, no news,—have you?

We talk about you forever and we all love you more than tongue can tell. I have such happy hours dreaming over my painting about you;—my *darling*! With love inexpressible,

Your own   Eileen.

ALS (WC, NjP).

[1] Frances Bunsen Trevenen Arnold, youngest sister of Matthew Arnold, mistress of Fox How, the Arnold family home near Ambleside.

Remarks at a Press Conference

September 18, 1913

What's your pleasure, gentlemen?

Mr. President, could you tell us anything about the visit of the Japanese Ambassador?

I would, if there were anything to tell that would constitute news. It was just a conversation about the last note of the Japanese government. It was merely by way of explanation of the situation on both sides. He was entirely satisfied, so there was nothing new that arose in it.

Was Japan pressing for a reply?

No, sir. No. On the contrary.

One of the New York papers, Mr. President, carried stories this morning that the Ambassador came here and was told he could not see the Secretary of State.

He expressed his regret that any such misrepresentation should have been made.

The Chinese situation was brought up in the conversation, was it, Mr. President, the situation in China with respect to the Japanese question?

No. No reference was made to that.

Mr. President, the discussion is not concluded, is it now?

Oh, no.

Mr. President, could you tell us anything about that last note from Japan?

Why, none of the notes has been made public, you know. It was just a thorough canvassing of all the aspects of the question, so as to see just exactly what our treaty relations will encompass.

Some time ago, Mr. President, you told us that you felt very much encouraged about the situation, looking forward to an amicable settlement of it.

I do still. I think that both governments are equally eager in their desire to come to an entirely satisfactory agreement.

Do you think you can find some definite ground for it?

I dare say we can, yes. . . . This is an interview I should have had with the Ambassador some time ago. It has been simply delayed by engagements on both sides, so there isn't any provocation.

Mr. President, has this government made to Japan any proposition at all that an amicable adjustment could be had?

No, no definite proposition.

Mr. President, there was a paragraph in one of the newspapers this morning which refers to a person formerly of Princeton[1] as having made a confidential inquiry into Philippine affairs.

Well, it was confidential in the sense that he was an old friend of mine who made it and wrote it for my eye.

And that he made some recommendations, suggesting a wider form of autonomy in the Philippine Islands?

There is no basis for that report at all.

There is no development in the formation of your Philippine policy as yet?

No further development.

Mr. President, could you tell us anything about the instructions which have gone to Mr. Lind?

None have gone to him. When do you mean? Recently?

Yes sir. I didn't hear myself, but I was told, that the Secretary of State said yesterday that he sent a telegram to Mr. Lind, a long telegram.

That was not in the nature of instructions. I doubt if he could have used that word. Mr. Lind was simply giving us his impressions of the day's end down there and the news of the day. That was all.

Mr. President, can you tell us how you regard that message, as to whether it was in keeping with your belief that a number of the proposals submitted by Mr. Lind would be accepted?

There was nothing in the message as it was cabled to us that was inconsistent with that last note and with the understandings which we interpreted that last note to convey.

JRT transcript (WC, NjP) of CLSsh (C. L. Swem Coll., NjP).
[1] Henry Jones Ford.

To Edward Mandell House

My dear Friend: The White House September 18, 1913

Your letter on the passage of the tariff bill gave me the kind of pleasure that seldom comes to a man, and it goes so deep that no words are adequate to express it. I think you must know without my putting it into words (for I cannot) how deep such friendship and support goes with me and how large a part it constitutes of such strength as I have in public affairs. I thank you with all my heart and with deep affection.

Your letter about the appointments in Massachusetts did not reach me at Cornish, but followed me here. I am entirely satisfied with the conclusions; I am only tied up for the moment by the desire to hear the Congressmen from Massachusetts with entire courtesy before acting. What you recommend with regard to Carroll as District Attorney and Reilley as Marshal strikes me very favorably, and I shall take the matter up with the Department of Justice at once.

Always

Faithfully and affectionately yours,   Woodrow Wilson

TLS (E. M. House Papers, CtY).

From Oswald Garrison Villard

Dear Mr. President: New York September 18, 1913.

I am most grateful for your kind letter of August 30th and the friendly spirit in which you accept my criticism. I note your recurrence to the fact that a number of colored men with whom you have consulted have agreed with you that segregation was in the interest of the colored people. I am being approached with many demands for their names and I wish I could obtain them—Bishop Walters is one, we are told; if the names are given out I veritably believe that these men will be driven out of the communities in which they reside, or at least held up to the scorn of the race, as has been the man Patterson whom you nominated for Register of the Treasury. I hope the message from the Northeastern Federation of Colored Women's Clubs, which represents nearly five thousand of the most advanced women in the race, protesting against segregation, was laid before you.[1]

To show how this situation is hurting the cause of good government, may I say to you that some of the best observers in this city say that the reform ticket, headed by Mr. Mitchel, will not receive a single colored man's vote in the coming election because they regard him as the New York representative of the Wilson Administration?

I note your statement that certain harshnesses in the segregation have been ameliorated, but this does not, it seems to me, touch the issue at all. The case has just been well stated by the Chicago *Public* in the following terms:

"This order places the Government of the United States in the position of endorsing a prejudice which some individuals feel toward a certain class of citizens. The government has no right to recognize social distinctions among citizens. Least of all has the Government of the United States a right to recognize an aristocracy of birth. The order should be rescinded and the official or officials responsible therefore given a much-needed lesson in sound democracy and true Americanism."

Believe me, it is not a question of handling segregation awkwardly or tactfully, or otherwise, it is a question of right and wrong. How I wish that your Administrative heads who have brought about this thing could for forty-eight hours be blacked up and compelled to put themselves in the negro's place—how differently they would feel!

May I call your attention to the fact that the National Association for the Advancement of Colored People, which wrote you the enclosed letter,[2] has had no reply from you save an official acknowledgement from Mr. Tumulty? May it not look for an answer before long? Later on, the officers of the Association, including myself, will formally and officially ask you to give us a hearing on this matter, and upon the general attitude of the Wilson Administration towards the colored man,—just as soon as the pressure of the tariff and currency bills is at an end. With all respect, it seems to me that the colored people of this country are entitled, before long, to have a statement of the Administration's position towards the colored man,—whether he is to be appointed to office, whether segregation is to go on, etc.

Of course, I am most grateful for your frankness in stating your decisions, and for your kind consideration of my letters.

Sincerely yours,   Oswald Garrison Villard.

P.S. I wish you might find time to read the splendid editorial protests in the Lexington, Ky, Herald,[3]—a Southerner's protest[4] and in the Congregationalist a copy of which I enclose.

O. G. V.

TLS (WP, DLC).

[1] Northeastern Federation of Colored Women's Clubs to WW, Aug. 15, 1913, T telegram (WP, DLC). This telegram is stamped "Ack'd Aug. 16, 1913 T[homas]. M Hendricks[.]" and carries the pencil notation "Will be brought to attention Pr"; however, it is doubtful that Wilson ever saw it.

[2] M. Storey et al. to WW, Aug. 15, 1913. This and the enclosures mentioned below are missing.

[3] "A Letter to the President," Lexington, Ky., Herald, Sept. 7, 1913. It began by quoting in full M. Storey et al. to WW, Aug. 15, 1913, and went on to argue that segregation was not only an injustice to blacks but also a "hindrance to the development of the white race." Moreover, it declared, "no greater calamity could befall this nation than to have included in its inhabitants millions of people of any race in whose face the door of hope is shut, who are not permitted to aspire to free and independent citizenship, and to strive for equal political, financial and industrial reward that brawn or intellect brings to those of any race." The

administration's action segregating federal employees could only encourage the plans of demagogues in the South and elsewhere to segregate blacks and deprive them of political rights. Such developments would be catastrophic not only for the South but for the nation as a whole.

⁴ Desha Breckinridge, Princeton 1889.

From Ellen Axson Wilson

My own darling,   Cornish, New Hampshire Sept. 18, 1913

I have'nt a single item of news for this veracious daily chronicle. It rained, I am glad to say, all night and tried (in vain) to rain all day. So we have had a quiet restful home day. I meant to do wonders in the studio but the mail kept me until eleven. Lucy[,] Mary and I went back to the studio after lunch prepared for an afternoon of reading & painting, but just as we were cosily started Coates appeared with the news that Ex-Ambassador White,¹ who had motored over from Dublin, wanted to call and pay his respects, at once, as he had a dinner engagement in Dublin tonight. So I had to shut up shop and go back to the house and dress. He came with his sister-in-law, Mrs. Ridgeley²—*the* Mrs. Ridgely of the famous Hampton Place near Balt., Mrs. Will Hoyt's aunt-in-law. We had a very agreeable visit. He says his son³ was at the pageant and found it *all* charming, but most of all Margaret's singing. I am glad he said that for the papers in their absorption in the more spectacular features scarcely mentioned the singing, and paid her no compliments.

There was a strong effort made by the Boston Audubon Society to get them to go & give the Masque at a private place in Milton. I declined to let Nell go,—which of course broke up the plan altogether. It was rather hard for me to take the stand so if you think it was right & necessary for me to do it I hope you will say so when you write, as I should like your moral support. She suggested telegraphing to you today to get your opinion. She was eager to go, but she was very sweet about it, and Mr. MacKaye behaved very well indeed.

One more question, a messenger went to you from N. Y. to urge you and all of us going to the first performance of "Evangeline," which is to be a Longfellow Memorial occasion. He reports that you were "non-committal",—which doesn't sound probable. You are *never* non-committal except for strictly diplomatic reasons. They are making a tremendous effort to get us, and we *will not* go all that way for no better reason. Margaret Howe⁴ is to play in it and she sent me 23 pages to-day on the subject.

We are all well & happy—and love you with all our hearts and talk, talk, talk about you all day long. I am very, *very* close to you in spirit my darling always. I wonder if you feel me! Always and altogether   Your own   Eileen.

ALS (WC, NjP).
  1 Henry White.
  2 Helen West Stewart (Mrs. John) Ridgely was the current mistress of Hampton, the Ridgely family estate. She was actually a cousin-in-law of Henry White.
  3 John Campbell White, son of Henry White.
  4 Marjorie Frances Howe of Hartford, Conn.

From William Jennings Bryan, with Enclosure

My dear Mr. President: Washington September 19, 1913.

I enclose herewith copy of a despatch just received from Minister Thompson,[1] at Bogotá, together with a copy of my reply.[2]

I shall be here early in the morning and shall remain at the Department until three o'clock. Tomorrow is the last of my Chautauquas for this season.

With assurances of respect, etc., I am, my dear Mr. President,
                 Very sincerely yours,   W. J. Bryan

The enclosed telegram is as O'Shaughnessy says very significant

TLS (WP, DLC).
  1 T. A. Thomson to WJB, Sept. 17, 1913, CC telegram (WP, DLC). Thomson reported that the Colombian Minister for Foreign Affairs had stated that any formal proposition from the United States should include the following points: an indemnity to satisfy Colombian claims relating to the Panama Canal and railroad, certain preferential privileges to Colombia in the use of the canal, a re-drawing of the Colombia-Panama boundary line, and "an expression of regret for occurrences of nineteen three." The most important of these was the settlement of the boundary line.
  2 WJB to T. A. Thompson [Thomson], Sept. 19, 1913, CC telegram (WP, DLC). Bryan replied that the United States could not propose preferential privileges without knowing what Colombia desired, and that it could not suggest a new boundary line without first consulting Panama. The United States was willing to submit a formal proposition of fifteen million dollars, or, if necessary, twenty million, in full settlement of all difficulties, without mention of special privileges or change of boundary. Colombia could then submit a counterproposition, stating its desires as to special privileges and the boundary. It would be "worse than useless" to raise the question of a new boundary line with Panama unless it was clear that there was a possibility of agreeing on the other terms.

E N C L O S U R E

Mexico City September 19 [1913]

. . . The Chamber's action[1] has resulted in the President's sending for Rodolfo Reyes and Jorge Vera Estenol, two of the leaders of the opposition, at one o'clock this morning and threatening them with momentary dissolution of the Chamber of Deputies if any further actions such as that of yesterday be taken. Deputy [Jesús] Urueta, the most brilliant orator in Mexico but a person of very doubtful reputation, who proposed the appointment of Tamaris, was arrested last evening when returning home. He has not been heard from since. Reyes, whom I saw this morning, is now in hiding. President Huerta was to have seen me at noon to-day but he has sent his adjutant to inform me that he cannot do so. In my opinion, the situation is very serious and if the Chamber of Deputies continues to oppose the President there will be a dissolution of the Chamber of Deputies and a military dictatorship established. The war Minister is firmly with the Chief Executive. Political passions are running very high, especially between clericals and liberals. Reyes tells me that the opposition in the Chamber of Deputies appreciates the attitude of the Government of the United States. This afternoon I shall report further in regard to this matter.

T telegram (WP, DLC).
1 On September 18, the Liberal members of the Chamber of Deputies blocked confirmation of Huerta's nomination of Eduardo Tamariz, deputy from the State of Tlaxcala, as Minister of Education.

John Lind to William Jennings Bryan[1]

Dear Mr. Bryan: Veracruz Sept. 19th [1913]

. . . You refer to my dispatches as valuable. I am gratified to think that they do not look ridiculous to you. I have often thought that they must look inconsistent and even contradictory. I have only this to say that when you are dealing with a people whose actions are neither measured or controlled by the standards to which we are accustomed it is difficult to analyze a situation and impossible to forecast. Politically, at least, the Mexicans have no standards. They seem more like children than men. The only motives that I can discern in their political action is *appetite* and *vanity*. This is harsh language, but I fear that it is accurate. Their talk about pride is all "rot." Their pride rarely compels action and is usually content with bluster and an exhibition on paper or in fiery speeches. Very few seek office to "make a record" or to realize political or social ideals.

It is this unfortunate situation as well as the complicated economic and social conditions—the result of three centuries of misrule religious, social and political—that make the solution of the present problem by the political and moral resources of the Mexican people seem almost impossible. I confess that I have almost given up hope, but I don't wish you to infer from this that

1 This letter, sent by mail, arrived in Washington about October 4. See WJB to WW, Oct. 4, 1913, and WW to WJB, Oct. 6, 1913.

I will relax my efforts one iota to accomplish what we all hope and pray for along the lines and in the spirit of my mission. My purpose in imposing this lengthy letter on you is to point out briefly the obstacles that seem to me so insuperable. I have already pointed out my want of confidence in the moral and political efficiency of the people—but here I must explain that it is the concensus of opinion of the hundreds of intelligent Americans (& other nationalities) that I have met that the Indians especially of the southern states give great promise of both moral and economic efficiency. Their potential capacity of development does not seem to be limited as is the case with the American Negro. In the valley of Mexico the race is inferior, debauched by pulque and vice and oppression. The judgment of the best informed—such men as Mr. Clark[2] general man. of the Mexican Rways—is that the hope of Mexico is in her Indian blood rather than in the mongrel progeny of the early moorish Spaniards. This however is mere speculation on my part and a repetition of what has come to me in various ways. I have already indicated by my cables that the agrarian question is a vital factor in the situation but I wish to review it more fully. In the State of Oaxaca the Indians generally are in possession of their ancestral domains. The village communities own enough land in common so that there is an outlet for the normal increase of the population. The people are fairly industrious in their own behalf and make most excellent workmen. They are capable of great industrial skill and 40% are sober, 60% are given to periodical sprees (usually the church fiestas), very few confirmed drunkards. As a rule they will not voluntarily submit to the contract labor system but they form groups of 12 to 20, select one of their number as spokesman and take contracts for the clearing of land, harvesting cane &c—very much like the farmers club together in your state and mine and take a "section" of work in railway construction. They are jealous of their rights and do not hesitate to sacrifice their lives in resisting for instance the appointment of an improper or unpopular man as "Jefe politico[.]" They have not been in rebellion at any time during the last three years and they are not likely to rebel if left alone. There are a few bands of marauding bandits in the State but no greater number than one might expect in our country if law and order had virtually been suspended or ceased to exist for a period of time. There are three or four other states where the conditions generally are about the same as in Oaxaca. In the State of Morelos, nearby, and having about the same climate and

---

[2] Even the *Annual Reports* of Ferrocarriles Nacionales de México from 1909 to 1913 refer to him only as "A. Clark, General Manager, City of Mexico."

aboriginal population and confessedly the richest and most beautiful state in Mexico the situation is radically different. The land was apportioned among the Conquerors and given to the Church in an early day. The arable part of the State is held in very large haciendas by a limited number of proprietors who reside abroad or in the City of Mexico. The indians were reduced to abject peonage generations ago. They live in huts about the haciendas as you undoubtedly observed in your travels. The overseer of the hacienda—frequently a brutal spaniard[—]exercises absolute control and has the power by law and custom to administer corporal punishment. If death results no questions are asked. The wage is 25¢ in silver and two pints of corn. Some of the peons are permitted to till a small tract of land "on halves" and to own and pasture a few goates and in isolated instances one cow. If they develop the least inclination to accumulate more property or to keep more than one cow they are deemed "undesirable citizens["] and are convicted of some trumped up offense or other and sent into the army. The haciendado keeps a "pluck me store" where the peons are entitled to credit and once in debt they are fixtures for life under the Mexican law. They have a process here, not unlike the old Common law writ of *ne exeat* by which an employer can prevent his laborer departing his service while in debt. The "contract" labor system that prevails on many of the large estates owned or operated by Americans does not differ in its practical operation from the Hacienda method outlined above except that the Americans as a rule are more humane and considerate in their treatment of their laborers and provide better food and sanitary conditions. In company with Admiral Fletcher I spent a day on an American plantation and observed the system in operation in its every detail. The manager —a Mr. Emory[3]—used to live in our state some twenty years ago. He was quite active in public life—a "democrat"—was a member of the Board of Regents of our University, is a New Englander by birth and blood. He is now nearly seventy years old but still a fine type of American manhood physically intellectu[a]lly and in point of general efficiency. But the admiral and myself were both astonished and dumbfounded to hear Mr. Emory discourse eloquently and persuasively on the benefits and advantages of the system to the men and to the proprietor alike. He showed us the men working in the cane fields in groups of 10 to 12 with an overseer over each group—armed with a very pliable and effective whip and a Colt's 44 at his hip. At the end of the rows, about

---

3 Sloan M. Emery, president and administrator of La Vista Hermosa Sugar and Mercantile Co., a large hacienda in northern Oaxaca. He had been a regent of the University of Minnesota, 1889-93.

20 rods ahead another man was stationed with a magazine gun. The discipline of the men even to the point of taking life is wholly in the hands of these overseers and they are never held to account for anything they do except in cases of "extreme abuse of power." It would be very unfair and unjust to Mr Emory, however, to use any language that would indicate that he abuses the system. On the contrary he has probably done more to make it tolerable as applied to his plantation than any man in Mexico. But what astounded us as I suggested above was his defense of the *system*. He is a very ardent supporter of General Huerta. So is Mr. Catlin[4] (who called on you) and *so is every* American similarly situated. They are absolutely sincere in their views. They have ceased to see things with American eyes but they don't know it. Mr. Emory, to me, deplored the frequency and the disturbing character of our elections. I have gone into the above details simply to demonstrate to you how difficult the task to convert the haciendados to see things in a different light—in the light of the 20th Century, when Americans and "democrats" at that, in the course of a few years become so entranced with this method of appropriating the toil and blood of human beings that they wantonly repudiate the noblest accomplishments of our people. But I must recur to Morelos. That State has been in rebellion constantly for more than three years. It is the home of the Zapatista uprising. The haciendas are in ruins. Mills and cornfields consumed by flames —the most beautiful State in Mexico, and the richest, utterly waste. No crops growing, no industry, hardly a goat to be found in the fertile valleys that abounded with the best cattle and horses in all Mexico a few years ago. The able bodied men are "bandits" in the mountains, the old, the very young and the decrepit have been "pacified." The women and the children who have survived have been and are now being deported. It is the plan of the present "regime" in and out of the government no[t] to leave "one person to the manor born" in the State of Morelos. Temporarily the helpless survivors are kept in Concentration Camps because of the interrupted R.R. communications but it is the ultimate purpose to transport them all to similarly depopulated areas in distant states and to bring the people from those sections to Morelos. *This is not hear say nor speculation.* I have this information from the highest officials in Mexico and the plan is now in process of execution. The immediate grievance that precipitated the Morelos rebellion was not the land situation so much as a dispute about water rights. Some of the Indians were still occupying a little land with pasture rights in the foot hills with certain

4 Unidentified.

water rights which they had enjoyed from time immemorial, but indian like they had omitted to protect their water rights by registry and as required by law. The *bishop* of the diocese quietly secured a cession of the water rights of the stream which supplied the community and immediately proceeded to collect water rates or cut off the supply. Under Zapata and other leaders the Indians rose in rebellion. Of course they were denounced by the government as traitors and they have all been excommunicated by the church. These "Zapatistas" have [*sic*] have been "conquered and subdued" en masse and in detail every week since my arrival, but to-day the government considers that they are as active as ever. In some form or other and in whole or in part the situation in Morelos has its counter part in more than eighteen States in Mexico at this writing.

But the situation is also embarrassed by what I will call a social question quite as acute as the agrarian. In any attempt at analyzing the present political and social situation in Mexico we must not overlook the effect of the contact of the Mexican peon with our civilization along the National boundary, in our schools, and along the lines of the National railways for upwards a quarter century. Many have tasted the sweets of personal independence and security and of a higher plane of living. Nearly all mechanical and operative positions on those railways are now filled by Mexican Indians. All agree that they are good mechanics trustworthy and fairly efficient in all lines of work. They have enough money to get formally married which is something of a luxury under the auspices of the church in Mexico. They lead orderly lives and they are very ambitious to educate their children in spite of the opposition of the church. They are breathing the atmosphere of the twentieth century in a rarified form. A middle class is in the making. They have become democrats by contact with democracy and the force of circumstances—very much like our own citizens have become aristocrats in temper and ideals on the plantations and in the large corporate undertakings, and in the degree that the Mexican of the North becomes a democrat his hatred grows against the social and economic conditions of the South and against the old 16th century regime. Huerta and his followers are the physical embodiment of all the evil in the State and in the church in the eyes of the North. But the new leaven is not alone at work in the North. It occurs in sporadic form in many sections of the Country. Right here at Veracruz there have been several strikes of the employes of the Terminal Company. The men employed in the yards are now getting $2.00 per day and those handling cargoes $3.00. The manager—an

American, a most excellent man—is of course a strong Huerta man. He does not want any more strikes—or a condition that makes them possible. It disturbs business and incidentally it affects dividends. It is the old, old story over again. Strikes by the way are quite common along the gulf coast.

If you have had the patience to follow my rambling tale of woe, you will understand by this time the reasons for my occasional lack of faith and my pessimism. I am not naturally a pessimist but the situation is so overwhelming when we look it squarely in the face that it is hard to be hopeful. With my best efforts I am unable to map out any positive program in my own mind predicated on Mexican resources. In a broad way the situation in Mexico to-day is not unlike our own in the days immediately preceding the civil war and when our nation with its vast resources of political experience and common sense found itself unable to solve the problem without resort to the last argument how can one reasonably expect these politically helpless people to accomplish by a policy of give and take and patient reform what we were unable to do. The long peace of Diaz' regime undoubtedly laid the foundation for the social and economic aspirations that are now awakened in the people of Mexico, but the absolute repression of all political activity for more than a generation left the people, as it seems to me, wholly unfitted to cope with the complex situation that now confronts them.

When I approach the question *negatively* certain propositions are very evident to me. The first is, that Huerta and Huertaism will not solve the problem. One of my favorite questions to the Huerta advocates has been "If the U.S. should recognize Huerta and enable him to get money to put down the present rebellion would that be the end of rebellions in Mexico?" in every instance that I can recall the answer has been "no." My next question has usually been "how long in your judgment would the peace last?" The estimates have varied from eighteen months to three years. Sometimes I substituted other names—Diaz, Caranza[,] Gamboa and with substantially the same result. All thinking men realize that there can be no lasting peace without judicious and substantial social and economic reforms. The old scientifico and church element will have *no reform*. Huerta denounced the Northern rebels as "socialists," to me, and all the other rebels as "bandits." The South would not tolerate a Northern man with any "heretical" ideas for a moment. They would rebel as Felix Diaz did and there is no one in sight giving more promise of political capacity than did Madero and he proved a failure politically. But I am digressing. Huerta is impossible and I am glad to say out of the way.

Intervention at this time unless forced upon us is not to be thought of—

1st because our own work at home makes it inexpedient to divert the public mind from the domestic questions that press for solution.

2nd The time is not opportune. The Mexicans have not yet demonstrated to the world the utter helplesness that I charge them with.

3 The estimate of their capacity which I have ventured to make may be erroneous. Providence may come to their rescue in some inscrutable way and besides it seems to me that fair play entitles them to another chance especially if they make a bona fide effort to comply with the President's suggestions.

Intervention eliminated, I see no course open but to press matters to an issue on the lines under way. I repeat that I am not sanguine as to the final outcome but I still deem it worth while to persist. Accordingly by the time this reaches you I will probably be back in the City. Mr. Gamboa has evidently been whispering to Mr. O'Shaug[h]nessy that it would be nicer for me to be nearer by but I feel that it would be unwise for me to make a move in that direction until Mr. Gamboa is prepared to commit himself unequivocally.

Congress is not going to be as pliable as some expected. The situation may reach a crisis before you get this. One of the possibilities in that event is a Huerta dictatorship and you will pardon me for outlining my views in that contingency. Two ways will be open—circumstances at the time to dictate the choice. If Huerta inaugurates a reign of terror and especially if all means of egress from Mexico are cut off immediate intervention is necessary; on the other hand if matters continue to drift with only occasional murders I am strongly inclined to the view that recognition of the rebels would be a wise preliminery step. The leaders of the rebellion may not rate very high as men but the movement as a whole has more merit than Huertaism and something good may be evolved out of it and in any event there are practical considerations that should not be ignored. If the U.S. should intervene now I am satisfied that some of the rebels would probably side against us. And while I do not look upon intervention as a serious matter from a military point of view it would be just as well to let them use up some more ammunition and exhaust their energies before we appeared on the scene. To preclude shocking you by these views I will tell you about my interview with the Rev. Mr. Vanderbuilt[5] a Presbyterian missionary the

[5] The Rev. William Evert Vanderbilt, Presbyterian missionary in Mexico since 1897.

other day. Mr. Vanderbuilt has been here upwards of twenty years, is a good observer and likes the Mexicans. At the end of an hours' talk I asked "What would you suggest?" "Well, he answered, I am a man of peace but if I had my way the rebels of the North would get all the guns and ammunition they needed" and strange as it may seem this was the remedy suggested by a delegation of native protestant ministers who called on me.

Well, I am tired writing and too lazy to revise. You will not read this with a critical eye under the circumstances. It is not intended as an official report. The heat is rather oppressive at times but Mrs Lind and myself are feeling pretty well. The admiral and officers of the fleet are very kind to us. Mr. Canada the Consul is one of the best and most level headed men that I ever saw in the service abroad. Kindly greet Dr. Hale from me. I congratulate the administration on the situation in Congress. It is splendid. It is good to be a democrat these days even down here in Veracruz   Yours truly   John Lind

ALS (W. J. Bryan Papers, DNA).

From Lindley Miller Garrison

My dear Mr. President: Washington. September 19, 1913.

I herewith inclose you a copy of my communication about the Philippines[1] for which you asked me this morning. Additional information which may be useful to you is as follows:

The legislation of the Philippines is now enacted by an Assembly composed wholly of native members elected by the people of the Islands, in conjunction with the Philippine Commission wholly appointive by the President of the United States. The Philippine Commission consists of nine members, five Americans and four Filipinos, namely: The Governor General and four Cabinet officers, one of whom is a Filipino; and four other members termed "legislative members,"—that is, they hold no Cabinet office, one of whom is an American and three are Filipinos. The three Cabinet officers who were Americans are, the Vice Governor, who is also the Secretary of Public Instruction; the Secretary of Commerce and Police; and the Secretary of the Interior. The Filipino Cabinet officer is the Secretary of Finance and Justice. The Governor General has under his immediate jurisdiction the Executive Bureau, the Bureau of Audits and the Bureau of Civil Service.

The positions of Secretary of Commerce and Police and Secretary of the Interior are now vacant. Mr. [Frank A.] Branagan is now the American legislative member, and Mr. [Newton Whiting] Gilbert is the Vice Governor and Secretary of Public Instruction.

If some scheme similar to the one I suggested is adopted, then we could give one of these Cabinet positions to a Filipino, which, with the one they already have and the three legislative members, would give them a legislative majority in the Philippine Commission.

It is probable that under existing legislation the Secretary of War has a veto on the Acts of the Philippine Legislature. Even if he has not, we have power of instant removal, and there is no grave danger from the effect of the operation of bad laws, if such were enacted, because we could immediately fill up the Commission and repudiate them. I do not think, however, that there is any question but what we could control that situation, and that there is a veto in the Secretary of War. In any event, Congress has authority to annul any laws.

I have made some little inquiry about Mr. Peters,[2] and I find that he was a member of the Committee on Insular Affairs at one time, and his attitude towards the Islands seemed to be an open-minded one, although he was evidently one of those who thought that we should never have taken them. He is, as you know,—or was—a member of the Anti-Imperialistic League, but does not seem to have ever been active.

Sincerely yours,   Lindley M. Garrison

Gov Harrison will be in Japan Sept 25th.

TLS (WP, DLC).
  [1] L. M. Garrison to WW, April 24, 1913, Vol. 27.
  [2] Andrew James Peters, Democratic congressman from Massachusetts since 1907.

From Ellen Axson Wilson

My own darling,   Cornish, New Hampshire Sept. 19, 1913

Oh, I am so delighted and excited over the passage in the House of the currency bill by so splendid a majority! To think of a clear 200 *majority*! isn't it wonderful?[1] The Senate surely cannot stand out against that,—whatever that abominable "Times" says. It insists that there is little hope of ever getting it out of committee there. And, as usual, "The World" did not come today. It always fails to come when we are mad to see it. The "Post" and the Boston papers simply say that "opinion in the Senate has not yet christallized."

We had an interesting guest for luncheon today, Norman Hapgood; (also his very beautiful little 16 year old daughter,[2] his only child.) He came over from Hanover to see us. It was such a comfort to your poor exiled wife to hear some intelligent *political* talk. He is so delightfully frank too in saying exactly what he thinks about both men and measures. I said nothing myself but just drew him out, and I had a great time. Oh yes, I did have and seize[d] the opportunity to defend Mr. Bryan against the charge of neglecting his duty. Mr. Hapgood had heard such varying reports that he did not know what to think about that. How atrociously insulting is "The World's" "offer" to Mr. Bryan![3]

I believe the drought has really broken. This has been "a rainy day,"—actually the first since we came to Cornish,—a soft, slow steady drizzle. Lucy, Mary & I have spent a good deal of it in the studio, Mary reading aloud. I have finished my picture, (I think) in fact two of it,—the little and the big one. The big one is the best, —as it should be,—has more freshness. So now I have four new large ones and will turn in and do more out-of-door sketching. The colour is beginning to be charming.

Jessie & Frank returned last night, Jessie looking much better in every way,—the "red in the eye" scarcely noticeable. They had a lovely time at the Garfields.

By the way, they brought from the Garfields, the report, which we had already heard from the little lame Miss Conover[4] and someone else, (I forget who,) that Mrs. Cleveland and her new husband[5] are very unhappy together,—in fact are *not* "together,"— very much of the time! He is said to be "going abroad" soon, and she is said to look most dreadfully. I don't really believe it and of course would not mention it except to you,—just as a curious rumour. We are all well & in fine spirits,—the more so because of your blessed note which reached me today. You darling! Everything you do & say makes me love you more and more and more! As always,   Your own   Eileen.

ALS (WC, NjP).

1 The House approved the bill on September 18 by a vote of 299 to 68.

2 Ruth Hapgood.

3 "The World to Mr. Bryan," New York *World*, Sept. 17, 1913. In this front-page editorial, the *World* offered to pay Bryan $8,000 a year during his incumbency if he would devote his full time to the duties of his office and refrain from delivering lectures and other addresses for which admission fees were charged. For the controversy over Bryan's lectures on the Chautauqua circuit, see Link, *The New Freedom*, pp. 111-12, and Paolo E. Coletta, *William Jennings Bryan* (3 vols., Lincoln, Neb., 1964-1969), II, 104-107.

4 One of the several Conover ladies of Princeton.

5 Frances Folsom Cleveland Preston and Thomas Jex Preston, Jr. Formerly engaged in the manufacture of linseed oil in Newark, N. J., Preston was graduated from Princeton in 1906 at the age of forty-three and received a Ph.D. in classical archaeology from the same university in 1911. He was Professor of Archaeology and Acting President of Wells College (his wife's alma mater) in 1911-12. After their marriage on February 10, 1913, he became a gentleman of leisure in Princeton.

Two Telegrams from
Viscount Sutemi Chinda to Baron Nobuaki Makino

5029　暗　華盛頓発
　　　　　本　省　着　大正2年9月19日　后5・00

牧野外務大臣

珍　田　大　使

第 277 号

往電第 273 号ニ関シ 9 月18日大統領ニ謁見シ貴電第 205 号
閣下カ米国大使ニ開示セラレタル御意見ノ要点ヲ繰返シ本
協約案ニ同意ヲ求メタル所大統領ハ元ヨリ本協約案ノ正理
ニ合スルヲ認メ其大体ノ趣旨ニ対シテハ何等異議ナキコト
ヲ明瞭ニ答ヘ唯上院議員中ニハ本協約案ヲ以テ「デモクラ
ット」党ノ根本政綱タル州権尊重主義ニ抵触スルモノトシ
強硬ニ反対スル者アルヘク事茲ニ至リテハ現ニ議会ニ繋属
スル二大法案ノ運命ニ影響ヲ及ホスヘキヲ以テ急速ニ決定
シ難キコトヲ説明シ追テ右法案カ予期ノ如ク臨時議会通過
ノ上ハ十分上院議員ヲ説得シ本協約案ノ成立ニ努ムルヲ辞
セサルモ之カ為メニハ尚時日ヲ要スヘク目下ノ形勢ニ於テ
ハ過日国務長官ヨリ本使ニ提議シタル如ク当該州ニ警告ス
ヘキコトヲ約スルニ止ムルノ外ナシ尤モ加州立法ニ関シ曩
ニ中央政府ノ斡旋其功ヲ奏セサリシハ事実ナリト雖必スシ
モ加州議会次回会期ニ於テモ同一ノ結果ニ陥ヒルヘキモノ
ト断言スヘカラスト述ヘタルニ付本使ハ右斡旋ノ結果ハ到
底日本国政府ノ満足シ難キ所ト信スル旨ヲ答ヘ本使ニ於テ
ハ敢テ急速ニ本協約案ノ調印ヲ迫ルモノニアラスト雖更ニ
幾多ノ時日ヲ経過シタル後上院議員ノ意嚮ニ顧ミ結局本案
ニ同意シ難キコトヲ回答セラル丶ニ止マルニ至ラハ本案交

渉ノ延期ハ畢竟無益ニ終ルノミナラス却テ不快ナル形勢ヲ
生スヘキヲ以テ上院ノ協賛ヲ得ルト否トニ係ラス行政部ノ
権限ニ依リ協約調印ヲ断行スヘキコトヲ保障セラレ以テ米
国政府ノ好意ヲ表明セラレンコトヲ切望スト述ヘタリ之ニ
対シ大統領ハ若シ行政部カ斯ノ如キ措置ヲ執ル場合ニ於テ
上院ノ協賛ヲ得サルニ至ルトキハ従来幸ニ一地方ニ限局セ
ラレタル問題ハ忽チ範囲ヲ拡大シ中央立法部ノ排日気勢ヲ
知ルニ足ルモノトシテ不良ナル感触ヲ日本公衆ニ与フヘキ
ヲ恐ルト述ヘ往電第273号国務長官ノ談ト同意見ヲ説キタ
ルニ付本使ハ又其当時国務長官ニ答ヘタルト同一ノ趣意ニ
依リ右危惧ノ理由ナキノミナラス反テ米国政府ノ友好ナル
態度ハ一般人民ノ諒トスヘキ所ト信スル旨ヲ説明シタルニ
大統領ハ之ニ耳ヲ傾ケ此点ニ付テハ尚篤ト国務長官ト協議
シテ意見ヲ決スヘシト述ヘタリ然ルニ国務長官ハ上院ノ協
賛ヲ得ル見込確実トナル迄ハ協約調印ヲ不得策ト認ムル意
見ナルコト既報ノ通リニシテ追テ大統領ヨリ同官ニ協議ス
ルモ満足ナル結果ヲ期シ難ク且国務長官カ本使ニ洩ラシタ
ル語調ニ依ルニ同官ニ於テハ時日ノ経過ニ従ヒ自然日本人
ノ心冷静トナルヘキコトヲ予想シ本件解決ヲ急カサルヲ得
策ナリトスルモノヽ如ク従テ同官カ本件商議延期ノ必要ヲ
説クモ要スルニ一ノ遷延策ニ外ナラサルカノ疑念アリタル
ニ付此際成ルヘク具体的ノ保障ヲ求メンカ為更ニ一歩ヲ進
メ若シ到底上院協賛ノ見込ヲ確カムル迄協約調印ノ途ナキ
モノトセハ勘クトモ過般「ニカラグア」保護条約案ノ例ニ
依リ不取敢本案全部ノ商議ヲ完結シ只調印ノ一事ノミハ之
ヲ延期シ右両国政府限リ協定ヲ遂ケタル成案ヲ上院外交委

員ニ附議シテ其同意ヲ経タル上調印スルコトヽスルモ可ナ
ラスヤト述ヘタルニ大統領ハ熟考ノ体ニテ此点モ亦国務長
官ト協議ヲ遂ケ同官ヲ経テ確答スヘシト答ヘタリ

Hw telegram (No. MT 3.8.2. 274-3, JFO-Ar).

T R A N S L A T I O N

Washington D. C., received, 5:00 P.M.
No. 277, Confidential.   September 19, 1913.

Concerning my telegram No. 273, I had a meeting with the President on September 18. I repeated the main points of the message which you had communicated to the American Ambassador and which appeared in your telegram No. 205, and sought his approval for this draft of the treaty. The President answered clearly that he recognized the righteousness of the purport of this draft and that he had no objection to its general principles. However, he said, there might be certain senators who would strongly oppose this draft of the treaty because they would think that it violates the principle of state rights, which had been one of the fundamental planks of the Democratic platform. In these circumstances, he explained, it was difficult to make an early decision because it might affect congressional decision on two other important bills which are now pending. He said that after these two bills could be passed in Congress, as was expected, during the extraordinary session, he would be willing to try to persuade the senators to approve the treaty. However, he went on, this would require some time, and in the meantime all that he could promise to do was, as the Secretary of State also mentioned the other day, to give warning to the state concerned. He said that, although it was true that the previous efforts made by the central government had not been effective enough to prevent legislation by the State of California, it should not be said definitely that the next session of the California legislature would necessarily do the same things. After answering that the Japanese government could not find any satisfaction in the outcome of their efforts, I said that I did not mean to ask for an immediate signing of the treaty. However, I added, if, after a long lapse of time, the United States Government finally replied that it could not agree to this treaty because of the opposition of the senators, the postponement of the negotiation of the treaty would not only prove fruitless but would also produce an unpleasant situation. In view of this, I urged strongly that the United States Government express its good will by pledging that it would exercise its executive power and sign the treaty without regard to whether the Senate would approve it or not. In answer to this, the President remarked that he feared that, if the Executive should take such action without the consent of the Senate, the problem, the effect of which had fortunately been limited until now to a certain area, would rapidly and widely expand so as to give an unfortunate impression to the Japanese public as proof of a heightened anti-Japanese feeling in the national legislature. His opinion was the same as that of the Secretary of State, which I reported in my telegram No. 273. I also replied in the same way as I did to the Secretary of State, explaining that I believed that the above-mentioned fear on the part of the President was unfounded, and that the friendly attitude on the part of the United States Government would be welcomed by the general public [in Japan]. The President listened to me carefully and told me that he would discuss more on this point with the Secretary of State before making a decision. But, as I have reported to you before, the Secretary of State did not consider it good policy to sign the treaty before making sure of the possibility of the Senate's cooperation and consent. Therefore, we cannot expect a satisfactory outcome of future discussions with the President and the Secretary. Moreover, judging from the impression made by the words of the Secretary of State, he seemed to think it better not to hasten the solution of this problem because he expected that the emotion of the Japanese would become calmed down naturally as time passed. Consequently, I suspect that his argument for the necessity of postponing the negotiation of this matter is nothing more than a dilatory tactic. Then I pushed my argument further in order to secure the most concrete pledge possible in the circumstances. I told the President that I thought, even if it was impossible for him to sign the treaty until he could make sure of the possibility of the approval of the Senate, at least it was possible, as seen in the previous case of the Nicaraguan Protection Treaty, to complete the negotiation of the entire draft of the treaty first, and postpone only the process of signing, which would be done after the draft agreed to by both governments had been submitted to the Senate Committee on Foreign Relations and approved by it. The President seemed to ponder the possibility and answered that he would discuss this point also with the Secretary of State and would give me a definitive reply through the Secretary.

5028　暗　華府発　大正2年9月19日　後4・00
　　　　　本省着

牧野外務大臣

　　　　　　　　　　　珍　田　大　使

第 278 号

往電第 277 号ニ関シ大統領ハ本使ノ退出セル後各新聞社代
表者ヲ引見セルガ其節一代表者ノ問ニ答ヘ日米懸案ハ双方
折衷案 (middle ground) ヲ求メ妥協ニ至ルヘキコトヲ信ス
ル旨簡単ニ述ヘ其所謂折衷案ナルモノニ付テハ何等説明ヲ
加ヘサリシカ胸中窃ニ成算ヲ有スルモノヽ如ク見受ケラレ
タル趣其席ニ列シタル一人ヨリ当館員ニ来報セリ

Hw telegram (No. MT 3.8.2. 274-3, JFO-Ar).

T R A N S L A T I O N

                                    Washington D. C., received 4:00 P.M.,
No. 278, Confidential.   September 19, 1913.

　　In reference to my telegram No. 277, the President had a press
conference after I had left. Answering a question posed by one
of the correspondents, the President said briefly that, as for the
pending problems between Japan and the United States, he believed that a compromise could be achieved by the effort of both
countries to seek the middle ground. Although he did not give
any explanation of the planned compromise, according to someone who attended the conference and brought this information
to the Embassy, the President seemed confident, as if he had
some plan in his mind.

From Ellen Axson Wilson

My own darling,   Cornish, New Hampshire Sept. 20, 1913

　　This has been another day which tried and failed to be a really,
truly rainy day. We elders have spent it peacefully and quietly
reading, sewing and painting. Nell & Margaret went horseback-

riding and then Nell did a really charming sketch. Frank & Jessie went on a long ride, picnicking in the car.

A Mrs Barnett[1] who asked some time ago if she might buy one of my small pictures, which she had heard I would sell for the school,[2] came in the morning and took two,—for fifty dollars each unframed. Rather oddly she choose the two from which I have just painted the large ones,—which of course suited me exactly. I told her I had used them in that way and she thought it added to their interest.

I have just discovered tonight that Frank sings well. He has just been singing some cowboy songs that are extremely interesting. He has a fine baritone;—so we really have a quartette in the family with you and Frank, Margaret and Nell.

"The World" is very cheerful, I note about the Senate and the currency. When do you think it will, or perhaps I should say "might, could or should" get out of the committee? As soon as you can form any idea as to whether or not you will be able to spend the latter part of October here, please let us know, dear, for it will soon be almost necessary for us to make some rather definite plans,—in view of the troussea[u]x, &c. &c.! And of course if you can't come here we will go to Washington the middle of Oct. at the latest. I note that the Washington paper says that Oct. is the best month in the year in Washingon as to weather.

In any event we must go to New York for two or three days week after next. Dear little Helen goes to Philadelphia next Thursday, and if we leave here the middle of the month will not return to Cornish.

We are all very well and love you devotedly. I would give "most anything" to have you here tonight my dear, *dear* love. Of course Sundays are the days when it is hardest to be apart. But of course I must not murmur. But oh! I love you passionately! As always.   Your own   Eileen.

ALS (WC, NjP).
  [1] Unidentified.
  [2] The Berry School, a preparatory and vocational boarding school with separate divisions for boys and girls, located at Mount Berry (near Rome), Ga., founded by Martha Berry in 1902. For a study of Miss Berry and her school, see Tracy Byers, *Martha Berry: The Sunday Lady of Possum Trot* (New York, 1932).

To Ellen Axson Wilson

My darling,   The White House 21 September, 1913.

Stockton is here. He turned up last night. The doctor and I found him here when we returned from our Saturday afternoon ride, exploring (this time very bad) roads. He is looking his best,

—radiates good health and vigour. It is delightful to see him so. He has evidently been greatly stimulated and refreshed by his renewed contact with the West, which he loves, and has some very interesting experiences to relate. I am expecting now to go up to Princeton on Tuesday to vote at the primaries, and probably he will go with me, but I shall try to bring him back with me. It is such a pleasure to have him, and he is better company than ever. We all three went to church together this morning, and he liked Mr. Taylor very much indeed. He preached one of the most interesting sermons I have heard from him. By the way, Stock. says that Dr. Fitch preached at Princeton last winter. He did not hear him, but he noted the unprecedented circumstance that the undergraduates discussed him and his sermon with the deepest interest not only throughout Sunday but for several days afterwards. He caught echoes of it all even in his preceptorial conferences. Do you wonder? Is he not just the sort to get under the skin of the average indifferent youngster? How he might spiritualize a college! Yes, that *was* a delightful lunch party at his little home up on the mountain. There was only one thing that disappointed me and made me feel uncomfortable (for with me, as you know, the keenest discomfort comes from self-consciousness). He had the bad taste to remind me again and again that I was President of the United States. I had expected him to have the right intuition about me and to know that I wanted, in such circumstances, to forget that and be his comrade. I did not feel that I was natural or spontaneous for a moment while I was there, as a consequence of my disappointment in that. But this is not criticism; it is *just* disappointment. How I hate the office when it holds me off from the people I want to get close to! As a barrier it is intolerable to me.

What a delight it is to have Sunday come and bring with it this chance to chat with my darling and take the strain off the longing with which thoughts of her sometimes almost overwhelm me! I cannot *really* tell her what is in my heart, but it is such fun, and such a relief, to try! My heart, dearest, in every sense, is the seat of my life. I cannot understand the lives of those men who seem to have fed on their minds,—on science, speculation, imaginative writing, the absorptions of scholarly research. They seem to me something less than human,—men like Herbert Spencer, for instance and a lot of the Germans. My happiness, my very life, depends on my relations with my fellow beings. And, ah! what an unspeakable pleasure it is to me to think of what God has given me, my incomparable little wife and wonderful daughters, compact of every charm of mind and heart and person! It is too wonderful to comprehend. And then dear creatures like Helen, for largess, and friends like Lucy and Mary, singular in any place or circle for their charm and interest and sweetness. I never did anything to deserve all this, but I could not have done what I have done without such support and subtle joy, such exhileration of deep enjoyment as I get from such associations. And how my heart leaps up when you tell me how much the girls and Helen and Lucy and Mary love me! That's tonic and joy enough for any man, and when added to your incomparable love and devotion is almost more than there are terms to reckon. My love, my love, my sweet, sweet love! how bright you make my way thro. every test and trial of my life! Your daily letters affect me like a breath of life. They remind me in the midst of weariness of everything that there is for my spirit to t[h]rive on. They fill my heart to overflowing, relax every strain, melt out of me what is harsh or touched with deep discouragement, because they breathe so perfect, so wonderful a love. It fills me with a sort of ecstacy, compensates for everything and leaves a margin of joy over and above the balance! Am I conscious of you? Indeed I am! As conscious as of the visable daily circumstance of what goes on about me. I am your debtor for all that makes the days go well and the nights seem sweet and wholesome. I am your lover, my sweet one, more deeply and truly than ever I was when I was a boy. I am every moment   Your own   Woodrow

See P.S. on other sheet.

I am perfectly well, and no piece of public business has altered for the worse.

I altogether approve your decisions about a performance of the masque in Milton and attending the Longfellow festival. The man who said I was non-commital simply lied. I told him we could not and would not come.

WWTLS (WC, NjP).

To Mary Allen Hulbert

My dearest Friend,   The White House 21 September, 1913.
The enclosed envelope was handed me this morning. Do you wonder that it startled me with its foreign postmark! does it not look like the handwriting of the dear lady who, when I last heard from her, was at Nantucket? It turned out to be the handwriting in fact of Mrs. Seymour Davis of Philadelphia,[1] and enclosed a clipping from the London Daily Mail about the passage of the tariff bill. The chief point with me is, that it was *not* from my

friend, last heard from at Nantucket, and that when last heard from she was by no means recovered from an illness which made me wretchedly uneasy about her. I have been waiting, waiting, with what anxiety and suspence she may imagine, to hear how she has fared. Will she not have someone drop me a note to tell me how she is, so that *this* anxiety may not gnaw at my thoughts while I strive to handle big things of state? I will bless her with all my heart if she will! For my heart is the organ by which I live and its loads are the only loads that are intolerable to me. If I must speculate whether my dearest friends are well or ill, in danger or out of it, I am in no shape to care as I should how the currency bill is shaped or handled. And so I cry out to her for aid. I must know how she is. I have been distressed by all sorts of conjectures and daunted by all sorts of doubts. My fear is, of course, that she is more ill than she cares to have me know, for fear of distressing me in the midst of public anxiety. If that is true, this is to tell her that it is kinder to tell me the real facts. And if, along with that, she can tell me what that I can do would help most to bring her back to health and strength, how it would cheer a man who chafes most at helplessness and inaction! I am perfectly well and strong, in spite of the strain which I had feared might be too much for me. Partly, perhaps, because so far all has gone singularly well in public matters. Do not believe anything you read in the newspapers. If you read the papers I see, they are utterly untrustworthy. They represent the obstacles as existing which they wish to have exist, whether they are actual or not. Read the editorial page and you will know what you will find in the news columns. For unless they are grossly careless the two always support one another. Their lying is shameless and colossal! Editorially the papers which are friendly (and some which are not) represent me, in the most foolish way, as master of the situation here, bending Congress to my indomitable individual will. That is, of course silly. Congress is made up of thinking men who want the party to succeed as much as I do, and who wish to serve the country effectively and intelligently. They have found out that I am honest and that I have no personal purpose of my own to serve (except that "If it be a sin to covet honour, then am I the most offending soul alive!") and accept my guidance because they see that I am attempting only to mediate their own thoughts and purposes. I do not know how to wield a big stick, but I do know how to put my mind at the service of others for the accomplishment of a common purpose. They are using me; I am not driving them. But I need not tell *you* all this. The joy of a real friend is that one need not explain *anything*: it is known and comprehended already. *You* will know just how I accomplish anything that I do accomplish. And what a pleasure it is, what a deep human pleasure, to work with strong men, who do their own thinking and know how to put things in shape! Why a man should wish to be the whole show, and surround himself with weak men, I cannot imagine! How dull it would be! How tiresome to watch a plot which was only the result of your own action and every part of which you could predict before it was put on the boards! That is not power. Power consists in one's capacity to link his will with the purpose of others, to lead by reason and a gift for cooperation. It is a multiple of combined brains. But you know that, too. The fact is that you are a very wise lady, because you instinctively comprehend your fellow beings, both singly and in the mass. That explains the hold you have upon individuals and the power you have in society whenever you have the chance or the wish to exercise it. To comprehend people is to rule them. At any rate that is the root and source of the whole thing. See the thing from the point of view of those with whom you are dealing and your influence is established, and is welcome. *But how are you*? That's what I am really thinking about. I spoke of the rest only because your own gifts suggested it. I am waiting more anxiously than you know to learn how my dearest friend is.

Your devoted friend,　Woodrow Wilson

WWTLS (WP, DLC).
¹ This letter is missing.

Viscount Sutemi Chinda to Baron Nobuaki Makino

5068　暗　華府発／本省着　大正2年9月21日　后5・10

牧野外務大臣

珍　田　大　使

第 280 号

往電第 277 号ニ関シ 9 月20日国務長官ヲ訪ヒ一昨日大統領ト会談セル始末ヲ通報シ特ニ大統領カ国務長官ト協議ヲ約シタル二点ヲ細述シタルニ同官ハ未タ右ニ関シ大統領ト会談セサリシ趣ニテ第一上院通過ノ見込アルト否トニ拘ラス

一旦協約ニ調印シテ上院ノ議ニ附スル考案ハ将来大統領ニ
重大ナル煩累ヲ及ホス虞アルニ付実行至難ナル旨ヲ述ヘ最
モ強硬ニ反対ノ意ヲ示シ第二両国行政部限リ商議ヲ完結シ
テ其結果ヲ上院外交委員ニ提出シ大体同意ヲ得タル上ニテ
調印スル考案ニ就テハ同官一己トシテ異議ナキ旨ヲ答ヘタ
ルモ右ハ尚大統領ト熟議ヲ要スルニ付本使ニ於テ暫ク帝国
政府ニ報告ヲ見合サンコトヲ求メタリ本使ハ右両案ハ畢竟
万々一上院通過ノ見込ナキ場合ニ対スル一ノ緩和手段タル
ニ止マリ主要問題ハ素ヨリ本協約ノ成立ニアルヲ以テ之カ
為米国政府ノ誠実ナル努力ヲ期待スルコトヲ反覆切言シタ
ル上右第二案ハ第一案カ到底不可能ト決セル場合ニ初メテ
詮議ニ上ルヘキモノニシテ本使ノ希望ハ素ヨリ第一案ニア
ルコトヲ説明シ置ケリ

貴電第224号本協約案カ土地以外ノ問題ニ付排日ノ立法ヲ
防止スルニ足ラサルコトハ本使ニ於テモ夙ニ考量ヲ加ヘタ
ル所ニシテ今少シク本案中ニ人民ノ生業職業ニ関スル最恵
国待遇ノ保障ヲモ包含セシメンコトヲ提議シタキ考ニテ折
角考案中ナリ右生業職業ノ問題ハ御承知ノ通一昨年条約改
正談判ノ際条約中ニ規定ヲ設ケン為帝国政府ヨリ極力主張
シタルニ拘ラス遂ニ米国政府ノ同意ヲ得サリシ所ナルモ今
日ハ同政府当局者モ一変シ形勢異ナルモノアルノミナラス
州権干渉非難ニ付テハ土地問題ニ比シテ幾分カ軽キコト丶
察セラルルニ付我ニ於テハ本協約ノ骨子ニシテ最モ近接ナ
ル土地問題ニ関シ商議ヲ進捗スルニ至ラハ更ニ其以外ノ問
題ニ亘リテ努力ヲ試ムルノ価値アリト思考ス

Hw telegram (No. MT 3.8.2. 274-3, JFO-Ar).

TRANSLATION

Washington D. C., received, 5:10 P.M.

No. 280, Confidential.   September 21, 1913.

In reference to my telegram No. 277, I visited the Secretary of State on September 20 and informed him of my meeting with the President the day before yesterday. Especially, I told him in detail about the two points which the President had promised to discuss with him. However, it seemed that he had not yet discussed these points with the President. First, he strongly opposed the plan of signing the treaty regardless of the possibility of its approval by the House of Representatives (the Senate?) and putting it to the discussion of the Senate afterward, for he thought that, because such a plan might cause great difficulties for the President in the future, it was extremely difficult to put the plan into action. Secondly, as to the plan of completing first the negotiations between the executives of the two governments and signing after submitting the outcome of the negotiations to the Senate Committee on Foreign Relations and gaining its approval, he said that he had no objection to it as an individual, though he added that he had to discuss this point further with the President. So he asked me to delay my report on it to the Imperial government. I said that these two plans were no more than palliatives in case the passage of the treaty in the Senate should become impossible. I emphasized that our main objective was of course the conclusion of this treaty and repeated that I expected the sincere cooperation of the United States Government. And I explained that, as for the two plans, I gave the first one much higher priority than the second. It should be considered only after it had become impossible to put the first one into effect. As for the other problems than those concerning land, which were referred to in your telegram No. 244 (?), I also have already thought that more remains to be done than to prevent anti-Japanese legislation. So I am now thinking about and planning to make a proposal to have the treaty include a pledge of the most favored nation treatment regarding jobs and occupations for our people. As for these problems of jobs and occupations, as you know, the Imperial government has urged that a provision be enacted concerning them during the negotiation for the revision of the treaty year before last, although it could not obtain the consent of the United States Government after all. However, not only because the authorities of the government have totally changed, and so the situation is different, but also because these problems could be thought less likely to evoke criticism on the point of violation of state rights than that concerning land,

I consider it worthwhile to make an effort to solve these problems after we have proceeded to negotiate about the land problem, which is the most urgent one and the main point of this treaty.

From Ellen Axson Wilson

Cornish, New Hampshire

My own darling, Sept. 20 [21], 1913.

We are just back from a lovely ride! The country,—beautiful before, is, now that the autumn colour has come, simply enchanting. Oh, how I longed for you. I hardly dare ask when you think you can come and see it! I suppose not until that bill gets out of committee.

Only Margaret and I took the ride. Jessie and Frank jogged off with the horse as usual on Sundays and the others refused to go out at all. It was a relief to get out in the open after the mornings experience at church. It was drizzling; there was practically no one there, and the minister dwelt at length on the statement that the people of Windsor,—or the churches,—(I forget which) were all ice-bergs! Amusing to relate, bad as our church is Jessie and Frank prefer it to his own[1] They went there two weeks ago and almost shudder at the experience.

Did you send me a *splendid* article about you from "The Westminster Gazette" called "President Wilson's first lap" by Edward Porritt? I simply found it in the mail. If you have not seen it I want to send it to you,—if you think it won't get lost! It is one of the finest things we have had.[2] I do so *love* to have good foreign ones, about you, to feel that all the world is beginning to know how great and good you are. The Mexican affair is worth all the trouble it is costing you because of the great opportunity it has offered to set a completely new standard in international morality. I am quite immoderately proud of all you have done and said, and refrained from doing. It makes one laugh to think how completely you must mystify the average diplomat. They can no more understand you than West can!

Goodbye, dear,—oh if I could only wish myself in Washington to-night how happy, happy I would be *I love you, dearest*

Your own Eileen.

I am investing $5500—$1300 of it being from coupons. We invested $3000 before, besides paying $6,000 for our debt & Sister Annie.

ALS (WC, NjP).

[1] That is, St. Paul's Episcopal Church in Windsor, the Rev. Parker C. Manzer, rector.

2 Edward Porritt, "President Wilson's First Lap," London *Westminster Gazette*, Sept. 1, 1913. Porritt emphasized Wilson's quiet but effective leadership of and cooperation with Congress, particularly in the struggle for tariff reform. Whenever a question of congressional wrongdoing arose, as in the matter of lobbying on the tariff bill, Wilson avoided personal attacks but effectively brought the matter before the court of public opinion, thus obliging senators and congressmen to stand up against the pressures. Porritt concluded that it was "faith in the President's straightforward honesty" that was winning the people to his support in dealing with all the complex issues, both domestic and foreign, facing his administration.

To Oswald Garrison Villard

My dear Mr. Villard: The White House September 22, 1913

I hope that you will try to see the real situation down here with regard to the treatment of the colored people. What I would do if I could act alone you already know, but what I am trying to do must be done, if done at all, through the cooperation of those with whom I am associated here in the Government. I hope and, I may say, I believe that by the slow pressure of argument and persuasion the situation may be changed and a great many things done eventually which now seem impossible. But they can not be done, either now or at any future time, if a bitter agitation is inaugurated and carried to its natural ends. I appeal to you most earnestly to aid in holding things at a just and cool equipoise until I can discover whether it is possible to work out anything or not.

Cordially and sincerely yours,   Woodrow Wilson

TLS (O. G. Villard Papers, MH).

To Oscar Solomon Straus

My dear Mr. Straus: The White House September 22, 1913

Your letter of September thirteenth[1] was very welcome, and I am sincerely obliged to you for your courtesy in enclosing the editorial from the Times.

I have had a great many very serious thoughts about the tolls exemption, and you may be sure that when the right time comes (at the regular session of Congress) I will try to find the wisest and most effective way of handling it. I am cordially obliged to you for your friendly suggestion.

Sincerely yours,   Woodrow Wilson

TLS (O. S. Straus Papers, DLC).
    [1] It is missing.

From Charles William Eliot

Dear Mr. President: Asticou, Maine, September 22, 1913.

Have you noticed that the instructions given by Mr. Lane to the Registers of the land offices were not that they divide the advertising fairly between Republican and Democratic papers, but that they advertise in newspapers "favorable to the Administration"? I venture to think that fair division between political parties of offices, advertising, and other patronage, although better than any onesided distribution, is not the guiding rule toward the building up of honest, effective, and patriotic Public Administration.

I have nothing but admiration for the way in which your Administration has dealt with the Consular Service. It is first-rate politics as well as first-rate promotion of efficiency; for American exporters have got firm hold of the doctrine that consuls should be active, intelligent, experienced promoters of American trade.

I confess that I am surprised that you have found any of the men in the Diplomatic Service, who entered it on examination intending to make it a life-career, unable or unwilling to adopt loyally and completely any new ideas about foreign affairs which your Administration wished acted on. To make such changes loyally when Administrations change is the fundamental idea of a trained diplomat who enters the Service for life. I should have thought that there would have been left over from the terms of Roosevelt, Taft, Hay, and Root, a considerable number of young men in the Diplomatic Service who would be simply delighted to have the chance to represent the moral and public considerations which ought to control the foreign policy of the United States, rather than the material interests of individual Americans or groups of Americans.

Congratulating you most heartily on the safe progress of the tariff and currency bills, and hoping to hear that you have established some regular exercise in the open air every day in Washington and frequent week-ends in the country, I am,

Sincerely yours,   Charles W. Eliot

TLS (WP, DLC).

From Samuel Gompers

Sir: Washington, D. C., Sept. 22, 1913

The Executive Council of the American Federation of Labor is now holding its regular session in Washington, and I am authorized by my colleagues to ask, and take pleasure in asking, whether you can find it convenient to meet us for the purpose of a conference upon matters in which we feel you are deeply interested.

If agreeable to you and to the Secretary of the Department of Labor, we respectfully suggest his participation in the conference.

Of course any time which you may designate will be entirely agreeable to us, but in order that the entire Executive Council might participate, I shall additionally appreciate it if you can meet us either Tuesday, Wednesday, or Thursday of this week.

I have the honor to remain,

Very respectfully yours,　Saml. Gompers.
President,
American Federation of Labor.

TLS (WP, DLC).

From Ellen Axson Wilson

My own darling,　　　Cornish, New Hampshire Sept. 22, 1913

Your lovely letter reached me just before dinner and made us *all* very happy,—for I read to the rest the dear things you said about them. Oh but you are sweet. It is delightful to have so good a report of Stockton, and to know that you are finding him good company. We knew he was due in Princeton about this time and are hoping to get him here for a few days before we leave. If he is still with you please ask him if he can't come. I suppose Princeton opens this week and I understand he is to lecture there this fall as usual,—but he might come for a weekend. I am very glad you found him so well, for he wrote to the Smiths that this summer out west had been a sad contrast to the last, when they were there, and they had all been so happy together. I fancy that it has not been good for him to be with Madge so much. He does not write a very good report of her condition.

Nell & Helen have gone to a dance tonight. The Smiths and I have been reading "Happy Acres"[1] the book dedicated to little Elizabeth Wilson,[2] the first copy of which came today. I think it is going to have a nice southern atmosphere. It rained *hard* all last night and much of the day. We took a long ride this morning in the rain much of the time, and it was perfectly beautiful. Wonderful effects both of colour and atmosphere,—I painted all the afternoon to make up.

Alas, I fear my good times in the studio are almost over, for I shall have no secretary here the rest of the summer. Helen goes to the hospital on Thursday, and Miss Hagner can't return, as she expected to do, on account of the family troubles. It is hard luck to have two secretaries and neither of them available. All the more reason for returning to Washington if you can't come here. But oh! I hope you can come once more; it is so perfectly lovely now. And the air is so sweet and fresh and soft, now that the drought is over. The little brooks are filling rapidly and are lovely. It seemed quite wonderful today to go splashing through pools of water.

I wish I could tell you, my darling, how happy your wonderful letters made me! But I can't! I think you must know without the telling. Believe me, dearest, as always in every heart throb,

Your own   Eileen

ALS (WC, NjP).
¹ Edna Henry Lee Turpin, *Happy Acres* (New York, 1913). This book is in the Wilson Library, DLC.
² Unidentified.

To Samuel Gompers

My dear Mr. Gompers: En Route, September 23, 1913

I have your letter of the twenty-second, and shall try, immediately upon my return to Washington, to arrange a conference such as you suggest for Thursday.¹

In haste   Sincerely yours,   [Woodrow Wilson]

CCL (WP, DLC).
¹ *The New York Tribune*, Sept. 26, 1913, reported that Wilson conferred with Gompers, the executive council of the A.F.L., and Secretary of Labor Wilson at the White House on September 25 "with regard to labor legislation pending in Congress." The only specific subject of discussion mentioned was a measure to increase the appropriation of the Department of Labor.

From Ellen Axson Wilson

My own darling,   Cornish, New Hampshire Sept 23 [1913]

I have been very naughty for I have put off writing until I am so sleepy and tired that I can hardly see the paper. My conscience pricks me, as it should,—and I wont do it again if I can help. I painted almost all day, spent the evening with the family, and then had to attend to a lot of business after I came up stairs before I could begin writing to you.

I will not have much more time to paint now and the colour is so lovely that I could not resist doing *two* studies,—morning and afternoon. Both are good,—for me. The conditions were favourable for working at the house here, for every body was away except Helen and me.

They all went at Mr. Baynes[1] invitation, to Corbin's Park to see the buffalos, &c. He wanted them to make it a picnic but preferred to do it all in the afternoon,—and as a consequence they did not get back until eight o'clock. They had to leave the car outside and go about the park with horses. They saw some 60 buffalos and had a very interesting time. They say it is an extremely beautiful place—really park-like.

Those inveterate picknickers Jessie & Frank are taking us off again tomorrow to go over the pass to Rutland and see the Green Mts. It is what we tried to do once before. This time they think they really know the way. Frank's holiday will be over on Sunday so they are making the most of it. It will be good for little Helen to have a last trip of that sort before she leaves on Thursday. I hate horribly to have her go to the hospital without any of the family. But of course it must be to avoid publicity. Miss Hagner insists upon going to Phila. that day, and that will be a great comfort to me. Fortunately Dr. Davis[2] himself is an old friend, and that makes a tremendous difference.

We are all well. The weather is gloriously bright today. The grass on the lawn is a vivid green all over. Hasn't it wonderful powers of recuperation? *Please* excuse this scrawl. I have a new pen, which won't work, & I *am* so sleepy. I love, *love, love,* you *darling!*   Your own   Eileen

ALS (WC, NjP).
  [1] Ernest Harold Baynes of Meriden, N. H., writer and lecturer on natural history. He played one of the roles in the bird masque discussed in earlier letters.
  [2] That is, Edward Parker Davis, Wilson's classmate.

To William Jennings Bryan

[The White House]

My dear Mr. Secretary: September 24, 1913

Professor Droppers is not only willing, but anxious, to go to Greece but feels that he would be acting in a way that would greatly embarrass Williams College if he gave up his classes there at this time, or, indeed, at any time before the end of the academic year. He wants to know if the appointment could be postponed until June next. What is your own feeling in the matter? He is a fine man and I should not like to lose him.

Faithfully yours,   Woodrow Wilson

TLS (Letterpress Books, WP, DLC).

From Ellen Axson Wilson

My own darling,   Cornish, New Hampshire Sept 24 [1913]

We carried out our schedule this time and really reached Rutland. It is 109 miles there and back and it was a wonderful trip. I feel almost *drunk* with colour. We were quite in amongst the Green Mts. for half the day, and they are very beautiful,—perhaps more *beautiful* than the White Mts.

We got back at 7.30 and it is now nine. We were detained by a little accident. We had our luncheon at one o'clock at the top of the pass then started down towards Rutland but had not gone on half an hour when we came upon three men with a team working on the road. They had dug a deep trench in which to put one of those huge round water drains; but they laid timbers across for us to pass,—the drain not having yet been put in place. The timbers were rotten and broke under our back wheels which went down their full diameter into the trench which was *very* deep. The two horses which the workmen had could not budge it of course, so the five men including Frank worked for an hour trying to insert some of the broken timbers under the wheels so as to ease it a bit; but it seemed pretty hopeless. In the meantime four other autos had gathered, and, of course, none of them could pass. It was an amusing scene. Being a mountain pass there were no alternate roads—no "long way around" such as we took to Balt.[1] I had asked the men if we could not get more horses somewhere, but they said there were none to be had for *miles.* Finally I got tired of hanging around and walked alone up the road,—a long gentle hill, winding to a bridge. At the bridge was a huge pile of timber and three wagons and *six powerful horses* loading up with it! I hired the two biggest horses & took them down the hill. They were hitched on and in three minutes the car was out of the ditch, very little the worse for wear, and we went on our way rejoicing.

Lucy says I must tell you that I looked like the Victory of St Gaudens in front of the Sherman statue[2] coming down the hill in a white dress with my long cloak open and flying and the two great horses walking behind me apparently of their own free will, —for they were unhitched, of course, from the wagon and the man walking behind was not visible.

We had meant to go to Mr. Stephen Parish's tonight to hear Mr. MacKaye read his new play but we are too tired, so only Nell and Margaret have gone. They were not with us today, as of course the car holds only six. Goodnight *darling!* I love you to distraction. As always

Your devoted little wife,   Eileen.

ALS (WC, NjP).

¹ A reference to Wilson's "long way around to Baltimore," when he escorted Ellen Axson to New York in 1884. See the Editorial Note, "Ellen's Visit to Wilmington and Her Trip with Woodrow to Washington and New York," Vol. 3, pp. 329-30.

² The equestrian statue of General William Tecumseh Sherman at the entrance to Central Park, Fifth Avenue and Central Park South, New York.

Remarks at a Press Conference

September 25, 1913

Well, gentlemen, I should think that even those who have been skeptical among you would begin to feel that the moral influence of the United States was counting for something in Mexico. I believe even Mr. Oulahan will admit that. Because you will see that really the course of events has justified my interpretation of that second note.¹ I have never varied, except for the outside news, in the impressions that I have had of what they meant, that they have yielded, of course, the two cardinal points of what we insisted upon— that General Huerta should not be a candidate, and that there should be guaranteed fair elections. Just how far the latter is practically possible, I can't judge; but they know that that must be their effort anyway. I think that the news from day to day confirms those impressions.

Would the candidacy of Gamboa² be more satisfactory to the administration than that of Huerta personally?

I don't feel that we have an opinion about candidacies outside the feeling that, I may say, we have already proscribed [Huerta].

You wouldn't pre-judge him as a creature of Huerta's administration?

I don't see anything that would justify our saying that.

Mr. President, the Constitutionalists today announced that under the circumstances they can't participate in this election. If that is true and they don't participate, would the condition by us, requiring a full participation in the election meet that condition, would that be satisfactory?

We didn't make that condition. We said that if these initial things were conceded, we would be glad to exercise our good offices to see to it that some sort of common understanding was brought about. But those good offices were declined, and there has been no opportunity for us to speak for the authorities in Mexico City at all in that matter. So that I don't think we can argue it, because it hasn't developed far enough.

Is there a positive assurance that Huerta won't be a candidate now?

As we understood it, there has been all along.

I believe there are dispatches in the afternoon papers today saying that he has accepted the resignation of Gamboa and approved his candidacy for the presidency. Interpreting that will prove that he will not be a candidate himself?

I think the proof will come to that effect, but, as I have said to you gentlemen several times, I understood all along that we had explicit assurances to that effect, in fact that he would not.

Mr. President, what should we do if the Constitutionalists refuse, if we see if they refuse—

I don't think it is wise for me to discuss any "if."

Mr. President, you did make a suggestion sometime ago, from which you drew the question that if an election was held in a representative portion of Mexico, it would be valid, and that you would so regard it.

My answer to that, Oulahan, would be this: We have got to see what actually happens. We have got to wait and see just how far the assurances are carried out before we make up our attitude about the result. . . .

Mr. President, it would be a great story for tomorrow morning if we were able to say or predict with assurance of realization that the efforts of the government would now be directed towards making the Constitutionalists tractable.

The field of prediction is very dangerous.

You have not been in communication with them at all, Mr. President?

No.

Mr. President, is it likely you would make any effort to get into communication with them, without saying so to the other government?

If we did, we wouldn't say anything about it. . . .

JRT transcript (WC, NjP) of CLSsh (C. L. Swem Coll., NjP).
1 Gamboa's note of Aug. 26, 1913.
2 About this matter see WJB to WW, Sept. 25, 1913, n. 1, below.

To Francis Burton Harrison[1]

[The White House, Sept. 25, 1913]

We regard ourselves as trustees, acting, not for the advantage of the United States, but for the benefit of the people of the Philippine Islands. Every step we take will be taken with a view to the ultimate independence of the Islands and as a preparation for that independence; and we hope to move towards that end as rapidly as the safety and the permanent interests of the Islands will permit. After each step taken experience will guide us to the next. The Administration will take one step at once. It will give to the native citizens of the Islands a majority in the appointive council and thus in the upper as well as in the lower house of the legislature. It will do this in the confident hope and expectation that immediate proof will thereby be given in the action of the council under the new arrangement of the political capacity of those native citizens who have already come forward to represent and lead their people in affairs.[2]

T telegram (Letterpress Books, WP, DLC).
   [1] This message to the Philippine people was read by Harrison as part of his speech upon his arrival at Manila on October 6, 1913.
   [2] There is a WWsh draft of this message in WP, DLC.

From William Jennings Bryan

My dear Mr. President: Washington September 25, 1913.

   The letter which accompanies this was dictated yesterday but was not ready to mail until this morning. In sending it to you, I beg to enclose a despatch from O'Shaughnessy which verifies the correctness of the report contained in the papers this morning.[1]

   I feel that we have nearly reached the end of our trouble. This eliminates Huerta, which is the first thing that we desired. I know of no objections that can be raised to Gamboa personally and we have, therefore, only to await the election to see whether it is fairly conducted.

   The injection of the religious question, while unfortunate from our point of view, will at least divert attention from the differences that have heretofore existed and tend to divide the country into two national parties, one of which must necessarily be dominant.

   Do you think it would be worth while to emphasize the significance of the action of Huerta in endorsing the candidacy of Gamboa (and thereby putting himself out of the race)—do you think it would be worth while to emphasize the significance of this by having Mr. Lind return in case we find upon inquiry that the Mexican Government has no more communications to make through him? I think it is worth while considering whether such a course might not give our country a sense of security in the belief that the crisis is now passed. And it might enable you to express the hope that, this end having been reached, the Constitutionalists would assist in securing a fair election and a full expression of the wishes of the people.

I shall see you tomorrow morning, but I submit this inquiry that you may have time to consider it before then.

With assurances of respect, etc., I am, my dear Mr. President,
Very sincerely yours,   W. J. Bryan

TLS (WP, DLC).
    [1] N. O'Shaughnessy to W. J. Bryan, Sept. 24, 1913, T telegram (WP, DLC). O'Shaughnessy reported that the Catholic party, on September 24, had nominated Federico Gamboa and General Eugenio Rascón as their candidates for President and Vice-President of Mexico in the coming election. He observed that both men had good records and that neither had been involved in the Huerta coup in February 1913. He mentioned also that Huerta had "given in to this move and promises uninfluenced elections."

From William Jennings Bryan, with Enclosure

My dear Mr. President: Washington September 25, 1913.

I enclose a copy of a telegram received from Governor Lind. He seems to share our confidence that Huerta will not be a candidate. Every day, I think, adds to the certainty of his not being a candidate.

The entrance of the church into the campaign tends to invalidate all former calculations because realignments are quite likely. The contest between the clericals and the anti-clericals is a deep rooted one, it having resulted in the routing of the clericals at the time when Juarez executed Maximilian. I would not be surprised if on both sides the feeling tended to obliterate the lines between the Constitutionalists and the Huerta Government, so that it would be difficult to calculate the result of an election where candidates represent the two sides.

You will notice that the President does not think it worth while for Lind to return to the City of Mexico at present. As I suspected, they are a little sore over our failure to receive Zamacona,[1] and yet I do not think that we could have done other than we did without the granting of the concessions which we asked. It seems to me that things are going along wuite [quite] well at present and we have only to sit tight and await the election. The hostilities seem to have decreased and we do not have so many reports of trouble down there. Our own Senators seem to be quiet, too, since your message. In fact, I feel that we are making as much progress as we could well expect.

With assurances of respect, etc., I am, my dear Mr. President,
Very sincerely yours,   W. J. Bryan . . .

TLS (WP, DLC).

¹ Manuel Zamacona, a career diplomat, formerly Ambassador to the United States, whom Huerta had wanted to send on a personal mission to Washington.

E N C L O S U R E

Vera Cruz, Mexico, September 23, 1913.

I feel confident Huerta will not be a candidate. They are now casting about for a candidate who will represent the Huerta policy. The Church will probably dictate the nomination and the Government will look after the election. The Church promised a loan of seven million dollars on condition that its nominees were appointed Minister of Public Instruction and Collector of Internal Revenue. The House balked on the nominee for Minister and now the nomination for President will be claimed and will probably be conceded. I suggested to O'Shaughnessy to sound Gamboa discreetly. He answers:

Quote. I have just seen Gamboa and talked with him again regarding your suggestion. Cannot give particulars. He informs me that he has approached the President in the premises and he says that he does not see any change in the situation which would warrant your coming. They resent Z not being received. There will be elections but I have my doubts if they will stand the test of a count by the Chamber of Deputies. End quote.

Of course I will not go until their attitude is different. . . . The rebels appear to hold their own and are occupying new territory. . . . Pressure should be applied and maintained at every point.

Lind

T telegram (WP, DLC).

From William Jennings Bryan

My dear Mr. President: Washington September 25, 1913.

I am in receipt of your letter in regard to President Droppers. I think it is all right to give Professor Droppers until next June to accept the appointment to Greece, but as Minister Schurman has already returned and there is a vacancy there, I think you had better appoint some one to hold the office temporarily. You will have no difficulty in finding some one, because it would be an honor that would be appreciated by many. We have so many deserving Democrats and so few places to give that I would like if all of them would be willing to serve for a short time so that we could pass the offices around. Have you any one in mind for this place during the short term intervening between now and June? Have you thought anything more about George Fred Williams? He might be willing to accept this short term as a compliment; at least, it would do no harm to offer it to him even if he declined it, provided you think he would be a proper person for the place and provided also you have no one else whom you prefer to him. If you do not approve of the suggestion in regard to George Fred Williams, would you like to have me look about for a good Democrat who would like a winter's stay in Greece?

    With assurances of respect, etc., I am, my dear Mr. President,

                    Very sincerely yours,   W. J. Bryan

O.K.   W.W.

TLS (WP, DLC).

From Ellen Axson Wilson

My own darling,   Cornish, New Hampshire Sept. 25, 1913.

    Another glorious day but spoiled for us by the necessity for going to a luncheon and an afternoon tea,—and also for me by having to settle down to desk work instead of painting. Alas, I am sadly spoiled by having secretaries to do things for me! Dear little Helen is busy packing as she leaves tonight. She is just as quiet and sweet and cheerful as if she were going off on a pleasure trip instead of to have an operation.

    Jessie, Nell and I go to New York on Tuesday the 30th, getting back either Friday or Saturday morning. Let us know if there is any chance of your coming up that week end.

    Margaret, Lucy and Mary go on the 1st (Wed.), to the White Mts. for a three days trip. It has been postponed until late because we expected Miss Hagner to return and go on it too.

    We are anxious to have Stockton come up and see this place and if possible take that trip with the girls, but we don't know where he is. If in Washington will you urge him to come, or have a night letter sent to him wherever he is. He would better not come before the 30th for Marguerite Walbridge[1] spends the week end here and returns with us to New York!

    We are delighted over the "free art,"—but will you please solve one riddle for us. The "N. Y. Post" said in its news columns that "all restrictions had been removed," and called it "free art" and then in its editorial said there was 15% duty,—which is right?

    I have ordered four more bonds from Webb & Prall, 5%,— and a 2500.00 6% mortgage from Dickinson. That makes 15000.00 invested in the six months, besides the $2400.00 to

Sister Annie and Wilson [Howe] and $4200 to pay our debt to the Princeton Bank,—the debt incurred before we went to Washington for our "trousseaux," the office in Trenton, &c. &c. That is $21,600 altogether in six months. We have $142,000 in all invested bringing an income of about $6400. By the way I have saved out less (that is I have invested more) than usual this month. Our balance now is about $1500.00 and I have just found that the other $1000.00 to Sister Annie is due her the 1st of Oct. So please deposit the salary promptly when you get it and let me know; when I will write to Ned Howe to send it to her in the form of American Express Co. checks; unless you prefer me to do it in some other way. Mary Smith thinks that is the most convenient form in which to have money when abroad.

I am finishing this at night. We have seen dear little Helen off, and I feel a bit heavy-hearted about her. She *is so* fine & brave.

We had a *very* good time at the Slades[2] at luncheon—no guests but the Smiths, Margaret & myself. Their view is too wonderful for words, especially now with the colour; and the house is adorable, not big like Miss Augusta Slades but still *perfection*. They too have lived in Italy for years so that it is almost an Italian villa in lines & furniture. The queer Miss Slade with the big man's voice is a remarkably interesting person when you get her to herself and with the most exquisite sensitiveness to *beauty* of all sorts, especially in music. It is a pathetic anomaly to have the face and the temperament match so ill. She and Mrs. Adams for instance are extreme opposites in that respect. Mrs. Adams *looks* all soul. She is doing very well indeed, by the way,—is sitting up.

Everybody sends oceans of love to you, dearest. I love you just as much as you want me to love you, and in every possible way. As ever   Your devoted little wife   Eileen.

ALS (WC, NjP).
    [1] About this rather mysterious woman, whom Stockton Axson once courted, see EAW to WW, April 10, 1904, n. 2, Vol. 15.
    [2] That is, Elizabeth and Fannie J. Slade.

To Walter Hines Page

My dear Page: The White House September 26, 1913
    Thank you with all my heart for the letter from Skibo Castle. You must know how glad such letters make me. I am so constituted that, for some reason or other, I never have a sense of triumph, but I do know in my mind that what we are accomplish-

ing with regard to the tariff is going to be just as epoch-making as you indicate and in just the way you foresee.

I, myself, had a couple of days once at Skibo Castle[1] and know how to sympathize with you.

In haste, with warmest regard,
                    Faithfully yours,   Woodrow Wilson

TLS (W. H. Page Papers, MH).
[1] From August 12 to August 15, 1908. See WW to EAW, Aug. 16, 1908, Vol. 18.

To Francis Fisher Kane

My dear Friend: [The White House] September 26, 1913

Thank you most warmly for your letter.[1] You may be sure that it gave me genuine pleasure to appoint you District Attorney.[2] How delightful it is to have a chance occasionally to show one's friends some real mark of trust and appreciation! I look forward with the greatest confidence to your successful administration of the office and shall watch your career in it with real pleasure.
                    Cordially and sincerely yours,   Woodrow Wilson

TLS (Letterpress Books, WP, DLC).
[1] It is missing.
[2] United States Attorney for the Eastern District of Pennsylvania.

To Lindley Miller Garrison

Personal.
                                        [The White House]
My dear Mr. Secretary: September 26, 1913

As you know, of course, Professor Ford has completed his errand to the Philippines. He brought down to me by his own hand the other day his reports. I am sending them to you in the hope that you may find the time (which I have not at present) to give them a careful reading. Will you not be kind enough to regard them as confidential until I see you concerning them?
                    Cordially and faithfully yours,   Woodrow Wilson

TLS (Letterpress Books, WP, DLC).

From William Jennings Bryan, with Enclosure

My dear Mr. President: Washington September 26, 1913.

I enclose copy of a telegram from Bogotá. I authorized Mr. Thompson to make a formal offer of fifteen millions. You will notice that his offer begins with an expression of regret "that anything should have occurred to mar in any way whatsoever the close and traditional friendship which so long existed, etc."

While I think that such an expression of regret as framed would not be construed as an attempt to apologise for the action of a former administration or to disapprove of it and while I think that we should go as far as we can without expressing disapproval, I have wondered whether this expression is framed, just as you would like it.

As this will be preserved down there as a public document and may be printed, it occurs to me that you might prefer to write it over so that it will represent your ideas exactly.

After conferring with the Colombian Minister, I am disposed to make the offer twenty millions rather than fifteen, since they refused to consider fifteen when put in the form of an inquiry. They know that we expect to offer more than the fifteen and that this is simply the beginning of the negotiations. Please let me have your idea as to the language of the offer.

With assurances of respect, etc., I am, my dear Mr. President,
Very sincerely yours,   W. J. Bryan

TLS (WP, DLC).

E N C L O S U R E

Bogot[a], Sep. 23, 1913.

Referring to your last sent[e]nce of your telegram of Sep. 19, 5 p.m. The Minister for Foreign Affairs[1] informs me that the President[2] is willing.

Subject to your approval will send the following: "Mr. Minister: The Government and the people of the United States sincerely regret that anything should have ever occurred to mar, in any way whatsover, the close and traditional friendship which so long existed between the United States and the Republic of Colombia, and my Government, earnestly desiring to remove the differences aroused by reason of the separation of Panama and wishing to make reparation to Colombia for the moral and material losses suffered by her, has instructed me to offer a sum of fifteen millions of dollars in full settlement of all claims and differences now pending between the Government of Colombia and the Government of the United States, and between the Government of Colombia and the Government of the Republic of Panama.

Jessie, Ellen, Eleanor, and Margaret

Ellen Axson Wilson

Wilson at Harlakenden

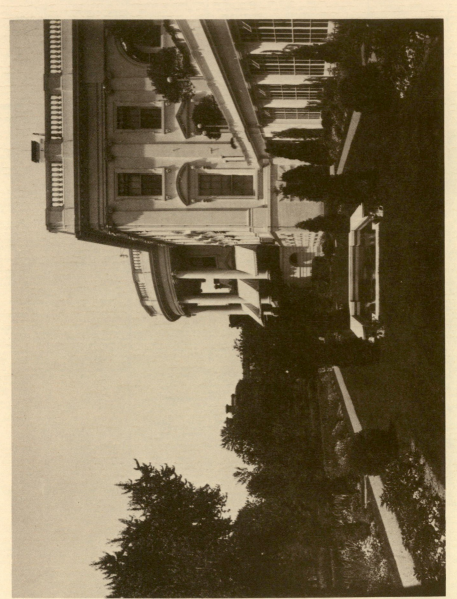

South side of the White House

Francis Bowes Sayre and Jessie Wilson Sayre

John Lind

Victoriano Huerta

Wilson reading his tariff message to Congress

In the hope that this offer will prove acceptable to your Excellency's Government, I avail myself of this occasion, etc."

Thomson.

T telegram (WP, DLC).
  1 Francisco José Urrutia.
  2 Carlos E. Restrepo.

From Ellen Axson Wilson

My own darling,   Cornish, New Hampshire Sept. 26, 1913

Did you see the editorial in todays "Times" on the Mexican situation? If not do make Mr. Tumulty produce it for you. What a triumph to have them forced, after all their outrageous criticism of you and support of H. L. Wilson, to take such a tone. "It must be admitted that things seem to be going President Wilson's way in Mexico." * * * "It must be admitted that all this looks enough on the surface like a successful outcome of our Mexican policy to justify a trifle of shouting." &c. &c.

But what do you think of Gamboa as a candidate? I suppose he will be a tool of Huerta's but I hope he will at least satisfy the technical requirements of the situation. I feel as if I *must* know how things really stand as regards Mexico and what you really think; so I have a bright idea. Tell Dr. Grayson and let him write it for me! I am sure he will be glad to do me that favour.

And please thank him for the very kind and comforting letter received from him yesterday. Tell him I can't express how much I was cheered by his good report of you and of things in general; and that I would write to him myself if the absence of both Miss Hagner & Helen did not make it almost impossible.

We have had another beautiful day. The touring car is out of commission for a few days owing to the accident; (nothing serious,—some part was hurt and they have to replace it,—I think they said "the clutch"). But we took a little ride in the landolet to get the sun and to take Mary & Margaret to a concert in Windsor. It was a guaranteed concert by professionals and very good, they said.

This morning the son of Mrs. Barnett[1] who bought two of my paintings came and bought one for himself. That makes $350.00 of the $1000 I want to raise myself for the "Berry School." Then I got in an hours painting and attended to my mail. The girls played tennis[,] read, horseback &c. &c. Margaret is in the highest spirits because she has finally achieved "high C., piannissimo,"—and in *songs*, not exercises. She could do it before but not softly. Well, it is late & I am very tired, so I must say, goodnight, my dear, *dear* love. I am ashamed of these scrawls! Always & altogether   Your own   Eileen.

ALS (WC, NjP).
    ¹ Like his mother, Mrs. Barnett's son is unidentified.

John Palmer Gavit to Oswald Garrison Villard

Confidential

Dear Mr. Villard: [Washington] September 26, 1913.

I have been so busy for the past week, trying to get out of my house here by the first of October, that today was the first chance I had to talk with Tumulty about the matters in which you are especially interested. I can see that he is a good deal distressed about the situation, and I can find no room for doubt of his sincerity. I have an appointment to talk with the President about the whole business next Wednesday, and Tumulty seems to be confident that I will come from it with an entirely different idea of the President's attitude on the subject from that which I have in large measure shared with you.

I can see that the peril of confusing the tariff and currency bills with a bitter controversy over a thing which is the subject of strong feeling on the part of every southerner (to say nothing of many northerners) has operated to palsy the hand of the President in this matter; though of course nobody will say that in so many words.

On the whole, I hope it will be possible to let the subject lie relatively quiet until I have had a chance to get the truth at first-hand. I do not know how much I shall be at liberty to write after my conversation next Wednesday; but I mean to give you a clear account of what I learn. After that you may see a bit more definitely what is to be expected. . . .

The fact that I am to see the President ought to be held as confidential until after it is over, anyway. I think it desirable that the subject should not be brought to any critical pass until I have had my talk. Perhaps you remember Billy McAllister's old minstrel song: "Never Push an Angle-worm, When He is Going Up Hill."
                    Sincerely,   J.P.G.

TLI (O. G. Villard Papers, MH).

From Ellen Axson Wilson

My own darling,   Cornish, New Hampshire Sept. 27, 1913

I have tonight a telegram from Miss Hagner saying the operation is over and Helen doing well in every way. Also that the conditions were as expected in every way,—that is not at all serious. All of which is a very great relief.

We have still the superb weather with the deep colouring of the week,—a perfect riot of blue mountains, violet shadows & red and gold trees. A little cold but otherwise perfection. It makes me wish that I were a good walker, for it is just right for that. But of course I must choose between walking and painting.

Marguerite Walbridge came today,—and will return with us to N. Y. on Tuesday. I am glad to know that Stockton is again with you over Sunday & so can get my message prompt[l]y about going with the girls to the White Mts. They will start early on the morning of Wed. the 1st. Please ask him to telegraph an answer.

I have just had a letter from Miss Dickson at Princeton.[1] She is so dissatisfied with the administration of things there that she thinks she, her four assistants and her housekeeper will all leave at the end of this year. She has been looking for another "field" this summer, perhaps social work, but finally decided to try it one more year. Her feeling about you and your work is beautiful. And she is also as usual very sweet to me—says my friendship and sympathy were the brightest spots in her Princeton life.

She encloses a long article about you, and incidentally about us, from one of her high-church English papers which is in parts very good and in parts very funny, with its odd English misapprehensions. You for instance are "the idol of Tammany," and my economy in dress "has greatly alarmed the modistes of Chicago and St. Louis"! and "the Christian ideals of Dr. Wilson & the late J. P. Morgan are not so widely apart as we might believe"!

Is'nt it perfectly terrible about Sulzer. It seems to get worse every day.

Are they really going to dispute over the tariff for another week. The papers says the conferrees are all at the point of nervous collapse.

Don't forget to make Dr. Grayson write me what you think of Gamboa's candidacy, and if it meets your conditions, and if it does what your attitude will be towards the still disaffected Constitutionalists.

Goodnight, my darling. Oh, how I love you, and how I *want* you! So much indeed that I hardly dare talk about it. With devoted love.   Your little wife   Eileen.

ALS (WC, NjP).

¹ Bessie Louise Dickson, in charge of the Isabella McCosh Infirmary at Princeton University.

To Ellen Axson Wilson

My precious darling,   The White House 28 September, 1913.

The fact that I do not read the newspapers gives your letters to me with [sic] a curious interest. You do read the newspapers, and your mind is occupied with questions and anxieties which seem new to me,—and also with interests which I do not share. For example, I did not read the editorial about Mexico in the *Times* to which you refer in the letter received this morning, and I cannot share your elation about it simply because it does not make the least difference to me, or excite even a mild interest, *what* the *Times* thinks or says about anything. As a matter of fact things do seem to have been effected in Mexico by our attitude which I must admit I did not expect. We have good reason to think that Huerta has actually elimin[a]ted himself from the field of choice for President chiefly through the influence of the Catholic party, whose candidate Gamboa has now become, and our chief object seems to be attained. It is by no means clear that Gamboa would be the mere *alter ego* of Huerta, if elected; and, besides, his nomination *may* bring about a genuine contest for the office; the Congress may not accept his candidacy; the liberal and progressive elements of the country are strongly anti-Catholic in the field of politics and may run some nominee of their own. We have sent word indirectly¹ to the revolutionists in the north that they cannot afford to stand aloof from a constitutional election, if they wish to retain our sympathy or tolerance. On the whole, therefore, I feel that real progress has been made, and the moral pressure has, after all, proved pretty powerful. If it should prove all-powerful, as there is reason to hope now, it will mean the beginning of a new era in the Latin American states. New forces are asserting themselves in Mexico at any rate, and there can hardly be a dictatorship.

As for my coming again to Cornish, my darling, that depends entirely on the Committee of the Senate on Banking and Currency. So soon as they report the bill out in a satisfactory form I may be able to run off for a week's end. Ah! how I long to! How deeply happy a glimpse of my dear ones would make me! How my heart needs them! But it is impossible, as yet, for me to predict what that unusual aggregation of wilful individuals will do. This, however, seems clear to me. I ought not to urge you to stay up there longer than the middle of October. The weather here now is wholly delightful, and you will need quite a month to get ready for the wedding. By the way, sweetheart, when you go down to New York to shop please take Murphy along[.] It will make me feel so much easier. You will then be safe against any kind of annoyance. Notice you cannot in any case hope to escape.

Of course you heard, as we did, from E. P. [Davis] that all had gone well with dear Helen. How my heart has gone out to her. She is indeed wholly admirable and lovable.

How I bless you, my incomparable darling, for the daily letter; and yet my conscience hurts me about them now that you have no secretary and must attend to all your own correspondence. Please do not write when you are too tired or too rushed or might snatch a little time for painting if you did not. I love *you* above all things, and shall feel unhappy if you drudge to give me this pleasure. Even as it is, you too often sit up after bedtime and force yourself when tired out to write. It makes me feel guilty and selfish! Stock. is here again to-day, after getting his classes started in Princeton. Unfortunately his classes come at the end of the week and he cannot get away to take the trip with Margaret and Lucy and Mary. He looked dreadfully disappointed when I gave him your message and he realized that he could not accept the invitation.

My visit to Princeton[2] was very interesting,—just how interesting probably no one outside the family could realize. The only call I made was on the Ricketts. Unfortunately I ran across Hibben just before leaving. Stock. says that I behaved pretty well, and did not freeze him as I did Richardson[3] who seemed, in his infinite stupidity, quite taken aback by my manner towards him. When we went in to the Mann house[4] I was for a moment taken aback. The first floor was so fully furnished and the rugs on the floors gave it such an occupied appearance that I could hardly believe that I was not walking unbidden into someone's home. How familiar it all looked, and how many memories it stirred up! And how my heart ached for the sweet lady of whom I was thinking all the while! Dearest, you seem at each step of my life to be a larger, more intimate, sweeter part of it. I think more and more in terms of myself *and you*! It is very wonderful how you have loved me. The soul of me is very selfish. I have gone my way after a fashion that made me the centre of the plan. And you, who are so individual, who are so independent in spirit and in judgment, whose soul is also a kingdom, have been so loyal, so forgiving, so self-sacrificing in your willingness to live *my* life. Nothing but love could have accomplished so wonderful a thing.

If I have not justified it, I have been deeply grateful. I at least have sense enough to know what treasure I have enjoyed and lived upon, and how pitifully poor I should have been without it. And, ah! my lovely dear, how my heart does yearn at thought of it all, and of you! Your beauty, so characteristic of the soul within, your gentleness, your tenderness, your sweet indulgences, your patience with me and the inexpressible gleams of joy and enjoyment that sometimes leap into your eyes! I have no words to express what all these evidences of your love mean to me, how they solace me and make me happy in my loneliness and in the daily routine and struggle of my task! God bless and keep you, and reward you as I cannot except by my deep and passionate love!   Your own,   Woodrow

Thank you for thinking of the money for sister. Please send it through Ed. Howe as you suggest.

WWTLS (WC, NjP).
1 Through William Bayard Hale, as will soon become evident.
2 Wilson had gone to Princeton on September 23 to vote in the Democratic primary election.
3 Ernest Cushing Richardson, Librarian of Princeton University.
4 That is, 25 Cleveland Lane in Princeton, the house owned by Parker Mann, where the Wilsons lived from October 1911 to March 1913.

To Mary Allen Hulbert

My dearest friend,   The White House 28 September, 1913.

It was a great comfort to get Allen's telegram yesterday.[1] I had grown very anxious and uneasy at not hearing in so many weeks; for when you last wrote it was evident that you were by no means so well out of your alarming attack as you wished me to believe. Maybe Allen will drop me a note to give a few reassuring particulars. Friends do not multiply as life lengthens; they grow fewer, rather, those whom one has had time to test and can tie to, and one feels his dependence upon them grow greater and greater almost week by week.

The struggle goes on down here without intermission. Why it should *be* a struggle it is hard (cynicism put on one side) to say. Why *should* public men, senators of the United States, have to be led and stimulated to what all the country knows to be their duty![2] Why should they see less clearly, apparently, than anyone else what the straight path of service is! To whom are they listening? Certainly not to the voice of the people, when they quib[b]le and twist and hestitate. They have strangely blunted perceptions, and exaggerate themselves in the most extraordinary degree. Therefore it *is* a struggle and must be accepted as such. A man of my temperament and my limitations will certainly wear himself out in it; but that is small matter: the danger is that he may be lose his patience and suffer the weakness of exasperation. It is against these that I have constantly to guard myself. How does the game look to you, and the actors in it, as you sit at a distance and look on at it? It is more important to me to know how it looks outside of Washington than how it looks inside. The men who think *in Washington* only cannot think for the country. It is a place of illusions. The disease is that men think of themselves and not of their tasks of service, and are more concerned what will happen to them than what will happen to the country. I am not complaining or scolding or holding myself superior; I am only analyzing, as a man will on Sunday, when the work pauses and he looks before and after. My eye is no better than theirs; it is only fresher, and was a thoughtful spectator of these very things before it got on the inside and tried to see straight there.

Perhaps you saw in the newspapers that I went up to Princeton the other day to vote at the primaries. To walk about the dear old place after these years in which my thought has of necessity been separated from it and after six months of actual physical absence from it was like revisiting my old self; and the experience was both sweet and bitter. As ill luck would have it, I saw both West and Hibben. I was not obliged to speak to West, but I met Hibben face to face and had to force myself to behave as I knew I should, not cordially (that was spiritually impossible) but politely. Those who looked on and understood, like Stockton Axson, say I did pretty well; but I suspect it was a rather shabby exhibition of manners struggling through feeling and infinite embarrassment. Do you remember how we used to sit on the shore in Bermuda and talk of West, in the days when he was showing himself so complete and able a Machiavelli and when my name was first being mentioned in connection with my present office? Do you think now that there were any elements of prophecy in those talks, so full of speculation and anxiety and of all that then perturbed me. *Your* contribution to those conversations was a serene, unreasonable faith in *me*, for which I blessed your heart with all the feeling that was in me but did not in the same measure admire your judgment or knowledge of the world. It would be impossible to say (would it not?) how much of a many-circumstanced man's success is made up, so far as its spiritual stuff is concerned, of the faith his loving friends have in him. It seems to make a standard for him to live up to, to interpret something ideal to him and oblige him to strive after it. In brief, it makes him just that much better than himself;

transfers and translates into him what is sweetest and most ideal in those who so trust him. To make a man who has the struggle of life to face feel the things you expect of him as a sort of compulsion on his spirit, a mandate in all his conduct, is to lift him where he could never climb by himself. And was ever man more blessed by such helping friends than I! It is such inestimable help and stimulation and revelation of what is best worth while gotten from you, my dear friend, that must make me now and always know myself

> Your devoted friend,   Woodrow Wilson

Love and thanks to Allen.

WWTLS (WP, DLC).
   1 It is missing.
   2 About the hard sledding of the Federal Reserve bill in the Senate Finance Committee on account of the opposition of Senators James A. Reed of Missouri, Gilbert M. Hitchcock of Nebraska, and James A. O'Gorman of New York, all Democrats, see Link, *The New Freedom*, pp. 227-31.

From Ellen Axson Wilson

My own darling,   Cornish, New Hampshire Sept. 28, 1913

Oh, how I wish and I wish you were here today! I am sure Heaven itself cannot be more perfect than this whole day has been for beauty and for the delicious fresh yet soft *feel* of it! And then the profound peace of this dear spot. Oh, I could weep because you are not here! It is the sort of thing that "soaks in,"— that rests one through and through.

We went to church,—six of us,—and then I took Marguerite to Mr. Vonnah's to see the picture. He leaves on Wed. I am glad I went today for I have not seen it since you were here and in the meantime he has done all the "still life,"—cups and saucers, silver &c &c., *beautifully*. They are in perfect relation to the rest. The colour scheme is really wonderfully fine, and of course it looks quite finished now. The whole Colony is rather excited over it. After dinner Marguerite, Margaret & I took a delightful drive returning at four for Nell, Jessie & Frank to call at the Maxfield Parish's. I then showed Marguerite my pictures, and since then we have been strolling about in this lovely air. It is now 5.30 —the car is just rolling up with the children and I must go down soon to see the last of Frank. He leaves on the 6.45 train. This is the end of his holiday. Those dear lovers have certainly had a perfect summer. Whatever comes to them later "they have lived and loved"!

We have just seen Frank off. We finished with the singing of hymns! Some dear old lady wrote Jessie begging her to have the family sing at a certain hour today "Guide me, oh, Thou Great Jehovah"! So they all did it,—also "Abide with me" and one or two others. It made us wish for you more than ever. But when are we not wishing for you! It is good to think that on this day at least you have time to consciously wish for *us*.

"I love thee with the smiles, tears[,] breath, of all my life.
And if God choose I shall but love thee better after death."

As always,   Your own   Eileen.

ALS (WC, NjP).

To William Jennings Bryan, with Enclosure

My dear Mr. Secretary: The White House September 29, 1913

I think the advice given by Hale in the enclosed memorandum is very good advice. I do not know how correctly he represents your own feeling about it, but I should like very much indeed to have a short talk with you on the subject. Would it be convenient for you to see me at the office tomorrow at twelve?

Cordially and faithfully yours,   Woodrow Wilson

TLS (W. J. Bryan Papers, DNA).

E N C L O S U R E

From William Bayard Hale

Mr President: [Washington] Sept 28 [1913]

Yesterday I submitted to you a telegram from Mexico City which suggested that Gamboa might be chosen President by popular vote, but be rejected by the Mexican Congress. I have this morning had a telegram from another source confirming this possibility—indeed, representing it as probable.

Under the election law (a copy of which I handed you) the Chamber of Deputies "counts" the vote; "counting" seems to be a very flexible and comprehensive process—indeed, the Chamber is authorized to "resolve itself into an Electoral College." In case no candidate has an absolute *majority* of all votes cast, the Chamber may elect one of the two leading candidates. Or it may, on any of several indicated grounds, invalidate the election.

My information is that Manuel Calero and Flores Magon, Liberals, now control Congress. Calero the other day succeeded in throwing out of the Cabinet the Clerical, Urrutia, for having put him, a Senator, under arrest. Since this success, the Liberal element in Congress appears to have taken the bit in its teeth.

It refused to let Huerta give the portfolio of Education to a Catholic, by a vote of 80 to 14. It is not likely to permit the Presidency to pass into the hands of the Clerical candidate, Gamboa.

Now, Manuel Calero has talked to me by the hour of the desirability of a real, country-wide election. Flores Magon has shown me letters he has sent to the northern Revolutionists urging them to take part in an election.

My suggestion is that the moment is propitious for the United States to take steps towards putting into force its original propositions for an armistice and an election to be participated in by the whole country. I believe that consent to this could now be secured, both from the Mexican Congress and from the Revolutionists; and that a stable basis of peace could thus be established. The mind of Manuel Calero and Flores Magon I know; that they could now carry through the proposition I believe. As for General Carranza—his most trusted friend and adviser, Senor Escudero, is now in Washington, and I have today learned that Escudero is strongly of the opinion that the revolutionary chief could be induced to enter into negotiations looking towards an armistice and a national election.

Why not move for a real solution of the Mexican problem?

I had a brief conversation with the Secretary of State last evening. Mr Bryan's attitude is that matters are going on so satisfactorily that further efforts are unnecessary—the policy of the Administration, which has for its chief aim the elimination of Huerta, is going to be vindicated, anyhow.

That happy result now indeed seems probable—though if the October election should be declared invalid, Huerta would still be in power. But, with all submission to Mr Bryan's judgement, it seems to me that to eliminate Huerta and yet leave Mexico in disorder is a small practical gain. The northern Revolutionists are not going to participate in an October election; here is Carranza today denouncing in advance as a traitor whoever assumes the Presidency as a result of it. The Mexico City people may come to some sort of a settlement among themselves, may even set up a government which we may recognize, but it may be set down as a certainty that the North will remain in revolt; we shall have months more of disturbances along the frontier, destruction of the property of Americans and occasional murders to provide material for intervention agitators, and, likely as not, before we are through with it, a secession of the northern tier of Mexican States, with all the embarrassments that would entail.

The one chance for peace, the only chance in sight, is to induce the Carrancistas to participate in an election.

It would mean a postponement of the election for some weeks. But it is a mere fact that no election worth dubbing such can be held October 26th, four weeks from today. The law calls for the final revision of the voting list by August 15th. Transportation and communication are demoralized every[w]here; couriers could not penetrate (if they were permitted to) into Sonora, Chihuahua, Durango, Campeche, in a month's time. A delayed election that would mean something would surely be better than a farcical performance on schedule time.

True, the Revolutionists declare that they will take part in no election so long as Huerta rema[i]ns in the presidential chair. Even that may be arranged, if only once the Mexico City government and the Revolutionists could be brought into negotiations.

The situation is precisely what it was three years ago when President Diaz was being slowly crowded to the wall. The Maderistas refused to take part in an election unless Diaz first resigned—Diaz, with thirty years rule behind him! The idea was preposterous. But with a Mexican everything is impossible the first time he hears of it. De la Barra was induced to meet and converse (here in Washington) with Dr Vasquez Gomez— negotiations were opened, in other words—and Diaz presently found it perfectly possible to resign, leaving de la Barra to preside over an orderly election in which the whole country voted.

I can see no reason why that history might not be repeated.

So far as I know, our government has made to no [sic] approaches to the Revolutionists. Ought we not do so? Peace can never be attained in Mexico until they are reconciled. More than two months ago, de la Barra said to me on behalf of Huerta, that though the Mexican government could have no direct dealings with the rebels, it could deal with them through us. It would be the greatest blessing to Mexico if the United States could somehow quietly bring the Mexico City government and the Revolutionists into communication with each other. The element that seems now to be in the ascendency in the capital desires, I know, an understanding with the North. The Liberals in the Congress cannot propose it, and indeed, it would be physically extremely difficult for either side to communicate with the other.

We could open physical channels of communication between them. We could set negotiations going. By means of suggestions, privaltly made, we could probably bring about an armistice and a real election—accomplish, not merely such a "vindication" of the Administration's policy as the crowding out of Huerta would be, but the complete success of restoring peace in Mexico.

Senor Escudero expects to leave for Hermosillo, to rejoin Carranza, within a few days. He would furnish an excellent means of reaching Carranza, if the idea is favorably regarded.

WBH

TLI (WP, DLC).

To William Jennings Bryan, with Enclosure

My dear Mr. Secretary:

The White House
September 29, 1913

I enclose a suggestion for our Minister at Bogota, in accordance with the request of your letter of the twenty-sixth of September.   Faithfully yours,   Woodrow Wilson

TLS (W. J. Bryan Papers, DLC).

E N C L O S U R E

The Government and people of the United States sincerely desire that everything that may have marred or seemed to interrupt the close and long established friendship between the United States and the Republic of Colombia should be cleared away and forgotten. My government, therefore, desires now to set at rest once and for all the differences which have arisen between it and the Government of the Republic of Colombia in connection with the question of proper reparation for the losses, both moral and material, suffered by the Republic of Colombia by reason of the circumstances accompanying the acquisition of the rights now enjoyed by the United States on the Isthmus of Panama. I am, therefore, instructed to offer the sum of twenty million dollars in full settlement of all claims and differences now pending between the Government of Colombia and the Government of the United States and between the Government of Colombia and the Government of the Republic of Panama. I hope that this offer will prove acceptable to your Excellency's government, etc., etc.

T MS (W. J. Bryan Papers, DLC).

From Oswald Garrison Villard

My dear Mr. President: New York September 29, 1913.

I have such a high opinion of your judgment and such a complete belief in your desire to do justice to all American citizens, that I am naturally greatly moved by your kind note of September 22nd. You may be sure that it is very difficult for those of us who feel towards the Wilson Administration as the officers of our Association do, and took the responsibility of counselling the colored people to vote for you, to assume a critical position which might eventually lead to direct opposition.

But our plain duty to these people compels us to ask you a few questions before we can decide the matter of policy which your letter raises. By "just and cool equipoise" we presume you mean that we should refrain from the policy of protest which we have conceived to be our duty since our protest against the segregation in the departments at Washington failed to bring us a definite statement of your policy, or any answer. Even during this period of protest the process of segregation goes on steadily. Thus, Mr. McAdoo tells me that he is taking every white clerk out of the Register's Division, and the spirit of segregation is rife under him as we know from our own observation. I know Mr. McAdoo's motive and respect it, but he does not see that in his well-meant desire to give the colored clerks an opportunity to contrast, as a group, more clearly with the white clerks, he is driving the entering wedge for a cruel and un-American segregation; that this division will immediately be called the "nigger division" and that the precedent thus established will be of the utmost danger to the colored people long after the motive has been forgotten and Mr. McAdoo has disappeared from public life.

Under these circumstances meetings of protest are beginning to take place all over the country—one in Cincinnati already, and others scheduled for Washington, Baltimore, Boston and other cities. Now if, as we take it you desire, we suspend, so far as lies in our power, such efforts to protest, will you not give through us to the country a clear-cut statement of what the attitude of your Administration is going to be, together with an assurance that so far as lies within your power the process of segregation now going on in the departments shall cease? Have not eleven millions of colored citizens a right to know your attitude in regard to them? They have had nothing since your assurance of October 16th, 1912 that they might "count on me for absolute fair dealing and for everything by which I could assist in advancing the interests of their race in the United States." The mass of the colored people knows only that segregation in the departments have been introduced by your Administration and that offices heretofore given to them have been given to white people, and that not a single Presidential appointment of a colored man has been made save one which was withdrawn.

As a result you have the condition described in Booker Washington's letter which I sent you in which he declared that never has he seen the colored people so depressed and embittered.

Our Association is but one of many. We have not the slightest idea that if we ceased our protest we could assuage this feeling of bitterness and humiliation, or induce them as a race to remain in "cool and just equipoise." They, unfortunately, know that they have been repeatedly urged to take precisely this position, only to discover that while they were thus in equipoise more and more of the rights and privileges to which they are entitled under the Constitution have been taken away from them by the race which vaunts itself superior, but is superior neither in justice nor humanity. Vardaman, Tillman, Hoke Smith, and the other demagogues of this type will never for a moment remain cool and just on this issue. I suppose you are aware that the Democratic majority is discharging all the colored men holding office in the Capitol, not now protected by civil service rules?

Finally, let me say as a deliberate judgment based on on [sic] nearly twenty years of experience in this work, that nothing but a vigorous confronting of such men as these, and a ceaseless battling for the colored people's rights will prevent further discrimination of vast proportions and undreamed of bitterness.

Will you not, therefore, let me hear from you again further as to your position, particularly how soon you will be able to clarify the whole situation by a characteristically strong utterance as Executive of this Nation, making it clear to the humblest negro what you propose to do on this vital question? Will you not, for the sake of a better understanding of the whole situation on both sides, grant a hearing to Mr. Storey, Dr. DuBois, myself, and other members of this association—at an early date?

Faithfully yours,   Oswald Garrison Villard

TLS (WP, DLC).

From Wesley Livsey Jones[1]

Washington, D. C.

My dear Mr. President: September 29, 1913.

I herewith hand you petition and protest with reference to the alleged segregation of the colored employes in the Departments of the Government here in Washington city for your careful consideration.[2]

It is hard to believe that any discrimination is being made by the officials of the National Government in regard to any of the citizens of this country. So far as the Government is concerned and its officials they cannot afford to practice any discrimination.

Hoping that this petition and protest will receive your careful attention, I am   Very respectfully yours,   W L Jones

TLS (WP, DLC).
  [1] Republican senator from the State of Washington.
  [2] G. B. Aldrich *et al.* to WW and members of the cabinet, Sept. 19, 1913, TLS (WP, DLC), protesting strongly against "the diabolical system known as 'Jim-Crowism'" in the several departments; urging Wilson and the department heads to "discontinue and discountenance" all attempts to introduce "Jim-Crowism" into the federal government; and calling upon the President to issue orders and instructions forbidding segregation on account of color, race, or creed.

From Ellen Axson Wilson

My own darling,   Cornish, New Hampshire Sept. 29, 1913.

Alas, I fear I absolutely must cut my letter short today, as there is a pack of them that I *must* answer before leaving for N. Y. in the morning. And of course it is not decent not to see a good deal of Marguerite when she is making so short a visit. I have been hoping to get a telegram from Stockton today saying whether or not he will come for the White Mt. trip.

Margaret went today to some remote place in the state to help organize a social centre. The train connections were impossible so she motored to Bellows Falls and the Smiths & Marguerite went with her,—leaving at 9.30 & getting back about three. They had a picnic luncheon and a lovely ride they say. I hadn't time to go with them,—and had taken that ride on our way to Williamstown. Margaret returns tomorrow and they start for the Mts. the next day. Then on Sat. she goes to Wilton to see Mrs. Sheridan,[1] so I will not see her until the middle of next week. She is a restless little piece. I am going to try and get through in N. Y. in time to return on Friday morning, but will stay until Sat. if necessary. How intensely I hate to go! I love the country so deeply that it is a sort of torture at first, to leave it in the fall and make the plunge into city ways,—shopping & all the rest of it. Fortunately one adjusts oneself later. What a stupid little scrawl. Absolutely nothing in it—but love! I love you intensely, tenderly, passionately. I am in every pulse of me,

Your own   Eileen.

Our address in N. Y. will be the Waldorf.

ALS (WC, NjP).
  [1] Sarah MacDonald Sheridan of New York, old friend of Mrs. Wilson and one of Margaret's singing teachers.

From William Gibbs McAdoo

PERSONAL.

Dear Mr. President: Washington September 30, 1913.

I enclose a letter from Senator Jones, of the State of Washington,[1] together with a petition addressed to you and the members of the Cabinet, which I bring to your attention because numerous protests are being received here, and it is evident to my mind that much misunderstanding exists about the alleged "segregation" in the different departments. I should like very much to discuss this matter with you when I next see you, because I think it is assuming proportions that may make a definite statement or announcement necessary.

Very sincerely yours,   W G McAdoo

TLS (WP, DLC).
[1] W. L. Jones to W. G. McAdoo, Sept. 29, 1913, TLS (WP, DLC). It virtually repeated Jones's letter to Wilson of September 29. The enclosure in McAdoo's letter is missing.

From Dan Voorhees Stephens[1]

Washington, D. C.

My dear Mr. President: September 30, 1913.

I am informed by a banker in my district that the big banks have their agents out ostensibly soliciting business, but as a matter of fact spreading poison against the currency bill. I have no doubt they are doing the same thing all over the country. Put this action with the attitude of the subsidized press of the country and the various repetitions of the action of the American Bankers Association by the State Bankers Associations, and we have before us clear as day the propaganda of the money trust to so amend our bill as to legalize the strangle hold the money trust now has upon the country.

I sincerely hope you will not retract one step by granting the demands of the bankers on any of the material points in question. Government control should be absolute and to amend that feature so as to weaken the control provided for in this bill would be dangerous in the extreme.

The Senate is in danger of yielding to this pressure and the House is sure to if the country can be pinched enough to frighten the people. Our hope for an honest currency bill lies with you, and I have the greatest confidence in your being able to make this fight for the people and win it.

With best wishes to you and congratulations upon the honor you will have in signing an honest tariff measure, I am,

Yours very truly, Dan V. Stephens

TLS (WP, DLC); P.S. omitted.
[1] Democratic congressman from Nebraska.

To Ellen Axson Wilson

My precious darling,   The White House 1 October, 1913.

I thought a little line from me might cheer you in New York; for I know how you hate to leave that adorable country and home up yonder for a shopping trip to New York.

How it makes my heart beat,—and ache,—to think of your being so much nearer to Washington and yet out of my reach! I wish I could tell you in adequate words how that wonderful letter you wrote on Sunday affected me.[1] There were tears running down my cheeks when I finished reading it, tears of tenderness not only, but tears that seemed to come from every fountain of emotion and of deep gratitude and happiness that was in me. Ah! my sweet one, that you should love me so and with such infinite sweetness! God bless you and keep you. I love you in like fashion, however far short of loving you with a like nature!

I am perfectly well, and all things go as well as could have been expected. Deep love to all.   Your own   Woodrow

The Sept. cheque was deposited to-day.

WWTLS (WC, NjP).
[1] Her letter of September 28.

To William Jennings Bryan, with Enclosure

My dear Mr. Secretary: The White House October 1, 1913

I suggest the enclosed as a telegram to John Lind, in accordance with our understanding of yesterday.

Cordially and faithfully yours,   Woodrow Wilson

TLS (SDR, RG 59, 812.00/9583, DNA).

E N C L O S U R E

Amconsulate, Vera Cruz

Please take steps to get into communication with the minister of foreign affairs and the leaders of the Mexican Congress and make the following representations to them: The government of the United States will not feel that a satisfactory constitutional settlement has been made unless an earnest and sincere effort is made to secure the participation and cooperation of the leaders in the north. This government hopes that its good offices may now be made use of for this purpose. It is as necessary in our view that this participation and cooperation should be striven for and secured as that a free election be held at which General Huerta shall not be a candidate. Has not the recent entire change of circumstances made action along these lines at last practicable? Hostilities should cease and peace be put upon a permanent basis by a return to regular and constitutional methods of action in which all can take part upon a footing of equality.[1]

CLST telegram (SDR, RG 59, 812.00/9583, DNA).
  [1] There is a WWT draft of this telegram in WP, DLC.

John Palmer Gavit to Oswald Garrison Villard

CONFIDENTIAL.

Dear Mr. Villard: [Washington] October 1, 1913.

I saw the President today, and had a fairly thorough-going talk with him. Partly as a result of that talk—though he gave me no syllable for publication, I am at work upon an article, which I hope to finish tomorrow, on the whole subject of the position of the negro in the federal service, and of the attitude of the present Administration in the matter. I shall try to make it candid, fair, and in a way final as setting forth the whole sad and tangled business. In my judgment—and I shall say so—as I said to Mr. Wilson today—it is the most difficult and embarrassing and dangerous subject with which he has to deal.[1]

I told the President frankly that I thought he had been wrong in failing to talk with *you* frankly, face to face; he had justified the feeling on the part of yourself and your associates in this matter that he was evading and avoiding a square dealing with the matter; that I regarded his attitude in that light myself. He saw, and substantially admitted, that I was right, and bade me say that he would "seek an interview" with you. He did not say when, but I am entitled to believe it will be soon. I pressed gently for a specific date, but dropped that as injudicious and likely to prejudice the matter unnecessarily.

It is perfectly clear to me that for the first time since the Civil War, we are at the point of conflict between two *utterly incompatible* ideas in this matter; that the issue cannot be avoided very long; but that the forcing of the issue will be fraught with momentous consequences. These two ideas, certainly clear in your own mind, are (1) that the negro is "a white man with a black skin," entitled to be treated in every way upon his individual merits, exactly as if he were white; (2) that he is of a different and presumably inferior race, to be treated with "justice" and all possible consideration, but kept apart racially, and compelled to make his progress on different, even though parallel lines. I see no middle ground. For myself, I hold the *first* view, as I suppose you do.

For the first time since the War, the Federal Government is in the hands of those who more or less frankly hold the latter view. Even the President is a Virginian, and *while he said nothing to me which would justify me in saying so*, I believe that what feeling he has inclines to that side of the case. Anyway, he has to deal with a Congress which in both Houses is dominated by men to whom this view is fundamental. Moreover, there is not the slightest room for doubt that the Southerners in Congress have the tacit support of a large proportion of men from the North and West. If he should now declare himself in opposition to this view, it would certainly precipitate a conflict which would put a complete stop to any legislative program. It is beyond question that the Senate *will not confirm* any nomination of a negro for any position in the federal service in which he is to be in command of white people—especially of white women.

When the Republicans were in power, it was necessary for them to pretend, at least, that they held to the first view of the negro's position; they needed his vote in a number of the big, doubtful states. The Southern Democrats care very little about his vote; but even if they cared much, they are all imbued with a racial prejudice which over-runs political expediency.

So far as the Federal Service in the city of Washington is concerned, the problem is complicated by the fact that Washington is essentially a Southern city; the great majority of the white people here hold the Southern view of the negro, and as for the Northerners here, it takes but a little while for them to become infinitely more anti-negro than any Southerner. The white men and women in the Government service always have resented being compelled to associate with the negroes. *Never before has there been an Administration that dared to cater to this feeling, except in surreptitious ways.* There has always been in the Departments in Washington a *wish* to do it, but not the *courage*.[2]

In point of fact, the extent to which "segregation" has been actually attempted has been much exaggerated. Even Miss

Nerney's report,[3] the accuracy of which I assume, confirms me in this. The story that one negro who could not be moved because of the importance of his work, was shut off by a screen, appears to be a lie out of whole cloth, or an off-shoot of the fact that in one of the Postoffice Bureaus *all* the negroes were separated by a row of lockers. But beyond a question the *spirit*, the desire, the intention, is present in varying degree. No policy has been adopted in any formal sense; no Cabinet officer has issued any instructions. In the case where signs were put up setting apart certain lavatories "For Colored Only," the signs were taken down as soon as the matter came to Mr. McAdoo's attention; I know of no other instance. Much of what has been done has been on the initiative of subordinate chiefs who would like to have done it long ago but dared not, or who, mostly newly-appointed Southerners, took the first opportunity.

I am not entirely clear in my own mind as to what the President ought to do. In the story that I am writing I intend to present the facts and the elements of the problem, and leave the expression of opinion to the editorial page. As I said before, I think the question by far the most difficult in all the circumstances, the most delicate, and perhaps the most perilous, confronting the President at this time.

But I am not in the slightest doubt, and I told him so, that he ought to talk about it frankly with you, and perhaps afterward with Mr. Storey, Dr. Dubois, and others as might seem advisable. The only practical suggestion I feel like making is that you allow him a reasonable interval during which to carry out his promise to "seek an interview." In the meanwhile, I shall send tomorrow, or next day at latest, an exhaustive discussion of the facts of the case, as I see them. That in itself will open the way for comment. I shall endeavor to furnish light, rather than heat; facts, rather than solutions. To me the thing is a meeting of the irresistible and the impenetrable; a tragic situation culminating the crimes and hypocrisies of three centuries.

　　　　　　　　　　Sincerely yours,　John P. Gavit

TLS (O. G. Villard Papers, MH).

[1] J[ohn] P[almer] G[avit], "The Negro at Washington," New York *Evening Post*, Oct. 21, 1913. With the necessary omission of the remarks Gavit had exchanged with the President, his article adhered closely to the outline of ideas set forth in this letter, with the addition of much factual detail on the extent of segregation in the federal service.

[2] About the gradual but steady spread of segregation in the departments during the Roosevelt and Taft administrations, see August Meier and Elliott Rudwick, "The Rise of Segregation in the Federal Bureaucracy, 1900-1930," *Phylon*, XXVIII (Summer 1967), 178-84.

[3] Printed as an Enclosure with O. G. Villard to WW, Oct. 14, 1913.

Remarks Upon Signing the Tariff Bill[1]

Gentlemen: [Oct. 3, 1913]

I feel a very peculiar pleasure in what I have just done by way of taking part in the completion of a great piece of business. It is a pleasure which is very hard to express in words which are adequate to express the feeling; because the feeling that I have is that we have done the rank and file of the people of this country a great service. It is hard to speak of these things without seeming to go off into campaign eloquence, but that is not my feeling. It is one very profound, a feeling of profound gratitude that, working with the splendid men who have carried this thing through with studious attention and doing justice all 'round, I should have had part in serving the people of this country as we have been striving to serve them ever since I can remember.

I have had the accomplishment of something like this at heart ever since I was a boy, and I know men standing around me who can say the same thing—who have been waiting to see the things done which it was necessary to do in order that there might be justice in the United States. And so it is a solemn moment that brings such a business to a conclusion, and I hope I will not be thought to be demanding too much of myself or of my colleagues when I say that this, great as it is, is the accomplishment of only half the journey. We have set the business of this country free from those conditions which have made monopoly not only possible but in a sense easy and natural. But there is no use taking away the conditions of monopoly if we do not take away also the power to create monopoly; and that is a financial, rather than a merely circumstantial and economic, power. The power to control and guide and direct the credits of the country is the power to say who shall and who shall not build up the industries of the country, in which direction they shall be built, and in which direction they shall not be built. We are now about to take the second step, which will be the final step in setting the business of this country free. That is what we shall do in the currency bill, which the House has already passed and which I have the utmost confidence the Senate will pass much sooner than some pessimistic individuals believe. Because this question, now that this piece of work is done, will arise all over the country: "For what do we wait? Why should we wait to crown ourselves with consummate honor? Are we so self-denying that we do not wish to complete our success?" I was quoting the other day to some of my colleagues in the Senate those lines from Shakespeare's "Henry V," which have always appealed to me: "If it be a sin to covet honor, then am I the most offending soul alive"; and I am happy to say that I do not covet it for myself alone. I covet it with equal ardor for the men who are associated with me, and the honor is going to come from them. I am their associate. I can only complete the work which they do. I can only counsel when they ask for my counsel. I can come in only when the last stages of the business are reached. And I covet this honor for them quite as much as I covet it for myself; and I covet it for the great party of which I am a member; because that party is not honorable unless it redeem its name and serve the people of the United States.

So I feel tonight like a man who is lodging happily in the inn which lies half way along the journey and that in time, with a fresh impulse, we shall go the rest of the journey and sleep at the journey's end like men with a quiet conscience, knowing that we have served our fellow men and have, thereby, tried to serve God.

T MS (WP, DLC) with editorial corrections from a reading of the CLSsh in the C. L. Swem Coll., NjP.
¹ Wilson signed the tariff bill at 9:10 P.M. on October 3 in the Oval Office of the White House before a group of some fifty cabinet members, senators, congressmen, political leaders, and executive and congressional staff members, most of whom had played some part in the enactment of the measure. For a full report of the ceremony, see the *New York Times*, Oct. 4, 1913.

To Dan Voorhees Stephens

Personal and Confidential.

My dear Mr. Stephens: [The White House] October 3, 1913

I am warmly obliged to you for your letter of September thirtieth, and you may be sure that there will be no budging here with regard to the essential features of the currency bill. I am sincerely grateful to you for giving me further evidence of the way in which the bankers are trying to poison the public mind against the currency bill. I think the whole matter will presently be made public and that it will help rather than hinder the legislation contemplated.

Cordially and sincerely yours,   Woodrow Wilson

TLS (Letterpress Books, WP, DLC).

To Oswald Garrison Villard

My dear Mr. Villard: The White House October 3, 1913

I should like very much to have a personal interview with you. I have had it in mind for some time and have only been awaiting the opportunity. Opportunities for real interviews do not seem to come to my office, so I shall just have to make a special effort to create a space when I can see you. I wonder if you can come down and take lunch with me on Tuesday next at one o'clock, so that we can have a talk afterwards, when business is less likely to intrude.

Cordially and sincerely yours,   Woodrow Wilson

TLS (O. G. Villard Papers, MH).

To Charles Richard Crane

My dear Friend: [The White House] October 3, 1913

I simply cannot adjust my mind to giving up the idea of having you represent us at the Court of Russia.[1] We are making a temporary appointment in the person of Mr. Pindell of Peoria, who is very glad to consent to the arrangement proposed that he later give place to yourself. May I not beg that we may at least leave this thing for consideration when you can free yourself a little from the obligations now pressing upon you? I cannot get my own mind to assent to a permanent disappointment.

I cannot tell you how warmly I appreciate the feeling you show in the matter, especially the feeling toward myself. I am deeply grateful to have such friends.

Cordially and faithfully yours,   Woodrow Wilson

TLS (Letterpress Books, WP, DLC).
  [1] Crane must have indicated in conversation with Wilson that he did not want to go to Russia. There is no earlier correspondence about his appointment.

From William Jennings Bryan

My Dear Mr President   Washington [Oct. 3, 1913]

I forgot to say, in writing you about the Brown Bros Loan, that I stated to Brown Bros that we ought to have some one in the bank, the R.R. & in the customs office upon whom the Dept could rely for accurate information as to what was being done. They agree to this. We could not well assist in protecting the interests of Nicaraugua with[out] some one who owes allegiance to the administration. With assurances etc I am my dear Mr President

Yours truly   W. J. Bryan

ALS (WP, DLC).

To William Jennings Bryan

My dear Mr. Secretary: The White House October 3, 1913

Thank you for your note about your understanding with Brown Brothers. You were quite right in suggesting that we ought to have someone in the bank, the railroad, and the customs office upon whom the department could rely for accurate information as to what was being done, and they were certainly sensible to agree to that suggestion.

Faithfully yours,   Woodrow Wilson

TLS (W. J. Bryan Papers, DLC).

From William Jennings Bryan

My dear Mr. President: Washington October 3, 1913.

Answering your favor of October third,[1] I beg to say that Mr. Leavell, of Mississippi, has been appointed to Guatemala, and I do not see how it would be possible to find a place for Mr. Herring.[2]

I have just received a telegram from W. W. Durbin, of Kenton, Ohio,[3] one of our most active Progressives, whom you will doubtless remember. He says that the Progressives will be pleased with the appointment of Mooney,[4] the man for whom Governor Cox asked. I wrote Cox in line with our conversation and told him to get the endorsements of the Progressives there for Mooney so that they would feel that they were being recognized. Durbin says:

> "Governor Cox has discussed with me the matter contained in your letter to him about Senator Mooney. The progressive leaders of this State are entirely agreeable to his appointment and would like to see it made. I will regard it as a personal favor to me."

I am very much gratified to have men like Durbin feel that their wishes are being considered.

George Fred Williams writes a very nice letter saying that he will consider the proposition, and from the tone of his letter I think he will accept. He is rather taken with the idea of making it a wedding tour and the short term would suit him better than the long one. I will let you know when I hear from him definitely, but it will please me very much if we can do this for Williams.

With assurances of respect, etc., I am, my dear Mr. President,

Very sincerely yours,   W. J. Bryan

TLS (WP, DLC).

1 WW to WJB, Oct. 3, 1913, TLS (W. J. Bryan Papers, DLC).

2 The letter cited in n. 1 refers to him only as D. W. Herring of Tennessee. The Editors have been unable to identify him further.

3 William W. Durbin, general manager of the Scioto Sign Co. of Kenton and long active in progressive Democratic politics in Ohio.

4 Daniel Francis Mooney, lawyer of Saint Marys, Ohio, member of the Ohio State Senate, 1908-10, 1912-13. Cox was urging his name (in letters to Wilson) as Minister to Belgium. He was named Minister to Paraguay on January 15, 1914.

From Ellen Axson Wilson

My own darling,   The Waldorf-Astoria New York. Oct. 3 1913

It is 7.45 A.M. I have had my bath early "to get out of the way," —for I have managed to secure a more modest "suite" this time with only one bathroom. Now I am writing in my wrapper, very much at my ease, while the others catch up.

It is a beautiful morning, bright and mild,—after the wild weather of the last two days. We had sunshine for a little while yesterday, then another storm. We are *hoping* it was a coast storm and so did not interfere with the plans of our White Mountain party.

We had a very successful day yesterday and will, I think be quite ready as well as willing to leave tonight. (Of course we are going whether we are ready or not!)

We will not have much time to [go] shopping today, as we are to have "Mimi" Brown,[1] Ed's wife, for luncheon, and after luncheon we go to see Dr Genthys[2] pictures of the bird masque (colour pictures). Ruth Hall, who is here, says they are lovely.

Mimi Brown is here for the winter, under treatment for her throat. We have not seen her yet;—will meet her this morning at the dressmakers.

Nell and I went to the theatre again last night. Jessie of course was with Frank. He met us when we arrived but went off immediately to be best man at Maynard Hazen's wedding[3] and had just returned last night. We saw two plays. One a rather dull little thing called "The Younger Generation,"[4]—a sort of "Bunty"[5] without the humour, and the other a strong but *terrible* one act play by Barrie.[6] We have seen two one act Barrie plays,—both good, but would much prefer a whole evening of him.

I am watching the papers most eagerly to see when you will be allowed to sign the bill. I had so hoped it would be over by the first. Now I am praying for tomorrow night. Please tell me if Hitchcock and O'Gorman are listening to reason. I am concerned by what I read about the Japanese situation,[7] and (if you have it) would like a word of reassurance on that subject too. Why don't you make the doctor write me as I suggested & so save you the trouble of alluding to politics in your letters. I know it bores you.

It was so very good in you to write me that *darling* little note which came yesterday. It certainly did accomplish its purpose of making N. Y. more cheerful,—for it made me *happy* through and through. Oh, but you are *wonderful* both in head and heart, and I *adore* you! The girls send dearest love. We are all perfectly well. I love you with all my heart and head and soul.

Your devoted little wife   Eileen.

ALS (WC, NjP).

¹ Mary Celestine Mitchell (Mrs. Edward Thomas) Brown.

² Arnold Genthe, German-born photographer and a pioneer in color photography, who at this time lived in New York. Genthe had photographed the participants in the bird masque during rehearsal and later made portraits of Wilson and other members of his family at the White House. See Arnold Genthe, *As I Remember* (New York, 1936), pp. 128-31.

³ Maynard Thompson Hazen, lawyer of Boston and son of Wilson's old friend, the Rev. Dr. Azel Washburn Hazen, married Marjorie Frances Howe on October 2, 1913. He and Francis B. Sayre were close friends both at Williams College and Harvard Law School.

⁴ William Stanley Houghton's "The Younger Generation: A Comedy for Parents" and James Matthew Barrie's "Half an Hour" opened as a double bill at the Lyceum Theatre in New York on September 25. Houghton's play dealt with the conflict between strict, Nonconformist English parents and their less inhibited children. For a review and summary of both plays, see the *New York Times*, Sept. 26, 1913.

⁵ Graham Moffat's "Bunty Pulls the Strings," a comedy about Scottish family life, had a successful run in New York in 1911. See the *New York Times*, Oct. 11, 1911.

⁶ In Barrie's play, a woman of aristocratic lineage attempts to escape from her wealthy but brutal middle-class husband by fleeing abroad with a younger man. However, her lover is killed in an accident, and she finds herself forced to resume her former role as dutiful wife while in great peril of being found out. The entire action of the play takes place in half an hour.

⁷ A brief news item in the *New York Times*, Oct. 1, 1913, stated that Japan had sent "another note of protest" in regard to the controversy over land ownership in California. On October 2, a slightly longer news report in the same paper said that Japan was seeking a new commercial treaty with the United States which would grant Japanese citizens the right of land ownership in any state of the Union on the same terms allowed to citizens of any other foreign nation.

John Lind to William Jennings Bryan

Vera Cruz, Mexico, October 3, 1913.

Trustworthy information from distinct sources would indicate the administration scheme as follows:

If elections are not postponed and I do not think they will be Gamboa will probably be given the plurality vote but the Liberal party which is in control of the House will not seat a Catholic candidate. Ample cause will be found for declaring election void and Huerta will be forced to continue against his will. Whether Gamboa is party to this scheme I have no information but it is significant that Moheno the recent appointee in the State Department was named Under Secretary. The Huerta Americans in Mexico City are very active again. A scurrilous petition circulated by Major Gillette is now on way to Washington primarily for publication in United States I think.[1]

Zamacona arrived today.   Lind

T telegram (WP, DLC).

[1] Under the leadership of retired U.S. Army Major Cassius E. Gillette, twenty-one Americans in Mexico drafted a petition to the President and Congress denouncing Madero, praising Huerta, condemning Wilson, and asking that the United States recognize Huerta. C. E. Gillette *et al.* to the President and Congress, Sept. 27, 1913, TS petition (WP, DLC).

From William Jennings Bryan, with Enclosure

My dear Mr. President: Washington October 4, 1913.

I am enclosing a letter from Governor Lind.[1] It is too long to read except when you have leisure, but if you can find time on Sunday, it will make good Sunday reading. If Lind had done nothing else than give us this review of the situation, his trip would not have been in vain. I shall be glad to discuss some of its suggestions to you when you have time.

With assurances of respect, etc., I am, my dear Mr. President,
Very sincerely yours,   W. J. Bryan

I enclose telegram from Lind. Will enquire about Major Gillette.

TLS (WP, DLC).

[1] J. Lind to WJB, Sept. 19, 1913.

E N C L O S U R E

Vera Cruz, Mexico, Oct. 4, 1913.

Negotiations opened informally some ten days ago may result in a tangible proposition which I may be able to report on next Monday. In the meantime it would be well to ascertain whether or not rebels would consent to a fairly constituted commission of which I would be a member constructively to formulate a basis for cessation of hostilities and permanent peace. Veracity is not a virtue in Mexico. I may have nothing to report and again I may.
Lind.

T telegram (WP, DLC).

From William Jennings Bryan

My dear Mr. President: Washington October 4, 1913.

I called your attention yesterday to contract No. 7 for a concession to build a short railroad between the Lake and the Pacific Ocean in Nicaragua. I do not like to have a concession connected with the loan and would rather leave it to be acted upon separately after the loan is made and when the Government is under no compulsion. The Government, however, seems disposed to give this concession, and I have inserted three amendments which I thought would protect Nicaragua; one limiting the franchise to the territory between the Lake and the Pacific, another making it subject to any canal or railroad rights which the Republic of Nicaragua may hereafter grant to the United States, and a third providing that in case of any sale of the road the new corporation shall give the Nicaraguan Government 49% of its stock —this amendment was suggested to prevent any sale that would deprive the Government of its present interest in the railroad. There are two other provisions which I think ought to go in, but which Judge Douglas thinks the bankers would not consent to. You will notice that the concession is exclusive. The fact that the Government has 49% of the stock makes the exclusive feature less important; still, I am not disposed to favor anything down there that I would not favor here and an exclusive franchise is abhorrent, especially when running ninety-nine years. It is impossible to look into the future and measure the value of such a monopoly and, therefore, no compensation can be secured for it even if it were proper for one generation thus to bind a succeeding generation. I shall not, therefore, consent to the exclusive feature unless you, upon consideration of the matter, express a desire that the contract should be approved in this form.

The second condition which I thought ought to go in there is one giving to the Government the right to purchase upon an equitable basis. This is the more important in case the concession is exclusive. It might not be so necessary for the Government to have a right to buy if it could build a competing line or permit a competing line; but while I think it would be unwise to permit an exclusive franchise under any conditions, it would be still more unwise to do so without a provision permitting the Government to purchase on equitable terms.

I would like to have your views also in regard to having a man connected with this enterprise upon whom we can rely for information as to what is going on. There seems to be a difference of opinion between Brown Brothers and myself as to what would be proper. My idea is that among their employees there should be one in the railroad, one in the bank, and one connected with the customs who would be designated by the Department, in order that he might be some one upon whose reports we could rely. He would perform the regular work of an employee and, therefore, there would be no extra expense. Brown Brothers seem to object to having one of their employees who would be under obligation to keep us informed and express a willingness to have an inspector who would receive proper pay and have access to the books. That, of course, would be an additional expense to the company and, to my mind, would not be so satisfactory as an employee working with the other employees. We are not in a position to ask anything of Brown Brothers at all except as they desire to use the moral influence of the Department to protect their interests. If they have a right to claim the moral influence of the Department, the Department ought to be in a position to know what is going on and I cannot see that there can be any reasonable objection to one of the employees in each branch of the service being known to be in contact with the Department. You will notice what Judge Douglas says on this subject. We are not asking that the Government of Nicaragua shall permit us to appoint any of her officials or inspect their work, but in so far as Brown Brothers send Americans there to do work for them I cannot see any inconsistency in allowing one of these officials in each department to be a means of securing the information that we need to enable us to know whether the conduct of the company is such as to justify us in lending it moral support.

With assurances of respect, etc., I am, my dear Mr. President,

W. J. Bryan

TLS (WP, DLC).

From Newton Diehl Baker

My dear Mr President: [Cleveland] October 4, 1913

I wish you all the health and strength your great task demands and all the happiness your great achievements deserve! I have waited just seventeen years for the pleasure of this hour—sometimes the waiting has seemed long but I never doubted that someday a democratic President would sign a democratic tariff law. It is a blessing my habits are so steady or the temptation to rejoice "too obviously" would be irresistable.

Gratefully yours, Newton D Baker

ALS (WP, DLC).

From Ellen Axson Wilson

My own darling,   Cornish, New Hampshire Oct. 4 [1913].

We had a very comfortable journey home reaching here on time this morning. We found it much less fatiguing to travel at night, for we all had a good night's sleep. Marguerite Walbrid[g]e & our Margaret left about half an hour after our return—Margaret to get back on Tuesday from her visit to Mrs. Sheridan. Oh, it is so good to be out of the city again and so enchantingly beautiful here!

The girls had, as we feared, very stormy weather for their White Mt. trip (two bad days and one bright one). But they are enthusiastic over their journey because of the gorgeous colour and the wonderful and endlessly varied cloud effects. In short it was Westmorland weather.

Mary & I went out just after lunch to ride and get the sun for ¾ of an hour. Now they are packing; I found a lot of important letters awaiting me and should have gone straight at them I suppose, but was so excited over the signing of the tariff bill that I could only devour the papers. Oh, my dear, how I wish I had been there! Your speech was *beautiful*! How happy you all must be! I am inexpressibly, profoundly happy & thankful. I hope for once you will break your rule and read the papers for the editorials are so fine. Also the two or three I have seen from English papers. *Please*, get Mr. Tumulty to make me up a "yellow book" of just editorials. The good ones are quite lost in that ocean of duplicate news articles he saves. More lost even than in my old trunks and boxes!

What about Hitchcock & the committee? Will they make it possible for you to come up on the 11th as Dr. Grayson intimated? I must let Mrs. Jaffray & Helen know at once about our plans. If you do not come we will leave here on the 15th, stay two days in N. Y. to have our clothes fitted reaching Washington on Sat. the 18th. The Smiths leave Monday, but will come to Washington, I *think*, the first of Nov. to stay until after the wedding.

They have just been telling me a good story from Maxfield Parish. It seems the Churchills[1] had a butler whom all the colony knew intimately. They had the Vanderbilts[2] up for a weekend & Mrs. C., who loves style, made "Charles" "announce" the guests. So when Charles called in a noble voice "Mr. Maxfield Parish," the latter said quietly "Well, Charles, what is it?" He says Mrs. Churchill explained later to the Vanderbilts that the Parishes were "dear, simple, little people."

Goodbye, you dear, splendid wonderful, adorable man! How

we all *ache* to get at you and make a fuss over you, and work off some of our excitement over the bill in that way. Love, *love, love* from   Your devoted little wife,   Nell.

ALS (WC, NjP).
   1 Winston Churchill and Mabel Harlakenden Hall Churchill, owners of Harlakenden House.
   2 Probably George Washington Vanderbilt II and Edith Stuyvesant Dresser Vanderbilt.

To Ellen Axson Wilson

My precious darling,   The White House 5 October, 1913.

I suppose you read about the scene at the signing of the tariff bill. It was really most impressive. I was very much moved and can only hope that the printed words of my little speech had something like the same effect that the spoken words had. I am told that there were tears running down the cheeks of even one or two of the reporters before I had finished speaking.

Are Hitchcock and O'Gorman listening to reason? No. Hitchcock never will. O'Gorman is showing signs of yielding, but not to reason,—to the force of opinion in the country and particularly among his colleagues in the Senate. A little patience, and a little *im*patience, will work the thing out. I shall exercise both to the utmost. I have practically a unanimous sentiment behind me among the Democrats of the Senate, outside the Committee.

There is nothing to be concerned about in the Japanese situation. The papers find out what is going on not only most imperfectly but also some weeks after it has happened and the situation has changed. The "new note" they have been speaking about the last few days is several weeks old and offers no additional difficulties. Mr. Bryan and I feel more confident now than ever before that we see a way out in the early future. Believe *nothing* you see on this subject in the newspapers, for they know nothing. It is hard work every day to keep things going, constant toil and trouble, but they go slowly forward. "Westward, look, the land is bright."[1] A stout heart and infinite staying powers will bring things to the right issue.

My thoughts have been very, very full of you, amidst all the hurry and preoccupation of the days, since you got to New York. The consciousness that you were in fact nearer to me in space,— only five hours' journey away,—seemed to accentuate my loneliness, my longing for you (which is with me all day and all night), the sense of separation. Ah! how you have wound my heartstrings about you, my little wife! I love you with all my heart!

I expected Stock. to come down last night and spend Sunday here, but at the last moment a telegram came saying that it was impossible. Dr. Grayson and I went to church together this morning. It was communion Sunday; and we had a most solemn, old-fashioned sermon and service, which did not make me miss you any less! There is something about the simplicity and homeliness of that little church which suggests the worship of a family, and makes a poor chap like me miss all the more keenly the dear ones who ought in such circumstances to be about him.

Do not be distressed by the little accident we had yesterday. As we were coming into town, returning from our Saturday afternoon ride, a messenger boy darted over from the opposite side of the street and ran straight into the front of our machine (with his head down, not noting where he went) before we could stop. Fortunately we were going very slowly. He was knocked down, of course, and pinned for a moment under his wheel under the front part of the motor; but he was very slightly hurt. We took him at once to the hospital, where I saw him this morning, and the worst that has happened is a stretching of one of the ligaments in front of his right ankle. We shall see that he is taken care of in every way, his bicycle mended, and his place kept for him. It was a great shock to me. For a moment or two I supposed that the wheel of the motor had crushed his leg. As a fact it did not touch him. He was very cheerful when I saw him this morning. He is in a fine Catholic hospital, where, as it happens, his own mother works as a charwoman.

What are your plans now, my darling? I am booked to go down the river to see the target practice and start on the evening of Friday, the seventeenth. Is it poss[i]ble that you will be here by that time? Shall I save a place, or places, on the "Mayflower"[2] for you or any of you? Ah! how it makes my heart beat to think of having you all here again. What a change it will make in the house. It will be home again, instead of merely a big empty lodging. At any hour I can look into my darling's eyes and be cheered and refreshed, take her into my arms and feel the thrill of her kiss, to make the day and its tasks seem easy and touched with beauty and peace. I have done bravely without you all these weeks, and should in fact have been unhappy had you insisted on staying here; but now I am reaching the limit of my powers in that matter. I *must* have you soon. How soon? I am well, and my heart is full to overflowing with love of all of you.

Your own   Woodrow

WWTLS (WC, NjP).
1 Arthur Hugh Clough, "Say Not the Struggle Naught Availeth."
2 The presidential yacht.

From William Jennings Bryan, with Enclosure

My Dear Mr President,   Washington [c. Oct. 5, 1913]
    This looks a little encouraging   With assurances etc
                                 Yours truly   W. J. Bryan

ALS (WP, DLC).

E N C L O S U R E

Copy of telegram from the American Embassy at Mexico City to the Secretary of State, No. 530, Oct. 3, 9 p. m.
    Confidential. For the Secretary of State.

I had a personal interview with President Huerta this afternoon. He requested an interview to confidentially inform you that in the event of the Chamber of Deputies passing a bill postponing the elections he would veto the same. During conversation he informed me that he quite understood the attitude of the President of the United States and that he did not wish him to believe that he (Huerta) desired to remain in power in defiance of the Constitution or by subterfuge. The general opinion continues to be that no candidate will receive a sufficient number of votes. He asked me to come to him if any matters were not speedily carried out by the various departments.
                                 Nelson O'Shaughnessy.

T telegram (WP, DLC).

From Ellen Axson Wilson

My own darling,   Cornish, New Hampshire Oct. 5 1913.
    We are back from one of the most beautiful drives we have had yet, and oh! how we did long for you. Just Jessie Nell & I went. It was to what is called "The Gulch," a deep mountain pass close to Ascutney. It is really almost sublime in its noble beauty. I have been hearing about it all summer and am glad to have seen it before we leave. The day too is absolutely perfect. Oh, it is hard that you are never here to enjoy all these things with us! But of course *we* are enjoying with *you* something much more splendid than "all these things"!
    I wish I could express the depth and soul-satisfying quality of the happiness I am deriving from the tariff victory. It is all-pervading—never out of my consciousness a moment. It is simply that now at last everybody in the civilized world knows that you

are a great man and a great leader of men. Also a great constitutional Statesman. "It is written." The sort of honour that is yours by right and that you "covet" *is* yours beyond a peraventure,— and you *have* won it for your friends and party as well as for yourself. How profoundly I thank God for giving you the chance to win such victories,—to help the world so greatly;—for letting you work for him on a *large* stage;—one worthy of the splendid combination of qualities with which He endowed you. It *would* have been tragic if such gifts had been even partially wasted, for want of the great opportunity. It has been the most remarkable life history I ever even *read* about,—and to think *I* have *lived* it with you. I wonder if I am dreaming, and will wake up and find myself married to—a bank clerk,—say! I love you, my dear, in every way you would wish to be loved,—deeply, tenderly, devotedly, passionately.   Your little wife   Eileen.

ALS (WC, NjP).

Remarks at a Press Conference

October 6, 1913

I see a dispatch this morning about the probable negotiation of a new treaty with Japan. Is there anything on that?

> No, nothing at all new. This whole thing in the papers puzzles me, because nothing has happened in, I guess, three weeks. There is nothing new about it at all that has been brought to my attention. Of course, it would have been brought to my attention, I think. What it is, as I suggested the other day, is simply negotiations that have been going on quietly and have been talked about.

Has the Japanese embassy offered to make any explanation?

> No. I haven't asked for it, at least.

Mr. President, are you receiving from the people, in any general sense, any comment of any kind on the currency bill as it stands, inquiries [that make] you think it is well understood?

> I should say so, and universally desired.

In what sort of form?

> It naturally wouldn't come in any analytical form, going into the features, but the country understands the main features of the bill. It naturally would not know all the details but thoroughly approves what the administration stands for, I have [stood for.]

Do you get letters from individuals?

> Yes, from every quarter, and a great many different ones from ordinary constituents, and very interesting comments

on the situation—and a great many from bankers who don't
want to be quoted. You can draw your own inferences.

Are you having a new conference, Mr. President, as to whether
or not and how they can bring the bill on?

No, that will be all right.

Are these bankers prominent bankers?

They range in size, so to speak. Some of them are big, but
the majority of them are the middle sized.

Bankers who are willing that they should be quoted? Do they
favor the bill?

Well, only the big ones are willing to be quoted. They don't,
for manifest reasons, want the absolute control of the country taken out of their hands, which no human being
should desire.

No self-respecting banker.

That is right. The thing is so manifest, I wonder the country doesn't [blank].

Are you confident, Mr. President, that you will be able to sign
the currency bill before this session ends?

I am.

Mr. President, has any proposition been put up to you for your
consent or for your discussion, with a view to the adjournment
of the House?

No, that has not been talked about with me.

How do you feel about that, Mr. President?

I don't know. I should think the House—

Mr. President, this long session is putting most of the congressmen in sanitariums and hospitals.

When we get through, we can all go together. I don't know
that it's any less hard on the President than it is on Congress, but I seem to be able to stand it.

JRT transcript (WC, NjP) of CLSsh (C. L. Swem Coll., NjP).

To William Jennings Bryan

My dear Mr. Secretary: The White House October 6, 1913

Thank you warmly for having let me see this letter of John
Lind's. It is a splendid letter and most instructive from every
point of view. It will furnish us much food for thought and conference.

Always

Cordially and faithfully yours,   Woodrow Wilson

TLS (W. J. Bryan Papers, DNA).

To William Gibbs McAdoo

My dear McAdoo: The White House October 6, 1913

I am sending you my revision of the inscriptions you asked me to look over for the new post office building. I hope you will like the changes.[1]

In haste   Faithfully yours,   Woodrow Wilson

TLS (TDR, RG 121, General Corr. and Related Records, DNA).

[1] Charles William Eliot had written the first version of the inscriptions. However, it was only later that McAdoo and Wilson learned of Eliot's authorship (see W. G. McAdoo to WW, Nov. 6, 1913, and WW to W. G. McAdoo, Nov. 7, 1913). Eliot's draft for the east pavilion of the building read:

    Carrier of news and knowledge
    Instrument of trade and commerce
    Promoter of mutual acquaintance
    Among men and nations and hence
    Of peace and good will

Wilson's revision read:

    Carrier of news and knowledge
    Instrument of trade and industry
    Promoter of mutual acquaintance
    Of peace and good will
    Among men and nations

Eliot's draft for the west pavilion:

    Carrier of love and sympathy
    Messenger of friendship
    Consoler of the lonely
    Bond of the scattered family
    Enlarger of the public life

Wilson's revision:

    Messenger of sympathy and love
    Servant of parted friends
    Consoler of the lonely
    Bond of the scattered family
    Enlarger of the common life

See also the *New York Times*, March 29, 1914. There is a WWT draft of his version in WP, DLC.

From Lindley Miller Garrison

Dear Mr. President: Washington. October 6, 1913.

We have spoken heretofore briefly on the subject of Porto Rico and its government.

I directed General McIntyre,[1] the Chief of the Bureau having this in charge, to prepare a memorandum giving the pros and cons with reference to citizenship and the form of government for Porto Rico. I attach hereto his memorandum,[2] with which I agree.

That is, I believe that we should extend citizenship to the Porto Ricans individually, but not collectively. The latter course would be fraught with too many dangers.

I believe that it is not necessary to go to Congress at this time with a recommendation for a change in the form of government, but that we may, as vacancies occur in the Executive Council and from time to time by the appointment of Porto Ricans, give them a greater participation in their government and, by just such steps as we propose to take in the Philippines, remove the grievance against the present government without risking a change in form which would destroy or injure its efficiency.

Sincerely yours, Lindley M. Garrison

TLS (WP, DLC).

[1] Frank McIntyre, brigadier general, U.S.A., Chief of the Bureau of Insular Affairs.

[2] "Memorandum for the Secretary of War. Subject: Porto Rico Citizenship," Oct. 6, 1913, CC memorandum (WDR, RG 350, BIA, Puerto Rico File, Nos. 114 and 115, File 1286, DNA).

Two Letters from Ellen Axson Wilson

My dear,   Cornish, New Hampshire Oct. 6, 1913.

I am sorry to trouble you with a domestic matter, but I do not know how to avoid it since the settling of it is not within my province, and I must write in a rather confidential way. It regards the difficulties at the garage here, which have now reached such a height that the Burlasqu[e]s[1] have refused to give White his meals; and as there is no where else for him to go I have to feed him here. It was settled before we came up that they would board him for the summer. The reason I *must* mention it *now* is that I understand Burlasque is in authority at the Washington garage as well as here, so that if any change is to be made it should be settled *before* our return.

My strong impression is that Burlasque is not fit to be placed in authority over other men,—that he has not enough self-control or force of character. He is rather a spoiled boy whose head has been turned by his very rapid promotion over the heads of older and more experienced men. It is not good for *him personally* to be the head man because he is evidently not an expert machinist; here he is dependent on his subordinate,—White. Yet because he is "the boss" he cannot or does not admit his deficiencies in that line but is always putting up a bluff. I think that both of them should be kept but neither in authority over the other. Would not Robinson[2] do for the chief? They have both been perfectly polite and obliging to us, never complaining of long hours or anything else, but White is the real expert. It is only his slow, dull manner that is against him.

In justice to Burlasqu[e] I think most of the trouble has been caused by his wife. He had orders to take the maids to a dance in Windsor every Wed. night. Mrs. Jaffrey settled that early in the summer. He tried to get out of it by telling Miss Hagner that it was not a suitable place for the maids. I made personal enquiries & found that all the best trades people in the town went. It was really a concession to their position & *our* servants that they were admitted. So I renewed the order & he "took it out on them" by driving them home at midnight at a madman's pace,— into ruts & over stocks & stones,—had them all screaming & praying with terror,—said he "would like to kill them." And of course to carry out my order in such a spirit was indirectly an impertinence to me. But of course he did not realize that. He was simply a boy in a violent passion. It may be that White has been sulky and ugly at having the youngster placed over him, but Martha the cook says he has been a miracle of patience. Mrs. B. refuses to board him because she says he does not treat her with proper respect. But enough of all this, I am so very sorry to trouble you with it. Just tell the proper person as much as you think wise (I don't know who he is) and dismiss it all from your mind. They are both good fellows, you understand, & I would not for the world injure either of them.

AL (WC, NjP).

¹ Mr. and Mrs. James Burlasque. He was listed in the *Official Register* . . . *1913* as a "laborer" at the White House.

² Francis Robinson, a chauffeur at the White House.

My own darling, Cornish, New Hampshire Oct. 6, 1913

The dear little Smiths have gone and Nell, Jessie and I are left rather "lonesome," as Ben says, in this big house. But we have had a beautiful day, as to weather, and a perfectly *wonderful* sunset,—two sunsets at once, so to say. On one side of the sky a silver moon and great rose pink clouds in a sky of tender blue, —and on the other side the real sunset, a gorgeous panorama of crimson & purple and gold. We went to tea at the Kings (our nearest neighbours, you know, at "The Churchill Inn")—the first time I have been in that house. They have, as I suspected, as unusually fine view—a perfect fore-ground. Miss Slade was the only other guest and we had a very "good time." Then we took Miss Slade home in our car and the sunset and moonlight from her hill were something to remember.

I have just had a telegram from Mrs. Jaffrey saying she will be here on Wed afternoon. So things are getting underway for our return. We want to take one more all day ride while the colour lasts to Lake Sunapee probably on Wed. or Thursday. Margaret returns tomorrow. I got in a little painting this afternoon before the tea—finished one of the two studies I had under way. But it is seven & I must close for I *must* make a long evening of it at my other neglected mail. With *devoted* love, believe me, dearest, always & altogether—   Your own   Eileen.

It is rather fine for a Republican to talk like this![1]

ALS (WC, NjP).
  [1] She enclosed an unidentified newspaper clipping in which one C. F. Mc-Kesson, Republican postmaster of Morganton, N. C., was reported to have told a convention of postmasters in Norfolk, Va., that Wilson was "the greatest chieftain the nation has ever had since the days of Thomas Jefferson."

From William Jennings Bryan

My Dear Mr. President: [Washington] October 7, 1913.

Before leaving, I thought it might be well to have a talk with Senator Reed, with whom I had promised an interview, on the currency question. He came out and I had an hour's conference with him. I feel sure that his position has been exaggerated by the newspapers. If he had been making the program, he would not have favored a general revision of the currency at this time, but he feels, now that the Bill has passed the House, it is necessary that there should be legislation at this session. There are some amendments which he would like to make. Some, in my judgment, have merit in them and some are, it seems to me, unnecessary. But I believe that he will content himself with presenting them and making an argument in their favor, whatever action may be taken in regard to them.

He thinks there will be no great delay in reporting the Bill, although he thinks that real benefit is being obtained from the hearings. I am satisfied, from conversation with him, that as to details he desires to support your views as far as he can bring himself to agree, and on the main principles of the Bill he is with you.

I did what I could to emphasize the merits of the principal features and the importance of early action. I believe it would be a good plan for you to call him into conference and get his views on disputed points and give your reasons for the provisions to which he objects.[1] While he is quite positive in his views, his sympathies are right and he recognizes the importance of united action.

The men with whom I have influence in the Senate—and I think I stand better with the Senate than with the House—nearly all seem to favor the Bill. If at any time there is anything you see that I can do, please let me know for I am intensely interested in the passage of the measure.

With assurances of my great respect, I am, my Dear Mr. President,   Very sincerely yours,   W. J. Bryan

TLS (WP, DLC).
    1 Wilson held separate conferences with Senators Reed, Hitchcock, and O'Gorman at the White House on October 16. According to the *New York Times*, Oct. 17, 1913, the conferences were cordial in tone but the senators all argued that the Federal Reserve bill would have to be extensively amended and that chances for its passage during the present special session were slim.

An Aide-Mémoire by Francisco Escudero

Washington, 7th October, 1913.

The Confidential Agent of the Constitutionalist Government of Mexico, in Washington, having communicated, by telegraph, to the First Chief of the Constitutionalist Forces, at Hermosillo, Sonora, that an expression was desired as to his possible willingness to participate in the elections fixed by the Mexican Congress for October 26, next, and if willing to so participate, under what conditions, is now instructed to make known the following:

That nothing in the present situation, can vary the previous line of conduct of the First Chief of the Constitutionalist Forces, as he considers that by such means only, can a firm and lasting peace be reached, and the Constitutional order restored in Mexico.

T MS (WP, DLC).

From Sydney Brooks[1]

Dear Mr. President,   Kensington, W. [London] Oct 7/13

As you will see if you can find time to glance through the enclosed articles[2] I have been often enough congratulating you anonymously on the somewhat dazzling start you have made in the Presidency; but I should like, if you will allow me, to do so now over my own name. What you have accomplished has been the most satisfying thing that has happened in America in the twenty years that I have tried to follow its affairs; & I hope you will feel that in these two articles I have done it & you justice & no more than justice. A quite extraordinary part of the work, the very difficult work, of interpreting America to England falls on my shoulders & I am therefore particularly anxious not to go too wildly astray.

It has been intensely interesting to watch your methods which anyone who knows your writings as well as I do could have inferred in advance. But I wonder whether I have analysed them, & the idea behind them, rightly? I may have imputed to you, though I don't think I have, a more definite & deliberate conception of the Presidential functions than you would feel like owning up to. One usually *does* get tripped up if one ascribes to an Executive or a party leader anything more than a determination to use commonsense in solving the problems of the next twelve hours. I remember McKinley saying to me—it must have been the only epigram he was ever guilty of—"Government is always crisis." So it is to the men who dare not or can not look ahead. But I mean, unless you peremptorily disavow it, to hold to my view that you are following a more or less carefully prepared ground-plan. That at any rate is why all you have done since you entered the White House, & the successes it has met with, seem to me so significant & stimulating.

But on these & many other topics I am hoping that before long I may be privileged to have a talk with you. Unless something goes very much awry at the last moment, I expect to be in Washington before the month is out; & there is nothing in my trip I look forward to more eagerly than the opportunity of paying my respects to you. Pray therefore do not on any account think of answering this note—or answer it only by allowing me the pleasure of seeing you when I present myself at the White House.[3]

May I be recalled to the Misses Wilson & will you, dear Mr President, believe me to me [be], with my warm regards & congratulations, Yours very sincerely Sydney Brooks.

ALS (WP, DLC).

[1] British free-lance journalist who had lived in the United States, 1896-1900, and often wrote on American subjects.

[2] "President Wilson's Record," London *Times*, Sept. 13, 1913, and "President Wilson's Triumph," *ibid.*, Oct. 4, 1913. These "articles" were actually unsigned editorials. Both praised Wilson for his effective leadership of Congress in the difficult process of enacting a tariff bill providing for meaningful reduction.

[3] Brooks had an interview with Wilson at the White House on October 30, 1913, and published a signed article: "President Wilson," *English Review*, XVII (June 1914), 372-84. If he published an earlier article based upon this interview, the Editors have been unable to find it.

From William Gibbs McAdoo

Dear Mr. President: Washington October 7, 1913.

Many thanks for your letter of the 6th instant, and for the revision of the inscriptions which you sent me, and which I think you have greatly improved.

Faithfully yours, W G McAdoo

TLS (WP, DLC).

From Ellen Axson Wilson

My own darling,   Cornish, New Hampshire Oct. 7, 1913.

Your delightful and interesting letter came today. Many thanks for the *whole* of it—the politics and the,—other! It is a relief to find you still confident about the currency. An article in one of the papers today must be more true than usual for it sounds like your letter. It said there was a smell of paint about the offices at Washington which one might suppose was due to the work on the building,—but it was really *war-paint*! Your "big square jaw was set," &c. &c.

Speaking of the papers, the accounts today of the new policy in the Phillipines, and of Mr. Harrison's arrival there, of his speech and the way it was received was thrillingly interesting. I am delighted with it all.

My letter saying we were to reach Washington on the 18th of course crossed yours. I note you say nothing further of the plan to come up for next Sunday. Monday being a holiday I thought possibly you would not have to watch the committee. I suppose they never meet on Saturday. However I must now assume that you are *not* coming and plan accordingly. We are delighted that you are going down the river, even if we are also taken aback at the thought of reaching Washington to find you gone. It will be at least a *little* better to get there just *before* you leave; so we will leave here on Tuesday the 14th (instead of the 15th,) and leave N. Y. on a very early train on Friday the 17th, which will get us to Washington about 1.30. You say you are leaving "Friday evening"—and as you are not such a Southerner as to say "evening" when you mean "afternoon," we can count upon seeing a little of you before you go. None of the girls wish to go on the trip down the river. Nell has been, and it does not seem to appeal to the other two. Of course I shall be too tired, after New York.

Margaret is back after a charming visit with the Chauncey Ryders[1] and Mrs. Sheridan. She says Wilton is lovely and the art colony there delightful,—much simpler, of course, than this, —more like Lyme. Also that Ryder's summer work is superb,—better than ever. Mrs. Sheridan is quite well again. She was really completely broken down by her humiliation over the divorce proceedings and the newspaper publicity. But now she has recovered her poise and put it behind her. By the way, her husband denied that he had told those lies about supporting her and sending her abroad to study. He has recently written to ask her for money because he wanted to get married again! He must be crazy. But at last she has got spirit enough to refuse even to read his letters,—they go to her lawyer.

Goodnight, dearest dear, I am *so* glad you want me. Can you imagine how I am longing for *you*? You don't mention when you return from that trip.

Oh how I envy those reporters who heard that wonderful speech & wept over it.   Devotedly,   Nell.

ALS (WC, NjP).
¹ Chauncey Foster Ryder, a painter of New York and Wilton, N. H. The Editors have been unable to discover his wife's name.

To the Editor of the *Washington Post*

Sir: [The White House] October 8, 1913

I am quoted in your issue of this morning as saying that any one who does not support me is no Democrat but a rebel.¹ Of course, I never said any such thing. It is contrary both to my thought and to my character, and I must ask that you give a very prominent place in your issue of tomorrow to this denial.²

                    Very truly yours,   Woodrow Wilson

TLS (Letterpress Books, WP, DLC).
¹ The *Washington Post* was referring to Wilson's impatience with Hitchcock, O'Gorman, and Reed and to his anger at the efforts of the banking lobby to split the Democratic party and prevent enactment of the Federal Reserve bill. About this, see Link, *The New Freedom*, pp. 227-31.
² This letter was published on the front page of the *Washington Post*, Oct. 9, 1913.

To James Fairman Fielder

My dear Governor: [The White House] October 8, 1913

I cannot refrain from giving myself the opportunity to say to you that you have begun your fight¹ along exactly the right lines. Undoubtedly, there is a portion of our party² which has been working, not for us, but against us, and which will do so at every opportunity. There can be no real truce or alliance between us and I believe that you never did anything to set your cause and ours forward more distinctly than to come out at the very beginning as you did in direct avowal of the facts. Along this line lies victory; along any other may lie defeat. The people of the State supported me in these things, and they will support you, for New Jersey is for clean, decent government, as you say.

Thank you warmly for your letter of October fourth.³

                    Faithfully yours,   Woodrow Wilson

TLS (Letterpress Books, WP, DLC).
  1 As the Democratic gubernatorial candidate in New Jersey.
  2 The Smith-Nugent organization in Essex County.
  3 J. F. Fielder to WW, Oct. 4, 1913, TLS (WP, DLC).

From William Joel Stone

Kansas City, Mo., Oct. 8, 1913.

I believe committee action on currency must be forced by caucus. Will arrive this week, ready to help.

W. J. Stone.

T telegram (WP, DLC).

From John Purroy Mitchel

My dear Mr. President: New York. October 8, 1913.

I beg hereby to tender my resignation from the office of Collector of the Port of New York.

The active and engrossing part of the work of the campaign for the Mayoralty of New York, in which I am engaged as a candidate, has set in, and, while the Collector's office is so well organized as to make it quite improbable that the Government's interests would suffer during the four weeks of the campaign, I feel that, as I am engaged in a local political contest, I owe to you the duty of offering my resignation.

The study of the organization and methods of the customs service at this port, instituted by me upon assuming the Collectorship, has made rapid progress. The reports and recommendations of the special staff will be in the hands of the Secretary of the Treasury not later than November 1st. It will then remain only to secure the approval of the Department and to make practical installation at New York. The results, both in economy of administration and in efficiency of the service, will exceed the estimate submitted to you at the time you gave approval to this work. It is also gratifying to know that we have worked out a basis for these reorganizations that will avoid the necessity of dropping from the employ of the Government any of the present staff of efficient employees. Neither does our plan contemplate salary reductions.

I take this occasion again to express my appreciation of the honor of having been allowed to serve under you. The privilege I have enjoyed of close official contact with yourself and my immediate superior, Secretary McAdoo, quite as much as the importance and attraction of the work of the Collector's office with its fine corps of public servants, makes it very difficult for me to resign. I feel strongly, however, that this is my proper course.

Respectfully,   John Purroy Mitchel

TLS (WP, DLC).

From Ellen Axson Wilson

My own darling,   Cornish, New Hampshire Oct. 8, 1913.

What exciting reading the paper is today as regards the currency bill!—the Clafin affair and all the rest of it.[1] I wonder how much of it is true. One thing that was said struck me as having force, viz. that it was a pity to be forced to make it a party issue; but that it was necessary because the Republicans (those, of course, who put *party* first,—before country,) felt that it would never do to let the democrats win the tremendous prestige of passing those two great bills in one session, and for that reason would fight it to the last ditch. It *sounds* like the sort of thing politicians would do!

I wonder if it is *hot* again in Washington. It is so warm here that I sat out of doors sketching all morning in a shirt-waist & bare-headed. *Delicious* weather, it is a luxury to be alive. And the beauty everywhere is thrilling. I really believe this is the lovliest country I have ever seen. It is partly of course that, thanks to the great splendid car I have *seen* it more completely than any other. The ride we took this afternoon is perhaps the most beautiful of all except the one over the mountains to Rutland. You take the river road about half way to Hanover and then turn up into the hills where you get views all the time that fairly take your breath away. I wish we had found it when you were here. But I don't feel as if you had really seen the country at all; it is all so different and so infinitely more beautiful with the autumn colour. It is really an exceptionally fine season for colour, Mr. Parish says,— more of the rich coppery reds, and less ordinary yellow. How would you like a little place here? I saw a nice looking farm house this afternoon on that hill road with magnificent views on practically *all* sides and 200 acres of farm & woodland all for sale for $4000. You remember the brick house you liked? It was sold with 140 acres for $3000. But it will take $5000 more to put it in shape. Prof Smyth of Harvard[2] bought it.

Mrs Jaffrey came tonight. She was due at 3.37 but was detained by another bad wreck on the road! She saw the cars all broken to splinters,—but it was a derailment—not a collision—and it is said no one was very seriously hurt.

I am very sorry, dear, you had such a shock as the accident to [the] messenger boy must have given you & oh so glad it was no worse! The girls, Margaret and Nell gave me a fright this morning by going *riding* at ten & staying out until nearly two. I was really in a panic for half an hour. But nothing was wrong. With love inexpressible I am

Your devoted little wife,   Nell.

I forgot to say that we will leave N. Y. on the midnight train on Thursday the 16th & be with you for breakfast on the 17th. The 16th is dear Nell's birthday,—am sorry we wont be spending it more appropriately.

ALS (WC, NjP).

1 In testimony before the Senate Banking and Currency Committee on September 17, John Claflin, president of a large dry goods store chain, had said that he represented merchants, not bankers, in suggesting that bankers have representation on the Federal Reserve Board. The story to which Mrs. Wilson referred appeared in the New York *World*, Oct. 8, 1913. It said that President Wilson had information that Claflin had been carefully coached by New York bankers before his appearance in Washington.

2 Henry Lloyd Smyth, Professor of Mining and Metallurgy since 1900.

John Lind to William Jennings Bryan

Vera Cruz October 8, 1913, two P.M.

The Huerta Government turns down the suggestion I made as impracticable at this time. On the ground that the administration believes that the election will be postponed by Congress and if not postponed it will be so conducted that Congress will declare it void. Huerta has determined to hold on. Lord Carden,[1] the new English Minister, arrived yesterday. He was received by Mr. Adams,[2] Lord Cowdrey's representative, whom I erroneously reported as having gone to England two weeks ago. I met the Minister at lunch given by Admiral Fletcher. We had long conversation. He impressed me as a man of great ability. He advocated the support of Huerta on the score of expediency because he is a strong man, a strong man being needed. Without entering into argument I pointed out certain facts in Huerta's career that do not indicate stren[g]th of character in the past nor give promise for the future. I suggested that our situation was different from that of European nations. They seemed content with any solution that temporarily enabled them to resume the production and shipment of oil and other products and to sell goods. We as neigh-

bors, while equally interested in the restoration of business, were
compelled to consider the future and that the President had
clearly indicated that he would sanction no attempted solution
that rewarded treachery and assassination with office and power.
In answer to the question as to what the United States proposed
to do in case of no election, I simply said that that contingency
had not yet been considered so far as I was advised. He then proceeded very adroitly to draw out my views to aid him as he said
in forming a judgment of the situation. I confessed to him that
the conviction had forced itself upon me that there could be no
settlement that ignored the people of the north; that they are the
most efficient part of the population, and that at times it seemed
to me that the most expeditious way might be to afford them a
fair opportunity to solve the situation and to pacify the country.
We parted. I did not expect to see him again. He returned at six,
in the meantime having been in conference with Adams. He
desired to know whether I thought that the President's conditions
had been if the elections are held as called. I said that I thought
that would depend on outcome. If a new man is elected and
seated: yes; if not; no. He argued that the country was in no
condition to have elections. I replied that Huerta had stated in
message and interview that the country was pacified. He said that
in any event neither of the two leading candidates before the
people, Gamboa and Diaz, were possible. The election of either
would complicate matters worse and it should not be permitted.
He renewed his advocacy of recognizing Huerta for balance of
term with assurances on his part as to the Cabinet and conduct
of affairs. I said that Huerta had by his own recent conduct made
such action impossible of consideration. His recent slap at the
South American Republics which had pursued the same policy
as the United States made it utterly impossible for the United
States to modify its position in any degree without incurring the
contempt of those countries. He then suggested as a possible solution that after election Huerta might resign after a proper man
had been selected to succeed him. That proposition I could not
discuss; it was such a remote possibility that I had given it no
thought. There are very persistent rumors that the rebels are
suing for peace. The man who brought Huerta's message this
morning assured me that Huerta is making every effort to induce
the rebels to surrender. He has won over the Maderistas in Congress by assurances of amnesty and official recognition for their
Constitutionalist friends. He wanted to know what I thought the
attitude of Washington would be if Huerta were able to truthfully
report a pacified country although the election had failed. I could

not say but I was sure that peace in Mexico would be welcomed at Washington by whomsoever secured.

Summary of my views: (1) Lord Cowdrey through Adams controls Huerta Administration absolutely. (2). I believe election will be postponed. If not postponed it will be set aside as void. The only thing all parties fear is the possibility of rebel success. Intervention is deemed preferable by Huerta for political reasons, by Adams as affording security.

With this situation it seems to me that there is little to be done except to watch developments. If I am expected to continue in Mexico indefinitely would it not be well for me to go to Washington for conference and instructions? I can leave here on October twelfth via Havana and Key West and return in time to reach Vera Cruz before election.   Lind

T telegram (SDR, RG 59, 812.00/9127, DNA).
  1 Sir Lionel Edward Gresley Carden.
  2 Fred Adams, the local agent for the Aguilar (Mexican Eagle) Oil Co., controlled by Lord Cowdray.

Remarks at a Press Conference

October [9] 1913

Mr. President, are you willing to make any comment on the suggestion that has been made that it doesn't make any practical difference whether the currency bill is brought to you and signed on November thirtieth, within the extra session, or on December first, after the beginning of the regular session, since the bill would lose no legislative standing during the recess?

It makes a great deal of practical difference. Time is of the essence. The business of the country is ready to settle down to the new legislation, inasmuch as business naturally quickens and accumulates in the autumn on the approach of winter. I think it is of the first consequence that the action should be as early as possible. While it makes no practical difference in the legislative standing of the bill, it makes a great deal of practical difference to the country.

Of course, you see, what lies behind my question, not to mention the words about it, there is a feeling I have seen expressed, that there was only a tactical question involved in the question, whether the bill was actually in the extra session, or the next day in the regular session.

I haven't made any point of what was first, but I have made a great deal of point of the time. If the regular session began tomorrow, I would wish it passed as early as possible. It is not a question of session, it is a question of time as being of the essence. I think it is of the first consequence that the question should be decided.

You are still as confident as you were that the result will be achieved?

Yes, sir, I am.

Has it been determined whether the bill that has come out of this committee is to be drafted with all Democratic members, or whether all of the members of the committee are to work on it?

Do you think we would get a bill if all of them do not work on it?

I don't know.

Well, you know as well as I do.

May I interpret that—that—

You are not to interpret it at all. You are to have your own thoughts about it. I will leave it to your judgment.

Mr. President, Senator Owen announced today that the hearings could not close before the twenty-fifth and that he could not tell the Senate as to when the report would be made by the committee. Do you think that makes for any unnecessary delay?

Certainly it does. All that these bankers have said has been said more than once before in the committees of Congress. It is going over old ground in which they are slowly shifting their position.

Do you think, Mr. President, that the resolutions adopted by the Boston bankers[1] are any more representative of general public sentiment than the resolution adopted at Chicago?

They are not representative of the general public sentiment at all.

You don't attach any more weight to those than the resolution adopted at Chicago?

I simply attach the weight I would attach to the utterances of men acting no doubt in entire honesty, who don't want their control of the business of the country altered.

Are these the large bankers?

I wasn't there. I don't know.

What do you mean by the bankers' shifting position?

I mean that some of them haven't said the same thing to the Senate that they have said to the House.

Can you give any specific instance?

No, I cannot. I have that at second hand, because I haven't read the testimony. That is what I was told by a member

of the Banking and Currency Committee of the House. . . .
Who fanned the fiction that I have abolished cabinet meetings?

I happen to be the one to write the story, Mr. President, that you had reason to do so for the summer.

No, the story I saw was in the *Sun*. It was said that I had abolished cabinet meetings and substituted individual conferences with members of the cabinet. Of course, that is done every summer, as you know.

It never has been done when the President was in Washington in the summer before.

I don't know anything about it. I know the summer meetings have been impossible because of the absolute dispersal of the cabinet. It is one of the most magnificent fictions that has been started. While I don't want to take it too seriously, I hope sincerely, gentlemen, you won't start reports of that sort, because it looks as if I were doing things that certainly would be detrimental to the best administration of the government. Nothing is more useful to me, speaking for myself, than the cabinet meetings and the interchange of views that we take up there, and the routine information that is exchanged, making it a sort of clearinghouse. I don't like the impression to get out to the country that anything so amateurish and silly as that is being done. When I relieve my mind, I can relieve yours.

JRT transcript (WC, NjP) of CLSsh (C. L. Swem Coll., NjP).
1 About the Chicago conference and the Boston meeting, see Link, *The New Freedom*, pp. 226, 229.

To Ellen Axson Wilson

[The White House] October 9, 1913

Alas, no chance of my getting away for Sunday. Delighted you are to arrive early enough on seventeenth for me to see you before I go down the river. I do not leave before evening. Shall be back Sunday or Monday morning at latest. Deepest love to all.

Woodrow.

T telegram (Letterpress Books, WP, DLC).

To John Bassett Moore, with Enclosure

My dear Mr. Moore: [The White House] October 9, 1913

Copies of Mr. Lind's last two dispatches[1] have been sent me and I write to suggest that if you approve, you send him some such message as the enclosed.

Faithfully yours,   Woodrow Wilson

TLS (Letterpress Books, WP, DLC).

[1] J. Lind to WJB, Oct. 8, 1913, 2 P.M., and J. Lind to WJB, Oct. 6, 1913, T telegram (WP, DLC).

ENCLOSURE

Suggestion for message to Hon. John Lind in Mexico, sent to Hon. John B. Moore, Department of State.

Your suggestion made to Huerta regarding negotiations with the northern revolutionists entirely approved. Please press these considerations as strongly as possible, always having it in mind that nothing that can be done by Huerta or the Congress will make it possible for the United States to recognize the legitimacy of his authority.

T MS (Letterpress Books, WP, DLC).

To Ralph Pulitzer

Personal.

My dear Mr. Pulitzer: [The White House] October 9, 1913

Now that the lobby investigation[1] is over, I must give myself the pleasure of expressing my deep appreciation of the service rendered by the New York World in making available the extraordinary testimony of Mr. Mulhall which did so much to throw light in a hundred directions upon the methods which have been used to influence legislation.[2] We are not unmindful, from day to day, of the great services which papers like your own render us in pushing forward the thing upon which all our minds are now concentrated.

Now for the currency. The influences which are working against it cannot be traced like the others, but they are very subtle and very powerful, and this is our opportunity to prove that we have the knowledge and the ability to set the business of the country free from the forces which have too long controlled it.

Cordially and sincerely yours,   Woodrow Wilson

TLS (Letterpress Books, WP, DLC).
    [1] An investigation of the alleged tariff lobby by a special Senate committee, about which see Link, *The New Freedom*, pp. 186-90.
    [2] Colonel Martin M. Mulhall, for many years a lobbyist, field worker, and strikebreaker for the National Association of Manufacturers, made public his experiences in a series of articles which appeared in the New York *World* between June 29 and July 8, 1913. Prompted by Mulhall's revelations, the House of Representatives, on July 9, adopted a resolution calling for an investigation of lobbying similar to the Senate investigation.

From William Jennings Bryan

My Dear Mr President   Ashville [N. C.] Oct 9 [1913]
    I had not seen your message to the Filipinos when I spoke with you Friday—allow me to congratulate & thank you for the promise of ultimate independence. It was admirable—just what they were waiting for. It is a great joy to me, my dear Mr President to have this country committed to independence—it has been on my heart for fifteen years.
    Am glad the cabinet meetings are to be resumed—they are an intellectual treat. We are having a delightful time here—you must renew acquaintance with Ashville[.] Our mutual friend Seely[1] has built one of the great hotels of the country[2] & the environment is magnificent. With assurances of great respect etc I am My dear Mr President   Yours truly   W. J. Bryan

Linds messages have been telephoned to me—Am afraid he is too pessimistic

ALS (WP, DLC).
    [1] Fred Loring Seely.
    [2] The Grove Park Inn.

From John Bassett Moore

My dear Mr. President: Washington Oct. 9, 1913
    The message to Gov. Lind, enclosed with your letter of today, has been telegraphed to him.
                              Very resp'y & truly yrs   J. B. Moore.

ALS (WP, DLC).

John Lind to William Jennings Bryan

                              Vera Cruz, Mexico. Oct. 9, 1913.
    Messengers of Huerta becoming more frequent. He is apparently getting anxious.
    The Torreon incident[1] may make the general situation very

grave any day. I become more and more convinced that if order and pacification can be accomplished by Mexican means it will be necessary to utilize the rebel organization in part at least for the work. Federal army, made up largely as it is of convicts, may vanish in other places as it did at Torreon. And if in addition a few rebel victories should be reported, the whole country will be a sinew of lawlessness and rebellion. I do not predict this as an immediate menace but it is a contingency that should not be ignored.

Recognition of the rebels may become a vital question as one of the instruments for establishing a semblance of law and order. If recognition were deemed expedient for that purpose, would it not be feasible to arrive at an understanding with the rebels that recognition is granted on condition that the rebels shall not regard the entrance of United States troops at points where there is no adequate protection for life and property as an invasion or in any other light than as a friendly act to Mexico? Once recognized and afforded a fair opportunity to contend, the rebels will easily prevail. The Huerta Government will crumble like a house of cards. The reason I venture above suggestion is because it would not surprise me to learn any morning that all means of communication between Mexico City and outside world have been severed. In such event a relief expedition would have to be started from the coast; should have good will of rebels.

Lind

T telegram (WP, DLC).
  1 Torreón, key to Huerta's defenses in the North, fell to the Constitutionalists on October 1. Huerta concealed news of the disaster for a week.

From Ellen Axson Wilson

My own darling.   Cornish, New Hampshire Oct. 9, 1913.
· We have been today on our last outing before we leave. We—four—went picknicking, to Lake Sunipee—a six hour excursion. It was 35 miles there and 26 around the lake. The latter was especially beautiful. It seems to be about a dozen different lakes connected by narrow channels, which gives it very great variety and charm. The road around it is fine and the shores beautifully wooded. It is all rather well developed & cared for too. It hasn't the majesty of my "ancestral lake" (New Found) for it has no high mountains about it, but it is *very* lovely. It was another perfect day,—like Oct. in Princeton,—a "delicate air" like the "maid" in the song.
Oh, how intensely we all longed for you! It would have been

so delightful to have had one such day all together—our whole family and no one else. I don't think I have ever been so *soaked* in beauty anywhere in the world as I have here in the last two or three weeks. It has really been a perfect orgy. It is almost too beautiful to be endured in such great draughts. But tomorrow we must turn our attention to business.

We had another little accident just before we reached Windsor, had to turn out for a great furniture-laden van and went into the ditch up to the hubs on the one side. The ditch was filled with mud and overgrown with grass so that it looked all right. But the horses attached to the van that caused the mischief stood by, and finally dragged us out. The car was not hurt and of course we were not in the least danger. We all simply stepped out over the sunken side.

I am still so absorbed in the currency bill and so eager to read every word in the papers about it, that it is now very late & I must stop. Mrs Jaffrey is largely to blame too for she talked half the evening. Largely about what an "abominable person" Mrs. Burla[s]que is; and about Burlasque's shortcomings! Goodnight my own dear love,—in one week and one night more I will be with you. I shan't try to tell you how happy the thought makes me. Dear & dearest love from all.

Your devoted little wife,   Eileen.

ALS (WC, NjP).

To John Lind[1]

Washington, October 10, 1913.

The President instructs me to say he feels that the circumstances and influences disclosed by yours of October 8th, 2 p.m., make it highly desirable that you should remain and keep a close watch on affairs preferably, if you find it feasible, at Mexico City itself. Your presence and constant moral pressure there might serve as a very useful corrective upon the inspired opinions of the new British minister who should be impressed as strongly as possible with our unchanged and unchangeable attitude towards Huerta and all that he represents. We demand a moral as well as a physical basis for government there. We thoroughly and entirely approve the course you have pursued in your interviews with the British minister and feel that the influence you are exerting will tell more and more, particularly in view of the revolutionary successes in the north. Hope it is your judgment also that you can be most effective just now at Mexico City.

Moore, Acting Secretary.

T telegram (SDR, RG 59, 812.00/9127, DNA).
¹ There is a WWsh draft of this telegram in WP, DLC.

To Henry De Lamar Clayton

My dear Mr. Clayton: [The White House] October 10, 1913

I am a great deal concerned at the thought of losing you from the working force of the House of Representatives.¹ As the chief direction of affairs in the present session has lain with the Committee on Ways and Means and the Committee on Banking and Currency, I foresee that the chief responsibilities of the next session will lie with the Committee on the Judiciary, of which you are chairman. I was looking forward with great satisfaction to working with you and having your experienced counsel and assistance in the work that is before us. It seems to me, indeed, indispensable in the carrying out of our party's programme.

I do not deem myself at liberty to suggest to you anything that would interfere with your own personal plans and I feel rather selfish in saying what I am saying, but I considered it a matter of mere public duty on my part to say how earnestly I had desired that I might have your aid and counsel as chairman of the Judiciary Committee during the next session and the next Congress,—for our work cannot be finished in a single session. If I accomplish no more by this than giving myself the pleasure of letting you know my personal estimate of you, I shall, at any rate, have discharged my conscience in the matter and said what was really in my mind and heart. If I dared, I would beg you to remain in the House.

        Cordially and sincerely yours,   Woodrow Wilson

TLS (Letterpress Books, WP, DLC).
¹ Clayton had announced his candidacy for the Democratic nomination for United States senator.

From Ralph Pulitzer

My dear Mr. President: New York. October 10, 1913.

I wish to thank you most sincerely for your kind words of appreciation of the service which we were able to render during the tariff fight. Now that that is over and the struggle has shifted to currency reform, I need hardly assure you that my own sympathy and the efforts of The World are with you in this fight.

    With kind regards   Faithfully yours,   Ralph Pulitzer

TLS (WP, DLC).

John Lind to William Jennings Bryan

Vera Cruz, October 10, 1913.

Yesterday a prominent Mexican from city called in behalf of Huerta and presented three propositions for my consideration: One, if elections were held as called would United States recognize the man elected. Two, the elections having been held and if the country were at peace would the United States recognize Huerta for remainder of his ad interim term? Three, would I secure the removal of the war ships from their threatening positions in the Gulf harbors? Each proposition was eloquently argued. It was pointed out that presence of ships more than anything else caused a public sentiment that made it impossible to meet the President's wishes with the frankness that could be done if they were removed.

As to the first I said that if a new man was elected under the conditions specified in the President's instructions to me of course he would be recognized. Second, I regretted that by its recent action against the Republics to the south who like the United States adhered to the Pan American resolution adopted in the City of Mexico the Huerta Government had made it utterly impossible for the United States to reopen the question of recognition under any circumstances. Third, I did not think that presence of war ships in itself had created much prejudice but I realized that the subject is one that readily lends itself to that purpose and I thought it had been freely exploited. I suggested that the maintenance of an army at the boundary was probably more offensive. The Colonel thought not, besides, it was needed for policing the boundary. I said that our government under the unsettled conditions also deemed it the part of prudence to have a force in the Gulf, but I suggested that whenever the Huerta Government would submit to me a request that the army be removed from the boundary zone I will be glad to recommend that the (apparent omission) be also withdrawn. The Maderista bloc in Congress is wholly under Huerta control. The bill to postpone elections was offered at his instance and he has resorted to every device to pass it. On this point I have absolutely reliable evidence. Yesterday it became evident that bill will not pass. This morning I received message from the City that the Maderistas in Congress are formulating a plan for settlement which they desire me to communicate to rebels. Messenger is to bring it to me tomorrow. I have no details as to this scheme. In my judgment rebels will accept no settlement at Huerta's hand at this late day. Detailed and accurate information obtained today through German sources as to the rebel situation confirms me more strongly in views expressed in yesterday's cable. The Huerta Government is not only owned and controlled, as I have indicated, but every one connected with the Government is hostile against the United States, whose attitude has foiled their plans. The *hacendados* and all big business interests are also hostile. Under these circumstances it seems to me that legitimate commercial as well as political considerations dictate that the United States do not neglect the opportunity to foster the good will of that section of the Mexican people which is inevitably bound to rule the destiny of the nation. The certitude of my connections on this point is my only excuse for repetition. The United States will probably be compelled to land troops in Mexico before long. If this becomes necessary I should like to see it done with at least the tacit consent of one section of the Mexican peoples. Lind[1]

T telegram (WP, DLC).

[1] Wilson's intended reply, which was forestalled by Huerta's dissolution of the Mexican Congress, is printed as an Addendum in this volume.

From Ellen Axson Wilson

My own darling, Cornish, New Hampshire Oct. 10, 1913

I am afraid I must write a short & hurried letter tonight because I have promised to give Jessie this evening for an exhaustive study of the lists for her announcement cards. It is getting time for that business to be under way. Just think it is only about six weeks.

I have been very busy all day so that I really could not get the letter in earlier. The morning was broken into by going at eleven to Maxwell Evarts[1] funeral. He has been very ill all summer. It is all extremely sad. He was only fifty and a very fine man, they say. He was adored by his young family of four children and so very necessary to them, for his wife is unbalanced mentally;—not really insane,—she is at home,—but there is something wrong with her.

We are already well on with our packing, and beginning to feel uprooted here—longing more and more to be with you. The stopping over in New York is for me a trial quite disproportionate to the plain facts of the matter. It seems the last straw, I suppose, in this long separation. Please thank Dr. Grayson for the very kind letter received today. It was a great comfort. And by the time this reaches you dear little Helen will be with you. Give her my dear, dear love & tell her how happy we all are at her good recovery. All send love beyond measure to our darling. I love you, dearest, with all my heart and soul. Always and altogether Your own Eileen.

ALS (WC, NjP).
[1] General counsel of the Southern Pacific Railroad, he was the son of William Maxwell Evarts (1818-1901).

A Draft of a Telegram to Walter Hines Page

[Washington, Oct. 11, 1913]

Sec'y of State: Suggested message to Ambassador Page at London.

The following correspondence between John Lind and the Department sent to you with this suggestion. It seems to us very important that Sir Edward Grey should feel to the utmost our conviction that moral considerations should be put before material at every point in the treatment of the Mexican situation and the re-establishment of genuine constitutional processes before the desire for order at any price. (Begin & end quote) We deem it most unfortunate that the new British Minister to Mexico should be guided in action and opinion by representations of Lord Cowdray, as unfortunate as it would be as to this government to determine its policy in Mexico upon advice of the Standard Oil Company or any other great interest. We feel confident that the British Foreign Office would wish its representatives to take a wider view. Now that you know Sir Edward Grey you will know how to approach him and open this subject for informal discussion.

T transcript (WC, NjP) of WWsh (WP, DLC).

To Walter Hines Page

Washington, October 11, 1913.

. . . The President directs me to send these[1] to you confidentially for your personal information and not for communication to Sir Edward Grey; but he deems it important that Sir Edward Grey should feel to the utmost the conviction which is expressed in the answer to Governor Lind and which has guided the course of this Government from the beginning, that moral considerations should be put before material at every point in the treatment of the Mexican situation and the reestablishment of genuine constitutional processes before the desire for order at any price. To this it is thought that material advantages should be treated as secondary, and it is confidently felt that the British Foreign Office would wish its representatives to take this wider view. Your acquaintance with Sir Edward Grey will enable you to know how to approach him and open this subject for information and informal comparison of views.

Moore, Acting Secretary.

T telegram (SDR, RG 59, 812.00/9127, DNA).
¹ J. Lind to WJB, Oct. 8, 1913, 2 P.M., and J. B. Moore (WW) to J. Lind, Oct. 10, 1913.

To John Sharp Williams

My dear Senator: The White House October 11, 1913

I have received and read your letter[s] about the currency bill¹ with the greatest pleasure and interest. I think there is a great deal of significance in all your suggestions, and I am going to take the liberty of handing them to the Secretary of the Treasury so that he may discuss them with Senator Owen, with whom he is in constant conference about the bill.

I note what you say about the indirect advantage of the delay which is being caused by the hearings, but I think that if you saw as clearly as I do the dangers which we are running in the delay, you would share some of my eager desire to have the bill pressed forward to report and passage. Things are going on in the banking world which are evidently based upon a desire to make the members of the two houses uneasy in the presence of the bankers' power, and it is possible that with expanding business and contracting credits a panic may be brought on while we wait. There is absolutely no excuse for the fall in the market value of the two-per-cents. It is being brought about by those who misunderstand or misrepresent or have not read the bill.

It delights me that you should have so favorable an impression of the bill and I am looking forward with the greatest pleasure to discussing it more particularly with you when an opportunity offers.

With warmest regard,
Cordially and faithfully yours,   Woodrow Wilson

P.S. I am going to take the liberty of sending your Life of Jefferson² back to you sometime for your autograph. It will greatly enhance its value for me.

TLS (J. S. Williams Papers, DLC).
¹ J. S. Williams to WW, Oct. 7 and Oct. 9, 1913, TLS (W. G. McAdoo Papers, DLC).
² John Sharp Williams, *Thomas Jefferson: His Permanent Influence on American Institutions* (New York, 1913).

To William Luke Marbury

Personal & Confidential.

My dear Mr. Marbury: [The White House] October 11, 1913

I was not able at once to take up the matter of your letter of October fourth.[1] Now that I have considered it carefully, I want to tell you how much it enhances my admiration for you and my confidence in both your character and disinterestedness.

I am exceedingly loath to have you withdraw from the Senatorial contest. I still think that you are the ideal man for the post, but, at the same time, I do not feel that I have the right to insist that you carry so heavy a burden as the contest would evidently be to you.

The feeling your letter leaves upon me is a feeling of regret that there are not more men who govern their own personal conduct by such high and unselfish motives.

I shall hope very soon to have a full talk with you.

With warmest regard,

         Cordially and faithfully yours,   Woodrow Wilson

TLS (Letterpress Books, WP, DLC).

[1] W. L. Marbury to WW, Oct. 4, 1913, TLS (WP, DLC), saying that he had decided to withdraw from the Maryland senatorial race since further prosecution of his candidacy would not be in the best interests of the party or of the Wilson administration.

To William Gibbs McAdoo

My dear McAdoo: [The White House] October 11, 1913

I should like very much to discuss the matter with you that Mr. Macrae[1] sets forth in the enclosed letter. I am interested very deeply and from of old in the matter of the importation of books. It is a sin and a shame that there should be any duty on them at all, and I should like to cooperate with you in making the duty as low as we can in conformity with the law.

         Cordially and faithfully yours,   Woodrow Wilson

TLS (Letterpress Books, WP, DLC).

[1] John Macrea, vice-president of E. P. Dutton & Co. of New York.

To Lindley Miller Garrison

My dear Mr. Secretary: [The White House] October 11, 1913

Thank you sincerely for having let me see the enclosed report and memorandum.[1] It is an extremely clear and interesting analysis and has helped my thought in the matter materially.

         Cordially and faithfully yours,   Woodrow Wilson

TLS (Letterpress Books, WP, DLC).
  [1] See L. M. Garrison to WW, Oct. 6, 1913.

From Henry De Lamar Clayton

Dear Mr. President: Washington, D. C. October 11, 1913.

Your letter of October 10 was duly delivered by special messenger. Of course it gave me great pleasure to know your kind opinion of my past services and the possibilities of usefulness you consider me capable of in the succeeding sessions of Congress. My work heretofore in its connection with you has been exceedingly pleasant. I have been in hearty sympathy with all your patriotic plans and purposes, insofar as I have known them.

I have consulted with such friends as I could reach and they have agreed with me that I should look upon the wish expressed by you, as the head of the party, as imperative. I will, therefore, give notice of my intention to remain in the House during the present Congress and retire from the race for the Senate from Alabama and submit the matter of my reelection as Representative to the loyal Democrats of the Third Congressional District of Alabama.

I want to say to you formally what I said to you in person in our conversation at the White House last night, that I am very deeply appreciative of, and grateful for, the great compliment you have paid me in your letter.

Sincerely yours,   Henry D. Clayton

TLS (WP, DLC).

From Ellen Axson Wilson

My own darling,   Cornish, New Hampshire Oct. 11, 1913

The papers are very exciting again today and I would give a great deal to know how the Huerta outrages on the legislators[1] are regarded by you—I mean as affecting the success of your policy, &c. &c. Was there ever in the world anything so vilely impudent, and idiotic both, as the conduct of those Americans in Mexico? The "World" editorial[2] does those gentlemen full justice. And then the great successes of the Constitutionalists. Oh, *how* I wish I knew if all this means a fresh "crisis" for you. I can't help being in sympathy with the Constitutionalists myself.

At any rate the currency matter seems to be going finely now according to the "World," and I am very happy over that. It even reports Hitchcock as showing signs of sense.

I finished my last little picture today, put things in order in the studio and left Henderson in possession to do the packing. I have had a good time there this summer. I don't know what I should have done without it. Probably worried myself sick as the result of mingled ignorance and suspense over the various political "crises," Mexican, currency and tariff. At three o'clock I took a little ride up the hill to Mrs. Louis St. Gaudens studio to see again the great vase she is modeling to celebrate the Bird Masque (I wonder if I wrote you about it before). The characters of the masque, in costume of course, move in procession around it, forming a wide frieze. It is really stunning. Nell had been posing for her this afternoon and the figure of her in low relief is very good. It is of course the central one,—the most prominent. But oddly enough Mr. Baynes is the best of all,—very picturesque. And you know how commonplace he looked really. But he has posed for her a great deal and so it is better artistically.

After I came back from there I lay down and rested and devoured the papers,—and now I must dress to go out to dinner!

Back from the dinner (11 P.M.) Where do you suppose it was? —at the Rublee's![3] Imagine my accepting an invitation there after all my fierce indignation over her bad behaviour. But she lured me by saying that she was having the Parishes—Maxfield & Stephen. Mr. Adams was also there and we had a charming evening. The Rublees are as enthusiastic about you as dear old Stephen Parish,—though Mrs. Rublee was an ardent Progressive and worked very hard to defeat you she says.

Goodnight, dear love, I am *mad* to see you,—I hardly see how I can wait even until Friday. We are all well & send fond love.

As ever   Your devoted little wife   Eileen.

ALS (WC, NjP).

[1] On October 10, Huerta imprisoned many of the opposition members of the Chamber of Deputies and dissolved Congress. For the complex circumstances surrounding these actions, see Charles C. Cumberland, *Mexican Revolution: The Constitutionalist Years* (Austin, Tex., and London, 1972), pp. 66-68, and Michael C. Meyer, *Huerta: A Political Portrait* (Lincoln, Neb., 1972), pp. 136-38, 143-49.

[2] "A Score of Benedict Arnolds," New York *World*, Oct. 11, 1913.

[3] George and Juliet Barrett Rublee. George Rublee had been until recently a lawyer with the Wall Street firm of Spooner and Cotton. He was a close friend of Louis D. Brandeis and associated with him in many of his public activities.

To Ellen Axson Wilson

My precious darling,   The White House 12 October, 1913.

How it makes my pulses jump, how it lightens my heart and changes the whole outlook to think that this is the last Sunday without my sweet one, my mate, the incomparable lady who is the centre of my life! It has been a long, long pull. I would not have had it shorter. I wanted it so. It would have been harder for me to see you sitting the heat through here, and all the dull strain of the vigil with Congress, than it has been,—much, much harder,—to know that you were in that adorable place, surrounded by everything that refreshes and pleases you; and amidst the sort of people you like best, and the sort of life! I have had what my heart most desired: you have been where it made my thought at ease to think of you, doing the things I most wanted you to do: and that is at the bottom of all happiness for me. And the dear ones with you! They have been doing what I would have picked out for them, for sheer love of them, because I am much better off when my loved ones are best provided for than I am when I am the centre and cause of the arrangement. But I am free now to admit that I have been desperately lonely. I am just realizing it in its fullness. So long as the thing was an established, accepted fact, made part of the programme by my own choice and insistence, I did not let my thoughts dwell on it one way or the other. I accepted it as part of the life I had devoted myself to, and let the business of the day swallow it up, not letting myself realize even that it took resolution to carry it through. And I was happy, with a deep satisfaction that things were right and that all was well with those I love much more deeply than I love myself. But now I can indulge what would then have been mere weakness and made me ashamed. I can now tell you of the deep longing that has filled the summer, the longing for you, my mate and sweetheart, and for the dear girlies. Now that it is all to end and there is almost immediately to be the happy home-coming, I have grown infinitely impatient and find it difficult to wait the five days that separate us! How shall I summon up the strength and courage to go away Friday night? That is particularly tough! The long embargo will begin to be lifted to-morrow, when dear Helen comes home. The dear little girl has come through splendidly. The best of it is that she will be free at last from even the vague apprehension which has so long depressed her, free in mind as well as in body. I predict that she will bloom out as she never did before. It makes me so happy to think of it. You arranged, did you not, with Davis, for us to pay the bill? She must not. Then on Thursday morning our precious Nell comes, does she not? Hoover tells me that that was the message sent him,— that she would be here in time for breakfast on Thursday. So that my contentment will steadily accumulate through the week, till all my dear ones are here. Ah! there will be a happy man, a grateful husband and father, in this old house on next Friday, if you all turn up safe and sound,—a fellow with overflowing heart! Do you realize that I have been alone (what I consider alone) in this old mansion for just about half of the time I have been President? "That's the h--- of a way to treat a President," isn't it? No doubt it was best for him, to begin with systematic discipline, but decidedly tough on him, nevertheless. He will require till next summer to recover and be thoroughly spoiled again. Then we shall have to resume the discipline, for the good of the nation. It does not do to indulge presidents for twelve months together. They lose tone and fibre, and begin to feel their oats too much. Their households are too apt to deem them great men and persuade them, by mere iteration, to entertain the same notion. Several months consorting with mere men, who have no such soft delusions, is wholesome for them, and should be administered in stiff doses. Just at this moment the medicine tastes bitter enough. I am rolling it upon my palate because I want by so much the more to enhance the sweetness of what I am to have at the end of the week. I shall be fairly drunk with the change, and may be unfit for serious business for a whole month to follow. I shall have the time of my life keeping my head! Ah! my darling, my darling! I am beside myself with the joy of it all! My exile is over. I am about to come out of the gray country of duty (fine enough in its way) into the sweet gardens where you are and all that you mean to me. God bless you and keep you and speed you! My heart is too full to go on,—full to overflowing with love for you all, but particularly for the sweetest wife in the world.

Your own Woodrow

WWTLS (WC, NjP).

To Mary Allen Hulbert

My dearest Friend,   The White House 12 October, 1913.

Did you write me a longer letter after the little note you scribbled just after the receipt of my telegram to Allen? If so, I did not get it. I ask, not with any implied complaint or criticism, but because from what you said in that note I fear that an earlier letter of yours did not reach me; and I began to wonder if it had happened again. I would like more than I can say to hear, directly from yourself, how you are, and to be assured that you are really improving, as the telegram said. I could tell, whether you talked about your health or not, by the tone and spirit of the letter. The delightful thing about close friendship is that your friend has only to speak and you know so much more than is said. And I long for the chance to read between the lines. The tone of the voice and the play of your mind in what you said would tell me everything. If you cannot write a real letter send me at least another little note, please. It would do me a lot of good!

I have been a bit under the weather myself for a few days, —perhaps a week; though getting better all the while and now practically well again. I have been under a terrible strain, if the truth must be told, and am still under it, and my little spell of indigestion (for that is what it was) was due, undoubtedy, to my being worn out and unable to run both my stomach and the government. I realize when I stop to think about it at all that I never before knew such a strain as I have undergone ever since Congress convened in April. The more I succeed in directing things the more I am depended on for leadership and expected to do everything, make all paths straight and carry every plan to its completion. I take the best care I can of myself. The doctor, who is one of my regularly appointed staff, is with me practically at all times of the day, and this summer, while the family has been away, has lived in the house here with me, being very watchful and very competent, and I shall fare very well; but I was a bit bored this past week to find myself so "poorly" that I almost lost interest in golf itself and lay down to rest instead of going out to play. When I did play I hardly had spunk enough to drive the ball a hundred yards. But that is all gone by now. For one thing the weather has changed. The lassitude that was in the air has been replaced, within the last twenty-four hours, by bracin[g] airs, and I am feeling very different,—all my spunk come back! So give yourself no concern about *this* public servant. He will feel entirely himself again when he hears that his dear friend in Nantucket is really well once more. Can you not supply that tonic?

This is indeed a complicated job I have undertaken down here. It uses up all the grey matter there is in my brain, and I have to borrow much of fellows as I go. What you read in the papers (If I may judge from what I read myself) is for the most part idle gossip, made up for the purposes of each particular paper. We shall get the currency bill through in due time, and the difficulties offered by the attitude of several of the Senators will in due process of argument and persuasion be overcome. But by that time we shall in all probability be in the regular session, and then we shall be in for many another struggle until the middle of next summer. I comfort myself with the thought that I am actually getting more or less used to it. My anxiety has not now quite the edge it had for the first months of the session.

What are your plans? Have you had the opportunity and the

strength to form any? Is it possible still that you will go to England and see some of your old Bermuda friends who have been wishing for you and planning for you for so long? My own idea is (and I think myself most unselfish to state it, though not *so* unselfish as if we could ourselves have you down here) that a complete change of scene and environment would be the best possible tonic and restorative for you. Even if you stay on this side the water, do please try to make some radical change from your old haunts and habits. That will set you up for another youth!

The family are coming back from New Hampshire this week, Gott sei Dank, and the period of my self-imposed exile from real home is almost at an end. Stupidly enough, I go down the river to see the battleships at target practime [practice] almost as soon as the dear ones arrive; but that will involve an absence of little more than thirty-six hours.

Give my love to Allen. God keep you and give you back to us your old self again!

Your devoted friend,   Woodrow Wilson

WWTLS (WP, DLC).

To Annie Josephine Wilson Howe

My precious Sister,   The White House 12 October, 1913.

What a delight it was to get your letter![1] I am going to steal time enough to answer it on my own typewriter, as in the old days. I have to *steal* it. Even Sunday (this is Sunday) is not my own. I lead a desperate sort of life, not free from the demands of public business day or night, with *no* time for my own things, my own thoughts, or my own people. I have actually been so absorbed during the three and a half months Ellen and the dear girls have been in New Hampshire (a full half of the whole time that has elapsed since I was inaugurated) that I have found the loneliness deadened and all but forgotten. It is as if the office swallowed up the individual life, whether you would or not, and used every nerve in you, leaving you only the time you were in bed, in the deep oblivion of utter fatigue. I am not complaining. It must perhaps be so; and I am not kicking against the pricks. I am only finding a way to tell you how I enjoy this indulgence of turning for a little while away from the whole thing to have a little talk with my dear sister. Did you know that Josie had given up his newspaper work in Nashiville and is now in Baltimore with a bonding company, a company that supplies official bonds for those who must give them in their business? It is the United States Fidelity and Guaranty Company. Its Baltimore office is on German Street. Alice has gone back to finish at the woman's college, Belmont, in Nashville, and Josie and Kate are living at the old Albion Hotel on Cathedral Street. Josie seems to be more than meeting the expectations of his new employers and associates, and looks better than I have seen him look in some years. And I have the great pleasure of seeing him here once in a while when he comes over on business errands or to spend a Sunday.

Jessie's wedding is to be on the twenty-fifth of November, as Ellen has probably written you before this, and we are now wrestling with the question who are to be invited—no easy or safe question for folks in public life, where there are so many sensibilities to be considered! Jessie did fall off her horse, but the stories of the accident were grossly wrong. She was taking one of her first rides *astride*, and while the horse was in a gallup lost her stirrups and slid off. She says she remembers merely having a half-amused feeling that she was slipping off and then she lost consciousness. Frank was just at hand, and so was the river. He quickly brought her back to consciousness with a little water on her face, took her to a nearby farmhouse, got a doctor who was passing to stop and look her over, and then brought her home. A few bruises were the net result. She had fallen on soft grass at the side of the road. The only conspicuous mark was a blacked eye, which she carried around for a couple of weeks under her veil.

Ellen wrote me a week or so ago saying that she was about to send you the thousand dollars in checques—American Express checques, I believe she said—so you need not worry about that. There will be no such impediment as there was about a letter from the Princeton Bank. I hope they will reach you in good season.

The introduction to Mr. Dawson[2] is all right, of course. I have not seen him yet. I do not know whether he has been in Washington since you gave it to him or not. Sometimes people seek me out and are headed off in the office without my knowing anything about it; but I am quite sure they would not treat anyone that way who brought a letter from you. I shall try to be nice to him when he comes. I say "try" because some days it is literally impossible for me to see anyone, outside the official visitors and conferees of the day. I hope it will not be so when he turns up.

It was good, *so* good to have news of you at first hand. Ellen had told me of her letter from you, too. We are all well. I have stood the extraordinary strain of the summer surprisingly well. There have been times, of course, when I have felt terribly fagged, and almost down and out, but I have come out of them at once all fit again. I am beginning to think that I am rather a tough customer, after all, physically, if not otherwise! It is good to hear that you and Annie and the baby[3] are all right! I suppose Josephine is beginning to talk French, rather than English, isn't she? I should like to hear it, whether I understood it or not.

I am sure all the dear ones would join me in deep love, if they were here. They will be here, God be praised, by the end of the week. Dearest love to all.

Your devoted brother, [Woodrow]

WWTL (WP, DLC).
[1] Annie J. W. Howe to WW, c. Sept. 25, 1913, ALS (WP, DLC). It was written from Paris.
[2] Francis Warrington Dawson, author, newspaperman, and lecturer, originally from Charleston, S. C., at this time living in Versailles. He was secretary to Theodore Roosevelt during his African trip in 1909.
[3] Annie Wilson Howe (Mrs. Perrin Chiles) Cothran and her daughter, Josephine.

From Ellen Axson Wilson

My own darling,   Cornish, New Hampshire Oct. 12, 1913

That troublesome Jessie has kept me another whole evening working over those wedding lists of hers! I hate to put you off like this until 10.30 when I am tired and sleepy. It seems very unfair, especially on Sunday,—and I have no good excuse. I wrote neglected business letters half the afternoon and rode the other half. After a day and a half of heavy rain it cleared this afternoon and was too irrisistably beautiful to stay indoors. We went again over the hill road which we have newly discovered and find so wonderfully fine as to scenery. Margaret's teacher, Ross David[1] wants a small farm and house up here and she has been looking about for him. It was in the course of those enquiries that she heard of the one on this road, of which I wrote you. It is to be sold at auction next week & we are urging Mr. David to come and see it. We interviewed an interesting young farmer named Charles Empey this afternoon about it and also about another deserted place near by. He told us a queer story about the latter. It seems that 25 years ago a prosperous young farmer of the neighbourhood built it with a view to marriage. He had been going to see a girl every week for nearly two years but never "said anything" to her. Then, the house being by that time almost finished, he ordered her to "name the day." I should say that all his visits had been made to the whole family; he had never tried to see her alone. So she told him she had no idea that he wanted to marry her, and in fact was engaged to a man in Lebanon. "If she had known in time she might have made other arrangements"! So the next day he ordered the painters and paperers out of the house, locked the door and has never been in it since, refuses to sell it and has never married. He still lives in the old family homestead close by, a rather handsome old place which in those days he shared with his parents. A real ["]Mary Wilkins" story. He seems to have considered himself very badly treated—wanted to know "what she supposed he went to her home for?"

It is good, dearest, to think that I am to see you *this* week. That makes it seem nearer. It is in fact only four whole days. I can hardly wait, for I want you so much that I cant bear to talk about it! Everything goes well with us and we are nearly ready to leave. With love inexpressible, I am, *darling*

Your own   Nell.

ALS (WC, NjP).
¹ Of New York, another of Margaret's singing teachers.

To Nelson O'Shaughnessy

Washington, Oct. 13, 1913

Call upon the Foreign Office at once and deliver the following message. The President is shocked at the lawless methods employed by General Huerta and as a sincere friend of Mexico is deeply distressed at the situation which has arisen. He finds it impossible to regard otherwise than as an act of bad faith toward the United States General Huerta's course in dissolving the Congress and arresting deputies. It is not only a violation of constitutional guarantees but it destroys all possibility of a free and fair election. The President believes that an election held at this time and under conditions as they now exist would have none of the sanctions with which the law surrounds the ballot and that its result therefore could not be regarded as representing the will of the people. The President would not feel justified in accepting the result of such an election or in recognizing a President so chosen.

Bryan

CLST telegram (SDR, RG 59, 812.00/9180A).

From Ellen Axson Wilson

My own darling,   Cornish, New Hampshire Oct. 13, 1913.

I am almost glad now that you did not get here for a final week end, for the weather is wretched, both cold and rainy, and of course the house is being "redd up" for leaving—though I must say there is *no* disorder or confusion. But evidently the autumn glory is past,—the play is over and the curtain is about to be rung down. There was a heavy frost last night, and the rains of the last few days have swept off half the leaves. One exquisite feature of our hill ride yesterday was the *road itself*,—in many places for long distances a solid untouched carpet of red gold.

All arrangements of every sort are made for our departure and I think we could leave now in two hours if it were necessary. We will, if we can get seats for Forbes-Robertson's "Hamlet,"[1] go to see it on the 16th, Nell's birthday, and go from the theatre to the train. It is the only night on which he gives that, and as he is leaving the stage, we are of course wild to see it. It will be Nell's birthday treat. I will get to you rather a wreck I am afraid; but then you are leaving at once, so it does not matter much. I will be rested when you return from up the river.

I did not see the Sunday papers until today so did not know the second chapter in the Mexican coup d'etat. Even "The Times" has given Huerta up at last,—says he has put himself on a level with Santa Anna. But oh! what next! If only a *man* would appear in that distracted country—a real leader, not a dictator. The event certainly justifies you before all the world in refusing to recognize Huerta, and also in advising the Americans to leave the country when possible.

Isnt it terribly sad that just as the long labour in Panama is ending "that good soldier of peace," Col. Gaillard,[2] lies unconscious & dying? It is growth in his brain, the direct result of overwork in a tropical climate. Poor Rose Dubose![3] It strikes her almost as heavily as it does Mrs. Gaillard.[4] He has been so wonderful to her. He was Mac's[5] double first cousin, you know.

But I am not writing a very cheerful letter. I must, to make up, tell you a tale about our funny little friends, the Maxfield Parish boys. They have all been ill & the other day his mother was brushing the crumbs out of the small one's bed. Suddenly he became *seriously* concerned as to "*who* brushed the crumbs out of Mrs. Woodrow Wilson's bed. If she were an ordinary lady she could do it herself,—but,—I *can't think*! Do you suppose that nigger feller does it?" "Oh, Max," said his mother, "who did you ever hear say such a word?" ["]Nobody! I got a toy named nigger jigger." I hope next summer you will know some of these amusing people, young & old.

Goodbye, dearest, and God bless you, I wish I could *know* that your burden was at least no heavier than usual today.

Your ever devoted,   Eileen.

ALS (WC, NjP).

[1] Actually, they saw two of Sir Johnston Forbes-Robertson's farewell performances—"Mice and Men" on October 15 and "Hamlet" on the next day, both at the Shubert Theater. Madeleine Lucette Ryley was the author of "Mice and Men."

[2] Lt. Col. David Dubose Gaillard, U.S.A., an Isthmian Canal commissioner. He had been in charge of the dredging and excavation of the central division of the Canal.

[3] Rosalie Anderson (Mrs. McNeely) Dubose, her classmate at Rome Female College and one of her life-long friends.

[4] Katherine Ross Davis Gaillard.

[5] The Rev. McNeely Dubose, an Episcopal minister, deceased.

To William Jennings Bryan

My dear Mr. Secretary: The White House October 14, 1913

The Secretary of War and I are very much interested, indeed, in securing an opportunity for some of the officers of our army to aid in training the army of China. This work is about to be placed almost exclusively, we understand, in the hands of German officers, and it seems to Secretary Garrison and me that it would be very appropriate if we also as such genuine friends of the new republic should have a chance to show our interest and render a service.

I am writing to ask if there is any proper diplomatic way in which we could suggest this as a manifestation of our friendship. I dare say it might be, personally and unofficially, taken up with the Chinese Ambassador.[1]

Always   Faithfully yours,   Woodrow Wilson

TLS (SDR, RG 59, 893.20/24, DNA).

[1] Bryan received assurances from the American Chargé in Peking, Edward Thomas Williams, that the Chinese had no intention of engaging any foreign officers and actually meant to reduce their army. See E. T. Williams to WJB, Oct. 20, 1913, T telegram (WP, DLC).

From Oswald Garrison Villard, with Enclosure

Dear Mr. President: New York October 14, 1913.

I take pleasure in sending you herewith a copy of the report of our investigator for which you were good enough to ask. I deeply appreciate your offer to see that the unpleasant features of the discrimination are put at an end, just as I hope with all my heart that you may yet come to the point of reversing this whole policy, particularly in the Treasury Department, if only because of the terribly dangerous precedents now being established. I also enclose as proof of the correctness of my statement to you that much dangerous work is being done by your subordinates without authority from above, a despatch from Atlanta which appeared last week in the New York *Sun*,[1] with the editorial comment which appeared the next day in that newspaper. I have already taken this up with Mr. McAdoo and he cannot believe that Mr. Blalock made this statement; but he is going to investigate it immediately. As I said to him, it seems to me that if this thing is correct Mr. Blalock should be removed. It is inconceivable to me that when, as we all know, an honest and efficient Administration like yours has to stand criticism anyway, its subordinates should seek to add to its embarrassments and entanglements by needlessly insulting one-ninth of the population and their white friends and sympathizers.

Faithfully yours,   Oswald Garrison Villard.

P.S. You will see by the enclosure[2] that Tammany is using the discrimination issue against Mitchel.   O.G.V.

[1] This enclosure is missing, but the controversy was caused by the alleged assertion by the newly appointed federal collector of internal revenue for Atlanta, Aaron C. Blalock, that there were no places for black men in the federal government.

[2] A flyer urging Negroes to vote for Judge Edward E. McCall and for the rest of the Tammany ticket who were "friends of the race," and to show contempt for Wilson's efforts to "segregate, degrade and dismiss colored federal employees" by voting against the Fusionist candidate, John P. Mitchel, who had Wilson's support.

ENCLOSURE

May Childs Nerney[1] to Oswald Garrison Villard

My dear Mr. Villard: New York 30 September, 1913.

In compliance with your request, I submit herewith a report of my investigation of the segregation of colored employees in government departments.

Segregation is no new thing in Washington, and the present administration cannot be said to have inaugurated it. The past few months of democratic party control have, however, given segregation a tremendous impetus, and have marked its systematic enforcement. It is becoming known as a policy of the present government.

[1] Secretary of the National Association for the Advancement of Colored People.

In saying they favor segregation, many white employees seem not to be expressing their own convictions so much as to be reflecting what they regard as the spirit of the new administration. Those who have been appointed in previous administrations apparently think that if they do not put themselves on record as approving this policy, the danger of losing their positions is thereby increased. How far this attitude is the result of official intimation cannot be ascertained. A social worker of prominence who is in touch with several government officials told the investigator that she had personally gone to the chief of one of the departments, an appointee under the previous administration, to urge him to segregate his colored employees because, as she put it, if he did not do it he might expect to be succeeded by someone who would. The immediate results bear witness that this man acted promptly upon this suggestion.

The investigator visited the following departments. Segregation may be more or less in force in other departments, such as the Bureau of the Census, but only those departments were visited where it was said to have increased considerably under the present administration.

BUREAU OF ENGRAVING AND PRINTING:

Here colored clerks are segregated in work by being placed at separate tables and in separate sections of rooms whenever possible. White guides told the investigator that it was to be the future policy of the Bureau to segregate all its colored employees, but that this could not be strictly enforced until the Bureau moved into its new building.

In both the Miscellaneous Division and Examining Division segregation has been increased. In the former Division, the employees operate perforating machines, one on either side, perforating the blocks of stamps. Here the workers have been paired according to race. In the same room the counters of these stamps have also been segregated according to color. In the Examining Division where tissue separating is carried on, the employees have been grouped according to color.

Colored girls no longer use the lunch rooms which for nine years they have been using in common with white girls. (See articles in LaFollette's Magazine, August 23, August 30.)[2] Though no official order was issued in regard to this, since Director Ralph told the three colored girls who had been eating in

2 Belle C. La Follette, "The Color Line," *La Follette's Weekly Magazine*, v (Aug. 23, 1913), 6; and Belle C. La Follette, "Miss Murraye's Dismissal," *ibid.*, Aug. 30, 1913, p. 6.

these lunch rooms that they must use a separate table, they have left and gone to the rooms assigned to them. These are most unpleasant, the wash rooms, lavatories and lunch rooms being all in one. One girl who objected has since been discharged.

POST OFFICE DEPARTMENT:

In the Dead Letter Office colored men and women have been segregated back of lockers in one corner of the room. The guide (Superintendent of the building) explained to the investigator that these lockers had to be moved because in their former position they had interfered with the ventilation of the room. He was unable, however, to give a satisfactory explanation of how it happened that the clerks behind these lockers all happened to be colored. At least the reason could not have been lack of efficiency, because the colored men here were doing a fairly high grade of work, that is, sorting letters and delegating them to the proper division. In another room where the purely mechanical process of opening letters was carried on, the clerks were all white.

The remainder of the colored force employed in the Post Office Building were in the janitorial or messenger service. The guide informed the investigator that the colored employees were classified as follows: 3 women laborers, 11 messengers and assistant messengers, 2 clerks.

No lunch room is provided for the colored employees in the Post Office Department. The white employees have a very attractive room. The guide advanced as a convincing argument in explanation of this condition that as no restaurants in Washington were open to colored people, the government could not be expected to furnish one. He further stated that only one colored man had "ever given them trouble" by trying to get his lunch in this room and that had happened but once.

TREASURY DEPARTMENT:

In the Treasury Department there are 270 colored employees. In the Treasury Building the colored clerks are scattered throughout the offices and have not yet been segregated, though it seems to be understood that an attempt is to be made to segregate as many as possible in the Registry Division. The investigator visited the following offices, finding in each the number of colored clerks indicated working with white clerks and in some offices working with white women:

Internal Revenue Division	Colored Clerks
Distilled spirits	6
Assessments	2
Filing rooms	2
Law	1
Stamps	1
Appointment Division	1
Books and Warrants	1
Files Division	1

(This man had recently been moved into this room. He works alone and receives a salary of $1400.)

United States Treasurer's Office:

Accounts—4 men, 1 woman (messenger), 1 stenographer

Redemption 1 woman

Registry Division

Loans 3

Note, coupons & currency 3 (with white women)

(This division has comparatively the largest percentage of colored employees.)

Office of the Auditor for the Post Office:

This office is a part of the Treasury Department but is situated in the Post Office Building. Here segregation seems to have been most successfully worked out. Mr. Kram, the Chief,[3] a holdover from the Taft administration, took pains to emphasize the point that he had been segregating colored employees for five years and that as far as his office was concerned, it was no new departure. He further stated that he would not lose an opportunity to perfect it. He admitted he had been able to segregate without interference with the work of his office because in the last few years he has been introducing a new system known as the tabulating system, which reduces many of the processes of the work to an absolutely mechanical level. If, for instance, he has one hundred clerks working on the "key punch," it is very easy to segregate the colored clerks and place them in a separate room or alcove. This has been done. In one room colored men operate what is known as the "gang punch" and in another room, all the force working at the "assorting machine" is entirely colored. White operatives doing the same work occupy separate rooms.

In one alcove which the investigator visited there were nine

3 Charles A. Kram.

colored women working on the "key punch." The light and ventilation were poor. These women had been moved several times but originally had been in rooms with white clerks where they had good light and air. While the new tabulating system was being introduced, Mr. Kram's office had been excused by Congress from making all of the audit of a certain year. As the omission of this audit has been brought as a criticism against his office, he has since decided to have it made. This, apparently, afforded the excuse for moving these colored women, since the rooms they occupied (with the white clerks) were necessary for the corps of bookkeepers who were to rush through this arrears in work. All the clerks, both white and colored, were moved out. The white clerks, however, were scattered in rooms where they have good light and ventilation, while the colored women were segregated in the alcove mentioned above. As usual, those segregated were placed in the poorest quarters.

In some of the rooms of this office white and colored employees still work together. For example, in the mail and files room there were six white and four colored employees. In two rooms which had been set aside for fourth grade bookkeepers colored and white employees were working together. There were no women in this room. The obvious intention is to segregate ultimately the colored bookkeepers in one of these rooms and the white in the other. As an indication of the feeling of the colored people in regard to this segregation may be cited the case of an old colored bookkeeper named Tyson who has recently been reduced from first to fourth grade bookkeeper with no change in salary. The reason assigned was that he could not do first grade work. This may be true. He resented the change bitterly and his chief told the investigator that he had cried like a baby when he was moved, not so much because of the reduction in work, but because he felt that taking him out of the room where he had sat for ten or more years with white people, including women, was a reflection upon him personally. The investigator overheard the chief of the Division, Mr. Kram, ask several of these women if they did not miss Mr. Tyson. They all replied they did and spoke of him in the kindliest manner.

One of the most interesting rooms in this department is where international coupons are audited. Mr. Kram explained that this was as difficult work as was done in his office and that he had found colored men more expert in it than white men. The investigator understood that the four men employed here, all colored, in charge of a fifth, also colored, had gradually been collected from other parts of the office. Those who advance the argument in favor of segregation that it will give the colored people a chance to demonstrate their efficiency as a race had better avoid this room, for the colored men here have proved their ability, not by competing with members of their own race but with white men whom they have beaten in a fair contest.

Another illustration of how economic efficiency refuses to follow the color line is the case of a young colored man who has become an expert operator on the adding machine. He is the only colored clerk employed in a room of white clerks doing the same work. Mr. Kram, when asked why he left him here, said he could not spare him as he was his most expert operator. It is trite to point out that here again the colored man is competing not with his own race but with the white man. Segregate the colored man and he will lose this opportunity to develop by competition, which is the foundation of all progress, and a principle to which the present administration has pledged itself.

That the basis of the whole segregation idea is caste and not race or lack of efficiency was amusingly indicated by the fact that both the Superintendent of the Post Office Building and the clerk who acted as guide in the Treasury Department repeatedly called attention to the absence of segregation in the cleaning forces, emphasizing the fairness with which the colored help is treated. When pressed for an explanation of this apparent inconsistency in policy, they stated that they had had no complaint from the "white scrub ladies." In answer to the question as to what would be the procedure should difficulty arise, they said it would be impossible to segregate without interfering with the efficiency of the work. The opinion of the investigator is that there will never be any difficulty. Should it arise, however, the solution would probably be the discharge of the colored part of the force, could this be done without interference with Civil Service rules.

Another difficulty in carrying out segregation by color consistently unexpectedly arose, to the great embarrassment of the clerk who was acting as guide in the Treasury Department. As he was taking the investigator into one of the rooms of the department, he remarked, "There are two in here, that man in the far corner of the room and"—turning to the white man at the door—"You are the other colored clerk in here, aren't you?" The reply was too emphatic for publication. It is significant that the man making it was considerably darker than some of the colored clerks who will have to be segregated if the present policy is perfected.

A Southerner in charge of one of the offices in the Treasury Building, mistaking the investigator for a sympathizer, confidingly remarked that they wanted to inaugurate segregation everywhere in the Treasury Department but were handicapped because they did not know how to go about it, it being most difficult to determine upon the best method. Before he could give more valuable information he was warned by the guide.

Although systematic segregation can only be said to have begun in the government departments, its effects are already startlingly in evidence. Those segregated are regarded as a people set apart, almost as lepers. Instead of allaying race prejudice, as some of the advocates of segregation would have us believe, by recognition, it has simply emphasized it. In fact, government approval in some cases has aroused it where it did not exist.

Competition in work has been eliminated so far as the colored employees are concerned. It is only a question of time before the few colored people who are now so expert as to prevent their being segregated, will leave the government service, and their positions, of course, will be filled by white people. Colored clerks, in other words, are practically limited to positions in a few offices which have been designated for colored help only. They have no real economic opportunity. Those who advance the argument that assigning a given division to colored clerks will give the latter a chance to test the efficiency of the race might as well test the comparative ability of women and men by insisting that the former devote themselves exclusively to the three K's and forbid their entry into any other fields of effort.

The same social worker already mentioned, referring to the segregation policy, said that the white people really do not object to the colored people as a race but are using this worn out prejudice as an excuse to get their positions. If the colored people protest against segregation, she says, it will only be a question of time before the present Civil Service Act is annulled and another passed, making it possible to deprive all colored people in the service of the government of their positions.

In Washington, history, as usual, repeats itself in relegating to those segregated what no one else wants or in failing entirely to meet their needs. For example, as has already been indicated, in the Bureau of Engraving and Printing the lunch room assigned to the colored women is unsanitary. In the Post Office Department there is no lunch room at all for colored help. In the Office of the Auditor for the Post Office, the colored women were taken

from light and airy rooms and segregated in an unpleasant
alcove. In the Dead Letter Office where the colored workers have
been segregated back of a row of lockers, the part of the room
chosen is the least desirable.

The way in which segregation has been effected so far without
official orders is worthy of study by experts in scientific management. Such delicate coordination on the part of officials is unusual. No orders have been issued segregating colored people in
their work, yet the practice goes on. Generally the excuse is a re-
adjustment in the work to increase efficiency. In this reorganiza-
tion clerks are moved from one room to another and when the
process is completed the colored clerks always find themselves
in some mysterious way together.

The only official order issued in regard to segregation related
to lavatories, and this is still in force in the Post Office Division,
the Treasury Department and the Bureau of Engraving and Printing. The signs originally posted in the Treasury Department have
been taken down. The investigator learned on reliable authority
that they are still posted on the inside and outside of the doors
of dressing rooms in the Bureau of Engraving and Printing. The
officials in Washington repeatedly call attention to the fact that
the colored people have protested against this order but have
made no objection to segregation in their work. The reason is,
of course, that the colored people are a sensitive people and
resent what they feel to be a personal affront; more important
is the fact that they cannot protest against segregation in their
work *when no official orders have been issued in regard to this*.
Should they make such complaint they would be merely asked to
cite a discriminating order and failing that would probably be
told that the changes that had been made had been necessitated
by exigencies in work, color having had nothing to do with it.
They would be unable to prove their case and might jeopardize
their positions because of "insubordination." Even the white
man is not fond of juggling with his bread and butter.

More dangerous to the colored people than segregation itself
is the subtle method by which its justification is being skillfully
spread. Friends of the colored people hear with comparative indifference the statement, "We are determined to reduce these
people to menial and subordinate positions." Such sentiments
cannot fail to arouse resentment among all believers in a democratic government. But the sinister equivalent of this blunt
declaration heard on all sides—"We cannot have colored men
working in the same room with white women or colored men in
charge of the departments employing white women"—is menac-

ing and much more difficult to combat, as those who promulgate it probably realize. Not only does this arouse latent prejudice but it tends to create it among large numbers of unthinking people where it does not now exist.

One white woman who has had considerable experience in office work has asked why the government should not segregate its women employees instead of the colored clerks. She failed to see why the entry of a comparatively few women into the economic struggle in Washington should disorganize the entire government service because any clerk, white or colored, who makes himself offensive toward his fellow clerks would soon find himself discharged. Then, after all, why discuss supposititious cases? With the resignation of Mr. [James C.] Napier, Registrar of the Treasury, there will be no colored men in positions of authority, the heads of all the departmemts being white, except Mr. Napier's successor, who is an Indian.[4]

A persistent rumor in Washington is that as soon as the fall elections are over a bill, already prepared, will be passed forcing "Jim Crow" cars on the District of Columbia.

Respectfully submitted,   May Childs Nerney

TLS (WP, DLC).
[4] That is, Gabe Edward Parker.

Nelson O'Shaughnessy to William Jennings Bryan

Sir: Mexico, October 14, 1913.

I have the honor to inform the Department that the new Minister of His Britannic Majesty, Sir Lionel Carden, was received by the Provisional President and that he has assumed charge of the British Legation in this Capital. Sir Lionel was British Consul in Mexico City from 1885 until 1894. He speaks Spanish fluently and his entire Consular and Diplomatic experience has been in Latin America. Sir Lionel is one of those European diplomats who sees the gradual progress which American ideas and commerce are making in Spanish America and who has done his utmost at every place where he has been to oppose the interests of the United States and to magnify the supposed desire of the United States for territorial aggression. I regret that at this time when the settlement of this question lies with the United States the representative of Great Britain should be a man entirely out of sympathy with the United States as the rulers of this country are very subservient to the advice and counsel of the Diplomatic representatives of great European powers. Personally,

I esteem Sir Lionel and he has been in every way cordial and courteous to me upon the occasions that I have met him. His last Post was that of Minister resident in Guatemala. Lady Carden is an American.

I have the honor to be, Sir,

Your obedient servant,   Nelson O'Shaughnessy

TCL (WP, DLC).

A Suggestion by William Bayard Hale

[Washington, c. Oct. 15, 1913]

THE MEXICAN QUESTION.

A Suggestion Submitted by Mr. Hale.

While awaiting the issue of events in Mexico, might not further efforts well be made to invoke pressure from abroad upon the Huerta Government?

Could not the leading European nations be led to take the position that their recognition of General Huerta was in his capacity of provisional president only and did not contemplate his retention of the presidential office—an ambition which, if persisted in, must cause a new and more serious scrutiny of the events of February.

I suggest that a strong statement of the objection of the United States to the permanent presidency of General Huerta (and other actors in the *coup* that overthrew lawful government in Mexico) be prepared and sent to our representatives at the capitals of the Powers which it is desired to influence;—this to be, not a formal document, but a warmly-written plea, including a narrative of the origin of the government of General Huerta, a description of the nature of his rule, an account of the condition of the country, and a statement of the troubles which will inevitably attend retention of office by the present dictators. The plea to be accompanied by instructions to the Ambassadors and Ministers to familiarize themselves with its contents and its spirit, and then, on high moral grounds, to urge the Governments to which they are accredited to support the United States in its efforts to reestablish peace in Mexico.

If Great Britain, France, Germany and Belgium could be persuaded to announce that their recognition of Huerta would terminate October 26th unless on that date a non-participant in the February conspiracy were elected President—that result would be pretty well assured.

I cannot but believe that we could secure this European cooperation if we went seriously after it. It might even be worth while for Governor Lind to make a rapid visit to three or four capitals in order to impress our diplomatic representatives there with the earnestness of the American Government and to present the facts at first-hand.

An inspection of the list of governments which (according to his message to Congress) have recognized General Huerta as President of Mexico reveals the fact that recognition is withheld by 12 of the 21 other nations of the Western Hemisphere:

> The United States
> The Argentine Republic
> Bolivia
> Brazil
> Chile
> Cuba
> The Dominican Republic
> Nicaragua
> Panama
> Paraguay
> Peru
> Venezuela

The above countries constitute an easy preponderance in the hemisphere.

Could not a great deal be made of the circumstance that the most settled and most powerful Latin American nations, conscious of the evils of violent political methods, refuse to admit the legality of the Huerta Government?

The Chilean and the Cuban Ministers near the Mexican Government are most outspoken in their denounciation of the crime of February. It would probably be not at all difficult to organize a Latin-American sentiment in support of the position taken by the United States.

T MS (WP, DLC).

From John Bassett Moore

My dear Mr. President: Washington October 16, 1913.

Having understood from Senator Burton[1] yesterday morning that he intended to speak to you concerning the so-called Seamen's Bill now pending in the Senate, I beg leave to state that three protests against the pending bill or one substantially similar to it have been presented by Great Britain, three by the Netherlands, two by Germany and one by Spain. The principal objections made to the bill are, first, that it proposes to invest our courts with jurisdiction to apply our laws concerning seamen's wages to all seamen without regard to their nationality or to the nationality of the vessel on which they serve, thus in effect denying to foreign nations any right to regulate the matter even within their own territorial jurisdiction and in respect of their own ships and seamen; and, secondly, that the bill proposes to do away with the consular supervision of ships and seamen which exists under existing treaties. There has also been some remonstrance against the doing away, as the bill proposes, with the arrest of seamen for desertion. This point is not deemed to be so important as the others, but in order that this change may be made, notice should be given in due form of the termination of our treaties providing for the arrest of deserters. These treaties are usually terminable on a year's notice, but the particular term is specified in each treaty.

Very respectfully yours, J. B. Moore.

TLS (WP, DLC).
[1] Theodore Elijah Burton, Republican Senator from Ohio.

From Ellen Axson Wilson

The Waldorf-Astoria New York.

My own darling, Oct. 16 [1913].

I hardly know whether this will reach you or not before we do. But I will send it on the chance. I havnt had a moment, *absolutely not one*—when it was possible to write a letter. And I am "holding up" the whole family to scribble this line. The trouble of course is that people come in, whenever we are not out. Mrs. Sayre[1] is here now!

But it will soon be over. Goodbye, my darling, I love you with all my heart. Your devoted little wife Nell

ALS (WC, NjP).
[1] Martha Finley Nevin (Mrs. Robert Heysham) Sayre, mother of Francis Sayre.

To Oswald Garrison Villard

My dear Mr. Villard: The White House October 17, 1913

Thank you sincerely for sending me a copy of the report. I shall make use of it as I told you I would.

I had a talk the other day with the Secretary of the Treasury about the alleged statements of Collector of Internal Revenue

Blalock of Atlanta. As the Secretary will inform you, Mr. Blalock disavows the interview. I am sincerely glad that it is so.

In haste   Sincerely yours,   Woodrow Wilson

TLS (O. G. Villard Papers, MH).

Two letters from Henry French Hollis

Dear Mr. President: [Washington] October 17, 1913

Since I saw you Thursday morning I have talked on a very friendly footing with Senator Bristow and with Senator Nelson. Both of them speak in the most encouraging way of a unanimous report on the bill.[1] They agree with me that there is not the slightest reason for handling the bill on a partisan basis, and they think we shall be able to report at about the date I suggested, November 10th.

I sounded them both on the matter of holding hearings in the evening next week, but they were both opposed to it. They have worked hard on tariff and currency matters, and in addition Senator Nelson (who is a veteran of the Civil War) has been on the Lobby Investigation Committee.

I am sure that your interview with Senator Reed brought good results. He spoke to me about the bill in a way which indicated that he considers himself in accord with the administration. I have not yet had a chance to talk with Senator Hitchcock. Senator Reed thought that I ought to tell you that I thought a unanimous report from the Committee was probable. I did not tell him that I had already seen you.

Sincerely yours,   Henry F. Hollis.

[1] The Federal Reserve bill.

Dear Mr. President   [Washington] October 17, 1913

I had a talk with Senator Weeks last evening. He expressed every confidence that there will be a unanimous report on the Banking and Currency bill and expressed much satisfaction with the fair treatment he was receiving from the Democratic members on the Committee.

I explained to you yesterday that the Committee would not vote to hold evening meetings next week to consider the bill, and that if some of us should meet the others would feel slighted, and it might hurt our chance for a unanimous report.

It has occurred to me that the situation might be met by having Senator Owen announce Monday that he should be at the Committee Room every evening at 8 o'clock to consider the bill and prepare necessary amendments: that he hoped the other members of the Committee would find it convenient to meet with him every evening: and that those who could not come every evening would be there as much as possible.

I have conferred with Senators Owen, Pomerene and Shafroth, and they think this will work well. We shall thus avoid the danger of having the Committee vote down a proposition to hold evening meetings: we shall make it evident that every member of the Committee is welcome: no one will have a chance to feel injured or jealous: and the real work will be advanced openly and naturally.

I feel more and more encouraged in my hope that we shall get a unanimous report about November 10th.

Sincerely yours,   Henry F. Hollis.

TLS (WP, DLC).

From Benjamin Franklin Shively

South Bend, Ind., October 18, 1913.

Your position in favor early action on currency both right and wise, delay mischievous and postponement hazardous. Will be in Washington before bill is reported.   Benj. F. Shively.

T telegram (WP, DLC).

Francis Burton Harrison to Lindley Miller Garrison

Manila. October 18, 1913.

I have the honor to submit resolution of the Philippine Assembly in answer to the President's message delivered upon arrival at Manila:

"We, the representatives of the Filipino people constituting Philippine Assembly solemnly declare that it is evident to us that the Filipino people have the right to be free and independent so that in advancing along the road of progress it will on its own responsibility work out its prosperity and manage its own destiny for all the purposes of life. This was the aspiration of the people when it took up arms against Spain and the presence of the American flag first on Manila Bay and then in the interior of the Archipelago did not modify but rather encouraged and strengthened the aspiration despite all the reverses suffered in war and difficulties encountered in peace. Being called to the ballot box the people again and again ratified this aspiration and since the inauguration of the Philippine Assembly, the national representative body has been acting in accordance with the popular will only, thus in the midst of the most adverse circumstances, the ideal of the people never wavered and was respectfully and frankly brought before the powers of the sovereign country on every propitious occasion. On the other hand, our faith in the justice of the American people was as great and persistent as our ideal. We have waited in patience confident that sooner or later all errors and injustices would be redressed. The message of the President of the United States to the Filipino people is eloquent proof that we have not waited in vain. We accept said message with love and gratitude and consider it a categorical declaration of the purpose of a nation to recognize the independence of the Islands. The immediate step of granting us a majority on the commission places in our hands the instruments of power and responsibility for the establishment of a stable Filipino government. We highly appreciate and are deeply grateful for the confidence reposed in us by the Government of the United States. We look upon the appointment of the Honorable Francis Burton Harrison as Governor General as the unmistakable harbinger of the new era in which we expect the attitude of the people to be one of decided cooperation and finally we believe that happily the experiments of Imperialism have come to an end and that colonial exploitation has passed into history. The epoch of mistrust has been closed and the Filipinos upon having thrown open to them the doors of opportunity are required to assume the burden of responsibility which it would be inexcusable cowardice on their part to avoid or decline. Owing to this a few days have sufficed to bring about a good understanding between Americans and Filipinos which it has been impossible to establish during the thirteen years past. We are convinced that every onward step while relieving the American Government of its responsibilities in the Islands will as fully demonstrate the present capacity of the Filipino people to establish of its own and guarantee in a permanent manner the safety under such government of the life, property and liberty of the residents of the islands, national as well as foreign. We do not wish to say by this that there will not be difficulties and embarrassments nor do we even expect that the campaign open or concealed of the enemies of the Filipino cause will cease soon, but we feel sure that through a conservative use of the powers entrusted to us the

Filipino people will with God's favor and the help of America emerge triumphantly from the test however difficult it may be."

Harrison.

T telegram (WP, DLC).

Remarks at a Press Conference

October 20, 1913

Mr. President, what is the situation on the currency bill at this time?

> Why, I think I can sum it up in this way: I think there is very good reason to expect a report not later than the first week in November, and I find every disposition to discuss it, without any attempt to delay it when it gets on the floor of the Senate, so that I should hope that two, or, at the outside, three weeks of debate would conclude the matter. I have been making some inquiries, and that is my general conclusion.

Will you have nonpartisan support for the bill?

> I think there will be a very considerable degree of nonpartisan support.

Does that involve any considerable change in the bill as it now stands?

> So far as I can see, no change that affects any vital part of the bill. I have found timely and unexpected agreement on the fundamental features of the bill.

Do you think it is possible to obtain a unanimous report?

> There are members of the committee who think that is quite possible. I, of course, don't know. I haven't conferred with a large enough proportion of the members. I have conferred with all the Democrats, but with only one or two of the Republican members.

That will be in a substantially unchanged form and not seriously amended?

> Amended only in particulars. . . .

Has any proposition been suggested to you in connection with that bill running to the establishment—I don't like to use the term, the term that occurs to me—of a central bank under complete governmental control?

> Oh, yes, there have been such suggestions, but I don't think any considerable number of senators have entertained them seriously.

Do you regard, Mr. President, the number of regional banks as fundamental? There is some doubt as to the number.

> One number is fundamental, of course, fundamental that there should be enough. That is a matter of debate.

Mr. President, is the presence of the Secretary of Agriculture and the Comptroller of the Treasury fundamental?

> In the act it is a question not of principle, you see, but of initiative, of breadth. Of course, I think we all desire that the system should have as wide a sympathetic connection with the business of the country, with the activities of the country, as possible. And that is all I think everybody is trying to work these details out on.

JRT transcript (WC, NjP) of CLSsh (C. L. Swem Coll., NjP).

To Henry French Hollis

My dear Senator: [The White House] October 20, 1913

Thank you warmly for your letters of the seventeenth. They afford me a great deal of encouragement. I will take pleasure in conveying to Senator Owen the suggestion you make about his meeting those who care to meet with him and keeping, as it were, open house for the Committee. I think it an excellent suggestion. Cordially and sincerely yours, Woodrow Wilson

TLS (Letterpress Books, WP, DLC).

To Benjamin Franklin Shively

[The White House]

My dear Senator Shively: October 20, 1913

I very much appreciate your telegram of the eighteenth. It has cheered me thoroughly. Indeed, the attitude of the Senators, particularly on our side of the chamber, in this matter ought to command and will command, I am sure, the admiration of the country. I have been conferring within the last few days with members on the committee of both parties and feel confident that we may expect action without further unnecessary delay.

I am delighted to know that you will soon be back.

> Cordially and faithfully yours, Woodrow Wilson

TLS (Letterpress Books, WP, DLC).

To Oscar Wilder Underwood[1]

[The White House]

My dear Mr. Underwood: October 20, 1913

Last week you called upon me and, in view of the very natural desire of the members of the House of Representatives to know why it seemed necessary to keep them continuously in Washington and when they might expect to be free to go home, if only for a brief interval of adjournment, asked me what I thought the prospects were with regard to the banking and currency bill in the Senate. As I then promised you, I have had conferences with members of the Senate Committee on Banking and Currency, both Democrats and Republicans. As a result of those conferences, I feel confident that a report on the bill may be expected not later than the first week in November. Most of the members of the committee with whom I have conferred have shown themselves keenly aware of the disadvantage to the country of any unnecessary delay. I believe that the action of the Senate upon the bill will follow within two or, at the most, three weeks after the report is made. I do not believe that there will be any attempt to delay its passage by dilatory tactics. Senators on both sides realize that the business of the country awaits this legislation, impatient of being kept in suspense, and display a most public spirited desire to dispose of it promptly. The passage of the bill is assured.

In these circumstances, I should like to confer with you, as you so kindly suggested, as to the action the House should take while awaiting the result.

Cordially and sincerely yours,   Woodrow Wilson

TLS (Letterpress Books, WP, DLC).
[1] The following letter was given to the press. There is a WWsh draft in WP, DLC.

To John Purroy Mitchel

Personal.

My dear Mr. Mitchel: The White House October 20, 1913

I am sure that Mr. House has already told you what my feelings are with regard to your resignation of the post of Collector of the Port, but I must not deny myself the pleasure of telling you how highly I appreciated your acceptance of the appointment and how much I have valued your services in the brief time that you have occupied the office.

I send this note merely as a personal message to interpret the routine letter of the Secretary of the Treasury, who, I am sure, feels as warmly and as cordially as I do.

Cordially and sincerely yours,   Woodrow Wilson

TLS (J. P. Mitchel Papers, DLC).

To Henry De Lamar Clayton

My dear Mr. Clayton: [The White House] October 20, 1913

Here are the anti-trust laws passed last session in New Jersey, known as the Seven Sisters. I am sure you will be interested in examining them.

Cordially and faithfully yours,   Woodrow Wilson

TLS (Letterpress Books, WP, DLC).

To John Bassett Moore

My dear Mr. Moore: The White House October 20, 1913

I am afraid that, unanimous consent having been obtained and being regarded as a very sacred thing in the Senate, it is not possible to prevent the consideration of the Seaman's Bill which Senator La Follette has brought up for action.[1]

I do not understand that the bill has passed the House of Representatives, at any rate, in the form in which it is now proposed in the Senate. I agree with you (much as I would like to see the bill passed and thoroughly as I believe in its principles and main provisions) that it would not be wise to have it made law before we know the results of the conference[2] which we, ourselves, called.   Sincerely yours,   Woodrow Wilson

TLS (J. B. Moore Papers, DLC).
[1] The Senate approved the measure on October 23.
[2] The conference on safety at sea, which was to meet in London on November 12, 1913.

Nelson O'Shaughnessy to William Jennings Bryan

[Mexico City, Oct. 20, 1913]

CONFIDENTIAL. FOR THE SECRETARY OF STATE.

The present British Minister is a firm believer that Huerta can settle the Mexican situation and lets it be known. The policy of Great Britain in Latin-America is purely commercial and forms of government matter little to her; she has no missionaries in Latin-America.

The British Minister has given me to understand in many conversations that he considers intervention as fatal to British interests and that our policy can only lead to it. Since his reception by Huerta on the 11th after the dissolution of Congress, he is all powerful here and seems to have the full support of his Government. See my despatch number two thousand ninety-two of the 14th instant.　　　　　　　　　　Nelson O'Shaughnessy.

T telegram (WP, DLC).

To James Aloysius O'Gorman

My dear Senator:　　　　　　[The White House] October 21, 1913

I have just read in this morning's World your admirable interview about the currency bill.[1] I want to thank you most warmly. It assists not only to clear the situation but also to assure the kind of action that we are all hoping for and expecting.

Cordially and sincerely yours,　Woodrow Wilson

TLS (Letterpress Books, WP, DLC).

[1] In this interview, O'Gorman said that he expected that the Senate banking committee would unanimously recommend the bill and was certain that it would be made law during that very session. He emphasized that the Senate hearings were extremely valuable since many of the controverted points were being thrashed out in committee; moreover, they were making it clear that the bill was no longer solely a Democratic party measure. He predicted that, after a few important amendments had been incorporated, the measure would establish "an ideal banking and currency system, making impossible financial disturbances such as the panic of 1907."

Walter Hines Page to William Jennings Bryan

London, Oct. 21, 1913.

Your Oct. 14, 7 p.m. Last night I had long interview with Sir Edward Grey. I gave the President's despatches of October twelfth and thirteenth to American Chargé in Mexico. Sir Edward said his Government would wait till Oct. 26th before deciding its next step and that then he would inform me what they would do. He expressed hope that there was no truth in the newspaper rumor that the President would raise embargo on arms to the "rebels in the North."

I again explained at length the President's policy and reasons therefore, saying that if he used the power of the United States in favor of one adventurer in Mexico or any other Latin American State merely because he seemed at any given moment stronger than his opponents, no progress towards stable government could ever be made and that there must be some moral foundation for our approval. I explained how we could not consider financial interests except as secondary to moral interests. I expressed my own belief that the President would never intervene for mere financial interests, however great or insistent, and that merely to restore order by force would not mean progress towards stable government by Mexicans but would be only another name for conquest which was abhorent. He expressed sympathy with this view and remarked that the trouble with intervention was the trouble of getting out. I reminded him that Mexico was only a part of Latin America and that the investments made there under Diaz did not change the fundamental problem.

He granted that the problem of the United States with Mexico was very different from the problem of any other Government. His direct comment was meagre but the general impression he made on my mind very distinctly was his appreciation of the difficulties and an increasing respect for the President's policy. My inference is that he is under strong financial pressure which is irksome.

At the end of this conversation Sir Edward himself brought up the Canal tolls which I make the subject of a separate telegram.

Page.

T telegram (WP, DLC).

From William Jennings Bryan

Dear Mr. President: Washington October 22, 1913.

I will have ready by this afternoon a rough draft of the paper which you asked me to prepare to be sent to such of the leading Powers of Europe as you may think best. I am not satisfied with it and have not yet submitted it to Mr. Moore. I thought I had better see first whether it conforms to your ideas before asking Mr. Moore to put it in diplomatic language.

In view of the fact that the election is only four days off and that it would probably be impossible for us to secure any affirmative answer on the part of other nations before the election, I find myself drawn more and more to the conclusion that we had better have the note ready and send it out the day after the election, so as to forestall any recognition of Huerta as an elected President. Great Britain has announced that her recognition was temporary and was only intended to extend up to the time of the election, and I think the British Foreign Office expressed the opinion that the other recognitions were of the same character. I think we would have a much better chance of securing cooperation if we asked them to refrain from recognizing than if we asked them to withdraw before the election the recognition already extended. When we say that the elections to be held next Sunday will have no moral weight and should have no legal effect, we are predicting, and prediction has not the weight of an assertion based upon an act already done.

The morning papers indicate that Diaz will be forced to retire and, according to Lind's despatch of last evening, Huerta's candidacy is likely to be announced today;[1] but as it is barely possible that he may prefer to be elected without being a candidate, instead of announcing himself, we might find our statement weakened if made before the election, if we had to assume his candidacy or allege it without any positive statement from him.

I submit these things for your consideration. If you desire the statement issued at once, please make such changes as you see fit, and then I will ask Mr. Moore to give us the benefit of his judgment as to phraseology.

I am staying at the house this forenoon and may not come down this afternoon, owing to a sore throat, which came on yesterday and now makes it difficult for me to talk.

With renewed assurances of my great respect, I am, my dear Mr. President,   Very sincerely yours,   W. J. Bryan

TLS (WP, DLC).
[1] J. Lind to WJB, Oct. 21, 1913, T telegram (WP, DLC).

From William Bayard Hale

Mr. President: Washington, D. C., Oct 22 [1913]

Would it perhaps be worth while to take advantage of the next few weeks to secure more accurate knowledge respecting the "Constitutionalist" leaders in northern Mexico?

The chiefs are now assembling in Hermosillo, Sonoro, apparently with some intention of closer organization.

I believe that I could get to Hermosillo without attracting attention. A fortnight spent there discreetly would enable one to arrive at something like a fair estimate of the proportions and prospects of the northern movement and of the characters of the men directing it.

I am, Mr. President,
                        Sincerely Yours   Wm. Bayard Hale

ALS (WP, DLC).

A Thanksgiving Proclamation

[[Oct. 23, 1913]]

The season is at hand in which it has been our long respected custom as a people to turn in praise and thanksgiving to Almighty God for His manifold mercies and blessings to us as a nation. The year that has just passed has been marked in a peculiar degree by manifestations of His gracious and beneficent providence. We have not only had peace throughout our own borders and with the nations of the world, but that peace has been brightened by constantly multiplying evidences of genuine friendship, of mutual sympathy and understanding, and of the happy operation of many elevating influences both of ideal and of practice.

The nation has been prosperous not only, but has proved its capacity to take calm counsel amidst the rapid movement of affairs and deal with its own life in a spirit of candor, righteousness, and comity. We have seen the practical completion of the great work at the Isthmus of Panama which not only exemplifies the nation's abundant resources to accomplish what it will, and the distinguished skill and capacity of its public servants, but also promises the beginning of a new age, of new contacts, new neighborhoods, new sympathies, new bonds, and new achievements of cooperation and peace.

"Righteousness exalteth a nation" and "Peace on earth, good will toward men" furnish the only foundations upon which can be built the lasting achievements of the human spirit. The year has brought us the satisfactions of work well done and fresh visions of our duty which will make the work of the future better still.

Now, therefore, I, Woodrow Wilson, President of the United States of America, do hereby designate Thursday, the 27th of November next, as a day of thanksgiving and prayer, and invite the people throughout the land to cease from their wonted occupations, and in their several homes and places of worship render thanks to Almighty God.

In witness whereof I have hereunto set my hand and caused the seal of the United States to be affixed.

Done at the City of Washington this 23d day of October, in the year of our Lord one thousand nine hundred and thirteen, and of the independence of the United States of America the one hundred and thirty-eighth.   Woodrow Wilson.

By the President:
W. J. Bryan, Secretary of State.

Printed in the *New York Times*, Oct. 24, 1913, with one correction from the transcript of a WWsh draft in WP, DLC.

To James Alexander Reed

My dear Senator: [The White House] October 23, 1913

I hesitate to ask you to break in upon what must be one of the busiest weeks you have had by requesting you to come to the White House in order that I may say what it is perfectly possible for me to say in a letter. I want to thank you very warmly and sincerely for your statement made through a New York newspaper.[1] I have felt all along the sincere honesty and independence of judgment you were exercising in this whole matter, and you may be sure that there has never been in my mind any criticism except an occasional difference of judgment. I think that things are now shaping themselves admirably, and I am quite willing to admit that the processes upon which you have insisted have contributed to that result. I feel that I can count on you from this time out to play a leading part in bringing this whole matter to a satisfactory issue, and I want you to know what satisfaction it gives me to feel that I can do this.

Cordially and faithfully yours,   Woodrow Wilson

P.S. Pray call upon me at any time that you would like to confer about any feature of the matter.   W.W.

TLS (Letterpress Books, WP, DLC).
  [1] The New York *World*, Oct. 21, 1913, reported that Senator Reed, long regarded as an opponent of the banking bill, had now joined the ranks of its supporters. He stated that he hoped that the Senate banking committee would submit a unanimously favorable report before November 10, adding that "the hearings that the committee has held and the consideration it will give the bill before the report is made will reduce greatly the amount of debate that would have been otherwise."

To John Sharp Williams

My dear Senator: The White House October 23, 1913

I hear from many quarters how helpful your interest in the currency bill is proving, and I want to thank you again for the interest you are taking in it and the impulse you are giving to the effort for early action.

I want, presently, to have a long talk with you on the trust question. I have been so much interested in the bills you have, yourself, proposed that it would clear my thought if we might have a discussion of the whole matter of the legislation. I see two ways open to us and I want to have my mind clear as to which is the better.

Cordially and faithfully yours,   Woodrow Wilson

TLS (J. S. Williams Papers, DLC).

A Memorandum by William Bauchop Wilson

Washington October 23, 1913.

MEMORANDUM for the PRESIDENT:

Referring to the Colorado Coal Miners strike situation:[1] On Tuesday afternoon I wired Mr. Ethelbert Stewart,[2] who had been detailed by this Department to act as a conciliator in that strike, for a statement of the steps he had taken in an effort to adjust the difficulty. His reply follows:

"Your telegram received. I first called on Mr. Bowers, of Colorado Fuel and Iron Company,[3] the dominant corporation getting from him his attitude toward the strike and its possible settlement. Then saw Governor Ammons[4] for general view of situation, saw spokesman of operators in Governor's office, then called upon local officers of Miners district fifteen.[5] I went into the strike district with the Secretary of State[6] and with State Commissioner of Labor[7] to study conditions, met and interviewed Hayes and John Lawson[8] at Trinidad and suggested that they offer to arbitrate the whole matter including recognition. They offered to arbitrate everything except recognition of Union. They contended that no settlement that did not include recognition would be of any final value. The operators had previously offered to let the Governor decide all other issues except recognition of Union. I interviewed Mine Superintendents and local miners in both strike districts, North and South, to satisfy myself as to the basis for the conviction among the men that without recognition no settlement would be permanent or satisfactory. Met District Attorneys, Sheriffs and business as to attitude of mine operators toward organization[;] returning to Denver I submitted to mine managers in presence of the Governor three propositions. First, that the managers of the mining properties involved in this dispute, hold a formal official conference with the officials of the miners' organization, at any place the operators might suggest. Second, that the managers meet the Governor, and these men named as individuals not as Union officials, together with myself in the Governor's office, in a purely informal way to talk the matter over such meeting to be unofficial not to commit anyone to any policy but simply to try in a gentlemen's meeting to induce each side to consider the claims put forth by the other. Third, that the mine managers should deliver to me any counter proposition they might have to offer for me to submit to the miners. The operators refused both of the first two propositions and declined to submit any counter propositions. I had become convinced that the local mine managers were not empowered to settle except on terms dictated from New York and hence stated to them that I would report the facts and suggest that a congressional investigation be recommended. Following this I was summoned before the Federal Grand Jury in Pueblo and found that attorneys for the managers had urged a Grand Jury investigation presumably to head off a congressional investigation. I urged the Grand Jury not to investigate as it was an industrial conflict not a criminal conflict. Since there seemed to be no possibility of a settlement at this time I left the state. I will be in Washington next Sunday and will report to you in person on Monday.   Ethelbert Stewart. October 22, 1913, 945 A.M."

The only part of the negotiations that is not included in this telegram is a trip Mr. Stewart made to New York to interview the Rockefeller interests there. At this interview he was informed that the New York office would not interfere with the situation unless requested to do so by their Colorado representatives. The Colorado Fuel and Iron Company, which is generally recognized as the dominant corporation in the Colorado Coal Fields, is said to be controlled by John D. Rockefeller, Jr. I have, however, no definite information on that point. The officers and directors of the company are as follows:

President—J. F. Welborn.

Secretary and General Auditor—J. A. Writer.

Chairman of Board, Vice President and Treasurer—L. M. Bowers.

Executive Committee: L. M. Bowers, Chairman; J. F. Welborn, Joseph Chilbert, S. G. Pierson and F. P. Gates.

Directors: H. E. Copper, F. P. Gates, George J. Gould, J. D. Rockefeller, Jr., E. P. Jeffery, J. H. McClement, S. J. Murphy, W. P. Ward, Joseph Chilbert, L. M. Bowers, J. F. Welborn, J. A. Writer.   (Moody's Manual).

W B Wilson   Secretary.

TS MS (WP, DLC).

[1] About the Colorado coal strike of 1913-14, one of the most traumatic labor disputes in American history, see George P. West, *Report on the Colorado Strike* (Washington, 1915), and George S. McGovern and Leonard F. Guttridge, *The Great Coalfield War* (Boston, 1972).

[2] Chief Clerk and Chief Statistician of the Bureau of Statistics of the Department of Labor.

[3] LaMont Montgomery Bowers, vice-president and treasurer of the Rockefeller-controlled corporation since 1907.

[4] Elias Milton Ammons, Democratic Governor of Colorado.

[5] Of the United Mine Workers of America.

[6] James B. Pearce.

[7] Edwin V. Brake.

[8] Frank J. Hayes, vice-president of the United Mine Workers, and John R. Lawson, ranking official of the Colorado district of the union and a member of its executive board. They were both leaders of the strike.

From Frank Arthur Vanderlip

Dear Mr. President: Washington, D. C., October 23, 1913.

I have been before the Senate Banking and Currency Committee today to elucidate a plan for currency and banking legislation which is the result of some suggestions made by various members of the Committee when I was last before them.[1]

In drawing this plan I have conferred with Mr. H. P. Davison, of J. P. Morgan & Co., and Mr. Benjamin Strong, Jr., of the Bankers Trust Company of New York. Both of these gentlemen are with me, and we shall be in Washington for several days.

My conviction is that the plan proposed is quite along the lines of your own thoughts, as I understand them. I would be glad to call upon you with Mr. Davison and Mr. Strong to more fully explain the plan if you have the time to give to us.

A note addressed to me at the Army and Navy Club will reach me promptly.   Very truly yours,   F A Vanderlip

TLS (WP, DLC).
[1] About the Vanderlip plan for a federally-owned and operated Federal Reserve Bank of the United States, see Link, *The New Freedom*, pp. 232-33.

John Lind to William Jennings Bryan

Vera Cruz, Mex., Oct. 23, 1913.

The military situation continues about the same—a see-saw from day to day. Being without artillery the rebels can hold places which they capture only long enough to levy tribute. It is questionable whether they can hold Torreon but they control the country generally in the north and in many localities in the south. This in connection with lack of labor has virtually suspended agricultural operations. The peons do not venture to accept work away from their homes and (?) places. All strangers in a community are captured on some trumped up charge and sent to the Army. The cotton is going to waste in the fields. The coffee is unpicked and little cane will be ground. Business is rapidly coming to a standstill. The radical fiscal changes decreed by Huerta are ruinous. His forced loans are becoming more numerous. The Banco Nacional paid the sum referred to in my last on Monday. It is provided in Huerta decree that certificates receivable for duties up to November tenth may be bought at a ten per cent. discount. He expects by this means and by forced loans to keep things going until December tenth. It is now confidently expected that Carden will recommend to the bankers that it is safe to exercise the option and take the bonds already authorized. I am of the opinion that he will so recommend and that the loan will be completed. Evidence is accumulating that Carden knew what was going to happen on the tenth and that the presentation of credentials was timed with reference to it. My evidence on this point is not complete but convincing to me. I also believe that Carden advised Huerta to strengthen his dictatorship by securing an endorsement at the polls. You observe that England now proposes to await the result of the election. In his interview in MEXICAN HERALD yesterday Carden justifies his stand against the United States on the ground of "our ignorance of Mexican affairs."[1] Lord Cowdray through his influence and family ties with members of the English Cabinet absolutely dictates the Mexican policy of England. He does not propose to take any chances of having his concessions scrutinized by unfriendly eyes nor does he want a form of Government which he cannot control. The way his domination works out in practice so far as our interests are concerned is illustrated by the recent fiscal regulations. Congress proposed to tax oil one dollar per ton—Congress goes to jail—Huerta as dictator instead levies the required revenue on industry and commerce. The United States the principal exporter is the principal sufferer.

Mrs. Lind[2] returns home today. I had a couple of hours confidential interview with Diaz last night. His staff is already in jail.   Lind.

T telegram (WP, DLC).
  [1] This was the *Mexican Herald*'s version of the interview which Carden gave on October 21. It set off an uproar in the American press, which denounced Carden as a second Henry Lane Wilson and a tool of the British oil interests. Carden's statements seemed to underscore the gap between American and British viewpoints regarding recognition of Huerta, the forthcoming elections, and the status of the Constitutionalists. About this, see Peter Calvert, *The Mexican Revolution, 1910-14, The Diplomacy of Anglo-American Conflict* (Cambridge, 1968), pp. 237-47. Carden vented considerable spleen against the United States and its policies in Mexico and Latin America generally in a memorandum which he sent to Sir Edward Grey on September 12, just before he left for Mexico. L. Carden to Sir E. Grey, Sept. 12, 1913, ALS, with typed memorandum (FO 371/1676, No. 43939, PRO). It was virtually a diatribe. Calvert, pp. 221-23, reproduces this memorandum.
  [2] Alice Shepard Lind.

A Statement on the Vanderlip Plan

The White House, Oct. 24, 1913.

When inquiries were made at the White House as to what the President's attitude was toward the proposals made by Mr. Vanderlip of the National City Bank to the Currency Committee of the Senate it was stated with the expected emphasis, that of course the President would not recede in any respect from the position he had already so clearly taken and which the whole country understands.

He has warmly and unqualifiedly indorsed all the main features of the Glass-Owen bill. He regards the plan provided for in that bill as excellently suited to the existing conditions of the business of the country, and in every essential particular sound and calculated to render the businessmen of the country great and immediate service, and he believes that the early enactment of the bill into law is expected and demanded by the most thoughtful business interests.

The evidences which have reached him of the support of the country are unmistakable and overwhelming.

Printed in the *New York Times*, Oct. 25, 1913.

To Frank Arthur Vanderlip

My dear Mr. Vanderlip: The White House October 24, 1913

Thank you for your note of yesterday, written from the Army and Navy Club.

I am at a loss to understand how you can have come to think of the bank plan which you proposed to the Senate Committee on Banking and Currency yesterday as "being along the lines of my own thought." It is so far from being along the lines of my thought in this matter that it would be quite useless for me to discuss it with you and Mr. Davison and Mr. Strong. I could in no circumstances accept or recommend it.

I thought I had made it clear to the whole country that I was earnestly and unqualifiedly in favor of all the main features of the bill recently passed by the House of Representatives and now in the Senate. The plan provided for in that bill I believe to be in every way suited to the existing conditions of the business of the country and in every essential particular sound and calculated to render the business men of the country a great and immediate service.

I am sorry to miss the pleasure of seeing you and the gentlemen accompanying you, but a conference such as you suggest would be of no advantage to any of us or to the ends the Congress is now seeking to serve.[1]

Sincerely yours,   Woodrow Wilson

TLS (F. A. Vanderlip Papers, NNC).
[1] There is a WWsh draft of this letter in WP, DLC.

To William Bayard Hale

My dear Hale: The White House October 24, 1913

Will you not see the Secretary of State at once about the suggestion you make apropos of the conference at Hermosillo? I conferred with him yesterday.

In haste   Sincerely yours,   Woodrow Wilson

TLS (received from William Harlan Hale).

A Draft of a Circular Note to the Powers[1]

Washington, October 24, 1913.

You will please call at the foreign office and deliver the following message: Quote

The President construes General Huerta's statement of yesterday[2] as an announcement of his purpose to overthrow constitutional government in Mexico and to convert that nation into a limited despotism in which force shall dominate regardless of either the wishes or the interests of the people. This government which, by reason of its position, is and must continue to be of paramount influence in the Western Hemisphere, cannot, without a sacrifice of its grave responsibilities, permit the ambitions of one man or group of men to check the upward progress of a sister republic or the development of its civilization. The people of Mexico have a right to determine their own destiny and they have intimated no desire to turn from the path of civilization back to the instruments and methods of barbarism. This Government refused to recognize the Huerta government because it was conceived in absolutism fastened upon the country by methods abhorrent to the conscience of the world and has been administered with contempt toward all that is good in modern civilization. The President, desiring to assist the unhappy people of Mexico, offered friendly mediation to secure a basis upon which peace could be restored and constitutional government reestablished with hope of endurance. These overtures were rejected and in due time the real aims and purposes of General Huerta became known and it scarcely required the dissolution of Congress, the arrest of its members and the assumption of autocratic power to prove to the world how utterly impossible it is for him to conceive or construct a government in keeping with modern times. This Government having, in the announcement and maintenance of the Monroe doctrine, shown its willingness to protect the people of this hemisphere from encroachment at the hands of European powers, having proven by its actions in the Venezuelaen contest its willingness to protect a little republic in its rights to have its controversies with great nations settled by arbitration rather than by force, is now prepared to assert with equal emphasis its unwillingness to have an American Republic exploited by the commercial interests of our own or any other country through a government resting upon force. If the influences at work in Mexico were entirely domestic, this Government would be willing to trust the people to protect themselves against any ambitious leader who might arise; but since such a leader relies for his strength, not upon the sympathy of his own people but upon the influence of foreign people. This Government, whether that foreign capital is from the United States or from other countries, would be derelict in its duty if by silence or inaction it seemed to sympathize with such an interference in the rights and welfare of Mexico. While this Government is glad to encourage in every legitimate way investments by its citizens in the countries of Latin America, these investments must be made with the understanding that our nation's interest in the advancement of these countries and in their working out of a great destiny, is greater than in any possible profits that may come from such investments. As in Cuba, the United States was willing to lend its assistance in the securing of independence from a foreign political power, so in Mexico this nation is willing to assist in maintaining Mexico's independence of foreign financial power. The President has confidence that the people of Mexico, if free to choose their own rulers, would choose men in sympathy with the nation's highest aspirations—men who would regard it a duty and a pleasure to carry out the will of the people. It will not, therefore, recognize as a legitimate government a government established by force and terrorism, whether the force and terrorism be exercised, as they were, in the establishment of the Huerta regime or are secured through the empty forms of a mock election. As this Government assisted the people of Cuba in securing free and fair elections, through which the voters could express themselves, so it is willing to assist the people of Mexico to give expressien to their wishes at a free and fair election, giving to the people of Mexico and the world its pledge of disinterestedness and of genuine friendship.

T MS (WP, DLC).

1 The following draft was the revised version of the rough draft referred to by Bryan in his letter of October 22. The rough draft cannot be found. The revised draft undoubtedly incorporated many emendations by Wilson; indeed, it is probable that Wilson wrote all of this version, for the vocabulary, phrasing, and style are his.

2 Huerta, accompanied by his entire cabinet, called in the diplomatic corps on

October 23. He explained the reasons for his dissolution of the Congress and imprisonment of certain members, asserted that he had reason to believe that some of his friends would propose him for the presidency, and declared that in no circumstances would he accept election. N. O'Shaughnessy to the Secretary of State, Oct. 23, 1913, *FR 1913*, pp. 848-49. Wilson interpreted this to mean, as did many American newspapers, that Huerta intended either to arrange his own election in order that he might repudiate it, or else to make sure that no candidate received a majority. In either event, Huerta would continue to exercise dictatorial power.

To William Jennings Bryan

My dear Mr. Secretary: [The White House] October 24, 1913

It seems to me that we ought, in order to be upon sure ground and gather no false impressions, to make immediate and direct inquiry of the British Government through Page as to whether the utterances attributed to Sir Lionel Carden were really made by him.

I notice by the papers this morning that there is some effort to speak of the Carden incident as closed. It certainly can not be closed until his utterances are disavowed or explained. It is a case much more open to severe criticism than Henry Lane Wilson's utterances, for which we immediately volunteered our apology, even after Mr. Wilson had retired from the active exercise of his duty in Mexico.[1]

In haste

Cordially and faithfully yours,   Woodrow Wilson

TLS (Letterpress Books, WP, DLC).
[1] On October 24, the British embassy made a formal disclaimer to the State Department of the British government's responsibility for the interview; it also repudiated its authenticity. *New York Times*, Oct. 25, 1913.

To John Bassett Moore

My dear Mr. Moore: [The White House] October 24, 1913

Knowing as I do that you are at work on a paper[1] which I feel will be of the greatest consequence in every way, I venture to suggest for the proper part of the paper phrases something like the following:

"The affairs of Mexico touch the commercial and material interests of other countries, but they touch our life and the happiness, the liberty, and the essential welfare of all the peoples of this hemisphere. Our interest and responsibility, therefore, stand in a case by themselves."

I know that you will pardon this suggestion. I am heartily glad that you are at work on this all important matter.

Cordially and sincerely yours,   Woodrow Wilson

TLS (Letterpress Books, WP, DLC).
¹ Wilson and Bryan, after completing the circular note just printed, had second thoughts about sending it and asked Counselor Moore to prepare a draft. J. B. Moore to WW, Oct. 28, 1913, conclusively indicates that Bryan did not give a copy of the Wilson-Bryan draft to Moore. Instead, Wilson typed out the outline, printed as the following document, and gave it to Moore on October 24 (possibly October 25).

An Outline of a Circular Note to the Powers

[c. Oct. 24, 1913]

This government most interested, most responsible.

The political fortunes and economic development of all Central America involved.

The government of Huerta, based upon usurpation and force, would long ago have broken down but for the encouragement and financial aid derived from its recognition by other nations, without regard to the wishes or purposes of the United States.

The continuance of that government is impossible with the consent of the United States.

Will the other governments cooperate with the United States, or is their policy and intention to antagonize and thwart us and make our task one of domination and force?

No joint intervention will be considered.   W.W.

Note: *As strong and direct as the courtesies and proprieties of pacific diplomacy permit.*

To England: The bottom was about to drop out when Sir Lionel Carden appeared upon the scene and took charge of its rehabilitation.

WWT MS (SDR, RG 59, 812.00/9625A, DNA).

From William Gibbs McAdoo

Confidential

Dear Governor: [Washington] Friday [Oct. 24, 1913]

I have concluded not to go to Philadelphia tomorrow as I think I should keep in touch with the Currency situation.

I hope that you may not have to go to Mobile.¹ It is a long, hard trip and I dont believe it is worth the Candle. Please excuse me if I am butting in. It is inspired solely by my concern for you.

Senator Owen is on the way here and is anxious to see you. I really think it important for you to see him for a moment. I shall do all that I can but he *may* need a little stimulus from you.

Reed left in fine spirits and urged me to urge you to send immediately (*invite*) O'Gorman & Hitchcock to see you. He says 20 minutes with them *now* may be worth days hereafter. I hope you may be able to do this. I am going to keep in close touch with all the members of the Committee.

Enclosed letter is a matter of importance & I dont want to send it without your approval.[2] Will you be good enough to read and return to me with a frank expression of your views. This is what I should like to do if it will not embarrass the administration.

Hastily & Cordially   McAdoo

ALS (WP, DLC).
[1] To address the Southern Commercial Congress on October 27.
[2] This enclosure has not been found.

An Address at Congress Hall in Philadelphia[1]

[[Oct. 25, 1913]]

Your Honor,[2] Mr. Chairman,[3] Ladies, and Gentlemen:

No American could stand in this place today and think of the circumstances which we are come together to celebrate without being most profoundly stirred. There has come over me, since I sat down here, a sense of deep solemnity, because it has seemed to me that I saw ghosts crowding in—a great assemblage of spirits, no longer visible to us, but whose influence we still feel, as we feel the molding power of history itself. The men who sat in this hall, to whom we now look back with a touch of deep sentiment, were men of flesh and blood, face to face with extremely difficult problems. The population of the United States then was hardly three times the present population of the city of Philadelphia, and yet that was a nation, as this is a nation, and the men who spoke for it were setting their hands to a work which was to last, not only in order that their people might be happy, but that an example might be lifted up for the instruction of the rest of the world.

I like to read quaint old accounts, such as Mr. Day[4] has read to us this afternoon. Strangers came then to America to see what the young people that had sprung up here were like, and they found men in council who knew how to construct governments. They found men deliberating here who had none of the appearance of novices, none of the hesitation of men who did not know whether the work they were doing was going to last or not;

[1] Marking the rededication of the building upon the completion of its restoration.
[2] Mayor Rudolph Blankenburg.
[3] John Wanamaker.
[4] Frank Miles Day, noted Philadelphia architect, who told about the restoration.

men who addressed themselves to the problem of construction as familiarly as we attempt to carry out the traditions of a government established these one hundred and thirty-seven years.

And so I feel today the compulsion of these men, the compulsion of examples which were set us in this place. And of what do their examples remind us? They remind us, not only of public service, but of public service shot through with principle and honor.

Then they were not histrionic men. They did not say, "Look upon us as those who shall hereafter be illustrious." They said, "Look upon us who are doing the first free work of constitutional liberty in the world, and who must do it in soberness and truth, or it will not last."

Politics, ladies and gentlemen, is made up in just about equal parts of comprehension and sympathy. No man ought to go into politics who does not comprehend the task that he is going to attempt. He may comprehend it so completely that it daunts him, that he doubts whether his own spirit is stout enough and in his own mind is able enough to attempt that great undertaking. But unless he comprehends it he ought not to enter it, and after he has comprehended it, there should come into his mind those profound impulses of sympathy which connect him with the rest of mankind. Because politics is a business of interpretation, and no men are fit for it who do not see and seek more than their own advantage and interest.

We have stumbled upon many unhappy circumstances in the hundred years that have gone by since the event that we are celebrating. Almost all of them have come from self-centered men, men who saw in their own interest the interest of the country, and who did not have vision enough to read it in wider terms, in the universal terms of equity and justice and the rights of all mankind. I hear a great many people at Fourth of July celebrations laud the Declaration of Independence, who in between Julys shiver at the plain language of our Bill of Rights. The Declaration of Independence was, indeed, the first audible breath of liberty, but the substance of liberty is written in such documents as the Declaration of Rights attached, for example, to the first Constitution of Virginia, which was a model for similar documents read elsewhere into our great fundamental charters. That document speaks in terms, in the uttering of which the men of that generation did not hesitate to say that every people has a right to choose its own forms of government—not once, but as often as they pleased—and to accommodate those forms of government to their own existing interests and circumstances. Not only to establish, but to alter in the fundamental principle of self-government, so that we are just as much under compulsion to study the particular circumstances of our own day as the gentlemen were who sat in this hall and set us precedents, not of what to do, but how to do it. Because liberty inheres in the circumstances of the day.

Human happiness consists in the life which human beings are leading at the time that they live. I can feed my own mind as happily upon the circumstances of the revolutionary and constitutional period as you can, but I cannot feed my thoughts with them in Washington now, because every day problems arise which wear some new face and aspect. I must fall back, if I would serve my conscience, upon those things which are fundamental, rather than upon those things which are superficial. I ask myself this question: "How are you going to assist in some small part to give the American people, and, by example, the peoples of the world, more advantage, more liberty, more happiness, more substantial prosperity; and how are you going to make that prosperity a common heritage instead of a selfish possession?" I came here today partly in order to feed my own spirit. I did not come in compliment. When I was asked to come I knew immediately upon the utterance of the invitation that I had to come, that to be absent would be as if I refused to drink once more at the original fountains of inspiration for our own government.

The men of the day which we now celebrate had a very great advantage over us, ladies and gentlemen, in this one particular: Life was simple in America then. All men shared the same circumstances in almost equal degree. We think of Washington, for example, as an aristocrat, as a man separated by training, separated by family and neighborhood traditions, from the ordinary people of the rank and file of the country. Have you forgotten the original personal history of George Washington? Do you not know that he struggled as poor boys now struggle for a meager and imperfect education; that he worked at his surveyor's tasks in the lonely forests; that he knew all the roughness, all the hardships, all the adventure, all the variety of the common life of that day; and that if he stood a little stiffly in his place, if he looked a little aloof, it was because life had dealt hardly with him? All his sinews had been toughened by the rough work of making America. He was one of the people, whose touch had been with him since the day he saw the light first in the Old Dominion of Virginia. And the men who came after him, men, some of whom had drunk deep at the sources of philosophy and of study, were, nevertheless, also men who on this side of the water knew no complicated life, but the simple life of primitive neighborhoods. Our task is very much more difficult. That sympathy, which alone interprets public duty, is more difficult for a public man to acquire now than it was then, because we live in the midst of circumstances and conditions infinitely complex.

No man can boast that he understands America. No man can boast that he has lived the life of America, as almost every man who sat in this hall in those days could boast. No man can pretend that, except by common counsel, he can gather into his consciousness what the varied life of this people is. So, the duty that we have to keep open eyes and open hearts and accessible understandings is a very much more difficult duty to perform than it was in their day. And yet how much more important that it should be performed, for fear that we may make infinite and irreparable blunders. The city of Washington is in some respects self-contained, and it is easy there to forget what the rest of the United States is thinking about. I count it a fortunate circumstance that almost all the windows of the White House and its offices open upon unoccupied spaces that stretch to the banks of the Potomac and then out into Virginia and into the heavens themselves, and that as I sit there I can constantly forget Washington and remember the United States. Not that I would intimate that all of the United States lies south of Washington, but there is a serious thing back of my thought. If you think too much about being re-elected, it is very difficult to be worth re-electing. You are so apt to forget that the comparatively small number of persons, numerous as they seem to be when they swarm, who come to Washington to ask for things, do not constitute an important proportion of the population of the country, that it is constantly necessary to come away from Washington to renew one's contact with the people who do not swarm there, who do not ask for anything, but who do trust you, without their personal counsel, to do your duty. Unless a man gets this contact, he grows weaker and weaker. He needs them as Hercules needed the touch of Mother Earth. If you lift him up too high, or he lifts himself too high, he loses the contact, and therefore loses the inspiration.

I love to think of those plain men, however far from plain their dress sometimes was, who assembled in this hall. One is startled to think of the variety of costume and color which would now occur if we were let loose upon the fashions of that age. Men's lack of taste is largely concealed now by the limitations of fashion. Yet these men, who sometimes dressed like a peacock, were, nevertheless, of the ordinary flight of their time. They were birds of a feather; they were birds of the forest; they were birds coming from simple breeding; they were much in the open heaven. They were beginning, when there was so little to distract the attention, that they could live upon the fundamental principles of government. We are taught them, but we have not time to absorb them. We have not time to let them into our blood, and thence have them translated into the plain mandates of action.

So the very smallness of this room, the very simplicity of it, all the suggestions that come from its restoration, are reassuring things—things which it becomes a man to realize. Therefore, my theme here today, my only thought, is a very simple one. Do not let us go back to the annals of those sessions of Congress to find out what to do, because we live in another age and the circumstances are absolutely different; but let us be men of that kind. Let us feel at every turn the compulsions of principle and of honor which they felt. Let us free our vision from temporary circumstances and look abroad at the horizon and take into our lungs the great air of freedom which has blown through this country and stolen across the seas and blessed people everywhere. And, looking east and west, and north and south, let us remind ourselves that we are all custodians, in some degree, of the principles which have made men free and governments just.[5]

Printed in the *Philadelphia Inquirer*, Oct. 26, 1913; with a few corrections from the text in *Celebration of the Rededication of Congress Hall . . .* (Washington, 1913) and in the Philadelphia *North American*, Oct. 26, 1913.
[5] There is a WWT outline of this speech in the C. L. Swem Coll., NjP.

A Talk at Swarthmore College[1]

Your Excellency, Mr. Clothier, Mr. President:[2] [[Oct. 25, 1913]]

That greeting sounds very familiar to my ears. It was quite like old times, and I am reminded of an anecdote told of that good artist but better wit, Oliver Herford, who, on one occasion, was dining at his club in London, when he was approached by a man who slapped him on the back and said heartily, "How are you, Ollie, old man? You're looking fine." And Herford, looking up at him, replied, "I don't know your name and I don't know your face, but your manners are very familiar." And so, just now,

[1] On Founders' Day.
[2] Governor John Kinley Tener; Isaac Hallowell Clothier, retired merchant, at this time a trustee of Swarthmore College; Joseph Swain, President of Swarthmore College since 1902.

your manners exemplified in that cheer seem delightfully familiar to me.

I find myself unaffectedly embarrassed today. I want to say, in serious thought, that I do not like to attempt an extempore address following such a distinguished orator as the Congressman[3] from your state who has just finished. Moreover, I am somewhat confused as to my identity today. I am told by psychologists that I would not know who I am today if I did not remember who I was yesterday; but, when I recollect that yesterday I was a college president, that does not assist me in establishing my identity today. On the contrary, this very presence, the character of this audience, this place with its academic memories, all combine to remind me that the greater part of my active life has been spent in companies like this, and it will be very difficult for me, in what follows of this address, to keep out of the old ruts of admonition which I have been accustomed to follow in the role of college president.

No one can stand in the presence of a gathering like this, on a day suggesting the memories which this day suggests, without asking himself the question: "What a college is for?" There have been times when I have suspected that certain undergraduates did not know. I remember that, in days of discouragement as a teacher, I gratefully recalled the sympathy of a friend of mine in the Yale faculty, who said that after twenty years of teaching he had come to the conclusion that the human mind had infinite resources for resisting the introduction of knowledge. And yet I have serious doubts as to whether the main object of a college is the mere introduction of knowledge. It may be the transmission of knowledge through the human system, but not much of it sticks. Its introduction is temporary; it is for the discipline of the hour. Most of what a man learns in college he assiduously forgets afterwards, not because he purposes to forget it, but because the crowding events of the days that follow seem somehow to eliminate it.

But what a man ought never to forget with regard to a college is that it is a nursery of principles and of honor. I can't help thinking of William Penn as a sort of spiritual knight who went out upon his adventures to carry the torch that had been put in his hands so that other men might have the path illuminated for them which led to justice and to liberty. I can't admit that a man establishes his right to call himself a college graduate by showing me his diploma. The only way he can prove it is by showing that his eyes are lifted to some horizon which other men less in-

[3] That is, A. Mitchell Palmer.

structed than he have not been privileged to see. Unless he carry freight of the spirit, he has not been bred where spirits are bred.

This man Penn, representing the sweet enterprise of the quiet and powerful sect that called themselves Friends, proved his right to the title by being the friend of mankind, and he crossed the ocean, not merely to establish estates in America, but to set up a free commonwealth in America and to show that he was of the lineage of those who had been bred in the best traditions of the human spirit. I would not be interested in celebrating the memory of William Penn if his conquest had been merely a material one. Sometimes we have been laughed at—by foreigners in particular— for boasting of the size of the American continent, the size of our own domain as a nation, and they have, naturally enough, suggested that we did not make it. But I claim that every race and every man is as big as the thing that he takes possession of, and that the size of America is in some sense a standard of the size and capacity of the American people. But the extent of the American conquest is not what gives America distinction in the annals of the world. It is the professed purpose of the conquest, which was to see to it that every foot of this land should be the home of free, self-governed people, who should have no government whatever which did not rest upon the consent of the governed. I would like to believe that all this hemisphere is devoted to the same sacred purpose, and that nowhere can any government endure which is stained by blood or supported by anything but the consent of the governed.

And the spirit of Penn will not be stayed. You cannot set limits to such knightly adventurers. After their own day is gone, their spirits stalk the world, carrying inspiration everywhere they go and reminding men of the lineage, the fine lineage, of those who have sought justice and the right. It is no small matter, therefore, for a college to have as its patron saint a man who went out upon such a quest. And what I would like to ask you young people today is: "How many of you have devoted yourselves to the like adventure? How many of you will volunteer to carry these spiritual messages of liberty to the world? How many of you will forego anything except your allegiance to that which is just and that which is right?" We die but once, and we die without distinction if we are not willing to die the death of sacrifice. Do you covet honor? You will never get it by serving yourself. Do you covet distinction? You will get it only as the servant of mankind. Do not forget, then, as you walk these classic places, why you are here. You are not here merely to prepare to make a living. You are here in order to enable the world to live more amply, with greater vision, with a finer spirit of hope and achievement. You are here to enrich the world, and you impoverish yourself if you forget the errand.

And so it seems to me that there is no great difference between the ideals of the college and the ideals of the state. Can you not translate the one into the other? Men have not had to come to college, let me remind you, to quaff the fountains of this inspiration. You are merely more privileged than they. Men out of every walk of life, men without advantages of any kind, have seen the vision, and you, with it written large upon every page of your studies, are the more blind if you do not see it when it is pointed out. You could not be forgiven for overlooking it. They might have been, but they did not await instruction. They simply drew the breath of life into their lungs, felt the aspirations that must come to every human soul, looked out upon their brothers, and felt their pulses beat as their fellows' beat, and then sought by counsel and action to move forward to common ends that would be crowned with honor and achievement. This is the only glory we seek for America, and let every generation of Swarthmore men and women add to the strength of that lineage that is yours, and glorify that greater life.

Printed in the Swarthmore, Pa., *Phoenix*, Oct. 28, 1913, with corrections from the texts in *Address of President Woodrow Wilson Delivered at Swarthmore College* . . . (Washington, 1913); the *Philadelphia Inquirer*, Oct. 26, 1913; the *New York Times*, Oct. 26, 1913; the Philadelphia *North American*, Oct. 26, 1913; and from a reading of the CLSsh (C. L. Swem Coll., NjP).

From Walter Hines Page

Dear Mr. President: London. Octr. 25. 1913.

I have talked with (and especially listened to) many sorts of persons this week about this wretched Mexican business and read columns and columns of comment and turned every conceivable phase of it back & forth in my mind; and I have not seen nor heard even an allusion to any moral principle involved nor a word of concern for the Mexican people. It is all about who is the stronger, Huerta or some other bandit, and about the necessity of order for the sake of financial interests. Nobody gives us credit for any moral purpose. Nobody recalls our giving Cuba to the Cubans nor our pledge to the Philippine Islands. But there is reference to the influence of the Standard Oil Company on the American policy. In a particularly offensive editorial in this morning's *Morning Telegraph* occurs this passage:

"President Wilson, on behalf of the American people, has

adopted a course which has not been appreciated by Europe generally. America has made her policy subservient to those residents in the Republic of her nationality who have embarked capital in the country. No blame, it may be, attaches to the United States Government on this account, but this attitude has naturally been resented hotly by Huerta."

This illustrates the complete divorce of European politics from fundamental morals, and it shocks even a man who already knew of this divorce.

In my last talk with Sir Edward Grey I drove this home by emphasizing with all my might the impossibility of your giving primary heed even to any American business interests in Mexico—even the immorality of your doing so: there are many things that come before business and there are some things that come before order. I used American business interests because of course I could not speak openly to him of British commercial interests and his own Government. I am sure he drew the inevitable inference. But not even from him came a word about the moral foundation of government or about the welfare of the Mexican people. These things are not in the European ruling vocabulary.

Still I cannot get rid of the feeling that when this Government recognized Huerta it did not foresee the consequences, that he seemed to them the only man likely to restore order (which is what they chiefly want) and that they now regard their recognition as a mistake. I have been trying to find a way whereby they may now avoid repeating this mistake and save their face. I have telegraphed one such plan to Mr. Bryan,[1] if you & he should approve of it—to put it to Sir Edw. Grey as squarely and as hard as may be prudent that one way lies a friendly act to us and that the other way lies an unfriendly. I think we can force him to show his hand, without the possibility of evasion. This Government will not risk our good will—if they are forced to choose & if it seem wise to you to put them now to a square test. I don't think they will. Our good will is a club they are afraid of. It's a wretched business, and the low level of European statecraft is—sad. It leaves to us the task of pulling the world up.

Very heartily yours,   Walter H. Page

P.S. But it is possible to extract some fun even from this sordid affair. The Prime Minister[2] came up to me at the royal wedding reception the other day and said:

"What do you infer from the latest news from Mexico?" (the Huerta coup d'etat in arresting the deputies)

"Several things."

"Tell me the most important inference you draw."

"The danger of prematurely making up one's mind about a Mexican adventurer."

"Ah!" and he moved on.   W.H.P.

ALS (WP, DLC).
    1 W. H. Page to WJB, T telegram (Oct. 24, 1913), WP, DLC. According to Page, the British government excused its failure to break with Huerta on the technicality that its original recognition bound it until the election. Page's plan was for the British to refrain from recognizing the person elected on October 26 until the United States had had time to consider its course of action and to communicate its decision to the British government.
    2 Herbert Henry Asquith.

From Festus John Wade

St. Louis, Mo., Oct. 25, 1913.

I am unalterably opposed to obstructing [constructing] any new banking and currency plan at this late date. I am confident the great masses of the American people are not willing to have a central bank inaugurated in this country. I commend in strongest terms your fixed determination and untiring zeal in endeavoring to pass financial legislation at this special session. I have every confidence the Senate Committee will revise the Owen-Glass bill as it passed the House so as to make it a practical workable law. I express sincere and earnest belief the measure will be properly amended and passed by Congress and signed by you before December first, next. Country needs it badly; consideration of any new bill now means only procrastination and delay.

Festus J. Wade.

T telegram (WP, DLC).

John Lind to William Jennings Bryan

Vera Cruz October 25, 1913

. . . After canvassing all the evidence available with the utmost care and reflection I have become convinced that the control and monopoly of the oil fields and oil business in Mexico is not only the aim of the Lord Cowdray interests but also of the English Government. England's Mexican policy for some time past has been shaped and exerted with this sole aim in view. The late Minister Strong was not deemed big enough to accomplish the work; hence Carden's appointment. The Madero Government suffered downfall not alone by reason of the hostility of the *hacendado* interests, but more especially because of its halting allegiance to Lord Cowdray. It is charged, and I assume truthfully, that the Standard Company financed the Madero rebellion in part, but however well disposed the Standard may have been to resort to corruption to further its aims it has utterly failed in accomplishing results as compared with Lord Cowdray. The Standard at this time has a Mr. Malbraithhead[—]a very nice man, probably an excellent business man, not overscrupulous I judge, but utterly lacking in political acumen as compared to Mr. Adams. Under Mexican law oil was originally deemed mineral, title in the State. Some years ago the Congress remitted the title of oil to the surface owner. The oil development to date has largely been under lease from surface owners and also under concessions in the public lands. About the time that I reached Mexico agitation was started for "nationalizing" oil. The legislation proposed to that end to cover all property not developed to the point of production. It was also planned or at least discussed in Huerta circles to prohibit the exportation of Mexican oil except for the use of the Governments of friendly nations. This latter proposition was much lauded as measure of conservation.

There has been considerable discussion in Government circles and also in the press of a scheme by which it was proposed by the Lord Cowdray interests to enter into a contract with the English Government to supply for Government use a very large stipulated tonnage of oil for a period of fifty or one hundred years and to assign the control of the corporations holding the Lord Cowdray interests to the English Government to insure the performance of the contract. The Congress now imprisoned was not wholly converted to these views. It is considered that Congressional legislation is necessary to carry out the scheme in its entirety, hence the disposal of the existing Congress and the call for the election of a new one. I feel morally certain that if the Huerta Congress is permitted to convene even for a day whether under Huerta or a successor the scheme above outlined will be sanctioned by formal legislation and additional concessions conferred. I have been convinced since the day after the coup d'etat that the principal object of that move was to facilitate the consummation of this scheme.

On the twenty second there appeared in NOTICIOSO MEXICANO published in City of Mexico, recognized as owned by Huerta's personal associates the following article:

We were holding the following information. The Government Secretary GARZA ALDAPE will shortly draw contract with the English, French and the German Government inasmuch as they offer hundred twenty million pesos annual rent for oil wells of the State of Tamaulipas. The understanding is that the project of GARZA ALDAPE after it is approved will affect the financial combination.

We do believe that this is the result of thoroughly intelligent plan by the Government.

As to whether the Governments of Germany and France are parties to this scheme I have not knowledge, but I have no reason to believe it authentic. There can be no question but that the Mexican elements represented by General Huerta are anxious to have the Government of England and perhaps other powers become contractually interested in the soil and in the most valuable and extensive production which Mexico has at the present time.

I shall not stop to discuss the possible political consequences that would necessarily result if these plans are not frustrated. Huerta's recent announcement of his intention to refuse election and to resign was made on the very day that his tools were circulating his confidential instructions for the conduct of the election. I have copies of these confidential instructions. They would make a Tammany chieftain green with envy. Will forward translation tomorrow. The whole plan is as follows: Huerta will resign. His successor Lord Cowdray's nominee will call a new election. Pending that election it is being considered whether or not Huerta should take the field. In due time he will announce his candidacy for the Presidency and with the prestige of an almost unanimous vote at the elections tomorrow he will of course be elected. Besides he will have a Congress of his own making to canvas and declare the result.

Yesterday I met Mr. Adams by appointment. We had a two hours' conference. I meet him again this afternoon. He deplored the lamentable situation in Mexico and said that Huerta's proposed resignation seemed like a ray of light and might afford a solution. He wanted to discuss with me earnestly plans for making the most of the opportunity etc. I said to him that as far as the Government of the United States was concerned recent developments coupled with Huerta's delay had made it a matter of utter indifference as to what Huerta did or did not do. I said further that before I would advise any participation on our part in constructive measures the boards must be cleared in toto of the whole Huerta regime; that it would be impossible to do any rational constructive work with such material as the Congress which Huerta was seeking to bring into being; that I personally would not, nor did I think that Washington would, give the question which he suggested any consideration whatever until the litter of political wolves which he proposes to turn loose tomorrow are politically strangled. If before his own resignation Huerta would denounce the election of members of Congress as utterly void and invalid, and direct his officials to refrain from making any returns of the election of Members of Congress, I would be glad to take the matter up in real earnest with reference to planning for the future. Our discussion generally was friendly. I was very conciliatory in regard to the matters recited above. Neither of us referred to Minister Carden's actions or speeches and I do not intend to discuss that question with him this afternoon. They know my views and that I have understood their moves in the past. Will report again tomorrow.

Lind.

T telegram (WP, DLC).

Walter Hines Page to Edward Mandell House

Dear House: Cambridge. England, Sunday, Oct. 26. 1913

Sir William Tyrrell, the Secretary of Sir Edward Grey, himself, I think, an M.P., has gone to the U. S. to visit his friend Sir Cecil Spring Rice. He sailed yesterday, going first to Dublin, N. H., thence, with the Ambassador, to Wash'ton. He has never before been to the U. S., & he went off in high glee, alone, to see it.

He's a good fellow, a thoroughly good fellow, in spite of his monocle; & he's an important man. He of course has Sir Edward's complete confidence, but he's also a man on his own account. I have come to reckon it worth while to get ideas that I want driven home into his head. It's a good head & a good place to put good ideas.

The Lord knows you have far too much to do; but in this juncture I shd. count it worth your while to pay him some attention. I want him to get the President's ideas about Mexico, good & firm & hard. They are so far from altruistic in their politics here that it would be a good piece of work to get our ideas & aims into this man's head. His going gives you & the Pres't & everybody a capital chance to help me keep our good American-English understanding. I think the chief thing in the way here is their slow density. Sir Wm. will bring straight back to Sir Edw. all that he hears & sees. Perhaps (I know you will pardon me) you'll have him fall into the right hands in N. Y. & Wash'ton.

Whatever happen in Mexico, I'm afraid there will be a disturbance of the very friendly feeling between the American people & the English. I am delivering a series of well-thought-out discourses to Sir Edw.—with what effect, I don't know. If the American press could be held in a little, that would be as good as it is impossible.

I'm now giving the For'n Office the chance to refrain from more premature recognizing.

                    Very hastily Yours,   Walter H. Page

ALS (E. M. House Papers, CtY).

An Address on Latin American Policy in Mobile, Alabama[1]

Your Excellency, Mr. Chairman:[2]   [[Oct. 27, 1913]]

It is with unaffected pleasure that I find myself here today. I once before had the pleasure, in another southern city, of addressing the Southern Commercial Congress.[3] I then spoke of what the future seemed to hold in store for this region, which so many of us love and toward the future of which we all look forward with so much confidence and hope. But another theme directed me here this time. I do not need to speak of the South. She has, perhaps, acquired the gift of speaking for herself. I come because I want to speak of our present and prospective relations with our neighbors to the south. I deemed it a public duty, as well as a personal pleasure, to be here to express, for myself and for the government I represent, the welcome we all feel to those who represent the Latin-American states.

The future, ladies and gentlemen, is going to be very different for this hemisphere from the past. These states lying to the south of us, which have always been our neighbors, will now be drawn closer to us by innumerable ties, and, I hope, chief of all, by the tie of a common understanding of each other. Interest does not tie nations together; it sometimes separates them. But sympathy and understanding does unite them, and I believe that by the new route that is just about to be opened, while we physically cut two continents asunder, we spiritually unite them. It is a spiritual union which we seek.

I wonder if you realize, I wonder if your imaginations have been filled with the significance of the tides of commerce. Your

---

[1] The occasion was the fifth annual convention of the Southern Commercial Congress. The Ministers to the United States from Costa Rica, Bolivia, Peru, and Panama, and the director general of the Pan American Union also spoke. Many of the sessions were devoted to exploring the trade benefits which would accrue to the South from the opening of the Panama Canal.

[2] Governor Emmet O'Neal of Alabama and Duncan Upshaw Fletcher, senator from Florida and president of the Southern Commercial Congress.

[3] In Atlanta. His address is printed at March 10, 1911, Vol. 22.

Governor alluded in very fit and striking terms to the voyage of Columbus; but Columbus took his voyage under compulsion of circumstances. Constantinople had been captured by the Turks, and all the routes of trade with the East had been suddenly closed. If there was not a way across the Atlantic to open those routes again, they were closed forever, and Columbus set out, not to discover America, for he did not know that it existed, but to discover the eastern shores of Asia. He set sail for Cathay and stumbled upon America. With that change in the outlook of the world, what happened? England, that had been at the back of Europe with an unknown sea behind her, found that all things had turned as if upon a pivot and she was at the front of Europe; and since then, all the tides of energy and enterprise that have issued out of Europe have seemed to be turned westward across the Atlantic. But you will notice that they have turned westward chiefly north of the equator, and that it is the northern half of the globe that has seemed to be filled with the media of intercourse and of sympathy and of common understanding.

Do you not see now what is about to happen? These great tides, which have been running along parallels of latitude, will now swing southward athwart parallels of latitude, and that opening gate at the Isthmus of Panama will open the world to a commerce that she has not known before—a commerce of intelligence, of thought and sympathy between North and South. The Latin-American states, which, to their disadvantage, have been off the main lines, will now be on the main lines. I feel that these gentlemen honoring us with their presence today will presently find that some part, at any rate, of the center of gravity of the world has shifted. Do you realize that New York, for example, will be nearer the western coast of South America than she is now to the eastern coast of South America? Do you realize that a line drawn northward, parallel with the greater part of the western coast of South America, will run only about one hundred and fifty miles west of New York? The great bulk of South America, if you will look at your globes (not at your mercator's projection), lies eastward of the continent of North America. You will realize that when you realize that the canal will run southeast, not southwest, and that, when you get into the Pacific, you will be farther east than you were when you left the Gulf of Mexico. (I am reciting these things because I recently discovered them, by myself, renewing my study of geography.) These things are significant, therefore, of this—that we are closing one chapter in the history of the world and are opening another, of great, unimaginable significance.

There is one peculiarity about the history of the Latin-American states which I am sure they are keenly aware of. You hear of "concessions" to foreign capitalists in Latin America. You do not hear of concessions to foreign capitalists in the United States. They are not granted concessions. They are invited to make investments. The work is ours, though they are welcome to invest in it. We do not ask them to supply the capital and do the work. It is an invitation, not a privilege; and states that are obliged, because their territory does not lie within the main field of modern enterprise and action, to grant concessions are in this condition—that foreign interests are apt to dominate their domestic affairs: a condition of affairs always dangerous and apt to become intolerable. What these states are going to see, therefore, is an emancipation from the subordination, which has been inevitable, to foreign enterprise and an assertion of the splendid character which, in spite of these difficulties, they have again and again been able to demonstrate. The dignity, the courage, the self-possession, the self-respect of the Latin-American states, their achievements in the face of all these adverse circumstances, deserve nothing but the admiration and applause of the world. They have had harder bargains driven with them in the matter of loans than any other peoples in the world. Interest has been exacted of them that was not exacted of anybody else, because the risk was said to be greater; and then securities were taken that destroyed the risk—an admirable arrangement for those who were forcing the terms! I rejoice in nothing so much as in the prospect that they will now be emancipated from these conditions, and we ought to be the first to take part in assisting in that emancipation. I think some of these gentlemen have already had occasion to bear witness that the Department of State in recent months has tried to serve them in that wise. In the future, they will draw closer and closer to us because of circumstances of which I wish to speak with moderation and, I hope, without indiscretion.

We must prove ourselves their friends and champions, upon terms of equality and honor. You cannot be friends upon any other terms than upon the terms of equality. You cannot be friends at all except upon the terms of honor. We must show ourselves friends by comprehending their interest, whether it squares with our own interest or not. It is a very perilous thing to determine the foreign policy of a nation in the terms of material interest. It not only is unfair to those with whom you are dealing, but it is degrading as regards your own actions.

Comprehension must be the soil in which shall grow all the

fruits of friendship, and there is a reason and a compulsion lying behind all this which is dearer than anything else to the thoughtful men of America. I mean the development of constitutional liberty in the world. Human rights, national integrity, and opportunity as against material interests—that, ladies and gentlemen, is the issue which we now have to face. I want to take this occasion to say that the United States will never again seek one additional foot of territory by conquest. She will devote herself to showing that she knows how to make honorable and fruitful use of the territory she has; and she must regard it as one of the duties of friendship to see that from no quarter are material interests made superior to human liberty and national opportunity. I say this, not with a single thought that anyone will gainsay it, but merely to fix in our consciousness what our real relationship with the rest of America is. It is the relationship of a family of mankind devoted to the development of true constitutional liberty. We know that that is the soil out of which the best enterprise springs. We know that this is a cause which we are making in common with our neighbors, because we have had to make it for ourselves.

Reference has been made here today to some of the national problems which confront us as a nation. What is at the heart of all our national problems? It is that we have seen the hand of material interests sometimes about to close upon our dearest rights and possessions. We have seen material interests threaten constitutional freedom in the United States. Therefore, we will now know how to sympathize with those in the rest of America who have to contend with such powers, not only within their borders but from outside their borders also.

I know what the response of the thought and heart of America will be to the program I have outlined, because America was created to realize a program like that. This is not America because it is rich. This is not America because it has set up for a great population great opportunities of material prosperity. America is a name which sounds in the ears of men everywhere as a synonym with individual opportunity because a synonym of individual liberty. I would rather belong to a poor nation that was free than to a rich nation that had ceased to be in love with liberty. But we shall not be poor if we love liberty, because the nation that loves liberty truly sets every man free to do his best and be his best, and that means the release of all the splendid energies of a great people who think for themselves. A nation of employees cannot be free any more than a nation of employers can be.

In emphasizing the points which must unite us in sympathy and in spiritual interest with the Latin-American peoples, we are only emphasizing the points of our own life, and we should prove ourselves untrue to our own traditions if we proved ourselves untrue friends to them. Do not think, therefore, gentlemen, that the questions of the day are mere questions of policy and diplomacy. They are shot through with the principles of life. We dare not turn from the principle that morality, and not expediency, is the thing that must guide us, and that we will never condone iniquity because it is more convenient to do so. It seems to me that this is a day of infinite hope, of confidence in a future greater than the past has been; for I am fain to believe that, in spite of all the things that we wish to correct, the nineteenth century that now lies behind us has brought us a long stage toward the time when, slowly ascending the tedious climb that leads to the final uplands, we shall get our ultimate view of the duties of mankind. We have breasted a considerable part of that climb and shall, presently—it may be in a generation or two— come out upon those great heights where there shines, unobstructed, the light of the justice of God.[4]

T transcript (WC, NjP) of CLSsh (C. L. Swem Coll., NjP); CLST transcript in *ibid.*

[4] There is a WWT outline of this address, dated Oct. 27, 1913, in the C. L. Swem Coll., NjP.

This transcript raises the interesting question as to whether Wilson had a photographic memory—a subject about which there has been a great deal of discussion among the Editors. Wilson, on one of the rare occasions in which he ever did so, went carefully through Swem's transcript and made fourteen changes in its wording. When we read Swem's transcript against his shorthand notes, we discovered that in every case but one Wilson's changes conformed precisely to Swem's own shorthand. Wilson's one change was simply literary.

It is obvious that Swem made his transcript immediately after Wilson delivered the address, for a copy of it was printed in the *Mobile Item*, an afternoon paper, on October 27.

We do not know when Wilson revised Swem's transcript, but it does not seem likely that he did so before his return to Washington at 10:45 p.m., October 28. Perhaps he revised it the following day. In any event, he was able to recall with absolute precision the exact wording of his address.

There is a larger question involved here, one which we raised in the Introduction to Volume 25, and that is how it was possible for Wilson to deliver speeches that were so perfect in syntax and majestic in language while speaking from only brief outlines. As we have said before, it was Wilson's practice, before giving a major address, to go to his hotel room or private compartment on a train for an hour or an hour and a half to think through what he was about to say. It now seems likely that our suggestion that he was able, so to speak, to compose a speech in his mind and then deliver it almost verbatim was correct. Of course Wilson did not always have the opportunity for such preparation, and the result was speeches obviously inferior to those which he had memorized beforehand.

There is other evidence that Wilson had a photographic memory. It was his practice, once the war in Europe began, to return letters and enclosures from Bryan and Lansing with his own reply attached, keeping no copies whatsoever of both sides of the correspondence. Many of the issues discussed were of a very highly complex nature, and yet he was able to refer days later to letters, dispatches, memoranda—in fact to keep the whole train of the nature of the correspondence in his mind—without having the documents before him.

There is an interesting episode in this connection. Wilson and House were together on December 12, 1913. Page had sent House a letter from a lady of the English nobility and asked him to read it to the President and then burn it. House's diary tells the story: "I started to burn it when the President remarked, 'let me see if I have the facts in the letter right.' He then repeated it almost verbatim, and I dropped it in the grate." House Diary, entry for Dec. 12, 1913.

William Gibbs McAdoo to Oswald Garrison Villard[1]

My dear Villard: Washington October 27, 1913.

Your letter of the 25th instant, with portion of your proposed remarks tonight on the alleged "segregation issue," containing references to the President and myself, was received today. I appreciate your courtesy in sending me this advance copy of your speech, as well as the sincerity of your motives and purpose, but I cannot permit you to make the numerous erroneous statements in your speech without first bringing them to your attention.

There is no "segregation issue" in the Treasury Department. It has always been a mischievous exaggeration.

The President and I agreed some time ago, from a desire to be just and generous to the negroes, that a negro Register of the Treasury should be appointed to succeed the then incumbent. Upon my recommendation, Adam E. Patterson, of Oklahoma, was nominated for that office. Opposition to his confirmation developed in the Senate, and Patterson withdrew his name.

Patterson is a fine example of the intelligent and educated members of his race. We discussed the advantages of making the Registry Division of the Treasury, under him, a distinctively colored division, with the idea that it would give the negroes an opportunity of national dimensions, to prove their fitness to run, unaided by whites, an important bureau of the department. We both agreed that it would have a stimulating and beneficial effect upon the progress and development of the negro race.

The failure of Patterson's appointment caused the abandonment of the experiment. In the Register's Division there is today about sixty per cent. of white and forty per cent. of colored employees.

There has been an effort in the department to remove causes of complaint and irritation where white women have been forced unnecessarily to sit at desks with colored men. Compulsion of this sort creates friction and race prejudice. Elimination of such friction promotes good feeling and friendship. In dealing with such cases negroes have been put at separate desks in the same room with whites, and there has been no discrimination against them in the matter of light, heat, air, furniture or treatment.

I cannot be a truer friend of the negro than to promote friendly relations between him and the whites and by seeing that he is justly and fairly treated. This I am doing. I know of no complaint. I cordially invite you to make a tour of the department in all of its divisions and see for yourself how unfounded are most of the statements and inferences of that part of your speech which you sent me.

For instance, you say, "In the Bureau of Engraving and Printing, colored girls are no longer allowed to use the lunch rooms which for nine years they have been using in common with white girls. They may eat in the toilet rooms, so gracious, so chivalrous, is the Federal Government."

Where, may I ask, do you get such information? There is no truth in this statement. Colored girls sit at separate tables in the same dining room at the Bureau of Engraving and Printing with white people. Your statement that "they may eat in the toilet rooms, so gracious, so chivalrous, is the Federal Government," while not a charge that they are *required* to do so, leaves the plain inference that the Government is forcing them to do so. I cannot too strongly condemn a statement so mischievous, unfair and unfounded.

In another part of your proposed speech you say that "the division of the Register of the Treasury will speedily be known as the nigger division; people will sneer at it; the finger of scorn will be pointed at its membership, etc."

This is merely an assumption on your part, and a violent one at that. It has been disproved entirely by the record of the negro in the United States Army. There we have four negro regiments. Every private in the ranks and every non-commissioned officer is a negro. Is the finger of scorn pointed at these regiments? Do people sneer at them? No. Their record and achievements on the field of battle have earned them the respect of the white people of America, just as honorable achievement in a responsible civil division of the Government would command similar respect.

Had these regiments been composed in part only of negroes, the race would not have secured the credit for their achievements.

Without prejudice against the negro, with every desire to help him, as is evidenced by appointments I have made of negroes in the Treasury Department, I shall not be a party to the enforced and unwelcome juxtaposition of white and negro employees when it is unnecessary and avoidable without injustice to anybody, and when such enforcement would serve only to engender race animosities detrimental to the welfare of both races and injurious to the public service.

In my humble opinion, a speech like the one you propose to make, containing so much that is misleading, and inaccurate, does infinite harm to the negro race.

I enclose a copy of the "Freeman" of October 11th, 1913, containing a correction[2] of some of the false stories that are being sent out about the Treasury Department.

Please excuse this long and hastily written letter. I do not so much care for any injustice that your speech may do me as I do for the wrong it inflicts on the President, than whom no truer, nobler, and braver soldier in the cause of humanity has appeared since the death of Lincoln.

You have my permission to make public use of this letter.

Very sincerely yours, W G McAdoo

TLS (O. G. Villard Papers, MH).

[1] The following letter is printed on the assumption that, because it was about a highly charged issue, and because McAdoo authorized its publication, he submitted it to Wilson for his approval after the President's return from Mobile on October 28.

[2] R. W. Thompson, "Thou Shalt Not Bear False Witness," Indianapolis *Freeman*, Oct. 11, 1913, reported as untrue the allegations that black employees of the Treasury Department would be demoted or dismissed.

From William Jennings Bryan

My dear Mr. President: Washington October 28, 1913.

From your speeches at Swarthmore and Mobile, I take it that you are revolving in your mind the statement which you are soon to make of your Mexican policy. I take the liberty, therefore, of presenting for you[r] consideration, the conclusions that have been running through my mind.

I was in doubt as to how our country's position could be so stated as to link the new position with the earlier statements of the Monroe doctrine, and did not see daylight until the publication of that statement then attributed to Huerta, but now believed to be entirely false.[1]

The first announcement of the Monroe doctrine was intended to protect the republics of America from the political power of European nations—to protect them in their right to work out their own destiny along the lines of self-government. The next application of that doctrine was made by Cleveland when this Government insisted that European governments should submit their controversies with American republics to arbitration, even in the matter of boundary lines.

A new necessity for the application of the principle has arisen, and the application is entirely in keeping with the spirit of the doctrine and carries out the real purpose of that doctrine. The right of American republics to work out their own destiny along lines consistent with popular government, is just as much menaced today by foreign financial interests as it was a century ago by the political aspirations of foreign governments. If the people of an American republic are left free to attend to their own affairs, no despot can long keep them in subjection; but when a local despot is held in authority by powerful financial interests, and is furnished money for the employment of soldiers, the people are as helpless as if a foreign army had landed on their shores. This, we have reason to believe, is the situation in Mexico, and I cannot see that our obligation is any less now than it was then. We must protect the people of these republics in their right to attend to their own business, free from external coercion, no matter what form that external coercion may take.

Your utterance in regard to conquest was timely. We must be relieved of suspicion as to our motives. We must be bound in advance not to turn to our own advantage any power we employ. It will be impossible for us to win the confidence of the people of Latin American, unless they know that we do not seek their territory or ourselves desire to exercise political authority over them. If we have occasion to go into any country, it must be as we went into Cuba, at the invitation of the Government, or with assurances that will leave no doubt as to the temporary character of our intervention. Our only object must be to secure to the people an opportunity to vote, that they may themselves select their rulers and establish their government.

It has occurred to me that this might be an opportune time to outline the policy which I suggested a few months ago in connection with Nicaragua, namely, the loaning of our credit to the Latin American states. They have to borrow money, and it is the money borrowed by those Governments that has put them under obligations to foreign financiers. We cannot deny them the right to borrow money, and we cannot overlook the sense of gratitude and the feeling of obligation that come with a loan. If our country, openly claiming a paramount influence in the Western Hemisphere, will go to the rescue of these countries and enable them to secure the money they need for education, sanitation and internal development, there will be no excuse for their putting themselves under obligations to financiers in other lands. I believe it is perfectly safe and will make absolutely sure our domination of the situation.

If, for instance, in the stating of your policy, you propose, with the approval of Congress, that the Government lend its credit, issuing its own bonds at three per cent., and taking the bonds of other countries at four or four and one-half per cent., the difference to be put in a sinking fund and used for the retirement of the bonds, we will offer what no one else is in a position to offer, and show that our friendship is practical and sufficient, as well as disinterested.

The loan proposition is not, of course, a necessary part of the policy you are preparing to announce, but I submit that it would be a valuable addition to it, because it would not only prove our real friendship and the depth of our interest, but it would offer to those countries an escape from the obligations which have brought them into servitude to European money lenders.

I believe that the country would respond instantly and with unanimity to the plan. The purpose, namely, (1) the desire to protect these countries from outside interference—whatever the character of that interference—is a practically unanimous desire. Second, the means of furnishing this protection will depend upon the conditions which we have to meet. It may be that the withdrawal of the encouragement given to Huerta by foreign governments may enable the Constitutionalists, with such encouragement as we can give them, to compel the holding of a real election. Third, in case of intervention, it should be temporary in its character and only for the purpose of aiding to secure an election, with the promise that we will respect the integrity of the Republic, and, Fourth, that we stand ready to assist in the maintenance and development of constitutional government by lending our credit to the lawful authorities, thus enabling them to secure, at a low rate, the money needed for their proper development.

I shall be at your command tomorrow and hold myself in readiness to call at the White House upon a moment's notice, but I thought best to put these suggestions in writing and have them ready for you on your return.

With assurances of my great respect, I am,

My dear Mr. President,

Very sincerely yours,   W. J. Bryan

TLS (WP, DLC).

1 He referred to the following portion of a report of an alleged address to the diplomatic corps on October 23: "Should the United States fail to recognize the established Mexican Government, Gen. Huerta declared, it would incur the risk of precipitating in this country a crisis, which might bring Washington face to face with the Governments at London, Paris, and Berlin, and which might lead either to the setting aside of the Monroe Doctrine, or to the appalling injustice of intervention by the United States in Mexico, bringing two friendly nations into hostile conflict, which the people of neither country wished, and which ought to be avoided." *New York Times*, Oct. 24, 1913. O'Shaughnessy reported on the following day that Huerta had said no such thing and that the report was "a gross exaggeration and misstatement." N. O'Shaughnessy to the Secretary of State, Oct. 24, 1913, T telegram (WP, DLC).

From John Bassett Moore, with Enclosure

Confidential.

[Washington]
My dear Mr. President: Tuesday, October 28, 1913.

I beg leave to enclose herewith a draft, made on Saturday,[1] of a telegram drawn, I believe, in diplomatic form, in the sense of your written instructions, handed to me by Mr. Bryan. (Enclosure 1.)

In handing to me your memorandum, I understood Mr. Bryan to suggest the inquiry whether, in connection with the course of the European Powers in recognizing the administration at the City of Mexico, the Monroe Doctrine might not be invoked, especially if it should be assumed that they acted under the influence of financial interests. I answered that the Monroe Doctrine did not appear to embrace this question. Recognition is an act performed in the ordinary course of diplomatic relations. As the independent States of America are not protectorates of the United States, we do not supervise their diplomatic relations; and it has therefore never been considered necessary for foreign Powers to ask our consent to their recognition of an American government, or to explain to us their reasons for such a step. Nor can there be any doubt that the American Governments would themselves deeply resent any attempt on our part to assume such a supervision.

They would as surely resent the attempt on our part to prevent them from obtaining European capital for their industrial development or for their governmental necessities. It is an elementary and well known fact that the United States cannot today finance even its own needs. To say nothing of the money that we have borrowed for governmental purposes, we have from the beginning developed our industries and are still developing them with foreign capital, invested under what we here call "grants" or "charters," and what the Latins call "concessions," the difference being one of language. Naturally, however, the conditions required by the investor vary with the risk. Whether a grant or concession might be of such a character as to raise a political question, as Brazil conceived to be the case with the concession made by Bolivia to the Anglo-American "Bolivian Syndicate" in the Acre territory (a territory then claimed and now owned by Brazil), would depend upon its terms. But, on the whole, in Latin-America as in the United States, the use of foreign capital has

---

[1] October 25.

helped to develop industrial and financial strength and has thus contributed to political stability and independence.

One of the latest definitions of the Monroe Doctrine is that which was given in 1901 by President Roosevelt, to whom it has not, I believe, been usual to impute undue or shrinking conservatism as a fault. It being understood that certain European Powers, particularly Germany, intended to take forcible measures in order to collect from Venezuela various pecuniary demands, President Roosevelt, in his annual message of December 3, 1901, said:

"The Monroe Doctrine is a declaration that there must be no territorial aggrandizement by any non-American power on American soil. It is in no wise intended as hostile to any nation in the Old World. * * * This doctrine has nothing to do with the commercial relations of any American power, save that it in truth allows each of them to form such as it desires. * * * We do not guarantee any State against punishment if it misconducts itself, provided that punishment does not take the form of the acquisition of territory by any non-American power."

On December 11, 1901, the German Embassy at Washington presented a pro-memoria, in which it was stated that the German Government, after delivering an ultimatum to Venezuela, intended in the first instance to institute a blockade of the more important Venezuelan ports, and that, if this measure should not be found to be sufficient, it would be necessary to consider the temporary occupation of such ports and the levying of duties in them. The German pro-memoria contained the following statement:

"We declare especially that under no circumstances do we consider in our proceedings the acquisition or the permanent occupation of Venezuelan territory."

Mr. Hay replied by a memorandum of December 16, 1901, which concluded as follows:

"The President of the United States, appreciating the courtesy of the German Government in making him acquainted with the state of affairs referred to, *and not regarding himself as called upon to enter into the consideration of the claims in question*, believes that no measures will be taken in this matter by the agents of the German Government which are not in accordance with the well-known purpose, above set forth, of his Majesty the German Emperor."

Before proceeding upon the assumption that foreign governments, in recognizing and continuing to recognize the administration at the City of Mexico, have acted in a spirit of subserviency to financial interests, it would seem to be expedient to consider the subject in all its aspects. One of these is the fact that that administration has since its installation been the only government at the Mexican capital, and that we have ourselves accordingly continued to conduct diplomatic relations with it, though without formal recognition. Nor is such a situation by any means unprecedented. The Diaz government was officially recognized by various European Powers in 1877, almost a year before its recognition by the United States, our recognition having been delayed for the purpose of bringing pressure to bear to secure the performance by the new government of certain obligations, particularly with reference to the suppression of border troubles and the payment of a large sum of money due under the Claims Convention of 1868. Our Government took no notice of the recognition of Diaz by other Powers, nor was it assumed that this was a question with regard to which other Powers were obliged to consult us.

The recognition by Great Britain of the present administration at the City of Mexico was sent out on the 1st of April and was officially presented on the 3d of May. That of Spain was also despatched on the 1st of April. Colombia gave her recognition on the 5th of May. That of France was given, as was also that of Austria-Hungary, on the 12th of May. Japan and Salvador gave their recognition on the 13th of the same month; Italy, Germany, Portugal, and China on the 17th; Belgium and Guatemala on the 21st, and Norway on the 25th. Russia recognized the government on the 1st of June. Switzerland and Honduras are stated to have extended their recognition in July. It thus appears that recognition was extended by seventeen governments, four of which were American; and our records indicate that other American governments would have followed suit if the United States had extended recognition.

There is nothing in the record to show that the governments that recognized the administration at the City of Mexico in May, June, and July last felt that they were doing anything unusual or requiring explanation, or that they were actuated by any other design than that of recognizing, in conformity with practice, what appeared to them to be the only governmental authority holding out the prospect of being able to re-establish order in the country. Nor had the United States said anything to indicate to them that it entertained a different view of their conduct. On the contrary, the first statement made by the United States of its own position was that which was conveyed to Mr. Henry Lane

Wilson, then Ambassador to Mexico, on the 15th of June; and this was a statement called forth by his urgent request. It appears by the records that Mr. Wilson tendered his resignation as Ambassador on the 5th of March. On the 17th of May he insisted upon its immediate presentation to the President. On the 9th of June, his resignation not having been accepted, he asked to be furnished with a statement by telegraph of the views and policy of the President, in a confidential way, in order that he might reflect them. It was in response to this request that Mr. Wilson was furnished with a "personal statement" of the President's position. This message was declared to be confidential and to be intended for his personal guidance in response to his request of the 9th of the month, and not to be intended as a message to the Mexican authorities. Nor was it communicated to foreign governments. The first public announcement of the policy of the United States was made in the President's message to Congress of the 27th of August. The circumstance that other governments have not since withdrawn their recognition is by no means remarkable. Recognition, once given, continues till the government falls or is replaced, or till severance of diplomatic relations, which is in itself an unfriendly act. The mere withdrawal of a Minister, leaving relations in charge of a secretary, does not operate as a withdrawal of recognition. Of these facts it is pertinent to take note in judging the motives and conduct of other governments, as well as in discussing the grounds on which they may be asked to reconsider their action.

A striking illustration of the spirit in which the governments have been acting has come to me only this morning. The Italian Ambassador,[2] calling on a matter of business, stated that a new Minister was on his way from Italy to Mexico and intimated the hope that this would not be considered as being in any way offensive to the United States, the press having intimated that we were offended at the presentation by Carden of his credentials. He said that the sending of a new Minister by Italy was in fact primarily due to his own suggestion; that when the government of the United States in August, in view of a possible crisis growing out of the sending of Mr. Lind to Mexico, invoked the aid of the European and other governments to impress upon Huerta the propriety and necessity of giving serious consideration to what Mr. Lind had to say, the Italian government was obliged to reply that it had no Minister at the City of Mexico and was able to speak only to the Mexican Minister at Rome. The Ambassador then suggested to his government that it was hardly

2 Marquis Cusani Confalonieri.

respectful to the United States not to be able to meet its wishes more directly, and that it ought to send out a new Minister, which has now been done. He seemed to be much disturbed lest he had misinterpreted our wishes and done something to displease us.

Before inferring that other governments, in failing to act in accordance with views which we subsequently announced, were actuated by motives that were either unfriendly or censurable, it is important to reflect upon our telegram of the 8th of August, above mentioned.

In considering the effect of a particular or special imputation to the government of Great Britain of improper or sordid motives for its course in Mexico, it may be expedient to view the situation somewhat broadly. I do not refer particularly to the fact that, while British oil interests are said to have given Huerta their support, certain oil interests in the United States have been equally pronounced in antagonism to him. There are still other matters to be taken into account. Among these may be mentioned the following:

1. The exemption by act of Congress of America "coastwise" vessels from tolls in the Panama Canal is regarded and is no doubt deeply resented by Great Britain as a violation by the United States of a solemn treaty. Without regard to the question whether this view is necessarily correct, account should be taken of the fact that the contention of the British Government has been unreservedly sustained by many persons of authority in the United States, including a former Secretary of State[3] of great distinction, who has in the discharge of his public duties had occasion to discuss the effect of the treaty. The exemption was advocated by the coastwise shipping interests, which constitute perhaps the closest monopoly in the United States.

2. Various arbitration treaties, of very limited scope, made for the purpose of simply renewing similar treaties previously existing, remain unacted upon in the Senate; and it is a notorious fact that this is due to the apprehension that the treaty with Great Britain embraces an obligation to arbitrate the tolls question.

3. On the eve of the meeting of an International Congress, which we ourselves were instrumental in convoking and in which we are to be ably represented, the Senate has adopted what is known as the Seamen's Bill, which not only embraces matters on which we have agreed to confer with other Powers but which proposes to deny to other governments the right to regulate even the terms of shipment of their own seamen on their own ves-

3 Elihu Root.

sels in their own ports, and to subject these matters to our own legislation. It is not denied that this strikes most directly at Germany and Great Britain.

4. Because of the opposition of local interests in Michigan and Puget Sound, our treaty with Great Britain of April 11, 1908, for the preservation of food fishes in waters contiguous to the United States and Canada, has remained unexecuted on our part, although it was carried into effect on the part of Canada two years ago.

The clause in the new tariff act providing for a five per cent discount on goods imported in American vessels opens to us the prospect of serious questions with the leading maritime powers.

These things are enumerated not for the purpose of offsetting a grievance on one side with a grievance on the other, but for the more important purpose of suggesting whether anything short of the clearest proof would at this juncture justify us in attributing to other governments, by means of a direct diplomatic communication, motives the imputation of which they would necessarily repel and resent. Expressions in the foreign press during the past week indicate a great reluctance in England and in other European countries to get into difficulties with us over Mexico under any circumstances whatever. It is not desirable to check this disposition.

With regard to the present proposed communication to foreign governments, there is, finally, one thought to be borne in mind. As we have, since the sending of Governor Lind to Mexico, held towards that country an attitude of interposition in its internal affairs, though not as yet in the physical sense, it may not be advisable too strongly to urge those governments to follow our example. For this reason they are not asked to "cooperate" with us.

I beg leave to annex hereto two documents relating to Mexican affairs in and prior to 1860. I mentioned them to Mr. Bryan yesterday, and, as he expressed an interest in them, I enclose them.

One is an extract from President Buchanan's Annual Message of December 19, 1859. (Enclosure 2.)[4]

The other is a summary of two treaties between the United States and Mexico concluded at Vera Cruz on December 14, 1859, for the purpose, among other things, of providing the Mexican Government with some ready cash. (Enclosure 3.)

These treaties were not approved by the Senate.

Very respectfully yours,   John B. Moore.

TLS (WP, DLC).
  [4] This and the following enclosure are not printed.

E N C L O S U R E

The Government of the United States desires in the existing critical situation in Mexico to lay before the other governments which maintain diplomatic relations with that country a statement of its views in the hope that they may find it practicable to act in harmony with the course which this Government feels obliged to pursue. The interests of other Governments in Mexico are chiefly commercial, but conditions in that country affect not only the material interests of the United States but also the life, the happiness, the liberty and the essential welfare of all the peoples of this hemisphere, and particularly of the peoples of Central America. The interest and responsibility of the United States as an American nation stand therefore in a case by themselves. It is the belief of the President that the Government of Huerta, based upon usurpation and force, would long ago have broken down but for the encouragement and financial aid derived directly or indirectly from its recognition by other nations. The United States has steadily refused to recognize that government or to give approval to its continuance. On the other hand, this Government has desired to avoid the adoption in Mexico of a policy of domination and physical force, and, while refraining from physical intervention, has sought to exert the pressure of moral force for the purpose of bringing about a better condition of things. This Government is not prepared to entertain the supposition that there has existed on the part of other governments an intention to antagonize and thwart its benevolent purposes, but the encouragement given to Huerta seems to have been his chief support in refusing to take such measures as would result in the establishment of a peaceful and constitutional order. Having in view the attainment of these ends, the Government of the United States would be glad to be assured of the disposition of other governments to act in harmony with its policy. It is proper to add that although this Government is not now contemplating armed intervention in Mexico, yet, if conditions requiring such action should arise, it would, in accordance with its traditional policy, assume full and sole responsibility for such measures as it might take.

You are instructed to confer with the Minister of Foreign Affairs and communicate to him the views set forth in this telegram.

T MS (WP, DLC).

From George Sibley Johns

Dear Mr President: [St. Louis, c. Oct. 28, 1913]

One Annabel Lee—I know not whether she is the lady embalmed by Poe in Poetic honey or not, but that she has a fondness for haunting verse is proved by her request for a collection of limericks, which she says, on your authority, were written in partnership by you and me in Princeton days.

I am ignorant of any such collection. I know of only one masterpiece of that age, written by me and preserved in memory by you. If you perpetrated limericks at Princeton they were carefully concealed, doubtless for a good reason. If they have been discovered and traced to their origin it is a great misfortune to the country. The Democratic regime is doomed. The Wilson mask of dignity and sense is off—all is lost.

I know the dictum that the king can do no wrong is applied to Presidents who have the privilege of shifting their mistakes, inanities, follies and unveracities upon others, but spare me in my obscure content the infamy of reputed fatherhood to your youthful villainies in verse.

Otherwise, I shall be compelled in self defense to publish this—

A Prex who with nerve was quite flush
Wrote verse that would make a dog blush
When charged with the stuff
He got in a huff
And swore that his friend penned the slush.

Yours sincerely   Geo S. Johns

ALS (WP, DLC).

Walter Hines Page to William Jennings Bryan

London, October 28, 1913

I have just come from an hour's talk with Grey about Mexico. He showed me his telegram to Carden asking about Carden's reported interview criticising the United States and Carden's flat denial. He showed me another telegram to Carden about Huerta's reported boast that he would have backing of London, Paris, and Berlin against the United States in which Grey advised Carden that British policy should be to keep aloof from Huerta's boasts and plans. Carden denies that Huerta made such boast in his statement to the Diplomatic Corps. Grey wishes for the President to know of these telegrams. I thanked Grey for his promise to wait until the President's statement should be received. Grey volunteered the information that Carden had not asked for warship and that none had been sent.

Talk then became personal and informal. I went over the whole subject, again telling how the press and people of the United States were becoming critical of the British Government; that they regarded the problem as wholly American; that they resented aid to Huerta whom they regarded as a mere tyrant; that they suspected British interests of giving financial help to Huerta; that many newspapers and persons refused to believe Carden's denial; that the President's ploicy [policy] was not academic but was the only policy that would square with American ideals, and that it was unchangeable. I cited our treatment of Cuba. I explained again that I was talking unofficially and giving him only my own interpretation of the people's mood. He asked if British Government should withdraw recognition of Huerta what would happen. I replied, "in my own opinion he would soon collapse." Grey said, "what would happen then, worse chaos?" I said, "that is impossible." "There is no worse chaos than deputies in jail, dictatorial doubling of tariff, suppression of opinion and practical banishment of independent men. If Huerta fell there was hope that suppressed men and opinion would set up successful Government." He asked, "suppose that fails, what then?" I have replied in case of continued and utter failure the United States might feel obliged to repeat its dealings with Cuba, and that continued excitement of opinion in the United States might precipitate this.

Grey protested he knew nothing of what British interests had done or were doing; that he wished time to think the matter out; and that he was glad to await the President's communication[.] He thanked me cordially for my frank statements and declared he understood perfectly their personal nature. I impressed him with seriousness of American public opinion.

I think he has complete confidence in Carden; that he credits his disavowals, and thinks that he, Grey, cannot and ought not to do more with this aspect of the matter. I have hope that the President's strong statement and mutterings of popular disapproval in the United States may cause withdrawal of recognition of Huerta. But British investors of every sort would doubtless complain and this Government is now in sore straits because of domestic troubles. Strong influences in Cabinet if not elsewhere will have to be overcome.   Page.

T telegram (SDR, RG 59, 812.00/9442, DNA).

Sir Edward Grey to Sir Cecil Arthur Spring Rice[1]

Private.

My dear Spring-Rice, London, 28 October 1913.

The American Ambassador came to see me to-day. After thanking me most cordially for my promise to wait before taking any decision about the result of the Mexican elections till I had received the expected communication from President Wilson, he proceeded to say that he would like to talk to me about the feeling in the United States. He had thought of asking his Government whether they would let him say to me all that was in his mind, but he considered that they would possibly answer: no; and he had therefore decided to talk to me unofficially and personally, without consulting them.

He said that he was made most anxious by the news that he received from the United States as regards the feeling that was rising there. It was producing, he would not say exactly ill-will, but a very critical mood as regards this country. The feeling was probably founded on misapprehension and misstatements; there was certainly nothing in the attitude of the British Government to cause it; but there it was. It was believed in the United States that British commercial interests in Mexico had financed Huerta.

I said at once that no British interests in Mexico had given me even a hint that this was the case, and I could only say that I knew nothing whatever about it.

The Ambassador said that it was very likely a misapprehension, and certainly a thing of which there was no proof. The trouble was that it had come to be believed in the United States.

He went on to say that there were articles in the British Press describing President Wilson's views as idealistic and fantastic. This was bound to give offence in the United States. To people there it seemed the most elementary thing that government must be based on the consent of the governed. The description of this opinion as idealistic and fantastic could arise only from a failure to understand the American point of view. Feeling about Mexico was rising in the United States with a rapidity and intensity that made him very anxious. It might sweep every thing before it, and lead to intervention. He had not so far had any sign of this in what he had received from his Government, and he had so far communicated to me every thing that he had received from them, but he had the impression that President Wilson was now for the first time beginning to fear that intervention might come. In that event, the United States would go into Mexico, and they would hold the elections with bayonets round every polling

station, to ensure that the people voted secretly and with freedom, so that the result of the elections might be the choice of
the people. There could be no question of the United States taking any Mexican territory: that would be resented by their own
people.

I said that intervention such as he suggested would be a very
big operation.

He replied that it would: but however many millions it cost,
if the American people decided to act, they would vote any thing
that was required.

I observed that, if there were in Mexico an element of sufficient
importance and of a sufficiently high moral standard to produce
the sort of government that the United States wished to see established, and American intervention put it in power, no doubt some
result would have been achieved. But, if no such element existed,
I did not see how intervention such as he outlined would produce
the result desired.

The Ambassador said that the United States had had to go
into Cuba twice to get the result there for which they wished,
but they had at last made the Cubans understand that they
must elect a government that had the consent of the people, and
that they must govern themselves in that way. It was true that a
similar operation in Mexico would be a much bigger thing. After
the elections had been held there, the Americans would
gradually withdraw. But, if necessary, they would hold elections
again and again in the same way, until they produced the same
result in Mexico as they had in Cuba. The President would have
the whole country behind him in an undertaking of this sort.
As a sign of this, the Ambassador told me that even the "New
York Sun," which was one of the most bitter opponents of the
President came out every day with a quotation from the Monroe
Doctrine, as a sort of intimation to the President that, however
much they might attack him in other matters, in this matter he
had the whole country behind him.

I observed that no one was countervening the Monroe Doctrine
as regards Mexico. We ourselves had not even sent a warship to
Mexican waters. Sir Lionel Carden would be perfectly right to
ask for a ship if it was necessary to protect British lives and property, but he had not yet done so, though it was the sort of thing
that he would have done if he had been pursuing a pushing or
forward policy.

The Ambassador admitted that no one was infringing the
Monroe Doctrine. He had given me this illustration only to show

how strong the feeling was in the United States, and the sort of excitement that existed.

He deprecated very much the statement in some British newspapers that financial interests in America dictated President Wilson's policy. This was ludicrous: because the financial interests had been hanged and quartered as far as the President's policy was concerned.

I said that I was quite sure that it was untrue that the President's policy was dictated by American financial interests; but the suspicion that Americans felt about British financial interests in Mexico provoked counter-suspicion here: that, for instance, American Oil Companies, who had not interests in Mexico, wished to see the chaos there continue, to prevent the export of Mexican oil that competed with their own.

The Ambassador spoke in a very friendly tone throughout, informally and unofficially, and evidently with great desire that the excitement in the United States should be allayed, but also with great anxiety as to how this could be done.

In the course of the conversation, I read to him the three telegrams that had passed between Sir Lionel Carden and myself, as recorded in my telegram to you, number: 291.

I gathered from the Ambassador that the Government of the United States would never recognize Huerta, that they believed he would have collapsed before now if European nations had not recognized him and that if we would withdraw recognition of him now, it would result either in his being displaced in Mexico by some one better or else in such an increase of chaos that the United States would have to intervene. Either of these alternatives seemed to the Ambassador to be better than the existing state of things. I said in reply to this that it was hardly reasonable that we should take a step to promote chaos.

Yours sincerely   E. Grey.

TLS (FO 800/241, pp. 351-54, PRO).
  1 The gist of this letter was sent via wire in E. Grey to C. A. Spring Rice, Oct. 28, 1913 (FO 371/1677, p. 357, PRO).

From Andrew Furuseth

Dear Mr. President: Washington, D. C. October 29, 1913.

It was indeed a surprise to me and to every seaman, that I was appointed a commissioner from the United States to participate in the International Conference on Safety of Life at Sea. Neither I nor any of the men whom I represent can understand it, except from the point of view that you desire the great body of seamen, the men before the mast, to be represented at that conference in order that the hopes, aspirations and experience of the seamen may be heard there. With this idea in my mind, I am profoundly grateful that you selected me. I shall try to serve to the best of my ability and above all to be true to the best interests of safety of life at sea; in so doing I shall be true to the highest hopes and aspirations of the seamen and, as I believe, to the best interests of our country.

Again expressing my profound gratitude, I beg to remain,
Respectfully and loyally,
Your obedient servant,   Andrew Furuseth

TLS (WP, DLC).

From John Franklin Jameson

Washington, D. C.
My dear Mr. President: October 29, 1913.

There are two historical matters about which I should like to be allowed to speak to you a few minutes, if you ever have any time to spare for such a purpose.[1] One is the matter of a National Archive Building, in respect to which I am charged by the American Historical Association to do everything that I can, but which has for some time hung fire in Congress. The other is the matter of a proper Commission on National Historical Publications, of which I wrote to you before your inauguration, sending a report of a provisional committee on the subject.

I have been either out of the country or out of Washington most of the time since your administration began, but have had great happiness in watching from afar its progress and its success.

Believe me, with the most abundant good wishes,
Very sincerely yours,   J. F. Jameson.

TLS (WP, DLC).
[1] On an attached note, Wilson wrote: "Please remind me to ask Dr. Jameson to lunch W.W." The White House diaries do not record when he came.

To Walter Hines Page

Washington, Oct. 29, 1913.
Am pleased with your reported conversation with Foreign Office. You followed exactly the right line. Watch for New York Herald of yesterday containing full report of President's speech at Mobile. It has been very enthusiastically endorsed in this country and indicates the President's line of thought. In conversa-

tions with British Chargé I have emphasized the same idea, namely, that the whole trouble in Mexico is due to the active influence of foreign investors who are denying to the people there the right to run their own government.   Bryan

CLST telegram (SDR, RG 59, 812.00/9442, DNA).

John Lind to William Jennings Bryan

Vera Cruz, Mexico. Oct. 29, 1913.

My evidence is growing stronger every day that Carden knew about coup d'etat in advance of its occurrence. The French Consul here in a written statement to me asserts that the four Vera Cruz Legislators who were taken from the MORRO CASTLE were apprehended and imprisoned because they refused to take action required in the interest of Lord Cowdary's concession in that State. I am investigating this question carefully. I trust you will not think me obsessed upon the subject.

I am so persistent in urging it upon your attention at this time is because I believe that it will save us untold complications if this Congress, conceived in fraud and corruption, is not permitted to convene on November fifteenth as is the plan. With adequate encouragement the rebels could be before the gates of Mexico before that time if no other plan is contemplated.

Lind.

T telegram (WP, DLC).

Remarks at a Press Conference

October [30] 1913

Mr. President, could you give us an idea of how long you are going to take before making your communication on the subject of the new policy?

You mean to whom?

I don't know, sir. Whether to us or to the foreign nations?

Why, as a matter of fact, what I have seen in the newspapers about my intentions was news to me. You are talking about my preparing a note for the foreign powers. Now that is not so, and I am very much instructed every day by what I learn of my intentions. But I am somewhat surprised and, therefore, that is one reason why I can't answer your question, Mr. Mann.[1]

Mr. President, not to betray the confidence of anybody at the head of the State Department, we certainly got the information over there the other day that you had asked all the powers or all the nations, rather, that had diplomatic representatives in Mexico, to defer action as a result of the elections until this government had an opportunity of defining a policy or communicating with them.

> Why, that is a very different proposition.

Yes, sir. I understand as to the form.

> You see, you asked me when I would be ready to make a communication. Now, whether I shall make any communication or not to anybody in particular remains to be determined. You see, there are two ways of handling a thing. You can talk or you can act. I don't mean to intimate either.

Mr. President, it is stated this morning in an Associated Press dispatch that you will present a plan or a new policy to the cabinet tomorrow.

> I can hardly do that, because there isn't going to be a meeting of the cabinet.

Mr. President, I did not think we were wrong in assuming that you were going to communicate to the powers what you are going to do.

> I am not trying, gentlemen, to play hide and seek with you. I am trying to convey to you the real situation, that I am waiting for things to come to me in definite shape, as the result of last Sunday.² I can't communicate, even to myself, what I am going to do until I am informed.

The foreign governments understand that?

> They understand that, and they are waiting for the same thing. Yes, we are entirely in touch with one another, and they are all waiting to see just what shape things take down there.

Mr. President, the United States is continuing to act independently, is it not, in this matter? It has entered into no arrangement of cooperative action?

> It has entered into no such arrangement.

In other words, Mr. President, there have been a number of reports of friction with other governments over this issue. Is there anything in that?

> No, sir, there is not. There hasn't been the slightest friction with any other government.

Well, Mr. President, then is it fair for us to say that the policy has not been formulated yet because it is dependent upon the result of certain things in Mexico?

> Well, I don't know just how to answer that question. It

would not be fair to make the statement in any such way as to imply that I didn't have very definite notions about it, but I dare say the right way to state it is that things are not in such shape as to make the announcement of our policy opportune.

In other words, you don't know, really, the result of these elections?

I don't want to set up a straw man and knock him down.

You don't know whether Huerta is going to retire or whether General Blanquet is to be president or Huerta is to go to the head of the army?

You see, they haven't declared what they understand the results of the elections to be.

Mr. President, to get a little bit deeper, the foreign nations won't know formally from you, or otherwise, what you are going to do until you do it?

Well, I am not making any promises at all.

I drew that distinction between now acting and telling people.

Naturally, they won't hear anything from us until we have something to say, but that is about all it comes to.

And there is no note?

None in my possession, nor in my head.

Mr. President, I am not quite clear yet as to whether—as to how you are going to make this known. I didn't quite understand what you meant by saying—

Of course, both the method and the action itself would have to go together. The best method of things must wait to be determined until the thing is done, so you see the form goes along with the substance necessarily.

Mr. President, are you awaiting a report from Mr. Lind on last Sunday's election?

Yes, we get reports every day from Mr. Lind. Nobody down there knows more than we do.

I saw on one of these bulletin sheets that Mr. Lind is forming a detailed statement to be mailed to you.

I dare say he is. He follows up dispatches with letters from time to time, but I don't know that that refers to anything in particular.

I thought, perhaps, you were waiting for this detailed report by mail? Mr. President, with reference to the foreign nations' acting, may we know a little more definitely how far their assurances have gone, and in return how far we have gone in promises of protection?

You gentlemen seem to think that there has been a very

lively conversation between us. You have heard all that I know already from the State Department, and heard during my absence, so that I got it by telegraph just at the same time you did. It was perfectly proper that you should learn that. But just as a matter of fact.

Mr. President, isn't that expression "cooperation" a misnomer? Isn't it a fact that there isn't any cooperation, simply because they are waiting and worried what we are going to do?

Well, of course, cooperation is mainly a matter of action and, to me, more a matter of counsel. They are certainly not standing in our way. . . .

Mr. President, has any one of the foreign nations, as we understand the term, conveyed to this government in any shape or form any concrete thing that it proposed to do in Mexico?

Well, now, gentlemen, do I have to go over that ground again and again? I have given you all that I know about the subject. There hasn't been any interchange of proposals at all.

They have made none?

I understand my language to mean that. I don't know how you interpret the English language. Really, I don't think it's quite good, going from a general to a specific statement, by making me repeat it in explicit details each time.

Mr. President, I think that your remark entirely concurs with nine tenths of the people here. I don't think you ought to be subjected—

I don't like to submit a bill of particulars after I cover a thing. . . .

Mr. President, has there been any communication with the Constitutionalists, particularly since Sunday's election?

Neither before nor since.

JRT transcript (WC, NjP) of CLSsh (C. L. Swem Coll., NjP).
  1 Unidentified.
  2 The Mexican election of October 26.

To John Bassett Moore

My dear Mr. Moore: The White House October 30, 1913

Thank you very warmly indeed for your letter accompanying the note which you so kindly drew up at my request concerning the Mexican situation, and also for the very interesting and useful enclosures. I had quite forgotten how close an analogy to the present situation existed in 1857.

May I not give myself the pleasure of saying how indispensable your counsel and assistance are?

Cordially and faithfully yours,   Woodrow Wilson

TLS (J. B. Moore Papers, DLC).

To Jesse Floyd Welborn

My dear Sir: [The White House] October 30, 1913

As you know, the Department of Labour of the federal government is empowered by act of Congress to exercise its good offices in trade and labour disputes for the purpose, if possible, of bringing about a just and amicable settlement. The attention of the Department having been called, as indeed, the attention of the whole country has been, to the distressing situation in the mines of the Colorado Fuel and Iron Company, Mr. Ethelbert Stewart, a trusted representative of the Department, was deputed to attempt to bring about conferences between the operators and the miners that would lay the basis for a settlement. His efforts were not welcomed or responded to in the spirit in which they were made, and he reports that he has met with complete failure.

I feel that the efforts of the Department are of so much importance to the country in matters of this kind, and I am personally so deeply disappointed that the Department's suggestions should have been rejected, that I now take the liberty of asking from the responsible officers of the Colorado Fuel and Iron Company a full and frank statement of the reasons which have led them to reject counsels of peace and accommodation in a matter now grown so critical. It will probably be my duty to report upon the case to the Congress and I do not wish to speak without full information.

Very truly yours,   Woodrow Wilson[1]

TLS (Letterpress Books, WP, DLC).
[1] There is a WWT draft of this letter in WP, DLC.

To George Sibley Johns

My dear Johns: The White House October 30, 1913

I have had a very good laugh over your letter about Miss Annabel Lee's request. I can't for the life of me imagine what she is thinking of, for, of course, I never told her there was any collection of limericks which we had jointly produced. I have been at some pains in recent months to convince people that I never wrote a limerick in my life, though I have given currency to some which I have taken great pleasure in repeating. You would certainly be justified in taking any revenge if I palmed off my "youthful villainies in verse" on you or anybody else. As a matter of fact, I at least had discretion enough not to try to write in rhyme.

Cordially and faithfully yours,   Woodrow Wilson

TLS (G. S. Johns Papers, MoSHi).

From the Diary of Colonel House

October 30, 1913.

I lunched at the White House. I sat by Mrs. Wilson. She is interested in the betterment of conditions surrounding Government employees, particularly the women. She thought mail bags should be disinfected; they were filthy and there was an unusual number of consumption [consumptives] in the Postoffice Department which was thought to have been largely brought about by the unsanitary conditions of mail bags. She said Burleson was opposed to doing anything in this direction.

The entire table was listening to us by this time, and I replied that Burleson had told me he did not fear microbes, that during the day he killed them with tobacco and at night he killed the tobacco microbes with whiskey. However, I promised Mrs. Wilson to take it up and see that something was done along the lines of her suggestion. . . .

After that, the President, McAdoo and I went into his study. . . .

We talked of the Mexican question which, for the moment, is absorbing his attention. He read us some memoranda[1] upon which he intended to base his message to Congress. He said this memoranda was "stripped to the bone" but when he wrote the full message he would elaborate upon it. His idea in brief is to insist that Huerta permit the status of affairs to go back where they began when Madero was assassinated, that is the former Congress should be restored and they should be permitted to elect his successor. He was determined not to allow the financiers control or supercede political control.

In other words in former years, the Monroe Doctrine was announced in order to keep Europe from securing political control of any of the states in the Western Hemisphere. The President thinks it is just as reprehensible to permit foreign states to secure financial control of these weak and unfortunate republics, and he will make that the keynote of his message. It is a new interpretation or elaboration of the Monroe Doctrine. I asked him if he had felt out the powers upon this point. He had not. He thought the British Government was undoubtedly backing Sir Lionel Carden in his efforts to maintain Huerta in order that Huerta in turn should maintain the present concessions to Lord Cowdrey's oil companies, and to legalize and grant him further concessions later.

The President is determined the British public shall know of this alliance between the Mexican Government and oil interests, and he believes British public opinion will be so strong against them that if it does not overthrow the present Ministry it will compel them to recede from their attitude.

When he said it was his purpose to build a fire back of the British Ministry through the English public, I thought of Philip Dru and of the suggestion I made there to do just this thing though for another purpose.

The President said the Huerta regime was practically at the end of its rope when Sir Lionel Carden gave it renewed life. He recalled the fact that when Dudley Malone was in Dublin, N. H. this summer, Sir Cecil Spring-Rice told him if his Government said or did anything we objected to about affairs recognized to be wholly within our jurisdiction, we should tell them frankly to remain quiet. I told him I had received a cablegram from Page requesting me to meet Sir William Tyrrell[2] who landed upon the Imperator yesterday, but that I did not receive the message until I was leaving for the Washington train.

I had called the British Embassy over the telephone and they said Sir William was going directly to Dublin, N. H. to be with Sir Cecil Spring-Rice. I promised the President I would get in touch with him and would feel out the situation.

I recalled to the President my conversation with Sir Edward Grey[3] in which I told him to bear in mind that the President's views and attitude of mind were quite different from Mr. Bryan's; that he, the President, was not only unafraid, but he did not look upon war in the same spirit as our Secretary of State, and he was not a man to be trifled with.

I asked the President how Mr. Bryan would feel about supporting such an aggressive policy as he had in mind. He said he was leading him gradually along and, up to the present, he had not baulked, and he thought he would consent to do every [thing] the situation demanded.

We discussed the feasibility of recognizing the Constitutionalists as belligerants in order that they might obtain arms and ammunition upon the same terms as the Federalists. The President has in mind to declare war against Mexico even though actual armed entrance into Mexico is not made. His purpose in this is to keep the powers from interfering and entirely out of the situation. He will first blockade the ports, thereby cutting off all revenue from the Mexican Government which will have a tendancy to break down Huerta's resistance.

He has in mind also throwing a line across the southern part of Mexico, and perhaps another line just south of the Northern States. He plans to send troops to the Northern States, if they consent, in order to protect the lives and property of foreign citizens. These troops would be stationed at strategic points, but would not be intended to contend against either the Constitutionalists or Federals unless some overt act was made by one or the other.

It is his purpose to send six battleships at once. A real crisis has arisen and I advised the President to go to the crux of the matter at once and say to Huerta he must restore the status of affairs as it was before he came into power or we would take forcible measures to bring it about. I did not think he should be given long to answer. I thought if he temporized with Huerta he would make promises, and conditions would drift along as now.

The President seems alert and unafraid. He realizes that his course may possibly bring about a coalition of the European Powers against this Government, but he seems ready to throw our gauntlet into the arena and declare all hands must be kept off excepting our own.

[1] Undoubtedly another copy of the outline for a circular note printed at Oct. 24, 1913.
[2] Tyrrell was coming, actually, to fill in temporarily for the ailing Spring Rice.
[3] House lunched with Grey at his London residence on July 3, 1913. They discussed, among other things, Bryan's "cooling-off" treaties.

A Draft of a Joint Resolution

[c. Oct. 31, 1913]

Resolved

[I] That it is the duty of the United States to demand, and the Government of the United States does hereby demand, that those who have thus usurped authority in Mexico, in contempt of her constitution and in disregard of the rights of her people, immediately surrender their force and authority into the hands of the Mexican Congress recently forcibly dissolved and make way in every respect for the restoration of the government chosen and sanctioned by the people of Mexico under their existing constitution.

II That the President of the United States be, and he hereby is, directed and empowered to use the entire land and naval forces of the United States and to call into the active service of the United States the militia of the several states to such extent as he may deem necessary to carry these resolutions into effect. III That the United States hereby solemnly disclaims any disposition or intention to exercise sovereignty, jurisdiction, or control over the states of Mexico except for the purpose of assisting in the restoration of the constitutional government therein, and asserts its determination, when that end is accomplished, to leave the government and control of the republic to its own people and their regularly constituted authorities, without dictation or interference of any kind.

T transcript (WC, NjP) of WWsh (C. L. Swem Coll., NjP).

A Draft of an Address to Congress

[c. Oct. 31, 1913]

Once more it has become my duty to call your attention to the unhappy posture of affairs in the Republic of Mexico, our neighbour, and to suggest the position which it seems to me we ought to take as her nearest friend, whose political and national interests are in many vital respects necessarily linked very closely with her own.

Mexico has no government. The attempt to maintain one at the City of Mexico has broken down, and a mere military despotism been set up which has hardly more than the shadowy semblance of national authority. It originated in the treason of Victoriano Huerta, who, after a brief attempt to play the part of constitutional president, has at last cast aside even the pretense of legal right and declared himself dictator.

This dictator, as he is without support of law or right, is also without force or means to establish order or give the nation a single controlling instrument of authority; and, even if he succeeded, could establish nothing but a precarious and hateful power which could last but a little while, and whose early downfall would leave the country in a more lamentable condition than ever.

The continuance of his command of an army and his unlicensed domination of the capital and the country immediately dependent upon it must certainly bring upon Mexico deep, perhaps irrevocable ruin, political, industrial, and social, whose effects will inevitably extend far beyond her own territory and create conditions under which neither her own people nor the citizens of other countries resident within her borders can be safeguarded even in even their most elementary and fundamental personal rights.

The paramount duty in the circumstances rests upon us, because of our long-established and universally recognized position with regard to the political development of the states of the western hemisphere and the legitimate and inevitable implications of that position.

We are bound by every obligation of honour and by the compulsion of sacred interests which go to the very foundations of our national life to constitute ourselves the champions of constitutional government and of the integrity and independence of free states throughout America, North and South. It is our duty to study the conditions which make constitutional government possible for our neighbour states in this hemisphere, as for ourselves, and, knowing those conditions, to suffer neither our own people nor the citizens or governments of other countries (if we may be so happy as to dissuade or prevent them) to violate them or to render them impossible of realization.

Again and again we have seen the same thing happen in those states of Latin America which have been so weak or so unfortunate as not to have governments at all times securely fortified against revolution. The ambition of some one man or of some small group of men has led to an attack upon the government and to its overturn, to the suspension of every guarantee of law or order, not in order to effect useful reforms otherwise impossible, but to afford the leaders of the revolution themselves an opportunity to grow rich by exploiting the resources of the country. Generally they have exploited those resources by granting to outsiders who were willing to pay for them in cash extensive concessions, unlimited private rights. Having got what they themselves wanted, they passed off the stage; but left their despoiled country to fare as best it might under the burdens their grants and concessions had imposed, and under the direction of foreign financiers, backed by foreign governments, rather than of their own regularly constituted authorities.

Revolutions just such as Victoriano Huerta has for the time effected in Mexico have been in the past the unmaking, or at least the serious and lasting embarrassment of constitutional government and national independence in other countries of

Latin America. The whole civilized world will wish to see the repetition of such things in Mexico prevented. In just such circumstances as those existing there may outsiders step in, whether from the United States or from elsewhere, and upon cheap terms of temporary financial assistance gain permanent rights and advantages for themselves which may embarrass the whole future of the struggling republic. Such men with such purposes may spring up from any quarter to feed upon the disordered country; and the injury they may do the free constitutional development of Mexico may be out of all proportion to their intentions or their immediate enterprise. Foreign financiers, from whatever quarter they come, our own people also, are but indifferent guardians of national independence.

It is our plain duty to hold our own citizens back from such undertakings, entered upon at such times, when caution and deliberation are out of the question, and it is equally our duty to do all that we can to safeguard our neighbours to the south against revolutions and personal usurpations of power such as will expose them to similar selfish and fatal enterprises on the part of citizens of other countries over whom we have no right of control and perhaps no influence of any kind. Constitutional development and material exploitation from without are absolutely incompatible if capital goes in when all the safeguards are down.

Therefore we must demand

a) the immediate and complete reconstitution of the national congress of Mexico recently dissolved;

b) the handing over to that body by General Huerta of the authority he claimed to derive from it and then took away from it by an arbitrary suspension of the constitution and the laws;

c) a declaration of amnesty by the congress and an invitation to delegates from the states now in revolution to join it;

d) the constitution by the body thus organized of a provisional government;

e) early elections under the direction of that provisional government for the choice of a new congress and a new executive to act under the constitution of Mexico as it stood before the usurpation of February.[1]

WWT MS (WP, DLC).
[1] There is a WWsh draft of this message dated "Oct., '13," in WP, DLC.

To Nelson O'Shaughnessy

[Nov. 1, 1913]

Convey the following, in confidence, to the Minister of Foreign Affairs, in view of his recent conversations with you, and the impressions you have received from them:

1. That the President of the United States feels that the recent coup d'etat was in direct contravention of the assurances that had been conveyed to his government by General Huerta;

2. That, unless General Huerta now voluntarilly and as if of his own motion retires from authority and from all attempt to control the organization of the government and the course of affairs, it will be necessary for the President of the United States to insist upon the terms of an ultimatum, the rejection of which would render it necessary for him to propose very serious practical measures to the Congress of the United States.

(Suggest here as of from your own mind, the countenance and active assistance of the constitutionalistas by the United States.)

3. That the government of the United States is anxious to avoid extreme measures, for Mexico's sake no less than for the sake of the peace of America, and is therefore willing to do anything within reason to spare General Huerta's feelings and dignity and afford him personal protection;

4. That it, therefore, suggests the following course: the choice of some man or small group of men, as little as possible identified with the recent troubles (elderly men now in retirement, for example, who enjoy the general public confidence) to constitute a provisional government and arrange for early general elections at which both a new congress and a new executive shall be chosen, and the government put upon a constitutional footing;

5. That some such course, approved by the government of the United States, is now absolutely necessary, that government being firmly and irrevocably resolved, by one method or another, to cut the government of Huerta off, if he persists, from all outside aid or countenance, and that Huerta will only for a very few days longer be free to act with apparent freedom of choice in the matter. His retirement and an absolutely free field for a constitutional rehabilitation being the least the United States can accept. This government cannot too earnestly urge him to make the inevitable choice wisely and in full view of the terrible consequences of hesitation or refusal.

6. That the attempt to substitute Blanquet[1] or any other representative of Huerta and the Huerta coup would lead to deeper

irritation on the part of the United States and the inevitable final rupture, as would also any attempt to carry out the pretended or apparent choices of the recent elections, either as regards the presidency or the congress.[2]

CLST MS (WP, DLC).
  [1] Aureliano Blanquet, Minister of War, and a write-in candidate for Vice-President on the unofficial Huerta ticket. See Charles C. Cumberland, *The Mexican Revolution: The Constitutionalist Years* (Austin, Tex., 1972), pp. 69-70, and Michael C. Meyer, *Huerta: A Political Portrait* (Lincoln, Neb., 1974), pp. 152-54.
  [2] This telegram was sent as W. J. Bryan to N. O'Shaughnessy, Nov. 1, 1913, T telegram (SDR, RG 59, 812.00/11443a, DNA). Attached to this telegram is a WWT draft.

To Mary Allen Hulbert

My dearest Friend,   The White House 2 Novemper, 1913.

Your note from the Manhattan has just been handed to me, and you may judge how glad I was to see it when I tell you that, except for the enclosed post cards of Nantucket, this is the first time I have seen your hand-writing since I received the little note you wrote me immediately after I telegraphed to Allen to ask how you were. Have I missed some? I have written three times to you since that little note came.

What a Relief it is to know that you are no longer lying ill at Nantucket, with nothing to do but eat your heart out! This letter from New York has sent my spiritual barometer up with a rush, and I thank you with all my heart. I need cheer just now, I can tell you, with all the influences of disappointment and obstruction I am struggling with, like one man against a thousand. I do not complain, but I do cry out for letters from those who can cheer me by the simple means of letting me know that they are thinking of me!

I must send this letter to the Manhattan, but will it get to you? Please tell me at once what permanent address will assure letters reaching you. We do not wish to lose you in the wide, wide world. It is much *too* wide! We might not be able to find you on short notice. Don't forget.

Yes, the beautiful table you were kind and generous enough to send to Jessie came. We did not know whom it was from until we found "Nantucket" on the wrappings. There was no card or name inside; but Nantucket told its own story of the thoughtfulness of a dear friend. Jessie was, of course, delighted, and will write to you presently herself.

I am feeling the strain of things a good deal these days, with all indications pointing to a crisis in Mexico. Many fateful pos-

sibilities are involved in that perplexing situation. I lie awake
at night praying that the most terrible of them may be averted.
No man can tell what will happen while we deal with a desperate
brute like the traitor, Huerta. God save us from the worst! I need
not expound to you what my feelings and anxieties are. Knowing me, you know them already, and just their kind. I have just
had a conference of an hour and a half with Senator Bacon, the
chairman of the Senate Committee on Foreign Relations, to keep
him posted, and get the advantage of his long experience. He
has been here ever since before our trouble with Spain.

In spite of everything I keep well. I take as good care of myself
as circumstances permit. The dear ones about me are all perfectly well, I am thankful to say. As the day for the wedding approaches there is more and more concentration of all thoughts
on the necessary preparations and even questions of state seem
to grow small by comparison! All join me in sending affectionate
messages. Try to get to Hot Springs. It would do you so much
good, and you need it so much! There is nothing in particular,
I hope, that makes you anxious about Allen.

How I wish we could see you. I grow more and more hungry
for the friends who are nearest to us. I shall await a letter, telling
us *all* that has happened and may happen to you, with the eagerness of one who has been starved.

Your devoted friend,   Woodrow Wilson

WWTLS (WP, DLC).

From Walter Hines Page

Dear Mr. President: London. Nov. 2. 1913

Out of your insisting on a moral basis of government for
Mexico must emerge a real policy for all the volcanic states in
Latin-America; and it will emerge, as all right policies do, from
proper & courageous action on a concrete case and not as a
mere abstract doctrine. That's the value of it. I never forget and
I never forget to say that Mexico is only part of the problem.
We have never had a South- and Central-American policy, worth
calling so, because we have never based our action in a given,
conspicuous case on a fundamental moral basis—except in Cuba.

It's hard to get this into the British head. They have a mania
for order, sheer order, order for the sake of order and—of trade.
They simply can't see how anything can come before order or
why anything need come after it. They are stupified by your concern about anything else in Mexico. What matter who rules or

how, so long as he keep order? These are the best policemen in the world, these English, in India, in Africa, everywhere; and, about outlying governments, they have policemen's ethics.

I don't know how to guess at their future action. This Government is most hard pressed at home, with the imminent danger of civil war in Ireland, with their land policy, and with their navy, presently in need of oil. If they offend anybody now—any strong trade or financial influence, they may be ousted.

On the other hand is their fear of losing our good-will, which they value. They will not risk it unless by risking it they think to avoid a greater, domestic risk. They await your communication with extreme eagerness. But they can hardly bring themselves to believe in any moral basis of government in Mexico. This is a new conception to these policemen of continents.

Yours very sincerely   Walter H. Page

ALS (WP, DLC).

Remarks at a Press Conference

November 3, 1913

Perhaps you can tell us something about the currency bill?

> Well, that was not the entire object of Senator Owen's visit, but I think I can say he reported progress and just came to inform me of what was contemplated. The committee has to adjourn over election day.

Is the four-bank plan acceptable, Mr. President?

> To me? Well, I think I have answered that already.

Have you talked, Mr. President, with Senator Owen, or anyone, about the proposals for public ownership of the banks?

> No. You mean public subscription of the stock?

Yes.

> No, I have not.

Would you care to express your opinion on that?

> Well, I stand for the bill. I never get on a pivot and swing around. I try to stay where I stand. The bill has an awful bony structure, but if altered would alter the whole thing. When I lay down a line, I don't mark it with chalk so that it can be rubbed out. Of course, I don't mean that there are not many debatable parts of the bill, but I say the bony structure is essential to the flesh that is on it.

Senator Owen didn't venture, did he, Mr. President, when he would bring out the bill?

> No.

Is the subject of Mexico still taboo?

> Well, apparently not. In reading the *Post* this morning, they, as usual, knew more about it than I did. I would be very much obliged if you would tell me what is going on in the State Department. Sometimes I get very excellent suggestions what I might do by an announcement of what I have heard.

Does that apply to the suggestion this morning in the *Post*?[1]

> There are a good many parts of it I could recognize.

There is a dispatch from Veracruz, Mr. President, to the effect that Mr. Lind will return immediately upon the arrival of the relief squadron.[2]

> That is one of the things I learned from the paper this morning.

Will it be necessary for him to do so, Mr. President?

> Certainly not.

You mean that the arrival of the battleships would put him in danger? I mean, the arrival of the battleships would cause him to feel like he had to come home?

> Not that I know of. He may have instances of uneasiness that I don't know anything about.

If I might, is there any report, Mr. President, of a conference with any other ministers down there?[3]

> Only to this extent: there was a conference, in which several of them came from Mexico City for the purpose of conferring with him, and they showed a disposition to cooperate with the United States.

Would you say whether they laid down any lines on which they made—

> No, he did not give the conversations themselves. He just reported that general impression.

Mr. President, there was a report this morning that a plea was to be made by General Carranza to be allowed to import arms from the United States. Has that reached you in any form?

> All that reached me when I saw in the paper this morning that they desired to make certain representations to us, and we of course replied that we could not receive any representations officially from them.

That wouldn't bar them from unofficially letting you know what they wanted?

> I suppose not, because it generally comes to us, you might say, one way or the other. . . .

Will we have the right to let Carranza have ammunitions?

> Why, of course Congress would have the right from time to

time to repeal that resolution, that joint resolution putting the whole thing upon the ordinary footing of neutrality.

Is there probably a necessity for an act of Congress?

Well, I suppose, on second thought, that that joint resolution does leave discretion with the Executive, as to whether arms shall be exported. . . .

Mr. President, there was a suggestion some time ago, with the House sitting there doing nothing, that you might send your trust program during November, so as to give the House something to do while they are waiting for the Senate?

I have no intention of distracting the attention of the country from the banking and currency situation. It is very usefully concentrating on that subject.

Mr. President, would it be out of the way to ask whether you have any other program besides trust to suggest now?

You know, my trust program is largely fiction. I mean that I have a definite program, armed to the teeth. Of course, I have certain ideas which I am earnestly [intent] on seeing carried out, and about which I have already conferred in an informal way with Senator Newlands and the chairman of the House committee. And I think from those conferences, that we really are, at any rate, thinking along very much the same lines, that it is very feasible to do what I have usually done in these matters. I haven't had a tariff program. I haven't had a currency program. I have conferred with these men who handle these things, and asked the questions, and then have gotten back what they sent to me—the best of our common counsel. That is what I am trying to do in this case.

JRT transcript (WC, NjP) of CLSsh (C. L. Swem Coll., NjP).

1 "Oust Huerta First," *Washington Post*, Nov. 3, 1913, reporting that the Wilson administration had worked out a plan for Mexico. A "supreme effort" was being made to bring about Huerta's retirement, as an indispensable preliminary to new elections in which the Constitutionalists might participate. Should Huerta not withdraw completely, then the United States might make definite proposals to assist in the political reconstruction of Mexico. It was also unlikely that the Washington government would make any move without sounding out the European powers. One remarkable fact, the story concluded, was that no administration official would deny that the United States was prepared to use drastic measures to oust Huerta.

2 Daniels had announced that four ships en route to the eastern coast of Mexico had originally been intended to relieve other ships, but that the latter had been ordered to remain off Veracruz.

3 Lind had recently conferred with the Russian, Norwegian, and German ministers to Mexico in Veracruz.

From Augustus Octavius Bacon

Washington, D. C.

Dear Mr. President: November 4th, 1913.

Referring to what was said in our personal conversation of Sunday last,[1] I beg to herewith enclose excerpts from newspaper publications of some interviews given by me. As stated by me to you, my object was to have these views presented to the public, and especially to the European public, without responsibility for the same being in any manner attributed to you. The two excerpts marked "New York Herald" appeared in that paper November 2nd, and were cabled to the Paris New York Herald.[2] The former interview of October 25th appeared in the papers served by the Associated Press and so much of the same as related to the question of the landing of marines in Mexico was also cabled to the Paris New York Herald.[3] I do not know that these interviews fell under your eye and I, therefore, enclose them to you as it may be of interest to you to know that these views have been made public in Europe.

With reference to the present Mexican complication, I think it important that I should also say to you that, without committing the Administration in any way, and without even suggesting what purpose may be in view, I have endeavored to sound members of the Senate to ascertain their opinions relative to the more desirable course to be pursued if necessity for action should arise. I find the opinion of Senators in such event to be generally in favor of the recognition of the belligerency of the Constitutionalists with the raising of the embargo upon the shipment of arms rather than any action in the nature of armed intervention by the United States.

I deem it important to give you this information and I may not have the opportunity to do so in a personal interview.

We have so industriously preached non-intervention during the past three or four months that the idea has taken very deep root and it may be difficult to effect a change of views in this regard.

I beg, Mr. President, to remain with the assurance of my highest regards,   Very truly yours,   A. O. Bacon

TLS (WP, DLC).

[1] From what follows, it is obvious that Wilson read his draft of a joint resolution and his draft of a message to Congress to Bacon at their conference on November 2.

[2] These paraphrases of Wilson's views follow:

"Such criticisms reveal a complete misunderstanding of the President's utterances and of the motives inspiring them. The President said not one word at Mobile that could be by any possibility be [sic] construed as indicating a purpose to discriminate against European concessionaires in favor of American concessionaires. He condemned the whole concession system, which so often has proved the chief inspiration of revolution in some Latin-American countries.

"The President intends that the moral influence of the United States shall be exercised to bring about a cessation of concession granting. His purpose is to protect the weaker governments on this hemisphere, which have so often been compelled to accept too harsh terms, and especially to give protection to the people of those countries who have suffered through the betrayal of their best interests by their own officials. It is, of course, notorious that the real inspiration of many revolutions has been the desire of individuals to obtain power in order to enrich themselves through concession granting. The 'patriotism' back of such revolutions has been the patriotism of the pocket, the patriotism of the 'rake off.'

"The President believes true friendship demands that the influence of the United States be exerted to assist the peoples of the weaker countries of this hemisphere in freeing themselves of the concession system. He has no idea, of course, of injuring any legitimate enterprise now in existence, whether this be European or American. The suggestion that he is working in the interest of the American 'trusts' is farcical. He is seeking to destroy a system that has been unjust to the people in many countries in whose welfare the United States has a deep interest, and he is against that system, both because of its injustice and because it is a fruitful source—perhaps the most fruitful source—of revolution.

"That he is as much against American exploitation of the weaker countries as he is against exploitation at the hands of Europeans was shown by his action in the matter of a loan recently negotiated by Nicaragua with American bankers. When the preliminary loan contract was submitted to him, he insisted upon less harsh terms for Nicaragua—and got them."

"Only one thing is needed to insure a peaceful settlement of the Mexican situation. This is for the governments of Europe to indicate in some positive way that they intend to leave in the hands of the United States the formulation of the policy to be pursued toward Mexica and that they will give their support to the po[l]icy of the United States. If this is made so clear that General Huerta will understand he will be compelled to accede to any demand made by the United States and a peaceful solution of the Mexican problem would very promptly be found."

3 This paraphrase follows:

"The interests of the United States in Mexico and Mexican affairs are in-finitely greater than the interests of the other great powers of the earth. The European nations are principally concerned in the protection of material in-terests wherever their subjects or citizens in Mexico have investments or in-dustrial enterprises, and they naturally desire to see them protected.

"With them it is not a vital matter who extends that protection. In other words, they are so far removed from the influences of the particular kind of government which may have authority in Mexico that that feature is not a matter of great vital concern to them. All they wish is protection for their property, subjects and citizens.

"With us it is a vastly greater and more important interest. Our citizens have, in the first place, more in the way of material interests than all of the other foreigners put together. In addition, we have great interests which a neighbor nation must have in the peace and good order of Mexico.

"These are immediate interests which concern the Mexican situation alone, but we have also the further interest in the promotion and maintenance of our governments of law in all countries on this hemisphere, particularly those of Latin-America in proximity to us.

"It is of the utmost importance that whatever is done in Mexico should have a good influence on all these other countries on this hemisphere in discouraging revolution and disorder and encouraging governments of law and order. In other words, we should not, by recognizing a government in Mexico founded on revolution and violence, put a premium on like methods of violence and usur-pation of power.

"The sending of warships by other governments is a recognized policy in cases of great disorder where the subjects or citizens of a country have great interests needing protection. I would not dispute the right under ordinary con-ditions to land marines wherever necessary for the protection of personal property, but I think it would be inadvisable under the present circumstances for them to land marines in Mexico, because that might lead to unfortunate complications.

"I have no authority to speak for anyone but myself, but I think if the subjects or citizens of any nation need protection in Mexico on account of which, under ordinary circumstances, marines would be landed, it would be far better to call on the United States for whatever protection is required; so that whatever may be absolutely necessary may be attended to by American marines.

"I say this because everyone must recognize that in the present delicate situation it is extremely important to avoid anything that would tend to produce the slightest conflict or friction between the United States and any one of these foreign countries."

To Edward Mandell House

My dear Friend: The White House November 5, 1913

Thank you with all my heart for your telegram.[1] The results of the elections are indeed most encouraging[2] and I take fresh heart from them.

It was a deep disappointment to me not to be able to go over to New York last night, but the developments in the Mexican situation are apt to be so rapid and unexpected that I did not dare to stay away, though, as a matter of fact, nothing of new consequence turned up.

In haste, with warmest regards from us all,

Affectionately yours,   Woodrow Wilson

TLS (E. M. House Papers, CtY).
   [1] It is missing.
   [2] Democratic, Progressive, and fusionist candidates swept the elections in most states. In the New York City mayoralty race, John Purroy Mitchel prevailed against Tammany Hall, and his fellow fusionists also won the presidency of the Board of Aldermen and the controllership. Former Governor William Sulzer was elected an assemblyman, twenty-nine of the forty-six Democratic assemblymen who had voted to impeach Sulzer were beaten, and anti-Tammany candidates won in many up-state races. In the New Jersey gubernatorial contest, the victory of James F. Fielder over the Republican candidate, Edward C. Stokes, supported by the Newark Democratic machine, was a notable victory for Wilson.

Two Letters from William Jennings Bryan

My dear Mr. President: Washington November 5, 1913.

I suppose that you have seen a copy of the despatch that has come from China.[1] It is a little startling. The President has dissolved the Nationalist Party and adopted something of Huerta's methods and given the same reasons. While it does not create any such situation as they have in Mexico it may temper our expectations somewhat of rapid progress in the Orient.

I do not know that we are in a position to take any action. If you have anything to suggest I shall be pleased to have your opinion.

With assurances of respect, etc., I am, my dear Mr. President,

Very sincerely yours,   W. J. Bryan

   [1] American Chargé d'Affaires to the Secretary of State, Nov. 5, 1913, FR 1913, p. 139.

My dear Mr. President: Washington November 5, 1913.

I take the liberty of enclosing a letter from Mr. Slayden,[1] which accompanies a resolution which he has introduced in the House. He suggests that this nation propose to the other nations of this hemisphere a treaty in which all shall join whereby the territorial limitations of the countries shall be observed.

I am inclined to think that such a proposition presented by us would emphasize our intention of respecting their territorial rights and it might lead to a treaty which would prevent wars between the countries. The proposition is, at least, worth considering. There are some unsettled boundary questions now, but the treaty could provide for the adjustment of these by reference of the disputes to the Hague Court or to some court to be established for hearing them. If we can once get the boundary lines fixed and then secure an agreement that these shall stand except where changed by mutual agreement and without resort to force, it would tend to make peace more certain in this hemisphere.

With assurances of respect, etc., I am, my dear Mr. President,
Very sincerely yours,   W. J. Bryan

TLS (WP, DLC).
[1] James Luther Slayden, Democratic congressman from Texas since 1897. His letter is missing.

William Monroe Trotter's Address to the President[1]

Nov. 6, 1913

There can be no equality, freedom or respect from others, in segregation by the very nature of the case. Placement of employees on any basis except capability is out of the usual course.

Segregation such as barring from the public lavatories and toilets and requiring the use of separate ones must have a reason.[2] This reason can only be that the segregated are considered unclean, diseased or indecent as to their persons, or inferior beings of a lower order, or that other employees have a class prejudice which is to be catered to, or indulged.

If the segregation is for the first or second reason, the Federal Government thereby puts an insult upon its own citizens, equal by law, unparalleled in the history of any nation since govern-

[1] Representative Thomas Chandler Thacher of Massachusetts led a delegation which presented to Wilson an anti-segregation petition with some 20,000 signatures of individuals from thirty-six states. William Monroe Trotter of Boston, secretary of the National Independent Political League which was primarily responsible for circulating the petition, addressed Wilson as follows.
[2] He referred to an order by Robert Wickliffe Woolley, auditor of the Treasury Department for the Interior Department, issued in July 1913 "by order of the Sec. of the Treas.," establishing separate toilets for white and Negro employees. The order is printed in the Boston *Guardian*, Nov. 15, 1913.

ments were established among men. If the last two are the reasons, the Government deliberately denies equality of citizenship, in violation of the Constitution and makes an inferior and a superior class of citizens. No citizen who is barred because of the prejudice of another citizen can be his equal in citizenship. By subjecting the former to the latter's prejudice, the Government denies equality. The indignity of such a segregation is indisputable, for the public have a right to draw their own conclusions as to the reason.

None other of the many racial elements of the citizens are thus treated. That they would regard it as an insult and an indignity will not be questioned anywhere. If separate toilets are provided for Latin, Teutonic, Celtic, Slavic, Semitic and Celtic Americans, then and then only would African Americans be assigned to separation without insult and indignity.

The separate eating tables admitted by Secretary of the Treasury McAdoo, likewise means a declaration of a foulness, indecency, disease, rudeness or essential inferiority, by the Government itself, or a decree that these citizens barred from the general tables shall be subjects of the race prejudice of all the others. This means inequality of citizenship.

All this is true of segregation at desks or in rooms, already notorious under the auditors of the Post Office, the Navy, in the Post Office Department, the Bureau of Engraving and elsewhere. Secretary McAdoo admits a rule against "enforced and unwelcome juxtaposition of white and Negro employees." This is segregation, and of African-American employees at the behest of the prejudice of all other racial classes of employees. It is clear and definite subjection of one element of citizens to the race prejudice of other citizens. It denies equality of citizenship to the former, in fact, unsettles their citizenship altogether.

For the rule is open to abuse and African-American employees are thus exposed to possible discrimination of any kind.

This segregation denies equal freedom and equal opportunity to employees of African descent as compared to all others, for it makes more difficult their placement and tempts to, if it does not insure, arbitrary limitations for race to advancement and promotion in a field more limited than that of all others in the reverse ratio of their numerical proportion.

If Scandinavian, French, German, American, Russian, Italian, Jewish and Irish employees are to be publicly subjected to this rule of "unwelcome juxtaposition" to employes of other races this discrimination would soften in its asperity.

Necessity can not be pleaded as an excuse for this affront

and injury. Afro-Americans and other American employees have been working together, eating at the same tables, and using the same lavatories and toilets for two generations. They have worked in peace and harmony and the Government's business has been well executed. Some of the very Afro-Am[e]rican clerks taken from rooms where Americans of other ancestries worked, or from seats in juxtaposition thereto have so worked for twenty-five and thirty years. They did so through two Democratic Administrations. These Democratic Administrations were nearer the abolition of the slavery of African Americans than yours, Mr. President. The same efforts to inaugurate this segregation in Government service were made under your illustrious predecessor, the late President Grover Cleveland, and were stopped by his order, as we trust they will be in short by yourself.

The inauguration of this policy therefore can be attributed to no cause but the personal prejudice of your appointees in the Executive Branch of the Government. Never before was race prejudice and race distinction made official under our National Government, never before incorporated in a National Government policy.

We can not believe that after this concrete evidence of its offensiveness to your Afro-American fellow citizens, you will permit this mistaken practice to continue. In the first place these, your fellow citizens, do not deserve this damning blow at your hands. Their class have helped build this nation from the very formation. They have defended it in every time of peril. Theirs was the first blood shed for the country's independence and it has been shed in every war to protect and preserve the Republic. They have been sore oppressed, but toiled on and struggled up and the semi-centennial of their liberation is most inappropriate of all times, for this National Government to which they have been ever loyal to inaugurate a new humiliation, a new handicap, a new slavery of caste, to resurrect incidents of the old slavery now happily forgotten.

They deserve it not from you, Mr. President, for never in their history did they so overcome traditional fear of party and section as they did last year in voting for you. Thousands upon thousands of them were your friends, and will so remain if there be no segregation and injustice, no stain upon your record and that of your Administration.

They did not expect and cannot believe they will receive this blighting blow from you, a blow such as no other of the varied elements of their fellow citizens have received, because of your assurances when their votes were wanted, that "if I am elected

President, I will enforce the Federal Law in its letter and spirit, nay more, in the spirit of the Christian religion. I shall be a Christian gentleman in the White House," and that you would accord equal rights and even-handed justice to all regardless of race or color.[3] No fair man would say that African-Americans could find these words of promise consistent with a new executive policy of separate toilets, separate eating tables, separate working desks, separate wash rooms for them and for them alone of all the many racial classes in this Republic. Nor would history's verdict be that they square with segregation of this element.

We told you in person before election our fear of Southern sectional prejudice and asked you then, as a condition of advising African-Americans to support your candidacy, whether you as Chief Executive would protect us from its extension and you said you would. In what was tantamount to an agreement with these ten millions you wrote to your "Colored fellow citizens," "it is my earnest wish to see justice done them in every matter, and not mere grudging justice, but justice executed with liberality and cordial good feeling. Every principle of our Constitution commands this and our sympathies should also make it easy."[4] Fairer words were never written and their readers could not possibly have expected their author to countenance the institution of any new policy in his own branch of the Government now admittedly based on racial prejudice against them, a policy of caste which no President would dare even hint for citizens of any of the many other racial extractions which make up our heterogen[e]ous and partly immigrant population.

It is preposterous to plead benevolence for such a policy. Oppressors from time immemorial have declared oppression good for its victims. The world is no longer thus deceived. As there is no benevolence in despotism and tyranny and subjugation, so there is none in segregation and caste. As you declare for action in the direction of greater freedom for the distant Philippino, so we appeal to you, not to permit a new policy of more limitation for citizens at home. Do not take from us now as President what you called us as candidate, "fellow-citizens," for segregation forbids "fellowship."

We confidently believe that the protest of African-American from east, north, west and south, from laborers, artisans, clerks, business men, professional men, from lodges, from churches,

[3] He was probably quoting from his report in the Boston *Guardian* of a meeting between Wilson, Trotter, and other Negro leaders in Trenton on July 16, 1912. No copies of *The Guardian* are extant for this period, hence Trotter's report has never been found.

[4] He was quoting from WW to A. Walters, Oct. 21, 1912, Vol. 25.

from men and women of high and low degree, such a protest as they have never made on any Federal policy, a protest only just begun,[5] convinces you that Colored Americans did not interpret your words to mean segregation; convinces you that they regard it as unjust, un-Constitutional, un-Christian and an undeserved limitation, degradation, a terrible injury, and by virtue of its influence for contempt, for mal-treatment, for race discrimination, for curtailment of industrial freedom and civil rights, a calamity.

There is no escaping the fact that to justify racial distinctions in citizenship, a treatment of Government employees on any basis but fitness, without any regard to race, on the ground of a benefit, is to insult the intelligence of the subjects of the treatment. No less is it true that for a President or a Government to maintain that any segment of citizens by racial extraction or ancestry can be expected to consider segregation in Government employment from all the other classes of citizens other than insulting, humiliating, unjust, intolerable, and hostile in itself, constitutes a declaration that they are innately inferior to all their fellow citizens.

Mr. President, segregation of one class for ancestry is a wrong and injustice, which no class can accept. It compels resistance forever. Nothing else, however good, can compensate or offset it. It poisons everything. There is no antidote.

Your administration has had, but for this, an auspicious beginning. Wipe out this blot, apostle of the "New Freedom," put no limitation on any being for race, advocate of "neighborliness all around," set up no barriers between citizens.

A preliminary endorsement has been given your cause by the elections just ended, but in New York and Massachusetts your party deplored this segregation.

Again we say, that our hope is in you, in your allegiance to your oath of office, your sense of justice, your personal integrity. For we cannot believe that you would stain your own honor or the record of your administration in history to satisfy sectional prejudice.

Printed transcript (WP, DLC).

[5] Trotter was not exaggerating, although Wilson had seen few of the letters and telegrams protesting against segregation. For an account, with numerous citations, see Link, *The New Freedom*, pp. 248-51.

Wilson's Reply and a Dialogue

[Nov. 6, 1913]

Of course, I need not say that an impressive petition like this will receive my most earnest and most careful consideration; but I want to say in partial reply to what you have said that some people have been interested to misrepresent the situation. Certainly nobody in my cabinet has expressed to me any feeling such as you have felt that they might entertain with regard to the people of your race. I do not think the spirit of discrimination has been shown in any essential matter; certainly not in the matter of promotions. There is not a single instance of that sort, and there will not be. This administration has but very slightly altered the conditions which obtained in the departments in former administrations. I was not aware of anything that justified the agitation, and this order from Mr. Woolley that you have shown me is the first that I have seen that could be called an order of segregation. There have been arrangements made in the Treasury which Secretary McAdoo honestly thought would be acceptable to everybody. The instances brought to my attention have been exceptional instances. They have not been the rule of the administration, and since they have been brought to my attention, we have been taking active steps to see that they were corrected.

I am particularly anxious that you should not go away with the impression that there is anything hostile in the attitude of my colleagues. I am slowly making myself familiar with the matter with the hope that I shall see my way clear to do the right thing all along the line. Therefore, I am not familiar with it at all. So I am slowly making myself familiar with it, with the hope of seeing the way to do the right thing all along the line. You know what my endeavors have been on certain occasions; and in one instance, for example, I could not get a nomination confirmed in the Senate. There are these difficulties of which we must be patient and tolerant. Things do not happen rapidly in the world, and prejudices are slow to be uprooted. We have to accept them as facts, no matter how much we may deplore them in their moral and social consequences. So that I want you to go away with the feeling that, in the first place, a great deal has been exaggerated, and that, in the second place, there is no policy on the part of the administration looking to segregation.

[Trotter] You say you could not get a nomination confirmed. Was such a nomination made and presented to the Senate?

[Wilson] The Senate told me they could not confirm it, and it was withdrawn not at my request.

[Trotter] Mr. Cleveland also made a nomination, which it refused to confirm, but the nomination was afterwards confirmed.

[Wilson] You know the circumstances in this case. I sent in the nomination. When it was found that it could not be confirmed, the man whom I nominated withdrew his name. He withdrew it at no suggestion of mine.

[Trotter] Mr. President, we believe that. Mr. President, we do not come here about a man in office, nor are we disappointed to see men in office, but, Mr. President, we do not [blank]. In this, Mr. President, is the thing that is unjust.

[Wilson] All that I can assure you at present is that what has been done—and a great deal less has been done than you imagine, so far as my inquiries have gone, a great deal less by way of contrast with previous administrations—has been done in the genuine desire to serve the convenience and agreeable feelings of everybody concerned. Now, mistakes have probably been made, but those mistakes can be corrected where they have been made, and you ought to assure those of your own people who are misinformed about these things that they must wait for the judgment of the long run to see what exactly happened.

[Trotter] Mr. President, we simply wanted an assurance that it will be worked out. This petition, Mr. President, is simply to show you that any sort of treatment based on color was never meant to be fair. All this we complained of also the year before. Never has a cabinet officer announced this sort of policy heretofore, earlier.

[Wilson] Never has any person announced this policy requiring action.

[Trotter] He said separate tables.

[Wilson] I beg your pardon. If a newspaper had made what we regarded as a gross misrepresentation, it was made in a statement to be announced, a policy to be announced. It was in defense of what was an inexcusable misrepresentation on the part of a certain newspaper that I made that statement. It was not a statement of policy, but it was a statement of fact.

[Trotter] Now, Mr. President, it is true in almost every case that we who suffer know as even you can't know. There would be things that come to us that couldn't possibly come to any other class of citizens. I have found by experience that the only way by which we could convince even our best friends that the things which we suffer would be to suffer things together—that they wear a face that is black or brown, as we do. And then they would see this democracy in a way which they have never seen it, in a light which they could not possibly see the day—differences, in a very real sense, experienced by us. We, the representatives of our race, have come from every section of the country to say to you that those who suffer know best because of their restrictions. It is in that spirit we came to you.

[Wilson] I assure you that it will be worked out.[1]

T MS (WP, DLC) and JRT transcript (WC, NjP) of CLSsh (WC, NjP).
[1] Trotter's Boston *Guardian*, Nov. 15, 1913, has the fullest account of this meeting. It prints Trotter's address but not the dialogue between Trotter and Wilson. A news story entitled "Petition Starts Presidential Inquiry," quoted the *Washington Post*, Nov. 9, 1913, as follows: "President Wilson, in response to a petition signed by 20,000 persons, mostly Negroes of the North and South, has instituted an investigation to determine whether Negro employes in government departments are being segregated." It also quoted the *New York Herald*, Nov. 9, 1913, as follows: "President Wilson is now facing the negro problem in a more serious form that it has been presented to any administration in recent years." *The Guardian*'s own reports described "this historic event" in some detail and said: "The President was impressed by the protest and commented on its strength and stated that it was deserving of, and should receive, his careful consideration."

John Lorance, a special correspondent of the *Boston Daily Advertiser*, which had been in the forefront of the fight against segregation in the federal bureaucracies (see, e.g., the editorial in its issue of Dec. 10, 1913), reported from Washington on December 9, as follows:

"Negro segregation in the Departments of the federal government has not only been effectually checked and therefore stopped, but it is rapidly being disintegrated—wiped off the slate, in other words. Somebody has seen a big light and as the start of negro segregation was very quiet so its demise is being conducted in a similarly noiseless way.

"President Wilson has yet to answer the petition of protest a delegation of prominent colored men, introduced by Congressmen Thacher and Peters, of Massachusetts, recently placed before him at the White House; this, he said, he would take under consideration.

"Judging from what is taking place in the Washington departments, it may be believed that the President has made personal inquiry and has given orders that wherever negro segregation has occurred it shall be undone to the very start, and presently the President will be able to report that in fact there is no negro segregation, it all having been eliminated in so far as there was any.

"A telling sign is what is taking place in the extensive offices of the auditor of the Post Office Department, under the direction of the Secretary of the Treasury, Assistant Secretary of the Treasury Williams, of Virginia, being the directing force. There has been more negro segregation here than elsewhere in Washington. Auditor Charles A. Kram, a Republican Northern hold over, seemed to revel in it. The segregation was outrageous at times. The auditor has his offices, and therefore his working force, in the Post Office building, with the Post Office Department itself, and the auditor's offices finally became the only place in the building where there was negro segregation.

"But Kram has heard something drop. He is undoing his work. Half of the colored people in some of the rooms where they were segregated have been taken out and distributed among the white people in other rooms, and the room vacated by the colored people has been taken by white people. So it is half and half at least. Thus is the negro segregation undone where it flourished most objectionably.

"There remains now the bureau of Engraving and Printing. This is presided over by J. E. Ralph. He is a Northerner. Doubtless there is going to be plenty of back pedalling there.

"Curiously all this has been in the Treasury Department, the head of which is Sec. McAdoo, who with sublime innocence and credulity wrote to Oswald Garrison Villard that it was untrue that there was any negro segregation in

Washington, especially in his Department, and that it was a shame thus to slander and injure President Wilson—especially that it should come from one who was a personal friend of the President. Well, Villard did not retract in the least; in fact he was more emphatic than ever. But Washington did have one big laugh at the expense of Sec. McAdoo.

"He seems to have become enlightened since, for somebody has given orders in the Treasury Department that are being obeyed, and it is also believed that Sec. McAdoo has come to learn that it was he, by the practices conducted under his nose, that was injuring the President, and not such men as Oswald Garrison Villard, who were lending a helping hand to the colored man discriminated against and persecuted.

"That the President has been very sensitive to the criticism of negro segregation in his administration is not open to doubt. He unquestionably meant well in his disinclination to believe that there was any. It had not been started by his orders, nor had he countenanced it in any way. He made his inquiries and the chiefs of his cabinet said there was none. Did not a man he much trusted, Sec. McAdoo, say so? All the same, incontrovertible testimony came pouring in upon the President and the resolutions and agitations of prominent bodies of people from Boston to San Francisco went straight to the attention of the President. There was no deceiving him.

"So, too, the cabinet heads became sensitive. There has never been any negro segregation under Sec. Bryan of the Department of State, under Sec. Garrison of the Department of War, under Sec. Wilson of the Department of Labor, under Atty. Gen. McReynolds of the Department of Justice, under Sec. Houston of the Department of Agriculture, and under Sec. Lane of the Department of the Interior.

"The most active segregation has been found under Sec. McAdoo of the Treasury Department, under Postmaster General Burleson of the Post Office Department, and under Sec. Daniels of the Navy Department.

"Sec. Redfield of the Department of Commerce has shown his sensitiveness in a letter he wrote in denial that there was negro segregation in the Bureau of Foreign and Domestic Commerce under him. There has been strong suspicion that there was a flagrant case there, but while positively asserted as a fact by some negroes in the Bureau, it is denied by other negroes. Some colored men have been put together for no particular reason that anybody could see. At all events a very minor official was responsible and he has apparently learned the error of his ways. Absolutely if there was a start toward negro segregation in the Department, it has been nipped in the bud. There can be no question but the idea is reprehensible to Sec. Redfield and that he will have none of it under him. But he must keep an eye on his subordinates.

"A bold attempt at negro segregation was planned in the Interior Department in the Pension Bureau. All the colored clerks were to be segregated in one or several rooms with colored chiefs over them. Everything was arranged in detail even though the colored clerks objected. But the thing never came to pass. It may be believed that Sec. Lane of the Department of the Interior, who is one of the finest men in Washington and as splendid a Cabinet head as ever there was, when he heard of it made short shrift of it. It is really inconceivable to think of negro segregation under Sec. Lane.

"Negro segregation has largely been a movement in the understrata of the Departments. The little fellows have tried to put into force an idea they had. It spread like smallpox contagion when it was found that the heads were not saying anything in opposition. But the opposition did come, though from without, and has made itself felt by impressing the authorities high up who were so incredulous.

"Negro segregation apparently is at an end, but those who have been fighting it are not going to sleep on that account. 'Eternal vigilance is the price of liberty,' is the watchword that is going to be practiced. An ounce of prevention is worth a pound of cure. It has taken six months of hard agitation and work to undo what was done. Any sporadic attempt to revert to negro segregation will be nailed at once.

"Miss Margaret Wilson, eldest daughter of President Wilson, has caused to be written a very pleasing letter to Archibald H. Grimke, the colored leader, in which she expresses great regret that colored societies were not included in the recent meeting in the East Room of the White House of the societies engaged in uplift work and meeting at the White House to extend their work. Miss Wilson lent her influence and high station because of her interest in welfare work.

"Miss Wilson is declared in the letter to have preferred it otherwise, but was not as a matter of fact consulted as to who would be invited, and that anyway she had only loaned the use of the East Room, and had accepted no further responsibility. She indeed regrets greatly the incident whereby colored societies were denied representation at this meeting.

"It looks as if Miss Wilson has unwittingly allowed herself to be 'used.' There is a great deal of social snobbery in welfare work and in negro segregation. Indeed it is declared that social snobbery is at the bottom of negro segregation, being instigated by ambitious women and men in Washington seeking to curry social and official favor with the administration, and believing that it could be obtained by pandering to Southern prejudices. These social climbers managed, it is said, very deftly to handle a situation in which they found Miss Wilson after all not prejudiced against the colored people. This they found out when some one in an unguarded moment asked if the colored people were to be represented and Miss Wilson replied: 'Of course, and why not?' " *Boston Daily Advertiser*, Dec. 10, 1913.

A "special dispatch" from Washington on March 6, 1914, to the same newspaper read:

"Colored people report that the last of negro segregation in the departments of the Government has come to an end in an order issued by Charles S. Hamlin of Boston, the senior Assistant Secretary of the Treasury. The segregation has hovered longest in the bureau of engraving and printing of the treasury, where some 300 negro girls were in the course of last summer ordered by Director Ralph to desist using the common dining room at the luncheon hour, but to use instead a small room containing the lavatories assigned to colored people. The crowding was terrible and there were other obvious objections.

"Ralph refused to make a change, however, and the former head of the fiscal division, Asst. Sec. J. S. Williams, a Virginian, did not make use of his authority, being in fact not a little responsible for the endorsement in the Treasury Department of negro segregation.

"Mr. Hamlin has now succeeded Mr. Williams and he has eliminated the last of the segregation, as reported, by ordering, now that the Bureau of Engraving and Printing is to occupy its new quarters, that all employees shall use the common dining room there provided.

"The colored people are very grateful to Mr. Hamlin. Today prominent negroes appeared in protest to a committee in Congress giving hearings on a bill purposing a legal enforcement of negro segregation in general in Washington." *Ibid.*, March 7, 1914.

For additional evidence on this matter, see Moorfield Storey *et al.* to WW, Jan. 6, 1914.

To Augustus Octavius Bacon

My dear Senator: [The White House] November 6, 1913

Thank you sincerely for your note of November fourth enclosing the clippings. I have already told you how much I appreciate your efforts to sow the right impressions and expectations in what you say for publication, but I want to tell you again how much I value your cooperation.

Cordially and sincerely yours,   Woodrow Wilson

TLS (Letterpress Books, WP, DLC).

A Memorandum by Joseph Patrick Tumulty

The White House.

Memorandum for the President: November 6, 1913.

Senator Bacon telephoned that he had been very diligently sounding the Senators and knew pretty generally what the sentiment among them is; that he talked particularly with the members of the Foreign Relations Committee and knew what their sentiment was; that he thought it important that the President should know this sentiment. The Senator said that he could tell the President about it over the telephone, but thought it rather dangerous to do so. He holds himself in readiness to call upon the President any time the President may wish to see him or to talk with him over the phone.[1]

T MS (WP, DLC).

[1] Wilson saw Bacon at the White House at 6:30 P.M. that day.

From William Gibbs McAdoo, with Enclosure

Dear Mr. President: Washington November 6, 1913.

Some time ago I begged you to review the proposed inscriptions to be placed on the new Post Office building in Washington. This you were good enough to do. I had no idea until the receipt of the enclosed letter from Mr. Anderson, of the firm of D. H. Burnham and Company, Architects, of Chicago, that Doctor Eliot had any part in this matter. I enclose (1) copy of Doctor Eliot's original draft, and (2) copy of Doctor Eliot's draft with your suggestions.

In the circumstances would it, in your opinion, be better to adopt Doctor Eliot's draft, or shall I take the responsibility myself of suggesting the changes to him, not necessarily as being upon your suggestion, but upon my own? I must say that you improved the inscriptions very much, and I should prefer to adopt your suggestions if it can be done without offense to Doctor Eliot.

With warm regards, always,

Cordially and faithfully yours,   W G McAdoo

TLS (WP, DLC).

ENCLOSURE

Peirce Anderson to Oscar Wenderoth[1]

Dear Mr. Wenderoth: Chicago. Oct. 23rd, 1913.

We are sending you today under separate cover prints of revised drawings of the inscriptions for the new Washington Post Office.

In this connection, I should like to have your advice on a matter of professional ethics. By agreement with the Treasury Department, the inscriptions were originally composed by Dr. Chas. W. Eliot, who was paid a professional fee for this service. The text of the inscriptions, as finally agreed upon with Dr. Eliot, was approved by the then Secretary of the Treasury, Mr. Mac-Veagh, and Dr. Eliot's name was placed on the drawings as the author of these inscriptions.

In view of the recent changes, is it proper still to consider that Dr. Eliot is the author of the inscriptions or would it be well to communicate with him with the idea of securing his approval of the recent changes in phraseology.

On one other occasion, i.e. that of the Columbus Memorial, Dr. Eliot has shown himself somewhat sensitive on the matter of changes in wording designed by him, and if the revised text is to be referred to him, it would perhaps be best to have this take place over the signature of the government officer who is responsible for the revisions.

I shall be greatly obliged if you will help us handle this somewhat delicate diplomatic matter.

Sincerely yours,   Peirce Anderson

TLS (WP, DLC).
[1] Supervising Architect to the Treasury Department.

A Draft of a Circular Note to the Powers

Foreign Legations.   Nov. 7, 8, 10 [1913]

You will please lay before the Foreign Office the following statement of facts and request:

The President directs me to say that the responsibilities of this Government as Mexico's neighbor and as the nation of paramount influence in the western hemisphere, compel him to lay before the various European governments which have recognized the Government of General Huerta the following facts:

On the 18 day of February, 1913, General Huerta, then in command of the army under President Madero, turned upon the executive and arrested and imprisoned him. A few days later he permitted the assassination of President Madero. He then assumed the authority of President. Whether the constitutional forms were observed or not, is a question in dispute, his friends affirming and his opponents denying, but duress was so plainly practised that the mere observance of forms would give no weight to his authority. His elevation to power came through methods so abhorrent to conscience and so destructive of constitutional government, that the President of the U. S. felt that a recognition of his Government would offend the judgment of the civilized world and put a premium upon lawless and despotic methods throughout Latin America. A large and increasing portion of the Republic of Mexico has been and is in insurrection against General Huerta's Government, and there is no prospect of his being able to restore peace and establish orderly government.

The President has tendered the good offices of this Government to assist in reconciling the differences on certain conditions, which were at the time made known to the world, the principal ones being that free and fair elections should be held at an early date and that General Huerta should not himself be a candidate. It is probable that these good offices would have been accepted and that the differences between the contending factions would have been adjusted but for the encouragement which General Huerta received from European nations. While this nation has larger material interests in Mexico than any other nation, and while more of its citizens are residing there, this Government has steadfastly refused to allow these material interests to control its course and, in company with the governments of nearly all of the Latin American countries, has given paramount consideration to the political and moral questions involved. European financeers, however, apparently in return for commercial concessions and aided by the recognition given by European governments, have supplied means whereby General Huerta has attempted to force himself upon his country and perpetuate his power. While the good offices of this country were formally declined by General Huerta, he afterwards, in addressing the Congress, pledged himself to fair elections and by encouraging the candidacy of others and in other ways gave assurances that he would not himself be a candidate for President.

In fact, he pointed out in his reply to the President that the Constitution forbade his candidacy.

However, on the 10th day of October, 1913, he suddenly dissolved Congress, arrested nearly one hundred of the members, suspended the Constitution, took unto himself the exercise of the functions of several departments of the Government, made himself dictator, and now holds office and usurps power resting entirely upon force when without the semblance of constitutional authority, and with a view to extending the reign of terror which he has established over his unhappy people, he is now being put fo[r]ward as a candidate for the presidency.

It need hardly be pointed out that an election held under such conditions would not be in any sense an election, but merely a farcical attempt to clothe tyranny and despotism in the livery of popular government.

Under these circumstances the President feels it his duty to bring to the attention of those governments which have recognized General Huerta the grave consequences which have followed the adoption of that course, and, in the name of the people of the western hemisphere, whose lands have been dedicated to free and constitutional government, ask them to withdraw that recognition which has exerted so baneful an influence, to the end that the people of Mexico may the more quickly put an end to arbitrary power and reestablish a government deriving its just powers from the consent of the governed.

CLST MS (SDR, RG 59, 812.00/9625a, DNA), with WWhw and WJBhw emendations.

A Note to the Powers[1]

Washington [Nov. 7, 1913]

Please say to the Minister of Foreign Affairs that, while the President does not feel that he can yet announce his policy with regard to Mexico in detail, he feels he should make known to the .... government confidentially in advance his clear judgment that it is his immediate duty to require Huerta's retirement from the Mexican government and that this government must now proceed to employ such means as may be necessary to secure this result. Also inform the .... government that this government will not regard as binding upon the people of Mexico anything done by Huerta since the assumption of dictatorial powers or anything that may be done by the fraudulent legislature which he is about to call together. The President hopes that the .... government will see fit to use its influence to impress upon Huerta the wisdom of retiring in the interest of peace and constitutional government.   Bryan

CLST MS with WWhw and WJBhw emendations (SDR, RG 59, 812.00/9625A, DNA).

¹ The following telegram was sent to various governments on Nov. 7, 8, and 10, 1913.

To William Gibbs McAdoo

My dear McAdoo: [The White House] November 7, 1913

I think the best way to handle the matter of the inscriptions on the post office building is to regard them as originating with nobody in particular. Doctor Eliot was most kind to make the original suggestions and has a special genius for the composing of inscriptions of this kind, but I honestly believe we have improved upon his suggestions and, yet, it might be distasteful to him to suggest alterations. I think I would authorize their carving without further ceremony.

          Cordially and sincerely yours,   Woodrow Wilson

TLS (Letterpress Books, WP, DLC).

To William Jennings Bryan

My dear Mr. Secretary: The White House November 7, 1913

Certainly Mr. Slayden's suggestion is a very striking one and thoroughly worth discussing. I hope we may have a chance to talk it over thoroughly after we get out of the throes of the present perplexities in Mexico.

          Faithfully yours,   Woodrow Wilson

TLS (W. J. Bryan Papers, DNA).

From William Jennings Bryan

My dear Mr President   Washington [c. Nov. 7, 1913]

I find that Gov Folk would be willing to go to Northern Mexico on a tour of investigation if you think it would help. If we had to confer with Carranza and arrange details he would be a good man —provided we need any one in addition to Hale. And by the way Hale has been discovered by a newspaper correspondent & the papers are enquiring about him. He is in seclusion awaiting instructions[.] Now that it is known that he is down there I think (following you[r] suggestion about his travelling incognito) that he might as well stay in Tucson and not try to conceal the fact that he is there. I await your opinion in the matter[.] With assurances etc I am my dear Mr President

          Very truly yours   W. J. Bryan

ALS (WP, DLC).

To William Jennings Bryan

                                            The White House
My dear Mr. Secretary: November 7, 1913

My judgment inclines to the conclusion that it would not be wise to have Governor Folk go to Mexico. He is officially connected with the Department of State and I am afraid that that official connection renders it unwise for him to represent us in Northern Mexico just at this time.

I agree with you, however, that Hale, having been recognized, might as well go to Tucson and await instructions there.

In haste   Faithfully yours,   Woodrow Wilson

TLS (W. J. Bryan Papers, DNA).

From James Bryce

My dear President   [London] Nov. 7th 1913

Thank you very much for the message you were kind enough to send through your Ambassador and which he read last night at a dinner given to me here.[1] It is an unusual honour, and one which my wife and I deeply appreciate.

I congratulate you heartily on your wonderful success with the Tariff Bill, to which there has been, I think no parallel in U. S. history for many & many a year. My wife unites with me in warm regards to Mrs. Wilson and your daughters. I am
                          Very sincerely yours   James Bryce

Page has won golden opinions here, as I gather on all sides and has every prospect of fully justifying your choice.

P.S. I am deeply concerned at the situation that confronts you in Mexico. From what I saw of that country when I travelled there and from what I have since seen of other Spanish American countries, I should fear that nothing can be done from outside to better their condition except at a dangerous cost to the benevolent neighbour. There is not now all through "Latin America" except possibly in Chile, such a thing as an honest election. Every Government 'takes care' of the elections, with fraud, or violence, or both; and the social conditions are such that this must happen. The best thing that can happen to one of these so-called republics is to get as soon as possible a dictator who will keep order and give a chance for material & educational progress. Porfirio Diaz did this, especially on the economic side; and if there had been a succession of such rulers for two or three generations, Mexico might be where Argentina is now, with the beginnings of a middle class capable of learning how to use free institutions. But Argentina has scarce any Indians: Mexico's population is two thirds Indian, & the mestizos little more advanced

ALS (WP, DLC).

1 The message read: "Few men have done more than James Bryce in strengthening the ties of friendship and brotherhood which unite England and America, and have been the cause of the common aspiration and high example to the whole world." *New York Times*, Nov. 7, 1913.

From Walter Hines Page

My dear Mr. President: London 7, Nov. 1913

Your kind message made public at the dinner to Mr. Bryce last night pleased him immensely, and it will have a most excellent effect. The audience, which included several important members of the Government, loudly cheered it. Old Lord Morley, next whom I sat, talked to me the rest of the evening about you and your thoughtfulness of Mr. Bryce.

Heartily Yours,   Walter H. Page

ALS (WP, DLC).

From LaMont Montgomery Bowers

Sir: Denver, Colorado. November 8, 1913.

Mr. Welborn, the president of our company, has requested me to reply to that portion of your letter in which you refer to the failure of Mr. Ethelbert Stewart to bring about a settlement of the coal miners' strike in southern Colorado. As briefly as possible I will review the efforts of Mr. Stewart to bring about a settlement, from the operators' standpoint.

As far as we are able to learn, Mr. Stewart did not seek an interview with any of the large operators or ask any of them to furnish him with any information whatever, with the exception of an hour's interview with the writer. Indirectly through Governor Ammons he undertook to arrange a conference between the officers of the United Mine Workers of America and three of the operators, the outcome of which Mr. Welborn will refer to in his letter to you.

Referring now to the conference of Mr. Stewart with the writer, I will say that after Mr. Stewart had been in Denver several days and, I understand, in conference with the union officials, he called at my office and we discussed the matter in a very friendly way. He, however, did not express any particular interest in anything but recognition of the union, as this was in fact the only item in the demands of the union leaders that had not already been granted to our miners without demand or solicitation on their part. We took up each item separately:

First, an eight-hour day.

Second, semi-monthly pay.

Third, their own checkweighman.

Fourth, liberty to trade wherever they wished.

Fifth, recognition of the union—which our miners had never asked for nor intimated that they had any interest in.

All but the latter, as above stated, had been voluntarily granted to our miners. I challenged Mr. Stewart, over and over again, to point out any advantage to our men in becoming members of the union, and the only reply that he made was that some times men gained points that they would not be likely to get otherwise.

I told him that the records of our stores showed that the average expenditure by our miners was between 20 and 22% of their earnings and that no pressure whatever was brought to bear in order to induce them to trade at our stores. I handed him the record for August, 1913, of the 22 mines in operation during that month, including our best and poorest mines, and the average earnings per day to each man was $4.15. Mr. Stewart questioned its accuracy, saying that he knew of no bituminous coal miners in the country showing such earnings. I offered to produce all the evidence he might desire, in addition to this official report which he saw, to satisfy him in this particular. Since then we have taken up this matter of earnings in more detail and in such a thorough manner that even the most biased labor union critic cannot dispute. We have taken several mines with the names of individual miners showing the number of days they worked and their earnings per day and per month for the month of August, the last month prior to the strike, and we find that the average earnings in some of our mines shows more than $4.40 per day each. These miners were all paid with checks, which were endorsed and cashed, and are subject to inspection by any one interested. Some of our mines working in September and since the strike average $4.70 for eight hours work by the miners.

Mr. Stewart also questioned my statement that our miners were permitted to have their own checkweighman. I told him that this had been their privilege during the entire management of the present officials and for many years prior to that time. He said he had been informed otherwise, and I secured the original notice that was posted at all of our mines, dated April 11, 1912, calling attention to the fact that our old miners were all familiar with our attitude toward checkweighmen, but many new men might not be, and this notice was for the purpose of stating that they were at liberty to employ their own checkweighmen. This, I think, was written and posted in six languages; and I will add that our company has not been accused in a single instance during the six years that I have been here, of any irregularity in regard to weights, so our miners decline to employ their own checkweighmen. I gave this notice to Mr. Stewart, which he took away with him.

One of the objections given Mr. Stewart why we refuse to recognize the union was that about 94% of our miners were non-union and the few who were members were old miners, some of them in our employ for twenty or twenty-five years, who had been members of the union in eastern states, probably having drifted west after being in strikes, and who had retained their membership largely as a matter of sentiment. Anyhow, at the mines where these union men worked, large numbers signed a protest against calling a strike.

When the matter of calling a strike was being provoked by Vice President Hayes and "Mother" Jones[1] (whose record is enclosed herein, the truthfulness of which has never been challenged), our miners repeatedly pressed the point that they had no grievances, that they were doing well and were satisfied. Later on when the convention was called, numerous meetings were held, and not in one of our mines did a majority vote in favor of a strike, neither did they elect a single delegate. Only six of our several thousand employes attended the convention, and but two presented themselves as delegates, though neither had been elected. One of them had recently come to one of our mines and worked a short time, earning $11. When spoken to by one of our men in regard to his small earnings, he said that did not count, as he was sent there by union officials who were paying him $5 a day for secret work.

As stated above, Mr. Stewart's discussion with me was almost entirely in regard to recognition of the union and our reasons for refusing to do so. I told him that thousands of our men had expressed their entire satisfaction in every particular; that they had been given all of the advantages secured by union miners,

1 Mary Harris (Mrs. George E.) Jones, who since the 1870's had aided working men and women in their struggles against low wages, long hours, and poor working conditions. She was especially active as an organizer for the United Mine Workers and participated in the anthracite coal strikes of 1900 and 1902. To dramatize the evils of child labor, she later led a caravan of child workers on a march from the textile mills of Kensington, Pa., to President Theodore Roosevelt's home in Oyster Bay, N. Y. She returned to West Virginia in 1911 to organize local mine workers' unions. She was eighty-three when the Colorado strike broke out. A recent biography is Dale Fetherling, *Mother Jones, The Miners' Angel: A Portrait* (Carbondale and Edwardsville, Ill., 1974).

which we had voluntarily given to them; that they were non-union men from choice, and to force them to join the union and to contribute from their earnings a large amount of money without receiving any benefit whatever for so doing, would be so unjust that if we had no other reason, this feature alone would cause us to flatly refuse to favorably consider the proposition. I pressed the point that the most cordial and friendly relations existed between our company and our employes; that they were prosperous and happy, and the coming of these agitators to stir up strife was almost, if not quite a crime. I challenged Mr. Stewart to show me wherein we were open to any criticism, and I offered to furnish him all the evidence he might care for, to prove to him the truthfulness of my statements. I told him that I would refuse, as would all of our officials, to recognize the union or the official representatives of the union in which 90 to 95% of our employes had no relation nor interest; that these officials had come here for the sole purpose of forcing this issue, and that, in my opinion, they had no interest whatever in these miners except to secure several hundred thousand dollars a year for their treasury.

Since receipt of your letter, diligent inquiry has been made and so far as we have been able to learn, Mr. Stewart did not take up the matter of mediation with any other representatives of the operators, as I have before stated. I referred him to the general manager of our coal mining department, Mr. [E. H.] Weitzel, then at Trinidad, where Mr. Stewart said he was going to visit some of the coal mines. Mr. Weitzel was instructed by this office to show Mr. Stewart every courtesy, to furnish him escort and the facilities of our railroad to make as thorough an investigation of the conditions as he desired. Mr. Stewart did not call upon General Manager Weitzel, or speak to him, though he had been pointed out to Mr. Stewart. Mr. Weitzel is acknowledged to be one of the best expert coal miners in the country, a man who has the respect and friendship of thousands of miners in Colorado and New Mexico because of his fairness and unceasing efforts for the welfare and success of the men under him. If Mr. Stewart was seeking for unbiased and truthful information, he could have secured it from Mr. Weitzel.

I was not aware at the time of Mr. Stewart's visit here, that the officials of the United Mine Workers of America had been in conference with Commissioner of Labor Wilson some time before the strike was called, neither did I know that Commissioner Wilson was for years the secretary and treasurer of this union, nor that Mr. Stewart was a leader in labor union circles. My notion of a mediator is that he should have an open and unbiased mind, which I have never known a man long connected with labor unions as an officer, to possess. My sense of fairness prompts me to say that an independent man should have been selected to act as mediator, providing there was any dispute existing between ourselves and our miners, demanding mediation, which there was not.

In my discussion with Mr. Stewart reference was made to an interview between Mr. Stewart and Mr. [Starr J.] Murphy, one of the attorneys in Mr. John D. Rockefeller's office, respecting the writer's attitude in regard to the treatment of the employes in the several companies in which I have represented Mr. Rockefeller's interests as a director and officer. Mr. Murphy informed Mr. Stewart that one of the important matters that I have been giving my personal attention to for nearly a score of years, has been the uplift and betterment of the thousands of men in our employ, and their families.

The writer reviewed some of my work in connection with The Colorado Fuel and Iron Co., during the six years I have been one of the executive officers, in improving the condition of our employes in the way of housing, schools, churches, Sunday-schools and in closing and lessening the saloons. I will say that we have excellent school buildings and employ the best of teachers in all of our camps, and I believe we do not stand second to any coal mining company in the United States in this respect. We have one or more salaried surgeons and physicians in every mining village, and at Pueblo, a convenient center, we have in some respects one of the best hospitals known in this or any other country. We have expended, during the past six years, for the betterment of our several departments, over $2,750,000. We have given steady employment since the panic of 1907-8 and during the depression of the past two years, to from 12,000 to 15,000 men—a record not excelled by any similar industry in America in continuous operation, and in all departments we have paid as high, and in some higher wages than is paid in similar industries in other parts of the country. The earnings of our coal miners are larger per man (as Mr. Stewart admitted) than is paid in any locality under the control of the United Mine Workers of America. We have made two advances of 10% each to our laborers during the past six years, and in both cases without demand or solicitation on the part of our employes.

We have been able to put this, the largest industry and employer of men in the west, upon a solid commercial and financial basis, and until this iniquitous strike was called, peace and prosperity were enjoyed by investors, officers and employes.

I believe I am justified in saying that no unjust or unfair treatment to our employes on the part of superintendents, bosses, storekeepers, or any other men in authority connected with this company, would be tolerated by the writer or President Welborn for a moment. Notwithstanding this well known fact, representatives of the United Mine Workers of America with "Mother" Jones, upbraid us without any regard to truthfulness or common decency. Their utterances prompted two religious organizations to send representatives into our camps to ascertain the true condition of things, one of them the Ministerial Association of the City of Pueblo, and the other, Rev. R. M. Donaldson, D.D., secretary of the Presbyterian Board of Home Missions in the Rocky Mountain states with other members of the synod just closed in southern Colorado. Both of these delegations unhesitatingly pronounced the charges as absolutely false, and Dr. Donaldson took pains to report to the writer personally that they were greatly pleased to find such good conditions everywhere they went.

It is reported that Mr. Stewart was heard to say that he found the mining camps of The Colorado Fuel and Iron Co. which he visited, as good as any he had ever seen. Whether this report is true or not, we know this to be the condition in all of the mining villages directly under our control. Where there is lawlessness and bad conditions, it is found in the open camps like Aguilar, which is one of the chief centers where union men and their sympathizers congregate.

You will pardon me, I am sure, in stating that the Scotch-Irish-Presbyterian blood coming down from my ancestors, becomes somewhat heated to know that such disreputable creatures as the self-named "Mother" Jones can secure the attention and cooperation of statesmen. Her vicious and blasphemous tirades upon the honor and fairness of our officers are too vulgar to repeat. I enclose herein a copy of an article published in a local paper of January 2, 1904,[2] and verified by scores of people who knew of this woman in red-light brothels of Denver, which corresponds to the records on file in the Pinkerton office. We have been unable to discover any attempt on the part of Mrs. Jones and her associates to deny the record of her immoral life. This vile woman hobnobs with the higher officials of the United Mine Workers of America and is under pay of that organization. She

2 This enclosure is missing.

occupies the same platform with Vice President Hayes, and is introduced to the ignorant foreigners and their wives as a model of goodness and near-saint. That she can get a hearing and the backing of men occupying important stations in the affairs of state, certainly indicates the low level that political ambition will bring men down to.

I am justified, I believe, in expressing to you, Mr. President, in this letter that you have so considerately invited the officers of this company to write you, my protest against the actions of Commissioner of Labor Wilson and Mr. Ethelbert Stewart in their effort to induce the coal mine operators of Colorado, together with their 14,000 employes, of whom all but 5 or 10% are non-union men without a grievance, to submit to the demands of Vice President Hayes, "Mother" Jones and their associates to join the union or be driven from their work. Those who have refused to submit to this unjust demand, have received black-hand letters threatening their lives and warning them that their wives and daughters would be assaulted, and some of the threats have been carried out to a surprising extent since the strike began. My self-respect forces me to resent the demands of the men back of this strike, to dictate the conditions and terms between ourselves and our employes, and I am sure you would never ask us to do so with the facts before you.

In closing, will you permit me to say for myself, that I am now over sixty-six years of age, with more than forty-six years of active, and by no means easy business life, that my sympathies have always been with the poor and the thousands of working men in my employ. I began life without a penny, and it has always been an important part of my every day life to do all that I possibly could for the uplift of mankind. I have secured, in most of the several industries in which I have been and am officially connected, many advantages in the way of generous wages, comfortable homes, and liberal educa[tion] for the children. Sunday work has been reduced to the lowest possible limit. I have insisted upon and established good schools with the best of teachers, established Sunday-schools and religious services in camps and villages. Since coming to Colorado we have secured two ordained Presbyterian ministers, who give their entire time to Sunday-school and religious work among our people. We have recently built a handsome church at one of our mines at our own expense, and turned it over to the Presbyterian Home Board in New York; and at the breaking out of the coal strike we were repairing another church that had been closed for years, but work has now been suspended. Besides this distinctively religious work, we have halls, sometimes in connection with our school buildings, where entertainments and social gatherings are held. These halls are used for Sunday-schools and are open to both Protestants and Catholics who care to conduct regular services. It has been one of my important activities and greatest pleasure for the past thirty years, to expend hundreds of thousands of dollars, including considerable of my own money, for the betterment of the thousands of men and their families in the employ of the several concerns with which I have been and am now officially connected. Our employes have never had any dictation as to their religious, political or fraternal relations.

In regard to labor unions, I have been governed very largely by the men themselves, although personally I prefer the independent and open shop, believing it best fits into our American industrial life and form of government. I have, however, directed managers and superintendents, when the matter of union has been under discussion, to take a secret vote with the understanding that the majority should rule where no injustice was likely to be done the minority, and I will say that where secret ballots have been taken in open shops, I have never had a majority favoring labor unions.

Since the beginning of the strike in northern Colorado three and a half years ago (where we do not operate), we have taken great pains to ascertain the sentiment of the thousands of miners in our employ in southern Colorado, and we know that not more than 6% in our employ were union men, and with all the efforts of solicitors prior to the strike in southern Colorado, not more than 4% additional were induced by these agitators to join the union. Therefore, I submit to you, Mr. President, that for this company to force upon fully 90% of our miners the financial burdens laid upon them by the rules of the union, would be so unjust and unreasonable that we could not possibly comply with their demand, even had the violence and outrages of their armed strikers during the past few weeks not been perpetrated.

I repeat that as every advantage enjoyed by union miners has been freely and cheerfully given our miners unasked for, there is nothing but recognition of the union that these disturbers of peace and destroyers of life and property are insisting upon, but there is no possibility of our considering this demand, however great the sacrifice we may be compelled to make.

Respectfully yours,   L. M. Bowers

P.S. President Welborn, of our company, is securing some additional data, and will write you in a day or two.

TLS (WP, DLC).

Walter Hines Page to William Jennings Bryan

London, November 8, 1913.

Your November 7, 10 p. m.[1] I informed Grey of contents at earliest possible hour today. He asked for time for answer, wishing to confer with Prime Minister. We made engagement to talk again Tuesday.

Meanwhile he asked if I would ascertain whether this telegram (yours of November 7, 10 p. m.) had been sent also to German and French governments. They had conferred with him concerning President's previous request to do nothing till the President's communication should be received, and he felt bound to inform them of his next action. Will you please instruct me what to say in answer to this question if possible on Monday.

In the informal talk that followed this difficulty in his mind became apparent. If the President should aid Constitutionalists and Grey should morally support the President such action by him would be equivalent to intervention and the British Government did not wish to intervene.

I assured him that the time for considering technical difficulties was past. If intervention became necessary the United States wished no aid and that the present effort was to prevent necessity for intervention.

He asked "Suppose Huerta be eliminated what then?" I answered he might consider Huerta's elimination certain, and have no doubt on that score. What would follow I could not definitely foretell but whatever followed it would be with the sanction of the United States and that the United States accepts the full responsibility of its action in eliminating Huerta. The question now is shall he be eliminated with or without the moral support of the British Government. His last words were "It is a very grim situation."

In reference to the notice that the United States Government will not regard as binding on the Mexican people anything done by Huerta or by forthcoming legislature Sir Edward Grey said that no British concessions had been asked for or received.

Page.

T telegram (SDR, RG 59, 812.00/10437, DNA).
[1] The circular note printed at Nov. 7, 1913.

To Walter Hines Page

Washington, Nov. 9. 1913

Have just read deciphered report of your conversation with Sir Edward Gray. You may say to him that we have made the same communication to Germany, France, Italy, Japan, Norway, Brazil, Argentina, Chile and Belgium. Also say that our despatches from Mexico indicate that Carden not only opposes the policy of this government but is even reported to have characterized our recent communication to Huerta as "bluff." Carden seems to be Huerta's chief reliance in opposing this government's demands. We cannot believe he is correctly representing his government's attitude. Our representatives confirm the newspaper reports to the effect that Lord Cowdry is assisting in the financing of Huerta's government with a view to continuing it.

Bryan

CLST telegram with WWhw emendations (SDR, RG 59, 812.00/10437, DNA).

Remarks at a Press Conference

November 10, 1913

Mr. President, what about Mexico? Is there anything that has developed?

> Why, no. The papers are wrong this morning in several particulars. For example, it is not my present purpose to make any address to Congress on the subject. Things are not in the shape that would give me anything definite to say. We have made certain representations to General Huerta and have received no reply of any sort yet.

Is it true, Mr. President, that Mr. Lind has recommended that all relations between this country [blank]

> Mr. Lind has made no recommendations. He has simply informed us of what was going on.

Have we set any time limit on Huerta, or anything of that sort?

> No, sir.

I suppose, Mr. President, with regard to communicating anything to the other European governments, the situation remains where it was last week; that is, you didn't know what you could communicate?

> No. There isn't anything definite to communicate.

Have they been acquainted with our representations to Huerta?

> Yes. They know just what is going on.

Then the communications with the European powers, as well as the communication to Congress, will wait upon the receipt of a reply from Huerta?

> They will wait upon the development of circumstances, necessarily.

Would you care to indicate whether you are considering the step of recognizing the belligerency of the Constitutionalists there?

> No. I am not ready to discuss it, one way or the other yet. I would very earnestly suggest this to you, gentlemen, that, having represented an act as more serious than it is, you are in danger of making it very serious, because nothing gives greater pleasure in Mexico City than to have intemperate things telegraphed from the United States as contained in our newspapers. It renders the task of the administration extremely difficult when the papers go very much faster than the administration goes.

Mr. President, has the text of the communication that Mr. Huerta is supposed to have made to the foreign representatives there been communicated to you?[1]

> No. That has made me skeptical as to the communication itself. I am quite sure Mr. O'Shaughnessy would have telegraphed us the text of it immediately, and yet we haven't received any. It must be a sort of patchwork of—it may be a sort of patchwork of rumor.[2]

The Mexican Chargé has received the same information from his government—that the statement was given out down there.

> I can only conjecture that there has been some delay.

He described it to me in the same general terms—that General Huerta had said that Congress would assemble and it would decide whether the election was void, particularly if some indications of public sentiment held that it was invalid, and there could be no election.

> Then what about the Congress itself?

That is sort of sloughed over.

> That would be an awkward situation. . . .

Mr. President, with reference to this Mexican question again, has the Huerta element in Mexico City made any representations to this government as to the atrocities committed by the Constitutionalists, with a view to moving the sentiment of this government, rather than—

> No, sir, and the fact that they have not leads me to hope that they have a sense of humor.

Mr. President, as a result of the proposed conference on the currency bill in the Senate, will that eventually result in making the bill a partisan rather than a nonpartisan measure?

No, sir, it will not. Of course, the Democratic party is responsible for legislation, and it is also responsible for seeing that there is legislation. And only in that sense will it be a party measure at all.

The corresponding Owen bill received some Republican votes in the House. Have you any information that it will receive Republican votes in the Senate?

No, I have no information on that subject at all. I should hope that it would, because, as I view it, it is not a partisan measure at all. It is either sound or is not sound. That is the only question.

JRT transcript (WC, NjP) of CLSsh (C. L. Swem Coll., NjP).
¹ A dispatch from Mexico City dated November 9, 1913, saying that Lind had recommended that all diplomatic relations with Mexico be terminated. It also quoted an alleged note from Huerta to "the foreign diplomats" saying that the presidential election of October 26 was invalid because not enough polling places were open, and that he would continue to work for the pacification of the country until new elections could be held. *New York Times*, Nov. 10, 1913.
² Wilson was right.

From Jesse Floyd Welborn

My dear Sir: Denver, Colorado. November 10, 1913.

I beg to acknowledge receipt of your esteemed favor of the 30th ultimo respecting the strike situation in Colorado and the visit of Mr. Ethelbert Stewart here in connection with it, and to assure you that it gives me pleasure to furnish the information requested on this subject.

Mr. L. M. Bowers, chairman of our board, has already written you at length with reference to his interview with Mr. Stewart, and it will be my purpose to recite for your information some of the details connected with this important matter.

So far as I know, the disposition of all coal operators was to show Mr. Stewart the courtesy due him as a representative of the Government at Washington. That was the attitude of Mr. J. C. Osgood, Mr. D. W. Brown¹ and the writer, who at Mr. Stewart's request, made through Governor Ammons, met him at the Governor's office on October 9th. We were, however, surprised and disappointed when informed by Mr. Stewart, at that meeting, that he did not care to listen to the operators' view of conditions and the causes which led up to the strike. His expressed purpose at the meeting in question was to bring the operators and the officers of the United Mine Workers of America into a conference; and as

¹ John Cleveland Osgood, chairman of the board of directors of the Victor-American Fuel Co., and David W. Brown, vice-president of the Rocky Mountain Fuel Co.

it had been the policy of The Colorado Fuel and Iron Co. and the companies represented by Messrs. Osgood and Brown, to treat directly with their miners, without prejudice, in matters affecting the relations between miners and operators, and as less than 10% of our employes were members of the organization in question, we advised Mr. Stewart that we could not meet the officials with whom he sought to bring us into conference. We hoped that, if he would but obtain the facts relating to the coal mining industry in Colorado, he would approve the policy maintained by the Colorado operators. We regretted that the meeting with Mr. Stewart was so barren of results, but in fairness to our stockholders and employes, we could not take a course that had for its ultimate purpose the closing of our mines to all except members of the United Mine Workers of America.

When Mr. Hayes, vice president of the United Mine Workers of America, came to Colorado about August 1st, he found a condition satisfactory to both miners and operators in the coal mines of southern Colorado. In the northern Colorado fields a strike had been in progress for about three and one-half years, yet notwithstanding this, the mines there were producing practically a full tonnage, though under heavy guard to protect men and property from frequent attacks made by the strikers whose places had been filled.

Most of the mines in the southern Colorado fields work about 300 days per year, with an average daily earning for miners of approximately $4. Those who work full time earn an average of over $100 per month. The men are charged 50¢ per month for sharpening their tools and $1 per month for doctor's services for themselves and families, which includes all medicine required and hospital treatment without additional expense when needed. These amounts and the cost of the powder purchased by the miners, representing a total of from 8¢ to 20¢ per day, or less than $4 per month on the average, are the only arbitrary deductions from the men's earnings.

Although our company and many other companies maintain modern, well-conducted stores at the mining camps, where supplies can be had at prices generally lower than in competing towns away from coal mines, the men have enjoyed the privilege of trading where they pleased, and in addition they also have:

(a) Semi-monthly pay day;   (covered by law)
(b) An eight-hour work day under ground, (covered by law)
(c) A check-weighman if and when desired, (covered by law)

Soon after his arrival in Colorado, Hayes told Governor Ammons that his demands upon the operators would be the four conditions named above, and a contract with his union, the terms of which in accordance with the universal custom of that union would require mine operators to employ only men belonging to the United Mine Workers of America and in addition, force the operating companies to collect from the workmen over the pay roll for the benefit of that union, all dues, fines and assessments that it saw fit to levy against its members. He stated that the operators had anticipated them somewhat by granting an increase in wages in 1912, but that the miners could secure their rights under the law, covering three of the other conditions named, only where mining companies were required to work under contract with the United Mine Workers of America.

When the Governor told me what the demands were to be, I advised him that our men were already working under all of the conditions named except a contract with or recognition of the union named; that the Governor might be the judge of the truth of this statement and right any wrongs he found; that we would not make a contract with the United Mine Workers of America and by so doing force the 90% or more of our employes who were not members of that organization to join and pay to it through us the dues, fines and assessments that the officers saw fit to levy; that we had not discriminated against men who belonged to a union, and we would not discriminate against men who preferred to remain out of the United Mine Workers of America. Furthermore, that organization is known to so disregard its contracts that it unhesitatingly breaks those made in one district when by so doing it can serve the interests of its officers or organizers there or elsewhere. Officers of the organization are at this time threatening to violate their contracts with operators in districts competing with Colorado if the shipment of coal from these districts into Colorado markets is not discontinued.

Our workmen were well acquainted with the fact that their earnings averaged 20% higher than were being paid in the Kansas and nearby coal fields whose product is the principal competitor of Colorado coals, and they were therefore well satisfied, and strongly desired that such conditions should be allowed to continue. The evidence of satisfaction on the part of our men had come to us frequently during the past few years through independent sources and from our mine superintendents, and had been strongly expressed at the time of our last voluntary wage advance in April, 1912, as well as at our later establishment of a semi-monthly pay day and an eight-hour work day in advance of the State statutory requirement.

Immediately after Hayes and his associates began agitating

the question of a strike, expressions of opposition to it or to being forced into the union, began to reach our office from the men, and continued to come to us daily up to the time the strike took effect. This opposition was most marked in the small sub-district known as the Canon field, where union tendencies were stronger than in any other field. They expressed the feeling (and in this they were right) that a contract between operators and the union which would force all mine employes to join that organization, meant an increase in their expenses and a corresponding if not greater reduction in net earnings.

Hayes was told by Governor Ammons and ex-Senator Patterson —both of whom have strong union sympathies—that conditions in Colorado coal mines were satisfactory to the workmen, and was urged by them not to call a strike. This advice, though coming from men who could be considered friends of the union officers, was not heeded, and they called what they chose to designate a convention of miners and operators to be held at Trinidad, September 15, 1913, for the expressed purpose of determining by vote of delegates whether or not a strike should be called. The so-called convention was composed of from 200 to 250 alleged delegates, more than half of whom had been out on strike in northern Colorado for three and a half years and were in no way connected with coal mining operations. With few exceptions, the remainder of the delegates were in the direct employ of the organization. Some of these delegates sought and secured a few days' work at various mines immediately preceding the date of the convention, then after leaving the employ of the mines where they had worked temporarily, attended the convention as delegates from those mines without any pretext of having been elected delegates by the miners. No delegates whatever were chosen by the men whose interest Hayes and his associates professed to be serving; and in one case a delegate impersonated a miner who worked for The Colorado Fuel and Iron Co. every day that the convention was in session.

The result desired by the agitators was the unanimous vote for a strike effective September 23d. When the convention adjourned it was found that the demands included an advance of 10% in wages. It was evident that the demand for such increase was an afterthought, as it had not been suggested by Hayes and his associates in their early discussions with the Governor, but on the contrary they made the statement in at least one interview with the Governor, that they were satisfied with the wages the men were receiving. There could be no purpose for this demand for an increase other than to give the agitators an argument that they were working for benefits to the men which they did not already have.

After the vote of the convention was made known, and prior to the date the strike took effect, our miners again indicated strong feelings of resentment and opposition to the action taken by the delegates, for the reason that they did not represent the men affected, who had no voice in the action. Two days before the strike date—too late to justify the charge of coercion by us— our men signed statements at many of the mines to the effect that they were satisfied with wages and conditions and did not want to strike. At one mine 189 men, representing 99% of the number employed there, signed this statement, and at many others a large majority expressed the same feeling in a similar statement. In addition, over 200 men at one mine, or about 75% of the employes at that property, held a meeting immediately before the strike date, and voted unanimously to remain at work.

Some of the men who had in various ways expressed opposition to the strike, responded to the call of the agitators for the reason that immediately after the strike was called, numerous letters threatening violence, and in many cases death, were sent to the men who had manifested a disposition to remain at work. Intimidation of this character and actual acts of extreme violence have continued ever since, causing a number of men who did not cease work the day the strike took effect, to leave our employment later. At one property about one hundred Austrians were employed. Most of these men had assured the mine superintendent that they would remain at work against all opposition, yet the intimidation was of such a character as to force practically all of them to leave their work within a week (the original letter of our mine manager on this feature of the subject is among the enclosures).[2]

The record of this organization in its conduct of strikes is one of extreme violence, and this record has been maintained in the present strike. Representatives of the organization began moving firearms and ammunition to their headquarters several days before their convention of September 15th, and at this time they were publicly stating that the calling of the strike would depend upon the vote to be taken at that convention. The first purchase of arms of which we obtained knowledge, representing an expenditure of approximately $1000, was made at Pueblo about September 12th, eleven days before the strike, for shipment to Walsenburg, one of the important stations in the strike district. Shipments of arms as well as ammunition into the strike district

2 They are ten items in all.

continued almost daily from that date up to October 28th, when the state militia were sent into the field.

The reign of terror commenced September 24th, the first day after the strike went into effect, when a marshal at Segundo camp was ambushed and killed in cold blood while making the arrest of three men engaged in an attempt to destroy some company property. Acts of violence have been of almost daily occurrence since, with at times from 1500 to 2000 armed strikers in the field. People in no way connected with coal mining operations or the strike, have been subjected to indignities, assaults, and in some cases death, while traveling on the public highways. Mine property and employes have been fired upon by large armed forces with the determination to kill those who remained at work. They have succeeded in their purpose to the extent of killing ten mine employes, while in the repulse of these attacks but one of their own number, so far as is known, has been killed. In no instance have sheriffs' officers or operators' employes fired upon the strikers until after they had been attacked by the latter; and the strikers have frequently gone several miles from their own camps to attack mining property and workmen.

Comparative quiet prevailed for a short time after the militia reached the strike district, but on Saturday, the 8th instant, a mine employe, while in charge of a town marshal at Aguilar, was ambushed and killed, and five employes of the Oakdale mine, while riding along the public highway in an automobile going to the mine from La Veta, were fired upon from a carefully prepared ambush and four of their number killed, the other one being seriously injured. In neither of these attacks did the men who were killed have any opportunity to defend themselves, and their deaths cannot be regarded as anything but premeditated murder.

It is the belief of the operators as well as of a majority of the citizens in the coal mining district who are not connected with mine operations, that had the state militia taken charge of the situation at the first outbreak of violence, most of the men would have immediately returned to work and that by this time the mines would have been operating at practically normal tonnage.

Many of the strikers have but recently returned from the Balkan War, and these as well as many others have been so inflamed by the speeches of the strike leaders and their raids on the mine properties, that they are imbued with the spirit of lawlessness and will not so readily return to work. However, more than 50% of our old employes are still at work, and as labor is plentiful over the western part of the United States, coal miners in other districts are anxious to come to Colorado where wages are so attractive when they feel that they can safely do so. The operators therefore feel that they are justified in the opinion that with the maintenance of law and order the production of coal will steadily increase and in a comparatively short time will be sufficient to take care of all demands on our fields.

Charges have been made through the press by the mine organization officers, that the operators refuse to comply with the laws regulating coal mine operations. In one of their recent advertisements they state that, "all the miners ask is a living wage and the enforcement of the state laws." At a conference had by certain of the operators with the Governor about two weeks ago, the charge of non-compliance with the laws was under discussion, and we then repeated assurances previously given him, to the effect that we not only would comply with the laws as heretofore, but we urged the Governor to see that these laws were strictly enforced against ourselves and other coal operators. A letter to the Governor confirming this declaration, which fully satisfied him, was mailed on November 5th, and a copy of same is enclosed. It and copies of our pay rolls (also enclosed) serve to answer the statement of the mine organization officers last quoted above.

In order to get the facts before the public, the operators have put out a number of advertisements, some of which are enclosed.

The attitude of the operators in this matter is one not of opposition to unionism, but of opposition to the United Mine Workers of America as it is conducted.

Our policy of open shop has been a consistent one, and independent of any views we might have had with respect to the U.M.W. of A., we could not have pursued a different course without unfairly treating most of our men, who have entered our employ with full knowledge of this policy.

Thanking you for the opportunity to present the facts in this matter, and with the hope that the information here furnished will meet your requirements, I beg to remain

Respectfully yours,   J. F. Welborn

TLS (WP, DLC).

From William Gibbs McAdoo

Dear Mr. President: Washington November 10, 1913.

To fill the vacancy caused by the resignation of Hon. John Purroy Mitchel, I respectfully recommend, as Collector of Customs for the District of New York, Hon. Dudley Field Malone, of New York.

Mr. Malone has not been a candidate for this office, and therefore, no recommendations are on file. I know him so well and favorably, as you yourself do, that I think no recommendations are necessary. I am sure that he will fill the office with satisfaction to the public and with credit to the Government. Naturally, I have not spoken to Senator O'Gorman about this matter, since the ties of relationship might disincline him to speak one way or the other about it. Senator Root tells me that he not only knows of no objections, but, on the contrary, thinks well of the appointment.   Cordially and faithfully yours,   W G McAdoo

TLS (WP, DLC).

To William Bayard Hale

[c. Nov. 11, 1913]

Confer with northern leaders and inform them that we contemplate permitting shipments of arms but before doing so desire you to make following statement. We desire above all things else to avoid intervention. If the lives and property of Americans and all other foreigners are safeguarded we believe intervention may be avoided. If not we foresee we shall be forced to it. We rely upon them to see to it that there is no occasion for it in their territory

WWhw telegram (WP, DLC).

Walter Hines Page to William Jennings Bryan

London, November 11, 1913

Your November 7, 10 p.m. I saw Sir Edward Grey at the Foreign Office this afternoon and began by expressing appreciation of the Prime Minister's statement in his Guildhall speech last night[1] to which you will have access by the press reports.

In giving his answer promised last Saturday as to the British Government's attitude towards Huerta, Sir Edward made the unhesitating declaration that they would lend no support to Huerta as against the United States. I repeat the dialogue.

Question. What do you mean by support?

Answer. Aid of any sort as against the United States.

Question. How would that be made effective?

Answer. If Huerta asked for our aid we shall tell him we cannot lend it.

Question. Suppose he does not ask it?

Answer. If he shows he expects it.

Question. Will you declare that to Huerta?

Answer. I will instruct Carden that if Huerta asks for aid or shows by act that he expects it he, Carden, is to inform him that he shall not have it.

Sir Edward stopped short of saying that without such act or request from Huerta he would instruct Carden to take the initiative in approaching him. It is possible that he may have in mind a wish to hear first from the other governments he is consulting. If from this consultation it should appear that a possible service may be rendered in enabling Huerta to retire with dignity he asked if the United States would receive such a suggestion. I replied that I had no authority to answer categorically but that my own opinion was that any help offered toward the peaceful elimination of Huerta would be acceptable. Please advise me definitely regarding this point.

Sir Edward repeated his declaration of the other day that no British concessions had been granted by Huerta and read me a paragraph from a letter from Lord Cowdray saying that he had secured no concessions.[2] I informed Sir Edward that it was widely believed in the United States that Lord Cowdray is giving financial assistance to Huerta. He again disclaimed any knowledge of this and remarked with a smile that he should think such aid a bad investment.

Sir Edward then said he would continue the conversation with me after he had heard from the other governments, mentioning in particular France, Germany and Spain. I venture to suggest for your consideration that he be queried whether it might not have a good effect in Mexico and the United States if you were to make public Grey's positive declaration that the British Government will not support Huerta as against the United States. Such a publication might put pressure on Carden.   Page.

T telegram (SDR, RG 59, 812.00/10438, DNA).

[1] Herbert Asquith categorically denied that Great Britain had entered upon a policy opposed to the United States and declared that the British government would never consider intervention in Mexico.

[2] "My attention has been drawn to a leading article in the 'Morning Post' of yesterday in which more or less credence is given to the statements in the American newspapers that Huerta was recognized by the British Government in recognition of Concessions that he had given to British interests, meaning ourselves. Of course such allegations are absurd on the face of them, but for your information I wish to say that neither I nor any of the interests with which I am associated have obtained any concessions from the Huerta Government." Lord Cowdray to E. Grey, Nov. 1, 1913, TLS (FO 371/1873, No. 50003, PRO).

William Bayard Hale to William Jennings Bryan

Tucson, Ariz., November 11, 1913.

Received your instructions and leave at once for Nogales, Hotel
Montezuma.   Hale.

T telegram (SDR, RG 59, 812.00/9668, DNA).

From the Diary of Colonel House

November 11, 1913. Washington.

When I reached Washington this morning a little after seven
I was surprised to find Mr. Bryan on the platform waiting for
me. He must have gotten up at six in order to have been there.
When we got into his carriage he immediately started to discuss
Mexico. I expressed the feeling that the oil interests were at war
there and were the cause of much of the trouble. I let him know
about Henry Clay Pierce[1] trying to force an interview with me
and of my having declined to see him. He spoke hopefully of
being able, if the worst came to the worst, of blockading Mexico
and not have to do any actual fighting. I regard this as a rather
optimistic view to take.

When we reached his home we had breakfast and he showed
me a dispatch which had just come from our Ambassador at
London, telling of an interview he had had with Sir Edward Grey.
It was satisfactory yet there were points in it that left one somewhat in doubt.

Mr. Bryan drove me to the White House and left me. He asked
me to say to the President that perhaps he would be a little late
for his engagement with him.

The President saw me at once, although I had no appointment. I expressed concern in regard to Mexico and explained
more in detail about Sir William Tyrrell. In talking to Sir William
we were practically talking to Sir Edward Grey, and I thought
it would be foolish not to exercise the opportunity in order to
bring about a better understanding with England regarding
Mexico. I told him of my luncheon engagement at the British
Embassy on Wednesday and thought if he would give me a free
hand I might do something worth while. He authorized me to talk
to Sir William as freely as I considered advisable.

We afterward discussed the appointment of a Third Assistant
Secretary of State in place of Dudley Malone. I told him Mr.
Bryan had in mind a man from Detroit. The President smiled and
replied "I have in mind William Bayard Hale." I do not like the

thought of Hale. A man like Billy Phillips of Massachusetts[2] would be an ideal appointment, though I did not make any suggestion.

¹ Financier of St. Louis and New York, involved in numerous ventures in Mexico. He was chairman of the New York board of the National Railways of Mexico, and chairman of the board of the Waters-Pierce Oil Co.
² William Phillips, Third Assistant Secretary of State, 1909, and First Secretary of the American embassy in London, 1909-1912. Wilson appointed him Third Assistant Secretary of State on March 4, 1914.

Two Telegrams from Sir Edward Grey to Sir Lionel Carden

CONFIDENTIAL.

Foreign Office, November 11, 1913, 8 P.M.

(No. 153.) R. to Washington.

My telegram No. 310

I presume Huerta knows that we cannot support him in any way against the United States, but if not you should make it clear to him.

Part of what I said to American Ambassador was in consequence of last paragraph of your telegram No. 137, in order to make sure that United States Government would be prepared to discuss conditions. I do not know, however, that Huerta is prepared to agree to any conditions of the kind, and we cannot do any more unless he wishes for mediation.

CONFIDENTIAL.

(No. 154.)   *Foreign Office, November* 11, 1913, 8 P.M.

I find that United States Secretary of State is under impression that prospect of getting British concessions from Huerta is the motive of our policy. I have therefore told American Ambassador that Lord Cowdray has informed me that neither he nor any of the interests associated with him has obtained any concessions from the Huerta Government.

I added that I thought it reasonable that foreign Governments should not support or regard as valid concessions obtained from a Provisional Government under such conditions as exist in Mexico at the present time. I also added that Lord Cowdray had, I understood, very large interests acquired in Mexico before the Huerta régime, and that these were a legitimate source of interest and anxiety.

(Repeated to Washington, No. 311.)

T telegrams (FO 371/1678, pp. 81, 84, PRO).

To Walter Hines Page

[Washington] Nov. 12, 1913

Reported interview with Sir Edward seems guarded. Sorry that he was not willing to direct Carden to notify Huerta without waiting for Huerta to enquire. Say to Sir Edward if he enquires that we shall be pleased to have Great Britain and other countries advise Huerta to retire if they volunteer to do so[.] We shall be pleased if agreeable to Sir Edward to give publicity to the assurances which he has given the United State[s] through you.

Bryan

WJBhw telegram (SDR, RG 59, 812.00/10438, DNA), undoubtedly dictated by Wilson.

William Bayard Hale to William Jennings Bryan

Nogales, Arizona. November 12, 1913.

In preliminary conferences Carranza and his Cabinet manifested great eagerness for the privilege of importing munitions of war and made a good showing of their prospects if permission were accorded.

They are anxious that action taken at Washington should extend to the full recognition of their character as bellegeients. They made one point of practical importance, namely, that not only should importation be permitted but the embargo should be raised on (?) arms and munitions of war now held in custody of our border authorities. A large amount of material would thus be made immediately available to them. I believe I was successful in impressing them with the necessity for respecting the lives and property of foreigners and in particular of observing the recognized usages of warfare.

This afternoon at a conference presided over by Carranza and attended by his four Cabinet Ministers Governor Maytorena of Sonora and Carranza's Aide-de-Camp, I conveyed this information and delivered the statement instrusted to me.

The purport of the message was absorbed slowly. At first there was evident perplexity caused by the language of the statement regarding the possibility of intervention. There was also delicate discussion of the precise purport of the word, "Contemplating." However, when the message was fully digested deep gratification was displayed and Carranza expressed himself in an eminently satisfactory reply which I shall transmit in plain language later.

Hale

T telegram (SDR, RG 59, 812.00/9685, DNA).

From the Diary of Colonel House

November 12, 1913.

Mr. Bryan again dropped me at the White House this morning. . . .

I saw the President as soon as he came from the White House proper. We took up the Mexican question. He told me, what I already knew, that it was suppose[d] Lord Cowdrey had furnished the money to buy the 80 000 rifles which were enroute from Japan to Mexico. He was about to show me Page's despatch but I told him Mr. Bryan had already read it to me.

I suggested again that in my talk with Sir William Tyrrell that it would be well to urge him to get England to bring the other powers to exert pressure upon Huerta in order that he might eliminate himself.

The President asked me to come to the White House and remain with him overnight. I told him I had counted upon returning home but my going depended upon the success of my interview with Sir William. I promised to get in touch with him, the President, as soon afterward as it was convenient to him, provided anything worth while developed. He said he had wished to get with me yesterday; he also told of how very tired he was. . . .

At one o'clock I lunched with Lady Spring-Rice at the British Embassy. . . .

Sir Cecil Spring-Rice was not well enough to appear and sent me words of regret. After lunch Sir William Tyrrell and I went into another room and discussed the questions uppermost in the minds of both. He began by showing me despatches from his Government and his own replies. He declared Lord Cowdrey had no concessions from Huerta and if he had them now, or could get them in the future, his Government would not recognize their validity. He thought a deliberate attempt was being made to connect Cowdrey with these matters in order to create a sentiment for intervention. He said Sir Lionel Carden was not antagonistic to America; he was fair, and would do in spirit, as well as in act, just what he was told to do by his Government. He admitted he was very pro-British but other than that no criticism could be made of him.

I replied that both the President and Mr. Bryan held very different views of Lord Cowdrey and Sir Lionel Carden and I was glad to hear the other side. He spoke of Sir Edward Grey's desire to bring about a cessation of armaments for he thought our present civilization would eventually be destroyed upon that rock. He thought, too, that an armament trust was forcing all governments not only to pay excessive prices, but were creating war scares, they being the only people having any interest in having the different governments keep up large expenditures for war purposes.

We talked of the Panama tolls question. Sir William said Sir Edward Grey's idea was that no possible good came to nations if either the letter or the spirit of a treaty was broken. He said the English people felt keenly upon this subject and no one more so than Sir Edward himself, and the only reason he held office was his desire to promote the peace of nations.

I replied that the President felt as keenly as Sir Edward did about the invio[la]bility of treaties and I thought when he talked with him, the President would make his position clear. I expressed the desire to immediately bring the President and Sir William together, and he was delighted to have the opportunity.

I went to the White House but the President had gone golfing not to return until six. I communicated this to Sir William who was waiting at the Embassy. At six I telephoned the President from McAdoo's house. He was taking his bath but sent word for me to come to dinner at seven. I dined with the family and two ladies, the Misses Smith of New Orleans. The ladies went to the theater and the President and I spend the evening in his study.

I told him of the progress the currency bill had made during the day, and afterward gave him in detail my talk with Tyrrell. It was a question whether to send for Sir William at once or to wait until morning. We decided upon the latter course because the President was so mortally tired.

He insisted upon sending for my things and my remaining the night at the White House. After we had finished our talk upon Mexico he read aloud one of Chesterton's "Little Father Brown" detective stories. He was very tired but seemed to become rested as we went along. We then recalled to each other some whimsical verses and fell to discussing the future tendancy of this Government and his own intentions and drift of mind. He said he believed in the Executive instituting or becoming the leader in putting into law the desires of the people. He thought there was no danger in this course for the reason that unless a President had the force of public sentiment back of him he could never get a law through. That the reason he, himself, had been successful with the tariff and the currency bills was because the people demanded them, and Congress knew it. It was not the pressure from him but the pressure of the nation back of him.

He read some extracts from his works on government in order

to better define his views. He expressed himself as being in sympathy with the movement for amending the Constitution with less difficulty than at present.

We talked until nearly eleven. He went to bed and I telephoned Sir William Tyrrell at the British Embassy to come to the White House at half past nine tomorrow. I also telephoned to New York to explain the delay of my coming home and then went to bed in the yellow room. This room, by the way, is the one I like best among the bedrooms of the White House, and perhaps because it is smaller than the others on the second floor.

November 13, 1913.

I was down at eight o'clock and the President a few moments later. We breakfasted together. He showed me his lest of engagements for the day and regretted that he had to go through with them. Most of his callers were Senators and they came largely concerning matters of patronage. While he dislikes the disposition of patronage yet he believes it is that which gives to a President much of his power to pass necessary legislation.

We talked of his anti-trust policy which will follow the currency bill. He is not yet clear as to what he will recommend. We also discussed his message and I urged him to make it short. He said he had no thought of doing otherwise and insisted that he could not write a long drawn out document when a short one would suffice. He intends to deliver it in person. He believed a half hour would be sufficient time for this.

We went to his study, but I left him with his stenographer and looked up Jessie Wilson so that she might show me her wedding presents. When I returned to the study the President had finished his correspondence and in a moment Sir William Tyrrell was announced. The President received him in the Blue Room. He had on a gray sack suit while Sir William wore a cutaway. They both appeared a little embarrassed. The President opened the conversation by saying I had told him of my conversation with him yesterday and then outlined the purpose of our Government regarding Mexico, very much as I had done the day before. Sir William replied much as he had to me. The President spoke frankly and well—so did Sir William. It was an extremely interesting discussion.

The President, of his own volition, brought up the arbitration treaty and the Panama tolls question and much to my surprise told Sir William what he had in mind, not only as to his views, but also how he expected to put them into force. He asked him to co[n]vey to Sir Edward Grey his sympathy with the view that our treaty with England should remain inviolable, but to ask him to have patience until he had time to develop the matter properly. He thought an overwhelming majority of our people held his views but there was an opposition composed largely of Hibernian patriots, both in the Senate and out, that always desired a fling at England.

We talked of the necessity of curbing armaments and of the power of the financial world in our politics of today. Sir William was just as earnest in his opinion regarding this as either the President or I. He said in England they owned and debauched the press. The President said, it is the greatest fight we all have on today, and every good citizen should enlist.

The hour was up and the President had to leave for other engagements. In bidding me goodbye he said I must come to them for the future and stop at the White House. I talked with Sir William for a moment after the President left. He was pleased over the interview and thanked me cordially. He said he had never before had such a frank talk about matters of so much importance, and the experience was new to him. We all spoke with the utmost candor and without diplomatic gloss. He said if some of the veteran diplomats could have heard us they would have fallen in a faint. Before leaving we agreed to keep in touch with one another. He is to telephone me whenever he receives dispatches which he thinks I should see and I am to go to Washington when necessary.

From William Jennings Bryan

My dear Mr. President: Washington November 13, 1913.

I have been waiting for a moment of leisure in which to report progress on the negotiations with Colombia.

The Colombian people have sent a reply to our proposition, but that reply contains some demands which seem to be quite unreasonable,—one in regard to the change in the boundary line. They have asked for a change that would give them nearly a third of Panama. This, of course, we could not consider except in conjunction with the Government of Panama, and, as it is not at all likely that they would consent, negotiations would be indefinitely prolonged without prospect of reaching a conclusion favorable to Colombia unless we were very insistent upon Panama. I take it for granted, therefore, that you will not think it wise to consider a change in boundary.

The monetary demand which they make is for fifty millions,

but this, of course, they do not expect. It is merely to have a starting point. Mr. Hannis Taylor, who is representing Colombia in the negotiations here, tells me that he thinks they will accept twenty-five millions and that he thinks they will also accept the present boundary line.

While some of the demands in regard to the Canal are excessive, I think there is little doubt that common ground can be found. The two points upon which there is likely to be difference of opinion—the only two—are the *amount* of cash payment and the *boundary* line. Minister Thompson, who has found it necessary to leave temporarily on account of his wife's health, informs us that the first clause in regard to the expression of regret is a very important one to Colombia. He thinks that if we can agree to some language substantially like that which they propose it will be comparatively easy to get over the other difficulties. I have laid the matter before Mr. Moore and he has prepared what he thinks could be offered as a substitute. It reads as follows:

"The Government of the United States of America, wishing to put at rest all controversies and differences with the Republic of Colombia arising out of the events from which the present situation on the Isthmus of Panama resulted, expresses, in its own name and in the name of the people of the United States, sincere regret that anything should have occurred to interrupt or to mar the relations of cordial friendship that had so long subsisted between the two nations.

"The Government of the Republic of Colombia, in its own name and in the name of the Colombian people, accepts this declaration in the full assurance that every obstacle to the restoration of complete harmony between the two countries will thus disappear."

It is not quite as strong as the statement proposed by Colombia but it contains the words "sincere regret," which are the words upon which they lay emphasis. I believe, with Mr. Moore, that we can afford to use those words in the guarded way in which they are used by Mr. Moore. It is not an apology for our actions but merely a sincere regret that anything should have occurred to interrupt or mar the relations of cordial friendship, etc. That "anything" may mean what they did as well as what we did. If you think it is safe to use those words, I venture to suggest that I be authorized to send a despatch to-night, about as follows:

"The President directs me to say that he is willing to agree to article one if changed to read as follows:

'The Government of the United States of America, wishing to put at rest all controversies and differences with the Republic of Colombia arising out of the events from which the present situation on the Isthmus of Panama resulted, expresses, in its own name and in the name of the people of the United States, sincere regret that anything should have occurred to interrupt or to mar the relations of cordial friendship that had so long subsisted between the two nations.

'The Government of the Republic of Colombia, in its own name and in the name of the Colombian people, accepts this declaration in the full assurance that every obstacle to the restoration of complete harmony between the two countries will thus disappear.' and that the cash compensation will be raised to twenty-five millions, *provided Colombia is willing to accept the boundary as it was established in 1855*. That will leave only for consideration the terms relating to the use of the Canal and as we feel quite sure that common ground can be found which will be acceptable to the United States and Colombia, the acceptance by Colombia of the definite terms above proposed will make practically certain a satisfactory settlement.

This partial answer is submitted at this time because the President has not yet had leisure for a complete consideration of the proposal in regard to the use of the Canal and as the Colombian Congress adjourns *Saturday*, we thought the President of Columbia might desire to report the agreement thus far reached.

We do not desire to have the above offer submitted unless you have assurance that it will be *accepted*,– that is, we do not want to make the offer of twenty-five millions unless we know beforehand that the President of Colombia will approve of the condition, namely, that the boundary line of 1855 be accepted as the basis of our agreement. If our offer of twenty-five millions was communicated as an offer without the other being accepted, they might demand a higher sum in consideration of the acceptance of the boundary."

If you are willing to endorse the article expressing regret and willing to have the twenty-five millions offered on the condition that the boundary of 1855 is accepted, I think it would be well to send this despatch tomorrow so that it can be presented to Congress before Congress adjourns Saturday, provided the President of Columbia is willing to accept the proposition thus far made.

I am sorry to present this as a matter requiring immediate attention, but Mr. Taylor thinks that it is quite important that this communication shall reach Colombia before Congress adjourns.

With assurances of respect, etc., I am, my dear Mr. President,
Very sincerely yours,   W. J. Bryan

Mr Taylor would like to have the above offer made without asking assurance in advance of its acceptance but I am afraid to make it unless they indicate in advance a willingness to accept. What do you think?

TLS (WP, DLC).

Walter Hines Page to William Jennings Bryan

London, Nov. 13, 1913.

Your November 12, 11 a.m. The abbreviated dialogue of my telegram of November 11, 7 p.m., I fear was misleading. Sir Edward Grey was definite, positive, exceedingly friendly, even cordial, and he seemed to me to give all we asked. I did not understand your instructions to mean that you wish him to take the initiative against Huerta and this he made plain, cordially and emphatically. He does not regard it as proper for his Government to take aggressive attitude because that would imply active British intervention; which the British Government does not regard as its duty nor does it regard such active intervention as desired by the United States. But if Huerta shows by word or act that he counts on British aid in any form he will be promptly informed that the British Government will not give it. This seemed to me wholly satisfactory. Any further course would imply British readiness for active intervention which as I understand it we do not ask for nor desire. Please inform me if I am mistaken. Sir Edward Grey left question of possible mediation between Huerta and the United States open till he should hear from other Governments, when it may be they will voluntarily advise Huerta to retire. I will promptly report what he says on that head. His talk was in letter and spirit in keeping with Prime Minister's Guildhall speech which Sir Edward inspired and possibly dictated. This speech has been enthusiastically received here by whole press and nation and a wave of cordial American friendship is now sweeping over the whole Kingdom. At many public dinners and gatherings intense satisfaction is expressed at cordial understanding as voiced by Prime Minister. We feel here that we have gained our whole wish and contention and the British Government and Nation understand that our whole contention has been granted.

My suggestion about publication was meant to change tone of American yellow press and to pull Carden's teeth. I will see Sir Edward at the earliest possible hour about consent to publication.

Only remaining difficulty as it appears to me is Carden about whom I sent separate telegram.[1] I heartily hope the British situation here seems satisfactory to you and the President. It is so meant to be by the British Government and by the Nation.

Cowdray publishes letter this morning denying any financial aid to Huerta except a small subscription through the Bank of Mexico (?) of his loans. General feeling towards Huerta has completely changed here. His elimination is regarded as certain and imminent and as desirable; but they regard this as the task of the United States with their cordial approval and not as their task.

Page.

T telegram (WP, DLC).
[1] WHP to WJB, Oct. 28, 1913.

To Walter Hines Page

[Washington, Nov. 13, 1913]

Your dispatch entirely satisfactory. We shall regard Great Britain's attitude as settled and in harmony with the President's plans.   Bryan

T telegram (WP, DLC).

Two Telegrams from Nelson O'Shaughnessy
to William Jennings Bryan

Mexico City. Nov. 13, 1913, 5 p.m.

Last night I called upon the Minister of Gobernacion regarding the unjust imprisonment of an American citizen by the name of Krause and took occasion to impress upon him the great danger and seriousness of the present situation and that I thought it his duty as a patriotic Mexican to take the matter in hand from that point of view.

The President's Private Secretary telephoned me this morning and requested me to come to his house at halfpast twelve. On arriving there I found also Garza Aldape, the Minister of Gobernacion. After stating the position of my Government to the best of my ability and foreshadowing to them the danger of refusing to come to acceptable terms with the United States, I said that while I had no authority to treat in the premises I would, however, transmit to my Government any proposition which Huerta might desire to make to the United States. Garza Aldape thereupon drew out of his pocket a document written by himself and signed by Huerta and stated that this was a proposition regarding Congress only and that he felt sure that if the United States could be brought about to see the matter, at least partially in the light that he did, that Huerta would follow out the suggestions of the United States.

The document in translation follows:

"First. Congress will convene for the purpose of deciding on the validity or nullity of the Presidential elections, it being understood that its decision must necessarily be for the annulment of such elections because the required number of polls were not in operation.

"Second. It shall also have for a purpose to confirm the extraordinary powers vested in the Chief Executive by the decree of October 11 last, until a new Congress is elected.

"Third. At the initiative of the Department of Gobernacion or of any Legislature or Congressional Committee, Congress shall declare that in order to eliminate any constitutional flaw which might affect its own election, because the call for the same was issued by the Executive and not by the Legislature, a call for new elections for President, Vice President, Representatives and Senators shall be at once issued and Congress shall then be dissolved. He stated that if an interim Government could be brought into being here, which the United States would recognize and support with the moral and material means at its disposal, the Federal Government would need no help from the United States in negotiating with the rebels as it would be able under such circumstances to suppress the revolution."

I told him that I would submit Huerta's propositions verbatim to you and at his suggestion I am to meet him at 3:30 tomorrow, Friday, in order to give him your reply. I went rather further than perhaps I should have in stating that the United States besides desiring the peace of Mexico through peaceful means would also under no considerations permit the legislative acts of the Congress which is about to meet to be considered as constitutional. Garza Aldape, although he endeavored to be calm, was very much overwrought and I believe that the administration here will fall in with your views rather than submit to the revolution of the north.

Please repeat this telegram to Governor Lind as the Embassy has no time to paraphrase and re-code it.

I send a commentary en clair for which please wait.

Nelson O'Shaughnessy

T telegram (SDR, RG 59, 812.00/9705, DNA).

Mexico City. Nov. 13, 1913, 7 p.m.

The British Minister has just called and informed me that he is ready to help in bringing about what you desire. I have informed him that I feel sure that if he will use his good offices to this end that you will not be displeased as you know his influence is great. He knows the general tenor of propositions.

Nelson O'Shaughnessy

T telegram (WP, DLC).

To Nelson O'Shaughnessy

Washington, November 14, 1913.

You will communicate the following to General Huerta immediately as the conditions on which negotiations will be resumed.

I.

The explicit agreement of General Huerta, First, that the Congress called tomorrow shall not assemble; and second, that General Huerta will absolutely eliminate himself from the situation immediately upon the constitution of an *ad interim* government acceptable to the United States the character and personnel of such a government to be agreed upon by negotiation; it being understood that Mr. Lind will return to Mexico City and will in conjunction with our Chargé conduct these negotiations with General Huerta himself or with any one whom General Huerta may fully authorize to represent and speak for him. It being also understood that the Government of the United States will do anything within its right and power to safeguard the personal dignity and safety of General Huerta throughout.

II.

Such a provisional government having been agreed upon, we will arrange for its prompt recognition by the Government of the United States and will at once come to an understanding with it with regard to the complete reconstitution of the Government of Mexico under the constitution of 1857 by means of free elections to be held at as early a date as possible.[1]   Bryan.

T telegram (SDR, RG 59, 812.00/9705, DNA).
   1 There is a WWsh draft of this telegram in WP, DLC, and a WWT copy of the second and third paragraphs in SDR, RG 59, 812.00/9707, DNA.

To Louis Freeland Post

My dear Mr. Post: [The White House] November 14, 1913
   Thank you sincerely for your information about the interurban settlement at Indianapolis and about the return of Mr. Stewart.[1] I shall hope very soon to have a talk with him. In the meantime, will you not be kind enough to refer to him the letter Mr. Tumulty will hand you which I just received from the president of the Colorado Fuel and Iron Company? I would like to know whether Mr. Stewart corroborates the statements contained in that letter.
                  Cordially and sincerely yours,   Woodrow Wilson

TLS (Letterpress Books, WP, DLC).
   1 L. F. Post to WW, Nov. 12, 1913, TLS (WP, DLC).

To Oliver Peck Newman

My dear Newman: [The White House] November 14, 1913
   I have read the enclosed bill[1] very carefully and have only two comments to make.
   On page eleven I have added a few words which seemed to me to be implied but not stated.
   But what chiefly struck me about the bill was that it made it mandatory upon the Commissioners, after acquiring the alley properties, to sell them in fee. Surely that is neither wise nor necessary. Would it not be better to leave it to the discretion of the Commissioners whether they shall sell or lease or themselves improve the property under municipal regulations such as have been adopted, for example, by the City of Glasgow in Scotland? My own judgment is that to part with the property outright might lead to a repetition of the abuses or of something else objectionable.
   For the rest, the bill seems to me excellent.
                  In haste   Cordially yours,   Woodrow Wilson

TLS (Letterpress Books, WP, DLC).
   1 This was the bill providing for the rehabilitation of alleys in the District of Columbia which was vigorously supported by Mrs. Wilson. See the article cited in EAW to WW, July 2, 1913, n. 6.

Five Telegrams from William Bayard Hale
to William Jennings Bryan

Nogales, Arizona. Nov. 14, 1913, 12 noon.
Carranza desired to revise my account of his remarks replying to your communication and is now working on revision. As spoken they were strong in declaration of purpose to protect lives and property of foreigners and of confidence in ability to do so in territory controlled by Constitutionalists.   Hale

Nogales, Arizona. Nov. 14, 1913, 2 p.m.
Carranza and his Cabinet strongly insist that they will go into no negotiations with Huerta or any remnant of his Government. They require its total extinction and then elimination from Mexican politics of the element that have made a Huerta possible. These men are plainly bent on a complete political and social revolution for Mexico. They are taciturn of speech but their moral enthusiasm is evident. They describe themselves as citizens in arms and declare their abhorrence of militarism. The only professional soldier among them is [Felipe] Angeles who, though one of the most conspicuous Generals of Mexican Army, is ranked here only as SubSecretary of War, not full Minister. They say they have resorted to arms as a result of intolerable conditions. Having done so they propose to stop at nothing short of possession of Mexico City and the Government. They declare they will destroy the taste of military element and landed aristocracy, restore peace thence as soon as possible hold a free, general election and hand over the Government to officials named by the people.   Hale

Nogales, Arizona. Nov. 14, 1913, 3 p.m.
URGENT. I have just learned that Carranza believes Washington is not sincere in its declared intention of allowing importation of arms. He strongly suspects he is being played off against Huerta. Cabinet is not in session. Failure to satisfy Constitutionalists' expectations now would cause profound resentment.
Hale

Nogales, Arizona, November 14 1913, 6 p.m.
I questioned Caranza in the presence of his Cabinet regarding the degree of organization existing throughout the revolutionary forces. His replies positive but carefully made indicated a unity far beyond anything with which the revolutionists here have been

generally credited. He asserts that not only is he in control of all troops in north but that practically every rebel commander throughout Mexico definitely recognizes him as Commander-in-Chief. While communication with the south is difficult couriers are constantly passing and general directions are given and obeyed. Zapata is among chiefs who acknowledge his authority. Carranza claims to command eighty thousand men actually in field. Whether or not Carranza's claims are fully sustainable, the admitted number of revolutionist troops actually in field duly uniformed and under responsible commanders and the vast extent of territory over which war is notoriously being waged, would seem amply to satisfy the demands of international law for the recognition of their belligerency. Inde[e]d on the merits of the case it would seem difficult to find reasons to justify longer withholding recognition of them in the character which in fact they completely possess.

I have not felt justified until today in reporting my impressions of personalities here. On the whole impressions are favorable. There is a total lack of accustomed Latin urbanity and of concern for plausibility. With few exceptions the leaders are plain men, their speech is remarkable for Quaker-like conscientiousness and precision. Carranza is positive character, huge, slow-moving of body and mind. He is deferred to absolutely. Carranza might be a somewhat more refined Oom Paul.[1] His capacity for silent deliberation is remarkable, though when he speaks it is with fluency and appositness. The Minister of Fomento, [Manuel] Bonillas, whom I esteem Carranza's ablest lieutenant, looks and acts like the best type of an old-fashioned Philadelphia Quaker. He is a Massachusetts Technology graduate with an American wife and household here respected by all. There is no mistaking the settled determination of these men and their completed confidence in ultimate complete success. At present there is much lack of orderliness in handling affairs. The Government is, so to speak, in Carranza's hat. He stands in need of more business-like secretaries.   Hale

T telegrams (WP, DLC).
[1] Stephanus Johannes Paulus Kruger, usually known as Oom (Uncle) Paul Kruger, pioneer leader and statesman of South Africa.

Nogales, Arizona. Nov: 14, 1913, 8 p.m.

Carranza and his Cabinet invited me to meet them this afternoon for the expressed purpose of going over with me the record of the Chief's language yesterday in reply to your communication. I found that they had prepared a version differing widely from the remarks actually made by Carranza yesterday. Today's version dwells much more strongly on their uncompromising objection to intervention. In addition to presenting this revised version General Carranza made a formal speech which was interpreted phrase by phrase and taken down by a stenographer in which he stated that he took occasion solemnly to reiterate and emphasize anew that the Constitutionalists refused to admit the right of any nation on this continent acting alone or in conjunction with European Powers to interfere in the domestic affairs of the Mexican Republic; that they held the idea of armed intervention from outside as unconceivable and inadmissible upon any grounds or upon any pretext. He desired to warn the United States that any attempt in this direction would rekindle old animosities now almost forgotten and be utterly disastrous. General Carranza feared that the Constitutionalists' attitude on this point was not clearly understood at Washington and charged me to make the representation of it emphatic. While Carranza several times spoke of "interference, mediation and intervention" he at one point explained that he desired always to be understood as meaning "armed intervention." He and his ministers have noted that your statement says "if the lives and properties of Americans and all other foreigners are safeguarded we believe intervention may be avoided, not will be avoided." Underneath their uneasiness on the subject of possible intervention is the suspicion which they strongly entertain, but have not expressed, that Washington is using the threat of lifting the arms embargo merely to unseat Huerta and to set up another President in Mexico City. This they would never forgive.   Hale

T telegram (SDR, RG 59, 812.00/9738, DNA).

The British Embassy to Sir Edward Grey

Private & Personal.   Washington, 14 November 1913.
Following from Sir W. Tyrrell:

At the suggestion of Mr. House, who is an intimate friend of the President and whom you met last Summer, I was sent for to White House, where the President gave me his views on Mexico for communication to you.

With the opening of the Panama Canal it is becoming increasingly important that the Governments of the Central American Republics should improve, as they will become more and more a field for European and American enterprize: bad government may lead to friction and to such incidents as Venezuela affair under Castro. The President is very anxious to provide against such contingencies by insisting that those Republics should have fairly decent rulers and that men like Castro and Huerta should be barred. With this object in view, the President made up his mind to teach these countries a lesson by insisting on the removal of Huerta. The mode of procedure which he proposes is that Huerta should convoke the Congress of last May, which he considers the only legal one in Mexico, and that he should proclaim a general amnesty so as to enable the contingents of the North to share in the election of a new President. If the latter refused to come in, they would be treated as rebels by the United States Government. The President assured me that, should Huerta agree to this, he would go almost to any length to enable him to save his face. After that, he does not propose to examine with a microscope what happens in Mexico, but he is under no illusion with regard to the capacity of Mexicans for maladministration. Huerta, however, exceeded the limit of what is permissible. The President is confident that the Mexican Congress would and could elect a President capable of maintaining law and order.

The President did not seem to realise that his policy will lead to a "de facto" American protectorate over the Central American Republics; but there are others here who do, and who intend to achieve that object. It seems to me that we have neither the intention nor the power to oppose this policy: the longer intervention is put off, the more distant the date on which this policy will mature. The Administration has, by its own mistake, got itself into a difficult position, as it wishes to avoid intervention if possible. If we can do any thing to help the President, he will be most appreciative.

The Prime Minister's speech, Lord Cowdray's statement to you, and his public announcement as to his share in financial assistance to Huerta,[1] and your attitude towards new concessions, as defined in your telegram number 154 to Mexico, have created an excellent impression both on the Administration and on the public, and have done much to dispel the suspicions aroused by the attitude attributed to His Majesty's Minister in Mexico and to Lord Cowdray. Mr. Hohler,[2] who was on his way home from Mexico, confirms the accuracy of the reports current here as to the pronounced attitude of Sir Lionel Carden in favour of Huerta on his arrival in Mexico and his disapproval of American policy; but the President agreed that these questions have now assumed a historical interest only. With all diffidence, I venture to submit that, if you could see your way to authorizing Sir Lionel Carden to move in the direction suggested in his telegram number 139, it would be highly appreciated by the President, who is a strong partisan of what Mr. House described to me as a sympathetic alliance with England. In his opinion, the present is the psychological moment for promoting it.

As regards the Panama Canal Tolls, the President volunteered the statement, for your personal and confidential information, that he is in entire agreement with your view on the subject, and that he is determined to overcome the opposition of the Senate which, as he told me, is partly due to the vanity of certain Senators and partly to the Hibernianism of others. With this object in view, he is even prepared to invoke the assistance of Republican Senators.

I thanked the President for his frankness and cordiality, which I felt sure you would appreciate very highly. I explained to him, as Mr. House had already done, that I was here in a private capacity, but that I was assisting the Ambassador, who wished me to remain in close and unofficial touch with the President. The latter expressed great sympathy with the Ambassador, and said that the present channel of communication suited him perfectly, and that he hoped that you would make use of it if you had any personal views to communicate to him, as he apparently did not wish to use the Secretary of State for the purpose.

He made on me the impression of great sincerity and force of character: every one is agreed that he is a man of his word, and the only man who counts in the Administration.

T telegram (FO 371/1678, No. 52367, PRO).

1 On November 12, Lord Cowdray issued from his home in Aberdeenshire this statement to the press:
"In common with most of the Banks, and leading Houses in Mexico my Firm and Allied Companies subscribed for a small proportion—less than three per cent—of the Government loan made through the National Bank of Mexico. Apart from this neither I, my Firm or allied Companies have in any way, directly or indirectly, assisted in a financial manner the present Provisional Government, nor, let me in justice add, have we been asked so to do." See Peter Calvert, *op. cit.*, p. 276.

2 Thomas Beaumont Hohler, First Secretary of the British legation in Mexico City.

William Bayard Hale to William Jennings Bryan

Nogales, Arizona November 15, 1913.

I feel I ought to say I am forced to the opinion that the Constitutionalists will be unswerving before suggestions that they parley with any Government whatever set up at Mexico City. They appreciate it highly that the thought of the United States Government has turned in their direction and they will be deeply grateful for permission to import munitions of war. But they are absolutely set on the total destruction of the old regime and their own *unencumbered* triumph. There is no limit to their detestation of the whole predatory aggregation at Mexico City, that is, not of Huerta alone, but of the interests which he has served. May I beg indulgence to suggest that while the elimination of Huerta might vindicate the policy of the Administration to some extent, it alone would go but a little way now to restore peace in Mexico. The Constitutionalists are totally irreconcilable toward the capitalistic and military elements which they hold would still be in power in the capital even with Huerta out of the Presidency. The Constitutionalists know their own minds perfectly, their programme is definite, their pertinacity is intense and their prospects bright. Do they not thus constitute the most powerful, single factor in the whole problem and is not any attempted solution which forgets that fact certain to fail to give Mexico peace?

Hale

T telegram (WP, DLC).

Louis Freeland Post to Joseph Patrick Tumulty

Dear Mr. Tumulty: Washington November 15, 1913.
   This is in reply to your request of the 12th in behalf of the President for such comments as I care to make regarding the statements of Mr. L. M. Bowers of Denver in his letter to the President under date of November 8th, which I herewith return.
   As I understand the strike situation in Colorado, to which the Bowers letter relates, Mr. Bowers himself is the one man whose simple word could at once bring that strike to an end. His extraordinary business abilities have made him absolute, so I am informed, as manager of the Colorado Fuel and Iron Company, even its president deferring to him in vital matters of administration, and the principal owner (Mr. Rockefeller) trusting him implicitly.
   Nor would it be necessary for Mr. Bowers, if he really possesses the great industrial power which is attributed to him, to use it otherwise than reasonably in order to end the strike. He could secure that result upon fair terms to all parties and without yielding any industrial advantage that he himself or his associates and principals in interest would frankly insist upon retaining. For nothing is asked of him but to submit the merits of the dispute to an unbiased board of arbitration.
   If the facts are as Mr. Bowers represents them in his letter to the President now before me, the award in such an arbitration could not fail to sustain his contentions. It would relieve him,

besides, of all suspicion of undue partisanship and his company of an odium that now attaches to it more widely and intensely than he seems to realize.

That part of the Bowers letter which relates to the conduct of Ethelbert Stewart, the mediator and commissioner of conciliation appointed by the Secretary of Labor, must be referred to Mr. Stewart if you desire specific comment upon the Bowers letter on those points. It will be so referred if you wish, and I suggest that Mr. Stewart really ought to have an opportunity to report upon it. Irrespective of this, however, it is due Mr. Stewart, I think, that I avail myself of the opportunity your request affords to say a word about his fitness for the mediation and conciliation service for which the Secretary of Labor chose him in connection with the Colorado affair. Mr. Stewart's reputation for wide and trustworthy knowledge of details regarding industrial problems is above reproach. This is so to my personal and intimate knowledge as to Chicago, where he has lived and long served the Federal Government. My impressions of his standing in Chicago might easily be verified through the City Club, Hull House, or the School of Civics and Philanthropy, or in any other centre of public spirited activities there. He is not a leader in labor union circles as Mr. Bowers implies, although he does command great confidence in those circles at Chicago as I personally know, and elsewhere as I have reason to believe. And he has earned this confidence by fairmindedness, industry and competency in the performance of official duties. I submit to your own sense of fairness that the readiness of Mr. Bowers to throw such a man into the scrap heap of the incapable and unfair adds no strength to the case the Bowers letter presents.

While refraining from comment upon those parts of that letter which relate to Mr. Stewart, and regarding which I am not yet sufficiently informed for a definite judgment, I think I should advise you nevertheless that I have reason to question some of those statements, and on other information than from Mr. Stewart either directly or indirectly.

Is Mr. Bowers quite correct, for one thing, in his contention that his company—the Colorado Fuel and Iron Company—has voluntarily granted to its men an eight-hour day, semi-monthly pay, their own check-weighman, and liberty to trade? Were not all these concessions secured by legislation which had been promoted by labor organizations and opposed by the Fuel and Iron Company?

Is Mr. Bowers sure, for another thing, that he is not deceived by his own statistics when he says that the average earnings per man per day in his company's mines is $4.15? It is stated to me that this statistical result is commonly produced by paying a group of miners in the name of one of them. However that may be in the present case, I am pretty confident (does it not seem so to you) that if $4.15 a day, as an average for average men, had been mining wages in southern Colorado, there would have been a stampede of miners to that field, and that not only would there have been no strike, but that no agitators could have made one?

Regarding Mr. Stewart's alleged neglect to confer with General Manager Weitzel, Mr. Stewart can doubtless explain; but whatever his explanation may be, I am assured through independent and trustworthy channels of information that when Mr. Stewart had talked with Mr. Bowers he had talked with Mr. Weitzel in effect; for Mr. Weitzel, a man who is generally liked in the mining regions where he serves his company as manager, is also regarded there as strictly the business agent of Mr. Bowers in all things.

In that connection, too, I am informed (and through similar sources) that there is a feudal system in the territory of the Colorado Fuel and Iron Company, benevolently paternal in some respects—schools, churches, etc.—but so absolute in all respects that freedom of opinion and action among its employees, even as to political affairs, is practically incompatible with continued employment. On this point both Senator Thomas and Congressman Keating[1] can give definite and positive information. But are not the probabilities of such a condition manifest from the Bowers letter? How else for instance is the refusal of the miners to employ a check-weighman, when they have the right or permission to do so and the expense would be only nominal, to be reasonably accounted for? The answer of the Bowers letter does not impress me as convincing.

Upon reading the reference to Mother Jones in the Bowers letter I was shocked; first, by the fact that Mr. Bowers could in such a letter be guilty of so base an insinuation even if there were ground for it, and, secondly, by what I believe to be its utter falsity. Even if the story were true it seems to me unworthy of any man and any purpose to assail the present good character of any woman, whatever her former record may have been, by raking up a career of immorality completely closed twenty-five years before. Is there no statute of limitations in our code of feminine morals? If there be none, then at any rate Mother Jones is entitled to a fair hearing on the question of whether or not her past is what Mr. Bowers assumes it was.

[1] Edward Keating, Democratic congressman from Colorado.

The gist of it is that in 1904 Mother Jones, accused in print of having been an immoral woman part of her life down to 1889, has never denied the accusation. Since having this matter brought to my attention, my regard for this woman has led me to inquire into her past, and I am informed that the story which Mr. Bowers transmits to the President but does not vouch for except by insinuation, originated in print with a notoriously irresponsible woman of Denver, who was at the time of its first publication the publicity agent of the Colorado Fuel and Iron Company. I am also informed that Mrs. Jones has taken the pains to deny the story whenever and wherever it has been circulated under circumstances reasonably calling upon her to do so. I am further informed that reprints of this story, identical with the reprint forwarded by Mr. Bowers to the President, are being circulated now in the strike region anonymously and that the Colorado Fuel and Iron Company is locally suspected of causing its circulation. As to the falsity of that story I find trustworthy men in the labor movement who have known of Mrs. Jones as active in that movement in ways and over a period which make it not only improbable but virtually impossible for the story to be true.

Having myself known Mother Jones since 1906 and of her for a longer time, I should from my knowledge of her reputation and course of life regard the story as highly improbable. Although her opinions and methods of agitation are in many respects not agreeable to me, I regard her opinions as sincere, her methods as well meant, and herself as a woman worthy of respect. She appears to be so regarded by nearly all who know her; and so far as I am advised, the exceptions may be accounted for by explanations that do not at all reflect upon her character. She is trusted, loved and idolized by scores upon scores of thousands of rough and ready men who do the heavy work of this country and whose wives and children she mothers in their distress. They find in her a sympathizer who thinks their thoughts and speaks their language—course language at times it may be to sophisticated ears, but a language nevertheless which those rough but by no means wicked men understand, and which to them rings true. I find, moreover, that Terrence V. Powderly's knowledge of Mother Jones goes back of the time when she is alleged to have closed her immoral life. He knew of her as active and to a considerable degree prominent in the American labor movement as long ago as 1877, twelve years before her alleged loose life had closed; and in 1887, two years before that, he knew her personally and has known her personally ever since. Mr. Powderly informs

me that the Denver story is utterly inconsistent with Mother
Jones' career since 1877 as he knows that career and of it.

And the Secretary of Labor, Mr. Wilson, who has known
Mother Jones personally for nearly seventeen years and by
reputation for a much longer period—long enough to have known
of the Denver episode if it were true—has expressed the sentiment
about her that prevails among all who know her. He did this in a
general letter under date of February 21, 1911, as follows:

"TO WHOM IT MAY CONCERN:

I have known Mrs. Mary Jones, known as Mother Jones, personally for fourteen years and by reputation for a much longer
period. During that time I have worked with her in many struggles of the coal miners in their efforts to better their conditions.
She has frequently been a guest at my home and also in the
homes of my neighbors.

I have been so closely associated with her in her work that I am
familiar with her hopes, her aspirations and her ideals. During
all the time I have known her I have never heard her express an
immoral thought and have never seen her do an immoral deed
and I do not believe her capable of either. On the contrary, of my
personal knowledge I have known her to endure hardships and
make many personal sacrifices in her efforts to promote the welfare of the workers collectively and relieve their distress in
individual cases coming under her personal observation.

Knowing Mother Jones as I do, I can say most emphatically,
she is not an immoral woman.

Respectfully yours,   W. B. Wilson."

But the Mother Jones phase of the Bowers letter is perhaps of
little concern except for the sake of fairness to this devoted woman. The important considerations are the strike itself and the
administration of the Department of Labor with reference to it.

As to the strike itself I am unable to reconcile some of Mr.
Bowers' contentions with the manifest facts. If Mr. Bowers is
correctly informed, at least 94% of his miners are not members
of a union and do not wish to be. If he is correctly informed,
there was not a majority vote for a strike in any of his mines, nor
did his miners elect a single delegate to the miners' convention,
although they acted in freedom. If he is correctly informed, his
miners are non-union from choice. If he is correctly informed,
the most cordial and friendly relations existed between his company and its employees and the latter were prosperous and happy
until the agitators came. Yet, in fact, Mr. Bowers' company is at

this moment involved in a terrible strike. Does it seem probable, then, that Mr. Bowers has been correctly informed?

As to the magnitude of that strike I am reliably advised (and through channels entirely independent of Mr. Stewart) that public opinion among all classes in and about Trinidad, places the proportion of strikers at 80% or more of the total number of miners. Is it reasonable to believe that agitators from outside could have brought on such a strike unless the great majority of the employees really wanted a strike as an alternative to the condition under which they were working? Is it not more probable that the prosperity, happiness and content, and the repugnance to unionization to which the Bowers letter refers, were only apparent?

With thirty-odd years of experience in observing labor controversies, I should judge that the true explanation of this strike may be read between the lines of the Bowers letter. Given a feudal system such as he describes, with power concentrated in a corporation controlling everything, from the natural deposits of coal to schools and churches and doctors and store custom and working opportunities and politics, as I am assured the fact is and as the Bowers letter implies—given that industrial condition, and a violent outbreak of "contented" employees is explainable. The fact that unionization is the insistent demand of the strikers testifies to the same effect. Their feeling evidently is that by unionization, and only so, can they defend themselves against the aggressions of their corporate employer whose power in respect of unorganized individuals is resistless.

It was to cope with this difficult situation, regarding which the employers reject all overtures, that the Secretary of Labor appointed Mr. Stewart as mediator and commissioner of conciliation under the organic law of the Department of Labor. Although Mr. Stewart has proved in his long and useful career in connection with labor problems that in the performance of his official duties he is a man of unbiased disposition, there would be no substantial reason for criticism if the fact in that respect were otherwise. What is required of a mediator in such a case is resourcefulness and tact in bringing opposing parties voluntarily together rather than the judicial fairness which is needed for rendering a decisive judgment.

Mr. Bowers appears to entertain a mistaken notion of the object of Congress in establishing the Department of Labor, and also of the functions of mediators and commissioners of conciliation under Section 8 of the organic act. His erroneous notions in that connection are expressed on page 3 of his letter, in the second paragraph, where he says:

"I was not aware at the time of Mr. Stewart's visit here, that the officials of the United Mine Workers of America had been in conference with Commissioner of Labor Wilson some time before the strike was called, neither did I know that Commissioner Wilson was for years the secretary and treasurer of this union, nor that Mr. Stewart was a leader in labor union circles. My notion of a mediator is that he should have an open and unbiased mind, which I have never known a man long connected with labor unions as an officer, to possess. My sense of fairness prompts me to say that an independent man should have been selected to act as mediator, providing there was any dispute existing between ourselves and our miners, demanding mediation, which there was not."

It was the Secretary's plain duty under the law to confer with officials of the United Mine Workers before the strike, for the purpose of averting it if that could be done. That he himself had for years been officially connected with that labor union, and that Mr. Stewart was a leader in labor circles (if the latter statement had been true) would have made no such difference as Mr. Bowers thinks it should make. His opinion that "an independent man should have been selected to act as mediator" rests, no doubt, upon his confusion of mediation with arbitration. But Mr. Stewart was sent to Colorado to arbitrate; he was sent there to bring the conflicting parties to some kind of agreement in the interest of industrial peace, one method among the hoped for possibilities being arbitration by arbitrators acceptable to both parties.

In other words, the functions of the Secretary under the organic law of the Department of Labor, and of his appointees as mediators and commissioners of conciliation, are analogous in industrial controversies to the functions of the Secretary of State and of Ambassadors respectively in international controversies. This analogy will commend itself, I think, to anyone who considers the organic act with any care. The purpose of the Department of Labor, which is, of course, the underlying and continuously applicable consideration in this connection, is prescribed in Section 1 of that Act. It is "to foster, promote and develop the welfare of the wage earners of the United States, to improve their working conditions and to advance their opportunities for employment." This means all wage earners of the United States, of course, and not organized wage earners alone; it means organized wage earners too. Even as to organized wage earners the labor organizations cannot be wholly ignored so long as the unorganized are as a mass inarticulate. For this Department to depend wholly upon organized employers like the Colorado Fuel and Iron Company for information as to the welfare and working conditions of their working men, would hardly meet the purposes of the organic act; and to consult the unorganized working men individually would be impracticable.

Mr. Bowers' strictures on the Secretary for conferring with the United Mine Workers prior to the strike would, therefore, seem to be not only without legal foundation but inconsistent with the Secretary's legal obligations. And so of his strictures upon the selection of Mr. Stewart as mediator. By Section 8 of the organic act the Secretary of Labor is empowered to "act as a mediator and to appoint commissioners of conciliation in labor disputes whenever in his judgment the interests of industrial peace may require it to be done." In cases in which either party to a labor dispute —whether the dispute be actually advanced to a state of industrial warfare, or be still in its beginnings—refuses to act reasonably in order to avert or end an industrial war by which whole communities are or may become chaotic, it is probably true that the Secretary of Labor may, and if so he ought to, exert the power Congress has reposed in him with a view to compelling industrial peace. In that event he should, of course, use his power fairly, both as to ends and means. And that the present Secretary of Labor would do this, no fairminded persons doubt who are at all familiar with his long and conciliatory career in the labor movement, whether those persons be working men or employers.

The exercise, however, of any such plenary authority should of course be avoided in every case so long as there is a reasonable possibility of voluntary adjustment through mediation. Diplomacy rather than power, for the maintenance of industrial peace, is the keynote of the act creating the Department of Labor; and it is in this spirit that Secretary Wilson has invariably administered Section 8 ever since my connection with the Department. It was in the same spirit that he appointed Mr. Stewart a commissioner of conciliation to the opposing parties in the present Colorado strike; not as an absolute arbitrator to decide conflicting claims, but as a conciliator to adjust them by means of voluntary settlement or arbitral agreement.

Had the Secretary's commissioner been met by the owners of the natural coal deposits of southern Colorado, in the spirit in which the Secretary of Labor sent him, and in which so far as I can learn he acted throughout, there would probably have been no strike, or if one had broken out it would most likely have been of short duration and free from the ugly phases it appears in fact to have assumed. Nor do I think I go beyond bounds in saying that the strike would end now if Mr. Bowers were to agree to a reasonable arbitration by unbiased arbitrators.

That industrial peace on fair terms was the Secretary's object in sending Mr. Stewart to Colorado is evident from the facts. From various sources he had been importuned to use the good offices of this Department in an effort to bring about a conference between the miners and their employers prior to the anticipated calling of the present strike. In response he had appealed to the miners to be patient while efforts to avert the strike were being made by the Department. On September 5th, nearly twenty days prior to the calling of the strike but when the conditions all pointed to an early call, he sent the following telegram to Frank J. Hayes, National Vice President of the United Mine Workers of America:

"I have today appointed Ethelbert Stewart, Chief Clerk of the Bureau of Labor Statistics, as mediator and conciliator in the impending trade dispute between the coal miners of southern Colorado and their employers. Mr. Stewart will proceed at once to get in touch with the eastern owners of the mines, and will later consult with the mine workers. I trust that the miners of southern Colorado will be patient, and that the situation may be satisfactorily adjusted without resorting to strike."

On September 10th the Secretary wrote Mr. Hayes in further reference to the Colorado situation, calling attention to his previous telegram, asking for continued patience, and, to promote peace, suggesting that there would be better opportunities for a successful conference if conciliatory proceedings were instituted before a strike should actually begin. A convention of miners had already been called, at which, as the Department was informed, a strike decision would be made. Thereupon the Secretary again directed the attention of the miners to the fact that Mr. Stewart would press the New York end of the situation—with reference, that is, to the interests at New York which own these Colorado coal deposits—as rapidly as possible, with the hope of getting definite assurances before the convention met, which might enable him to make a satisfactory adjustment of the impending controversy without any strike. But the owners of those coal deposits, or their representatives, were immovable. This you may infer without further evidence, I think, from the tone of the Bowers letter and from its explicit intimation of persistent refusal to submit to arbitration the questions which made the strike and keep it alive, but which as they assert, in spite of its inconsistence with the fact of the strike, do not exist.

This Department did everything possible to bring about an amicable adjustment, as you may see from Mr. Stewart's report as soon as it can be put into written form; and when contrary to the wishes and efforts of the Department the strike had been called, the Secretary of Labor sent the following telegram to Mr. Stewart at Denver under date of September 29, 1913:

"Cooperate with Governor Ammons or any other person whose influence you can utilize towards bringing about a satisfactory settlement of the strike."

This telegram was in response to Mr. Stewart's written report of September 25th, the next day but one after the strike call, in which he said of his visit to the Governor of Colorado upon the day of that call that he found the Governor to have "the most complete and apparently impartial information on the whole situation."

By the same report it appears that Mr. Stewart had called upon Mr. Bowers on the 24th, the day before his report, and had found him "very bitter." This judgment would seem to be confirmed by an undertone of Mr. Bowers' letter to the President. That Mr. Stewart was reasonably and fairly disposed, seems clear enough from that part of his report of the 25th, now in the files of this Department, in which he says: "Of course, I have not gotten sufficient hold here to be sure of my ground, but I am of opinion at present that if an agreement which did not recognize the union (something after the order of the Anthracite Commission agreement)[2] could be secured, the union ought to accept it as the best thing obtainable at present. The organization is thus preserved without recognition. Frankly it looks to me like a strike for organization purposes with recognition of the union as its sole objective point; and frankly again I do not now believe this can be achieved. I believe a safeguarded open shop agreement is all that can be secured." That does not read like the report of an unduly biased man. Neither does Secretary Wilson's telegraphic acknowledgment quoted above imply that he had any other purpose than to make a fair and peaceable adjustment—satisfactory to reasonable employers and reasonable workmen alike— of a labor dispute, which he knew from advance information would involve, as in fact it has involved and still does involve, industrial warfare in Colorado. To accomplish this end it was necessary to secure, and only decent to deserve, the confidence of the organized workmen. Any other course would have made

[2] The Anthracite Coal Strike Commission appointed by President Theodore Roosevelt to arbitrate the strike of 1902. See Robert J. Cornell, *The Anthracite Coal Strike of 1902* (Washington, 1957), pp. 215-59.

mediation impossible. To be sure, it was necessary also to secure, and only decent to deserve, the confidence of the employers. That the Secretary did secure the confidence of the organized men is true, I am sure. That he deserved the confidence of both, I am also sure. If he has failed to get that of the employers, the reason must be that such as they are accustomed to exacting unquestioning and undivided loyalty to themselves as the price of their confidence, an estimate which the Bowers letter to the President goes far to verify.

Would it be overleaping the limitations of your request, dear Mr. Tumulty, if, by way of concluding comment on the Bowers letter, I suggest that a broader public policy than acquiescence in the feudal overlordship and arrogant attitude of such employers as the Colorado Fuel and Iron Company indicate themselves to be by the Bowers letter, must be adopted in order to secure industrial peace in such cases. This company owns some of the rich natural resources of the people of the United States. That ownership is in the nature of a trusteeship. There could be no justification, political, industrial or moral, for allowing a few men to turn those natural deposits into private property, were it not that private tenure seems to offer the most expedient method for the utilization of natural resources under existing social policies. Such ownership is, therefore, in the nature of a trust for the common good, the beneficiaries of that trust being the whole people, and its condition the maintenance of industrial equity and peace in the utilization of those natural deposits. If industrial war comes, such war as that which now exists in Colorado—the fault must be attributed to the trustees, the owners for a peaceable public purpose, of the natural deposits over the utilization of which that warfare arises, unless they affirmatively show that they are not in the wrong. And in making this showing they ought not to be allowed—if there is any law to meet the case, and if there is none one should be enacted—to "stand pat" upon their own ex parte testimony in the determination of that issue. If they refuse to consent to a fair arbitration of disputed questions which vitalize such a strike as this, or refuse to propose some other reasonable mode of adjustment, but insist upon settling the matter according to their own code of ethics and by means of their own industrial power, which springs largely from their monopoly of natural resources, then they should be made to realize that they have misapprehended both the powers of the Government and the temper of the people.

Faithfully yours,   Louis F. Post

TLS (WP, DLC).

To William Bayard Hale

Washington, November 16, 1913

Your despatch of seven last evening raises several questions to which the President desires answer before taking further steps. He has no thought of regarding as binding on the Mexican people any thing done by Huerta since assuming dictatorial power, neither will he consider as binding anything done by the new congress in case Huerta resigns. The President will not accept as provisional authority any one connected with Huerta or in sympathy with his purpose and methods. The President's sole desire is to assist in restoring Constitutional Government in Mexico and all steps taken by him will be taken with this end in view. He does not desire to use force and will not resort to it unless conditions compel it. He does not expect such conditions to arise and should they arise guarantees will be given as to the disinterestedness of our Nation's purpose by a declaration that will preclude the possibility of our asking either land or money indemnity or continuing oversight or authority. This outline of the President's plans is given you that you may be able to remove any fears that the Constitutionalists may entertain and thus be in position to secure a frank expression of their views on the following subjects. Are the Constitutionalists willing to have Constitutional Government restored by peaceable means or do they prefer force? If assured of a free and fair election would they submit their cause to the ballot or do they still insist on the sword as the only available weapon? Are there any men outside of their army in whose wisdom and patr[i]otism they have confidence? If so secure as many names as possible? If the Constitutionalists succeed in setting up a government by force do they intend to give the people an early opportunity to elect a president and congress at a free and fair election? If so would they be willing to surrender the government into the hands of those selected by the people at such an election even though the persons elected were not the one preferred by those in power? These questions are suggested that the President may be informed as to the views and plans of the leaders of the Constitutionalists. He is deeply disturbed by the impression he gets from your last telegram that the leaders of the Constitutionalists would trust no one but themselves. He would not be willing, even indirectly, to assist them if they took so narrow and selfish a view. It would show that they do not understand constitutional processes.[1]

CLST telegram (SDR, RG 59, 812.00/9759, DNA).

[1] Wilson dictated this telegram to Bryan, whose handwritten draft is in SDR, RG 59, 812.00/9759, DNA.

William Bayard Hale to William Jennings Bryan

Nogales, Arizona. November 16, 1913.

Following is the declaration made by Carranza in response to your communication. It was originally made ex tempore but has been under revision for several days. In addition they are, I believe, preparing a formal, written reply. In all this there is a considerable element of gallery play. These documents bring [being] in large part designed to make a record for home consumption. Carranza, First Chief of the Constitutionalists, declared that: He considered the determination which the Government of the United States contemplated relative to the passing of arms and munitions as an act of justice. This same act, besides being just, would arouse a wave of sympathy not only on the part of the Constitutionalists who are actually in arms, but of all the Mexican people who favor the cause which he represents. If, at this moment, the struggle appears to be undetermined it is because the Constitutionalists have not been able to arm themselves as they desire since the Constitutionalist movement is sustained by the great majority of the Nation. This would be seen by the greatly hastened triumph over the usurper and the prompt and secure peace that would follow the free passage of arms. He has always followed the policy of respecting the lives and property of foreigners having publicly declared this on divers occasions. His orders in this respect have been obeyed by all the chiefs except in those cases in which, because of the interruption of communication or because of the great distances which separate military operations, these orders have not been received or have not arrived in time. But these difficulties are going to be corrected promptly as the Constitutionalist forces consummate their triumph and restore communication. The aforesaid policy of respecting the lives and interests of (#) ought to be extended to those foreigners who observe a conduct (characteristic) of such and not to those who take a material part in the present struggle or who intervene in it in any manner. With regard to (the possibility) that the United States might under certain circumstances believe itself obliged to intervene, Mr. Carranza delivered himself as follows: In no case and for no motive should this hypothesis, inconceivable to the Constitutionalists, be even considered; it should not be considered either by the United States alone or by them in accord with any European Powers. Moreover, the rancor and resentment which existed between us for so long a time following the war of 1848 and which have been gradually giving away to a friendly and cordial relations between the two neighboring Republics teach that it would be very lamentable even to discuss a question which would result only in kindling a fire that is extinguished and which would surely carry us to an ending struggle. The whole responsibility would rest upon the United States if upon the ground of protecting the interests of foreigners they should attempt an act of this sort, because no one denies that European interests are very much smaller than those possessed by the United States in our country.

Hale

T telegram (WP, DLC).

Remarks at a Press Conference

November 17, 1913

I see by the papers this morning that Mr. O'Shaughnessy is coming back, but has not been told to come back, and has not been given his passports down there. In short, the whole thing is a fake so far as I know.

Mr. President, the hopeful elements of which you spoke last Thursday have been dissipated by subsequent events?

No, sir. The mills of the gods grind very slowly, but they grind exceeding fine.

Has this government made any representations or sent any warnings to the Constitutionalists with regard to the execution of Federal prisoners?

We are investigating those reports. They haven't been verified yet. You notice that in the dispatches they vary very greatly in details and even in general import. . . .

Have you information, Mr. President, from Mr. Hale, or otherwise, as to Carranza personally—what kind of man he is?

Why, no. I was reading, with a great deal of interest, the other day, an article that appeared in the London *Times* from a correspondent, which gave a very interesting and apparently a rather intimate picture of the man.[1] But we have no independent—we have made no independent investigations or inquiries.

I have been wondering where we here could get some idea. It has been very hard for us to get a notion of the kind of man he is.

Very, very indeed. One gets varying accounts of him. It is very hard, I suppose, because he is always inaccessible during his constant movements.

Mr. President, have you been advised that he has refused any offers of mediation from this government, with the prospect of any mediation by this government?

I haven't heard of that, because he can't have refused them because none was made. I don't know where that thing got started. He is said to have made utterances declining all mediation, but no one has offered any mediation. That's a bolt shot into the air.

Mr. President, I think that after Mr. Hale's visit there, if you could, tell us something more definite with regard to Mr. Hale's purpose.

Well, if I could, Mr. Hale certainly wouldn't make any offer to him. He wasn't authorized to do so.

Mr. President, has there been any change of conditions since you told us what the outlook was and you were encouraged for an immediate settlement?

I don't know that I can answer that question, Mr. Lowry.[2] The thing is kaleidoscopic. It seems to change in its detail most unexpectedly. So there have been changes, but they have been changes rather in the personal attitude of Huerta than in the circumstances. The circumstances haven't changed at all. . . .

Can you tell us anything about your reports from Dr. Hale?

No, sir. There is nothing to tell.

JRT transcript (WC, NjP) of CLSsh (C. L. Swem Coll., NjP).
  1 [Henry Hamilton Fyfe] "Troubled Mexico. A Visit to the Stronghold of the Rebels," London *Times*, Oct. 27, 1913, a highly flattering portrait of Carranza as a man of principle and honor.
  2 Edward G. Lowry.

From John Sharp Williams

My Dear Mr. Wilson: [Washington] November 17, 1913.

From some things I saw in the Washington Post this morning, I have become a little afraid that you might launch your anti-trust legislation bolt too early. For heaven's sake wait until we get the currency bill through. Rome was not built in a day. Let us get through with one thing at a time and then tackle the next thing in line. I am inclined to think that you and I agree in the fundamental ideas as to the management of the trust question, but please do not precipitate it until we are through with the other things. After all, it is the *pièce de resistance* of Democratic legislation, and must be husbanded.

I am, with every expression of regard,

Very truly yours,   John Sharp Williams

TLS (WP, DLC).

William Bayard Hale to William Jennings Bryan

Nogales, Arizona. Nov. 17, 1913. 9 p.m.

Since the receipt of your instructions of this morning I have spent hours endeavoring to persuade Constitutionalists by every argument which I could bring to bear that their hope lay in accepting constitutional processes. They do not swerve from their position that no triumph will be secure which is not secured by arms. They are unwilling to accept the idea of Provisional Government even though its personnel were believed by Washington to be unconnected and unsympathetic with Huerta or Huerta methods. They look upon themselves as a body of men inexperienced in public affairs, namely farmers, unsophisticated people of small ways of life, whom the past has taught, it is feared, the keener wits and extensive influence of the Scientifico class. The leaders here dwell on the statement that they would not be able to carry the people with them in any arrangement looking towards an interim Presidency. They hold they [that] they must abide by the plan of Guadeloupe. This was a compact in which the military chiefs associated in it mutually pledged their honor to fight until complete victory were achieved, then to entrust to one of their own number temporary authority under which he would, by a decree, enact social and political reforms which they agree upon as fundamental; then only to call general election which they guarantee to be free and fair; install as President the indicated choice of the people and to submit all the acts of the revolution to the Congress chosen at some election. Their model in this programme is the Mexican patriot Juarez. Their answer to your question as to their intention to give the people an early opportunity to elect President and Congress at free and fair election is an earnest affirmative and they further affirm that they will surrender the Government into hands of those selected by people at such election even though persons elected were not preferred by them.

I am still engaged with Constitutional leaders and shall be probably until late tonight.   Hale

T telegram (WP, DLC).

Sir Edward Grey to Sir Cecil Arthur Spring Rice

Private

Foreign Office, November 17, 1913, 7.20 P.M.

Please communicate following to Sir W. Tyrrell:

"Your private and confidential telegram of 14th November.

"I am much gratified by frank exposition of views that the President has given you. This, and demands of United States of America reported in Sir L. Carden's telegram No. 141, repeated to you, answer my question reported in my telegram No. 316 to Sir C. Spring-Rice; and my telegram No. 167 of 17th November to Sir L. Carden will give you the latest instructions sent to Mexico.

"The object of securing better Government, which the President has set before before him, is one with which every one should sympathise, but I doubt whether there is any means by which the President can carry it out except direct intervention. I hope you will find an opportunity of expressing to the President how cordially I appreciate what he has said to you, and the various telegrams sent to Washington and Mexico will enable you to inform him of the line we are taking."

Printed telegram (FO 371/1678, p. 209, PRO).

Sir Edward Grey to Sir Lionel Carden

CONFIDENTIAL.

(No. 167.)   *Foreign Office, November* 17, 1913, 7 P.M.

Your telegrams Nos. 140 and 141 of 15th and 16th November.

I had heard that what President of United States would require is that Huerta should convoke the Congress of last May, which President of United States of America considers the only legal one in Mexico, and that Huerta should proclaim a general amnesty to enable contingents of the north to share in the election of a new President. If the latter refused to come in, they would be treated as rebels by the United States Government. Should Huerta agree to this, the President of the United States of America would go almost to any length to make it easy for Huerta to retire. But demands of United States Chargé d'Affaires reported in your No. 141 seem to be somewhat simpler and easier.

You will of course report any statement or proposal that Huerta makes to you, but Government of United States of America are now irrevocably committed to resort to any means, even force if need be, to secure retirement of Huerta, and the only chance of a peaceable solution is for him to arrange terms with them.

(Repeated to Washington, No. 325.)

Printed telegram (FO 371/1678, p. 186, PRO).

To LaMont Montgomery Bowers

My dear Sir: [The White House] November 18, 1913

Allow me to acknowledge the receipt of your letter of November eighth. I do not feel that I can at this distance enter into any discussion of the questions involved in the strike. I can only say this, that a word from you would bring the strike to an end, as all that is asked is that you agree to arbitration by an unbiased board. This is not only a reasonable request, conceived in the spirit of the times, but is one the rejection of which, I am sure, would be universally censured by public opinion. Whatever may be the history of recent negotiations or the impressions you have gained during their progress, it remains true that what the Department of Labor of the Government of the United States requests you to do is only what ought to be done in any circumstances. The questions at issue ought to be submitted to some body of men who can make an impartial determination of the case on its merits. If the investigation led to nothing more than a full understanding of both sides of the case by the public, the air would be cleared and the basis of settlement would, I venture to predict, become obvious.

The Department of Labor is acting under a statute which is only permissive, but it carries great moral weight, and I feel it my duty as the head of the Administration to back its request with the greatest earnestness and solemnity.

Very truly yours,   Woodrow Wilson

TLS (Letterpress Books, WP, DLC).

Two Telegrams from William Bayard Hale to William Jennings Bryan

Nogales, Arizona. Nov. 18, 1913, 12 noon.

Carranza is now excusing himself from seeing me on the ground of press of affairs, referring me to Escudero and Bonillas. Going fully into matters discussed in your last despatch I am now insisting on seeing Carranza himself, further argument with his Ministers would be fruitless. Constitutionalist position with regard to provisional Government that which I have reported in previous despatches.   Hale.

Nogales, Arizona. Nov. 18, 1913, 7 p.m.

After a day of evasive excuses for Carranza's inability to see me personally, Escudero today informs me in a lengthy speech that the original subject of the lifting of the arms embargo has been broadened by the introduction of your inquiries relative to the Constitutionalists' position regarding a Provisional Presidency; that Carranza must ask me hereafter to communicate in writing with his Minister for Foreign Affairs.

I replied that the withdrawal of Carranza from conferences upon which he had embarked with professions of perfect frankness and the tardy raising of questions of formality was incomprehensible, except upon the supposition, which we should dislike to entertain, that on certain features of his policy Carranza was unwilling to communicate to the President of the United States a speedy and candid reply.

I observed that this sudden change of method savored of a lack of candor in matters really vital and indicated a spirit of delay and evasion which I feared would create an unhappy impression at Washington as most unsuited to a critical moment and unworthy of men who aspired to govern a great nation.

If you desire me to communicate with Escudero in writing I presume you will advise me under what style to address him and in what character to subscribe myself—matters which they regard as of high (importance?). In my opinion this new assumption rises in part from an exaggerated sense of their own consequence inspired by recent Constitutional victories; in part is a shrewd effort to secure formal recognition; but chiefly is a method of evading giving an immediate authoritative answer to your inquiries respecting a possible Provisional Presidency.

Carranza's attitude is accurately represented by my despatches of November 15, 6 [7] p.m., and November 16, 11 p.m.: he hesitates to state it boldly. If we press him in writing for an answer he will probably reply that the matter is one of purely internal policy which Mexicans cannot discuss with another Government.   Hale

T telegrams (WP, DLC).

From the Diary of Colonel House

November 18, 1913.

Sir William Tyrrell called me from Washington to say he had an important despatch from London regarding the Mexican situation. He wished to know if I was coming over and I told him not until Monday. He said it was important that he communicate the contents of the despatch to the President and he did not know how to reach him. I offered to make an engagement for him by telephone.

I called up the President and asked him to see Sir William at his earliest convenience and in a way that would not be known. He was pleased to hear that Sir William had good news and said he would see him at once.

Sir Cecil Arthur Spring Rice to Sir Edward Grey

CONFIDENTIAL. *Washington, November* 18, 1913.

Following from Sir W. Tyrrell:

"Your telegram of 17th November.

"President asked me to thank you very warmly for communicating to him your instructions to His Majesty's Minister at Mexico, as contained in your telegram No. 167 of Nov. 17 to Sir L. Carden.

"He would be very grateful for earliest possible communication to him of statement which Huerta proposes to make to-day to Sir L. Carden, for transmission through you to President.[1]

"The latter quite realises that premature leakage has handicapped Huerta, and he assured me again that he would act with great patience.

"On leaving, he bade me convey to you his warmest thanks and high regard."

Printed telegram (FO 371/1678, No. 52477, PRO).
[1] See C. Barclay to WJB, Nov. 25, 1913.

To Mary Allen Hulbert

My dearest Friend, The White House 19 November, 1913.

I wish with all my heart that we had know[n] that there was even a possibility that you could come to the wedding.[1] We would have kept a place open for you in the house as well as in our hearts. But we knew how you have felt ever since your dear one went, and how far from well you have been lately, and sadly took it for granted that you could not and would not venture upon the excitements and fatigues involved. So that now the house is to be full to overflowing. And, if you were to come and *not* be in the house, we could literally see nothing of you, because of our necessary absorption in our houseful. We are deeply grieved to have missed the *chance* even, as apparently we have.

I am sure you understand why we have not written oftener. We are living amidst distractions such as I never dreamed of. As for myself I did not know that a man *could* live under such pressure of tasks and responsibilities as I am staggering under. I can *think* of my friends, thank God, and be refreshed by the thought of them, and my affection for them keeps green and constant, but I am in despair about writing regularly. Last Sunday, for example, I spent the whole day at the dentist's,— simply because there was literally no other time I could go, or think of my own personal or bodily needs at all. Fortunately the friends we love understand,—understand everything and every word.

All join me in affectionate messages.

Your devoted friend,   Woodrow Wilson

WWTLS (WP, DLC).

1 Jessie Woodrow Wilson and Francis Bowes Sayre were married in the East Room of the White House on November 25. For descriptions of the event, see the *New York Times*, Nov. 26, 1913; Francis Bowes Sayre, *Glad Adventure* (New York, 1957), pp. 45-48; and Eleanor Wilson McAdoo, *The Woodrow Wilsons* (New York, 1937), pp. 259-64.

To Walter Hines Page[1]

Washington, Nov. 19. 1913 1 P.M.

President directs me to say for your information

First, That Sir Edward's attitude is now entirely satisfactory.

Second, that Carden has been instructed to cooperate and is obeying instructions.

Third, The President feels it his duty to force Huerta's retirement, peaceably if possible but forcibly if necessary[.] The steps which he has in mind are (A) withdrawing of diplomatic representatives (B) raising of embargo on arms shipped to Constitutionalists. C Blockading of ports (D) use of army[.] This is the order contemplated but subject to change to meet new conditions[.] He still hopes that Huerta can be induced to retire or, if not, that Constitutionalists can compel his retirement without necessity for employment of force by us.   Bryan

WJBhw telegram (SDR, RG 59, 812.00/9817a, DNA).

From John Bassett Moore

My dear Mr. President: [Washington] November 19, 1913.

I beg leave to enclose herewith a copy of a memorandum left with me at half-past-four this afternoon by Mr. Colville Barclay, the new Counselor of the British Embassy.[1] This memorandum, as Mr. Barclay advised me, embodies the substance of telegrams which were sent from London yesterday evening and which were received in Washington this morning. In it the British Government mentions, as it has done on previous occasions, the importance of timely notice to foreign governments of any step on the part of the United States which might result in danger to the lives of British subjects and other foreigners. The fact is also stated that, in view of the danger with which British subjects are at the present moment threatened in Puerto Mexico and the region about Tampico, the British Government is sending two ships to those ports to protect British lives and property and to take off refugees; and the hope is expressed that pending the arrival of those ships recourse may again be had to the aid of our men-of-war in affording British subjects such protection as may be possible. I told Mr. Barclay that such action on our part would only be in line with what we had done in similar cases previously.

I avail myself of the present occasion to enclose herewith a copy of a letter addressed by me this morning to the Secretary of State, incorporating a communication which the Secretary of the German Embassy had, in the absence of the German Ambassador, just made to me in relation to our course in Mexico.[2] Probably the Secretary of State has acquainted you with the contents of this letter, but, in his absence this afternoon, I take the precaution of enclosing a copy of it.

Very respectfully yours,   J. B. Moore.

TLS (EBR, RG 130, DNA).

[1] T memorandum dated Nov. 19, 1913 (EBR, RG 130, DNA). Moore summarizes it below.

[2] J. B. Moore to WJB, Nov. 19, 1913, TLS (EBR, RG 130, DNA). The communication, from Baron Kurt von Lersner, said that the German government had tried to follow the lead of the United States in Mexico but had not yet been informed of plans contemplated by the Washington authorities. The Imperial German Government was particularly eager to know the name of "the American candidate for the Presidency in Mexico, since the retirement of Huerta seems possible only after a successor has been found who would guarantee the establishment and maintenance of peace and order in Mexico."

Three Telegrams from William Bayard Hale
to William Jennings Bryan

Nogales, Arizona. Nov. 19, 1913, 10 a.m.

URGENT. Carranza informs newspaper men that he intends returning to Hermosillo today at 2:00 p.m.

Unless otherwise instructed I shall leave at 1:30 for Tucson and await your instructions there at Hotel Santa Rita.

Hale

Nogales, Arizona. Nov. 19, 1913, 11 a.m.

Constitutionalists doing everything in their power to express indifference to your action. They are much elated over recent military successes.   Hale

T telegrams (WP, DLC).

Nogales, Arizona, Nov. 19, 1913, 1 p.m.

Learning that Escudero remains here today I shall wait here for your instructions. I could leave this afternoon for some near-by point if so instructed.   Hale.

T telegram (SDR, RG 59, 812.00/9825, DNA).

William Jennings Bryan to William Bayard Hale

Washington, Nov. 19, 1913.

The President thinks you had better return to Tucson at once and await further instructions.   Bryan

Hw telegram (SDR, RG 59, 812.00/9825, DNA).

Remarks at a Press Conference

November 20, 1913

Mr. President, Mexico seems to be in [the news].

> Well, I sincerely wish as much as you could wish that there were some news, but we are absolutely dry today. And it was a mistake I saw in one morning paper, but I saw a statement, in that it seems instructions had been sent to Mr. O'Shaughnessy. That is not true. I mean fresh instructions recently they haven't heard of.

Were any instructions sent to Mr. O'Shaughnessy as to whether or not to attend the reception given by President Huerta?

> He didn't. I would know whether any [reports] were sent to the State Department or not.

The afternoon paper said Mr. O'Shaughnessy was there, they played the Star Spangled Banner, and Mr. Huerta embraced Mr. O'Shaughnessy.

> I wish he had embraced his opinions.

Mr. President, might we know something more of Dr. Hale's mission now?

> Well, you know as much as there is to know. Dr. Hale has come back, I believe, from [Nogales]. I haven't heard that definitely, but I understood he was coming.

I presume back to Washington?

I think he is coming back to Washington.

Might we know whether those negotiations have resulted in anything?

Well, don't think of them as negotiations because they were—

Communications, or whatever they were?

No, they weren't communications. We simply wanted to have some method of knowing what was in the minds of the principals.

Has any information come of the result of that visit of Dr. Hale changed any terms of your Mexican policy?

We were not there debating with them what we should do at all for negotiations.

Mr. President, were possible conditions for a provisional president in Mexico discussed?

Certainly not. Nothing was discussed, no part or intimation of a plan was discussed.

Mr. President, is it true that Carranza asked Dr. Hale for credentials?

We haven't had that verified. That was in the public dispatches. I doubt if that was true. There was something done, I think, about it, brought out in the Mexican press, both from there and persons up here.

Is there any such policy that was in contemplation under any contingency?

Oh, well, I don't look forward. I live from day to day.

Do recent reports of occurrences encourage you to believe, Mr. President, that a solution of the Mexican situation may be found through the Constitutionalists, or through using them as instruments?

Well, we haven't chosen to use anybody, either party, or anybody as instruments. And on that, all I can say is, from dispatch to dispatch there is evidently a thing that is very slowly [blank] about all I can say is to be drawn from the dispatches. . . .

Mr. President, I think the most interesting question, perhaps, is whether any further action is being taken by this government in a positive way?

Well, you gentlemen will understand, of course, that it may be that if we took positive action of one sort or another, it would be wisest not to speak of it. But I can say at this hour that none has been taken, none further that you now know about.

With regard to Dr. Hale, Mr. President, would it be fair to say he went down there to see men, then?

    The latter part would be. It would have to be an absolute negative on the other. He didn't go down there to map out anything. He went down there for information.

Was the information supplied by the Constitutionalists, Mr. President? All the indications and dispatches from down there, and certain questions were written as if questions on future activities were in the nature of pledges, but the answers were not forthcoming.

    Oh, that was largely imaginary. All the information I desired was what he could get to us for our eyes and ears. It would not matter what they said to him at all. If you go down there and know what you are looking for, you can see it. I would know what he was looking for.

Perhaps you can tell us, then, did Dr. Hale make a report to you about the [blank] messages?

Mr. President, have you had any report of the massacre at Victoria recently, when it had been captured by the rebels—some six hundred Federals killed?

    No, I haven't. Of course, a battle is not a massacre. We must allow for some killing in a fight.

Yes sir, but the report was that these people were killed after—

    This is an interesting circumstance. We just received within a day or two the detailed report of one of our consuls at Torreón.[1] You know, we had the most extraordinary tales of barbarities at Torreón. I was only this morning reading his narrative very carefully of that series of days that preceded the capture, and while the facts were all very sad, I don't think that anything went on that one wouldn't expect in such circumstances. You see, we must remember that when these forces touch, there is a fringe of disloyalty to both, or treachery to both, so they naturally want to cut off that fringe when the other gets the upper hand in the contest; and there are, of course, a considerable number of persons who have played fast and loose on both sides— I mean, citizens of Mexico. But they treated Americans with respect and gave them protection in Torreón and other signals to stay.

JRT transcript (WC, NjP) of CLSsh (C. L. Swem Coll., NjP).
  [1] George C. Carothers, "Conditions prevailing in Torreon from Sept. 25 to October 11, inclusive," T MS (WP, DLC).

From Edward Mandell House

My dear Friend,   [New York] Nov. 20 [1913].

I am hoping you will come here on Friday in time to dine and go to the theatre with me, and do the same thing on Saturday. This will give you a real rest if you stay until Sunday afternoon. We could motor in the country a part of the time, or do whatever you liked best. A few days away from Washington will make you anew. It will make me very happy if you will do this.

Your devoted,   E. M. House

ALS (WP, DLC).

To John Bassett Moore

My dear Mr. Moore: [The White House] November 21, 1913

Thank you for the memorandum left at the Department by Mr. Colville Barclay, the Counsellor of the British Embassy, and the communication from the German Embassy, concerning our course in Mexico.

We have sent word to the naval commanders at the Mexican ports to act in the interest of the safety of British lives and property and, indeed, of the lives and property of all foreign subjects, as they would act in the case of our own citizens, and I hope sincerely that they will be able to render adequate assistance.

The request of the British and German governments that they be informed beforehand of any decisive steps taken on our part is most reasonable, and, of course, we have had it in contemplation to do so.

Cordially and sincerely yours,   Woodrow Wilson

TLS (Letterpress Books, WP, DLC).

To James Bryce

My dear Mr. Bryce: The White House November 21, 1913

I wish that I might have been present at the dinner given you instead of merely sending a message, and you may be sure I sent the message with the warmest feeling of friendship and admiration.

I am a bit daunted by your opinion of Latin-America and the possibilities of development within it, and I must admit that there is much to be said for your thesis. We are laboring through rather blind ways in Mexico but I have considerable hope that a solution may come which is not altogether inconsistent with ideals of constitutional development.

Mrs. Wilson joins me in the warmest regards to Mrs. Bryce and yourself. We have been very sorry indeed about the illness of Sir Cecil Spring-Rice.

Cordially and sincerely yours, Woodrow Wilson

TLS (J. Bryce Papers, Bodleian Library).

To Walter Hines Page

My dear Mr. Page: The White House November 21, 1913

Thank you for your little note about the Bryce dinner. You may be sure the message was sent with the greatest pleasure. I hope if you get a chance you will give my regards to Lord Morley, whom I once met at Skibo Castle.

In haste

Faithfully yours, Woodrow Wilson

P.S. I hear nothing but the finest sort of reports of the impression you are making in London.

TLS (W. H. Page Papers, MH).

From William Jennings Bryan

My dear Mr. President: Washington November 21, 1913.

The Colombian Minister[1] is very anxious that we shall make a counter proposition before the Congress adjourns. It took a recess for a few days and is to adjourn, I believe, about the last of this month.

You have the papers in the case and in our conversation over the telephone you expressed a willingness to have the first article of the treaty changed as suggested by Mr. Moore, the change retaining the word "regret." I am very glad that this is agreeable to you, for I think we can properly make that concession.

The Minister here feels hopeful that twenty-five millions will be accepted, together with the present boundary, provided the concessions as to the Canal can be satisfactorily agreed upon.

I know you are very busy, but I think the papers that you have contain a memorandum by Mr. Moore covering the various concessions asked and I believe that you can in a few minutes satisfy yourself that the concessions as phrased by Mr. Moore are reasonable. If you can find time to examine them and to send the papers back with your opinion on the same, I think we can take up this question with a prospect of an early conclusion.

    With assurances of respect, etc., I am, my dear Mr. President,
Very sincerely yours,   W. J. Bryan

TLS (WP, DLC).
  1 Julio Betancourt.

From Sir William Tyrrell, with Enclosure

Dear Mr. President,   Washington. November 21, 1913.

    I have received from Sir Edward Grey a telegram[1] the substance of which is embodied in the enclosed memorandum. I venture to send it to you instead of encroaching upon your valuable time by a request for a personal interview.

    May I add that I feel sure that Sir Edward would appreciate very highly if a public announcement could be made here on the lines of the suggestion contained in his telegram?

    I should be very grateful if you would authorise me to reply in a favourable sense to his enquiry.

    It is by Sir Edward's special instruction that I have the honour to address myself to you.

    As regards the final paragraph of the enclosed memorandum, Sir E. Grey has already been informed by telegraph of the welcome news that United States ships would continue, in the absence of British ships, to afford all possible protection to British subjects.

    Sir Edward also desires me to inform you very confidentially that the interview between Carden and Huerta which was to have taken place on Tuesday night has been deferred at the latter's request to tonight. I shall lose no time in communicating the result as soon as it reaches me.

    Carden anticipates that the principal difficulty will be in connection with the Congress question.

    Believe me, Your's very sincerely,
With the highest respect,   W. Tyrrell

TLS (EBR, RG 130, DNA).
  1 E. Grey to C. A. Spring Rice, Nov. 19, 1913, printed telegram (FO 371/1678, No. 52685, PRO).

ENCLOSURE

MEMORANDUM.

Sir E. Grey has had most urgent appeals from British and Canadian interests representing some forty million pounds of investments in tramways, railways, light and power works and oil in Mexico under concessions or contracts of many years' standing.

They ask practically two things:

1. That the United States Government should make it clear that they do not merely wish to force Huerta from power, but also intend to secure that Mexico eventually receives better government.

Sir E. Grey replied to this that the information he had received was to the effect that the whole object of the United States Government was to see that Mexico received better and more stable government.

But some public announcement by the United States Government of this intention would undoubtedly help credit and enable some of those commercial interests which are of a most legitimate character and old standing to survive bad times.

2. That property should be protected.

Sir E. Grey has replied that nothing can be done by His Majesty's Government in the interior, but that they are sending two ships as soon as possible to the ports.

It would be very desirable meanwhile if instructions could be given to the United States ships now in Mexican waters to give what protection they can and use their influence when appealed to for the protection of British lives and property. Sir E. Grey would be very grateful if President Wilson would authorise this.

British Embassy, Washington, November 20, 1913.

T MS (EBR, RG 130, DNA).

To Sir William Tyrrell

My dear Sir William: [The White House] November 22, 1913

I am more than willing to comply with Sir Edward Grey's suggestions as conveyed to me in your letter of yesterday, which has just been placed before me. My only embarrassment is this, whenever I make any public announcement, it is met by some form of defiance or some indication of irritation on the part either of the Huerta people or the Constitutionalists in Mexico, and the things which are in course of being handled are put back a little and embarrassed.

I beg that you will assure Sir Edward Grey that the United States Government intends not merely to force Huerta from power, but also to exert every influence it can exert to secure

Mexico a better government under which all contracts and business and concessions will be safer than they have been.

It has taken every possible step, also, to see that property is protected. Again and again every consul of the United States in Mexico has been instructed to warn the authorities, whether at Mexico City or in the North, on this score, and as often it has received assurances that the property of all foreigners would be protected as far as military operations made it possible.

For example, we have just received from the Constitutional commander at Tuxpam the following message:

"I am governing on a constitutional basis, my attitude being to guarantee the interests of all foreign and domestic oil corporations existing in the regions I occupy, fulfilling in this manner the demands of civilization, and not being governed by caprice or vengeance."

We have also instructed our naval commanders on the coast to render every possible assistance not only to our own citizens but to the nationals of other countries.

I hope that Sir Edward Grey will feel free to convey the contents of this letter to those British and Canadian investors for whom he, naturally, feels a sympathetic anxiety.

With much respect,
Cordially and sincerely yours,   Woodrow Wilson[1]

TLS (Letterpress Books, WP, DLC).
[1] This letter was repeated in C. A. Spring Rice to the Foreign Office, Nov. 23, 1913, printed telegram (FO 371/1678, No. 53167, PRO).

From Walter Hines Page

Personal and Confidential

Dear Mr. President: London. Nov. 22. 1913

The Mexican problem, so far as it touches the British Government, seems to me to fall under these three heads:

(1) Making this Government understand precisely what you are driving at and deny Huerta any help or comfort whatsoever and tell him so. This latter they have done very clearly, somewhat tardy as they were for lack of a quick understanding. About the obligations and inferences of democracy, they are dense. They are slow to see what good will come of ousting Huerta unless we know beforehand who will succeed him. Sir Edward Grey is not dense—very far from it—but in this matter even he is slow fully to understand the new policy. The Lord knows I've told him

plainly over and over again and, I fear, even preached to him. At first he couldn't see the practical nature of so "idealistic" a programme. I explained to him how the policy that we all too easily have followed for a long time of recognizing any sort of an adventurer in Latin America had, of course, simply encouraged revolutions; that you had found something better than any mere policy, namely, a principle, that policies change but principles do not; that he need not be greatly concerned about the successor to Huerta; that this is primarily and ultimately an American problem, and so on and so on. His sympathy and his friendliness are beyond any possible question. But Egypt and India, rather than Cuba, are in his mind. He said one day with a smile that it might take two centuries to bring the Mexicans to self-government. "Well," said I, "the United States will be here for two centuries." He still sees no escape from armed intervention.

But he is learning. And many men are seeing the new idea. (I wonder if you are conscious how new it is and how incredible to the Old-World mind?) and they express sincere admiration for "your brave new President." A wave of friendliness to the United States swept over the Kingdom when the Prime Minister took his stand in his Guildhall speech. Such hitherto unusual experiences as these are almost common now: At a dinner of the Titmarsh Club—a little group of Thackeray enthusiasts, to which I belong—[William Leonard] Courtney, the editor of the *Fortnightly Review* proposed your health in a capital little speech. The very next night at the big dinner of the largest of the guilds —successful business-men—your health was given most heartily; and, when I arose to speak they cheered longer than I had ever heard a British dinner-audience cheer. There is, among the people (the shipping people excepted) a positive and definite enthusiasm for the U.S.

But they are simply dense about any sort of government for "dependencies" or backward people, but their own. I have a neighbor who spent many years as an administrator in India. He has talked me deaf about the foolishness of any other plan of dealing with Mexico than by the sword. He is wholly friendly but wholly incredulous. And for old-time Toryism gone to seed, commend me to *The Spectator*. Not a glimmering of the idea has entered [John St. Loe] Strachey's head: I doubt if it ever does. The London *Times*, however, now sees it very clearly. Their editors have had much talk with me and they have written good 'leaders' out of our conversations. They are about to publish a South-American edition in Spanish, and in that they have made a clear explanation of the new principle. I am having many conversations with Central & South-American ministers here. In fact, I am having the whole staff of the Embassy incidentally to see as nearly as possible every Latin-American in the diplomatic corps and incidentally explain the whole thing—how this applies to our whole continent. Your Mobile, or Swarthmore, declaration against our acquiring new territory interests them all. I am having the principal Latin-American Ministers to lunch with me, one at a time; and I shall have something interesting to write you later, perhaps. Doing such work "incidentally" (they become talkative when grog & cigarettes are passed & the ladies have gone from the table) is exceedingly interesting

I get some interesting back-door news, too, now and then about this Government and the Mexican situation. I hear, for instance, that if you had declared in March that you would not recognize Huerta, this Government would have followed that cue. When you answered that you had not made up your mind or had not taken the subject up (it was during your first weeks in office) the commercial interests here used all their influence and this Government followed its old habit. Of course they now see their mistake.

Again, a back-door report comes to me from the reputable newspaper world, that several sensible members of the Cabinet sought the Prime Minister and Sir Edward Grey and, having demanded to know what I had said to Sir Edward, insisted on an unequivocal declaration—surprised them by hinting at grave danger from public opinion in the U. S. if they were not prompt. The inference was that other members of the Cabinet were influenced by the great oil interests here. (I do not know.) This Cabinet, you know, is an odd kettle of fish, and some of them are under suspicion at least by their opponents.

Lord Cowdray has as good a poker countenance as old John D. I met him soon after I came here, and I've run across him at intervals. When he sought me the other day, he was dead in earnest—exceedingly polite, inscrutable, but greatly concerned about his endangered property. He is an interesting man—that much is certain. The next day (the papers here having caught him at the Embassy) a lady of high station in political & social life, who has been very kind to Mrs. Page, called at my house and said to her: "You must never forget nor permit the Ambassador to forget, that all the Cowdray tribe are—liars. I know them all. My son married one of them. My daughter-in-law is the only one who knows how to tell the truth."

But I am dropping into gossip. Under the first general head, you may be sure of the enthusiastic friendliness of these people, and of the square deal and firm stand of Sir Edward.

(2) Carden. It seemed to me better tactics to take up these heads in order—to get the general situation clear before making complaints against Carden, especially since I have received only the most general complaints. But I have already "poisoned" Sir Edward's mind somewhat, and we are to take the subject up more fully when he returns in a few days from his visit to the King, in the country. Two years ago Mr. Knox and Mr. Reid made a bad blunder in sending merely general complaints against Carden—against his "anti-Americanism."[1] The result was a success only for Carden. I shall take him up informally and use all the ammunition I have. My own impression is that he is the root of most of the trouble. But the State's Dp't has sent me only one new thing to accuse him of—his reported saying that the U. S. was using only bluff.

(3) British commercial interests never sleep. We shall have more dealings on their account. But the way now seems clear and we can "tackle" them when they come. It seems to me that it may be worth something in the future—Cowdray's asking protection and his declaration that he has neither sought nor accepted any concession from Huerta. He is, by the way, very grateful for the prompt sending of one of our warships to the danger-point of his property. He informed me in a very confidential manner that the Waters-Pierce people are the "head-devils" in the whole trouble.

The upshot of it all so far is that this Government and this people feel that there is a new hand at the helm in Washington; and we can drive them hard, if need be; for they will not risk losing our friendship. I have the utmost confidence in Sir Edward, but not in the same degree in all his cabinet associates—on a pinch. I have discovered that infallibility, wherever she lives, dwells not in Downing Street: they make many mistakes. In this Mexican business they have made two bad blunders—recognizing Huerta (they see that now) and sending Carden, who lacks political imagination amazingly (they may be brought to see that, if he makes another "break.")

And I never expected to have the holy joy of putting the British

[1] In April 1911, Ambassador Whitelaw Reid complained informally to Sir Edward Grey about the alleged "anti-United States attitude of Mr. Carden." In October of the same year, Grey, in a formal note, defended Carden. See Warren G. Kneer, *Great Britain and the Caribbean, 1901-1913: A Study in Anglo-American Relations* (East Lansing, Mich., 1975), pp. 181-82.

Government through an elementary course in the meaning of Democracy!

Yours, Mr. President, with congratulations on the historic Wilson doctrine—no more territory, no more tyrants, no stealing of American governments by concessions or financial obligations (that's fixed now: no successor can set aside a righteous principle once clearly formulated).

Yours most heartily and faithfully—   Walter H. Page

ALS (WP, DLC).

From William Gibbs McAdoo

Dear Mr. President: Washington November 22, 1913.

Some time ago you wrote me about the duty on foreign books. The Board of General Appraisers has just decided that where foreign books are imported in sheets, unbound, and later bound in the United States, a royalty being payable only when, and if, the book is finally sold by the publisher, such royalty is not a part of the foreign market value. This decision was rendered by a board of three General Appraisers, and, consequently, it is final.

While there are many other questions pending regarding the importation of books, I think this question is, perhaps, the most important. The book publishers will be very much pleased with this decision, and I hope it satisfactorily disposes of the question you brought to my attention.

Faithfully and sincerely yours,   W G McAdoo

TLS (WP, DLC).

William Bayard Hale to William Jennings Bryan

Tucson, Arizona. November 22, 1913.

Upon reviewing all the words and acts of Carranza and his advisers I note that they maintain the attitude of being now indifferent to raising of the arms embargo, rejecting the idea of moral aid from the United States, refusing to entertain suggestion of nominating for Provisional President and ? us to recognize the Carranza "ministers." In part this attitude is insincere. Carranza is afraid of giving other chiefs a pretext for disputing his leadership. It is possible that if Carranza were confronted with the actual necessity of participating in the choice of Provisional President or of seeing such Provisional Presidency pass in to other hands, he might yield his scruples. It might be well to keep possibility of communication open against sudden events in Mexico City. Yet my judgment is all against submitting to Carranza's assumption that we will deal through his ministers. On the other hand if it should still be determined to permit Constitutionalists to import arms we should doubtless do well to take this step not grudgingly but with complete grace even to the extent of recognition. Escudero and Bonillas are tonight still at Nogales.   Hale

T telegram (WP, DLC).

Louis Freeland Post to Joseph Patrick Tumulty, with Enclosure

Dear Mr. Tumulty: Washington November 22, 1913.

Pursuant to request of the President by letter of November 14th, and through yours of November 17th, the papers inclosed in your letter—namely, the letter from the president of the Colorado Fuel and Iron Company and the accompanying exhibits —are herewith returned with the comments of Mr. Ethelbert Stewart of the Bureau of Labor Statistics.

As to your suggestion that I also make such comments as I may care to, I see no occasion for adding to my letter to you of November 15th on the same general subject, anything further than Mr. Stewart's letter now inclosed.

Trusting that Mr. Stewart's letter may prove to be sufficiently complete for all the purposes of a response, and assuring you and through you the President of any further information that may be desired that I may be able to procure, I am,

                Faithfully yours,   Louis F. Post

TLS (WP, DLC).

E N C L O S U R E

Ethelbert Stewart to Louis Freeland Post

Dear Mr. Post: Washington November 21, 1913.

You have done me the honor to refer the letter written to the President of the United States by Mr. J. F. Welborn of the Colorado Fuel and Iron Company, with the request that I indicate whether or not I can corroborate the statements in that letter.

Taking the matters therein in their order: In the conference in Governor Ammons' office October 9, there was no necessity for getting involved in a labyrinth of detail which had been thrashed over and over again. There were but two propositions to discuss: i.e., would the managers meet the representatives of the organizations either formally or informally to discuss terms of settlement; second, had they any counter propositions to make to me to convey to those representatives. To each of these proposals, they entered a negative. As a matter of fact, I had heard Mr. Bower's and Mr. Brown's statement of the causes that led up to the strike. I had their reports to the Governor, and knew all they had to say, as well as what the other side had to say, and there was only one question to ask: i.e., were they ready to take some step toward getting together, and certainly the step I asked them to take was the least offensive one possible. The managers all along insisted upon taking the position that I was sent there to investigate the strike statistically, as an Agent of the Bureau of Labor Statistics would do. I had emphatically told them to begin with that I was sent only to be helpful in securing a peace-pact or arbitration agreement. The only investigating I felt called upon to do, was to determine what compromises, if any, could be insisted upon, and which party ought to give or take the more. In other words, while I was there primarily to get the parties together upon any terms both would agree to, I did feel warranted in making such a study of the situation, as would enable me to urge what seemed to me fair to both. I had made this investigation; the least that the managers could do, would be to meet the men in charge of the strike, officially if they would, if not then as informally as men. When the managers refused to do even this, there was nothing more could be done in the form of mediation.

To get at once to the heart of this matter Mr. Post, let me say that, in essence, it is a strike of the twentieth century against the tenth century mental attitude, as to the industrial relations that should obtain between employers and employees. The mines have been filled with the greatest possible conglomeration of nationalities—there being twenty-one languages spoken in one mining camp. That this had been done deliberately, was the statement to me of the highest official of this company located in Colorado. The purpose was, of course, to produce in advance a condition of confusion of tongues, so that no tower upon which they might ascend into the heavens, could be erected. The managers felt that the animosities of race, nationality, and religions, would prevent union upon any line. Then the men were subjected to armed guards while at work, and while in their daily life in the camps. These armed men were called "marshalls" by the companies; "gunmen," by the workers. The real splinter under the skin, which caused the festering sore culminating in the strike, was this irritation caused by the "gunmen," kept up for years. Theoretically, perhaps, the ease of having nothing to do in this world but work, ought to have made these men of many tongues, as happy and contented as the managers claim to think they were. To have a house assigned you to live in, at a rental determined for you; to have a store furnished you by your employer where you are to buy of him such food stuffs as he has, at a price he fixes; to have a physician provided by your employer, and have his fees deducted from your pay, whether you are sick or not, or whether you want this particular doctor or not; to have churches furnished ready-made, supplied by hand-picked preachers whose salary is paid by your employer; with schools ditto, and public halls free for you to use for any purpose except to discuss politics, religion, trade-unionism or industrial conditions; in other words, to have everything handed down to you from the top; to be not only not called upon, but prohibited from having any thought, voice, or care in anything in life but work, and to be assisted in this by gunmen whose function it was, principally, to see that you did not talk labor conditions with another man who might accidentally know your language,—this was the contented, happy, prosperous condition out of which this strike grew. The companies created a condition which they considered satisfactory to themselves, and ought to be to the workman, and jammed the workman into it, and thought they were philanthropists. That men have rebelled grows out of the fact they are men, and can only be satisfied with conditions which they create, or in the creation of which they have a voice and share. To illustrate: churches are usually built up from the people,—grow out of the contributions of many, many families. They develop with, for, and by the people around them, and these through the elected church organization select a minister. Not so in the "closed" mining towns of Southern Colorado. There, they are ready-made, "hand-me-down" institutions, preachers and all, so far as the miners and mine laborers are concerned. I talked with the ministers of some of these churches which are owned and operated as a part of the coal shafts in and around Trinidad.

I submit that if the wage-system is to have a fair trial it must be humanized and not terrorized, and that this is the essence of the Colorado fight—to get the wage-system of the twentieth century out from under the mental attitude toward labor that obtained in the tenth century, before the wage-system was instituted.

I submit that under a gunman regime, the company does not know whether their men are 10 per cent organized, or 80 per cent; that under such a system, the sullen worker tells the gunman what he thinks he wants him to say, lies about being satisfied, lies about belonging to the union, lies whenever he says anything about his relations to the company.

I submit that the gunman as a spy and a detective, is an ideal system to keep the officers of the company constantly deceived as to the real feelings of the men. Admittedly, the men signed papers stating how happy they were, and within two days struck work.

I submit that under the methods that have obtained in the Colorado Coal mines, no statement of the attitude of the men on any subject coming from the company officials, is competent or valuable as furnishing possible facts.

I submit that the wages earned in coal mines by miners, as stated by the companies, is open to serious doubt; besides, Mr. Hayes stated to me that if the company could prove such earnings he would ask the men to withdraw their demand for 10 per cent increase in tonnage rates. That the day rates should follow the Wyoming rather than the Kansas scale, seems fair to me, but could be easily adjusted in any event.

The claim that the men after the strike, or even before, got guns, may be true. I do not know. If Calaban learns his master's language, and uses it to curse him, the blame can not all be Calaban's. For Calaban will and must learn something, and the only language common to all, and which all understand in Southern Colorado, is the voice of the gun, and Calaban did not invent or introduce it.

Frankly, Mr. Post, I can not find it possible with my knowledge of the situation to corroborate any of the statements in Mr. Welborn's letter; certainly not in the terms and tone of his statements. He states that many of the demands of the men are already a part of the State law. It is not the first time men have had to strike for what the law, but not their employer, conceded them. The right to have unions has been the law since 1908, and certainly Mr. Bowers, Mr. Brown, numerous mine superintendents, State officials, and common knowledge assured me in the early days of this strike, that unionism had been forbidden always in the mines of Southern Colorado. The State has good mining laws with no machinery for their enforcement. A good agreement with a strong union, having within itself the machinery for enforcement of the agreement, said agreement to cover no more than is now written into the laws of Colorado, would, in my judgment, be accepted by the men, and end the strike in an hour. In other words, if the managers would make such an agreement directly with the men, as they offer to make with Governor Ammons to hand down to the men, the men would accept it, and end the strike. But here is precisely the trouble. The managers will agree to anything with the Governor, but will not come into direct touch with the parties directly in interest. They can not be brought to admit that fuedalism is no longer acceptable, and that Southern Colorado is, or eventually will be—if not under their ownership, then the title must change—placed industrially where it is geographically, as a part of the United States, and not of the Hanseatic League.

Neither the Governor nor the State has any machinery in the mines for carrying out the agreement or the laws. The union is such machinery for the men. Collective agreements are the rule in the coal mines of the United States; they spell a humanized wage-system and peace. The whole subject, with the details Mr. Welborn refers to, would make a letter too long for perusal, and I can only hope that some time when you can find it convenient, we can give an hour to personal discussion of the Colorado situation.

While in Colorado, of course, I heard the cry of the suffering of the innocent public, but I confess I was not deeply impressed, or convinced of the massive innocence of a public that sits supinely by for thirty years, and sees the fungi of mediaevalism overspread the industries of the State without a protest. To be sure, there has been some protest against Peabodyism[1] in politics, but no protest against the same thing in industry, and it was the gunman in industry that produced Peabodyism in politics, and the evils that are permitted to generate, unmolested in industry, must always, sooner or later, assert themselves in politics, or cry out to the military arm of the State for defense.

I am, very truly yours,   Ethelbert Stewart

TLS (WP, DLC).

[1] A reference to the attitude and policies of former Governor James Hamilton Peabody of Colorado who, during his term of office from 1903 to 1905, repeatedly sent the state militia to intervene in mining strikes in an avowed effort to drive organized labor out of the state. "Peabodyism" was also the principal issue in the bitter Colorado gubernatorial campaign of 1904 and its dénouement in March 1905, when Peabody and his followers succeeded in removing Alva Adams, the duly elected Democratic governor, from office. See James Edward Wright, *The Politics of Populism: Dissent in Colorado* (New Haven, Conn., 1974), pp. 235-47.

To William Jennings Bryan, with Enclosure

[The White House]

My dear Mr. Secretary,   23 November, 1913.

As you know, the German government is asking very earnestly, as other governments are also, to be taken into our confidence with regard to our Mexican policy. It should be our pleasure, as it is certainly our interest, to comply with that request. I am therefore sending you, for your comment and criticism, a suggested note, to be sent practically to all the governments which may be likely to exercise influence in the circumstances.

May I know what you think of it, and what you would suggest to add or subtract?

With warmest regard,

Cordially and faithfully,   Woodrow Wilson

WWTLS (W. J. Bryan Papers, DNA).

E N C L O S U R E

International Note.

OUR PURPOSES IN MEXICO.

The purpose of the United States is solely and singly to secure peace and order in Central America by seeing to it that the processes of self-government there are not interrupted or set aside.

Usurpations like that of General Huerta menace the peace and development of America as nothing else could. They not only render the development of ordered self-government impossible; they also tend to set law entirely aside, to put the lives and fortunes of citizens and foreigners alike in constant jeopardy, to invalidate contracts and concessions in any way the usurper may devise for his own profit, and to impair both the national credit and all the foundations of business, domestic or foreign.

It is the purpose of the United States, therefore, to discredit and defeat such usurpations whenever they occur. The present policy of the Government of the United States is to isolate General Huerta entirely; to cut him off from foreign sympathy and aid and from domestic credit, whether moral or material, and so to force him out.

It hopes and believes that isolation will accomplish this end, and shall await the results without irritation or impatience. If

General Huerta does not retire by force of circumstances, it
will become the duty of the United States to use less peaceful
means to put him out. It will give other governments notice
in advance of each affirmative or aggressive step it has in contemplation, should it unhappily become necessary to move
actively against the usurper; but no such step seems immediately necessary.

Its fixed resolve is, that no such interruptions of civil order shall
be tolerated so far as it is concerned. Each conspicuous instance in which usurpations of this kind are prevented will
render their recurrence less likely, and in the end a state of
affairs will be secured in Mexico and elsewhere upon this continent which will assure the peace of America and the untram-
me[le]d development of its economic and social relations with
the rest of the world.

Beyond this fixed purpose the Government of the United States
will not go. It will not permit itself to seek any special or exclusive advantages in Mexico or elsewhere for its own citizens,
but will seek, here as elsewhere, to show itself the consistent
champion of the open door.

In the meantime it is making every effort that the circumstances
permit to safeguard foreign lives and property in Mexico and
is making the lives and fortunes of the subjects of other governments as much its concern as the lives and fortunes of its
own citizens.[1]

CLST MS (W. J. Bryan Papers, DNA).
[1] This note was dispatched verbatim on November 24. See, e.g., W. H. Page to
E. Grey, Nov. 26, 1913, TLS (FO 371/1678, No. 53702, PRO).

Walter Hines Page to Edward Mandell House[1]

Dear House: Hassocks, Sussex. Sunday. 23d. Nov. 1913.

Your letter telling me about Tyrrell & the President etc. etc.[2]
brought me great joy. Tyrrell is in every way a square fellow,
much like his Chief; and, you may depend on it, they are playing
fair—in their slow way. They always think of India and of Egypt
—never of Cuba. Lord! Lord! the fun I've had, the holy joy I am
having (I never expected to have such exalted and invigorating
felicity) in delivering elementary courses of instruction in
democracy to the British Government. Deep down at the bottom,
they don't know what Democracy means. Their empire is in the
way. Their centuries of land-stealing are in the way. Their un-
sleeping watchfulness of British commerce is in the way. "You
say you'll shoot men into self-government," said Sir Edward.

"Doesn't that strike you as comical?" And I answered, "It is comical only to the Briton and to others who have associated shooting with subjugation. We associate shooting with freedom." Half this blessed Sunday at this country house I have been ramming the idea down the throat of the Lord Chancellor.[3] *He* sees it, too, being a Scotchman. I take the members of the Government, as I get the chance or can make it, and go over with them the A.B.C. of the President's principle: no territorial annexation; no trafficking with tyrants; no stealing of American governments by concessions or financial thimble-rigging. They'll not recognize another Huerta—they're sick of that. And they'll not endanger our friendship. They didn't see the idea in the beginning. Of course the real trouble has been in Mexico City—Carden. They don't yet know just what he did. But they will, if *I* can find out. I haven't yet been able to make them tell me at Washington.

But, whether they tell me or not—(Washington is a deep hole of silence towards Ambassadors), I'm going to get that fellow's scalp—not suddenly, perhaps not soon; but I'm going to get it. By gradual approaches, I'm going to prove that he can do—and in a degree has already done—as much harm as Bryce did good— all about a paltry few hundreds of million dollars worth of oil. What the devil does the oil or the commerce of Mexico or the investments there amount to in comparison with the close friendship of the two nations? I'll get that fellow transferred or translated or put into the House of Lords or otherwise disposed of—see, if I don't. He can't be good long: he'll break out again presently. He has no political imagination. That's a rather common disease here, too. Few men have.

It's good fun. I'm inviting the Central & South American Ministers to lunch with me, one by one, & I'm incidentally loading them up. I have all the boys in the Embassy full of zeal & they are tackling the Secretaries of the Central & South American legations. Some of them are queer fish, but they'd just as well begin to learn. We've got a *principle* now to deal by with them. They'll see it after a while

The English people are all right, too—except the *doctrinnaires*. They write much rank ignorance. But the learned men learn things last of all.

I thank you heartily for your good news about Tyrrell, about the President (but I'm sorry he's tired: make him quit eating meat & play golf); about the Panama tolls; about the Currency Bill (my love to McAdoo); about my own little affairs.

We're looking with the very greatest pleasure to the coming of the young White House couple. I've got two big dinners for them

—Sir Edward, the Lord Chancellor, a Duchess or two (they're getting a little easier: they'll be human after a while), some good folk, Ruth Bryan,[4] a couple of Ambassadors etc. etc. etc. Then we'll take 'em to a literary speaking-feast or two, have 'em invited to a few great houses; then we'll give 'em another dinner, and then we'll get a guide for them to see all the reforming institutions in London, to their hearts' content—lots of fun.

Lots of fun: I got the American Society for its Thanksgiving dinner to invite the old Lord Chancellor to respond to a toast to the President. He's been to the U. S. lately & he is greatly pleased. So far, so good. Then I came down here where he, too, is staying. After five or six hours' talk about everything else he said, "By the way, your countrymen have invited me" &c. &c. "Now what would be appropriate to talk about?" Then I poured him full of the New Principle as regards Central & South America; for, if he will talk on that, what he says will be reported and read on both continents. He's a foxy old Scot, & he didn't say he would, but he said that he'd consider it. "Consider it" means that he will confer with Sir Edward. I'm beginning to learn their vocabulary. Anyhow the Lord Chancellor is in line

It's good news you send always. Keep it up—keep it up. The volume of silence that I get is oppressive. You remember the old nigger that wished to pick a quarrel with another old nigger? Nigger No. 1 swore and stormed at nigger No. 2, and kept on swearing & storming, hoping to provoke him. Nigger No. 2, said not a word, but kept at his work. Nigger No. 1, swore & stormed more. Nigger No 2 said not a word. Nigger No 1 frothed still more. Nigger No. 2, still silent. Nigger No. 1 got desperate & said: "Look here, you kinky headed, flat-nosed, slab-footed nigger, I warns you 'fore God, don't you keep givin' me none o' your damned silence!" I wish you'd tell all my friends that story.

Always heartily Yours,   Walter H. Page

ALS (E. M. House Papers, CtY).
1 House read this letter to Wilson on December 12, 1913.
2 EMH to WHP, Nov. 14, 1913, CCL (E. M. House Papers, CtY).
3 Richard Burdon Haldane, Viscount Haldane.
4 Ruth Bryan (Mrs. Reginald Altham) Owen. The eldest daughter of William Jennings Bryan, she had married a British army officer in 1910 and at this time was living in London.

William Jennings Bryan to William Bayard Hale

Washington, Nov. 24 1913

The President thinks you had better come to Washington at once.   Bryan

WJBhw telegram (SDR, RG 59, 812.00/9825, DNA).

To Albert Sidney Burleson

My dear Burleson: The White House November 25, 1913

The Junior Senator from New York[1] was in to see me yesterday and had this to say about the post office appointment at Buffalo: It seems that he recommended a German Lutheran and that upon some impression he gained at your office he permitted it to be announced in Buffalo that his candidate would be appointed, whereupon the said candidate was serenaded, etc., by various Lutheran societies and his not being appointed has caused him considerable mortification. I mean the candidate.

I remember that we have several times alluded to Buffalo but I do not know that we have discussed the actual condition. I write this because the Senator is obviously anxious that I should acquaint myself with the situation.

Faithfully yours,   Woodrow Wilson

TLS (A. S. Burleson Papers, DLC).
[1] That is, Senator O'Gorman.

From LaMont Montgomery Bowers

Sir: Denver, Colorado. November 25th 1913

Your valued favor of the 19th is at hand. Allow me to say in reply, that we appreciate to the fullest extent the importance of laws intended to lessen friction between employers and employes.

The arbitration law, to which you refer, has the approval of the writer and we would invite arbitration in the present disturbance in this state, if there were any differences between the company and its employes.

To satisfy the public, we have had committees from the Bankers association, the Chamber of Commerce of this city, also the Editors of the most important news papers of the state, irrespective of party, make a thorough investigation and they each report, that the only question of importance, is the demand of the United Mine Workers of America, for recognition of their union and the abandonment of the open shop policy.

To this demand, we shall never consent, if every mine is closed, the equipment destroyed and the investment made worthless.

I may say, that this strike is now at the point where its local importance or that of its thousands of stock holders and the owners of its bonds, is being rapidly over shadowed by a far more vital matter, viz; the avowed purpose of the labor unions to force at whatever cost, the open shops of the country to cloes [close] and their workmen to become members of the unions, or continue work at their peril.

The threats made by representatives of the United Mine Workers of America during the past few weeks in Colorado, fully justifies this view of the intentions of the labor leaders. Their speakers have frequently referred to the backing of the government, which has aroused intense interest on the part of employers of non union labor throughout the country; in this state this boast has had especial emphasis in the close relations between Mr Ethelbert Stewart and the officers of the union during his several weeks stay in Colorado.

Perhaps more concern has been expressed by thinking men of all classes in the address of Commissioner of Labor Wilson during the convention of the Federation of Labor, at Seattle a few days ago.[1] Some statesmen do not hesitate to say, that this outspoken and important utterance will force employers who run open shops together with their millions of employes, to make the rights of the open shop a national issue without delay, as the liberty loving american people will not submit to any organization forcing men to quit earning a living whether they belong to a union or not.

We will assist you Mr President in every possible way that we can, to make a thorough investigation of the riot and destruction that has been going on in the coal mining districts of this state for two months and by men entirely free from bias, so operators, employes and the representatives of the United Mine Workers of America, may all be included.

We promise out [our] best endeavors and cordial cooperation especially in bringing the assassins and all violators of law and order to trial, that they may receive the punishment that their crimes merit.   Respectfully yours   L. M. Bowers.

TLS (WP, DLC).

[1] Secretary Wilson addressed the convention of the American Federation of Labor in Seattle on November 12. He said many things that conservative businessmen like Bowers would have found offensive, beginning with his salutation to the audience: "Fellow Unionists." However, Bowers here refers to the Secretary's comments on his conception of the role to be played by the new Department of Labor:

"The Department of Labor as now organized and directed will be utilized to co-operate with the great trade union movement in its effort to elevate the standard of human society.

"One of the general duties imposed on the department is that of promoting the welfare of wage-workers. The one great specific duty imposed on the department is to act as a mediator and to appoint Commissioners of Conciliation in trades disputes. There can be no mediation, there can be no conciliation between employers and employes that does not presuppose collective bargaining, and there cannot be collective bargaining that does not presuppose trade unionism." New York Times, Nov. 13, 1913.

Colville Barclay to William Jennings Bryan

MOST CONFIDENTIAL.

Dear Mr. Secretary,   Washington. November 25, 1913.

Sir Edward Grey has received a telegram from Sir Lionel Carden, the purport of which I am instructed to communicate to you.

Sir Lionel has had an interview with General Huerta in which he informed him that, according to his understanding, the President of the United States desired three things, namely:

(1). That General Huerta should retire from the Presidency.

(2). That he should reassemble the late Congress, which the Government of the United States considered the only legal one.

(3). That he should proclaim a general amnesty so that the northern contingents might participate in the new Presidential election.

After considerable discussion General Huerta authorized Sir Lionel to make the following statement:

(1). Congress will at once proceed to the revision of the returns of the Presidential election. The election will certainly be nullified and a new election convoked. General Huerta will then retire from the Presidency, will appoint a substitute who will offer the necessary guarantees, and will devote himself entirely to the pacification of the country.

(2). General Huerta stated that the late Congress could not possible be recalled since many of its members were so hostile to the Administration that they had conspired with the Northern rebels and had rendered government impossible. He went on to say that after all he was bound to maintain his Government which was the only one in the country and the downfall of which would result in chaos. He did not wish to act unconstitutionally but had been forced for these reasons to convoke a new Congress.

(3). General Huerta said that general amnesty to the rebels was impracticable for many of them had committed atrocious crimes against foreign subjects as well as Mexicans and that he could not take on himself the responsibility to foreign Powers of a general amnesty. A cessation of hostilities which would be regarded by the rebels as a sign of weakness was equally impossible, but if the States in revolution would take part in the election he was prepared to suspend operations so far as to enable them to do so, and also to discuss means whereby the rebel leaders might be informed of this offer.

In reporting this conversation Sir Lionel says that if the above is regarded as affording a satisfactory basis for arrangement he has no doubt that the details can also be arranged to the satisfaction of the President of the United States provided that he is willing to consent to their being arranged, not in a direct agreement with the Government of the United States, but in a declaration of intention by General Huerta conveyed through Sir Edward Grey.

Sir Lionel also expresses the opinion that a prompt and satisfactory settlement would be facilitated by the withdrawal of some of the United States ships now at Vera Cruz.

In communicating to you, dear Mr. Secretary, these last two paragraphs which embody Sir Lionel's views, I am directed by Sir Edward Grey to say that he thinks it right to communicate them to you most confidentially for your information since they evidently convey the impressions created in Sir Lionel's mind during his conversation with General Huerta, but that Sir Edward Grey does not feel at liberty to endorse any suggestion that United States ships should withdraw from Mexican waters at a moment like the present when there is reason to fear that danger to the life and property of foreigners might occur suddenly and force foreigners to take refuge at the ports, and when His Majesty's Government have already asked United States ships to give protection, if necessary, and have themselves sent two British ships to Mexican ports.

I am dear Mr. Secretary,
Yours sincerely,
(for the Ambassador) Colville Barclay

TLS (WP, DLC).

From Sir William Tyrrell

Dear Mr. President,   Washington. November 26, 1913.

I telegraphed fully to Sir Edward Grey the contents of your letter to me of November 22nd and I have now received a telegram from him in reply desiring me to express his sincere thanks to you for your message, the friendliness of which he very highly appreciates.

I am, Dear Mr. President, with the highest regard
Yours very sincerely   W. Tyrrell

TLS (WP, DLC).

Walter Hines Page to Edward Mandell House

Dear House: London. Nov. 26. 13

Won't you read the enclosed[1] & get it to the President? It is somewhat extra-official but it is very confidential, & I have a special reason for wishing it to go thro' your hands. Perhaps it will interest you.

The lady that wrote it is one of the very best-informed women I know, one of those active and most influential women in the high political society of this Kingdom, at whose table statesmen and diplomats meet and important things come to pass. Her husband, a Liberal and now in the service of the Government, comes of one of the most illustrious of the great families. I am sure she has no motive but the avowed one—except, of course, the unconscious scorn of the old gentry for the newly rich, which alone wd. not have caused her to write this letter. She has taken a liking to Mrs. Page & this is merely a friendly and patriotic act.

I had heard most of these things before as gossip—never before as here put together by a responsible hand.

Mrs. Page went to see her & as evidence of our appreciation & safety, gave the original back to her. We have kept no copy & I wish this burned, if you please. It wd. raise a riot here, if any breath of it were to get out, that would put bedlam to shame.

Lord Cowdray has been to see me for four successive days—eats out of my hand. He's scared to death. I have a suspicion, too, (tho' I don't know) that instead of his running the Gov't, the Gov't has now turned the tables & is running him. His Gov't contract is becoming a bad thing to sleep with. He told me this morning that he (thro' Lord Murray[2]) had withdrawn the request for any concession in Colombia. I congratulated him. "That, Lord Cowdray, will save you as well as some other people I know a good deal of possible trouble." I have explained to him the whole New Principle *in extenso*, "so that you may see clearly where the line of danger runs." Lord! how he's changed! Several weeks ago when I ran across him accidentally he was humourous, almost cynical. Now he's very serious with hints of abjectness. I explained to him that the only thing that had kept Southern America from being parceled out as Africa has been is the Doctrine and the U. S. behind it. He granted that. "In Monroe's time," said I, "the only way to take a part of South America was to take land. Now finance has new ways of its own." "Perhaps," said he. "Right there," I answered, "where you put your 'perhaps,' I put a danger signal. That, I assure you, you will read about in the histories as 'The Wilson Doctrine.'"

You don't know how easy it all is with our friend & leader in command. I've almost grown bold. You feel steady ground beneath you. They are taking to their tents. "What's going to happen in Mexico City?" "A peaceful tragedy, followed by emancipation." "And the great industries of Mexico—" "They will not have to depend on adventurers' favors." "But in the meantime, what?" "Patience, looking toward justice."

Yours heartily & in health, (you bet!)   W.H.P.

ALI (E. M. House Papers, CtY).
    1 About this letter and its destruction, see the extract from the House Diary printed at December 12, 1913.
    2 Alexander William Charles Oliphant Murray, First Baron Murray of Elibank, former Liberal party leader in Parliament. For his activities in Colombia, see Peter Calvert, *op. cit.*, pp. 174-75.

Sir Cecil Arthur Spring Rice to Sir Edward Grey

CONFIDENTIAL.

(No. 203.) R.   *Washington, November* 28, 1913.
    Your telegram No. 359 Following from Sir W. Tyrrell:

On my taking leave of the President previous to my departure next week, he asked me whether you expected a reply to communication from Huerta. I said that no instructions had reached Ambassador on the subject of an answer, but that I felt sure that if President decided to send an answer to proposal by the same channel, you would be happy to forward it.

From casual remarks which he made on merits of the proposal, I do not gather that he intends to reply to it; he seemed to regard it as a futile proposal put forward with the object of gaining time.

Printed telegram (FO 371/1678, No. 53930, PRO).

From the Diary of Colonel House

November 28, 1913.

The President was scheduled to arrive at 5.56 but did not get in until a half hour later. . . .

The President and I dined alone. We had some profitable discussion during the meal. The main thing we talked about was the number of important appointments he had to make in the near future. There will probably be four Supreme Court Judges to appoint within the next two years, three Interstate Commerce Commissioners to be named now, and the Federal Reserve Board when the currency bill is passed.

I suggested that he appoint McReynolds to Justice Lurton's

place.[1] This is proper as they both come from Tennessee. The President thought if this were done, Garrison perhaps should be given the Attorney Generalship. I had this place in mind for Gregory, but it might be better to put Garrison there and give Gregory the War Portfolio, unless another man is thought of who comes from a better locality. Texas already has one place in the Cabinet, and Houston is practically from there, and the President might not like to appoint another Texan if he could find a suitable man elsewhere.

The only reason for transferring McReynolds from the Department of Justice is on account of his lack of political acumen. He is a great lawyer and will probably bring to successful conclusions the various suits in which his Department is now engaged.

I talked to the President about Dudley Malone. He expressed a deep affection for him, and shared my opinion as to his unusual ability. We also spoke of Joseph Davies of Wisconsin, and I asked why some members of the Cabinet and Tumulty thought he was not fitted for Governor General of the Philippines. I had met him but once and had talked with him for an hour only but did not have a bad opinion of him. The President remarked that he thought he had more ability than Burton Harrison whom he finally appointed.

We went to Cohen's [Cohan's] Theater to see Potash and Perlmutter.[2] When we entered the orchestra began to play the Star Spangled Banner and the audience cheered heartily. There is nothing of the "grandstand player" about the President. He does not come in late, after the audience has assembled, and make a spectacular entrance. He always arrives well before the play begins and generally before the theater is half filled.

Loulie, Eleanor Wilson, Dr. Grayson and Mr. and Mrs. Dudley Field Malone and George Martin[3] were in our party. After the theater the President and I had our usual sandwiches and a few minutes talk before going to bed.

[1] Horace Harmon Lurton, sixty-nine years old, had recently fallen ill, prompting rumors of his retirement from the Supreme Court. However, he returned to his seat in April 1914.

[2] A comedy by Montagne Marsden Glass based upon his own short stories in the *Saturday Evening Post*. It dealt with two Jewish partners in the clothing business. *New York Times*, Aug. 17, 1913.

[3] Unidentified. Those New York newspaper reports which listed the members of the President's theater party do not mention him at all.

November 29, 1913.

We breakfasted at 7.30 in order that the President might go to the North German Lloyd Pier in Hoboken to see his daughter,

Jessie and her husband off on the George Washington which sailed at ten o'clock.

At breakfast I talked to him about unfettering the railroads and corporations. I went into detail as to how impossible it was for them to thrive when many of them were throttled by the hands now controlling them. I particularly condemned the iniquity of directors of corporations profiting in any way by dealings with the corporations. This is [I] held was as reprehensible as a trustee of an estate profiting by his trusteeship, and the one should be made as impossible as the other.

I did not go to the George Washington as I had too much to engage me at home. He returned at eleven o'clock and a few minutes afterward we took a walk. We found the quiet streets like Lexington and Park Avenues more impossible than Fifth Avenue because a small crowd followed us and we attracted attention. When we were on Fifth Avenue the following crowd was not noticeable among the many thousands already there, so we took that as our route.

Upon our return to the apartment we tried to get Tumulty who was stopping at the Knickerbocker Hotel. Dudley Malone told me last night that Tumulty was in a bad humor and he thought it was caused by his not having been invited to go to the theater with us last night. I telephoned this morning to invite him for tonight but was unable to reach him. I mentioned what Dudley had said to the President, but he did not think Tumulty had any feeling of jealousy. I differed from him and thought he had plenty of it in his composition.

Failing to get Tumulty after repeated calls, the President got on the telephone himself and at last got in touch with him. Tumulty had no notion of going to the ball game or of playing with us in any way. The President insisted upon his going to the game and also to the theater tonight.

At luncheon Dr. Grayson, Eleanor and Loulie were present and we all went to the Army-Navy Football Game afterward. I had some talk with Tumulty. I found he had considerable feeling and yet I could not develop it. He said he would tell me the whole story when he had a proper opportunity. As a matter of fact, I think I know it. Dr. Grayson seems to be his trouble and I unwittingly aggravated it by consulting with him regarding this trip.

At the game many people of distinction came to our box to pay their respects to the President. Among them were Governor Glynn, Senator O'Gorman and many others.

I suggested to the President after our return that he lie down and sleep for awhile. I waked him at half past six so that he might dress for dinner. When he was lying in bed he asked if I had also rested. I answered that I seldom had the time to rest, that, in a way, I was as busy as he was. He said he was sorry for this, but I declared I deserved no sympathy because I enjoyed my work thoroughly and was in better health than I had been in twenty years.

Before dinner I explained my plan to counteract O'Gorman's influence in the Panama tolls question.

We discussed the currency measure slightly and also some appointments of minor interest. We talked of the French mission. He wanted to know what I thought of George Harvey for it. I felt we had better wait and see what Harvey had to say in the forthcoming number of the North American Review. He made no mention of Hugh Wallace but spoke of Untermyer, saying that McCombs had suggested him. He was quite emphatic in his decision not to appoint him. I said, in my opinion, Untermyer was trying to do right and was accomplishing a great deal of good; that he had made all the money he desired and was now devoting himself to public and charitable purposes. I related a discussion I had heard concerning Untermyer, one man taking the stand that his success had a bad influence upon the youth of the country, the other contended that his failure to obtain public recognition was in itself a good lesson to the youth of the country. The President thought both gentlemen were correct. Personally I am not certain, for Untermyer has done many things of great public value.

We dined alone with Dr. Grayson; the President's Aide, and then went to the Astor Theater to see "The Seven Keys to Baldpate."[1] We were met at the theater by the rest of the party, Loulie, Eleanor, Nona McAdoo,[2] Janet, Secretary McAdoo, Tumulty, Dr. Grayson, Gordon and his brother Rex.[3] After the theater the President went directly to his private car and took the midnight train for Washington.

[1] A "mystery farce" by George Michael Cohan. See the *New York Times*, Sept. 23, 1913.
[2] Nona Hazlehurst McAdoo, daughter of William Gibbs McAdoo.
[3] Gordon Auchincloss, House's son-in-law, and Reginald LaGrange Auchincloss.

To Mary Allen Hulbert

Dearest Friend,   The White House 30 November, 1913.

Your letter from Boston has cheered me. It showed you so much nearer your own normal spirits, with its enjoyment of the trip from Pittsfield and its thought of interesting plans of work and play in Boston (where, if anywhere in America, you should find the things your tastes and your vivid interest in people and what they are doing and thinking about most crave and are most nearly satisfied with,—you really belong on the other side of the water, preferably in Italy) and spoke in so sweet a tone, that it made me less anxious about you than I have been. I believe that the entire change of plan, the interesting place, and your constant contact with your son and his interests will do wonders for you; and that your freedom from the cares of housekeeping will enable you to recover your old physical elasticity again. All of which I am very deeply content to think and hope. For there is no concealing the fact that we have been really anxious about you.

And, do you know, I have come to think that Trenton is the worst possible place for you. You always come away from your visits there, and your inevitable contact while there with that little circle in which malicious gossip is always rife, very downcast and morbid. Those particular people[1] so like to be disagreeable and to smirch everything that is fine, and know so many things that are not so, that I do not see how any wholesome person could live long amongst them without losing his spirits and his generous thoughts about his fellow men. I have not Mrs. Roebling in mind, for she seems to me to be naturally a fine and generous creature, but the people she is surrounded by. I am glad their atmosphere cannot reach as far as Boston. It is poisonous.

You speak of *three* letters written from New York. You mean one, I suppose, written before you went down to Trenton, and two afterwards, one of the latter enclosed to Helen? If so, I received them all. I tried to answer them in my last, sent you just before the wedding. They are the text of my comment on Trenton and its influences.

The wedding went off beautifully. I do not know what you may have read about it in the papers, but the fact is, that it went off with a combination of dignity and simplicity which even I, who had to play a part and could not get the detached impressions of a looker on, could appreciate and rejoice in. The dear bride was as sweet as she could be. I saw her off yesterday (for I was in New York to see the army and navy game,—one of the bounden duties of the President), and she had spent Thanksgiving with us; so that I can testify that she is radiantly happy, dear thing, and starts her life journey as propitiously as even Ellen and I could wish. I need not tell you what effect it has had upon our spirits to part with her. But Ellen has acted with noble unselfishness in hiding her distress, and I have tried as best I could to emulate her example. It is easier for me, of course, than for her. She lives in the home from which the dear one is now gone, for good and all, while I am in the office the greater part of the time and busy with a thousand things from which I *cannot* withdraw my attention. My very burdens are at such a juncture my blessings.

It must be said that they do not grow less, but greater, rather. Now the prospect is that I shall have *no* vacation at all, till summer at all events. The Senate has suddenly begun to show extraordinary diligence, at least the Democratic members, and has resolved to keep at work till the currency bill is passed, without a vacation for the usual Christmas holidays. I had been counting on those holidays to get my own first respite from the continuous strain. But I am far from complaining. I would a great deal rather have the legislation than the holiday. Holidays will come some time, and will be infinitely more enjoyable and more profitable if they come after things achieved than before them.

We missed you sadly at the wedding. Though we could have seen little of you in the rush and absorption of it all, it would have been a deep pleasure to have you at hand and part of it. And yet, knowing what was in your heart, about your own loneliness and bereavement (a thing irreparable) it would have been too much to ask of you, and you would simply have had to force yourself to seem light-hearted.

All join me in affectionate messages. Keep to the mood rest and Boston have bred in you and we shall be happy.

Your devoted friend,   Woodrow Wilson

WWTLS (WP, DLC).
¹ That is, the household of Washington Augustus Roebling and Cornelia Witsell Farrow Roebling of Trenton.

From William Bauchop Wilson

Denver, Colo., Nov. 30, 1913.

Proposition for settlement will be submitted to vote of miners.¹ I do not think it will be accepted, but negotiations will still be open. I will remain here while there is the least hope of adjustment.   W. B. Wilson

T telegram (WP, DLC).
¹ About the "proposition for settlement," see the memorandum by Secretary Wilson printed at Dec. 10, 1913.

Remarks at a Press Conference

December 1, 1913

It was a good game, wasn't it?[1]

It depends upon the viewpoint, Mr. President.

How about Mexico, Mr. President?

Well, they seem to be running their own affairs down there in a very interesting way just now. There is no development, so far as we are concerned at all.

Have you heard from Dr. Hale since his return?

No. I got a note from him this morning saying that the Doctor was at my service for a conference, but I haven't seen him.

There have been no reports from him? He hasn't written?

No, he hasn't written anything. . . .

Is it true, Mr. President, that Lord Cowdray has given up his concessions in Colombia?

I don't know anything more than is in the press about that.

So then there is no basis for the report that adduces, directly or indirectly, that this government was responsible in part?

Certainly not directly, and not by any indirect suggestion. Of course, that the policy of this government may have had something to do with it is all I know.

It is suggested that the speech that you made at Mobile is probably responsible.

I have seen that suggestion, but of course I don't know whether it was or not.

Mr. President, did you indicate to Mr. Hale when you would be willing to see him?

No, sir. I haven't had a chance to study my calendar when I will be free to see him. . . .

Mr. President, in view of the fact that Congress should pass the currency bill, have you given up your idea of a vacation?

Unless they pass it in time to get away, of course I am not going unless they go. They determine my vacations as well as their own.

Have you seen the draft of the bill the Democratic caucus has been working out?

Not with the results of the conference in it. I have read what the Senate had printed containing the original House [bill] and the so-called Owen suggestions and the so-called Hitchcock suggestions.

Which of those do you prefer, Mr. President, the Owen—the so-called Owen bill—or the House bill?

I am in the middle of studying them. I interrupted myself
to come over here this morning.
Do you get any assurances whether that will pass before Christmas or after?
No, I won't get any direct information on that subject, I
suppose, until the Senate really gets down to work. As for
the Senate, you can't tell. But there are not as many persons
equipped for opposition on the currency as on the tariff.
Does that make any difference, in the number of opponents?
I don't know. That depends upon the discretion of the members.

JRT transcript (WC, NjP) of CLSsh (C. L. Swem Coll., NjP).
1 In what the *New York Times*, Nov. 30, 1913, described as the "most
spectacular game the two service branches of Uncle Sam's have ever played,"
Army defeated Navy, for the first time in four years, by a score of 22 to 9.

To William Bauchop Wilson

[The White House] Dec. 1, 1913.

Thank you warmly for the efforts you are making. Leave no
stone unturned.   Woodrow Wilson.

T telegram (Letterpress Books, WP, DLC).

Sir Edward Grey to Sir Cecil Arthur Spring Rice

No. 360   [London] 1.15 p.m. December 1, 1913.
Your telegram No. 203, of November 28: Mexico.

I should be glad if you could ascertain definitely whether it is
the intention of the President to reply to Huerta's proposals. As
they were made through Sir L. Carden and Huerta knows they
have been communicated to U. S. Government, we ought in due
course to let Huerta know what is thought of them. I infer that
he must be told that there is no chance of his proposals being accepted, but I should like to know whether the President wishes to
give any further indication of what would be acceptable, or
whether Sir L. Carden should simply repeat what he said in the
2nd paragraph of his telegram No. 149, of November 21.

T telegram (FO 371/1678, p. 391A, PRO).

ADDENDUM

To John Lind

[The White House, c. Oct. 10, 1913]

Please take steps to get into communication with the minister of foreign affairs and the leaders of the Mexican Congress and make the following representations to them. The government of the United States will not feel that a satisfactory constitutional settlement has been made unless an earnest and sincere effort is made to secure the participation and cooperation of the leaders in the north. This government hopes that its good offices may now be made use of for this purpose. It is as necessary in our view that this participation and cooperation should be striven for and secured as that a free election be held at which General Huerta shall not be a candidate. Has not the recent entire change of circumstances[1] made action along these lines at last practicable? Hostilities should cease and peace be put upon a parmanent basis by a return to regular and constitutional methods of action in which all can take part upon a footing of equality.

WWT telegram (WP, DLC).

[1] That is, the change in the course of the war caused by the capture of Torreón by the Constitutionalists.

INDEX

NOTE ON THE INDEX

THE alphabetically arranged analytical table of contents at the front of the volume eliminates duplication, in both contents and index, of references to certain documents, such as letters. Letters are listed in the contents alphabetically by name, and chronologically within each name by page. The subject matter of all letters is, of course, indexed. The Editorial Notes and Wilson's writings are listed in the contents chronologically by page. In addition, the subject matter of both categories is indexed. The index covers all references to books and articles mentioned in text or notes. Footnotes are indexed. Page references to footnotes which place a comma between the page number and "n" cite both text and footnote, thus: "624,n3." On the other hand, absence of the comma indicates reference to the footnote only, thus: "55n2"—the page number denoting where the footnote appears.

We have ceased the practice of indicating first and fullest identification of persons and subjects in earlier volumes by index references accompanied by asterisks. Volume 13, the cumulative index-contents volume is already in print. Volume 26, which will cover Volumes 14-25, will appear in the near future.

The index supplies the fullest known form of names and, for the Wilson and Axson families, relationships as far down as cousins. Persons referred to by nicknames or shortened forms of names can be identified by reference to entries for these forms of the names.

All entries consisting of page numbers only and which refer to concepts, issues, and opinions (such as democracy, the tariff, the money trust, leadership, and labor problems), are references to Wilson speeches and writings. Page references that follow the symbol △ in such entries refer to the opinions and comments of others who are identified.

INDEX

WOODROW WILSON

APPEARANCE

APPOINTMENTS

CABINET MEETINGS

FAMILY AND PERSONAL LIFE

FOREIGN POLICY

HEALTH

LEGISLATION

OPINIONS AND COMMENTS